CW01276502

Pianola

The History of the Self-Playing Piano

By the same author

COLLECTING MUSICAL BOXES
PLAYER PIANO
CLOCKWORK MUSIC
MECHANICAL MUSIC
PERPETUAL MOTION
BARREL ORGAN
MUSICAL BOX – A HISTORY AND COLLECTORS' GUIDE
RESTORING MUSICAL BOXES
JOSEPH HAYDN AND THE MECHANICAL ORGAN
RESTORING PIANOLAS AND OTHER SELF-PLAYING PIANOS

Pianola

The History of the Self-Playing Piano

ARTHUR W. J. G. ORD-HUME

Illustrated by the author

London
GEORGE ALLEN & UNWIN
Boston   Sydney

© Arthur W. J. G. Ord-Hume 1984
This book is copyright under the Berne Convention. No reproduction without permission. All rights reserved.

**George Allen & Unwin (Publishers) Ltd,
40 Museum Street, London WC1A 1LU, UK**

George Allen & Unwin (Publishers) Ltd,
Park Lane, Hemel Hempstead, Herts HP2 4TE, UK

Allen & Unwin Inc.,
9 Winchester Terrace, Winchester, Mass 01890, USA

George Allen & Unwin Australia Pty Ltd,
8 Napier Street, North Sydney, NSW 2060, Australia

First published in 1984

British Library Cataloguing in Publication Data

Ord-Hume, Arthur W. J. G.
　Pianola.
1. Player-piano – History
I. Title
789′.72　　ML1070
ISBN 0–04–789009–6

Library of Congress Cataloging in Publication Data

Ord-Hume, Arthur W. J. G.
　Pianola: the history of the self-playing piano.
Bibliography: p.
Includes index.
1. Player-piano.　　I. Title.
ML1050.O728　1984　　789′.72′09　　84–6216
ISBN 0–04–789009–6

Set in 11 on 12 point Plantin by Nene Phototypesetters, Northampton
and printed in Great Britain by
The Alden Press, Oxford

The most valuable commodity
in the whole wide world
comes in three pieces –
understanding,
information and
experience.
Put together
they make one priceless whole –
knowledge.

Contents

		page	
	List of Plates		xi
	List of Line Illustrations		xv
	Acknowledgements		xvii
	Preface		xix
	Introduction		1
1	The Rise and Fall of the Automatic Piano		9
2	The Barrel Piano and Its Development		51
3	From Mechanical to Pneumatic Action		79
4	The Evolution of the Player Piano		105
5	How the Pneumatic Player Piano Works		127
6	The Perfection of the Player Mechanism		155
7	The Reproducing Piano		173
8	The Nickelodeon		193
9	Other Roll-Playing Musical Instruments		199
10	The Post-War Revival of the Player Piano		215
11	Music for the Player Piano		229
12	How to Play the Player Piano		255
13	An Assessment of the Capabilities of the Reproducing Piano		263
14	List of Principal Makers, Patentees and Agents		269
	Appendix A Player piano pot-pourri		319
	B The player piano in flying training		355
	Bibliography		359
	Picture Credits		363
	Index		365

List of Plates

For the convenience of the reader, the photographic illustrations are arranged in three sections and in groupings as follows:

Early and rare mechanical instruments: Plates 1–8
Simple barrel pianos: Plates 9–29
Barrel piano orchestrions: Plates 30–34   } Between pages 44 and 45
Mechanical piano players: Plates 35–55

Pneumatic piano players: Plates 56–65
Player pianos, upright: Plates 66–77
Electric piano-playing systems (early): Plates 78–82   } Between pages 172 and 173
Player piano, grand: Plate 83
Reproducing piano players: Plates 84–87
Reproducing pianos: Plates 88–111

Pneumatic piano orchestrions: Plates 112–139
Key-top piano-player devices: Plates 140–144   } Between pages 268 and 269
New generation instruments: Plates 145–150

Picture credits and acknowledgements appear on page 363.

1   16th century clockwork-driven mechanical spinet
2   Mechanical spinet believed to have been owned by King Henry VIII
3   Mechanism of a clockwork-driven spinet of the 16th century
4   Clockwork spinet made in Augsburg by Bidermann
5   Dr Haspels and the author inspect a clockwork spinet in Utrecht
6   Massive longcase clock with dulcimer
7   Detail of the barrel-operated dulcimer
8   Clockwork dulcimer clock from the Black Forest, c.1800
9   London-made upright clockwork barrel piano, c.1800
10 Interior view of the London-made clockwork piano
11 Mid-19th century domestic barrel pianoforte
12 Mechanism of the domestic barrel pianoforte
13 Domestic barrel and finger upright pianoforte
14 Interior view of the barrel and finger piano
15 Nilsson's Pianoharpa made in Sweden
16 The small proportions of the Andersson Pianoharpa
17 Andersson's Pianoharpa with the lid raised
18 The simple dulcimer action of the Pianoharpa
19 Belgian coin-freed clockwork café piano
20 Coin-freed clockwork piano, Keith Prowse, London

21 Café piano by Crubois of Granville in France
22 'Have a tune, Miss' – Rejlander's street musician picture
23 Danish portable street piano
24 Interior view of a Danish portable street piano
25 Greek portable piano with part-iron frame
26 Portable street piano with animated scene
27 Spanish street barrel piano by Luis Casali
28 Typical London-made 48-key street piano
29 32-note Pasquale street piano with original cart
30 Central European weight-operated barrel piano
31 Clockwork café piano by Vanroy
32 Lochmann hollow-cylindered piano orchestrion
33 Projectionless hollow metal cylinder used by Lochmann
34 Detail of Lochmann piano orchestrion showing xylophone strikers
35 Ehrlich Orpheus cardboard-disc-playing miniature grand piano
36 Ehrlich cardboard-disc-operated piano player
37 Detail of the Ehrlich piano player showing key fingers
38 Piano Melodico in the shape of a baby grand piano
39 Small rectangular Piano Melodico
40 Book-playing Piano-Orchestrion powered by a hot-air engine
41 Hupfeld Clavitist mechanical barrel and finger piano
42 Hupfeld Patent Player Attachment in playing position
43 Hupfeld Player open to show mechanism
44 Pianotist-type player with music roll in place
45 Music rolls for the Pianotist were made of thin card
46 Pianotist mechanical player attached to a Steinway upright
47 Pianotist mechanism showing mechanical keyframe
48 Mechanism of the kicking-shoe player action
49 Keyboardless Debain Piano Mécanique
50 Piano Mécanique showing planchette music on the keyframe
51 Piano Mécanique mechanical piano in detail
52 Piano Mécanique mechanical and manual pianoforte
53 Piano Mécanique showing the two sets of hammers
54 Polyphon Rossini mechanical piano played by card rolls
55 Unidentified early keyless mechanical player upright piano
56 The Farrand Cecilian cabinet piano player
57 Operator's view of the Themodist Pianola piano player
58 Cabinet panels removed to show workmanship of Pianola
59 Pianola showing striking pneumatics and mechanical fingers
60 Smith Lyraphone piano player
61 Operating controls of the Smith Lyraphone
62 Theodore P. Brown's Simplex piano player
63 Hupfeld Phonala piano player showing controls
64 Development of the cabinet player – the reproducing push-up player
65 The Wilcox & White Angelus Orchestral combined reed organ and player
66 Poyser's Classic interior player in an ordinary upright
67 The compact Classic showing the folding takeup spool
68 Slimline Classic top action would fit into any ordinary upright
69 Kastner Autopiano showing 65–88 note tracker bar and theme holes
70 Bansall's Universal piano-playing attachment

LIST OF PLATES

71 Hupfeld Phonola controls showing palm control for pedal
72 Steck Pianola upright piano
73 Pianola action installed in an Ibach upright
74 Boyd Pistonola showing neat and compact installation
75 Roll motor cylinders of the Pistonola
76 Angelus Brinsmead upright piano showing controls
77 Upper action of the Angelus Brinsmead showing roll drive motor
78 The Telektra electric piano-playing control unit
79 The Tel-Electric electric piano-playing control unit
80 The special thin brass music rolls for the Tel-Electric player
81 The Telektra attached to a Chickering upright
82 Wolverhampton electrical exhibition of 1912 showing Hopkinson Electrelle
83 The author playing a Hupfeld Solophonola grand
84 Welte Vorsetzer reproducing piano player
85 The mechanism of the Welte Vorsetzer showing the fingers
86 Welte Vorsetzer showing the bellows linkages and roll motor
87 The only known Duo-Art reproducing piano player
88 Keyboardless Feurich piano playing 'red' wide-paper rolls by Welte
89 Special tuners' detachable keyboard for Welte keyboardless pianos
90 The Welte-Mignon-Piano keyboardless reproducing piano
91 Steinway Welte-Mignon reproducing grand piano
92 Eugen d'Albert recording a roll for Welte on a special piano
93 Hupfeld's answer to the Welte – the Dea of 1905
94 Welte-Mignon (Licensee) in a Bauer grand of 1924
95 The mechanism of the Hupfeld Dea reproducing piano
96 Electric drive mechanism of the Welte-Mignon (Licensee) action
97 Hupfeld Solophonola player grand
98 Early Steinway Duo-Art Pianola upright
99 American Steinway Duo-Art grand installation showing controls
100 English Steinway Duo-Art pedal-electric grand
101 Steinway Duo-Art pedal-electric grand showing controls
102 Operator's view of the Duo-Art grand
103 Duo-Art grand in a Spanish-style case
104 Duo-Art grand in a Louis XVI style case (a)
105 Duo-Art grand in a Louis XVI style case (b)
106 Duo-Art grand in an early Sheraton-style case
107 Percy Grainger 'playing' Grieg at an October 1972 concert
108 Grotrian-Steinweg Ampico Model A installation
109 Marshall & Wendell Ampico Model A grand piano
110 Marshall & Wendell Ampico Model B of 1931
111 William Knabe Ampico Model B installation
112 Pierre Eich Solophone made in Belgium in the early 1930s
113 Detail of the instrumentation in the Solophone
114 Kuhl & Klatt piano-orchestrion with xylophone, interior view
115 Weber Grandezza piano orchestrion with mandolin and xylophone
116 Weber Unika piano orchestrion with mandolin and violin pipes
117 Weber Brabo piano orchestrion with violin pipes and xylophone
118 Popper Salon Orchestra made between 1912 and the late 1920s
119 Catalogue illustration of the Philipps Pianella Orchestrion No. 43
120 Kuhl & Klatt 70-key piano orchestrion of 1920

121 Philipps' automatic roll-changing mechanism as fitted to the Paganini
122 Weber Grandezza modified by Berckelaer of Antwerp
123 Popper Happy Jazz-band piano orchestrion of about 1920
124 Seybold Piano-Accordion Jazz made in France
125 Popper Violinovo piano orchestrion with violin of 1930–31
126 Detail of the Violinovo showing the arrangement of the violin
127 Close-up of the violin-playing mechanism of the Violinovo
128 Hupfeld Phonoliszt-Violina, a Rönisch piano with three violins
129 Blessing Polyvox jazz band orchestrion, c.1920
130 Philipps' automatic roll-changer or 'Revolver System'
131 North Tonawanda Musical Instrument Works Pianolin 44-note piano
132 Link Model 2-E electric cabinet piano and xylophone with endless music
133 Operator's Piano Company Style X Orchestrion
134 Operator's Piano Company Reproduco piano and pipe organ combined
135 Seeburg E Special piano orchestrion, upper work
136 Seeburg E Special piano orchestrion, electric drive and xylophone
137 Link Style A orchestral piano
138 Cremona Style G Flute piano orchestrion by Marquette Piano Company
139 American Photoplayer Company Fotoplayer cinema orchestrion, c.1921
140 Key-top piano players: the Electrelle and the Dynavoice
141 The portable Dynavoice piano player
142 Detail of the Dynavoice piano player
143 Detail of the Electrelle piano player
144 The Maestro key-top piano player
145 The Stonehills Duo-Art Robot piano player
146 Detail of the Duo-Art Robot
147 Harpsichord fitted with Marantz Pianocorder cassette player
148 Aeolian Musette player piano, 1968
149 New spinet-action upright fitted with Pianocorder cassette player
150 The latest keyboards produce piano tone and have solid-state memories

List of Line Illustrations

1	Notation and mechanical music	page	14
2	Portable street piano in 'Christie's Old Organ'		16
3	Debain's Antiphonel piano player of 1850		21
4	Votey's first Pianola piano player		25
5	Votey's first Pianola at the Smithsonian Institute		27
6	The early gramophone recording studio		33
7	Advertisement from 1912 showing the Pianola in use at a concert		38
8	The reproducing piano in the home – a full-colour advertisement from 1919		40
9	The Aeolian Company's 'great removal sale', 1930		47
10	Details of the Hicks style portable street piano		53
11	Various types of barrel piano		55
12	Two trade labels from Hicks-type barrel pianos – Joseph Hicks and John Baylis, both of London		56
13	Schmidt and Potthoff & Golf's patents for combined barrel and finger pianos from the 1880s		58
14	DeKleist's Tonophone electric barrel piano		61
15	Mandoline effects on street pianos		62
16	Typical tremolo gearing		63
17	Luigi Villa's advertising barrel piano		63
18	Lochmann's hollow-cylinder clockwork piano		64
19	Peters' clockwork barrel and finger piano		66
20	1909 advertisement for Marteletti's café pianos		67
21	1895 advertisement for Mina's New York street pianos		67
22	Patent drawings for the Andersson Pianoharpa		69
23	Bohemian style of piano orchestrion action		72
24	Street piano tune changing system		77
25	Ehrlich's mechanical piano played by endless band		82
26	Fourneaux's Pianista pneumatic piano player		84
27	Types of player on the European market in 1900		85
28	Kicking shoe piano playing action		87
29	Lacape's combined barrel and finger player		88
30	Leipziger Musikwerke's Daimonion		89
31	Pneumatic action book playing Pianista Thibouville		92
32	The mechanical action book playing Piano Melodico		93
33	Perforated paper mechanical keyless piano by Crasselt & Rähse		95
34	Leipzig and Berlin-made electrically-driven mechanically-played pianos		96
35	New York-made electric piano with kicking-shoe action		99
36	Heilbrunn's Virtuoso electric piano of 1905		100
37	The Electrelle piano player from 1908		101
38	The Tel-Electric piano player from 1912		102
39	The Harper electric piano		103

PIANOLA

40	Four early types of piano player	108
41	The Angelus diaphragm pneumatic action	114
42	Comparison of upright and grand pneumatic actions	115
43	Action of ordinary upright piano	126
44	Principles of pneumatic control and operation	131
45	Section through basic player action	134
46	Two-valve action and Aeolian single-valve action	135
47	Section through upright Pianola player piano	138
48	Section through the Hupfeld upright player piano showing double valve chest under keyboard	139
49	Section through typical roll drive wind motor	140
50	The tempo governor	142
51	Principles of automatic roll tracking	144
52	Methods of controlling piano functions	147
53	The Standard Player crash valve	149
54	Standard Player action	152
55	Four other types of player piano action	153
56	Operation of the Themodist theming system	163
57	Example of themed notes on a music roll	167
58	The Welte *Vorsetzer* cabinet reproducing player	177
59	Schematic illustration of the Duo-Art system	187
60	Sir Henry Wood conducting the Queen's Hall Orchestra at a Duo-Art concert	188
61	The Rolmonica	211
62	The Maestro key-top piano player	216
63	The Dynavoice key-top piano player	217
64	Principles of the computerised player piano	222
65	Types of music roll spool end	244
66	Types and widths of player music rolls	246
67	Perforated Music Company advertisement, 1915	247

ADDITIONAL ILLUSTRATIONS

p. 8: An alternative to mechanical playing was practice and Bohrer's 'Automatic' Hand Guide (1878) was promoted as a teaching aid. **p. 50**: Imhof & Mukle advertisement for automatic instruments c.1860. **p. 78**: Battery-operated pianos by Heilbrunn & Söhne from an advertisement of 1908. **p. 125**: Metzler's 'Humanola' advertisement, October 1905. **p. 154**: Kastner's Autopiano promoted as playing 88 notes in November 1913 and Higel's metal player action, May 1917. **p. 171**: The Rialto player of January 1913 fitted to the front of the keyboard. Poyser's 'Classic' action could be fitted to any upright (October 1915). **p. 172**: The 'Pistonola' of Boyd was widely promoted in 1913. **p. 192**: Maxfield's 'Duplex' (March 1913). **p. 198**: A testimonial for North Tonawanda's Model G theatre orchestra. **p. 214**: Zuleger's 'Tanzbär' roll-playing concertina; Berthold's music-roll machinery, both from 1908. **p. 228**: Two notices for Hupfeld players – Bluthner 1917 and the 'Solophonola', 1913. **p. 254**: Simplex music roll sale advertisement, May 1912 and Kastner's Triumphauto piano roll label. **p. 261**: Farrand Organ Co. notice for the Cecilian player, March 1902. **p. 262**: July 1912 advertisement for the Welte Mignon 'Vorsetzer' reproducing player. **p. 268**: Kastner Triumphauto advertisement, 1921. **p. 354**: Another player action was the Stradola (April 1913). **p. 357**: Musical box makers Polyphon introduced this orchestrion in 1909. **p. 362**: Paderewski was one artist who commended the 'Pianola' (1921). **p. 364**: Music roll advertisement from Colleys, April 1908.

Captions to the advertisements reproduced in Appendix A appear on p. 353.

Acknowledgements

With the compilation of a work of this complexity, it is inevitable that I have had to call upon others for encouragement and, more importantly, assistance in matters both historical and technical. Accordingly, I would like to express my sincere gratitude to all those who have aided me so ably and who have shared so freely with me their own knowledge and skills. As with my earlier book, *Player Piano*, I express my great thanks to J. C. Allen of Steinway Pianos, L. K. Busby of Blüthner Pianos, D. F. Andrews of Boyd Pianos, and to the staff of Broadwood Pianos for their co-operation in allowing me to use material from their archives. Mr Phelps Snr and Mr Phelps Jnr of Phelps Pianos, and D. R. Heckscher and M. R. Heckscher of Heckscher & Company have also aided me, as have W. J. Bassil of J. & J. Goddard, the late S. J. Murdoch of Harrods Piano Department, and H. R. Goodall of the Aeolian Corporation, New York. Special assistance in connection with his work with both advanced reproducing piano mechanisms and the use of the player piano in flying training has come from Gorden Iles of the Artona Music Roll Company, an introduction to whom I owe to Gerald Stonehill, London.

Members of the Player Piano Group have proved a fund of invaluable information and assistance, particularly the founder of that group, Frank Holland of the British Piano Museum. Tony Morgan, late of Harrods and of Kemble Pianos, has allowed me access to his own collection of ephemera.

Dr Jan-Jaap Haspels and Dick van Minnen, respectively conservator/director and technician/restorer of the Nationaal Museum van Speelklok tot Pierement in Utrecht, have likewise been of immense help and have allowed me access to much archival information in this, Holland's unique museum of mechanical musical instruments.

While on the subject of archival material, my special thanks go to Dr Paul D. Ottenheimer of New Jersey who graciously allowed me access to his valuable and extensive collection of American advertising ephemera. Others who have assisted in this connection include Gustave Mathot of Brussels, Bill Edgerton of Darien in Connecticut, Q. David Bowers, late of California and now in New Hampshire, and Mary Belton, late of the Original Pianola Shop in Brighton, Sussex. All these have made available to me original literature from their extensive collections and other sources. Frank Adams of Seattle, Washington, and Harvey Roehl of the Vestal Press, New York, have assisted me by providing copies of service manuals and advertising literature long out of print. My good friend Douglas Berryman has also unearthed much valuable old material for me.

A word of special thanks goes to André Baumes, former managing director of Grundig International Ltd (now in charge of Grundig France) and to his personal assistant Jörg Lässig (now president of Grundig Panamericana in Miami) for the very particular help and assistance which they and Grundig International have given me, particularly over travel and research in Germany. Jörg Lässig has also allowed me free access to material in his private collection of archival material in Pfronten, Bavaria.

Professor M. S. Kastner of Lisbon, son of Maximilian Kastner, has also been of help to me, as has Bill Lindwall of Sweden, who researched so thoroughly the history of the Pianoharpa, Peter Georg Schuhknecht of Hanover for access to material and instruments in his collection, and for information in general Jens Carlson of Braunschweig, Werner Baus of Fuldatal, Jan Brauers of Baden-Baden, and Danny Dekyndt of Aalst in Belgium.

My many fellow members and friends in The Musical Box Society of Great Britain and the Musical Box Society International, the French society and the two in Germany, have allowed me to benefit from their knowledge and experience. Thanks are also due to the Musical Box Society of Great Britain for allowing me to make use of material which has appeared under my own name and various pseudonyms in the journal, *The Music Box*. Other material has appeared in various forms in the Bulletin of the Musical Box Society International and also in *Music & Automata* of which last periodical I am currently editor.

Great assistance has been provided by the staff of the Patent Office Library in London and the New York Public Library (Patents Division). To the various museums and galleries who have provided illustrations and details, specific acknowledgements appear in the proper places, but particularly I would acknowledge the help received from the Victoria and Albert Museum, London, the Metropolitan Museum, New York, the Smithsonian Institution, Washington, the Franklin Institute in Philadelphia, the Deutsches Museum, Munich, the Kunsthistorisches Museum, Vienna, Walt Bellm's Cars & Music of Yesterday Museum, Sarasota, Florida, the former West Cornwall Museum of Mechanical Music, Marazion, and many others.

To those whose just credits I may have omitted, my apologies. To those who have expressly requested that their names not be mentioned (which includes some Eastern European contributors and also some friends and enthusiasts behind the Iron Curtain), my thanks also go.

While on the subject of credits, I never have any objection to the use of my material so long as its source is fully acknowledged. I am prompted to make this normally unnecessary observation following the recent arrival in Britain of an exhibit from a Central European museum which was extensively illustrated with material from my other books, none of it bearing any form of credit. The subsequent unwitting involvement with one of our national museums served only to make matters worse.

Preface

My first book on the subject of self-playing pianos was written in 1967. This was called *Player Piano – the History of the Mechanical Piano and How to Repair it*. This was published three years later and was intended to serve as a primer for collectors, restorers and anybody else who might have an interest in these instruments and their preservation. At the time the book appeared, ordinary player pianos had virtually no market value, and demand and interest were at their lowest. Even the reproducing piano had only a small devoted following and second-hand instruments could be bought for $250 or so – about £100 at that time. And the wholesale destruction of unwanted pianos was still something widely practised at bonfire parties up and down the country.

Player Piano served its original purpose well, I think, and inspired owners to preserve their instruments. It also, I am told, played some small part in the reawakening of interest in these devices and, in consequence, I must assume some responsibility for the increase in prices of player pianos in recent years. Very soon, though, this first book on the topic was out of print – and in increasing demand!

Since the preparation of that first book, interest in player pianos has multiplied fantastically. A good proportion of this has resulted from people's increasing awareness of just what this instrument can do. Interest has been fostered by the 'live player piano' concerts staged in London by the Player Piano Group, and by the issue of numerous hi-fi records of piano roll music following the sudden discovery, in musical circles, that the reproducing piano roll could, with certain reservations, actually teach something about the techniques and styles of former pianists and times long past.

One result of this resurgence of interest is that whereas fifteen years ago you could not give away a player piano for love or money, instruments were incinerated at an alarming rate, and player piano rolls were used to stoke furnaces, today things are very different. Instruments command good money and rolls are saleable commodities, albeit with a high degree of ignorance in many cases. It is a fact that certain rolls are very valuable, and those for some reproducing pianos, such as the 'red' Welte rolls, are worth a great deal of money in the London salerooms, but the plethora of metrically cut dance rolls, emetic song rolls and cathartic medleys from best-forgotten musicals are still worth only a few pence. Even so, many vendors apply a sort of flat-rate price structure of several pounds for anything on a spool.

Another result is that owners now appreciate good music and players in good condition, and thus demand an increasingly high level of knowledge on the maintenance of their instruments. As for the instruments advertised as 'fully restored', well, there are several interpretations of this description of which only one is accurate. More on this one in the proper place.

In recent years a number of new books have been published on the piano and its history. It is a cause of great surprise that the player piano receives such scant reference in these works, and that it is usually referred to in somewhat derogatory terms. For an instrument that was once produced in greater numbers than ordinary finger-played pianos, this is something of a shock. The serious piano historian who quests for information from the modern bibliography of the piano will find himself denied reliable and accurate information on matters relating to the self-playing variety of the instrument. The student who perseveres with his inquiries will no doubt be forced to conclude that the modern studies of the piano were in the main compiled by people largely ignorant of this important section of piano history.

It is always gratifying for an author to find that his book is sought after, and so, with interest in pianos that play by themselves ever increasing in both Britain and America, it was decided to produce a second edition of *Player Piano*. However, this was not a proposition which I could really justify since, while the first book was written to suit the somewhat arbitrary mass interest of the late 1960s, today people are far more aware of the player and its potential and the sort of information they need is well beyond the scope of the first slim volume.

And so I decided that there would have to be a new book, not just a revised edition of the old, but a wholly fresh work with new text where needed and fresh illustrations wherever possible. Because it was not a good idea to use the same title for a new book, I decided to use the present title, *Pianola*, which, as everybody knows, is the registered trade name for the instruments made by the Aeolian Company. Although but a trade name for the instruments made by one company, the fact remains that this name has become synonymous with the player piano. I use as my authority the *Shorter Oxford English Dictionary*.* I could have called this book, Angelus, Simplex, Auteola or Pleyella by the same token; yet these words, equally renowned trade names for specific marques of player mechanism, have not one fraction of the charisma of that great company name. It is thus not quite as bad as saying that I drive a Ford made by Chrysler. . . .

Barrel pianos are seldom found in good condition today and the vast majority of player pianos can benefit from careful overhaul or rebuilding. All this work is within the capability of the average enthusiast and I would draw your attention to the companion volume to this book which is called *Restoring Pianolas and other self-playing pianos*. This gives step-by-step instructions on restoring the normal player piano and also the barrel piano, with important guidance on the associated instruments such as piano orchestrions and player organs (there is a whole chapter devoted to the Aeolian Orchestrelle, for example). There is also a section on understanding the reproducing piano action and guidance on how to restore it using the original makers' instruction manuals.

With these two books, the enthusiastic owner of a self-playing piano has at his fingertips the salient information he needs both on its history and development and on its repair and overhaul.

ARTHUR W. J. G. ORD-HUME

---

* **Pianola.** 1901 (app. intended as a dim. of PIANO.) Trade name for a mechanical attachment for playing the piano; also a piano equipped with this.

Introduction

Ever since man first set out on the course of musical appreciation and enjoyment – presumably from the moment he first pursed his lips, blew and whistled – music has had a fascination for people in all walks of life. Of all the arts, music is the one which is most desired, the one which is considered the most beneficial with which to be associated and the one which is available to everybody at a wide variety of levels of participation. The expert may compose his own melodies, play them on musical instruments of his artistic bent, or make his mark as a critic or musicologist by carefully dismantling the works of others and putting his own interpretation on them. The non-skilful can listen to others making music without themselves undertaking the toil of learning music, practising an instrument, or having to translate a printed page of tangled crotchets and quavers into muscular action on a keyboard or other instrument.

Between these two poles of musical appreciation and participation, there lies a multiplicity of other levels of appreciation. There are the musical instrument makers – craftsmen for whom performance is not as important as the making of the device to perform upon. Then there is the gramophone record collector, the musical instrument restorer and historian, and the collector of rare and exotic musical manuscript, for whom the paper and its attribution are of greater significance than the conductor of the latest phonograph disc.

Musical appreciation is a wide and all-embracing field. It admits those who do not play an instrument or even read music. As for the accomplished pianist, his technique may not always be entirely faultless – one of the finest pianists of the era of the reproducing piano noted to his embarrassment no fewer than 360 incorrect notes in a single performance, while Camille Saint-Saëns (1835–1921) is reputed to have said: 'I have heard piano salesmen get a better tone from an instrument than a professional pianist.'

There is also another area between the non-performing musical appreciator and the ace artist – a hinterland which has seldom been without music of one sort or another, be it created automatically either by an entirely self-acting and random instrument such as the Aeolian harp, or by a mechanical musical machine such as a barrel organ or player piano of one sort or another. The subject of our study is the latter instrument – the piano which plays (more or less) by itself or, to be more precise, a piano wherein the fingering of the correct notes does not demand the services of a skilled musical performer.

The mechanical piano quickly advanced to a position in the forefront of popular musical enjoyment. It was easy to use, it could play an immense variety of music from a choice of thousands of different piano rolls, and it was not desperately expensive.

Just as today every new technology is greeted by at least one dissenting voice, so it was with the pianoforte player. An un-named Viennese writer, quoted in *Musical Opinion* for November 1904, is said to have commented: 'For a year or two it will occupy a few minutes' chat in every drawing room, and a few columns in every magazine; and it will then, to borrow the elegant language of the playbills, be withdrawn to make room for some other novelties.' Of course, he was basically right, but his 'few years' extended to several decades.

The capabilities of the player were not overlooked by Sir Edward Elgar (1857–1934) when he presided over the inaugural meeting of the Birmingham University Society in July 1907. In acknowledging the gift of a piano, he remarked:

> You won't expect me to say much practical about a piano. Some people do gush over a piano; but I cannot. The instrument is useful and we cannot do without it, but some day, no doubt, pianos will be looked upon as curiosities. The multiplication of mechanical players is proceeding in such vast numbers that the human player will disappear. I am reminded of a story of the late Dan Leno when he visited the House of Commons. Looking at the very serious proceedings he said: 'It is all very well, but the show would go better with a piano.'

Sir Thomas Beecham, surprisingly, seems never to have commented on the mechanical piano. He had already dismissed the upright as 'a musical growth found adhering to the walls of most semi-detached houses in the provinces'.

There was the serious side to the player piano, though. It offered the amateur a unique opportunity to explore the somewhat esoteric world of music – a world from which lack of even a basic standard of musical knowledge might otherwise exclude many. The novice could see how music was put together; he could watch his rolls unfurling as he played, and see more than the finest musical score might teach him. Musical knowledge of a pretty acceptable sort was readily available to those prepared to work at their piano rolls.

The industrious musicologist and dictionary editor Percy Scholes (who compiled the first *Oxford Companion to Music* and countless other musical literary excursions) was a frequent writer on the player piano and a staunch advocate of its role as a musical educator. In several works sponsored by the Aeolian Company, he extolled its virtues in glowing terms. Another and no less important musical character of the time, Sir Landon Ronald, was also a strong believer in the instrument. Sir Landon (1873–1938) was the highly esteemed guest conductor of, among other European orchestras, the Berlin Philharmonic, before becoming the mainstay of the New Symphony Orchestra, later to be known as the Royal Albert Hall Orchestra. He was a man whose musical opinions were respected and whose talents earned him a knighthood in 1922. Two years later he wrote:

> I have a great belief in the educative power of the player-piano, and I think that it has done, and will do, much to spread the knowledge of good music.

The London firm of Chappells produced a special upright player for King Edward VII, who thereby added his endorsement to the long line of royalty, nobility, statesmen and churchmen who at some time or another enthused over the player and its capabilities. Among these, the most extraordinary has to be the story of the 93-year-old Pope Leo XIII, who, just one month before his death in July 1903, apparently greatly rejoiced over the arrival at the

INTRODUCTION

Vatican of an Apollo push-up. The exertion, one feels, may have been too great for him.*

The player piano gained in respectability. It also became an accepted part of life and in so doing had to take its share of satire. A writer in the magazine *Punch*, on reading that before Paderewski played the piano at a recital he immersed his hands in hot water, claimed that before playing music on his player piano he soaked his feet in a bowl of hot water. A cartoonist depicted two frowzy women discussing a child whose pianistic efforts could be heard from another room. 'Your daughter's got a good foot for music!' was the caption. And a Disney cartoon showed a 'player piano' producing music from a thin slice of holey cheese! In H. G. Wells's story *Tono-Bungay*, someone asks about a piano-player: 'Does this thing play?' The reply he receives is: 'Like a musical gorilla, with fingers all of one length. And a sort of soul.'

Aside from all the comic aspects which one could find for the instrument, the famed music critic and writer Ernest Newman (1868–1959) was one who recognised the attributes which were positive when he wrote:

> To have absolutely perfect technique at one's command is, as every artist knows, the indispensable pre-requisite for artistic playing; only when you can forget your fingers can your brain be perfectly free. It surely stands to reason, then, that the ready-made technique of the player-piano sets the musician's brain free to attend to the purely artistic side of the performance.

This same writer fired a broadside at the anti-mechanical-piano brigade in his book *The Player-Piano and its Music*, when he wrote:

> The commonest complaint against the non-human piano-player is that it is 'mechanical'.
>
> Where, in truth, is the non-mechanical musical instrument? Start with the indispensable minimum – say a few pieces of metal or gut stretched across a hollow piece of wood, and plucked by the fingers. Does man stop there? By no means! The

---

* The incident with the Pope seemed to misfire from the word go and the Apollo company bombarded the press with corrections. Sadly all this was to no avail with the death of the Pope on 20 July. I wonder, did his successor, Pope Pius X, take over pedalling the Apollo? Or was it cast out? The following letter, headed 'The Pope and Apollo', was published in *Musical Opinion* for July 1903:

> Sir, – On June 7th, our Mr C. H. Wagener, director general of the Apollo Companies (New York, Boston, Chicago and London) in conjunction with Mr Spencer Lorraine (managing director of the Apollo Co., London) had a private audience with his holiness Pope Leo the Thirteenth, in his apartment at the Vatican, on which occasion an Apollo attached to a Melville Clark piano was played before his holiness and a number of church dignitaries. The Pope expressed himself delighted with the instrument, pronouncing it to be 'molto miracoloso'. The Apollo and the Melville Clark piano remained in the private apartment of his holiness, being his property. The Apollo is the only piano player which has been played before his holiness, and is the only instrument in his apartments at the Vatican.
>
> This audience has been reported throughout the world, and we find that in some papers a mistake was made, and *The Daily Chronicle* had an article headed 'The Pope and the Pianola'; through some mistake of the correspondent in Rome, the word 'Pianola' being substituted for 'Apollo'.
>
> We have tried our best to rectify this matter, and the press have taken due notice of it. At the same time we fear that some careless dealer might take advantage, showing *The Daily Chronicle* report as it was first reported, thereby causing us damage and annoyance. We therefore feel bound, through the columns of *Musical Opinion and Music Trade Review*, to notify the music trade at large of this mistake; and, in case the question should arise, we should be pleased if this letter would be shown to any intending purchaser and a request made to them to ask us for further information.
>
> Yours etc.,
> THE APOLLO CO. (LIM.).

119 Regent Street, June 13, 1903.

anti-piano-player puritans are always horrified at the substitution of mechanism for the hand of the performer; they miss 'the human touch'. Well, string instruments have only become as expressive as they are in virtue of this substitution. Man first of all replaced the finger-tips by a plectrum; then he elongated his fingers, and softened the pressure of them, by means of a bow. The history of the best of the single instruments – the pianoforte – is the record of an incessant piling up of mechanism. After all, what is a pianoforte, in essence, but a dulcimer? Why all this elaborate mechanism for the mere striking of a piece of wire? Why not be satisfied with a little hammer held in the hand? Simply because the complicated mechanism of the pianoforte hits the wires better than the hand could do – is, in fact, an intensification of the human hand, as the wheel and the gun are intensifications of the human leg and arm. The anti-piano-player pianist is, in fact, a million removes from mere nature; he would be helpless without the huge box of mechanical tricks in front of him. In decency and reason, then, he ought to be less vehement against the mechanical piano-player.

Another playful little dodge of the anti-piano-player extremist is to doubt whether anyone who commends 'mechanical instruments' can be a real musician. That also one can face quite cheerfully. If to praise the piano-player is to work one's own damnation, one has at least the consolation of being damned in excellent company. Perhaps I ought not to drag in the names of mere composers – such as Strauss, Grieg, Elgar, Scriabine, Max Bruch, Fauré, Humperdinck, Mascagni, Max Reger, Saint-Saëns, Max Schillings, Balakirev, Debussy, Glazounov, Liapounov, Rimsky-Korsakov and Sinding who have sung the praises of one or other of these instruments. Their evidence may be tainted; these abandoned fellows, together with conductors like Nikisch, Colonne, Chevillard, Landon Ronald and Sir Henry Wood, may also be, or have been when they were alive, in the pay of 'the makers'. But when we are told, especially by amateur pianists, that the piano-player is a soulless machine that no self-respecting musician would be seen sitting down to, we may remind them that some of the warmest commendations of it have come from pianists of the front rank, such as Busoni, Harold Bauer, d'Albert, Backhaus, Carreño, Dohnanyi, Arthur Friedheim, Gabrilowitsch, Mark Hambourg, Josef Hofmann, Frederic Lamond, Wanda Landowska, Pugno, Sauer, Stavenhagen, Szanto, Rosenthal and Leschetizki. Many people will remember, again, a concert at Queen's Hall in 1912, at which the London Symphony Orchestra, conducted by Nikisch, accompanied Mr Easthope Martin in the Grieg Concerto, Mr Martin playing the solo part on a piano-player, while later Miss Elena Gerhardt sang some songs to the accompaniment of the maligned 'mechanical instrument'. In 1913 a similar concert was given in Paris with Chevillard, the Lamoureux Orchestra and a piano-player. It is evident, then, that whatever the average amateur or teacher may think of the piano-player, it is taken seriously enough by the composers, pianists, conductors and singers who stand at the head of their profession.

While the player piano became an accepted musical interpreter, its predecessor the barrel piano or street piano, dubbed so erroneously by contemporary writers as the 'piano-organ', came in for some pretty adroit abuse from the public who sought to eradicate the street musician. For him, with his portable piano or donkey-cart piano, or, in poorer times, himself between the shafts, the piano was a means of earning a living and for those within earshot it was often anathema.

INTRODUCTION

In a manner strangely reminiscent of that adopted today (more justifiably, I hasten to add) to improve what we prosaically call 'the quality of life', there were many attempts to rid our streets of these things. *Musical Opinion* of June 1902 reported as follows:

> *The Medical Press and Circular* is attempting to lead an outcry against the piano organ. It pictures the agony which the 'damnable iteration' of these music hall melodies inflicts upon nervous and sick people, and it does so with the aim of having the Italian and his music excluded from holiday resorts where invalids chiefly congregate. The matter has our hearty sympathy. But it is not the invalids alone who have to be considered. Among the furniture of the street piano there is sometimes an 'encradled baby'. Fancy the unkind fate which condemns an unhappy infant to listen at close range to the same tunes, from street to street and from day to day! We should say that this torture is a fitting case for the Prevention of Cruelty to Children.

By comparison, only a few months earlier* the same magazine was asserting on the one hand how good the player piano was for business, while at the same time questioning, no doubt quite rightly, the value of such an instrument to the genuine keyboard artist:

> *The Chicago Indicator* says that there can be no doubt that the 'piano players' have given a fillip to business in the more expensive pianos. The self-player absolutely calls for a good instrument, otherwise the beautiful tones which it makes possible are marred. In the opinion of experienced men in the trade the vogue of the self-player will last here about five years; not more unless their price is considerably reduced. At present it is only the rich – who are usually the least talented – who can afford self-players. That the self-player will ever commend itself to the musician is doubtful. Even the poorest player would rather make his music for himself than rely on mechanical means; although, of course, the genuine musician is not always a pianist, and must derive advantage from hearing the classics played in faultless style.

A mere dozen years later, Europe was in the grips of a war which, even in the light of subsequent conflicts, remains the bloodiest and toughest war ever fought. Men, among them piano makers, craftsmen of the finest calling, were laid waste on a frightful scale. Again, *Musical Opinion* had something to say about its effect on the 'piano-organ' in its issue for April 1917:

> A correspondent asks: 'Have you noticed the effect of the war on the piano-organ man?' Yes, I have noticed it: he is conspicuous by his absence from the streets. But there is no doubt that he has given a good account of himself, fighting for one or other of the allies. It is (for us) a pity that he was not allowed to take his organ with him! . . . I must confess that I had some affection for the man and his instrument, if only for the undoubted pleasure given to many people and children, these latter being known often to follow an organ for long distances to hear it once again. In many of the humbler streets, this was the only music they heard from one year's end to another, and indeed it was often better music than the German band monstrosities, with their clarinets, double basses and

---

* *Musical Opinion*, January 1902.

female cornet players. The gramophone has no doubt found its way into many a home that could not afford to buy a piano or an organ; and, if only a mouthorgan, it encourages the music trade. So we need not grumble.

Woven between the pneumatic player of the masses and the Italian street grinder of the piano-organ, there was the reproducing piano, the domestic or drawing-room barrel piano, and the barrel-and-finger piano – all instruments which were, in the true sense of the words, 'self-acting'.

And so this book relates the story of the self-acting piano. Probably one's first reaction to the reading of that as a title, unless aware of the proper and intended meaning, is to visualise some supernatural or magical powers bestowed upon that 'household god', as Charles Dickens referred to it, or to picture some electronic marvel coupled to a computer in a broadcasting studio. Or, most probably, to consider the statement carefully, admit confusion to surface, and remain unimpressed and none the wiser.

In truth, supernatural or magical properties there could well be, for with the reproducing piano you can have a long-since departed maestro of the keyboard emerge before your very ears and play your own piano for you. As for computers and electronics, well, this is the very latest player piano technology which is with us in an age becoming increasingly dominated by the micro-processor and its heart, the silicon chip. Oh, what wonders could player-piano man have created had he had the magical sliver of silicon a century ago! Although self-acting pianos existed at the time of Chopin, the technology had yet to be perfected whereby he might have been able to record his memorable performances for us to cherish today.

Perhaps it is my last postulated reaction which is the best one – the clear, unfettered mind of he who knows not the player piano from a motorised lawnmower, save that one probably makes a more melodious sound than the other.

But if I qualify the description of 'self-acting piano' by adding the word 'pianola' or 'pianola piano', then perhaps my reader may be a little wiser. The fact is that 'pianola' is a trade name registered by one maker of these instruments. However, in the same way that 'meccano' has come to be accepted as a word in the dictionary, having started life in a like fashion, so has Aeolian's coined name 'pianola' come to mean the genus player piano. I shall not fight the case further, only urge my reader never to refer to his player piano as a 'pianola' unless it bears that name on the keyboard fall. Reason? Well, your pianola could be by Angelus, which to the player piano expert is rather like saying that you have a Dutch street organ made in Germany, or a Hoover vacuum cleaner made by Electrolux.

Now that I have, I hope, established that this book is something to do with player pianos, I wonder just how many today have seen one, let alone enjoyed pedalling through a roll of music. Even fewer have ever sat back and marvelled at the faithful performance of a reproducing piano playing music recorded in perforated paper by a great pianist of the past whose technique and talent have gone with him to the grave. Back to the supernatural again, for we can bring back his ghost!

The first player piano I ever saw was when I was at a very impressionable age. As a child I could not imagine that it was a real piano and I recall vividly concluding that it must be a synthetic instrument and thus something to be avoided. As its keys went down by themselves, it must be an evil instrument and so, in fear, I fled. My next encounter was with a superb reproducing piano in a stately old mansion near where I lived as a schoolboy. This played through open French windows to numerous croquet parties on the lawn. I used to

INTRODUCTION

lurk unseen in the hedgerow marvelling at the skill of that wonderful piano which could play Chopin with such panache and accuracy. Then one stormy night that fine old house took fire and I watched, heart pounding, as the magic piano died in the flames.

The barrel piano is a different instrument entirely. Purely mechanical in operation, the simple street piano is very basic: no great subtlety of pneumatic valves went into its making. Barrel pianos could still be heard in their multitudes in London right up to the 1950s and as a youngster I recall very many of them. My father, who, in his later years, was a writer and dramatic critic and thus a professional theatre-goer, occasionally took me with him to theatreland, as that area of the West End is dubbed. One particular street musician could always be found in those courts off Charing Cross Road close to where, in another age, the young Mozart lodged above a barber's shop. This man's handle-operated piano used to dispense a diet of *Lambeth Walk*, *I do like to be beside the Seaside* and other, similar ditties, all at the same volume of sound and brisk tempo. My father explained how these men could be found in the small hours pushing their instruments all the way back to Saffron Hill near Farringdon – no mean walk for an unencumbered athlete, let alone a wheezy middle-aged or old man with an ungainly wooden piano on two cart wheels.

The lowest point in the popularity of the player piano was probably reached ten or so years ago. However, in more recent times, interest in the instrument has increased and they are now sought after not only by collectors and enthusiasts but also by a growing number of people who, tired of piped entertainment and the modern environment with all its undesirable trappings, seek respite in music and ownership of a piano.

The current generation, with its general hatred of preservation, has deprived us of countless pianos and many a splendid instrument has ended its days prematurely on a bonfire, or been wantonly broken up in one of those demented and pointless piano-smashing competitions. Such public demonstrations of destructiveness, accompanied by dancing and chanting, are reminiscent of the sacrificial ceremonies of primitive tribes and seem an anachronism in twentieth-century England. However, it is these people who grow up to extend their destructive tendencies to fine buildings and the countryside and thus they are the very creators of the tasteless, characterless city environments which engender in sane people a greater than ever need to seek salvation in the arts of better years.

Because today everything which savours of quiet pleasure tends to be termed 'escapism', he who seeks to enjoy music in his own home is probably thought unusual, but these conditions have insidiously spread a love of music to an ever-widening circle of ordinary people who suddenly think that they would like to own a piano. Possibly the long-term effects of the pianola of the twenties still remain with them in that they were products of the generation which was never taught to play; perhaps they can play but, as in my own case, 'just hate the sound of themselves practising'. It is this band of devotees who are calling for the ultimate in high-fidelity – the sound of a real piano in their homes.

When it comes to the interpretation of music using means other than musical skill, it is only in the mechanical musical instrument that one may determine to one's own satisfaction the speed or tempo of the performance. With the accepted means of producing music in the home – the gramophone or tape recorder – any variation in speed destroys pitch and an attempt to continuously vary the tempo makes it quite impossible to enjoy the music. How often have we criticised a work by saying to ourselves 'That section should be played slower.' The mechanical musical instrument, on the other hand, possesses true and, to all intents and purposes, inviolate pitch. The speed at which the music is played upon such a machine and the number of variations in tempo during the performance have no effect whatsoever on the pitch of the sound. It is this characteristic which makes possible a different and personalised rendition of a music roll with every performance and enables the player performer to achieve the utmost involvement with his music rolls and the greatest satisfaction from his playing.

History is a dull subject usually, but the story of the evolution of the mechanical piano within which the player piano and the barrel piano are the star performers is rather interesting and thus I have set this out briefly. I have dealt at length with the development of the barrel piano and the pneumatic piano and described their actions in detail because these points need to be known and understood if the owner or restorer of these instruments is to become anything of an expert.

BOHRER'S "AUTOMATIC" HAND GUIDE.
(PATENTED.)

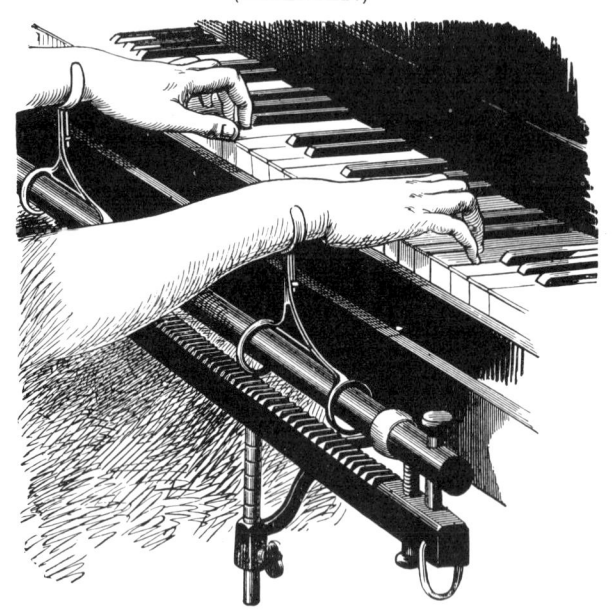

Price Two Guineas.

From the Directorium of the Conservatory of Leipzig.

The Directorium and the College of Professors of the Conservatory of Music at Leipzig have examined the "Automatic Piano Hand Guide," invented by Mr. Wm. Bohrer, of Montreal, Canada, and testify that it is a most ingenious invention, being not a mere assistance to inattention and absence of mind on the part of the pupil, but a most excellent means to compel careful study. It will also prove very useful to beginners on the pianoforte.

It will, therefore, be introduced in the Royal Conservatory of Music at Leipzig, there being nothing in the action of this Guide, or in the principle upon which it is constructed, to prevent such introduction.

CHAPTER 1

The Rise and Fall of the Automatic Piano

Long before the first pianoforte was made, the art of programming music for automatic playing was fairly well developed. The pinned wooden barrel represented the highest development of the art and its use and capabilities were understood at least as early as the eighth century AD. And the oldest surviving barrel organ still in playing condition is dated 1502.* So when Christofori of Florence built his first *gravicembalo col piano e forte* in about 1709 the technique for automatic playing was already in existence. Indeed, if one delves further into the history of the piano, we find a Dutch-made instrument constructed a century before that of the Italian. This had small hammers attached to the keys, but no dampers. This was said to have been made for a French nobleman and was probably no more than an isolated example of experimental work. And a rare manuscript in the Bibliothèque Nationale in Paris appears to describe an instrument of the pianoforte type, that is to say with hammers to strike the strings. This is dated 1430, an incredible three centuries before Christofori made his first instrument and became the accredited inventor. Yet even as early as this the pinned barrel, the pinned wheel and similar if more primitive means of mechanical playing were understood. The piano thus grew up in an era when it was virtually inevitable that sooner or later it would receive the same treatment as the pipe organ and become capable of automatic playing.

There was, of course, nothing new about stringed instruments and the dulcimer was mentioned in literature as early as *circa* 1400 and the virginal was well established by the sixteenth century. The couched harp or spinet was developed in the seventeenth and eighteenth centuries. These early string instruments featured just one string to each note. The first application of the pinned barrel to their playing seems to have come at about the beginning of the seventeenth century. A famous maker of musical automata, Samuel Bidermann, was making spinets in Augsburg which could be played either by a pinned wooden barrel or from a keyboard. Marin Mersenne (1588–1648) wrote in the year 1636:

> One can still recall in our time the invention of drums or barrels employed to play several pieces of music on spinets without the use of the hand, for the Germans are so ingenious that they make them play more than fifty different pieces by means of several springs which, when set in motion, ballets with several figures leap and move to the rhythm of the songs without any need to touch the instrument after having wound the spring.

Mersenne, one concludes, had observed such instruments but had not entirely understood the operation or principle of pinning tunes on barrels: fifty tunes probably refers more to the

---
* See Ord-Hume, *Barrel Organ*.

scope of an individual tune-pinner's repertoire than the number of sets of pins he could hammer into a small barrel.

Erhard Weigel (1625–95) asserted some sixty years later of such instruments of automatic music: '. . . especially at Nahe-Kussen near Augsburg, desks, chests and all kinds of decorative cabinetwork are made and sent far and wide throughout the whole world.'

The pre-eminence of Augsburg at so early a date is not difficult to explain. The principal seat of commerce in southern Germany, it was a place where wealthy merchants and their masters met and could expand cultural ties between the states of Germany. It thus enjoyed a rich trade in artefacts such as watches, jewellery, instruments and musical automata.

The Bidermann family was closely involved in the making of musical automata including automatic spinets and there is evidence that the family co-operated with other members of automaton-making families such as the Langenbuchers and the Runggels.* Samuel Bidermann was born at Ulm in 1540 and died in Augsburg in 1622. He was a renowned organ builder and maker of spinets known as *ottavinos* – clockwork-driven, automatically-played instruments. After his death his work was continued by his sons, Samuel the younger (1600 until at least 1653) and Daniel (1603–63).

It is related that amongst the fine collection of musical instruments left by Henry VIII was such a device. The item is described in detail in the catalogue prepared at the time of his death in 1547. Some doubt as to its classification must have existed, for it is included amongst the 'virgynalles' and is listed as being:

Item. An Instrumente that goethe with a whele without playinge uppon, of woode vernisshed yellowe and painted blewe with vi round plates of siluer pounced with anticke garnisshed with an edge of copper and guilte.

Whether it was at this time a unique specimen or merely the representative of a class can never be discovered, but it was clearly a barrel instrument.

A very early instrument of the mechanical spinet type is now in the collection of Lord Howard de Walden at Dean Castle, Kilmarnock. This was restored to playing condition in 1957 by Fritz Spiegl (to whom I am grateful for these notes) in collaboration with Roger Fisk and John Sebastian Morley. There is a distinct possibility that this is the instrument which belonged to King Henry VIII, or was at least made by the same craftsman. It corresponds in almost every detail with the description given in the catalogue of the musical instrument owned by Henry VIII, even down to the fact that there are six silver medallions decorated with painted figures. The costumes worn by these figures suggest Flemish origin and, indeed, the Keeper of Henry VIII's musical instruments was Flemish.

There is a possibility that a mechanical instrument of this type was in fact used by Shakespeare in an early performance of *Cymbeline*. In the cave scene (Act IV, Scene 2) one may well have been used to accompany the famous dirge 'Fear no more the heat of the sun'. This must originally have been sung but, in the text as we have it, Imogen's brother Arviragus says of himself and his brother Guiderius, 'And let us, Polydore, though now our voices have got the mannish crack, sing him to the ground', implying that their voices have broken and so they are unable to sing. Perhaps the mechanical instrument was thus

---

* See 'The Bidermann-Langenbucher Lawsuit' by Eva Groiss in *Music & Automata*, Spring, 1980, pp. 10–12.

introduced because the boy actors' voices broke and the dirge had to be spoken whilst the instrument provided the solemn music called for in the stage direction. Belarius says: 'My ingenious instrument! Hark, Polydore, it sounds! But what occasion hath Cadwal now to give it motion? Hark!'

Although made more than three and a half centuries ago, a number of these instruments survive to this day – and some of them are still in playing condition. The surviving examples include one, which is undated, in the Germanisches Nationalmuseum in Nuremberg. This is from the collection of Dr Rück and bears all the characteristics of Bidermann instruments. Dr van der Meer believes it to be the work of Bidermann Junior, dating from about 1640.

A second is dated 1606 and is in the Fürstlich Oettingen-Wallenstein'sche Bibliothek und Kunstsammlungen at Schloss Harburg near Donauwörth which is near Augsburg. This is signed Joannes Bidermann MDCVI on the jackrail. A third dates from 1627 and is in the Institute for Scientific Research on the Theatre and Music, Leningrad. This is signed Samuel Biderman Augusta,* 1627. This has a compass of three octaves, F–f, and 37 keys. In the same collection is a second, undated, specimen playing three octaves and a sixth, E–c, 45 keys.

A 45-key automatic spinet with a short-octave C–c compass is in the Schlesisches Museum, Breslau. The barrel is pinned with six tunes, the titles of which are written on a label beginning with 'a joyful procession announced by the blowing of the trumpeter (by Jr. Kay, May; the procession held in Nuremberg). This no doubt refers to the reception of the Emperor Matthias by the city of Nuremberg in the year 1612, and this suggests that the instrument was made shortly after 1612 and was made by Samuel Bidermann the elder. It bears a printed label reading *Samuel Bidermann, Instrumentmacher, Augsburg.*

The Kunsthistorisches Museum in Vienna has an instrument which bears this selfsame label. It is reputed to date from *c.* 1625–30 and is thus probably the work of Bidermann Junior. This museum has another undated automatic spinet claimed to date from the second half of the sixteenth century. This has a C–c four-octave compass and plays six tunes which are transcribed in Schlosser. Originally in the Amras collection until 1880, this has four labels each reading *Samuel Biderman, Instrumentmacher in Augsburg.*

The signature *Samuel Biderman Augusta*† appears again on a spinet in a case which was in the Old Savoye Collection, Paris, and which is thought to be the same one which is now in the Tagger collection in Paris. This has a compass described as 'two-octaves and eight notes'.‡

An unsigned and undated instrument also exists in the collection of Gustav Adolf in Uppsala. This was acquired by the City Council of Augsburg in 1632 from Philip Hainhofer and presented to the King of Sweden. Although unhappily a victim of the Second World War, mention should be made of an instrument in the Carolino Augusteum Museum, Salzburg, which, according to descriptions, must have strongly resembled Bidermann workmanship.

It will be observed that the clockwork spinet exists in three distinct forms: as a barrel-and-finger instrument for either automatic or manual playing, as a mechanical

---

* Biderman spelled his name sometimes with one 'n', other times with two. See also 'The Bidermann-Langenbucher Lawsuit' by Eva Groiss in *Music & Automata*, Vol. 1, pp. 10–12.

† *Augusta* is the Latin name for Augsburg. The city took its name from the Roman Emperor Augustus, who set up a Roman colony named Augusta Vindelicorum in about 14 BC.

‡ Donald H. Boalch, *Makers of the Harpsichord and Clavichord, 1440–1840.*

instrument on its own, and as a mechanical instrument operated by a clock or at will in the same manner as a clockwork table organ.

Both the specimen in the Silesian Museum, Breslau, which we shall identify as Item 1, and the specimen in the Kunsthistorisches Museum, Vienna, which we shall call Item 2, are square virginals of normal size with folding front keyboard fall and compartments to the left and right. The Ruck specimen in the Germanisches Nationalmuseum, Nuremberg, which we shall call Item 3, is an octave virginal. Item 1 has a richly inlaid ebony case, the inside of the lid being decorated with a painting of Apollo and the nine Muses. Written on the wood above the printed label is the date 1651, which probably denotes the date of a repair. Item 2 also has an ebony case inlaid with different woods. A full description of this is printed in Schlosser. This instrument has a veneered and inlaid stand with two small drawers left and right. The case of Item 3 is also of veneered ebony and stands on four feet fixed to the underside. The case slopes upwards towards the back. The sides are panelled with incised mouldings and the front panel hinges downwards, serving as the key-fall lid. The top of the case is hinged and bears a green velvet panel with a gold border. On the right is a nest of drawers lined with red silk. Dr van der Meer attributes this to having been made in Nahe-Kussen and on the front of the key-fall lid are the emblems of Augsburg. In the inside of the lid is a mirror (not original) with the arms and motto enclosed in a moulded frame. Oil paintings on wood panels are set to the right and left of the mirror; that on the left being of a woman and that to the right the portrait of a man. They are painted in the style of Anton van Dijcks. In all three instruments, the whole casing can be lifted up and off the mechanism.

In all three, the soundboard is of pine glued to a frame which stands on four short legs on the case bottom. The soundboard displays flowers and fruit painted in water-colour (in the case of Item 2 there is also a scroll). Delicate ornament in fine line engraving surrounds the central rosette and runs parallel to the edge bridges and the row of action jacks in Item 3 and to the row of pins in Item 2. The geometrical rosettes have a herringbone pattern. The base stands on supporting mouldings, partly of hornbeam wood, the right-hand table (the left-hand table on Item 1) as well as the soundboard being decorated with mouldings. The action jacks pass through the soundboard in a special guide.

By removing the soundboard with bridges and jacks as one unit, the instrument can be operated from its barrel, the keyboard remaining separately in the case.

The naturals of the keyboard are overlaid with ivory (in the case of Item 2 not original), the sharps being of black-stained pear wood with ebony veneer. The compass of Item 1 and Item 2 is $C/E-c^3$; that of Item 3, the octave instrument, $c/e-c^3$ without d^3.

All three instruments have a wooden barrel for the automatic mechanism. These bear the characteristic ruling and dividing practised by the Bidermanns, the surface of the barrel being scored laterally and circumferentially to produce a grid of small squares. Each of these squares is divided between the six tunes of Items 1 and 2 and the four of Item 3. Vertical markings show the lengths of four crochets and the divisions numbered around the circumference in indian ink. The pins of the quavers and the repeated crochets are of steel whilst those of the shorter notes are of brass, the longer values having brass pins bent over into a hooked shape.

In all three instruments, a spring in a brass spring barrel drives the movement. Winding is by catgut fusee and the actual gear train differs between the instruments.

The six compositions on the barrel of Item 1 are given in Protz; the six on Item 2 in Nettl and Schlosser. The four pieces of Item 3 have been transcribed by Dr van der Meer.

I mentioned that there was some evidence of collaboration between the Bidermanns and other makers of automata. One maker with whom joint work appears to have been created was Matthäus Runggel, also of Augsburg. Runggel is known for several pieces, perhaps the most interesting and complete of which is the automaton clock known as *Der Hottentottentanz* (Dance of the Hottentots) which is in the Staatliche Mathematisches und Physics museum in Dresden. This is described in *Barrel Organ** and is unusual in that it incorporates a clockwork-driven barrel organ as well as a spinet action, both having the same compass of 16 notes. This is pictured in Bassermann-Jordan.† This selfsame feature of a coupled barrel organ and spinet, again of 16 notes, appears in an unsigned Augsburg musical clock now in Switzerland and illustrated in Chapuis's *Automata*.‡ This piece includes a rotating stage upon which small automaton figures gyrate and Chapuis describes in detail the many features of this piece, which include a most interesting and unusual method of moving the central figure on the principle which came later to be known as the Roskopf watch barrel.

In 1979, a mechanism described as 'constructed by Rungel of Augsburg' was sold by auction in Geneva.§ This is described in the sale catalogue as having both spinet and organ mechanism plus a clock, although the clock is not to be seen in the illustration. Sadly, one of the two pictures illustrating this particular lot is taken from Chapuis and is thus not of the same instrument. Both mechanisms, though, share a strong family resemblance.

Bearing a strong likeness to these two pieces, both as regards the mechanism and the external appearance, is a small temple-like musical clock in the Nationaal Museum van Speelklok tot Pierement in Utrecht (see Plate 5). This piece bears the monogram of Viet Langenbucher which is particularly interesting since the style and construction of the barrel and the shape of its pins are in accordance with those of Bidermann. Viet Langenbucher's monogram is a large letter V to the right-hand stroke of which is attached a slightly smaller letter B. The apex of the V is extended rightwards to underscore the letter B. Again this piece has 16 notes and plays three tunes on a small rectangular spinet.¶

All of these instruments pluck their strings with properly contrived plectra. A variation on the clockwork spinet was the harp clock (*Harfenuhr*) or dulcimer clock in which the strings, instead of being plucked, were struck by small hammers. The wooden-framed, lightly-strung dulcimer was arranged vertically behind the clockwork and the hammer mechanism was directly comparable to that used in the carillon clock and its music was pinned to a barrel in the same way.

Essentially an adjunct to the clock and so far not found on its own as an automatic musical instrument, the harp or dulcimer clock was made in Germany and also in the Low Countries more or less contemporaneously with its more popular cousin, the flute-playing clock. Its period appears to have been from the first half of the eighteenth century through to the middle of the nineteenth century. Even so, very few examples survive, no doubt because of the fact that they needed fairly constant retuning and thus were probably considered by their owners to be more trouble than they were worth. They also had the disadvantage that, as with the flute-playing clock, they were frequently very tall and could only stand in a room with a high ceiling: no use in the modern home with its 8-foot-high plasterboard.

---

* pp. 71–2.
† *Uhren*, p. 166.
‡ pp. 91–4, figures 88–98.
§ Galerie d'Horlogerie Ancienne, Vente aux Enchères XIII, 6 October, 1979, lot number 137.
¶ See illustration in *Music & Automata*, Spring, 1983, p. 13.

PIANOLA

The mechanical keyboard instrument stemmed as we have seen from the pipe barrel organ and the earliest surviving mechanical organ seems to date from the late fifteenth or early sixteenth century. The mechanical organ at Salzburg was made in 1502 and the barrel organ really came into its own in the first half of the eighteenth century, when it was developed into an instrument suitable for the mechanical production of music to accompany hymns and chants in church.

MECHANICAL NOTATION

The knack of transcribing music from ordinary notation into a forest of short, thick pins on a wooden barrel was described by The Rev. Father Engramelle of Paris during the latter half of the eighteenth century and, before him, by Athanasius Kircher. The first written words on the subject can be said to be those of an Oxford doctor of medicine at the beginning of the seventeenth century – Robert Fludd, alias de Fluctibus – who described four different types of cylinder in his book *De Naturae Simia*. Contemporary with Fludd, a French engineer, Salomon de Caus, illustrated part of his book *Les Raisons des Forces Mouvantes* with a drawing of a cylinder pinned with the first six bars of a madrigal by Alessandro Striggio (1535–90).

In the eighteenth century several inventors, among them Johann Friedrich Unger, sought to make a machine which could aid the technique of pinning cylinders or barrels (see Chapter 11). These devices were intended to record the fingering of a performer on a keyboard to produce something which could be used as a pattern for pinning. This technique subsequently came to be called 'melography'. At a much later epoch, melography came to be used not just for the barrel type of musical programme but for the later developments of punched-card and paper music. The work of Charles Abdank and, separately, Jules Carpentier, which made this goal a possibility at the end of the last century, is well documented.

Music set on a barrel is transcribed in a notation virtually at right-angles to that of printed

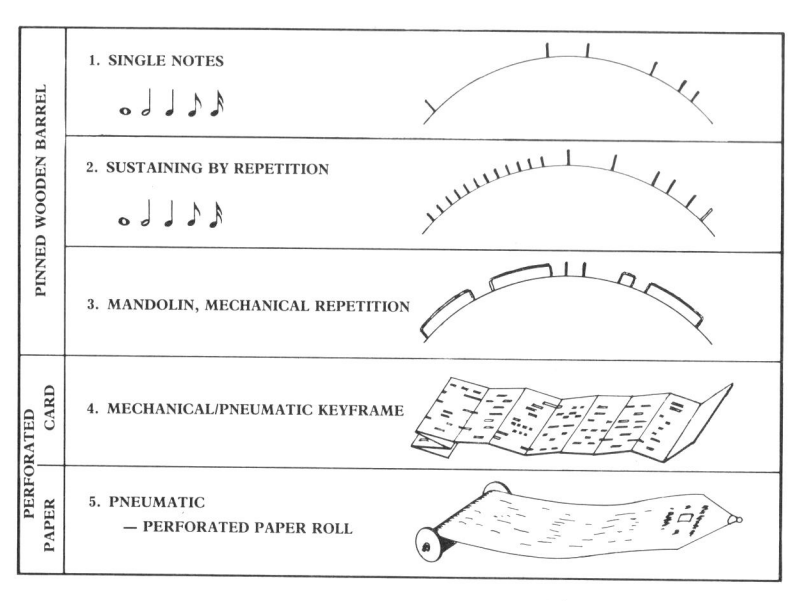

Fig. 1
Different types of mechanical music notation. The first three show styles of operation using a mechanical key raised and lowered by pins or bridges in a rotating wooden barrel. The fourth one shows a perforated cardboard programme used to operate spring-loaded keys which may either operate a mechanical or a pneumatic servo action. The fifth style shows perforated paper used as a sliding valve in a purely pneumatic system.

music. The length of the music, as measured by the number of bars, becomes the length of the piece of paper. The bars thus run horizontally across the paper, and the various notes and their lengths are represented vertically. To set a piece of music of, say, forty bars length on to a barrel, the circumference of the barrel is taken as the length of the paper pattern. This length is then subdivided into forty horizontal spaces. The paper is then subdivided again, this time vertically and at a spacing equal to that of the fingers or keys of the playing mechanism. This grid is now marked in accordance with the musical notation, after which it is stuck to the barrel and the pins or bridges (in the case of an organ) inserted. In practice, more than one tune is pinned to each barrel, and therefore the paper is then marked over with different tunes, each one being displaced laterally a given distance equal to the lateral shift of the barrel needed to bring another set of tune pins under the keyframe.

Again, once the ruled paper pattern has been created, it can be used as a master for marking similar pieces of paper, either by 'pricking' the location of each pin or by lithography, only the position of the musical notes being transferred, not the redundant ground ruling.

The technical difficulties in reproducing in any way faithfully the tones and colours of stringed keyboard instruments by mechanical means were far greater than those needed to achieve the same ends for the mechanical organ. When in 1817 Flight & Robson of London completed their remarkable Apollonicon organ, they were confident in proclaiming that it could perform with a degree of perfection at least equal to that of an accomplished performer. This organ was equipped with sets of barrels which played whole overtures and lengthy operatic selections. Many great organists also performed on this manual and self-acting instrument, which was provided with no fewer than five separate co-lateral consoles. Later rebuilt on an even larger programme with six separate keyboard consoles, the Apollonicon always included in its performances a popular operatic overture performed from its three barrels. These were claimed by many to be note-perfect when compared with the orchestral scores.*

An acceptably high degree of perfection from the barrel-programmed pipe organ had thus become a practical reality by the time Queen Victoria came to the throne. European makers such as Blessing, Welte, Kaufmann and others took the art to a very high level during this period.

Yet still, at this time, the mechanical piano was labouring away, trying hard to do something to offset its uncompromising tone and its unworthiness to any claim towards perfection of interpretation or purity of tone. It could not be a pianoforte – only a mechanical string-hammerer. Sophistication and subtlety did not come into it.

Devices were invented in an attempt to improve the quality of its performance. These, in being reliant on the state of the musical engineering of the time, tended to be of indifferent effect, some working to a greater or, more frequently, lesser extent. Most suffered the defects of incorrect theory and inherent impracticability.

The main drawback hinged on nothing more difficult to appreciate than the basic dynamics of the barrel organ versus the barrel-playing piano. With the barrel organ, all the barrel pins had to do was to lift a free-pivoting key, depress a light wooden sticker and open a small wooden pallet in the windchest. The sound was made by the passage of wind through an organ pipe connected by a windway to the opened pallet.

* The history of the Apollonicon is related in considerable detail in *Barrel Organ* by Ord-Hume.

PIANOLA

The barrel-operated piano, however, asked considerably more from its variant of the barrel organ mechanism. It was necessary for the musical strings to be struck with comparatively considerable power to produce the musical sound and this had to be accomplished through the interaction of the barrel pins and a key linkage. Appreciably more force was needed to work a piano compared with that needed to play an organ.

STREET MUSIC AND ITS LEGACY

At the more mundane end of the spectrum, the barrel piano and the barrel organ merged into a sort of audible blur as far as the general public were concerned. The barrel organ was part and parcel of the street scene. But just what was meant by the term 'barrel organ'?

The words 'barrel organ' represent perhaps the largest misnomer in the whole field of mechanical music, for a barrel organ is a pipe instrument – a real organ – played with a wooden barrel studded with pins instead of with a keyboard. But, to all and sundry, a barrel organ was a large box on a handcart. A swarthy character would stand beside it, turning steadily at a handle emerging from its front. From the box would come popular honky-tonk piano music in a seemingly endless flow. A colourfully dressed monkey would often be seen sitting on top of the box holding a hat out to passers-by who would be expected to drop in their small change in appreciation of the music. The man who turned the handle was called the organ-grinder, sometimes grinder for short, and the whole story would be further confused by the introduction of another name for the instrument – a hurdy-gurdy. Now the

Fig. 2
When Mrs O. F. Walton wrote her 19th century religious novel *Christie's Old Organ*, her story centred on a poor street musician and his small boy benefactor. The instrument which was the centre of the story was a Hicks-style street piano as seen in this illustration from the original novel.

hurdy-gurdy was a stringed instrument in the form of a violin played by the rotation of a rosin-coated wheel. The strings droned continuously and the performer would make his music by playing on a little keyboard on the side of the belly of the instrument. The keys operated tangents which stopped off the strings, so altering their pitch.

What, then, was that instrument which once played such a part in town life and which may still be seen today as a charity fund earner? Barrel organ? Hurdy-gurdy? It was, in fact, a *street piano*. A large wooden barrel, resplendent with thick pins like headless nails and similar to that found in the real pipe barrel organ, was turned by a worm gear on a handle and, as it went round, the pins engaged in sprung hammers which, when drawn back by the pin, would be let loose to fly forward and strike tuned strings stretched across a soundboard in a piano frame.

The street piano on its handcart, sometimes with shafts for a donkey to provide forward power, was a development of a much smaller, portable street piano which first appeared during the early years of the nineteenth century. This instrument was carried by a strap which passed around the operator's shoulder, and steadied on a single pole protruding from its base as he played it.

In 1793, a Londoner named Charles Clagget published a little booklet in which he described his Aiuton or ever-tuned organ which played on a series of special tuning-forks. Similar in concept to the Dulcitone invented by the Scotsman Machals and manufactured and sold by him in various styles between the years 1910 and 1936, Clagget's Aiuton would also be played by a barrel like a barrel organ. Its inventor thought that it might replace both piano and organ. It didn't and no example is known.*

Since the earliest times, attempts had been made to play the piano by using some sort of frame or set of mechanical fingers which could be used to strike the piano's keys. The pinned barrel, though, emerged as the most practical solution at this stage of development. The direct association of the barrel and the keyboard, however, was not the answer to improving quality of tone.

An item appeared in *Musical Opinion* for April 1916 under the heading 'Early Mechanical Pianofortes'. This stated:

> The following advertisement appeared in *The Times* a century since, – viz, Wednesday March 6th, 1816, '*A Newly Invented Musical Instrument.* – Two handsome cabinet pianofortes, that play themselves in a most brilliant and correct style all the fashionable country dances, waltzes, reels, etc., one of which will be parted with on reasonable terms. Would particularly suit a foreign market, as a great curiosity. Apply to A.B. 82 Newgate St.'

An early mechanical piano was that produced in about 1820–5 by Clementi, Collard & Co, the musical instrument makers, in London. Muzio Clementi was born in Rome in 1752 and was a many-sided man. Infant prodigy, keyboard virtuoso, he is known for his sonatas for piano and harpsichord. He came to England at the age of fourteen and was a concert performer until he was almost sixty, at which point he abandoned public performances, joined the London firm of Longman & Broderip and took to the manufacture of musical instruments, among them some fine church and domestic barrel pipe organs. Upon the

---

* A single copy of Clagget's booklet on his Aiuton and other of his instruments is known to exist. Formerly in the Galpin collection and now in the British Museum, this was reproduced in facsimile in *The Music Box*, Volume 4, pp. 498–509.

dissolution of that firm, he manufactured under his own name until he teamed up with Collard. As well as making barrel pipe organs and ordinary pianofortes, he made the 'Self-Acting Pianoforte'. This was a combined manual and mechanical instrument so that, if desired, the two functions could be performed together, one played by hand and the other by a 'horizontal cylinder similar to that of a barrel organ and set in motion by a steel spring', which latter was capable of performing the 'most intricate and difficult compositions' and of playing for half an hour without rewinding. The self-acting mechanism acted upon only eighteen of the piano notes.

Describing this machine, Thomas Busby, in his *Concert Room Anecdotes* (1825), relates:

> The time in which it executes any movement may be accelerated or retarded at pleasure; and while by the delicacy and perfection of the mechanism the *piano* and *forte* passages are given with correctness and effect, the *forzandi* and *diminuendi* are produced by the slightest motion of the hand applied to a sliding ball at the side of the instrument.

Another maker of barrel organs of this era was the Londoner John Courcell, who was later to become well known in the Commonwealth for his church organs. Many were sent to Australia, for example. Courcell in his early days turned his attention to the mechanical piano and produced a machine called the Cylindrichord in which the piano keys were depressed by a mechanical escapement set in motion by a pinned barrel and keyframe.

Dr Busby classified the Cylindrichord as an 'admirable and efficient substitute for a first-rate performer on the pianoforte' and says of it:

> In small or family parties, where dancing to the music of the pianoforte is practised, a person totally unacquainted with music, a child or a servant, may perform, in the very best and most correct style, quadrilles, waltzes, minuets, country dances, marches, songs, overtures, sonatas, choruses, or indeed any piece of music, however difficult. This instrument is extremely simple and differs altogether from the barrel or self-playing pianoforte; it can be accommodated to the height or dimensions of any pianoforte, and when not in use for that purpose, forms a piece of elegant furniture.

How effective these instruments were we have only the eulogies of Dr Busby from which to judge. The fact remains that it was not possible to make a mechanical piano which was a faithful interpreter. Certainly the direct linkage of a barrel to the mechanism of the piano was not good enough. The barrel pin even at its best was not up to providing the motive force on the hammer action of the period.

It may well have been instruments made by Clementi that formed the collection of mechanical pianos owned by Benjamin Flight Jnr (1767–1847) at his home at 101 St Martin's Lane. When Flight & Robson, famed barrel organ builders, dissolved their business partnership in 1832, the whole premises and stock were auctioned, including these unnamed but interesting pianos. The auction catalogue* lists four consecutive lots and the numbers given must refer to serial numbers. That all the items must be by one maker seems obvious by the disposition of these numbers. Flight & Robson are not known to have produced barrel pianos. I quote from the catalogue of the sale of Wednesday, 14 November 1832:

---

* This complete catalogue is reproduced in an Appendix to *Barrel Organ*.

Lot 20   A ROSE-WOOD SIX-OCTAVE SELF-PERFORMING and FINGER-KEYED CABINET PIANO-FORTE, made on the latest and most improved principle, with Cylinder Front, Columns in the top and bottom part, Ionic Carved Caps and Bases, Carved Legs and Cornice, Radiated Silk Curtain, French Polished, &c. – No. 2795. The Self-performing part has 49 Keys, Shifts from Forte to Piano, and takes off the Damper as set by the Composer. One Spiral Barrel. No. 2815. Set to the Water Witch Quadrilles.

Lot 21   No. 2796 A MAHOGANY SIX & HALF-OCTAVE DITTO. The Self-performing part has 61 Keys, Cromatic [sic] Scale and Shift, &c. as the foregoing. One Spiral Barrel. No. 2721. Set to CLEMENTI'S Celebrated Duet.

Lot 22   No. 2781. A SEVEN-OCTAVE DITTO. The Self-performing part as the foregoing. One Barrel plays Eight Popular Airs, (No. 2791) viz. Green Hills of Tyrol, Mazourka, Stop Waltz, WEBER'S Last Waltz, La mi Aspada, Gallopade, Der Freschutz Waltz and March in Oberon. Cromatic Scale.

Lot 23   No. 2728 A MAHOGANY DITTO, without the Finger Keys, has 61 Keys, &c. as the foregoing, with 1 Spiral Barrel, No. 2810. Plays PAGANINI'S Set of Quadrilles.

NOTE. The Cromatic Scale has this advantage, that it performs exactly as the Composer has wrote it; whereas in the smaller Barrels they have not room to get it in as it is written, and are obliged to transpose, which loses the effect intended by the Composer.

In 1832 a mechanical piano (and a 'grand' at that) was in use at the Grecian Hall (later the Royal Grecian Saloon), Eagle Tavern, City Road, London. The instrument was used to open the evening's performances and, in the programme for 17 February 1832, we read that 'The Self-Acting Grand Piano Forte will commence every evening at 7.0 precisely'. An undated newspaper cutting in the Enthoven Collection (Victoria and Albert Museum) refers to the fact that the self-acting pianoforte 'has now been repaired and sounds very much better'. Was this one of Clementi's instruments? Can it be one about which Thomas Busby wrote so glowingly? Alas! history does not relate and, some time before 1836, the instrument had been replaced by a more conventional and probably more acceptable band of instrumentalists.

CLOCKWORK PIANOS

The clockwork piano with its ability to produce music – especially popular music – without effort, became popular not just with the more genteel middle classes, but in places of working-class entertainment and the seamier sides of life. Whereas the self-acting pianoforte at the Grecian Saloon played for the entertainment of those who journeyed out to the edge of London in the 1830s, by the time the century was closing places far less fashionable housed such instruments. One notorious place was the old Hotel de Provence on the corner of Cranbourn Street in Leicester Square. In the 1890s and the early 1900s it was a popular place for night-time entertainment with a downstairs café featuring a long bar and marble-topped tables. All the waiters, somewhat surprisingly, were German and fights were commonplace. The police raided the establishment regularly and could reckon on six or so patrons being arrested nightly. A clockwork piano was one of the more moralistic attractions to the scene. The old building, changed and rendered respectable in the 1930s, disappeared during an air raid in April 1941.

The clockwork piano, or, as the continentals preferred to call it, the café piano, was capable of playing quite involved music and, by the diligent use of special barrel pinning and levers controlling a simple action, a degree of primitive expression could be imparted to its performance. But even as the twentieth century turned and the First World War came and went those makers who still made the piano orchestrion, later variant of the clockwork barrel piano, chose to concentrate much more on the things it could do best of all rather than to try to make it emulate the best pianists of the age. Those features which were best developed were its abilities in rhythm, noise and percussion – not, one must openly admit, all against the instrument for it did have strong merit points.

But before the piano could attain any real degree of passing expression it had to progress considerably further and along different avenues. One of the early attempts at doing just this came from a Frenchman named Fourneaux who, in 1863, decided to employ another feature of the barrel organ besides just the barrel in an attempt to play the piano. He used the bellows, keyframe and sticker assembly from the barrel organ in his Pianista. Each note of the music on the barrel raised the organ-type finger keyframe and depressed a wooden sticker into a windchest. This opened a pallet which sent air rushing not, as in the organ, to a pipe but into a small expanding bellows. It was this bellows assembly that actually caused the piano key to be struck. To play a piano, the Pianista had to be pushed up in front of it and aligned with the keys. All the performer had to do was to turn the handle which rotated the barrel and pumped the bellows.

PIANO MÉCANIQUE AND ANTIPHONEL

A device which would not really be considered a serious contender for the advancement of the mechanical piano was that patented by a Frenchman, Alexandre Debain, in 1846. His mechanism was made to fit across the keyboard of a harpsichord or spinet and was a peculiarly shaped frame containing levers and stickers which rested on the keys. The music was represented by strips of wood or *planchettes* which were studded with pins. These wooden strips were fed along a channel in the top of the mechanism. Called the Antiphonel, Debain's device was a hark-back to more primitive days and was certainly far less practical than even Courcell's push-up player of more than twenty years earlier.

Debain went on to make pianos which incorporated the Antiphonel. His earliest was a 'keyless' model which could only be played using the planchettes, but, by the time of the Great Exhibition, he was producing combined Antiphonel and manual instruments. Quite long pieces of music could be played, the planchettes being numbered as sections of the music to show in which order they should be played. The mechanically played compass was 61 notes.

The catalogue of the Great Exhibition of 1851 (vol. III, page 1233) described this device as follows:

Piano mécanique or antiphonel pianoforte, an instrument which has been applied with success as a substitute for organs and harmoniums, it is said to be superior to the barrell [sic] used in church organs, and less costly.

The flat surface of the upper portion of the antiphonel is covered with a metal plate, pierced across its width with a series of openings, which admit through them a corresponding number of metal points, projecting about 1/8th of an inch above the plate. These points are the extremities of small levers, which communicate with the action, then the upper level surface of the machine forms a complete keyboard, the

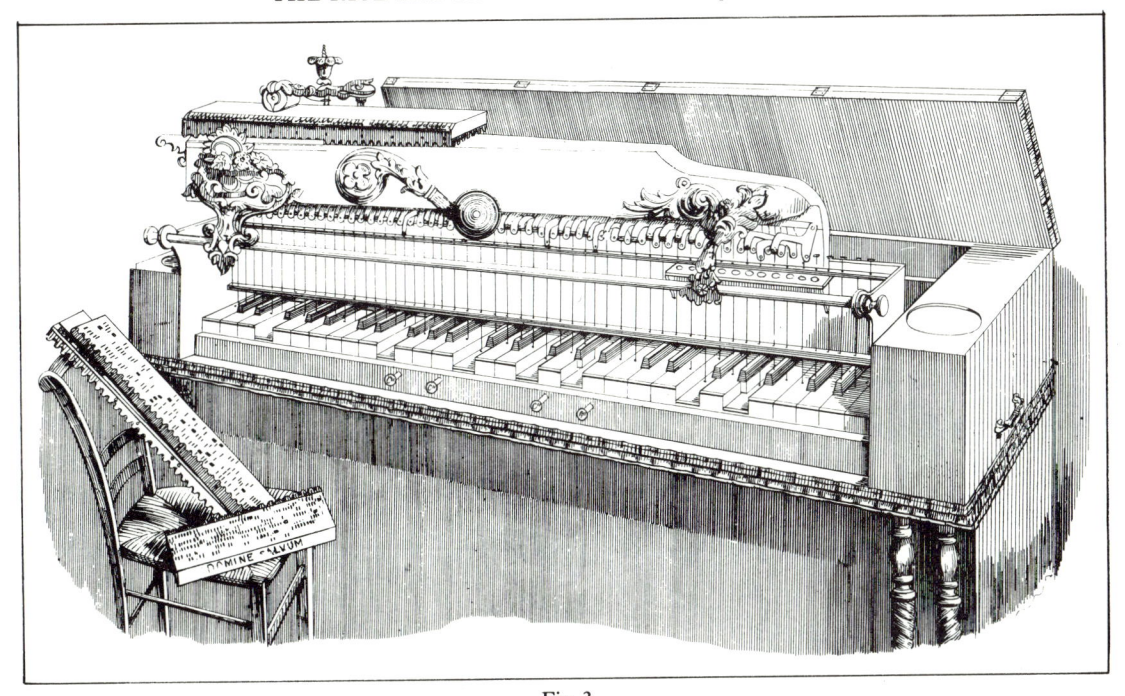

Fig. 3
Alexander Debain's Antiphonel was first patented in 1846. A key-top mechanical player, the Antiphonel appeared in many styles and could also be obtained built in to a special piano or harmonium. The music was set as a pattern of studs in wooden boards called planchettes which were drawn across the mechanical keyframe by a rack and pinion system.

projections are pressed down to perform the music by a piece of hard wood, studded with pins, which is forced over the level surface already mentioned. The piece is held down by a bar placed over it, and the pressure regulated by springs. Having placed the piece on the antiphonel, it is passed over the key frame by turning a handle, and as the pins on the plank come into contact with the antiphonel keys, the notes are struck, which are loud or soft as required.

The pieces studded with pins may be from 4″ to 24″ long; 8″ will contain as much as is written on a page of music paper, any number of pieces may be used for compositions of greater length. While one piece is playing; another should be had in readiness immediately to succeed it; until the piece of music is concluded.

The mode of studding the wood with pins, to produce the various effects required, is very simple and easily executed.

The Antiphonel can be placed on the pianoforte as a cover, and by a simple contrivance, on opening the pianoforte, the antiphonel action is removed, and on touching the keys the tone of the instrument is not affected by the attachment. In closing the pianoforte the antiphonel resumes its place, and is ready for use.

When applied to the organ etc., as pressure on the keys is only required, the antiphonel is placed over the key frame and appears like fingers pressing down the required notes.

The Antiphonel was, in fact, available in three forms. The first was as a key-top player which was fitted on a keyboard and played by moving an ingeniously thought out lever up and down, the music planchettes being advanced evenly on either stroke. An arrangement of double-ratchet levers imparted continuous forward motion to the music drive pinion. The second version was as an automatic keyboardless piano shaped like a small upright and having the player action arranged on the horizontal platform where the keyboard might normally be expected to be. The third version was the combined manual and automatic Antiphonel piano. This was a most ingenious device for it incorporated two complete and independent piano actions. The first was that of the normal piano and was used for hand playing. For mechanical playing, a large lever under the keyboard was pulled across from one side to the other. This bodily raised the whole upper portion of the piano from a telescoped, closed position, at the same time moving clear the keyboard hammer action and bringing into position the hammer action for mechanical operation. The operator then lifted the piano top lid, revealing the steel table and guides for the planchettes. The crank handle was then pushed home through its hole in the front (and secured in position by a 'secret' catch only released by pressing a flush button in the planchette table) and the first planchette, numbered 1 for a given tune, engaged in the guide. Briskly turning the handle advanced the planchette over the protruding keys of the mechanical keyframe and the operator's assistant would keep the operator fed with the correctly numbered planchettes. Each one bore a number stamped into its front edge and repeated sections were indicated by the numbers. For example, a board bearing the numerals '1, 5, 8, 10' meant that the planchette board marked '1' was the first to be played and was played again after number 4, number 7 and number 9.

PERFORATED CARDBOARD MUSIC

Perforated cardboard music originated in 1842 from the invention of punched cards to operate weaving machinery – the Jacquard card system for looms. The new system was variously applied over the years without much success until it came into its own at the start of the 1880s, at which time it appeared likely to oust the wooden barrel for both organs and pianos which worked automatically.

Names of instruments often recur in the annals of the mechanical piano player and one of the early ones offered on the market was another Pianista, this one manufactured in Paris by Jérôme Thibouville-Lamy. There is an interesting story about this device which I told in the pages of *The Music Box* some years ago.* Thibouville-Lamy's Pianista played the keyboard by means of perforated cardboard music books. A version was made for use on the pipe organ or harmonium and this was called the Organista.

In 1884 there was staged a furniture exhibition at north London's Agricultural Hall, a now deserted and crumbling building which stands plaintively plastered with placards in Islington. This was the age of exhibitions, of well-patronised trade shows, and the many suitably appointed venues ranged from the Earls Court upwards and downwards. Here at Islington, however, the apparent mundaneness of a furniture exhibition was relieved by the fact that musical instruments were at that time popular and abundant enough to rate high on the list of furnishings. And so amongst the tallboys, sideboards and wardrobes stood a Chickering grand piano and in front of it a cabinet player called the Miranda Pianista. A contemporary scribe takes up the story:

* 'Miranda and the Pianista', *The Music Box*, volume 6, pp. 92–3.

Projecting from one side of the 'Miranda' is a series of wooden levers or fingers exactly the width of the pianoforte keys to be operated upon. These levers are moved in accordance with holes in perforated cards, as in the Jacquard loom, a series of small pneumatic valves (worked automatically by a reservoir bellows) producing the motive power. On placing the Miranda in position in front of the piano and turning a handle, the perforated cards are drawn through, and the mechanical fingers are moved with an exactness not always obtained even by expert pianoforte players. The matter of expression is secured by a little lever controlled by the left hand, on moving which a stronger or weaker touch is possible, to the extent desired by the performer. Further, the ordinary pedals of the pianoforte are extended and carried through to the front of the invention so as to be under the control of the performer.

The instrument was patented in all countries in Europe and an organisation formed to market it – The Automatic Musical Instrument Company, 27 Penton Street, London, N. This was headed by a man called Ellis Parr, musical instrument dealer and occasional inventor, who ran the agency for several German pianos and who was the co-patentee of the Symphonion musical box.* From the summer debut of the Miranda in London until the end of that year – 1884 – the AMIC was quietly at work arranging its outlets and the manufacturing of the Miranda. In January 1885, it announced that Mr Ellis Parr had been appointed the agent for the instrument and that its manufacture was to be undertaken in Germany by the Hanover piano makers Karl Haake (established in 1836 and then managed by Herman Feldmann). Parr already had the agency for Haake pianos in London and it was promised that instruments would be placed 'very shortly' before the trade.

In July 1885 the first advertisement was put out for the Miranda Pianista by Ellis Parr of 99 Oxford Street. This drew an unexpected reply directed at the music trade from none other than Jérôme Thibouville-Lamy from its address in Charterhouse Street, London:

> I beg to state that I bought the patent of the instrument named the 'Pianista' in 1872. Since then I have improved the instrument in many ways: my last patent is dated 1883. The Miranda pianista is simply a variation of my old system. Yours very truly,
> J. Thibouville-Lamy (10 August 1885).

I have been unable to trace any reference to the Miranda after that date. Obviously such a revelation must have killed off the instrument as surely as a stab in the bellows would have done. It must have been a red-faced and saddened Parr and Haake who received this bombshell, for only in April of that year they had confidently predicted in the press a dividend of nearly 30 per cent on the projected first year of trading. And so the handling company, named Automatic Music Company with offices at 3 Copthall Buildings, London, EC, quietly folded.

During the history of mechanical pianos, many companies were to lose money through inadvised ventures, and this was an early example of just that.

Meanwhile, Thibouville-Lamy's Pianista was something of a moderate success and sold fairly well by all accounts. It is related that if the operating handle was turned quickly the music came out loud and fast; if it was turned slowly the music came out soft and slow. There

---

* See Ord-Hume, *Musical Box, A History and Collectors' Guide*, 1979.

was apparently no reliable method of regulating volume and speed independently.

The next significant development owed its origins to a somewhat earlier invention. During the period 1878–90, the first of a number of table instruments playing free reeds appeared in America. The first of these was called, not unnaturally, the Organette. Precursor of a very large number of different makes, designs and styles, this was a pneumatic instrument which controlled the speech of its reeds via a strip of perforated paper or card. The operator turned a small handle to feed the music through the machine and also to reciprocate a pair of small bellows which continuously drew the air out of the case. When a perforation in the paper engaged with a passage leading to a particular reed, the suction of the bellows or exhausters would draw air through the reed, so making it speak.

The invention, however, was not entirely American in origin for as early as 1846 a Londoner, Anthony Baynes, had taken out a patent for the playing of a pipe organ using a perforated paper roll. The concept was not developed, though, and it was not until the advent of the organette that the clue to the pneumatic playing of a piano was understood. The table organette was built in Germany, England and America in a large variety of shapes and sizes, some playing perforated metal discs similar to those used on the disc musical boxes. In these the projections on the disc engaged in levers which opened pallets over the reeds. The true pneumatic organette, playing a paper roll which was fed over a perforated tracker bar, was the first step towards the pneumatic action already being exploited in organ construction* and its application to the piano.

When in 1887 the Welte Company of Freiburg im Breisgau perfected and patented a piano-playing system using a pneumatic action controlled by a perforated paper roll, the stage was set for the ultimate in piano mechanism.

PAPER USED TO CONTROL AIR

Up to this time, the barrel piano and most of the cardboard playing pianos had employed, to a greater or lesser extent, a mechanical action. The new discovery was the power of air. Used in conjunction with a method of modifying the pressure of air in a vessel relative to that surrounding the vessel, air could be made to perform a variety of operations quickly and positively. The pressure modification was achieved by bellows or exhausters, and the performance of duties by small bellows also called 'pneumatic' motors, and valves. The music sheet was no longer expected to make physical contact with a lever or to do any work other than to control the access of air to a small wind passage in the fashion of a sliding valve. It could thus be made of a thinner substance – paper.

The paper-roll pneumatic action was used mainly in the production of orchestrion organs

---

* The application of the pneumatic motor in organ building came about through the inventiveness of a young man born in Bath on 10 October 1806. Charles Spackman Barker was destined to enter the medical profession until one day he chanced upon the erection of a church organ close to his home. The work was by the famous organ builder James Bishop, who had been an apprentice to Flight & Robson. Barker decided that organ building was to be his chosen occupation, apprenticed himself to Bishop in London and later returned to Bath to set up in business. Around 1832 the newly built large organ at York Minster attracted his attention and so, in particular, did the amount of force required by the organist in depressing the keys. Working in an old mill in Gloucestershire, Barker set about experimenting with ways of easing the organist's lot, the outcome being the celebrated 'Barker pneumatic lever'. Attempts to interest British organ builders in his invention proved unsuccessful so he went in 1837 to Paris where Cavaillé-Coll promptly adopted it in his new organ for the church of St Denis. Barker later worked extensively in Paris, with, among others, Merklin, until the uprising of 1870 forced him to leave Paris and return to England, where he died at Maidstone in November 1879. Interestingly enough, it seems that the Edinburgh organ builder Hamilton invented the pneumatic lever separately at the same time as Barker and he subsequently contested Barker's patent although without success.

AN IMPORTANT AEOLIAN INVENTION

Two views of the earliest model of the Pianola—later reduced in size and greatly improved—invented by E. S. Votey, now Vice-President of The Aeolian Company

Fig. 4
Edwin Scott Votey's first Pianola was a large and cumbersome instrument of almost the same size as the instrument it was intended to play. Votey was made Vice-President of The Aeolian Company.

in Germany by Welte, who later expanded their interests to America where they set up a factory. The next major advance came in 1888 when William D. Parker of Meriden, Connecticut, devised a player reed organ called the Symphony which was produced by the Wilcox & White Company. He followed this in 1891 with a combination manual and paper-roll-operated piano. In England, the paper-playing Maxfield reed organ was perfected. Alfred Dolge, one time head of a great piano manufacturing empire and American piano historian, suggests that R. W. Pain produced the first self-acting pneumatic piano in 1880 as a complete unit for Needham & Sons. This had 39 notes and was followed in 1888 by an electrically operated 65-note instrument.

In 1896, Edwin Scott Votey invented a piano-playing machine which he called the Pianola. The first experimental model was sent from Detroit where it was built to New York where it was shown in the factory of the Roosevelt Organ Company. This device was the first provenly successful example of a whole number of piano-playing devices which, although short-lived and soon discarded in favour of subsequent improved players, played a vital part in the history of the self-acting piano. The Pianola was intended to make any piano into an automatically playable instrument. It was, in fact, a completely separate appliance which was stood in front of an ordinary piano. Known as a cabinet-style player or, in the vernacular, a 'push-up', it consisted of a set of exhausters worked by the feet of the operator, a paper-roll-transporting device which fed the perforated music over a tracker board containing small windways leading to a set of pneumatic valves, and a row of small fingers at the back of the player which rested on the piano keyboard. Votey's prototype, which played on only a few of the keys, is preserved today in the Smithsonian Institute, Washington.

Large and unsightly though it was, this first model embodied the flexible, elastic touch and the varying degrees of wind pressure that made possible the contrasting dynamics, the basic principles upon which the success of the Pianola was based. Votey's first patent application was not filed until 25 January 1897, and was granted on 22 May 1900.

The elemental production Pianola was a cumbersome device and while it only played on 58 notes of the piano (much later 65) it was so large that it obscured even the largest and most grandiose of uprights. In due course, development resulted in a smaller and much more compact instrument.

Backed by the enormous drive and business acumen of William Barnes Tremaine (1840–1907) and his son Harry B. Tremaine (born 1866), plus the facilities which were later to add up to the largest player-piano manufacturing organisation in the world, Votey's Pianola piano player was soon in production and on sale virtually all over the world. So were the similar products of many other firms who wheedled their various ways around the Votey patents to build virtually the same mechanism.

The importance of Harry B. Tremaine's part in the Pianola scenario cannot be overstated. Originally he had worked in the company his father set up in 1878 to market Mason J. Matthews' Orguinette – this was the Mechanical Orguinette Company which later made the Celestina organette and the Aeolian organ of 1883. W. B. Tremaine acquired in 1888 the patents and stock-in-trade of the Automatic Music Paper Company of Boston and united the two into the Aeolian Organ & Music Company, boosted again by the purchase, in 1892, of the Monroe Organ Reed Company of Worcester, Massachusetts. In 1895 he introduced the Aeriol self-playing piano. It was while Harry B. Tremaine was working at the Mechanical Orguinette & Music Company that he suddenly declared that he had an idea for the benefit of those who liked music but who couldn't play. His father had already taken out several patents for players, including one with R. W. Pain, and now Harry B. began working on similar devices. It was at this time that the Tremaines conceded that Votey had done a better job, although the Tremaine patents were later embodied in the Pianola. Harry B. went on to become general manager of Aeolian until 1898 when he became president. Much later, in 1927, he perfected what was called the 'Audiographic' music roll which had a system of commentaries and directions printed on the player rolls. He died in 1932 while visiting his daughter in Washington.

The Tremaines' early faith in the piano player boosted efforts to combine the mechanism with the piano. The separate player was at best a cumbersome contraption, tricky to position at the keyboard and with the ever-present risk of damage to the slender, felt-covered fingers at the back. After a life of but six or seven years, Melville Clark's new interior player captured the market. By 1908, player sales had dropped almost to nil in favour of the latest developments. And this was in the face of the belief firmly held by experts such as William Braid White that the cabinet player would not lose its popularity in favour of 'the inner player'.

Nevertheless, and although push-ups were still made in small numbers until at least 1910, the advantages of this sort of machine paled into insignificance in the face of one instrument which could be both player and played upon manually.

Notwithstanding the claim by Dolge of the existence of a single-unit player piano of 1880, Melville Clark – another American – had discovered a method of packing all the player action

Mr. E. S. Votey at the right, inventor of the Pianola, is here shown in Washington, with the original model, which will be preserved among the other important musical instruments of our National Museum

ORIGINAL PIANOLA MODEL PRESENTED TO SMITHSONIAN INSTITUTE

A UNIQUE and fitting ceremonial took place during Tribute Week when E. S. Votey, Vice-President of The Aeolian Company, and inventor of the Pianola, presented the original model of this instrument, pictured above, to the Smithsonian Institute.

Officials of the National museum represented by Dr. Walter Hough, curator in charge of the musical instruments department, said: "The Smithsonian Institute is a storehouse of all our endeavors in inventions, especially prior to the mechanical age.

"The invention of the Pianola has added so much happiness to humankind that we cannot fail to be thankful to its originators.

"We are happy to receive this original Pianola instrument as one of the most important contributions made to our collections."

Fig. 5
The prototype Pianola now rests in the Smithsonian Institute. Here Votey presents the instrument to Institute officials in the 1920s.

components inside the piano by 1901. He produced the first documented player piano and, within a year, the Aeolian Company in New York had been forced to follow suit, advertising 'The Pianolo Piano – The First Complete Piano'. Clark was also the first person to produce a pneumatic player action in a grand piano in 1904.

So was born the pneumatic roll-playing piano, and with it all the trappings of a new industry. In America, specially modified Ford trucks were produced which had piano-loading attachments so that the piano salesman could take an instrument to a prospective client, offload it, demonstrate it and, he hoped, clinch the sale on the spot. Some 2½ million player pianos were sold between 1900 and 1930.

In England, where such methods of direct selling were considered distasteful to say the least, refined advertisements in the best newspapers and family magazines such as *Punch*, *The Illustrated London News*, *The Royal* and *Harpers*, together with displays of instruments in piano showrooms, produced a comfortable growth in sales.

Chicago was a major centre of the player industry in America and so it is not surprising that the local newspapers considered that the industry in their midst was worth reporting on. The leader in the British periodical *Musical Opinion* for January 1903 was given over to a verbatim quote from the Chigaco *Indicator*. This is a first-rate and well-written assessment of the state of the instrument and the contemporary American market:

THE PIANO PLAYER VOGUE

The increasing vogue of the piano player is causing widespread comment, not only in musical circles but in the private homes of American citizens who possess no musical education. This vogue is now regarded – and rightly regarded – as one of the most significant phases in the life and advancement of this mechanical age. It is heralded by the enthusiastic as a portent of the dawning of a new epoch, when machinery will still be the motive power of civilisation, but will be applied to uses hitherto deemed sacred from its invading banners. In other words, these persons – dreamers, perhaps, the conservative may call them – regard as now near at hand the day when mechanical inventiveness will invade the precincts of art and will fix its ensign in the very altar of that domain. If this vision is to be realised, the piano player will certainly be the most prominent factor in its accomplishment. The public in general will be pleased, and the piano trade will certainly not lag behind the rest of the world in similar feelings; for it is plain that, when the day of the player arrives, the field of piano enterprise will be greatly enlarged.

The public in general are fonder of music to-day than they were twenty-five years ago. Musical comedy is now the most popular form of stage attraction, and the musical comedy of the day is far in advance of the childish affairs that passed for such in an earlier period. But how to reach, if possible, the causes of the vogue of the piano player as distinguished from the causes of the vogue of music in general?

First, we must recognise the popularity of the piano as an instrument for the home. It has always been great, but never greater than at present; and in view of certain qualities possessed by the piano, which we need not discuss here, it is not likely at any time within the next hundred years to recede from its position. From the piano to the piano player is but a step; a public pleased with one will be pleased with the other.

Another cause of the rise of the player proceeds from our American habits of economising time. Our citizen loves music, but he has no time to spend in studying a complex technique. His daughter, perhaps, who would be the proper person to fill this want in his household, is busy working in a store or factory, or goes to high school and must study her Caesar or geometry when she gets home. And then there are many people who have no daughter, or none of the proper age. These matters seem trivial, but they nevertheless have a potent influence.

The third fact is this: With a piano player in your house you can give a friend musical entertainment and discourse with him at the same time. Or if you have nothing to talk about – and this is a contingency that happens with remarkable frequency at social gatherings, especially small ones – you may set your piano at work.

Still another cause lies in the admiration of the public for anything which acts, talks or plays automatically. They wonder at the thing. A wonder is a good thing to subdue and make your own. It pleases you; it will please others. Perhaps it will make them envy you; and what so sweet as envy to the envied? Again, the piano player is a novelty. In all ages novelties have been eagerly sought for, but never has there existed such a craving for them as now. Finally, we must not forget the preparative influences of certain other automatic pleasure making devices that found their way into American households before the general introduction of the piano player. These are principally the music box and the phonograph.

But doubtless, while the present writer has been setting down these reasons, its readers have evolved as many more; and it is remarkable how manifold are the reasons that bring an invention like the piano player into the forefront of public approval.

The quality of players and the effect poor mechanisms might have on the piano industry was the subject of another article which *Musical Opinion* 'lifted' from another Chicago paper – this time the *Presto* – and republished in October 1905:

INTERIOR PIANO PLAYER

Whatever may be the influence of the interior player upon trade (says the Chicago *Presto*) there can be little doubt as to its effect upon the pianos themselves unless the mechanism of the former be reliable and as nearly perfect as anything made by human hands can be. This is a horn of the dilemma that has not been discussed seriously by the trade papers for obvious reasons; but it is nevertheless a point of view that should occupy the careful attention of the piano manufacturers and of the dealers also. When the piano players first appeared as separate instruments collateral or auxiliary to the piano, there was no imminent danger to the musical instrument itself; the fame of a musical instrument was not jeopardised by the possible failure of the player. The latter might operate well, and so the combination prove rather a help to the piano's distinction than otherwise; or the player might prove unsatisfactory or troublesome and be set aside as a bad bargain, in which event the dealer had his troubles and in turn the player manufacturer came in for his share of them. But the piano itself took no chances in the final verdict. With the interior player the case is very different. It is easily possible for a piano of great distinction to suffer loss of prestige in a community by the failure or by the fragile character as to durability of a single interior player. The piano is certain to bear the brunt of it, for the distinguished name on the fall board will certainly suffer almost incurable injury if the interior player prove a failure even in partial degree. This makes it a matter of serious consideration from the point of view of all piano manufacturers who have consistently worked for distinction and whose pianos bear names representing a valuable asset in fame or in selling influence. Possibly the interior players are as good, as durable and as perfect in every way as their makers proclaim. Certainly some of them are marvelous creations: but not all of them. Some of them are not at all good specimens, and they are sure to drag down the pianos into which they are placed.

This is so important a matter that the piano manufacturers cannot consider too carefully the character of the mechanism that is placed in their cases. There seems to be no vital part of the player that is protected securely by patents: this makes it easy to infer that 'they are all alike'. But they are not all alike, and this fact alone should warn piano manufacturers whose products have influence that there is danger in applying the interior players unless there is ample security that the result may not tear down within twelve months the results of the work of a lifetime.

And so it was that, as with many a new product in a new industry, many makers entered the field, some of whom for a variety of reasons were less able to survive than others. It became a market where, indeed, only the fittest would make the grade. Company failures and take-overs were commonplace. One such event was reported in the pages of *Musical Opinion* for April 1905 as follows:

A telegram announces the purchase of the Playano Manufacturing Company of Boston by the Story & Clark Piano Co. of Chicago. A new piano with interior player, to be known as the Story & Clark player piano, will be put in work at the factory as soon as possible. A player department will be established, whose purpose will be the manufacture of this new interior attachment and also of the cabinet Playano. 'I have read the handwriting on the wall,' says Mr E. H. Story. 'I am convinced that the player piano has come to stay; so are my associates in the ownership of the company. We feel that the future prospects of the player business are good enough to warrant us in buying a player business outright, and that the Playano Co. was the concern to buy.'

The opportunities for the masses to make music without formal training had begun with the little organette reed organ with its dozen or two dozen notes. Now the self-playing piano was available in increasing numbers to a public hungry for music of all types. Many new to music derived a genuine and sincere musical appreciation from having a piano initially as a novelty and then finding that they actually liked the increasing repertoire available to them. That excellent barometer of musical progress, *Musical Opinion*, reported in November 1907:

At the recent Leipzig Fair the chief interest from a musical point of view was the large number of mechanical pianos shown. E. Dienst sent one each of his Capella and Perla orchestrions; also an Ariophon mandolin piano. Popper & Co. exhibited orchestrions and electrical pianos. The house of Hupfield was a prolific exhibitor of orchestrions and of electric instruments. Phillips & Son sent a Tremolant piano orchestrion. Lochmann, amongst other items, a 'string orchestral instrument'. Bruno Geissler, a self playing harmonium.

THE RISE AND FALL OF THE AUTOMATIC PIANO

On the same page was a description of another British-made player – one which made (or tried to make) a feature out of being the cheapest on the market!

> We looked in at the Musicus Piano-Player Co. at Salisbury Road, Highgate, the other day and found the company busy. They manufacture an inexpensive piano, in which is fixed their 'player' mechanism of sixty-five notes. There are several good points in this internal player which were duly explained to the visitor. The treadles are hinged and can be folded in out of the way; the 'player' can be quickly removed for tuning or for replacing a string; the tuner has full opportunity without being encumbered; the music roll is actuated by a three-throw noiseless crank; and there is plenty of room everywhere. A cleverly arranged 'stop' also permits of prompt accentuation; and, finally, it is claimed that 'nothing so cheap has previously been placed on the market'.

It is worth recording that within a few short years, this company found itself bankrupt.

In 1912, a concert was held at the Queen's Hall in London at which the London Symphony Orchestra conducted by Arthur Nikisch played Grieg's Pianoforte Concerto in A Minor, the solo part being played by Easthope Martin on a player piano. Elena Gerhardt sang several songs to 'pianola' accompaniment at the same concert. The programme was repeated a year later with Camille Chevillard conducting the Lamoureux Orchestra.

Among the many devices employed to popularise the instrument in England besides many concerts such as these were the early endeavours of Britain's largest manufacturers of piano rolls, the Perforated Music Company. In 1913 they started their 'Riddle-Roll' competition in which an unlabelled roll (usually an abstruse piece of music) would be supplied to subscribers for identification. Together with their 'Popular-Puzzle-Roll' contest, the first prize was a year's free subscription to the roll library.

There was still the ultimate in player pianos to be invented – the reproducing piano. The ordinary player piano would produce all the notes, but left the actual expression (soft and loud, pedalling, theme expression and phrasing) to the performer, who achieved these effects by small levers on the piano which operated pneumatic bellows controlling the actual action of the piano and quite independently of the musical playing action.

REPRODUCING PIANOS

The problem of making the whole system automatic was not insurmountable by any means. It just demanded that the roll of music be provided with some extra perforation to control special action pneumatics directly. As early as 1904, the German firm of Welte built a reproducing piano known as the Keyless Welte since it had no keyboard but was purely mechanical. Hupfeld followed with an electric reproducing piano of more conventional layout in 1906. However, it was not until just before the First World War that the Duo-Art reproducing action was perfected in America, followed soon afterwards by the Ampico.

So absolutely perfect were these instruments claimed to be, and so perfect the interpretations which they could give, that each roll was specially recorded by an artist who would add his name to the roll. Many famous pianists did just this and, thanks to their co-operation and to the reproducing piano, we can actually hear today the performances of such masters as Edvard Grieg, Claude Debussy, Theodor Leschetizky, Josef Lhevinne and Rachmaninov, to name a glittering handful.

Thanks to the reproducing piano it becomes possible today to gain some fair impression of how a pianist of the past used to play. More to the point, though, and dwelling for a moment on this point of realism, the reproducing piano enables us today to hear what was considered (at the time the particular roll was made) to be an acceptable interpretation of a piece of music. Many of the pianists recorded on piano roll never made gramophone records and those that did were confronted by the technical limitations of the recording studio. Phonograph recordings not only depended on acoustic microphones and recording apparatus which was distressingly primitive by today's standards, but the range of sound frequencies capable of transfer on to the cylinders was very limited. In practice, this meant that the performer could not play *pianissimo*, but had to pound out the music, largely with disregard for the soft pedal. Also, each cylinder played for a set time, and so the performance had to be tailored to that duration. The reproducing piano roll had no such shortcomings as far as duration was concerned, for it provided a timeless, mute transcription, faithful in every respect to the day it left the studio with the artist's signature and, presumably, his blessing. For reproduction, all it required was to be placed on a similar reproducing piano. Not that we should allow ourselves to be deluded too greatly by these recorded rolls, for they were not without their own very special inherent shortcomings. These are examined in Chapter 13.

The importance of the player piano during its life cannot be overemphasised. It was certainly regarded as of greater interpretational significance than the gramophone by such famous pianists as Leschetizky – who firmly averred his disappointment that it had not arrived on the musical scene a century earlier – and Busoni, who is reputed to have thought it as important an invention as the cinematograph.

There is no doubt that during its lifetime the player piano was in no small measure responsible for the growth and development of musical knowledge amongst people who might otherwise have never had their latent musical interest aroused. A spokesman for the Perforated Music Company said, in 1913, 'A man buys a player, and the first month he plays rag-time. Then he goes rapidly through the comic opera stage, till he reaches Chaminade and MacDowell. Often he gets no further than that, but an increasing percentage go on to the classics.' Certainly more people were inclined to take 'the classics' into their homes when they could 'play' themselves and it has been averred that the reputation of MacDowell in this country was largely due to the influence of the player piano.

The potentials of the music roll are best demonstrated in a story told some years before the First World War by a well-known American roll manufacturer. A famous singer was about to take part in a piano-player promotional recital and, the preceding afternoon, was taken on a conducted tour of the factory. She showed such a great interest in the roll-making department that after a while she was invited to sit at a piano and sing one of her own songs. At the conclusion she was asked if she would sing that particular song in the recital due to begin a few hours later. 'But it isn't even in manuscript,' replied the artiste. 'I haven't had time to write it down and no one could accompany me and I cannot do both satisfactorily.'

She was then told that, although the new song was not written down, she had in fact just cut the master roll by playing upon the recording piano. The song was performed that evening.

A foretaste of later trends in public libraries occurred in 1914 when the library in Kansas City, Missouri, added 500 player-piano rolls to its music library. Non-musical ratepayers, however, had little cause for grievance; the rolls were the outcome of a gift from a private individual.

THE RISE AND FALL OF THE AUTOMATIC PIANO

An appreciation of just why player-piano rolls and, later, reproducing rolls may be able to give us a far better idea of musical interpretations of these early days than the surviving phonograph and gramophone recordings can best be deduced from the following extract from a letter which Busoni wrote to his wife in November 1919:

My suffering over the toil of making gramophone records came to an end yesterday, after playing for 3½ hours! I feel rather better today, but it is over. Since the first day, I have been as depressed as if I were expecting to have an operation. To do it is stupid and a strain. Here is an example of what happens. They want the Faust Waltz (which lasts a good ten minutes) *but it was only to take four minutes!* That meant quickly cutting, patching and improvising, so that there should still be some sense in it; watching the pedal (because it sounds bad); thinking of certain notes which had to be stronger or weaker in order to please this devilish machine; not letting oneself go for fear of inaccuracies and being conscious the whole time that every note was going to be there for eternity; how can there be any question of inspiration, freedom, swing or poetry? Enough that yesterday for nine pieces of 4 minutes each (half an hour in all) I worked for three and a half hours! Two of the pieces I played four or five times. Having to think so quickly at the same time was a severe effort. In the end, I felt the effects in my arms; after that, I had to sit for a photograph, and sign the discs. – At last it was finished!

Fig. 6
The limitations of early gramophone recording are shown in this old engraving of a pianist recording on a cylinder phonograph using a horn.

In a later letter, just before he gave his last public concert in 1922 at the age of fifty-six, he wrote from his London hotel to his English manager:

The conditions are most unfavourable. The room, the piano, the chair not inviting. I have to start like a racehorse and to end before four minutes have elapsed. I have to manage the touch and the pedal differently from how I do it usually.

What, in heavens name! can be the result of it? Not my own playing, take it for granted!

Busoni was, admittedly, best described as an interesting if unconventional performer whose personality and creative imagination often coloured his renditions to such an extent that, as Claudio Arrau once said, 'very often the composer was almost totally lost'. Be that as it may, his comments on the techniques and demands of the recording studio remain extremely valid and demonstrate forcibly the enormous value of the reproducing piano and its music and, albeit to a slightly lesser extent, the ordinary player piano.

These highly sophisticated reproducing pianos and their actions were expensive and followed a number of attempts over the years at achieving partial expression from music rolls by simpler methods. Electric 'expression' pianos with up to half a dozen steps in 'expression' were popular in the 1920–30 period. These offered what might be called ungraduated pedalling as compared with the Duo-Art, which provided no fewer than sixteen different 'shades' of dynamic intensity to cover all extremes of *fortissimo* and *pianissimo* and to produce finely graded crescendos and diminuendos.

The Aeolian Company used the Duo-Art action in its pianos, both grand and upright. In the course of its advertising campaign, Aeolian promoted a series of concerts at Aeolian Hall, New York, at which the New York Symphony Orchestra performed piano concertos with the piano solo part being supplied by a Duo-Art playing a roll. These rolls were always signed by the artist who had originally recorded them, and it was widely publicised that the soloist at one such concert – Harold Bauer – would be in Chicago at the time of his New York 'performance'.

At a London concert, a performance of a Liszt rhapsody was shared between the pianist Cortot playing 'live' and a previously recorded music roll by Cortot. The effect, we are told, was so dovetailed that music critic Ernest Newman said: 'With one's eyes closed, it was impossible to tell which was which.'

HOW PIANO-ROLLS WERE RECORDED

The system by which piano-roll recordings were made was ingenious. The celebrated pianist performed upon a grand piano, which, in outward appearance, was no different from an ordinary instrument. However, from the piano ran a multicore electric cable carrying two different sets of wires, one from contacts beneath each piano key and one from positions near where the hammers struck the strings. The cable led out of the recording studio into a soundproof room in which was situated the recording apparatus. Here the wires were attached to electromagnets which operated paper punches in a perforating machine, each punch corresponding with its proper note on the piano. As the pianist played so the punches cut the master roll and made a permanent recording. Different systems varied the technique: on Welte, for example, a melographic trace was produced for subsequent punching and on others an engineer was responsible for noting the performer's dynamics.

This method of recording thus secured accuracy of replaying, the length of the perforation being determined by the duration that the recording pianist held down the particular keys. The punches in the machine repeated at the rate of 4,000 cycles per minute, so making possible the accurate recording of the most rapid staccato notes struck by the pianist. The resultant punched hole for the briefest note would be just 1/32 inch in diameter.

Rhythm of the music was determined by the spacing of the markings or perforations in the master roll as it passed through the recording machine at a constant speed, which was normally eight feet a minute. So long as the rolls made from the master so cut were played back at the same speed, faithful *tempi* would naturally result.

With the Duo-Art, the touch of the pianist was similarly recorded and reproduced, using the same technique of perforations in the music roll following electrical impulses from contacts within the recording piano. With four dynamic controls, sixteen different degrees of touch could be produced (see Chapter 7), extending over the whole range of finger power from the lightest *pianissimo* to the strongest accent. In combination with the Themodist device already mentioned, the melody could be differentiated from the accompaniment, each having its own set of dynamic controls and full range of touch.

When the original recording was made, it more than likely contained stray wrong notes which no pianist may entirely avoid when playing passages requiring speed and force. One of the finest pianists of the time noted to his chagrin no fewer than 360 false notes in a single performance!* Fortunately, these wrong notes could be detected and corrected under the supervision of the artist himself. Every blemish to the performance could be removed and omitted notes cut into their proper places. Even the touch and rhythm could be improved upon if the artist was dissatisfied with his recording.

It is obvious that, with such revision carefully carried out with the artist, the result was a most polished interpretation. While with a modicum of such 'editing' a fine performance could be produced, too great a dependence on the editor with his correcting pen, sticky paper and hand punch could destroy the very spontaneity which the reproducing system sought to preserve. This explains the statement of Percy Grainger (who studied with Busoni) that his records on Duo-Art represented him not merely as he did play, but as he 'would *like* to play'. Possibly the greatest tribute to the Duo-Art came from Paderewski, who, speaking of the music roll of one of his compositions, said that listening to it gave him the same feeling in his heart as when he played it himself.

REED ORGANS AND A DEVELOPING INDUSTRY

The American company Aeolian produced a range of player reed organs between the later 1890s and 1914. These were the Aeolian Orchestrelle marque initiated with the Aeoline and the Grand and closing with the Solo Orchestrelle. The major part of this production played 58-note music rolls although the Solo instruments featured double tracker bars playing 116-note music. The instruments were voiced to produce different sounds from each rank of reeds in the same way as the developed American reed organ. Instruments ranged in size from a large upright piano to 9-foot high monsters in richly ornamented cases with as many as twenty-eight different speaking stops. The Wilcox & White Company of Meriden, Connecticut, built a similar range of player reed organs called the Symphony. As with the Orchestrelles, the Symphony played paper rolls and the performer was left to use his own discretion as to the stops to use, guidance on speed and expression only being provided.†

The reproducing piano technique was applied to these reed organs and also to special pipe

---

* It was said, somewhat uncharitably, that people used to travel miles to hear the pianist Cortot and his wrong notes.

† In America, however, Aeolian issued a special series of 'Orchestrated' rolls which gave the player an accurate guide to recommended stops to use. These rolls were not, to my knowledge, offered to the UK market.

organs made by a number of American companies, including Aeolian. These were very beautiful instruments, both in tone and appearance, and they played 176 notes on two manuals. All functions of the organ, including the swell shutters, could be operated automatically from the paper roll as well as the stops.

Wilcox & White reflected the trends with their early reed player instruments and one of their Angelus models could be pushed up to a piano keyboard in the same manner as the contemporary piano-player. Playing from the music roll, the organ would perform on a small number of stops – usually about seven – and, when a stop-knob marked 'Piano' was drawn, it would let down upon the piano keyboard a set of fingers which would then function in the same way as those on a conventional player. The device could thus play a piano and organ duet, a 'dual solo' or whatever the performer demanded just by the arrangement of the stop knobs. It assumed that organ and piano were tuned to the same pitch.

In America, the electrically driven nickelodeon – basically an expression player piano to which was added percussion effects and sometimes a few ranks of organ pipes – became the rage. Both in Germany and in the United States, many varieties of these instruments were made for bars and cafés, dance-halls and amusement arcades. The centres of production were, respectively, Leipzig and Chicago. With the coming of Prohibition in the 1920s, the market for these diminished considerably and many makers went out of business or changed to the manufacture of cinema 'Photoplayers' (see Chapter 8).

The complexity and intricacy of some of these devices bring home the fact that it is not just the present-day technician who knows how to pack a large number of pieces into a small space. The only difference lies in the fact that components packed into a player mechanism tended to be larger than those packed into, say, a modern electronic watch.

The player-piano inventors of the period were not short of ideas and a great number of patents were taken out for various improvements to the instrument, its action and construction. Some were of lasting value, such as the invention by the Aeolian Company in 1901 of the printed *tempo* line on the ordinary music roll, and the primary pneumatic action. Others, such as the electromagnetic player using sheet-metal music rolls, were destined not to make the grade.

A vast industry had been created and the number of player-piano manufacturers is impossible to estimate. Almost every maker fitted either his own player action or, more commonly, a recognised action available as a kit or unit from a player action maker. The psychological impact of the instrument on the public was profound and sales boomed. Pianos with player capabilities went to ocean liners, troopships, dance-halls, hospitals and private homes. Interest and demand for the player piano spread throughout the world and by 1920 Japan had a thriving industry manufacturing *ji-do pianos* (player pianos, literally 'self-moving piano') which cost from 1,400 yen to 3,800 yen for a player grand. Also in full manufacture at this time in Japan were electric coin-freed barrel pianos for cafés.

The popularity of the player piano can in some measure be judged from the fact that the 1922 *London Trades Directory* listed agents and manufacturers for no fewer than fifty-two different types of instruments, including reproducing pianos. Some of these were inferior instruments but these figures prove the existence of a very considerable demand in Britain. Since the demand here was but a fraction of the American sales, the number of makers in the United States was extremely large and, in the way of things, the precise figure may never be known.

Considerable artistry could be employed in the playing of a music roll and, indeed, a performer who had both flair for musical interpretation and an understanding of the mechanism of his instrument could produce a performance of extremely high quality using the manual expression controls fitted to an ordinary player piano. The logical argument was that, with all the musical notes ready to play and requiring no mental effort, the performer could concentrate all his skills and faculties on the method and style of interpretation. The serious player-piano operator could produce a perfect interpretation from an ordinary roll, given a good piano and the desire to master it and to learn the roll.

Notwithstanding the two more obvious elements of the player piano which were responsible for its popularity – entertainment and personal gratification – the instrument could be used by the serious music lover for the analysis of a piece of music. Even the accomplished pianist could learn much from the music roll that the musical score and his interpretation might otherwise pass over. The Aeolian Company's introduction of 'annotated rolls' was engendered by just this demand. Considerable explanatory text and a wealth of detailed information – including the musical score – was actually printed on the rolls to 'educate whilst playing'.

Indeed, in one interesting experiment to demonstrate the art of the contrapuntal as employed and developed by J. S. Bach, a piano roll of one of his compositions was reversed so that the high notes became the bass and the low notes the tenor and treble. The result, so it is related, sounded just as melodious as before! The qualifications of the listener on that occasion are unknown.

This more serious side to the player piano is further demonstrated by the activities of the German Honorary Committee for the Promotion of Musical Studies, by means of the Duo-Art and Pianola. Although savouring strongly of a publicity gimmick, this group held its inaugural meeting in Berlin on Wednesday 18 May 1927, and included such musical personalities as Max Bauer, Siegfried Wagner, Bruno Walter and Percy A. Scholes. The objectives of the Committee were (a) to further the educational use of Duo-Art and Pianola instruments and music rolls; (b) to comment technically on the music available from the Aeolian catalogue, and (c) to recommend to the company a choice of new compositions to record.

Also at this meeting, Percy A. Scholes introduced 'The World's Music' series of music-rolls in their various forms. These included the Biographical Roll, the Analytical Roll, the Running Commentary Roll and rolls with explanatory introduction. Aeolian was certainly the most enterprising of the roll makers. Little could the company have imagined on that day that the world's economy was on the brink of the worst slump of the age and that the decade would end in world-wide misery.

Early in the 1930s, more in an attempt to stimulate the dying market following the Wall Street crash than to foster perfection, American dealers organised player-piano proficiency contests for students. Two authoritative books were written by musicologists on the techniques of playing the player piano and the British Broadcasting Company (as it then was) employed a reproducing piano to play not only interval music but also a few scheduled piano music programmes. The instrument had not only become accepted, it was most definitely acceptable.

True as this was, the player piano had a profound sociological effect on the community. As Roehl* reflects, a whole generation grew up without the need to learn to play the piano.

---

* *Player Piano Treasury*, Vestal Press, New York.

Hitherto, piano playing was part of home life, part of growing up. Almost everyone could perform to some degree. With a self-acting instrument, there was no longer any call for tiresome five-finger exercises. All that was wanted was a roll of music, for technical competence had been superseded by rubber tubing, valves and air motors. The *Saturday Evening Post* cartoonist summed up the situation in one sentence. His cartoon showed a young girl rather stolidly pumping her way through a roll of music. A woman, in conversation with her mother, comments: 'Your daughter's got a great foot for music.'

The president of Aeolian, H. B. Tremaine, was honoured for his work with the company and, indeed, for his pioneering work in the field of the player and reproducing piano, by the staging of an International Duo-Art Week on 20–25 November 1922. Commemorating Tremaine's twenty-five years' service, Duo-Art recitals took place in many parts of the world and they included Paderewski's Duo-Art performance of his 'Minuet' to mark also his return to the concert platform.

One hundred distinguished musicians under the chairmanship of Walter Damrosch and including all the famous Duo-Art pianists formed the Tremaine Tribute Committee to arrange the events. Tremaine received many awards, including one from the Pope (as 'purveyor to the Papal Palace'), the Belgian Order of Leopold and the French Legion of Honour.

Fig. 7
From *The Connoisseur* of April 1912 comes this advertisement showing a Pianola push-up being played at London's Queen's Hall. This venue seems to have been an early mecca of self-playing pianos in concert use – see also Fig. 60.

THE RISE AND FALL OF THE AUTOMATIC PIANO

The London Duo-Art concert was held at the Queen's Hall with Sir Henry Wood conducting and the Duo-Art as soloist in Saint-Saëns's G Minor Concerto. Photographs of Aeolian Halls and showrooms in Australia, New Zealand, Capetown, Johannesburg, Gibraltar, Java, Gothenburg and Trondheim (Norway), Denmark, Holland, France, Germany, Spain, Italy, China, Japan, Argentina, Brazil, Chile, Venezuela, Colombia, Ecuador, the West Indies, England and North America were on show.

An interesting display was mounted which traced the history of the player piano and organ from 1885 through the organette, Aeolian organ (46 notes), Aeolian Grand (58 notes), Aeolian Orchestrelle, Pianola Cabinet (65 notes) to Pianola Piano (65 and 88 notes) and thence to the electric Duo-Art grand piano.

The arrival of the phonograph was considered a threat to the success of the player piano. Just as with the disc-playing musical box which rapidly incorporated a device whereby it could play either musical box or phonograph discs (see under *phonopectines* in *Musical Box*), so the player piano was considered a possible mate for the gramophone. During the late teens and the twenties a number of players were produced which had gramophones built into them. Most of these heralded from Germany and the United States and were hermaphroditic precursors of the later wireless-pianos – ordinary pianos which incorporated wireless sets in the same cabinet.

Amalgamating the player piano with a gramophone may be seen as a simple endeavour: in fact the methods suggested were as complex as those laid out in the early days of the player for playing a piano from perforated paper. Powering the gramophone from the piano pedals and the roll motor were tried, springs and electric motors were used and even descending weight mechanisms were patented.

However, more enterprising if less realistic inventors decided to try to make player piano and gramophone into a mechanism with one programme source by engraving the record track along one edge of the player roll. The advance of the cinematograph inspired applications of optical soundtrack and as late as 1928 one A. E. Zoppa was granted a British patent for a piano roll with an optically scanned music track down the right-hand edge. If any of these odd devices were ever made, certainly none is known to survive. Yet, strange to relate, the operation of the modern Pianocorder with its compact cassette of magnetic tape bears a passing relationship to this primitive type of endeavour.

THE SOCIAL HISTORY OF THE PLAYER PIANO

It is interesting to look back and reflect upon all these events in the light of the years which were to follow. By 1929, the world was plunged into the depths of a financial crisis heralded in America by the Wall Street crash. The cold reality of unemployment spread across America and Europe and in the few short years which followed the London Duo-Art concert not only did Tremaine's empire crumble but the player piano itself, considered invincible by many, lost stature and withered away.

The player piano remained popular until that economic crisis. It died in America in about 1932, was dead in France by the following year and, in spite of strenuous efforts in Britain as I shall relate in a moment, it was a non-seller by 1935. The peak of its popularity lay between 1910 and 1925. Almost every manufacturer of pianos in America and in Europe fitted player actions to their instruments. There was no question of its being beneath the dignity of the great names amongst makers to build players. Indeed some of the finest instruments bore

> ## Lean Back and Listen
>
> THIS very evening, in the quiet of your own home, you may summon for your delight such artists as Beryl Rubinstein, Herma Menth, Harold Bauer, Yolande Mero, Doris Madden, Gabrilowitch and Godowsky.
>
> Lean back and listen. They will play your favorite compositions. Science and art have struck hands to make your dreams come true. They have created
>
> ### THE ARTRIO ANGELUS REPRODUCING PIANO
>
> In itself a superb example of craftsmanship, the electrically operated Artrio brings to every home the true pleasure of hearing music as the artist himself first played it.
>
> The Artrio is also a beautifully constructed and beautifully toned grand piano that you may play yourself. There are no projections to interfere with playing found in other reproducing grands.
>
> *We are makers of the Angelus Piano, The Angelus Player Action, The Artrio Angelus (electrically operated) and Angelus Artistyle Rolls. Send for our interesting catalog number 34.*
>
> **THE WILCOX & WHITE CO.**
> MERIDEN, CONN.

Fig. 8
Expensive full-colour advertising was rarely used in player piano promotions but here, from the *Atlantic Monthly* of 1919, is a lush presentation for the short-lived Artrio Angelus made by Wilcox & White. *Paul Ottenheimer collection.*

such gilt-edged names as Steinway, Blüthner, Chickering, Mason & Hamlyn, Broadwood and others. Naturally the better the piano the better the player action fitted and, understandably, it was the practice of these top-class makers to fit reproducing actions such as Hupfeld, Welte, Ampico and Duo-Art.

The peak years had long since gone. E. H. Story's words quoted from 1905 took on a hollow sound as the industry ground to a halt. Let's take a retrospective look at the golden year of 1914 when the player piano was still in the ascendant.

THE RISE AND FALL OF THE AUTOMATIC PIANO

In January 1914, the *Piano Player Review*, a sixpenny monthly publication, issued its sixteenth number. Ernest Newman was then its editor and in his editorial for that month he dealt with an attack by the *Yorkshire Observer* on mechanical music. Then he discussed the subject of player-piano classes at competition festivals. Interesting replies were received from Harry Evans (the then well-known music adjudicator) and from Landon Ronald (later to become Sir Landon Ronald), who was wholly in favour of player-piano classes.

The *Manchester Guardian* had an interesting and outspoken leading article on this subject, wholly in favour of the innovation, as was J. A. Rodgers of the *Sheffield Telegraph*. In that month, a classical song recital was given at Wolverhampton when every item was accompanied on the player piano. Sidney Grew was agitating for barred music rolls (music rolls on which the music notation and bars was printed to aid musical understanding), a campaign which he waged, largely unsuccessfully, for many years. Messrs Boyd gave a player recital in the Town Hall at Ilford; pianola recitals took place in seven large provincial towns; the Perforated Music Company staged its Riddle-Roll Competition; *The Times* revealed the fact that the Orchestrelle Company had made a net profit of £171,603; and the *Financial Times* gave particulars of the failure of another company marketing a new kind of player piano, with a £28,184 deficiency.*

In February, Sir Henry Wood came into the question of player-piano classes at competition festivals. He wrote:

> Your idea of a class for player-piano performances at musical competition festivals is excellent. It would cause a lot of young people to grind away at the classes – a thing they would never hope to do if left to their own fingers: and it would do more to bring out their interpretive abilities than anything else.

Ernest Newman wrote an article for *The English Review* which caused a great stir in the professional world, and that journal published supplements dealing with each make of player piano then being made. Player piano concerts in this month were held at Worcester, Wolverhampton and Dublin.

In March the piano trade expressed surprise at the growth and grip of the player piano manufacturers. Recitals were given at Tunbridge Wells and Wolverhampton, and Ernest Newman was again dealing with the player piano at competition festivals. A London newspaper, the *Globe*, on the 26th of that month, started a player-piano page in every Thursday issue.

In April, the alarm of the piano trade mentioned among the March events had been transformed into hostility towards the *Player-Piano Review*, which journal had come under some sort of trade boycott. It was thought, unjustifiably, that this journal was being run by a powerful syndicate or company for the exploitation of its own particular make of player piano. The journal defended itself simply and effectively: there was not a shadow of reason for the fears of the trade. It was at the time running a competition among its readers for the best selection of a hundred music rolls. A new piano player appeared in the preliminary stages, its chief claims being sensitiveness and smallness. Part of the player was a permanent fixture under the keyboard of the piano, the other part (in cabinet form) was detachable (this was, one imagines, the Universal Piano Player of Messrs Bansall – see Chapter 14 and

---

* This was the failure of the New Trist Player Piano Co. Ltd (details in Chapter 14).

Appendix A). Recitals by various makers were given at Reading, Wolverhampton (yet again), Wells and Grimsby. In that month, Dr Smith, principal of the Hull College of Music, ventured to say in an address that 'in the not far distant future the various mechanical piano-players would dominate the musical world to such an extent as to create a slump in piano study'. The *Dundee Advertiser* had an article dealing with the abuse of the player piano – the writer had been on the receiving end of a player-piano fiend next door. During April, also, the daily press was very active in player-piano matters – encouragingly so. The *Daily Chronicle* came out with a strong article, 'Pianists All: The Printing Press and the Player-Piano', by 'Crotchet', an apt sobriquet; the *Daily Mail* joined in with 'No More Pianists: the Perfection of the Machine' by 'A Musician'; the *Globe*'s subject headings included 'Music for the Player-Piano', 'Treasure Trove', 'The Player-piano from its Educational Aspect', 'A Susceptible Instrument', and so on; a paper called *Civil & Military* printed an interesting article called 'The Player-piano: Variations in Performers'; and five firms were advertising their issues of music rolls.

In May, a correspondent in *Musical Opinion* had had a glorious smack at the wickedness in player-piano advertisements. The mechanics' journal *Work* had some articles on 'How to build an Up-to-date Player'. The *Pall Mall Gazette*, under the title 'Music and its Makers: Expression' by E.E., pointed out how a pianola can become a bad form of musical self-indulgence 'not far removed from that which consists in eating too many sweets at a time'. W. R. Hall Caine in the *I.O.M. Weekly Times* advised boys and girls to 'keep away from the piano stool'. 'Girls, I say, leave music to those whose business it is, and crowd not into a profession already crowded and one wherein mechanical arts threaten to outrival the very highest technical skill.' The *Globe* still continued its weekly page for the player piano. One interesting section appeared, 'The Case for Literature', in which the writer pleaded against a sham pretence of enjoyment that he noticed at piano recitals – and he advocated for player-pianists an honest declaration as to the kinds of music that, fashion apart, really interested them individually. The *New Age* made reference to the piano players – 'A source of misery or delight according to the fitness or otherwise of the performer on it'. 'Crotchet', again, in the *Daily Chronicle*, said: 'It is this scope for personal skill that has made the pneumatically-controlled player-piano so popular.'

In June, the trade journals all seemed preparing for combat. There were exhortations, accusations and general activities surrounding the player piano and its distributors. The *Music Student*, which had arrived at a player-piano page, printed some advice to player-pianists, obviously written by someone who did not possess an instrument. Even so, this paragraph remains good for all time: 'The pianist who, after ten years or more hard labour on the keyboard, imagines he will *straightaway* obtain full satisfaction from the new mechanical medium is the victim of a grave delusion.' The *Globe* busied itself in preparing some excellent player-pianists' programmes and had an article, 'What it means', that sensed the progress of the player piano in the years ahead. But how different the immediate year ahead proved to be!

The *Piano Player Review*'s last issue was July 1914. It had served to mirror an activity in relation to the player piano – a progress of that instrument so steady and definite that perhaps only the war and its subsequent turmoil could have interrupted it.

The depression of the 1929–32 period did more to kill off the player piano than did wireless or the gramophone, both of which suffered just as severely. The size of the problem can be judged from the simple fact that in America unemployment soared to 13·7 million in 1932 and was to rise to 15 million the following year (it was down to 8 million in 1937). Germany was hit just as hard with 5·6 million out of work and Britain, with an estimated working population of 18·5 million, had 2·8 million on the dole.

The Wall Street crash in October 1929 preceded the abandonment of the gold standard in America by four years. Britain abolished the gold standard in September 1931, the value of the pound falling from $4·86 to $3·49.

Although luxury goods suffered a sharp setback and many people were forced to move into smaller homes where space was at a premium, the player piano did not die without a struggle. It was championed by a number of dedicated player men, not the least being Reginald Reynolds (see Appendix A), who, having seen his employer Aeolian go to the wall, had the courage to stay in the player business to the bitter end.

In 1930, in an attempt to revitalise the interest in player pianos, *Musical Opinion* published a small booklet called 'Converting a 65-note Player' which told how a 65-note model could be made to play standard 88-note rolls by the dubious expedient of changing the tracker bar, adjusting the roll drive chucks and T-jointing the upper and lower notes of the 65-note scale to play all the notes of the piano. A simpler method was to tee in all the bass and treble notes of an 88-note stack so that 65-note rolls could appear to play all the notes on the keyboard – in octaves at each end, of course. This little booklet, responsible for modifying and mutilating a number of pianos at this time, proved so successful that during the next six years it ran to four reprints. It was written by Harry Drake, whose player articles were a one-time feature of *Musical Opinion*.

It was in *Musical Opinion* of July 1932 that another bastion of the player piano, Harry Ellingham, wrote:

> There are unmistakable signs that the player-piano, after sixteen years' partial eclipse, is coming back out of the shade into clear vision. Wireless, the gramophone and the reproducing piano caused the shadow that covered the true player-piano from view; and how dark has been the shadow can well be gauged by the [prominence that the instrument attained up to the time of the Great War and what has happened since].
>
> But none of these things – the war, wireless, the gramophone, the reproducing piano – killed the player-piano. Its ultimate use as the home instrument cannot be doubted. Perhaps the saturation point of listening to wireless and potted music generally is being reached; or it may be that this very element of listening to much music is inducing people to seek personal performance. Whatever may be the cause, no sane survey of the present situation can leave any doubt that the time is here again when the player-piano is emerging from partial obscurity. The demand for the instrument will grow, as people have little inclination and less time to face ordinary piano playing; and it will grow the more rapidly, much more rapidly, in proportion as the instrument is manufactured and presented as a sensitive musical instrument that can with advantage be studied seriously by every untrained lover of good music and taught by professional musicians.

A man who contributed a great deal of effort to the attempt at resurrecting the player-piano industry in England was Charles W. Bannister, who, in the autumn of 1932, urged the industry to unite and present a common advertising campaign. In admitting that a problem still lay in the relatively high cost of piano rolls, Bannister was of the opinion that if demand could be increased then these costs could be reduced. He put forward the idea of National

Player-Piano week. The problem of roll cost was not one which had escaped the attention of the roll makers and, indeed, the Muvis piano roll, a standard 88-note introduced in the autumn of 1931 at a price of 2/6d regardless of the type of music, was a conscious effort to re-establish the popularity of the player by offering an extensive catalogue of good-quality low-cost rolls readily available.

On 26 September 1932 a meeting was held at Pagani's restaurant in London's West End. Piano and player-piano makers, store buyers and dealers all sat down to discuss what to do to drum up trade which, it was postulated, had suffered at the hands of the motor car (people were travelling about more for leisure and the car was beginning to assume importance in the range of domestic durable goods) and the increase in the number of people buying their own homes, not to mention the attractiveness of wireless and the gramophone. Meeting organiser Charles Bannister sounded a clarion call to the industry to make the best of the slowly returning prosperity. Why, he told the meeting, he had heard of people who were selling their motor cars because the cost of petrol had just been increased. Bannister proposed that everybody should pull together in staging a national week to promote the instrument and that the emphasis should be on the player piano and not on brand names. He recalled that before the 1914–18 war opinion had said that the American organ took the place of the harmonium, and the piano superseded the American organ and now it was time for the player piano to oust the ordinary piano.

Bannister's move was greeted with unanimous approval and at once a committee was organised chaired by Plymouth dealer Sidney Moon. It resolved to stage the first Player Piano Week, to canvas makers to support (one immediately pledged £1,500!), to get the BBC to broadcast more player-piano concerts and to try to get Europe's commercial radio station, Radio Paris, to advertise the event on Sundays. The date of the special week was finally fixed as 21–26 November and the BBC agreed to broadcast a player piano recital by Reginald Reynolds on the National programme on 24 November between 8 and 8.25 in the evening.

The committee, which included Messrs F. H. Saffell of Triumph-Auto, Findley of Aeolian, E. H. Aird of Harrods, Pinfold of Godfreys, A. H. Fawn of the Universal Music Company and Watts of Monington & Weston, proved itself an enthusiastically strong and effective means of promotion and meetings were held up and down the country to spread that enthusiasm.

A meeting of the North-Western Division of the Music Trades Association held on 26 October agreed unanimously to support all moves to re-establish the player piano and was reminded by Bannister that the very first general radio broadcasts in Britain were made from Manchester's Trafford Park using a player piano and a gramophone. And that was in November 1922.

The initial success of the player-piano week was encouraging and dealers hoped that the three or four-year old slump, during which time many had been forced to take pianos in part-exchange for new gramophones and wireless sets, was well and truly behind them. Even the Prince of Wales was prompted to respond that 'His Royal Highness, as you know, is intensely interested and keen on the betterment of all industry. He hopes that the steps taken for a national player-piano crusade will prove a great success.' And dealers were reminded of the Cromwellian dictum: 'Don't wait until the iron is hot – strike until you make it hot!' A second player-piano week was promptly scheduled for 6–11 March 1933.

As an indication of the position of European trade, an examination of the export figures from Germany makes interesting reading. Where once Britain had been a major importer of

▲ PLATE 1
The earliest stringed instruments to be mechanised were the small table spinets or octave-spinets. This is probably the oldest surviving example and comes from the collection of Lord Howard de Walden at Dean Castle in Kilmarnock, Scotland.

▲ PLATE 2
This clockwork spinet bears a remarkable resemblance to one which was described in the catalogue of the collection of musical instruments owned by King Henry VIII, at the time of his death in 1547, as follows: 'An Instrumente that goethe with a whele without playinge uppon, of woode vernisshed yellowe and painted blewe with vi round plates of siluer pounced with anticke garnisshed with an edge of copper and guilte'. Whether or not this is actually the King's instrument, there appears some evidence to suggest that it emanated from the same craftsman.

▲ PLATE 3
The component parts of a clockwork spinet showing the fusee-wound motor and the pinned wooden barrel. The keyboard has 36 notes of which just 20 can be played from the barrel. The soundboard and strings are formed in a separate unit which stands over the barrel and is shown here separated.

PLATE 4 ▶
The clockwork spinet shown in detail above complete in its cabinet. Once the property of the German musicologist Dr Rück of Nuremberg, this was made around 1575 by Samuel Bidermann and is preserved today in the Germanisches Nationalmuseum, Nuremberg. The design follows a popular style of the period and resembles a writing case.

PLATE 5 ▶
Dr Haspels of Utrecht's Nationaal Museum van Speelklok tot Pierement points out features of a clockwork spinet to the author. This tiny instrument bears the monogram of Veit Langenbucher of Augsburg and dates from the early part of the 17th century. Besides playing music from its pinned wooden barrel, it includes an automaton scene in a cupola on top.

▼ PLATE 6
Musical clocks incorporating dulcimers, mistranslated from the German *Harfenuhr* as 'harp-playing clocks', were popular between the last quarter of the 18th century and the first quarter of the 19th century. Their often prodigious size combined with the need for frequent tuning did not ensure lasting favour. This mammoth Dutch example houses spare wooden barrels in one cabinet while the other opens out to form a set of steps to enable the barrels to be exchanged almost eleven feet above ground.

PLATE 7 ▶
The mechanism of the dulcimer clock seen above showing the barrel. There are 76 hammers in this remarkably large musical clock. The strung back for the dulcimer extends almost all the way down the back of the case. The musicwork is driven by a descending weight – another reason for needing steps to reach the top.

◄ PLATE 8
Another dulcimer clock, this one of unusual format, is to be found in the Deutsches Museum, Munich. Made in the Black Forest by an anonymous craftsman, the piece plays 18 notes on a horizontally-arranged upright strung back and in some ways reminds one of the Andersson (see Plate 18). The date of manufacture is around 1800.

▼ PLATE 9
The handsome upright clockwork piano, below left, was made in London at the beginning of the last century by John Longman of Cheapside who claimed a patent on his action. This particularly rich example, formerly in the de Vere Green collection, is now in the museum in Utrecht.

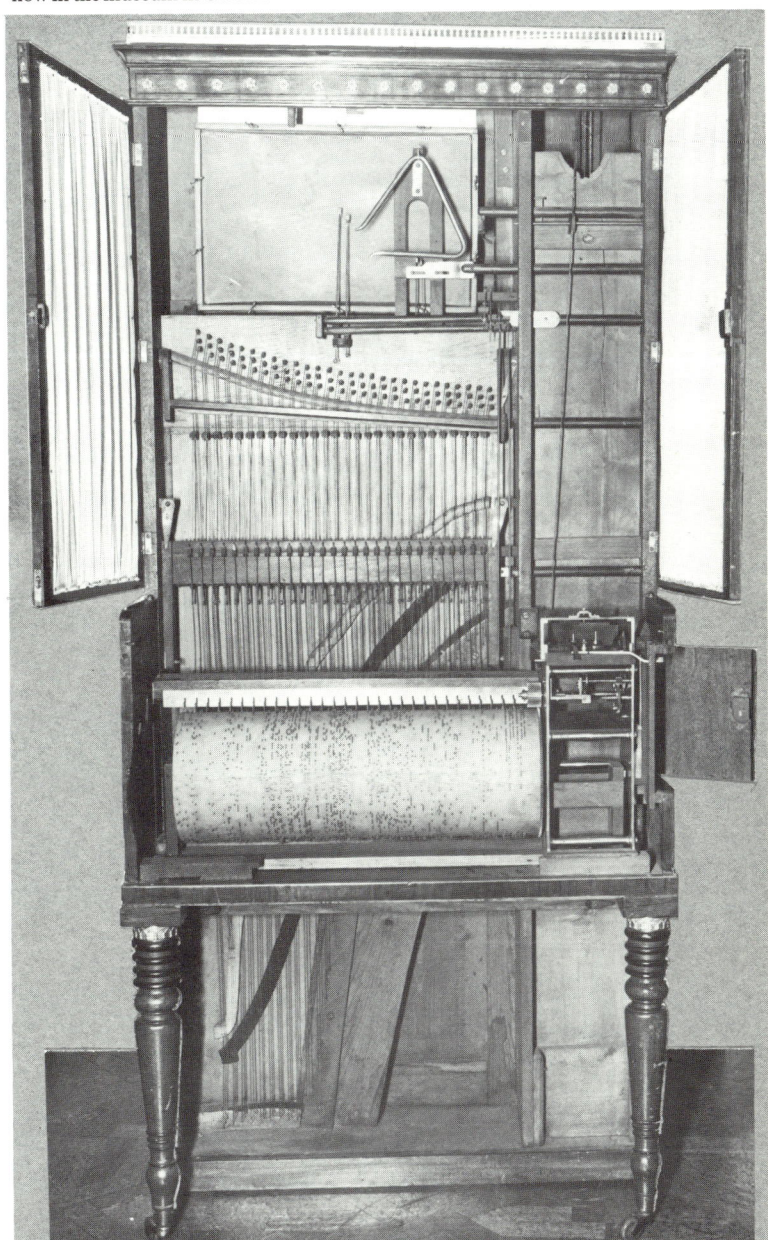

PLATE 10 ▲
The mechanism of the Longman clockwork piano reveals the rectangular drum placed behind the triangle. Down the right side, behind the clockwork, is the compartment for the driving weight and across this can be seen the five stop control rods whose knobs can be seen in Plate 9 (left). These operate drum piano or forte by moving the drum closer to its beaters, triangle on or off, drum on or off, sourdine (a felt-strip mute between hammers and strings), and piano or forte by moving the keyframe. There are 28 notes in trichords. Ten dances are pinned to the barrel.

◀ PLATE 11
A particularly fine and handsome piece of furniture is presented by this barrel piano made in the Black Forest by Imhof & Mukle during the first half of the 19th century. Playing 54 notes, the instrument is provided with a sustaining pedal and the action is based on the contemporary design used in normal upright pianos.

▼ PLATE 12
Removing the front panel and the top falls reveals the action in detail. Barrels are changed by opening a long vertical door in the right hand side of the case and the spare 10-tune barrel is housed in the bottom of the case. This view also shows the gravity dampers over the bass notes which were a common feature of barrel pianos of the period. Each of these wooden blocks hung from a pivot wire and the part which touched the string had a felt pad glued on. A piece of lead set into the wood kept the damper at rest on the string but this light pressure was such that when the string sounded, it bounced clear, returning to silence the string a moment later.

◄ PLATE 13
Early barrel-operated pianos were often arranged in the style of so-called barrel-and-finger instruments so that they could also be played by a normal keyboard when desired. There were many patents for such actions and some are reproduced elsewhere in this book. This is a particularly attractive specimen of the breed. Made in Central Europe around 1800, only the greater depth of the lower case suggests that it is other than a normal upright. The glazed panels are probably not original, fretted falls or pleated silk fronts being used to conceal the mechanism.

PLATE 14 ►
This view of the barrel-and-finger pianoforte shows what is basically a conventional sticker-type upright piano action. The mechanical action comprises a keyframe similar to that of a barrel organ which is placed above the barrel. A system of levers transfers the key motion to that of a pitman or plunger which pushes up against the back of the manual keys. To play the piano mechanically, the handle protruding from the righthand truss is turned. The handle on the right flank of the piano is used to change the tune. The instrument is in the Gustave Mathot collection in Belgium.

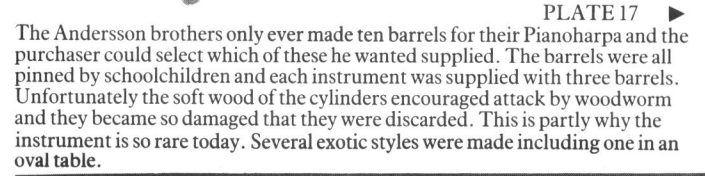

▲ PLATE 16
The brothers Anders Gustaf and Jones Wilhelm Andersson patented the Pianoharpa in 1889. A very simple instrument and one which is little more than a mechanical dulcimer, surviving serial numbers suggest that around 1,000 or so must have been made.

◄ PLATE 15
Inventor of the Pianoharpa appears to have been I. F. Nilsson of Öster Korsberga, Lemnhult, Saxhult. Twelve tunes are played on the wooden barrel which is 25¼ inches long and 4⅜ inches in diameter.

PLATE 17 ►
The Andersson brothers only ever made ten barrels for their Pianoharpa and the purchaser could select which of these he wanted supplied. The barrels were all pinned by schoolchildren and each instrument was supplied with three barrels. Unfortunately the soft wood of the cylinders encouraged attack by woodworm and they became so damaged that they were discarded. This is partly why the instrument is so rare today. Several exotic styles were made including one in an **oval table.**

◄ PLATE 18
Detail of the very simple construction of the Pianoharpa. This example belongs to museum owner Bill Lindwall in Stockholm who has researched the history of the instrument. Generally speaking, the musical arrangements are very simple and not oustanding.

PLATE 19 ▶

Coin-freed café pianos were very popular from the turn of the century right up to the start of the Second World War. Whereas English examples were not especially ornate, those made in Europe were often richly embellished with decoration. This example was made around 1925 by Charles Luche, automatic piano manufacturer of 70 rue des Tournelles in Paris. The piano plays 36 notes and includes drum, cymbal and castanet percussion effects. The case is of carved oak in *art nouveau* style.

▲ **PLATE 20**

The English style of clockwork barrel piano was, by comparison, little different from that of the cart-mounted street piano. The case was carved, an etched mirror top panel fitted, a pediment with panel for the list of tunes, and the whole given a polished black finish. This example bears the name of Keith Prowse & Co. of London, a well-known early instrument maker, but may well have been branded from Chiappa whose style it follows closely.

PLATE 21 ▶

The clockwork barrel piano industry in France developed into one of the most important in Europe. While Central Europe developed the upright form of barrel orchestrion of the type shown in Plate 30, other than products by makers such as Brun of Saint-Étienne, the majority was of the basic barrel piano format. Crubois of Granville made this impressive 51-note 'automatic' around 1930. It has drum, triangle and castanets. It is interesting to note that café or public-house pianos retained the pinned wooden barrel long after perforated card and paper had assumed supremacy in mechanical music as a whole.

▲ PLATE 22
Victorian photographer O. G. Rejlander took this endearing picture of a boy with a Hicks-type street piano *c*. 1872–4. Called *Have a tune, Miss*, it portrayed the 'grinder' in a light which cartoonist John Leech and mathematician Charles Babbage – both anti-street musician campaigners – might not have agreed with.

PLATE 23 ▲
Top right: Danish portable street piano of similar type to the Hicks style.

◄ PLATE 24
Left: Simple interior and mechanism of the Danish street piano seen top right.

PLATE 25 ►
The Hicks style appeared also in Italy and in Greece. This is a modern Greek street piano with part-iron frame. The compass is 39 notes, the lowest nine of which have gravity dampers (see Plate 12).

◀ PLATE 26
Street musicians, both barrel-organists and barrel-pianists, were all dubbed 'organ-grinders' by the often long-suffering public. The performers themselves resorted to all manner of ruses to gain attention. It was not enough just to play music. The pet monkey who would perform in gaily-coloured clothes could be relied upon to take the collecting cap round an appreciative audience. For the performer without a monkey, he could resort to an instrument with animated or automaton scenes. This piano has a tableau of musicians, magicians and conjurors all worked from special barrel pins. This type of mechanism was made in two areas – London and Berlin. Many portable street organs of the 1800–1850 period had such additions.

PLATE 27 ▲
Spanish street pianos often had part-iron frames and were much heavier than their London or New York-made counterparts. Luis Casali succeeded Barcelona's long-established family of barrel-piano makers (that of Pombia) and could thus claim to have been established in 1800. This piano plays 10 tunes and, like many Spanish instruments of the type, has five bells. The piano was made about 1920.

◀ PLATE 28
Typical London-made street piano on handcart. This one has 48 notes and is a mandolin style. The upper notes are each provided with five strings to add brilliance to the tone – and to provide a tuner's nightmare.

PLATE 29 ▶
If the sound of a good zither-banjo piano could, as Canon Wintle claimed, carry for a mile, a straight piano with a good soundboard could guarantee attention without quite so much volume. One very bright piano was the little 32-note Pasquale seen here on its original handcart.

▲ PLATE 30
Central Euorpe was the breeding ground for a whole range of barrel pianos extending from weight-driven through to spring-powered clockwork models, from simple automatic pianos through to machines with extensive percussion accompaniments, with ingenious mechanisms for realistic drum-roll and re-iterating or tremolo actions. Makers abounded in centres such as Vienna and Prague. Said to be the largest manufacturer of them all was Gustav Stingl in Vienna. In the same city were the workshops of Machinek and Gössl. Prague was the home of the family Klepetář whose many pieces demonstrate both quality and originality. There was also Diego Fuchs and many others. Outside this area there were others such as Johann Thim in Trautenau and the Lüneburg-Musikwerke in Altona but it is to Bohemia and Austria that we must look for the classic Central European style. Almost all demonstrate a bright sound and excellent musical arrangements. This unidentified example of an early weight-operated piano with drum and triangle dates from around 1905.

PLATE 31 ▶
The café piano in Northern Europe (but excluding Great Britain) underwent some interesting stylistic changes during its lifetime. Belgium was the centre of some of the most artistic developments, even if today the products of the era may be considered vulgar. The ordinary barrel piano was decked out in a façade of ornamental carved mirrors in *art nouveau* and *art deco*. While Gavioli in Paris was producing charming and flamboyant cases for his show organs, Belgian makers of automatic pianos were following suit. Here is an instrument made around 1930 by Pierre Vanroy of Aalst and reflecting the gradual trend towards more sober casework that followed the riotous 'twenties.

◀ PLATE 32
Piano orchestrions were also made in Leipzig and this one comes from Symphonion musical box inventor Paul Lochmann. Featuring a hollow steel cylinder, the Original Walzen-Orchestrion appeared in several styles. See Fig. 18.

▲ PLATE 33
Detail of the hollow cylinder which, like some disc-playing musical boxes, is projectionless. Notes are sounded by the keys dropping down into the holes in the cylinder surface. The series of machined cams around one end work percussion-selecting keys.

PLATE 34 ▶
This instrument, which belongs to Bill Lindwall of Stockholm in Sweden, also has a wood-block xylophone or marimba besides drum, triangle and cymbal. It is operated by weights which can be seen on the floor in front of the instrument in the top picture. Lochmann was not alone amongst disc musical box makers to turn his attention to pianos. His original company, Symphonion, also produced mechanical pianos while rivals Polyphon made a tall disc-playing piano with percussion, a variant of which was also built in America by Regina. The same two companies both made tall pianos played by perforated card rolls (see Plate 54). America's F. G. Otto company, makers of the Capitol musical box, also produced a disc-playing piano called the Pianette.

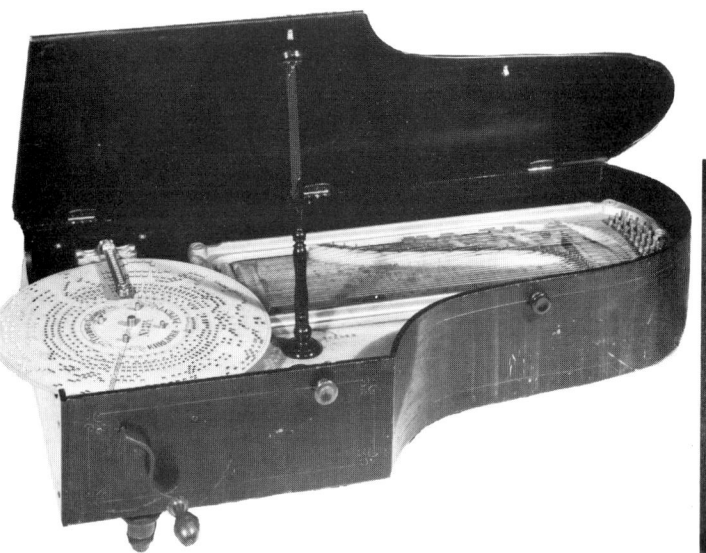

◀ PLATE 35
Leipzig musical box and organette maker Paul Ehrlich made a large number of mechanical pianos. The Orpheus was a small, attractive grand piano with an iron frame and a Christofori-type dulcimer action which played Ariston-type perforated cardboard discs.

▲ PLATE 36
Ehrlich also made a mechanical piano player, again using Ariston organette discs, which could be placed in front of a piano in order to play on the keys. The instruments were also made or factored by J. M. Grob, later to become Hupfeld, who marketed it as 'Hupfeld's Pianoplaying Apparatus No. 10'.

PLATE 38 ▼
Italians Giovanni Racca and W. Seward of Bologna patented the Piano Melodico in 1886. The instrument played book music – early ones used a pinned barrel – with a tremolo or vibrato hammer action shown in Fig. 32. There were several different sizes and shapes, this, the largest, costing £52 10s complete with 150 feet of music to play on 73 notes.

▲ PLATE 37
Rear view of the cardboard-disc piano-player. Note the fingers for the piano's black notes are colour-coded to aid positioning the player to the keyboard. Gaps at the bass end reveal the non-chromatic scale.

▲ PLATE 39
Piano Melodici models ranged from four to six octaves in compass. This is the smallest, seen with the playing desk open ready to receive the book of music.

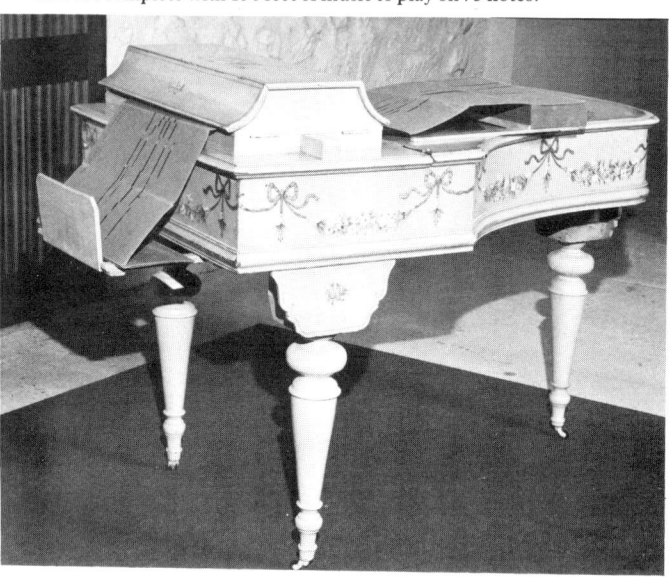

◀ PLATE 40
The so-called Piano-Orchestrion was an automatic variety of the Piano Melodico which could be operated by an electric motor and battery or by a hot-air engine. This can also be played by hand-turning the wheel. Other styles of cardboard-playing pianos were also made by Hupfeld probably under licence. These were named the Concerto, two models of the No. 11 style being known. This has 15 bells, drum and triangle. Racca also made a similar, tall cabinet piano called the Verdi.

▼ PLATE 41
Clavitist was, for a short while, the generic term which Hupfeld tried to introduce for its automatic pianos. The name was used from the earliest models through to the early 1920s. Here is an early Hupfeld Clavitist using a kicking-shoe-type player action from a perforated paper roll housed beneath the keyboard. This rare survivor is another from the Gustave Mathot collection in Belgium.

▲ PLATE 42
Hupfeld patented a kicking-shoe player attachment for pianos. Here it is seen fitted to a 1902 upright by F. Geissler of Zeitz. It is shown in the playing position.

PLATE 43 ▶
Here the player drawer is pulled out to show the mechanism of the roll transport with the mechanical keyframe and its grooved pressure roller treble of centre. The lever at the extreme right behind the crank handle locks and unlocks the drawer.

◄ PLATE 44
The Hupfeld player attached to a piano by Gebruder Perzina of Schwerin dating from 1905. The music roll is placed on the left-hand spindle and is wound across the keyframe by a central row of sprocket holes. The basic Hupfeld system was improved upon several times by the inventors. It was also taken up by an American company, Adek Manufacturing Co. of New York as the Pianotist.

▲ PLATE 45
The Pianotist Company opened in London although, as these special Pianotist rolls clearly proclaim, all the music was cut in America. Roll number 15 (left) of *La Paloma* cost 4s, Rubenstein's *Melody in F*, number 9, cost 5s 9d and the overture to *The Merry Wives of Windsor*, number 137 (right) cost 14s 6d.

◄ PLATE 46
The Pianotist was smaller, neater and better engineered than its Leipzig-made counterpart but it was still a system plagued with mechanical problems which put its manufacturers out of business. Here the Pianotist is fitted to a Steinway of about 1908. The kicking-shoe roller can just be seen at the bass end of the piano.

PLATE 47 ►
Detail of the Pianotist action drawer. The angled pressure rollers are to overcome tracking problems. In this picture, incidentally, the piano's keys have been removed. The Pianotist itself appeared in several forms one of which included a set of small folding foot pedals situated right at the treble end of the keyboard. These served to rotate the kicking-shoe roller. The Pianotist was developed between 1903 and 1905. According to American historian Q. David Bowers, a commercial version was also made which was called the Nicklin. This was electrically-powered and coin-freed.

PLATE 48
Detail view of the kicking-shoe action of the Pianotist. This mechanical piano-playing principle was first devised by the Frenchman Lacape and was subsequently used in a variety of ways. While obviously mechanical in its operation, the signalling of the system was achieved in a number of ways over the years. Electrically-operated versions were made and even pneumatically-cued models were patented by inventors in both Europe and America. The kicking-shoe was not, it would appear, favoured by British inventors of piano-playing actions.

PLATE 49
Alexander Debain patented a system of mechanically playing a piano using wooden boards studded with projections. These he called *planchettes* and the instruments were styled Antiophonel pianos. A wide variety of styles was made ranging from key-top players for pianos, harmoniums and pipe organs to complete Antiophonel pianos. Here, dating from about 1860, is a rare example of the keyless Antiophonel automatic piano. The instrument is in the Nationaal Museum van Speelklok tot Pierement, Utrecht.

PLATE 50
Detail of the playing system of the Debain Antiophonel piano. The pinned wooden planchette is here seen upside down to show its principles. In normal use, this is placed the other way up on the playing deck and its toothed rack engaged in a drive cog. Turning the handle draws the planchette across the mechanical keyframe, setting in motion the hammer action.

PLATE 51
The Debain Piano Mécanique Antiophonel piano with the doors open to reveal the clean and simple lines. This instrument must be considered a rarity since pianos for domestic use which could only be played mechanically have never enjoyed a strong following with the public.

◀ PLATE 52
The complete Piano Mécanique of Debain could be played by hand or by the use of the sets of pinned planchettes. Here can be seen the combined instrument with the Antiphonel player on the top. This operates its own separate set of piano hammers.

▼ PLATE 53
In this view of the Piano Mécanique, the set of hammers controlled by the automatic player can be seen in a frame along the top of the strings with the hammers extending downwards. For mechanical playing, the normal hammers are drawn back out of the way and the mechanical ones lowered into place as in this view.

◀ PLATE 54
The Polyphon Rossini piano orchestrion played a 73-note perforated roll made of thick, durable paper or card. Early examples were barrel-operated.

▼ PLATE 55
This keyless mechanical player looks as if it has been converted from a normal keyed piano. There is neither name nor indication of origin, yet it may be Italian.

German-made musical goods, in particular automatic pianos, the position was now very different. In October 1932, Germany exported 107 automatic pianos to Italy, 90 to Switzerland, 638 to Czechoslovakia, 71 to Sweden and 121 to Austria. None to Britain. In the month of December 1932 Germany exported only 8 pianos to Britain – three of them grands and none of them players – yet it sent 67 players to Switzerland, 49 to Italy, 142 to Sweden, 22 to Japan, 12 to Denmark, 225 to Czechoslovakia (which had just begun its own obviously successful player-piano push), and 52 to Austria. Its entire export to the last-mentioned five countries in that month were players.

In *Musical Opinion* of April 1933 the second player week was reported enthusiastically thus:

> Despite the severe economic depression, unprecedented in the whole history of the world, dealers and the big stores entered enthusiastically into making the second player week a bigger success than the first, the general opinion being that any kind of movement or activity is better than stagnation.

The report went on to relate the support promised by the BBC (it never came), Radio Athlone, Radio Paris and Norway. A quarter of a million circulars were distributed free by committee members by courtesy of the Universal Music Company. The front showed a typical surburban home and the message 'Why is this a Happy Home?' The answer turned out to be because it had a player piano 'on which the latest song rolls' could be enjoyed. Large-scale production which had helped lower costs to something approaching those of the ordinary piano, plus the availability of deferred terms, made the player piano universally attractive and promised to put its owner firmly on 'the road back to the personal participation in music'.

The British player trade received a side-blow when, in 1933, import duties on German pianos (not automatic ones) were reduced from 33⅓ per cent to 20 per cent. The Pianoforte Manufacturers' Association, under its outspoken chairman William Evans, protested that this move could flood the British market with cheap German instruments, so forcing our factories out of business. 'We had nearly two hundred firms producing pianos in this country,' he said. 'As a result of the depression of the last five years the number has already been halved. Another "bump" from Germany would mean that another fifty would go out.'

By the summer of 1933, people in the know were beginning to detect the changes in the way in which people spent their money. Although there was rather more money about, it was going on other items. This was the age of the cinema and the age of motoring for everyman. The £100 private car had arrived and the building of dream-palace cinemas with their very own version of *art deco* was in full spate. The piano *per se* had lost its popularity, they said, and was no longer fashionable. Addressing the Scottish Music Merchants' Association at Pitlochry on 6 June that year, pianomaker W. H. Strohmenger said:

> It is estimated that during the present year the number of pianofortes manufactured in this country [the British Isles] will amount to some seventy per cent less than those manufactured in the peak period, which, when you consider that we have suffered the total loss of the export trade, the forced sale by many private owners, and the enormous shrinkage in all incomes, coupled with the fact that the piano is a luxury, is not a very

serious matter. It is very interesting to know that the figures of the last few months would go to show that the recovery is starting, slowly, but still advancing.

The American Society of Composers, Authors and Publishers meanwhile was most concerned at what was happening to the music trade and, in particular, to the popular song. It found that the life of a song, measured in terms of how long it was saleable as a printed sheet of music in the store, had been seriously diminished by the introduction of radio. It went so far as to publish a little leaflet called *The Murder of Music* which contained some interesting statistics, some of which I reproduce as follows:

The growth of the Radio Audience

1925	16,000,000		1929	38,000,000
1926	20,000,000		1930	46,000,000
1927	26,000,000		1931	52,000,000
1928	30,000,000		1932	60,000,000

Total Sales of Pianos (in US dollars – £1 = $3·49)

1925	93,670,000		1929	38,000,000
1927	67,000,000		1931	12,000,000

Sales of Gramophones (Phonographs) (in US dollars)

1925	22,600,000		1929	31,656,000
1927	46,000,000		1931	4,869,000

Total Sales of Radio Sets (in US dollars)

1925	165,000,000		1929	592,068,000
1926	200,000,000		1930	332,198,000
1927	168,750,000		1931	212,040,000
1928	388,000,000		1932	124,860,000

Total Sales of Sheet Music (in US dollars: compiled from three leading firms)

1925	2,639,351		1929	2,130,722
1926	3,447,775		1930	1,261,137
1927	2,797,518		1931	861,383
1928	2,790,862		1932	827,154

Employment of Musicians in Motion Picture Theatre Orchestras

1925	19,000		1932	3,000

Meanwhile in Britain plans were laid for a further player-piano week, this one to be merged with the Music Trades Association's National Music Week. The event was held from 9 October 1933 and, whereas at the first player-piano week some 300 dealers arranged displays of instruments and the second week saw this number increased to 400, the hopes for a turn of the tide were so great that the nationwide campaign involved even more dealers up and down the country.

The success of this October meeting was such that several makers who had ceased making players were inspired to reopen their production lines. And Charles Bannister said again that he was optimistic about the future of the player piano. The next National Player Piano Week was fixed for 5 November 1934.

Meanwhile the Americans had been watching events in Britain and were impressed by the united efforts of the industry towards re-establishing sales. In the early part of 1934, the Chicago *Piano Trade Magazine* discussed the possibility of revival of the instrument in America, commending the work of Charles Bannister in Britain. Many American makers, it said, immediately got out of the business at the onset of the depression, so accelerating the

> AN OUTSTANDING FEATURE OF THE
> # AEOLIAN CO.'S
> # GREAT REMOVAL SALE
> OF THEIR ENTIRE BOND STREET STOCK
>
> A GROUP OF
> ## GRAND AND UPRIGHT
> # 'PIANOLA' PIANOS
> WITH 'DUO-ART' REPRODUCING ACTION
> THE INSTRUMENT DE LUXE OF THE PIANO WORLD
> ## MARKED DOWN
> TO LESS THAN HALF PRICE TO ENSURE CLEARANCE
>
> *Your Great Opportunity*
> to secure one of these magnificent instruments
> at little more than the cost of an ordinary piano.
>
> *Call or write for particulars*
> ## THE AEOLIAN COMPANY, Limited
> AEOLIAN HALL, 131-7, NEW BOND STREET, LONDON, W.1
> 'Phone: MAYFAIR 7095

Fig. 9
By May of 1930, The Aeolian Company had embarked on a clearance of stock as a prelude to the closure of its London operation. The company took large spaces in daily newspapers to offer players at bargain prices (see *Clockwork Music*, p. 278). This notice appeared in an unidentified magazine of that year. *Paul Ottenheimer collection.*

decline in the market by cutting off the supply of instruments at source.

This same year a controversial article appeared on the Continent. Commenting on the early demise of the French player-piano industry and the stoic efforts of the British at resurrecting trade after the depression, the publication *Musique et Instruments* had some interesting remarks to make on the reproducing piano:

> The player piano, as at first developed, aimed chiefly at facilitating the playing of the piano. To a certain extent it took charge of what may be called the physical part of playing, leaving to the performer the task of phrasing and expression. People were able more easily to become players, but musical qualities were not excluded. On the contrary, these remained, and it was possible to obtain from the instrument all that could possibly be expected. The owner of the player did not become a passive listener, but rather satisfied his musical tastes by musical expression personally applied.
>
> The American player makers erred when they changed the instrument into something more automatic. The reproducing piano was introduced, and while a marvel of mechanism, it was inimical to the interests of players. With appropriate rolls, the 'reproducer' could certainly imitate the art of Paderewski and other virtuosi, and this by persons with no knowledge of music whatsoever. The new instrument gained popularity rapidly, but it was short-lived, for there was something psychologically false about the suggestion that the operator was responsible for the result.
>
> The reproducer, entirely automatic, captivated at first those disposed to make little or no effort: it also secured the adherence of some true lovers of music who found in it real opportunities for hearing performances better than they could produce on a foot-blown player. They were satisfied for a time, until indeed they were satiated with the store of rolls at their command, and then they realised that they were no longer making music. They had again been reduced to a state of passive listeners with a stale repertoire: and their taste for the player and its music faded away. These people realised that the radio with its loud speaker offered something more to their taste and in increasing variety.

In 1936, the National Player-Piano Publicity Committee came into action again, publishing a pamphlet called 'Plea for the Player'.

In February 1937, what was probably the last of the player pianos to be produced in England was revealed at the British Industries Fair by the London makers Barratt & Robinson. This was the Minstrelle Autopiano, which measured a mere 1 ft 5½ in. deep and 3 ft 3 in. high. This used a single-valve action placed under the keyboard. The player controls were accessible with the key fall closed and a transposing tracker bar (which was viewed as vital if the piano was to be used to accompany singing) was fitted. At this same B.I.F. an exhibitor called Bush Radio displayed models of a thing called the Bush Televisor Type T5. Selling at 55 guineas and only usable in the area covered by the BBC television station at London's Alexandra Palace, this object caused fresh unease amongst the piano trade. Will it, they asked one another, affect the piano industry as the invention of wireless did not so many years ago?

How insignificant it all seems now when one looks back to that year. Europe was boiling for war, America and Canada experienced the first sit-down strikes in the huge General Motors dispute – and, while Wallace Carothers (1896–1937) was making the first nylon stockings, Frank Whittle was testing the first jet engine. The world was preparing for the ill-fated 1940 Olympic Games in Tokyo and fifty seats were booked in advance on the Hindenburg airship which was to visit the games. After its 1936 season refit, the giant German dirigible sported a Blüthner piano in its spacious lounge. This special piano, a 5 ft 5 in. grand, weighed only 326 lb instead of the usual 530 lb thanks to the use of duralumin for the frame and all other metal parts (save, of course, the strings). The piano case was covered with light yellow pigskin. It perished along with thirty-six souls at the Lakehurst mast on 6 May 1937. The world was being swept up on a whirl of accelerating technology.

And yet, in April 1937, a New York trade paper revealed that there was now a campaign afoot in America to try to revive the player. Several makers were making new models. And in Britain Charles Bannister's National Player-Piano Publicity Committee was also detecting a resurgence of interest – again.

With the progress of radio and the widening interest in television during the years immediately prior to the 1939–45 war, not to mention improvements in the gramophone industry, the hoped-for revival was not to be. Although as the world climbed out of the depression there was more money and ordinary pianos began to sell again, players were no more. Production had long since tailed off and many makers went out of business or were absorbed by larger firms. The onset of war marked *finis* to the era. In the short space of about forty years, the pneumatic player piano had developed from a rather primitive and somewhat impractical machine to a set of production components which fitted inside the piano and by means of which something close to perfect reproduction might be obtained. As with so many great inventions, having gone through the processes of evolution it emerged as the quintessence of its designed specification only to find that standards had been altered so much that it was no longer required. Thus in its very prime it became obsolete.

In certain quarters, though, the player piano's following has never really waned. In Australia, for example, the instrument is almost as popular now as it ever was, there never having been any marked recession in interest or demand. Indeed, Melbourne's branch of Aeolian, The Orchestrelle Company, was still selling new Duo-Art and other rolls right up to the time of its closure as late as 1976. There is still a rich trade in restored player-pianos and also in new rolls which are still being produced in quantity. In both England and America there exists small firms, often one-man outfits, who will produce new ordinary rolls, or make a copy of an old roll for reproducing piano or nickleodeon. And the QRS company still survives in the States along with Mastertouch in Australia. There is an interesting tale about Mastertouch which I am sure they will not mind my telling. Some years ago, the proprietors decided to close the business and advertised all the plant and equipment for sale. So great was the response and so positive the regrets that this action was being considered that Mastertouch decided to remain in operation!

The use of modern techniques in roll-copying has made possible a number of commercially-available roll-punching machines for the enthusiast. Some use pure mechanical means, others electro-pneumatic or electro-mechanical. The computer-controlled roll-perforator may yet come . . .

Interest in player pianos is mounting daily now. They are becoming more and more sought-after; their ownership, once considered a liability, is now being cherished and owners are taking a second look at their pianos and even taking the trouble to learn the proper way to make them perform a roll. Even so, as an industry, it is still precarious and one may confidently predict that it may never again be so lucrative a line as it was half a century ago.

EUTERPEON ROOMS,
547, OXFORD STREET, W.C.
IMHOF & MUKLE,

GERMAN ORGAN Builders, MUSIC PUBLISHERS,

PIANOFORTE Manufacturers, MUSIC IMPORTERS,

AND PATENTEES.

THE ONLY MANUFACTURERS IN ENGLAND OF SELF-ACTING INSTRUMENTS.

ORCHESTRION, the largest self-acting instrument ever made, possessing all the effects of a full orchestra, including Drum, Triangle, &c. .... from 800 to 1,000 guineas.
EUTERPEONS, self-acting instruments, with Flutes, Oboes, Clarinets, Bassoons, &c. .... ,, 150 to 700 ,,
Self-acting FLUTE INSTRUMENTS, having all the pipes voiced like the Orchestral Flute, and of a beautifully rich tone (this class of instrument can never get out of tune) .... ,, 30 to 400 ,,
Self-acting ORGANS and MUSICAL CLOCKS of every description .... ,, 20 to 100 ,,

HANDLE ORGANS.
GERMAN HANDLE ORGANS, of a sweet, soft tone, suitable for Schools, Nurseries, &c .... from 90 shillings.
PORTABLE ORGANS, with Trumpets, Flutes, &c .... ,, 20 guineas.
HANDLE ORGANS, with mechanical figures of every description .... ,, 2 ,,

PIANOFORTES, &c.
Self-acting PIANOFORTES, Upright Cottage size, with six barrels, which are removed from the top of the instrument; quite a new model, and differently made from any other, having also the usual finger action .... ,, 170 ,,
HANDLE PIANOFORTES in handsome cases .... ,, 10 ,,
COTTAGE PIANOFORTES, full compass, and all the latest improvements .... ,, 36 ,,
PICCOLO PIANOFORTES, full compass, cylinder fall, and all the latest improvements .... ,, 25 ,,
CONCERT FLUTES, with 8 German Silver Keys and Fittings .... ,, 1 ,,
FLUTE FLAGEOLETS, combining Octave Flute and Flageolet, with the Old Flute Fingering .... ,, 1 ,,
OCTAVE FLUTES, PICCOLOS, FLAGEOLETS, DUET and TRIO FLAGEOLETS, made to order.
ENGLISH CONCERTINAS, full compass, G to C, 48 Keys .... ,, 4 ,,
ANGLO-GERMAN CONCERTINAS (own manufacture, with the German Style of Fingering) .... ,, 30 shillings.

IMPORTERS OF NICOLE FRERES' MUSICAL BOXES.
MUSICAL SNUFF BOXES, playing 2, 3, or 4 airs .... ,, 14/6
MUSICAL BOXES, large size (from 1½ inches to 22 inches long), playing 4, 6, 8, 10, or 12 tunes .... ,, 4 guineas.
PIANOFORTE MUSICAL BOXES .... ,, 8 ,,
MILITARY MUSICAL BOXES, with Drum and Peal of Bells, playing 6 tunes .... ,, 16 ,,

Every description of Musical Boxes repaired on the premises.

Importers of ALEXANDRE'S HARMONIUMS and ORGANINES, ORGAN MELODIUMS, ORGAN ACCORDEONS, TREMOLO FLUTINAS, ORGANOPHONES, FLUTINAS, GERMAN CONCERTINAS, VIOLINS, VIOLAS, VIOLONCELLOS, GUITARS, WIENER ZITHERS-EMMYLYNKAS, ROMAN and NEAPOLITAN STRINGS.

BARRELS marked with any selection of Music for German, French, or English Instruments.

ALL INSTRUMENTS manufactured by Messrs. I. & M. warranted to stand SEA VOYAGE and TROPICAL CLIMATES.

INSTRUMENTS BUILT TO ANY DESIGN.   **REPAIRS DONE FOR THE TRADE.**

CHAPTER 2

The Barrel Piano and Its Development

The barrel piano appeared as a direct application of the principles of the mechanical pipe organ and was the result of a logical progression from the mechanical spinets, described in the previous chapter, and the barrel organ of pre-Christian origin.* Its main parts were a wooden barrel studded with metal pins corresponding with the music to be played, a piano frame or strung back, and a means of rotating the barrel, usually hand crank, worm shaft and cog-wheel. Between barrel and piano strings was a rudimentary set of sprung hammers mounted transversly across the instrument in a keyframe.

As detailed earlier, stringed instruments struck by hammers go back at least to the sixteenth century and long case clocks with barrel mechanisms which played on dulcimers were not uncommon in the eighteenth and early nineteenth centuries. However, the introduction of the earliest identifiable 'street piano' appears to be attributable to a piano maker named Hicks in Bristol in the first few years of the nineteenth century. This seems an unusual location for the instrument but the roots are almost certainly Italian. Many Italians came to Britain through the ports of both London and Bristol and one might imagine that an enterprising piano maker might have seen the familiar portable street organ and decided to try to make a small street piano along similar lines. Alternatively, he may have seen an early Italian instrument and copied it with an edition of his own. The true answer may never be known. However, the Hicks family were prolific workers and, from 1805 up to at least 1850, they produced many such instruments in Bristol and, later, in London as well. One of the Hicks family was still pinning street organ and piano barrels well into the second half of the last century. A member of the family travelled to America and established a branch of his art and craft in New York. Similar instruments were produced, also in Bristol and London, by Distin. These were technically and stylistically virtually identical. There is also a like-styled barrel piano in the Marino Marini collection in Italy which is said to date from around 1810 and to have been the work of Volontè Pietro of Como. This reinforces the confusion as to whether Hicks invented the style or anglicised a product of Italian origin. While I am inclined to consider that the barrel piano ought first to have seen the light of day in Italy, lack of dated evidence makes it impossible to prove that Italian-made 'Hicks-style' pianos predated the work of the great Bristol family.

So, then, Joseph Hicks appears to have been the inventor of the instrument which has subsequently come to be called variously cylinder piano, barrel organ (incorrect), street piano, piano-organ (travesty), hurdy-gurdy (incorrect), grinder organ (incorrect), mechanical dulcimer (perhaps the most apt). Even the word 'piano' must be adopted with reserve for,

---
* *Barrel Organ*, p. 41ff.

certainly at the beginning, it was incapable of varying its sound output and was far more *forte* than *piano*. Although 'mechanical dulcimer' is thus nearer the truth terminologically speaking, cylinder piano or barrel piano may more readily be understood.

The date of the invention is claimed by Percy Scholes* as 1805; John Clark† says 1810. Without doubt the techniques and skills necessary to construct such an instrument were known well before that time and I feel inclined to suggest that the earlier date is more probably correct.

Joseph Hicks was the son of a famed cabinet-maker named Peter Hicks, who was admitted a freeman of Bristol on 12 October 1812. The last entry in the Rates Books which Langwill has traced for Joseph is 1847.

A specimen of this type of small street piano exists in the George Brown Collection, New Jersey, and bears the mark: 'George Hicks, Hand-Organs and Cylinder Pianos, Brooklyn, L.I.' This instrument is identical to those made by Hicks in England and, in the absence of concrete evidence, it may be suggested that George was either the brother or the son of Joseph Hicks, emigrating to America probably about 1820.

One John Hicks of Clerkenwell, London, was building the same type of instrument *c.* 1850 and it is more than likely that he too was related to Joseph. The name of Joseph Hicks crops up again on a much larger instrument in which the barrel paper watermark is 1846. The address given is Pentonville, London. Whether this implies that Joseph (of Bristol) died in 1847 and Joseph (of London) was a son, or whether Joseph left Bristol in 1847 and came to London, remains unknown. There is a close similarity between all the instruments bearing the name Hicks and the trade of cabinet-maker is certainly evidenced in the good workmanship and appearance of their cases.

With the apparent exception of the large one by Joseph Hicks in London, referred to above, these early pianos were intended for use by street musicians. Street music is as much part of life as any other form of music and was particularly so at this time. Indeed, a study of this subject, its sociological influence and its general effect on the public at large would itself require a large monograph.‡ The wandering musicans either played ordinary musical instruments (where they had the ability) or relied upon mechanical ones.

The small barrel pianos, barrel pipe organs and the barrel harmoniums of later years were extremely popular – at least with their players. This enthusiasm was not always shared by the town residents, however, and the mass exposure of citizens in their homes to noisy musicians in the road outside, invariably playing the same tune over and over again, jarred nerves, encouraged high blood pressure, fostered questions in Parliament, engendered ineffectual by-laws – which still did not stem the remorseless tide of mechanical music in the streets. The Victorian writer, John Leech, was sent to an early grave because, he apparently claimed shortly before his demise, he was being driven mad by the noise of 'organ grinders'.§

Professor Charles Babbage, mathematical visionary, inventor extraordinary and a cantankerous genius to boot, justly earned the title of the organ-grinder's Public Enemy Number One. Like Carlyle, his concentration was extremely sensitive to distracting sounds and he considered that a quarter of his life's working power was destroyed by the audible nuisance of 'organ-grinders' and other street musicians performing outside his house in

---

* *Oxford Companion to Music*, 8th edition, 1950.
† *Musical Boxes*, 2nd edition, 1952.
‡ See T. J. Wyke, 'Street Music', *The Music Box*, Vol. 9, pp. 162ff.
§ T. J. Wyke, *op. cit.*

THE BARREL PIANO AND ITS DEVELOPMENT

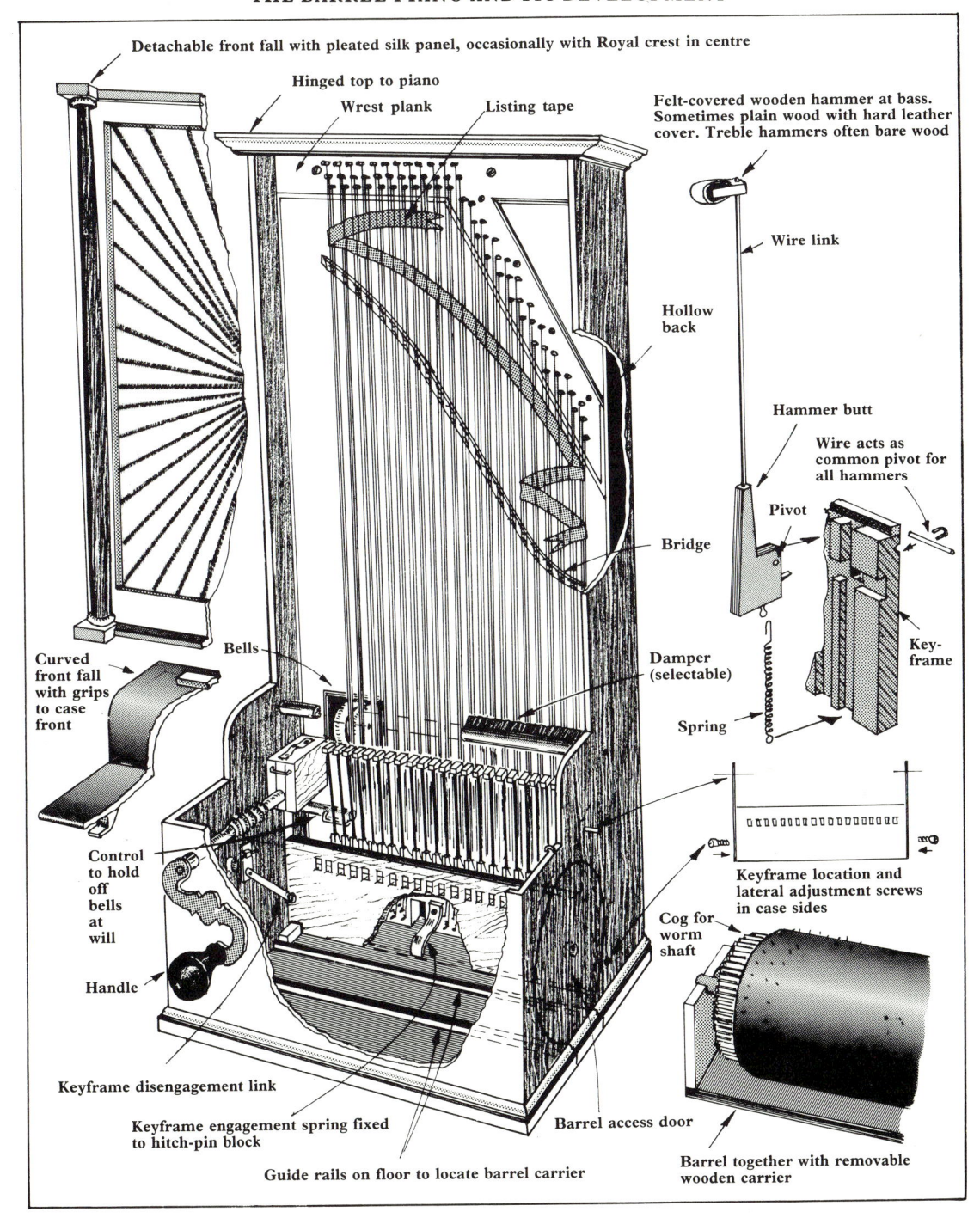

Fig. 10
Details of the construction of the Hicks style of English portable street piano.

Dorset Street, London. Babbage took up petitions against them, complained to his Member of Parliament, badgered the police to arrest them and, so it is related, once pursued a fleet-footed member of this maligned fraternity for a mile across London before finding a policeman who was willing to run him in.

Nevertheless, the closing years of the reign of George III saw the resurgence of street music using mechanical barrel pianos. Pall Mall in London was the first street to be illuminated by gaslight in 1807, breaking for the first time the Stygian gloom of London's nightlife. The itinerant musicians could now play after dark and gain revenue from the theatre-goers and promenaders.

When Joseph Hicks died, his teachings survived in the hands of his one-time apprentice, Henry Distin. He produced instruments very similar to those of Hicks, playing eight or ten tunes on 23 notes. All these pianos had wooden frames; indeed, with the exception of the hammer shafts and the sundry brass springs and steel linkages, they were made entirely of timber. The barrel was made of poplar, the wood used for almost all organ and piano barrels on account of its even grain and consequent suitability for pinning. The iron frame for normal pianofortes, an American invention, did not come until 1825, so there was nothing unusual in this style of construction. With the pianoforte, the total pull of all the strings on the wooden frame was often as much as 30 tons and thus it was not uncommon during the interval of a concert or piano recital for the tuner to come to the rostrum and retune the instrument. The smaller street piano suffered, to a lesser extent, from the same inherent problem and thus there was plenty of work to be had for the Distins and the Hickses, maintaining their products in service. The fact that these street pianos went out of tune so quickly and also that their operators usually either couldn't care less or, quite probably, were not musical enough to notice only fanned the rising distaste of the public for this sort of music. Henry Distin later moved to Philadelphia, where he was still alive in 1898 – his eightieth year.*

Other makers who produced this type of portable piano included Baylis, Sharp and Taylor. Since all these made virtually identical instruments, the probability is that these men were at some time associated with Hicks, possibly, like Distin, employees or apprentices.

There was a trend for the musicians to favour the street barrel organ playing pipes rather than the barrel piano. Although its initial cost was probably greater, it did not require frequent attention and, with normal use, remained in tune. Jos. W. Walker, a parlour apprentice organ-builder George Pike England, was prompted to manufacture a barrel organ almost identical in appearance to the Hicks/Distin type of barrel piano. Only one of these has ever been seen and the average street barrel organ tended to be a smaller, more compact instrument taking the best advantage of the ability of organ pipes of excessive length to be mitred into compact shapes.

The strong similarity between the concept of the barrel piano and the barrel organ led to the manufacture of mechanical pianos by several barrel-organ makers. William Rolfe of Cheapside, London, built both barrel organs and normal square pianos. His son, Thomas Hall Rolfe, concentrated more on the mechanical piano and, in 1825, took out patents for

---

* An interesting story concerns Distin's father, who was a solo bugler in the Grenadiers. In that capacity he was supposed to test all the musical instruments for the British bands. One day he chanced to try a bugle which had been sent down from the Tower. It had been badly packaged and a nail from the packing case had been driven through it. Distin tried the instrument and found that it played a new note (bugles at this time, in keeping with most horns, had no pistons). Thus inspired, he bought an old bugle and filled it full of holes until he found the new notes which would be usable. Henceforth, the keyed bugle was perfected.

THE BARREL PIANO AND ITS DEVELOPMENT

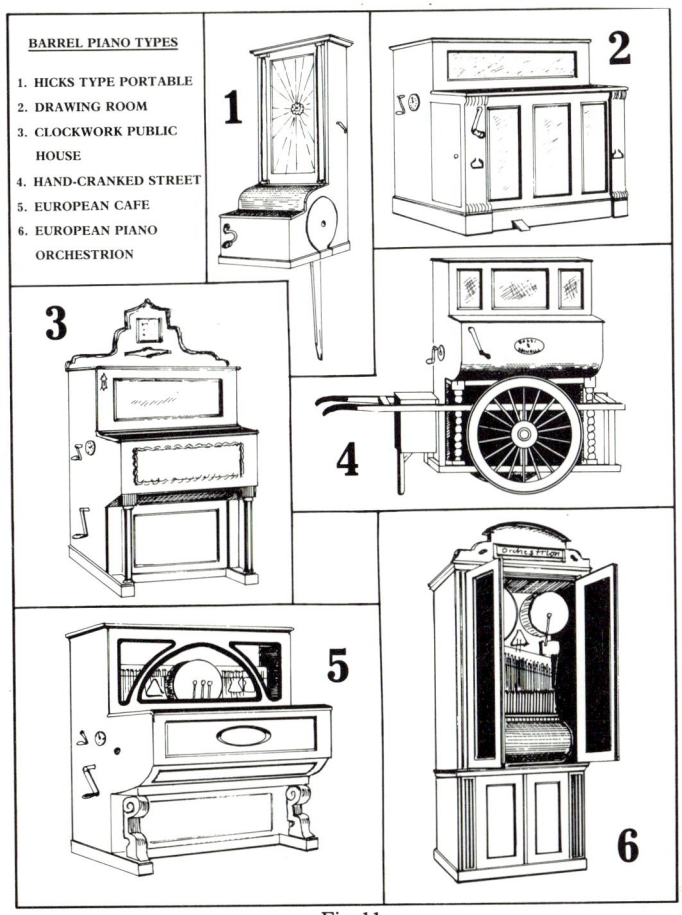

BARREL PIANO TYPES
1. HICKS TYPE PORTABLE
2. DRAWING ROOM
3. CLOCKWORK PUBLIC HOUSE
4. HAND-CRANKED STREET
5. EUROPEAN CAFE
6. EUROPEAN PIANO ORCHESTRION

Fig. 11
Six basic types of barrel-operated piano.

improvements on the self-acting pianoforte which comprised a method of pinning the barrels to produce loud or soft notes by regulating the length of the pins – a device later perfected by Schmidt in Germany, as we shall see further on.

Perhaps it was one of these instruments which was the subject of the following diary item published in *Musical Opinion* in September 1912 – a time when the player piano was very much in vogue:

> There is, indeed, nothing new under the sun. Attention has recently been called to the fact that even the automatic piano player is not such a novel invention as most people suppose it to be. *The Manchester Courier* for March 15th, 1828, has an advertisement headed 'Self-Performing Pianoforte'. It describes some of those beautiful and valuable instruments which, besides all the usual properties of a pianoforte, possesses the peculiar and pleasing addition of a mechanical arrangement by which several approved pieces of music are performed in the most brilliant style without the assistance of any performer, while at the same time it may be accompanied by the performer at the keys if desirable. The advertisement adds that 'for quadrille parties, assemblies or ball-rooms,

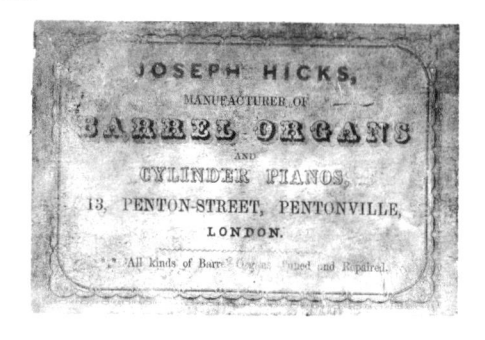

Fig. 12
Makers of portable street pianos often affixed their trade labels to their soundboards. Little is known of John Baylis but note that he says 'Old Barrels re-set to Modern Music'. Joseph Hicks was certainly much earlier and his 'parlour apprentice' Henry Distin succeeded him as a maker in Bristol.

and in all situations where a performer is not present it proves a valuable acquisition'. It would be interesting to know if a specimen of this 'self-performing pianoforte' is extant.

William Youens built a mechanism patented in December 1859 which could be placed on the keyboard of a piano or harpsichord for mechanical playing. Unlike Alexandre Debain's Antiphonel playing mechanism of 1846, which used flat, studded wooden boards or 'planchettes' to produce movement via stickers to the keys, Youens used the time-tested barrel as the musical provider. This was fixed in a frame with a set of weighted levers, one for each piano key. The music was represented not by pins on the barrel but by holes or depressions. When the ends of the levers dropped into these openings in the barrel surface, their opposite ends contacted the keys. The force of contact, and thus the volume of sound produced, could be varied by the form of the barrel note holes. This keyboard player could be operated either by hand or by clockwork.

During the 1850s, thoughts were turning towards larger barrel pianos and two other famous barrel organ manufacturers – Imhof & Mukle and T. C. Bates – directed their attentions to the making of fine instruments which would blend with the fashionable styles and decor of the period.

Imhof & Mukle made some particularly attractive hand-wound pianos in ornamental cases richly endowed with ormolu decoration. These had 54 notes and were provided with storage space for a second barrel in the bottom. Extra cylinders could be bought for £10 and many were pinned for dance and popular music of the time. One example I have seen plays selections from *The Bohemian Girl* by Balfe (1843). The tone of these Imhof instruments was comparable to that of the contemporary pianoforte.

T. C. Bates & Son of Ludgate Hill, London, produced a clockwork cylinder piano which stood 7 feet high, was 4 feet 7 inches wide and 2 feet 3 inches deep. It played 85 notes and had a manual keyboard. The 3 foot 9 inch long cylinder for mechanical playing was placed in the bottom of the case along with the action. Bates also built weight-driven pianos standing 4 feet 6 inches high and playing 3 foot long cylinders.

William Gillet and Charles Bland improved the Hicks system in 1869 when they devised a barrel piano having continuously-beating hammers, allowed to contact the musical strings only when the correct key was lifted by a barrel pin. Their invention was not a success, though, and in 1874 Daniel Imhof devised a combined damping and sustained device for barrel pianos played with ordinary Hicks-type hammers.

Daniel Imhof had amassed a tremendous amount of experience using pinned barrels for the orchestrion organs which his firm, Imhof & Mukle, manufactured at Vöhrenbach in the Black Forest, and he devised a number of improvements to the basic mechanism, particularly with regard to the tonality.

Instead of a crank handle, the manual mechanical piano made by J. Lecape & Co. in 1882 was operated by a foot treadle which turned the barrel for mechanical playing.

ITALIAN INFLUENCE

For the major developments in the barrel piano we have the Italians to thank. During the second half of the nineteenth century, a large number of Italian musicians and artisans came to England to find work. A number of these settled down to producing large barrel pianos for the street musician.

In the years which followed, history can become confused because these Italian artisans formed many different partnerships and companies, frequently changed their addresses, re-formed with colleagues from other firms and re-organised time and time again. Practically every one of the Italian makers in London, for example, worked at some time or another with his contemporaries. We have therefore to steer a path through this period by examining some of the improvements which these men made and commenting on their influence on the progress of the barrel piano.

One of the Italian migrants was Giuseppe Chiappa who founded a street-organ and piano works in the Clerkenwell district of London in 1864 with a fellow Italian, G. Fersani. This particular quarter of London, the Farringdon Road area of the watch- and clock-making district of Clerkenwell, was to become the home of the street barrel-piano industry and practically all of the subsequent firms made their homes either here or in near-by Warner Street and its environs. In the immediate vicinity were the lodging houses of Saffron Hill, where the street musicians, mainly Italians, made their homes.

Chiappa and Fersani produced large barrel pianos which were transported on handcarts or donkey-carts. Whether or not they were the first to make these large street instruments is unknown, but they were certainly among the earliest of the London builders. In 1878 they took out a patent for a combined street piano and organ played by one barrel. Half the instrument was a piano played by pins on the wooden drum, and the other half played a 'cornet accompaniment' from pins and bridges over that half of the barrel. In true barrel-organ fashion, the worm-gear which drove the barrel also manipulated bellows through reciprocators to provide wind for the pipes. No such instrument has been seen and it is to be assumed either that few were manufactured or that the difficulty of keeping them in tune rendered them short-lived.

In the following year, J. Y. Smith patented a method of controlling the action of barrel organs and pianos but it fell to Alexander Capra, J. B. Rissone and S. Detoma jointly to make the first worthwhile improvements to barrel piano action in 1880.

The instrument of this period comprised a vertical wooden frame, substantially built to resist the enormous strain of the combined string tension, a pivoted keyframe or, more properly, hammer-frame which supported one sprung hammer for each note, and a pinned wooden drum. Each drum would play eight or ten tunes and was advanced manually by a snail cam controlled from the outside end of the case. This cam was linked to the hammer frame so that when the barrel was shifted the delicate hammer-tails were lifted clear of the barrel pins to prevent damage. Unlike the cylinder musical box, to which there was a mechanical family likeness, the tune could be changed at will, even in the middle of a performance, by indexing the cam with the handle provided.

Each musical note was represented by wire strings as in the ordinary pianoforte. The base strings were copper-covered and usually the extreme two or three bass notes would be represented by single strings. The remainder of the wrapped strings would be bichords, that is to say that there would be two strings tuned in unison. The central portion would be represented by trichords – three strings in unison. Some makers later used four or even five strings in unison for the extreme treble register. This was due to the fact that thin strings, of short length to produce a high note, are weak in volume for a given hammer force. Volume can be increased by increasing the number of strings which sound that note.

Alexander Capra devised a barrel piano with 'mandolin harp' effect in 1890. Each string was plucked by a rotating cylinder holding three spring-wire plectra. The plectra throughout the piano compass were kept in rotation by a linkage from the crank handle and were brought into contact with the strings by the normal function of the barrel key and connecting levers.

Capra was an inventor who also gave thought to the possibilities of automating the ordinary pianoforte and in 1880 he was granted British Patent number 4725 for 'improvements to the piano action for playing either manually or from a pinned wooden

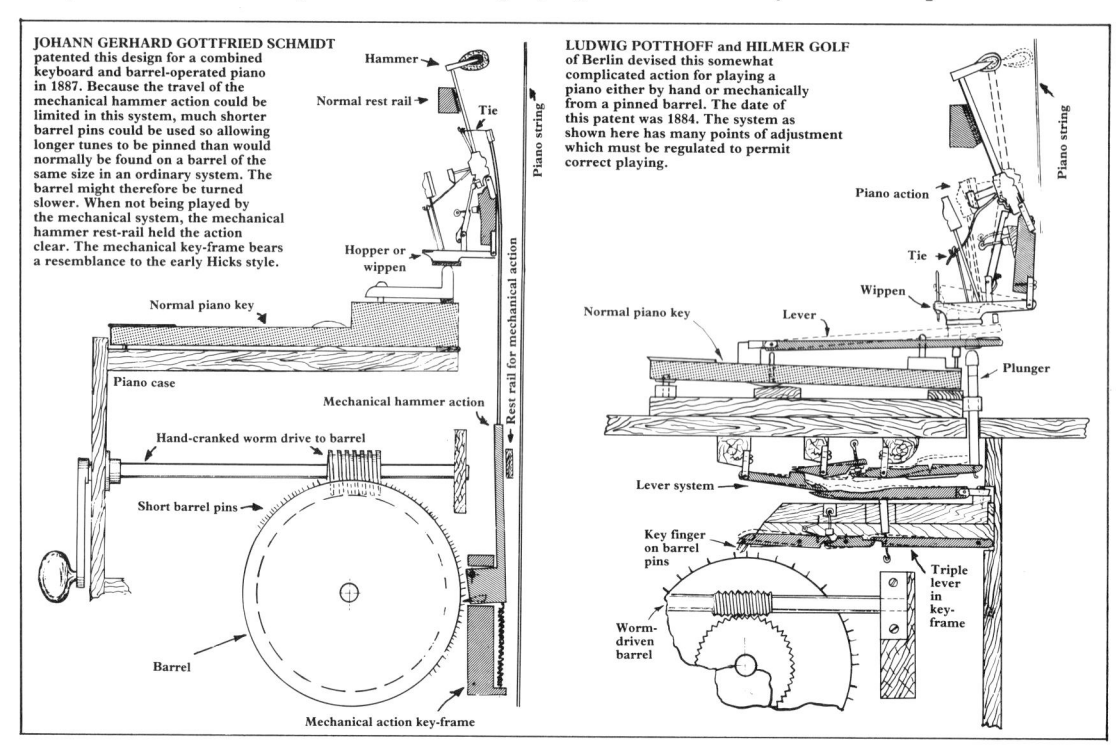

Fig. 13
Two inventors' approaches to the barrel-and-finger piano. On the left is Schmidt's relatively simple system of 1887 while on the right is the very complex design of Potthoff & Golf in 1884.

barrel'. The outcome was the Per Omnes Pianoforte, advertised in 1881 by Capra, Rissone & Detoma. This was a rather bulbous-fronted piano with a keyboard, a barrel and a handle for turning. 'The Per Omnes arrangement', said the advertisements, 'can be attached to any piano as at a small cost.' None is known to survive. The following year, 1882, Capra devised a piano player using a pinned barrel and stickers which could be used to play on an ordinary piano keyboard. Again this seems to have been a short-lived development.

Capra and Rissone now turned their attention towards the other possible markets for the barrel piano. The public house was an obvious choice and for such use they devised the first clockwork-driven barrel piano. This was powered by a fusee-wound spring motor and would play a tune to order without the need for cranking a handle all the time. The first of many such clockwork pianos, termed 'automatics', this appeared in 1884 and proved an immediate success.

Just as Bidermann had mechanised his keyboard spinets by the addition of a barrel mechanism, so did similar solutions receive consideration from inventors. Ludwig Potthoff and Hilmar Golf of Berlin devised a most complicated barrel attachment to a keyboard piano which they patented in 1884. The barrel mechanism was mounted under the keyboard and, when played mechanically, the barrel pins operated a linkage of primary and secondary levers and cams, terminating in a secondary piano key which set in motion the piano action in the same manner as the pianist's fingers.

Johann Gerhard Gottfried Schmidt of Köpenick near Berlin was soon to realise that his compatriot's endeavours to set in motion the piano action via the barrel was rather like burning down the farmyard to achieve bacon. All that had to be moved was the actual hammer, not the action, and so, in 1887, he perfected a simple barrel mechanism, again under the piano keys, to do just that. He also patented the principle, first registered by Rolfe in 1825, that the volume of the note depended on the force exerted on the hammer-tail by the return spring and thus the intensity of a note could be varied by the distance which the pins protruded from the surface of the barrel.

In Bologna, Italy, Giovanni Racca and W. Seward were making barrel pianos for use in indoor public places, and Francesco Getto of Ivrea, Italy, produced small portable street pianos similar to those of Hicks. Getto, however, improved on the detail of Hicks's concept in many ways, not the least of which was the use of thinner music strings to produce a brighter and more singing tone.

DEVELOPMENTS AND PROBLEMS

When Gillett and Bland contrived their design for continuously-beating string hammers in 1869, they were on the threshold of perfecting what was later to be known as the 'mandolin' effect in which, when a note is sounded, the hammer strikes the strings several times in quick succession. With sustained notes, the effect is supposed to resemble the sound of a mandolin.

Precursor of the great Hupfeld organisation, J. M. Grob & Co. of Eutritzsch near Leipzig was the first to devise a practical mandolin effect from a street piano. A fluted steel shaft was arranged between specially shaped sprung hammers and the piano strings. The hammer-tails, which were not rigidly attached to the hammers themselves, were moved by bridges on the barrel, in the same way that a barrel organ works. The bridges raised the hammer-tails and held them for the appropriate length of musical time, drawing the actual hammer against the rotating shaft by means of a spring. The result was the staccato striking of the string.

Some two years later, in 1890, Capra improved on Grob's invention and so successful was this modification of the barrel piano that during the next twenty years almost every manufacturer of consequence perfected his own system of achieving this effect.

The clockwork barrel piano found a ready market now just in England but throughout Europe and was now being built by many makers. In an endeavour to break fresh ground, Gregori Pasquale & Co., which firm comprised Charles Romano and Pasquale Amato at this time, placed the clockwork motor actually in the end of the wooden barrel and wound it through a hole in the barrel access door. This was in 1898. It was obviously necessary to let the spring run right down before attempting to remove the barrel for changing and it meant that each replacement barrel had to have a spring motor built into it.

The following year, P. Rossi, C. Rossi and Loreto Spinelli made a barrel piano which could be either hand-turned or clockwork-driven and this included tuned bells and a drum. The spring motor was again in the barrel.

Most serious of the many problems which faced the street piano during its necessarily arduous life was the climate and the effects of wind, rain, hot sun and rapid changes from one extreme to the other. Warping of the frames, separation of the glued joints and splitting of the timbers were commonplace. The most common defect in service was the tendency of the wooden wrest-plank or pin-block to split along its length and tip forward as a result of the string tension. Because the instruments were cheaply and quickly built, this sort of problem marked the end of the life of an instrument. Even if it survived these problems, loosening of the tuning pins (wrest-pins) through expansion and contraction of the wood and exacerbated by the string tension was frequent. At its best the street piano seldom could stay in tune for long and its life was short.

It was in an endeavour to cure these shortcomings that Rossi and Spinelli produced some clockwork pianos having iron frames. These were intended for indoor use but they were not a success since the tone suffered badly due to poor design of the soundboard.

The iron frame was never adopted for the street instrument. This was primarily due to the greater weight which it would have entailed. However, if any application of the barrel piano called for an iron frame it was certainly the poor street model with its erroneously supposed stoic disregard for climatic changes and the exigencies of the weather.

In America, Eugene deKleist of the North Tonawanda Barrel Organ Factory near New York was devising a barrel piano, later to be known as the 'Tonophone', for the Wurlitzer company. DeKleist, who came from Dusseldorf in Germany, went back to Fourneaux's system in that he used a barrel and key frame system combined with pneumatic bellows. The pins on the barrel lifted a key which connected with a tracker to a wind chest, admitted air into a small pneumatic motor or bellows and thus allowed the string to be struck by a hammer connected to one of the bellows boards. Driven by an electric motor, deKleist's Tonophone was patented in July 1901.

The coin-freed piano had been in existence for some time and was probably the invention of Gregori Pasquale who set up his firm in London in 1895 and remained in business until 1940. This attachment to a clockwork barrel piano allowed a tune to be played by the insertion of a penny. It was usual for the tune to be played twice for one coin and it speaks well of the design and execution of these instruments that, although there was only the smallest gap in the pinning between the beginnings and ends of the tunes, the mechanism always stopped in the right place after its two revolutions. Chiappa made improvements to this mechanism in 1901 and became one of London's largest manufacturers of this type of

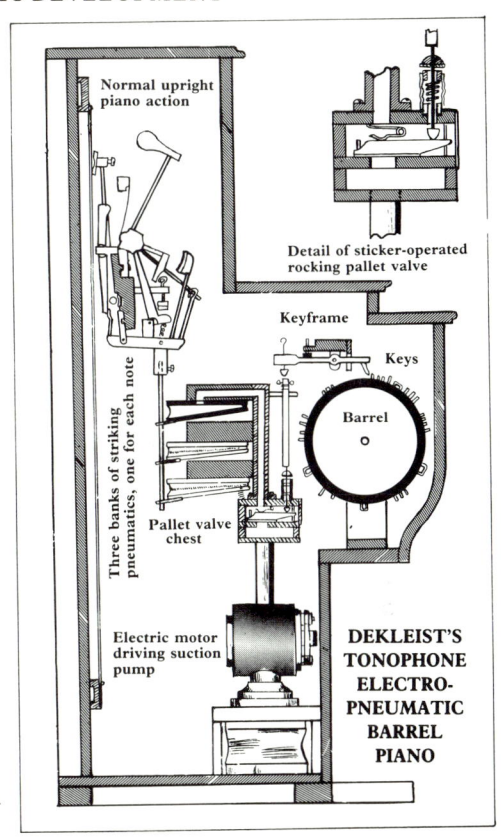

Fig. 14
DeKleist's Tonophone dates from the turn of the century and was an electrically-driven pneumatic-action barrel piano.

instrument, probably ranking very close to Pasquale, who was a prolific maker.

Because the power of the wrist remained in excess of that afforded even by the best clockwork motor, the clockwork automatic barrel piano was unable to strike more than five strings at once without 'jumping'. The hand-wound piano, however, could strike eight or more notes at once and thus manufacturers were able to make the street piano into a more florid interpreter of music by employing many more barrel pins and exercising their transcription skills to the full.

Several of the London makers had branches elsewhere in the country and the two cities most favoured were Manchester and Glasgow. At some time or another, a number of the larger manufacturers opened works in these places, as did some of the barrel-organ makers. Gavioli, for example, was making organs in the Great Ancoats Street part of Manchester.

One piano maker who, it seems, remained in the Manchester area was D. Antonelli, who specialised in clockwork barrel instruments. He patented in November 1901 a method of removing the barrel for changing without disturbing the rest of the mechanism. This was a very great step forward and the Antonelli improvements were to be felt throughout the entire industry in a short space of time. Hitherto, to change a barrel was a fairly lengthy business, demanding, for example, great care in realigning the new barrel. Antonelli retained his barrels in a fixed location in the piano case, pushing them into the right position with a leaf spring on the access door.

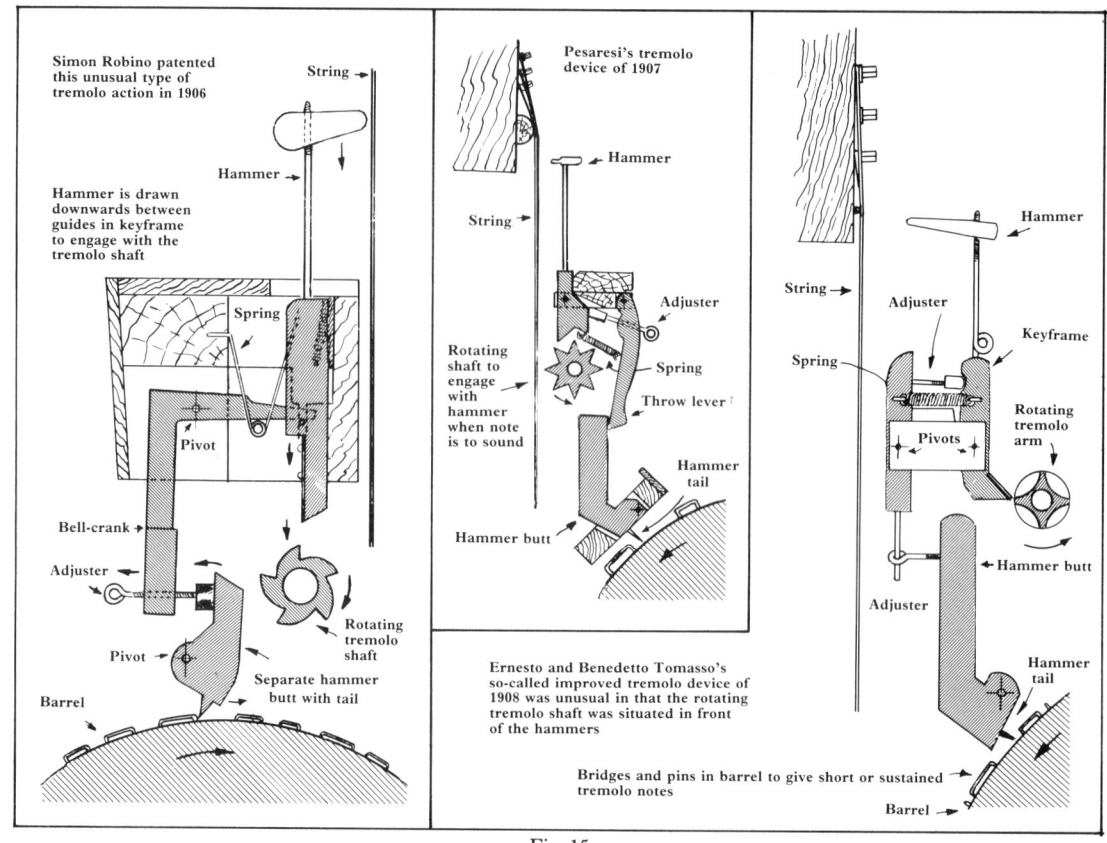

Fig. 15
Three different approaches to producing the mandoline effect on a street piano.

Joseph Piana Canova of Clerkenwell was one of the many makers who thought up improvements to the beating-hammer tremolo or mandolin effect in 1902. In the following year, Luigi Pesaresi coupled a fortune-telling device to a street piano, which consisted of a wheel set spinning inside a window in the front fall of the piano case.

Another maker in Clerkenwell, Luigi Villa of Granville Square, Farringdon Road, also directed his inventive thoughts to utilising the piano case for secondary purposes – this time with strong commercial leanings. In April 1903 he took out a patent for a method of displaying advertisements through a large window in the front fall. A system of levers and links, intermittently moved by pins in the end of the music barrel, converted the continuous rotary motion of the barrel into an intermittent rotation of vertical rollers at each end of the case. These rollers carried a travelling blind upon which were mounted advertisements. This was a variation on the moving picture fronts which appear to have dated from the end of the last century. Operation was from the same two vertical rollers, but they received a steady motion from bevel gearing on the end of the winding handle. The canvas blind portrayed a continuous scene either of country life or the bustling city (the former seems to have been the more popular) and these were almost always very finely painted. Their durability was poor, though, for the continual flexing of the fabric over the rollers ultimately cracked and flaked the oil paint.

THE BARREL PIANO AND ITS DEVELOPMENT

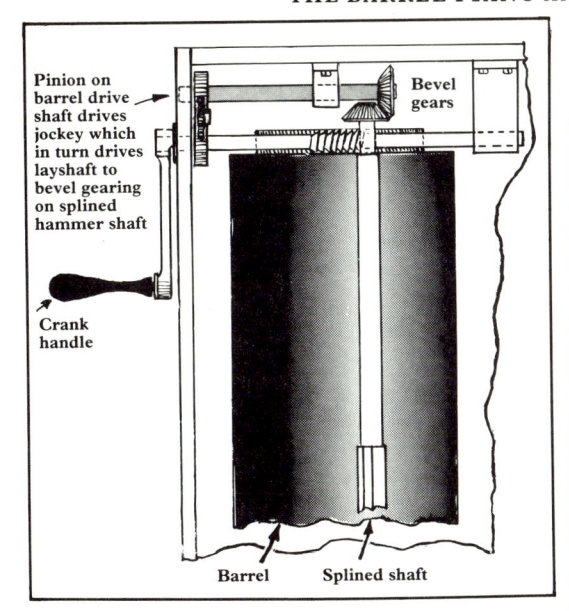

Fig. 16   Typical tremolo or mandoline gearing.

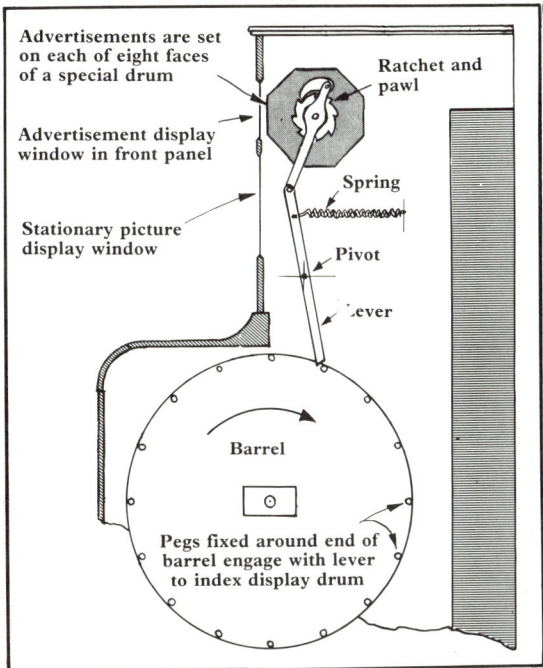

Fig. 17
Luigi Villa devised this method of displaying advertisements in the upper part of the piano case while music was being made.

The developments in England were rapidly expanded across Europe and by the early years of this century there was a thriving business in the manufacture of clockwork barrel pianos for use in cafés and other public places. Belgium, Holland and France became the European centres of mass production and very many makers were employed in supplying what today seems to have been an insatiable demand for these relatively low-cost instruments. In Belgium, the instruments were frequently built with street-organ-type proscenium fronts, richly carved and sometimes provided with mirrors. Some of these were of very large proportions and included an octave or more of nested hemispherical bells, wood-block percussion, drum and triangle, and occasionally xylophone.

Although the instrument was largely finished in Britain by the outbreak of the 1914–18 war, it was to remain in production in Europe, particularly southern France, well into the 1930s when, to all intents and purposes, it might have been expected to have been superseded by the pneumatic-action piano.

But to return to the early years of this century: across the Atlantic, deKleist's Tonophone pneumatic barrel piano was selling well, sponsored by Wurlitzer. He improved his original mechanism and took out subsequent patents covering his new thoughts in both 1902 and 1903.

Rose, Coop & Rissone of Regent Street, London, applied the coin-freed mechanism to a pneumatic piano-player which they made in 1903 and, after that, they seem to have discontinued barrel instruments. Pesaresi & Son concentrated mostly on 40- and 44-note automatic street instruments, usually fitted with tremolo or mandolin effect, but they were made only in small numbers – for some reason they were unpopular with users.

The clockwork barrel piano was in wide use in cafés, public houses, and suchlike. In the same way that the modern juke-box may be controlled remotely from customers seated at their tables in a café, so did Thomas Linforth Jones contrive to set clockwork pianos playing in 1905. He used 'electro-magnetic energization' by the insertion of a coin in a remotely mounted coin-slot box to free the detent on the piano's clockwork mechanism. Any number of such coin-slot boxes could be connected to the one instrument.

Fig. 18
Peters of Leipzig was the distributor for the hollow-cylindered barrel piano orchestrions devised by Paul Lochmann.

THE BARREL PIANO AND ITS DEVELOPMENT

The so-called mandolin or tremolo effect on a street barrel piano seems to have been very popular and every maker of consequence devoted efforts to perfecting the system. The general concept remained virtually the same as that which appears first to have been used by Grob in Leipzig in 1888. The hammer was made in two parts, usually connected by a spring. Between the two parts rotated a splined shaft. A sustained note on the string was represented by a bridge or staple on the barrel, instead of the usual pin. This bridge held the lower part of the hammer in such a way that the hammer arm and head was placed in engagement, under the load of the spring, with the rotating shaft, thus imparting a staccato beating to the string.

A drawback to the rotating-shaft system for creating a mandolin effect was the appreciably greater wrist-power needed to play the instrument. Even when in good order, more than twice the force was required and one can imagine that after a few hours' playing the operator would be somewhat fatigued.

In 1905 Julius Carl Hofmann of Vienna again modified the beating-hammer system and, in the same year, Spinelli built the first split-bridge mandolin piano. This had a soundboard with two treble bridges which effectively divided it so as to provide two sets of strings for the treble notes, allowing two hammers to be used to sound one note. By pinning the barrel to work each hammer alternately, a mandolin effect could be achieved without the complication of bevel gears and beating hammers.

Simon Robino, described as a musical instrument maker of Manchester, patented his own version of the beating-hammer tremolo in 1906 but his system involved a complex movement of the hammer as compared with the contemporary trends. His hammers were drawn down by bellcrank-shaped hammer-tails until they engaged in a starwheel which kicked them against a return spring.

Clerkenwell's Warner Street was, as we have seen, a haven for the barrel-piano makers and another maker there was Vincenzo Pozzouli. He shunned the complex trappings of the tremolo devices of his contemporaries and made, in 1906, a mandolin piano having four bridges – the first being a mandolin, the second a piano, the third a second mandolin, and the fourth a bass piano. He also used hardwood hammers.

Even so, this cannot have proved very successful, for still the rotating-shaft tremolo method was being improved upon by the larger makers and, in April 1907, Luigi Pesaresi registered another patent for yet another different system.

One would think that there would have been a limit to the variations on the same theme but the ultimate had, so it seems, still not been reached, for in the following year Ernesto and Benedetto Tomasso, who made barrel pianos in Leeds, devised another such system. This one was different insomuch as the rotating shaft was in front of the hammers as distinct from being between hammers and strings.

SOME UNUSUAL TYPES

A type of barrel piano introduced about 1910 was the 'zither-banjo', which produced a distinctive, clear sound not at all unlike that of a banjo. It was, however, very loud and Canon Wintle asserted 'that it could be heard a mile away'. The secret lay in the mandolin-like duplication of strings and a very thin soundboard.

At this particular time the book-music piano was in vogue. Chiappa was probably the first to change to this type of instrument in the mid-1890s. Whilst the barrel continued to have its staunch devotees, cardboard music was favoured on several counts. To begin with, the piano was not so bulky and certainly lighter in weight. Furthermore, the music was readily available and could be carried or stored with ease, as compared with the heavy barrel together with its limited repertoire represented in pins which were liable to damage.

The cardboard-music street piano was not, however, a success, for it carried with it its own individual shortcomings. The Italian musicians soon tired of the books of music which rapidly wore out, tore or got lost. Whilst book music was fine for an indoor piano or even a fair organ, the street piano was an instrument exposed to rough use, the exigencies of the weather and the wear of continual movement along cobbled streets. Moreover, the barrel makers offered a very quick and cheap repinning service and could set new music on existing barrels with great finesse. It is thus perhaps not surprising that few, if any, of these cardboard-music instruments for street use have survived.

A barrel piano of singular design is one surviving at present in unplayable condition in the collection of Walt Bellm of Sarasota, Florida. In shape and proportions, the case is no different from that of a normal barrel piano. The normal type of circular barrel access door is featured on the right side and a clockwork motor is in the conventional left-hand position inside. The piano back is straight-strung on an iron, unmarked frame. In place of the wooden barrel, however, there is a cylinder of perforated metal. Both ends of this hollow cylinder are provided with square-shaped drive perforations which engage with drive cogs. The start/stop mechanism is operated from cut-outs in the extreme outer edges of the metal, as also appear

Fig. 19
An early clockwork barrel and finger piano again distributed by Peters.

to be other features such as damper and mute. The keyframe is made of very heavy channel-section iron on the front edge of which are mounted the keys. These are of stamped punched steel with an escapement action. A damper for the lower half of the strings is operated by slots and in places large square holes pierced around the centre of the cylinder's length. A felt-covered mute is fitted which can be swung up under the hammers by means of a knob in a slide hole on the right side of the case. There is no indication as to the maker of this unusual piano although as it was bought in Copenhagen it was almost certainly European in origin. The mystery would have remained unsolved had not a piano orchestrion been identified in the collection of a Stockholm collector as having precisely the same mechanism. It was then but a short dig amidst the patents to identify both instruments as coming from the factory of Lochmann.*

Fig. 20
Marteletti of Casale Monferrato in Italy advertised these clockwork café pianos in 1909.

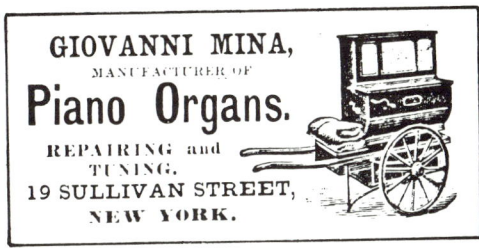

Fig. 21
1895 advertisement for street pianos by Giovanni Mina in New York.

The clockwork barrel pianos did not reach as high a state of perfection in England as in other parts of the world. Probably related to the popular trends in entertainment in public places, they were to reach their zenith in Europe and in America, where they proceeded onwards through the whole gamut of mechanical musical instrumentation. The Wurlitzer company, which first commissioned deKleist's Tonophone pneumatic barrel piano, went on to make mechanical banjos, harps, zithers, guitars and even jazz bands. The call for musical entertainment has always been greatest in America and the later machines made to accompany silent films in picture theatres achieved a remarkable degree of perfection and flexibility. The Photoplayers of the twenties combined a wide range of effects in a basic roll-operated pneumatic piano mechanism and Wurlitzers constructed an incredible number of full-orchestra theatre organs, some of which were installed in this country.

The clockwork barrel piano, other than for the entertainment of the British working classes as they drank, never ascended very far above its street hand-cranked brothers.

In Italy, Austria, Belgium, Holland and France, however, mechanical pianos with percussion accompaniment were popular in cafés and restaurants. Rossi made a number of these in Italy, as did makers such as Crubois in France during the second decade of the twentieth century. Crubois continued making these pianos at least until the late 1920s and they featured a partial iron frame, drum and triangle and castanets. These were coin-freed and driven by clockwork motors.

---

* A detailed description of this latter instrument, identified as a Lochmann's Original Walzen-Orchestrion, appeared in *The Music Box*, Vol. 9, pp. 270–4. In this article is reproduced the original Lochmann advertisement for this type of instrument.

In the same way as the barrel-piano industry was established in England by Italian immigrants, so were similar industries established in other parts of Europe at more or less the same time. Spain in particular possessed a large and flourishing manufacturing industry.

An Italian named Apruzzese came to Salamanca, Spain, in 1883 and began making barrel pianos. The firm he formed moved to Madrid in 1906 and, in the same year, the present owner, Mr Antonio Apruzzese, was born. He is today the last remaining member of the family to be engaged in piano work and he is also the last surviving barrel-piano restorer in Madrid.

Perhaps the best of the Spanish makes were the instruments built by Luis Casali, another Italian. He came to Barcelona and set up business early in the 1880s. The firm comprised three partners – Casali, Pombia (who was responsible for the actual construction), and Subirands, whose job it was to transcribe music for the wooden barrels. So successful were their instruments that they were awarded gold medals at the Brussels Exhibition of 1895, having earlier received a similar award in Spain in the year 1886.

Spanish instruments usually included percussion instruments such as the drum, bells and, most common of all, the castanet. Triangles were sometimes to be found as well. It is interesting to note that the instruments built in various countries by these Italian emigrants rapidly became musically acclimatised to their area and developed distinctive regional identities. The Spanish piano invariably included at least one *pasodoble* in its programme and these dances and other music of similar *tempi* came over particularly well.

The Spanish barrel piano was built with 30, 35, 40, 45, 56 and 60 hammers and the larger models were made to be fitted to a donkey cart. Felt-covered hammers, then common to most other European makers, were soon dispensed with in favour of plain walnut hammers when it was discovered that they produced a brighter and louder sound. Wooden, unfelted hammers had, of course, been used by Hicks, Distin and others in England for tenor and treble notes and twentieth-century tremolo pianos were all to make use of uncovered wooden hammers.

While the barrel piano only appeared as an indoor instrument in a few isolated instances alongside its street variety, it was in Sweden that the instrument appeared solely as a domestic music machine. Sweden's contribution to the history of mechanical musical instruments is small but not insignificant since the machines produced were radically different from those to be found anywhere else in the world. Johan Petter Nyström of Karlstad produced the Reform-Orgel in 1891. This was an unusual variant of the genus American organ (i.e. it sucked its reeds instead of blowing them as in the harmonium) which could also be played automatically by means of a perforated disc.*

The other instrument to emerge from this part of Scandinavia was the Pianoharpa, which is said to have been the invention of I. F. Nilsson of Öster Korsberga, Lemnhult, Saxhult. This looked rather like a deep-topped table with a lift-up lid. Musically, these were not particularly inspiring machines and not many were built. However, on 13 August 1889 a Swedish patent number 2239 was issued in the names of Anders Gustaf Andersson and his brother, Jones Wilhelm Andersson, for improvements in the Pianoharpa type of instrument.

As Bill Lindwall related in his scholarly article in *The Music Box*,† the Andersson brothers lived in the tiny village of Näshult outside the small town of Vetlanda in the south of Sweden.

---

* See *The Music Box*, volume 8, pp. 2–6.
† ibid., pp. 330–4.

They were carpenters and had a workshop where they produced domestic furniture and similar utilitarian articles. At this time, Sweden was still a somewhat impoverished nation whose economy centred on its agriculture. So hard was the peasant style of life that many Swedes left to seek their livelihoods elsewhere. This was the time when the migration of Swedish people to America began. Most people lived poorly and under extreme circumstances.* It was at this time when the Anderssons produced their Pianoharpa.

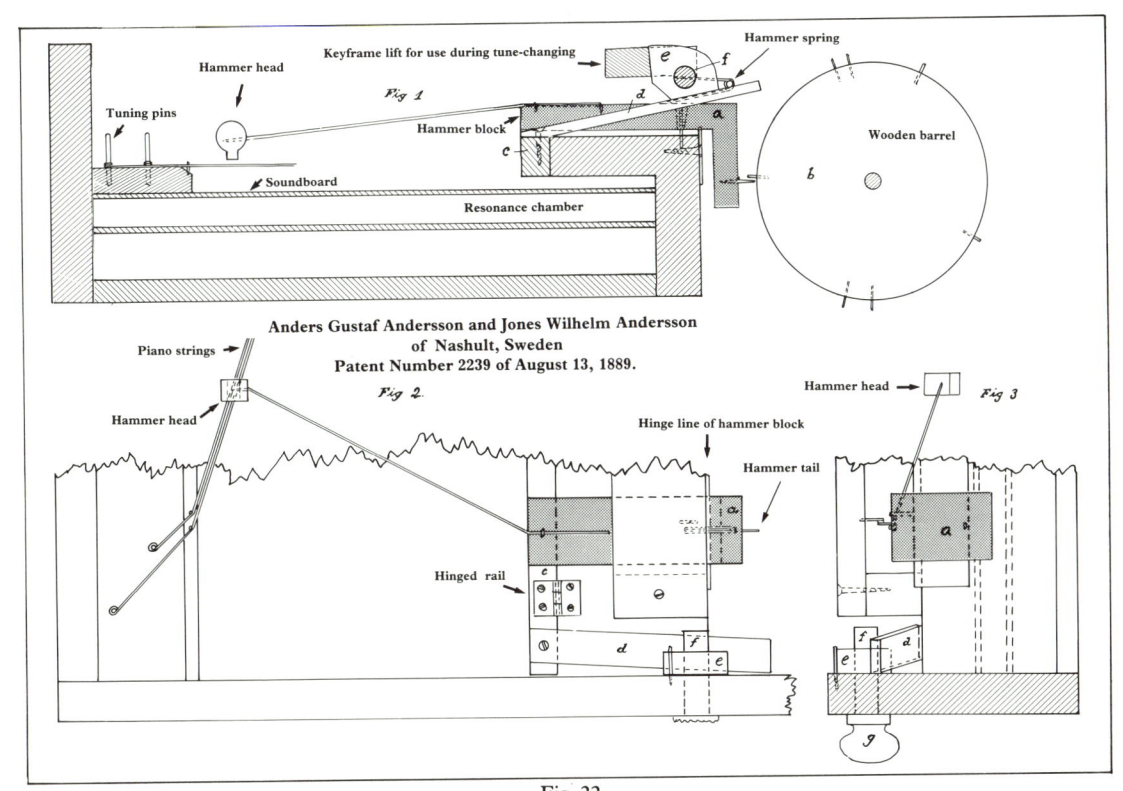

Fig. 22
Taken from the original Swedish patent drawing, this shows the principle of Andersson's Pianoharpa, a barrel-playing table piano.

When these conditions are understood, it is easy to appreciate just why the appearance of the Pianoharpa was so unattractive. Possibly the lack of technology and experience also explain why the instrument suffered from poor sound production. This is not to decry the efforts of Andersson but simply to state the fact.

With such a dubious national economy, one might feel that the Anderssons' venture into mechanical musical instruments would have proved unwise but, in fact, the opposite was the case. Demand for the instrument turned out to be rather big for those days and quite a number were produced.

Andersson actually called his instrument 'street piano', which probably is a more accurate name. It is, in truth, possible that the Pianoharpa had been produced over many years before

---

* See *Music & Automata*, Vol. 1, pp. 134–40.

1889 and it is also possible that the principle for the design was copied from similar instruments. It is significant that patents were not applied for for the instrument itself, but for two specific mechanical features that Andersson designed himself.

The instrument was very shallow in depth and for this reason the design employs a style where the keys are in effect bent downwards to minimise the total height. This was the first improvement patented.

The second concerned a rotatable bar which enabled the keys to be depressed slightly so as to increase the distance between the hammers and the strings. In fact this operated as an adjustable rest-rail, making it possible to moderate the volume of sound produced. An examination of the patent drawing shows how this bar (f), turned by knob (g), depresses the strip (d) by means of the cam (e). The strip (d) is attached to the hinged rail (c) which runs beneath all the trailing ends of the hammers. By raising this rail, the ends of the L-shaped hammers (a) are lifted up, so backing the key-points away from the barrel pins slightly. The sound is thus softened through the shorter stroke applied to the hammer by the barrel pin and the softer blow occasioned by the weighted hammer on the end of its hammer wire (Fig. 22 refers).

The Pianoharpa measures 76 cm high, 93 cm wide across the front, and 49 cm deep from front to back. The keyboard has 18 notes, these being g, a, h, c, d, e, f, g, a, h, c, d, e, f, g, a, h, c.

The crank handle at the front of the case rotates the pinned wooden barrel which has a diameter of 10·5 cm and a length of 64 cm. The barrel can be moved laterally via a knife and bolt system as found in the early street piano or barrel organ so as to change the tunes, of which there are twelve to the barrel.

Most barrels featured the popular music of the period but there were exceptions: for example there were barrels with only hymns or Swedish folk tunes. Interestingly enough, only ten programmes of music were ever provided for the Pianoharpa and an index of tunes shows the titles available.*

The production of the instrument was characteristic of the cottage industries of the time and was a time-consuming business. The task of hammering the pins into the barrel, for example, was carried out by schoolchildren. The Piano Harp was designed to look like a table and thus it was exactly the right height for anybody who wanted to play it. Its appearance might possibly account for the reason why it came to be used as a central place upon which to place the family china.

How the soundboard was made can be seen from the patent drawing. The wrest-plank and hitch-pin block were of heavy timber: there was, of course, no metal frame. This means that it was a difficult instrument to keep in tune and it was affected by changes in temperature and humidity.

At the time Bill Lindwall was researching the history of this piece, he made contact with an aged collector (then in his seventies) who lived not far from Vetlanda. He knew a nephew of the Andersson brothers who himself was seventy years old and who died in the spring of 1978. This man had passed on some of the early history of the Pianoharpa and recalled that as a young boy he had helped to pin the barrels after finishing school for the day. He was certain that only ten barrels had ever been designed and said that when an instrument was sold it was accompanied by three barrels. Unfortunately the soft wood from which barrels were made

---

* ibid.

was prone to infestation by wood worm and many instruments became so damaged from worm holes that they were thrown out. This is why only a few are known today.

At some time the Andersson brothers appear to have tried to produce a domestic barrel organ using the same basic principles as those of the Pianoharpa. This used a similar-shaped table-like case and housed 50 speaking pipes and a pair of bellows. Only one of these is known to survive and that is in the Lindwall collection in Sweden.

The Pianoharpa was a surprisingly original concept, although its realisation lacked finesse, partly due to the obvious fact that the builders possessed insufficient understanding of the properties of the soundboard and the science of scaling.

But while the Swedes were producing these rather primitive instruments, the barrel piano had become stylised as regards construction throughout the rest of the world. Durable instruments for street use in all weather now replaced the exquisitely subtle tones of the drawing-room instruments conceived much earlier in the century by craftsmen such as Rolfe. And at the other end of the scale, so to speak, the new indoor instrument was the handsome example of cabinet-maker's skill housing the weight-driven iron-framed instrument often with a performance embellished with drum (sometimes bass and side-drum), triangle, xylophone and bells. This was the piano orchestrion, so called because the instrument often included an automatic damper or long and short pins, so producing a true *piano-e-forte* effect.

In Germany and Central Europe as a whole, the piano orchestrion underwent considerable refinement and some magnificent instruments were produced which were barrel-operated and quite often had iron frames of superb quality. The early ones sometimes incorporated clocks: others were made for use in cafés and other public places. Ultimately, these were the progenitors of the pneumatically played piano orchestrions which were complete orchestras in themselves.

AUSTRO-HUNGARIAN IMPROVEMENTS

It was in Bohemia and the Austro-Hungarian empire that the piano orchestrion reached its zenith of musical and mechanical perfection. Almost all of these instruments were weight-driven and incorporated a variety of effects such as xylophone, drum, cymbal and occasionally wood blocks. In their developed form, they achieved hitherto unheard goals in musical expression, producing piano and forte effects with panache from the special programme pins on the barrel.

The division of the barrel piano frame into two halves was an early accomplishment. This enabled the uncluttered arrangement of percussion and effects controls, taking commands not only from each end of the barrel but also from the centre where special bridges, some of great length, controlled the operation of dampers and a simplified form of action rail. These very long bridges frequently wear thin in the middle and even although some were supported under the span of the bridge with single pins, worn pianos with vague effects can usually be diagnosed as suffering from thin bridges, age having caused them to wear and bend in the middle, so letting the key waver between 'on' and 'off'.

One of the most impressive developments achieved by these makers was the solution to the problem of the drumroll effect. Back in the days of the orchestrion organs it had been the practice with large instruments to have a special, separate drum motor with its own driving weight. A keyframe key freed the stop-start detent on this unit and the descending weight

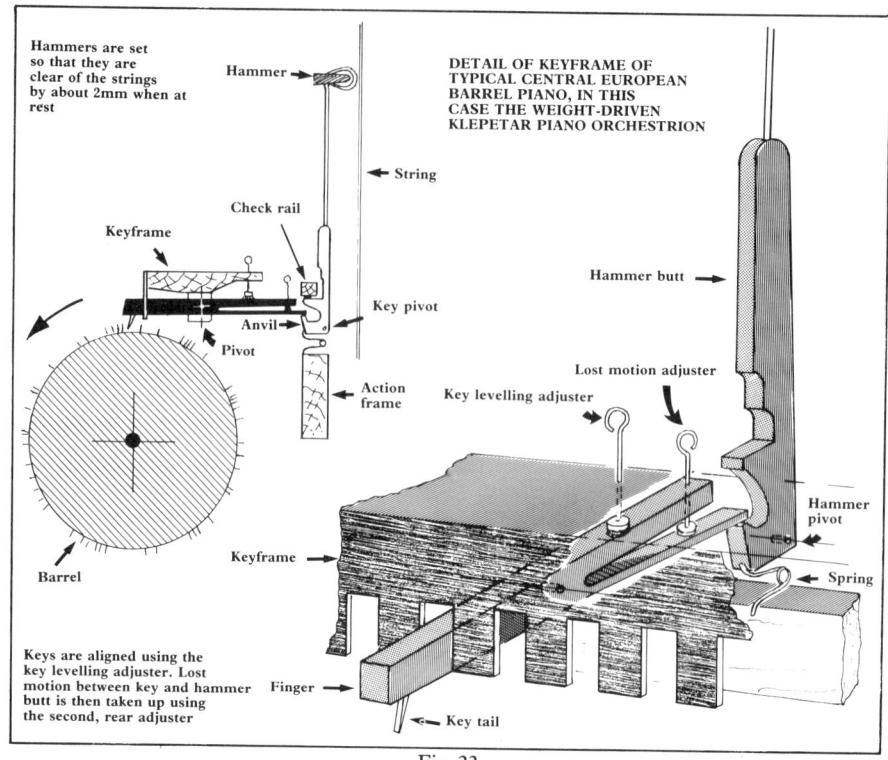

Fig. 23
The Bohemian style of piano orchestrion action taken from the instrument made in Prague by Klepetar.

caused a multi-cammed shaft to rotate, a series of spring-loaded hammers sequentially striking the drum as the shaft turned to produce a drum roll. Sometimes the drum-roll clockwork would run down before the end of the music and need rewinding. Later pneumatic versions used the forerunner of the pneumatic reiterating motor in the form of a pair of balanced valves effectively linked by a coiled length of tubing with an expansion or buffer air reservoir in the middle. American makers were left to devise the neat repeating motor used on coin-freed pianos made by firms such as Link, Nelson Wiggin and Wurlitzer.

The Bohemain solution was elegantly simple. Most of these instruments used a steam-engine type flying-ball governor rather than the usual speed-regulating air-brake. On the very top of this governor was fitted a small brass wheel with an offset pivot hole to which was connected an eccentric link. This in turn was connected to a long link arm on a very thin, low-mass cross shaft extending the width of the instrument at a position above the strings but below the drum. The drum sticks were attached to this cross shaft using a leaf spring and the hammer was checked during the no-play part of the music by a simple escapement. When a drum roll was required, a barrel bridge would free the hammer which at once came under the influence of the very rapidly oscillating axis rod, its movement being imparted from the eccentric on the governor. The result was a high-speed drum roll of great precision. So precise, in fact, that one single pin in the barrel was sufficient to produce a short, sharp, definable repetition.

Among the many makers who produced barrel piano orchestrions and clockwork barrel pianos was the Prague maker J. Klepetar, who made a large number of fine and imposing machines. One style featured a 34-note iron-framed piano, two drums, a triangle and a cymbal. Power was provided by a clockwork mechanism using an iron weight of about 60 kg which was wound up to the top of the case back. As it slowly descended, it transmitted its kinetic energy to the driving train through pulleys and gears. All but the four lowest strings on this style featured trichords, the very lowest ones being bichords. Like most of these instruments, this one was coin-freed, playing twice or three times on one coin. This Klepetar played a barrel 9½ inches in diameter and 25½ inches long.

Other makers in Prague around the turn of the century included men such as J. Stychs, Wenzel Hrubés and Jan Rubes. Later, Diego Fuchs formed the 'Erste Prager Musikwerke- und Orchestrionfabrik' in the Wenzelplatz and became a prime supplier, while Ignaz Klepetar became a main agent for many makers in Prague's Eisengasse. By this time, though, the barrel piano orchestrion was losing favour to the new electric pianos.

Édouard Jacques Bourquin of Paris was to contribute the last significant improvement to the barrel piano in the summer of 1922 when he made use of the revolver-barrel mechanism first used by barrel-organ maker James C. Bishop, and later by Forster & Andrews and T. C. Bates on some of their church barrel organs. Bourquin mounted a large number of tune barrels between the flanks of a pair of large wheels. Each barrel was indexed in turn against the piano-string hammer-tails and was played. The barrels turned on a spiral as they played, thus enabling quite lengthy tunes to be performed from one barrel. On the completion of a barrel, the mechanism would disengage, rotate sufficiently to bring the next barrel into place, and then play again.

CANON WINTLE'S ENTERPRISE

No account of the barrel piano and its history would be complete without reference to the contribution of the late Canon A. O. Wintle. During the agricultural depression following the 1914–18 war, he provided employment for men home from the war in the repairing and restoration of barrel pianos at the Old Rectory, Lawshall, near Bury St Edmunds in Suffolk.

He founded the East Anglian Automatic Piano Company and specialised in the restoration, tuning and repinning of old and new barrels. No new pianos were made and the instruments which were rebuilt were either sold or hired out to charitable organisations.

Canon Wintle unquestionably gave a new lease of life to many instruments which would otherwise have fallen into decay and been destroyed. However, in so doing he almost always saw that the name of the original maker was obliterated and replaced by that of the E.A.A.P.C. – usually in the form of an oval blue rubber stamp applied to the barrel paper prior to repinning. When Wintle died in 1959 the firm closed and the remaining stock of sundries was destroyed.

Many people believe that the existence of a barrel piano today reveals the survival of an instrument dating from the turn of the century. In truth, this is probably far from the case since the life of these instruments was comparatively short in service. They were still being built in the 1930s and the late Canon Wintle extensively rebuilt many, many instruments up to the end of the 1950s.

After the death of Canon Wintle, his pianos changed hands several times and ultimately ended up in store in a warehouse in Hull. I was requested by a museum to examine the instruments with a view to their acquisition and this I prepared to do. The sight in that warehouse was one very hard to describe. There were so many pianos, stacked three high and many rows deep, that it was not even possible to count them! Some were extremely early ones with beautifully veneered and inlaid cases, others were black-painted pub-type pianos. The lot was finally sold and transported in truck-loads down to Cornwall to await the lengthy job of restoration. Sadly a number of pianos, barrels and parts of others were destroyed in store when fire broke out in an adjacent building, but enough remains to ensure that the work Wintle so enthusiastically started will, in part at least, be completed.

As for barrel pianos in general, the majority of surviving examples date from the years between the wars and, with a few exceptions, earlier models just have not survived. The Italians who worked on these to keep them playing on the streets were under no delusions as to their worth. They were cheap to build and maintain but once they ceased to become an economic proposition they were burned. For a description of the making and operation of street pianos, see the *New Penny Magazine* for 12 January 1901, which contained an article entitled 'All About Piano Organs' (this is reprinted in *Clockwork Music* by the present author, pp. 293–8). One must remember that the life of these machines was arduous to say the least. They were out in all weathers, usually stored in the open, and generally misused. As the discerning reader will already have gathered, the close relationship of makers and the inevitable swopping of workers all engendered instruments of similar appearance and performance. Where no original name survives, or where it has been removed, it is almost impossible to discover the true maker and date. The tunes a barrel piano plays are also of no use as a clue to its date because barrels were frequently repinned or replaced.

THE MUSIC PLAYED

And what of the repertoire of these instruments? The late Canon Algernon Wintle (who, as a boy, used to spend much time with the 'organ-grinders' as well as Simon Robino, the Manchester manufacturer of street pianos) analysed their music. Of the ten tunes pinned to each barrel, the first two were invariably waltzes, the third a quickstep in two-four time, then a jig, hornpipe or Scottish reel followed by a foxtrot in four-four time. The sixth would be a two-step in six-eight time whilst the seventh was usually reserved for a special tune to suit the customer. This might be a pop song or something more exotic – Wintle once set Mozart's *Eine Kleine Nachtmusik* on one! The eighth tune on the barrel would be another waltz or perhaps a march whilst the ninth could again be a march or perhaps an aria from the opera. The tenth and last tune might be from the opera, a hymn or a sentimental song. Musically speaking, the street piano catered for a wide variety of tastes and it was nothing uncommon to find so-called 'classical' music on the clockwork pianos used in public houses.

The art of barrel-pinning was jealously guarded amongst the various makers, 'the secret of the clock-face', as it was termed, being passed on only to their own children.

While there is little doubt that the earlier barrel pianos were all pinned using the index and pointer method (this is described fully with examples in my book *The Mechanics of Mechanical Music*), there is evidence that the marking out of barrels was also done on the drawing board. In his article 'Toni Pins a Barrel',* George Eves described the process as follows:

> Now a piano barrel starts off as a slab of well-seasoned beech or birch. This first of all gets a steel spindle in its centre, and it is on the centres the ends are provided with that

---

* First published in the *World's Fair* and reprinted in *The Music Box*, Volume 7, page 328.

the drum is turned to the length and diameter the particular instrument demanded. On to it then was glued a sheet of brown paper, which just met end to end, which carried the seven, nine or eleven tunes in the form of hundreds of little black dots.

Toni bought the sheet music of the tunes he wanted in the Charing Cross Road and posted it back to his native country, where the musical maestros translated crochets, quavers, semi-quavers, etc., into myriads of black dots on the master copy. These were then printed off on a hand press and sent back in the form of copy. To look at these sheets and the faceless dots was to marvel at the ability of the man who could convert music to dots. The sheet glued on, it was rubbed down hard with a 'boner' and then a calico bandage four inches wide was wound tight over it all like a sleeve. This was then set aside for a week after which time the cocoon was removed.

The next job was to key on one side of the steel spindle the bronze gear wheel, which would, in due course, mate with the worm wheel on the turning handle spindle. Next the paper-covered drum was set up in a stand, which was nothing more than the innards of a discarded street instrument, and up to this the 'pinner' drew a high stool after providing himself with a box of pins, a special 2-oz hammer, a depth punch and a sharp bradawl. And there he was, all set for a week's or maybe two weeks' work driving in hundreds of cast steel pins.

On every dot the bradawl made a starting hole for the pin, which was then hammered in gently until it was in roughly far enough. Then the depth punch was set to get the pin down to its precise homing. This punch had a hole drilled in one end which accommodated the pin snugly and in depth it gauged the correct amount the pin should stand out from the drum.

This job would go on for days on end. Some 'pinners' worked in bands round the drum; the gearing answered to a couple of turns on the handle. Others worked in lines across the drum but whichever method, by the time all those hundreds of pins had been inserted, it reflected music. The whole art of this job was that the pins had to be dead upright, as a pin leaning either forward or backwards meant the note sounded either early or late; excruciating to the ears of these professionals.

New barrel pianos are being produced today in Spain and these are usually small instruments having 32 notes, two clappers and one triangle. Featuring nylon and plastics in their construction, they are pleasing little devices and are referred to as *'pianos a manubrio'*.

To all intents and purposes, though, the barrel piano has departed from the street scene for ever and remains only as a curio – a nostalgic memory of the hansoms, trams, fog and the 'twopence-a-pint' pubs of the early part of this century.

The mechanism of the barrel piano is extremely simple and the illustration readily shows the primary parts (Fig. 24 refers).

The case of the instrument comprises a solidly built back, of heavy-section framing, with a spruce or clear pine soundboard upon which is set the bridge (in the case of some pianos, the bridges). The top member of the piano frame carries the wrest-pins for the strings, the other ends of which are hooked on to sprags (hitch-pins) driven at the lower end.

The side-boards to the frame, as well as forming part of the enclosure, also locate the action parts, simple that they are. A wooden block positioned on each inside face of the side-boards holds the keyframe on a pivot, so that the entire frame can be rotated towards and away from the strings. This keyframe carries the hammer tails which are usually formed in two parts lapped and glued together from close-grained ash or beech. A flat-sectioned iron pin is provided in the lower part of this tail to engage with the barrel pins. From the top of the hammer tail projects a stiff wire which carries the actual hammer head, usually of wood wrapped with felt, often with a sheepskin overwrap. Some makers used plain wood hammers, leather faced or not, particularly in the treble register where a much more percussive sound was required to enable the note to sing out above the more resonant bass strings.

Each hammer was pivoted on a continuous wire hinge and fitted with a safety-pin-type spring beneath to keep it firmly engaged with a felt strip-covered fixed rest-rail when the hammer was not in use striking the string.

The tune barrel, sometimes mounted on a wooden carrier to facilitate loading and in the same manner that barrel organ barrels were usually made, was slid into the case through a circular removable door in the right-hand side panel. With hand-cranked pianos, the left end of the barrel was equipped with a broad wooden gear-wheel which engaged in a brass worm-shaft fixed in the case at the left side of the front. Later pianos employed a cast gear ring screwed to the end of the barrel. Pianos which were driven by a clockwork motor – automatics, as Pasquale and others preferred to call them – had, in place of the wooden or cast-iron gear, a thin iron gear-wheel to mesh with a broad pinion on the motor which was usually fixed below the barrel at the left side of the case.

To allow for the changing of the tunes (most barrels were pinned for eight or ten tunes), a snail cam was fixed to the left end of the case and against this rested the steel axis of the barrel. In the same way that a musical box changes its tune using a snail cam, so did this cam serve to shift the barrel laterally to bring another set of barrel pins to bear on the iron pins in the hammer tails.

This snail was controlled by a handle on the outside of the case. To avoid damaging the hammer-tail pins and the barrel pins, operation of the snail cam control-handle served also to rotate a cam which automatically lifted the keyframe well out of the way. In this way, it was possible to change the tune at any time – even in the middle of a melody – without risk of damage to the instrument.

Those familiar with the musical box will know that, after playing the repertoire of tunes pinned on the musical box cylinder, the final change of the snail is to let the cylinder move back from the furthest tune position to the first again – usually a distance of little more than an eighth of an inch. The musical box cylinder, moving laterally against a spring to effect such a change, makes this jump with a slight bang. On some larger musical boxes, the probable deleterious effect of this hammering of the cylinder against the snail on this large change was minimised by the provision of a short intermediate step so that, as the snail turned, the cylinder made two jumps in rapid succession.

With the barrel piano, however, the barrel was much heavier and the distance from the first tune position to the last was more in the order of an inch. To have the barrel jumping back that distance could only lead to a loud bang and ultimate danger through wear and so the change snail was designed so that it moved up for half the number of tunes, and back again for the other half. On an eight-tune barrel, the changes would be 1, 3, 5, 7, 8, 6, 4, 2, and then back to 1 again. This made for smoother action as well, for the barrel was shifted by a large and powerful leaf-spring contained in the barrel access-door on the right of the case. Naturally this sequential change was purely of mechanical necessity, the tunes being numbered according to the turn of the tune-change handle.

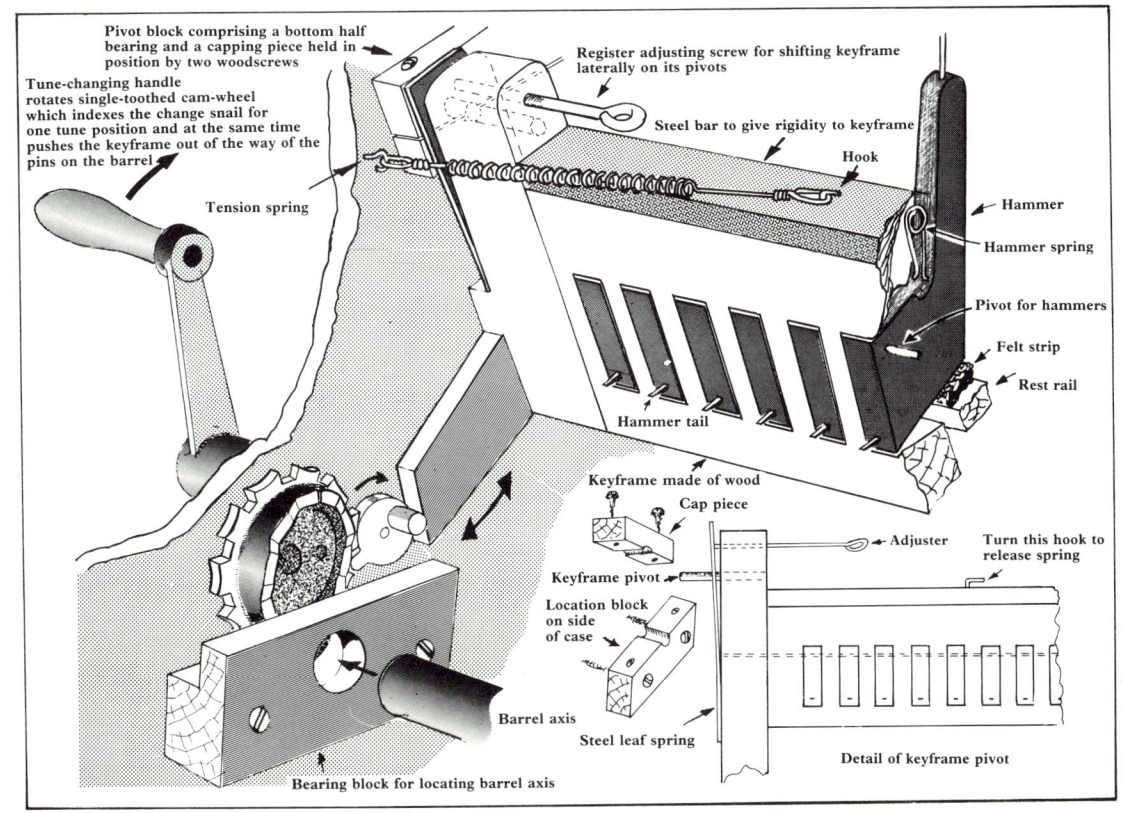

Fig. 24
The tune changing system of the English street piano.

The small barrel pianos, it should be added, together with the earlier instruments, employed the barrel-organ change system – a completely manual movement of the barrel using the notch-plate and knife.

Coin-freed automatic pianos used a counter balanced coin tray which freed a sprag from the governor on the motor. At the end of the tune (they frequently played twice for one coin), the coin would have tipped out and the balanced tray would rise up and re-engage the motor governor.

The clockwork motors were most commonly wound directly from a handle on the outside of the case. Sometimes, though, chain-driven winding handles would be used in cases where the motor was mounted too low in the case for practical direct hand-winding.

Since the inventions and improvements of Antonelli and others, the majority of street and clockwork barrel pianos employed the same basic mechanisms. These and how they relate in the production of music are outlined in the companion volume to this book, *Restoring Pianolas and other self-playing pianos*.

PIANOLA

Grand Prix Brüssel 1905.   Goldene Medaille Leipzig 1905.

Chicago 1893.   San Franzisko 1894.   Berliner Gewerbe-Ausstellung 1896.

Wien 1892   London 1891.

MUSIK-FACHAUSSTELLUNG 1906

Preis-Liste

über

selbstspielende Pianos

mit selbsttätiger Rückrollvorrichtung der Noten
„Patent HEILBRUNN".

D. R.-Patente

No. 86748

„ 103744.

D. R. G. M.

No. 84171
„ 137675
„ 145165
„ 145728
„ 193906
„ 193907

K. Heilbrunn Söhne

Keibel-Strasse 39 ◦ Berlin N.O. ◦ Keibel-Strasse 39.

CHAPTER 3

From Mechanical to Pneumatic Action

So far, all the instruments we have been looking at have been operated by purely mechanical means – a barrel with projections so arranged that as they rotate by means of some intermediary action they strike musical strings. The automatic playing of both the organ and the piano depended from the earliest times on the wheel. The primitive automatic instruments such as the chime or forerunner of the carillon employed a wheel around the periphery of which was arranged a number of projecting pegs. As the wheel rotated, so these engaged in suitable linkages to operate the musical sounding parts. By extending the wheel in thickness, that is to say laterally, more circular tracks of pins could be employed. From this it was but a short step to the evolution of the barrel.

The pinned brass cylinder was a refinement of the barrel and was to be used in musical clocks from the 17th century onwards; prior to this a miniature carillon barrel of iron or bronze was provided with pegs which, as in the case of clocks such as the Trautmanndorf piece, could be reset to make different tunes. The brass cylinder also became standardised in the musical box and indeed it remains so: present-day Swiss and Japanese musical movements use this old but reliable principle.* Of course, the musical box produced its offshoots in the way of those variants which played metal discs or perforated card strips, and even one worked by a perforated paper roll. The disc musical box was an undoubted success, offering changeability of music easily, quickly and for little cost. However, this important feature of the later musical box was effectively killed, as was the need for the musical box industry itself, when the phonograph was introduced. Musical boxes then degenerated into devices to produce soothing tinkling rather than the more serious business of interpreting a melody, and thus the cylinder with its fixed, take-it-or-leave-it programme was reverted to.

Pianos and organs, though, called for barrels of such large dimensions that they presented a serious disadvantage. Indeed, on the large barrel-playing orchestrion organs and military bands the barrels reached such prodigious proportions that it required two men to change the music and needed a large amount of space in which to store the barrels when not in use.

A form of music programme for such instruments which would be less cumbersome and less liable to damage through careless handling and bad storage was needed. A solution was to come from a completely different direction and one far removed from music.

Lyons, France, was the home of a straw-hat maker named Joseph Marie Jacquard (1752–1834). He was to become a highly respected weaver in silk, a position he gained by seeking to improve the existing looms upon which patterned cloth was woven. The looms

---

* The modern mass-produced miniature musical novelty movement of today, however, often uses a folded metal barrel of steel with note projections punched out.

were made to weave different designs in different colours and the selection of the proper colour controls on the loom had to be executed deftly by highly trained personnel. Jacquard worked on the idea that if he could bring all his loom controls together as small keys on a control board they could be selected in any prearranged order by passing across them a strip of cardboard, suitably punched with holes or slots. By feeding long strips of cardboard across these keys, intricate and varied patterns could be woven accurately by semi-skilled operators.

Jacquard's control system for looms called for the design of the cloth for weaving to be set out on graph paper in such a manner as to represent a greatly magnified plan of the finished cloth, showing the weave interlacings in detail. The design was then transferred to cards into which holes and slots were punched on a machine known to this day as a 'piano machine' worked by a foot treadle.

The complete bundle of cards was then laced together into an endless chain and fixed to a square drum on the Jacquard machine normally situated above the loom. As each card was presented to a matching set of needles or tiny levers, the interlacing of one pick of weft was completed according to the instructions passed on by the perforations in the card.

Jacquard is credited with this invention between the years of 1801 and 1808. He was awarded a medal at the Paris Exhibition of 1801, and, after interviews with Napoleon and Carnot, he was seconded to work at the Conservatoire des Arts et Métiers in Paris. Here he worked on his loom, incorporating ideas from a loom conceived in 1745 by Vaucanson (who is perhaps better known as a maker of spectacular automata). Messrs Bouchon and Falcon had done similar work in 1725 and 1728 respectively.

Having perfected his special loom and its method of control, Jacquard returned to his native Lyons only to be given a hostile reception by the local silk-weavers, who feared redundancy should his machine be adopted. Just as James Hargreaves had seen his spinning-jenny smashed up by those who gave vent to similar sentiments in England in 1764, Jacquard witnessed the burning of his loom by the angry mob. As with most revolutionary inventions, there is always an initial predominance of hot-headed pessimists whose misplaced loyalties and passions can generate such conduct. Today, though, labour forces go on strike as a more civilised method of taking up the cudgel against things which might upset the fine balance of industrial relations.

Once the initial fury regarding Jacquard's loom had died down, the importance of its capabilities and the increased trade potential created by its adoption were gradually recognised and Jacquard lived to see happier times with his looms in almost universal use and bringing prosperity to his native city. The new loom could weave delicate patterns in carpets and could make fine cloth quicker and cheaper than the old hand methods. Napoleon, ever appreciative of any technical genius that would further the industrial reputation of his country, rewarded him with a pension of £60 and a royalty of £2 on each loom erected, along with the Cross of the Legion of Honour. Jacquard died in 1834 and, six years later, a statue of him was erected in Lyons on the spot where his first loom had been publicly burned.

The casual reader may ponder on the connection between the weaving industry and the mechanical piano. The answer lies in the ability to correlate a pattern of behaviour to a set of keys. Axminster carpets, rugs, complicated stitches – all were being automated by cardboard strips which passed over the control keyboard of looms. The keys were held firmly down as the strip moved steadily along. When a hole or a slot came up to a key, the key would rise through the cardboard and some mechanical linkage at its opposite end would control a function of the loom. The fact that a spring-loaded key could be made to rise and fall by the passage of a perforated card strip was the making of mechanical music to come. Whether the end of the key was connected to a loom shuttle control, or to an organ windchest, or to a pneumatic lever to strike a musical string was of no consequence. The cardboard could still be made to move the key.

Jacquard had no interest in playing musical instruments from his improved weaving machinery, so it fell to others to see the capabilities of the perforated card programme. The first to look specifically at player actions was Alexander Bain of Hampton Wick, Middlesex, in England. In 1847, Bain was granted a British Patent number 11,886 for an instrument controlled by a perforated paper roll in which the holes directly controlled the passage of air through reeds. Bain was far-sighted enough to suggest that his system might also be used with an electromagnetic device so that more than one instrument could be played simultaneously. However, Bain's invention related solely to the control of musical production by a pattern of holes in paper which corresponded to a musical score: it did not specifically mention pianos, nor could his system of direct interaction be employed, as it stood, for playing a piano.

Duncan Mackenzie was granted a British Patent number 12,229 in August 1848 for improvements to the Jacquard system whereby it might be employed for playing musical instruments. The patent law requirements were such that at this time in their history it was not necessary to provide other than sketchy details as to how the device for which the application was made might work. This is even more demonstrable in the patent taken out by Charles Dawson of Islington (then in Middlesex, now north London). His patent, number 12,307 of 1848, described his occupation as professor of music, and in it he sets about describing how to play instruments which can be played mechanically or automatically. There is a flute, keyboard instruments and a mechanical organ. The mechanical organ was actually built and he exhibited it in the musical instrument section of the Great Exhibition of 1851. By that time he was describing himself as an organ builder with premises at 395 Strand.*

Although in itself it was hardly a successful instrument, Dawson's mechanical organ was historically significant. Writing in his *Musical Instruments in the Great Exhibition of 1851*, historian William Pole tells us:

> Mr Dawson exhibits a mechanical organ on a new construction which he calls an autophon, and for which he has a patent. This instrument has no wind chest, valves or keys, but the wind is conveyed directly from the bellows to the channels of the soundboard by a row of passages, which are cut through transversely by a long horizontal slit, just large enough to admit a sheet of pasteboard. The pasteboard is pierced with a number of holes, corresponding to the given tune to be played, and is drawn through the slit by rollers, turned by a winch; when, therefore, the holes come opposite the passages in succession they admit wind to the soundboard and cause the corresponding notes to play. This instrument might be called a *jacquard* organ. It is simple, and does away with barrels, and many other expensive parts; but it has the disadvantage of admitting the wind gradually into the pipes, and cutting it off gradually from them; the effect of which is a disagreeable wavering at the commencement and termination of the note.

---

* Dawson's descriptive leaflet on his Autophon Improved Organ is reproduced in facsimile in *Barrel Organ*, page 144.

Adoniram F. Hunt and James S. Bradish of Warren, Ohio, were granted an American Patent number 6006 on 9 January 1849 for a means of playing an octave in a piano using perforated cardboard strips passed between rollers and over a keyframe. There was even a system for emphasising certain notes so that a theme or melody would stand out from the accompaniment. It is very unlikely that this went beyond the patent and model stage and no further information exists outside the patent specification.

Much the same sort of comment can be made about many of these early patents. There was that of Jean-Henri Pape of London. A Frenchman and a master piano builder, he was in business between 1844 and 1848 in New Bond Street and also for a time in Little Newport Street, Leicester Square. He was awarded French Patent number 5923 of 1850 for an unusual system centring on the use of a barrel containing a large number of spring-loaded pins. This was rotated in conjunction with a perforated cardboard sheet. When a pin found a hole, it passed through and so could strike the piano mechanism or an organ key.

In a surprisingly incomplete, inaccurate and unsympathetic brief section on the mechanical pianoforte in her book *The Piano Forte*, Rosamond E. Harding (p. 283) refers to Jean-Henri Pape's invention of 1851 and says:

> His mechanism was worked by means of a handle, weights and springs, but it is unnecessary to describe it, as Debain's 'piano mécanique' was by far the most perfect mechanical contrivance for this purpose at that time.

This singularly ill-informed statement on the one hand omits to note that Debain's instrument, described in Chapter 1, had a compass of 61 notes and was provided with no facility for rapid repetition of notes, and on the other that the barrel as a means of programming music for the pipe organ and, indeed, the pianoforte had attained a high degree

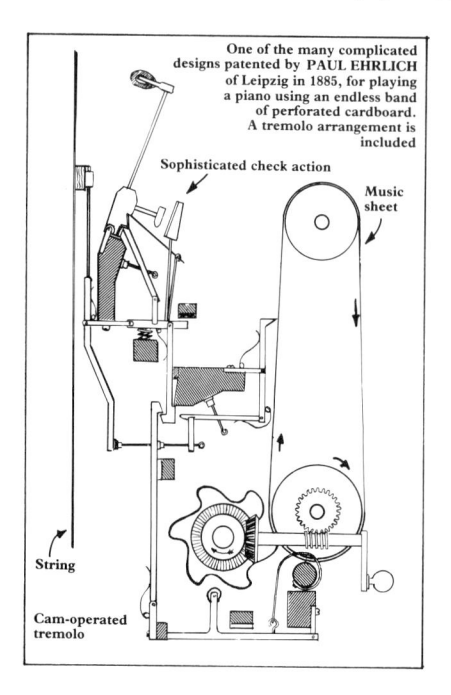

Fig. 25
Ehrlich invented a number of different ways of playing the piano and this one, patented in 1885, is for an endless band system using a band of cardboard. The cam system is intended to operate as a tremolo mechanism on the note being played. As with so many of these systems, it is unlikely that they were ever actually manufactured.

of perfection. Thomas Rolfe's instrument of 1824, for example, would play the whole compass of the piano.

The 'self-acting piano or seraphone' patented in 1849 by William Martin was also played by a system of Jacquard cards.

Joseph Antoine Teste applied the Jacquard system to the playing of mechanical organs in 1863 and improved upon it during the next year, taking out several patents. J. Amman, two years later, produced an electromagnetic piano-playing system using a Jacquard card moved between the two contacts of a primitive solenoid. In England, Alfred Barlow played a reed instrument using an endless band of paper which had holes punched in it. This was one of the forerunners of the reed instruments later to be called organettes and the date was 1870. An electromagnetic system was used in the following year by E. Molyneux to open the pallets of his reed organ which played a perforated paper strip.

Determined not to permit one chink in their patent specification, Charles Abdank de Laskarewski and Thomas Herbert Noyes specified either the pinned barrel or the perforated card or paper strip on their mechanical musical instrument of 1873 which played on tuning-forks rather like Clagget's Aiuton.

Paul Ehrlich of Leipzig was a prolific inventor of improvements in both the musical box and organette field. He patented a system of perforated tune sheets for organettes in the summer of 1876. These were intended for the mechanical playing of 'automatic organs, harmoniums &c' and had wedge-shaped holes so that the keys passed slowly through the slots and the opening of the pallet could be controlled to produce louder or softer notes. The system, Ehrlich claimed, could also be used for musical boxes and pianos.

Ehrlich produced a disc-playing piano-player using cardboard discs of exactly the same style and appearance as those used on his Ariston organette and Orpheus disc piano, only they were $16^{11}/_{16}$ in. (423 mm) in diameter.

From this point forward, the use of perforated music advanced steadily towards the ultimate goal of full pneumatic action. The player developed in three stages, the steps between which were seldom clear. The use of perforated tune sheets initially served directly to admit and cut off wind to the musical production components: in other words, it was a direct valve and hence had serious shortcomings. Next was the interposing of a servo mechanism between tunesheet and musical components, most frequently in the form of a mechanical keyframe or a set of sprung buttons normally held in the 'off' position by the music tune sheet. The third was the full pneumatic action between sliding valve and musical component. With this, the paper was required to suffer no forces other than to regulate the supply of power to a set of valves and secondary parts which themselves were called upon to do the work of physically causing a sound.

So it was a little surprising to find that in the two French patents taken out by J. B. Napoleon Fourneaux of Paris in 1863 and 1871 for a pneumatic piano player all the mechanism comprised was a pinned barrel which operated pneumatic motors to sound the piano keys. The machine was, furthermore, larger than the piano! Fourneaux's instrument, named the Pianista, was widely publicised at the time, actually crossing the Atlantic to be shown at the Philadelphia Exposition of 1876.

The possibilities of the perforated tune sheet had now been determined. A cardboard strip could be made to push small levers up and down. Perforated paper was easier to make and to store, but it was impossible to use it to do mechanical work. It could, however, be used to open and close a small air passage leading to a reed or musical pipe.

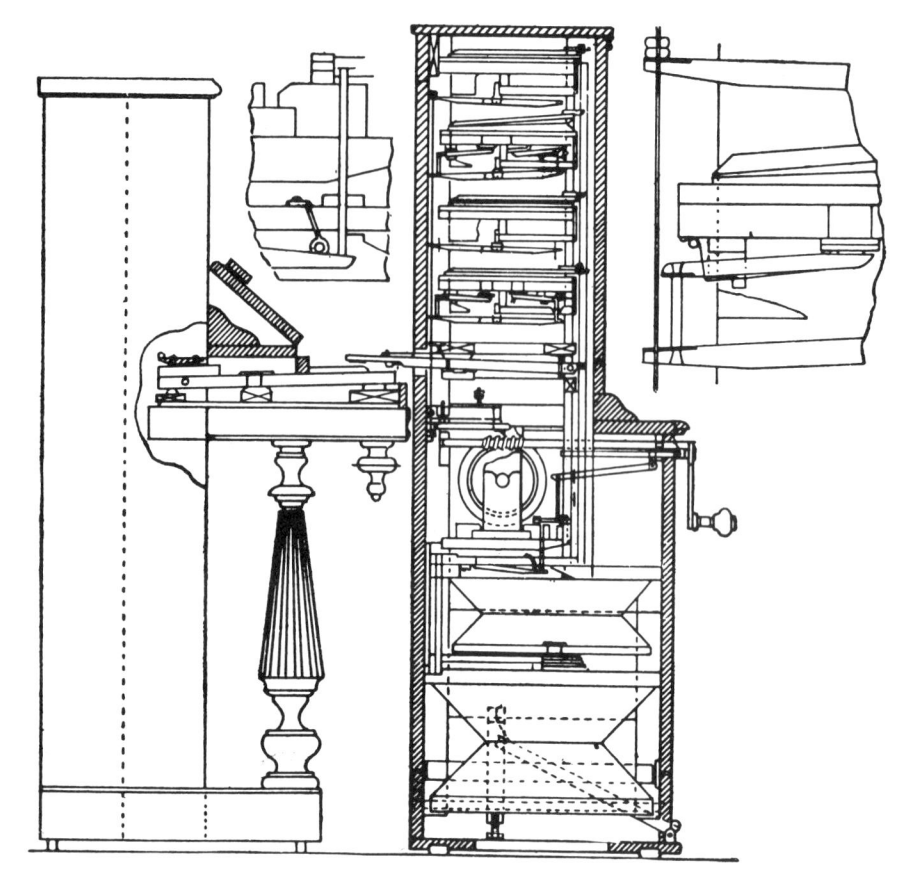

Fig. 26
Even larger than Votey's first Pianola was Napolean Fourneaux's Pianista of 1863, demonstrated at the Philadelphia Exposition of 1878. Four banks of rather complicated pneumatic motors were set in operation from a pinned barrel. Foot-operated bellows provided air at pressure to work this, possibly the biggest push-up ever made.

THE DEVELOPMENT OF PNEUMATIC ACTIONS

At this time there were thus two distinctive methods of producing music using a perforated substance as compared with the traditional barrel. As we have shown, there was on the one hand perforated paper used to operate a pneumatic valve. On the other hand, perforated card could be used to move a mechanical lever.

The earlier use of pneumatic principles in playing music was the work of a mechanic from Lyons in France, C. F. Seytre. His Autophon, patented in 1842, played 'all kinds of melodies by means of perforated cards with square or oblong holes according to the length of the notes to be played'. The holes were connected by tubing which led air pressure from pedal-operated bellows to small cylinders attached by each key in the keyboard. In each

J. M. Grob & Co., Eutritzsch bei Leipzig

empfehlen als besonders absatzfähig ihre patentirten Neuheiten:

Klavierspieler 36 Töne neue Construction

eignet sich zum mechanischen Spielen auf allen Tasteninstrumenten, wie Pianino, Flügel, Harmonium etc., mittelst der bekannten runden Noten des Riesenaristons. Repertoir, ca. 500 verschiedene Stücke, wird täglich vermehrt.

Klavierspieler 61 Töne!! grossartiger Effect!!

spielt mittelst durchlochter Pergamentnoten Musikstücke von beliebiger Länge, kurze Tänze, vollständige Ouverturen etc. Beide Apparate sind mit Leichtigkeit an jedem Tasteninstrument anzubringen. Ferner bitten wir nicht auf Lager fehlen zu lassen:

Ariston, Aristonette, Riesenariston, Orpheus und Symphonion in den versch. Grössen und Ausstattungen. Alle von uns geführten Artikel übertreffen in ihrer Güte und Leichtverkäuflichkeit alles Andere dieser Branche und werden jedem Händler besonders durch den fortwährenden Notennachbezug guten Gewinn bringen.

Cataloge und **Notenverzeichnisse** in allen Hauptsprachen stehen zum Gebrauch oder Versand an die Kundschaft in mäßiger Anzahl gratis zur Verfügung.

Heilbrunn's Kunstspiel-Pianos „VIRTUOS"

Patentiert.   Patentiert.

sind Pianos normaler Beschaffenheit, welche mit den Händen, mit Fussbetrieb oder elektrisch gespielt werden können. Dieselben reproduzieren die von Pianisten gespielten Stücke mit allen Nüancen und Wechsel der Tempi

selbsttätig.

Der Spielapparat kann in jedes Piano und jeden Flügel eingebaut werden.

Es ist jedoch volle Freiheit gelassen, nach eigenem Empfinden Nüancen und Tempo zu verändern, derart, dass jeder einzelne Ton zur vollen Geltung gelangen kann. Das eigene Notenrepertoire ist unbegrenzt, jedes gewünschte Stück kann rasch geliefert werden. Unsere Apparate können auch für **jedes** beliebige andere Notensystem (65 Töne) eingerichtet werden. Man verlange Prospekte. Die einzigen Fabrikanten

K. Heilbrunn Söhne, Berlin NO, Keibelstrasse 39.

Filiale: Hamburg, Kaiser Wilhelmstrasse 46.

Fig. 27
Types of player on the market in Europe around the turn of the century. At the top are two mechanical players by Grob, forerunner of Hupfeld. One is disc-operated and the other plays from a punched roll of thin card. Below are two of Heilbrunn's electric pianos, both operating with a kicking-shoe type of mechanism. All of these are mechanical players.

cylinder was a small piston which, when subjected to air pressure, could move a jack to engage with the tail of a hammer striking the string from below.

Probably the first satisfactory method of utilising air was devised by another Frenchman, J. Carpentier, who, as related by Buchner, constructed his first pneumatic instruments for the International Electricity Exhibition in 1880. His 'repeating melograph', first used for the harmonium, punched holes directly in paper strips which were then used to play the music in a specially constructed electrically operated harmonium. Carpentier developed two more instruments in 1887 – the Melograph and the Melotrope – which he put before the French Academy. The Melograph recorded music performed on any keyboard instrument whilst it was being played. It worked by means of electrical conductors leading from contacts beneath the keys of the instrument. As the key was pressed down, current passed to the Melograph which operated along similar lines to a teleprinter. A wooden plaque with a row of flexible metal strips was attached to the instrument in such a way that the strip of metal came beneath each of the keys, forming the contact when the keys were moved. The strip of paper upon which the music was recorded was moved along by an electric motor with a speed-regulating device. Underneath the paper was a perforated cylinder inking-roller which was kept wet with black ink. Above the paper was a row of vertically mounted impression rods which could be actuated by electromagnets which caused the rods to press down on the paper whenever particular magnets received the current. There were thirty-seven magnets to play thirty-seven keys on the instrument. The recording thus produced consisted of inked lines and the distance between these marks and the edge of the paper indicated the notes to be played and also their duration. In order to obtain from this Melograph perforated strips for use in suitably equipped mechanical instruments, Carpentier invented a hand-driven perforating mechanism equipped with punches. The punched strip thus obtained was used to make large numbers of copies in a mechanical perforating machine. To play these strips, Carpentier invented a crank-driven mechanism – the Melotrope – which was placed on the keyboard of the instrument to be played. It was in the form of an oblong box and contained thirty-seven mechanisms for the playing of that number of piano keys. At the right-hand end, the perforated tune sheet held down lightly sprung metal fingers. A slot in the music allowed one of these fingers to lift up into a grooved brass pressure roller above it in the manner which Anselme Gavioli was to use on his book-music-playing show organs in later years. The Melotrope's levers were each connected to rocking levers spaced along the length of the box. The wooden plungers which sounded the piano keys were themselves spring-loaded and loosely attached to the rocking levers by a cord which also passed twice around a rotating wooden shaft running the length of the instrument. When a key was raised by the music slot, the rocking lever would cause this cord to be drawn tightly against the rotating shaft. The friction would at once cause the plunger to be pushed downwards on to the piano key. Musical expression was obtained by using the pedals (in the case of a piano), and the volume of sound was controlled by a lever which raised or lowered the key plungers. Both the Melograph and the Melotrope were very popular at the end of the nineteenth century and a large number of pieces of music were 'recorded' in this way.

This mechanism, which I have dubbed the 'kicking-shoe' type, was used quite widely by mechanical players for some years. Hupfeld in Germany also used it and it featured in many patents. In terms of practicability, it certainly allowed very thin punched card to initiate a blow of considerable force by inducing cork-soled shoes or quadrant levers to touch against the surface of a rotating shaft and so gain movement from them. However, these were fiddly devices to assemble and maintenance posed a great headache, for the check strings which were used to disengage the shoes at the end of each note-strike were prone to breaking and fraying from the high loads imposed on them.

The mechanical player of the period used long and sometimes endless card bands, strips

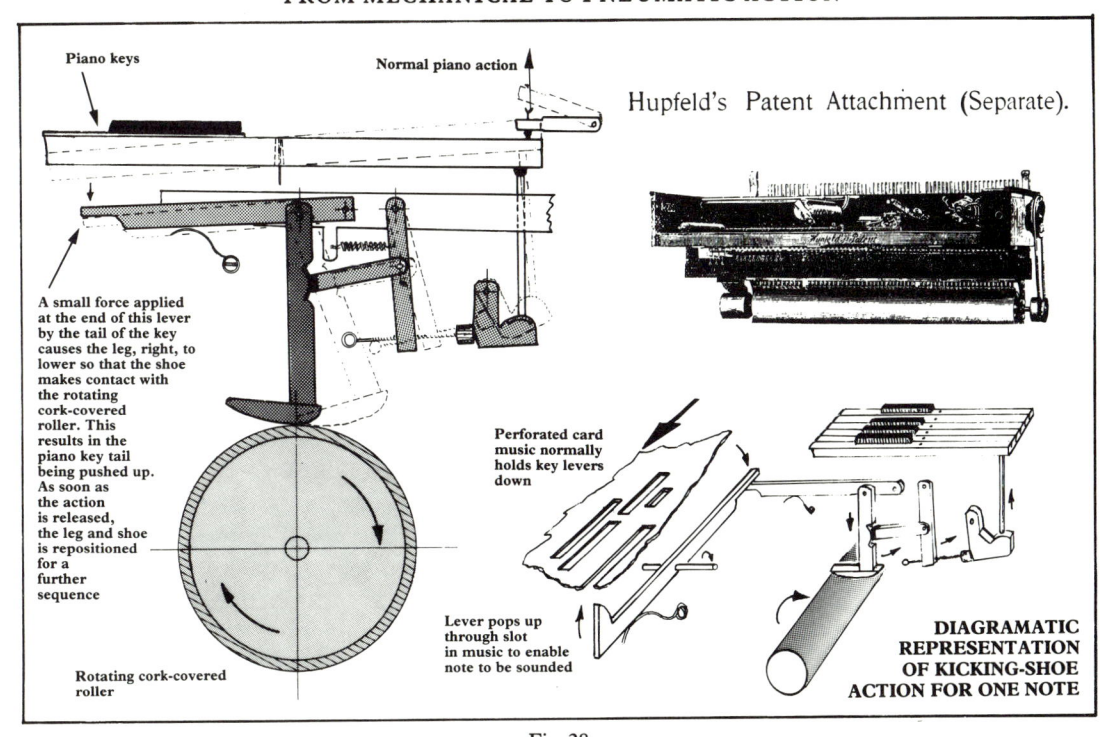

Fig. 28
The kicking shoe piano playing action. This schematic drawing shows the principle of operation and, inset, is part of an advertisement for Hupfeld's kicking shoe player attachment which could be fitted to any piano.

and discs. J. M. Grob of Leipzig was one maker who favoured the cardboard disc and his player was a neat little box affair which stood on spindly legs in front of the piano, small wooden fingers protruding from behind being caused to play on the keys while the operator turned a handle at the front which rotated the disc against a mechanical keyframe.

The 1880s were the period of introduction of these, and *Musical Opinion* for May 1888 announced one as follows:

> Mr. Alfred Lengnick, of Oxford Street, is the sole wholesale agent, for the United Kingdom, of the 'piano player', an attachment which will fit any piano, and by means of which any piece of music may be performed on the pianoforte by putting on a perforated disc and turning the handle of the instrument. It is claimed for this ingenious invention that it has the advantage of not being purely mechanical, time and expression being within control of the player, and with very little practice the crescendo and diminuendo can be exactly rendered. Prices will be, we are informed, forwarded on application.

The same publication, in August 1883, announced the appointment of a London agent for the invention of a Frenchman, J. Lacape (his name is mis-spelled in the news item). Lacape's barrel-operated mechanism fitted under the keyboard and appears to have owed some of its detail design to the sewing machine, since a foot treadle was used to turn a large-diameter flywheel to turn the pinned barrel. The report reads:

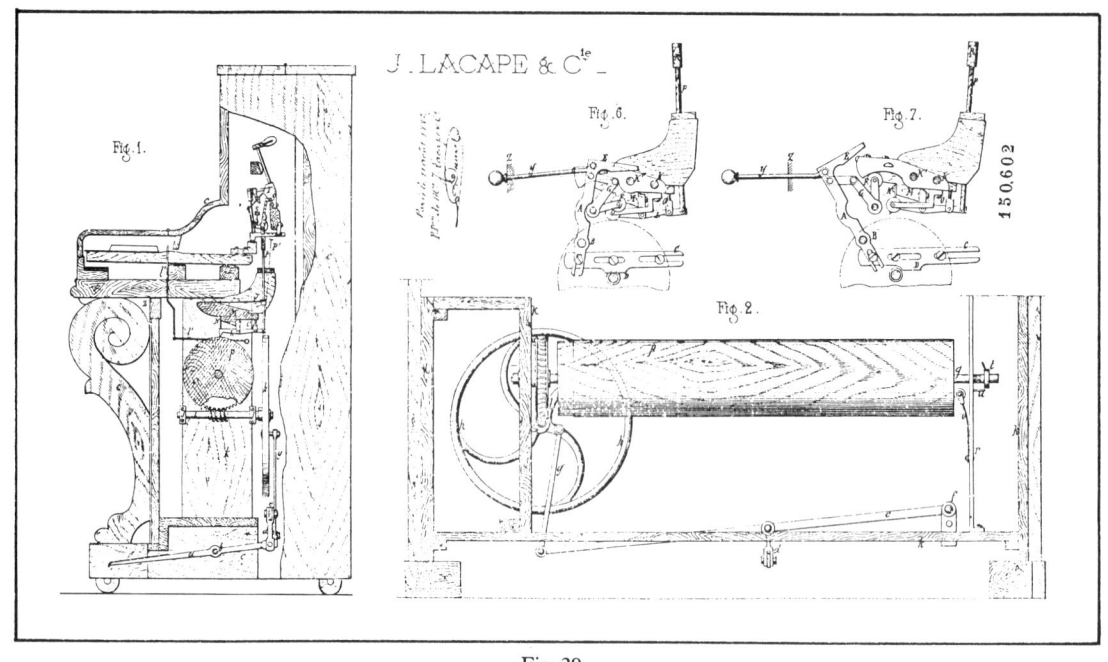

Fig. 29
J. Lacape of Paris patented this treadle-driven barrel in 1882 and was awarded a bronze medal for barrel pianos at the 1883 Brussels Exposition.

Another mechanical pianoforte! Messrs. Metzler & Co. are the agents for Lacafé's clever invention, by which a simple piece of mechanism is adapted to the interior of an upright pianoforte, to play which a special pedal (placed at the side of the ordinary pedals) is put in motion, each stroke of this pedal marking the measure of the air that is being played, and by that means a more artistic rendering is capable than when a continually revolving handle is used for the purpose. The instrument, possessing a key-board, can be played in the ordinary manner. Messrs. Metzler have also brought out a folding harmonium, which, when closed, takes the form of a book. It is worked by a treadle, and is designed for use on a table, being only two feet wide and six inches deep.

Shortly after this, Gavioli invented a book-playing mechanical piano. This was shown at the Barcelona Exhibition of September 1888, and the correspondent of *Musical Opinion* wrote as follows:

The sole piano forwarded by Messrs. Gavioli & Co., Avenue de Taillebourg, Paris, will be found very useful by persons desiring to play the piano, but not knowing how. For, by fixing and turning a handle in the slot projecting from the upper front panel, after laying the long strip of cardboard music, folded as a book, therein, and fixing as directed, the result is music by the yard, or by the hour, churned out as in a regular piano-organ. This is an idea which occurred to the writer many years ago, and the marvel is that so simple an instrument was not produced ten years back. The 'piano executor' will be found valuable.

FROM MECHANICAL TO PNEUMATIC ACTION

Das neueste und epochemachende Erzeugniß auf dem Gebiete der mechanischen Musikwerke ist unstreitig das

Daimonion
(Δαιμόνιον).

Dasselbe stellt Alles, was bisher auf dem Gebiete der Drehpianos geleistet wurde, vollständig in den Schatten. Die Ausstattung des Instrumentes ist eine hochelegante, die Mechanik so sauber und solid gearbeitet, wie bei dem theuersten Salonflügel. Das Instrument hat

vollständigen Eisenrahmen und widersteht jedem Witterungswechsel.

Reparaturen sind fast gänzlich ausgeschlossen.

Die Tonfülle ist geradezu großartig und befriedigt auch den verwöhntesten Musikliebhaber. Es ersetzt vollkommen ein Klavier mit Streichinstrumenten-Begleitung. Zum Spielen werden die uns patentirten kreisförmigen Notenscheiben benutzt. Das Repertoir ist außerordentlich reichhaltig und wird täglich vermehrt. Bestellungen bitten wir möglichst frühzeitig zu machen, damit die Lieferung rechtzeitig geschehen kann.

Daimonion (Δαιμόνιον).

Orchestrionettes,
mit endlosen, bandförmigen Noten zu spielen.

Non plus ultra,
mit und ohne Deckel, in verbesserter Construction.

Außerdem empfehlen wir:

Klavier-Automaten
in vorzüglich sauberer Arbeit.

Aristonettes,
19 tönig.

Preis-Verzeichnisse u. Noten-Cataloge stehen zu Diensten.

Fabrik Leipziger Musikwerke
vorm. Paul Ehrlich & Co. zu Gohlis bei Leipzig.

Fig. 30
Leipziger Musikwerke, successors to the business of Paul Ehrlich, advertised the Daimonion keyless piano in 1903.

The reporter, who takes the opportunity to display his foresight for such an instrument, seems to have been unaware of similar instruments, admittedly playing wooden planchettes, which had been around then for more than forty years. His description of a slot projecting from the instrument is an indication that he was no technical man. Gavioli's Piano Executant, to give it its proper name, is a rare instrument today and I know of only one instrument – this was in a sale in France early in 1979 and was acquired by a British collector.

Imhof & Mukle perfected what they termed their 'leaf-system' for playing pianos and orchestrions. This was a roll of stout manila paper or thin card which was wound onto a large drum and drawn across a mechanical keyframe so as to operate mechanical key action. The card was often up to 100 feet in length (30 metres) and because it travelled slowly it was possible to encompass a long piece of music in this manner. Imhof produced many fine piano orchestrions which featured quite complex automaton scenes. Frequently these involved a 'back projection' system where the front of the case, or part of it, would be painted as an opal screen behind which was a travelling transparent belt with figures and suchlike painted upon it. Behind this would be an electric lamp and when the instrument was switched on a small belt drive from the mechanism roll and bellows operating mechanism would set the effects in motion. One such model had a waterwheel, a hot-air balloon which apparently crossed and recrossed the vista (by means, one imagines, of an ill explained and rather wayward wind direction!), a train which passed over a bridge between two hills, a windmill and a waterfall. This whole effect was achieved in silhouette on the translucent glass painted scene. Imhof pianos, along with many other of these very large orchestrion pianos, could be tuned by swinging out the strung back and action: it was hinged at the bottom at the back so that it could be moved down into the horizontal position.

Elias Parkman Needham, in America, exploited the paper-roll system and, from 1877 onwards, presented many improvements in the development of the pneumatic system. He invented the upright player action used in reed organs, which was the step that paved the way for the entire later development of paper-controlled music.

The first person to make significant improvements to the simple pneumatic system was John McTammany of Worcester, Massachusetts. He was a far-sighted inventor who patented a remarkable series of improvements to the paper-roll system from 1868 onwards. He applied his techniques to the manufacture of organettes but the venture was not a success. Unable to pay the renewal fees on his patents, he had to see each one taken up and successfully exploited by other companies. McTammany, whose name is almost forgotten today, did much to give us the player organ and organette as well as the player piano, yet he was to die penniless in 1915.

THE FIRST PNEUMATIC PIANO

The kudos for the invention of the very first pneumatic self-playing piano, however, should probably go to R. W. Pain, who, in conjunction with Henry Kuster, built such an instrument for Needham & Sons in 1880. This had a 39-note compass. In 1882 he constructed for the Mechanical Orguinette Company (later to become the Aeolian Company), an inner player with a range of 46 notes, and then in 1888 he produced an electrically powered 65-note player.

Merritt Gally of New York patented in 1881 a pneumatic device for use in playing pianos. In concept, this was some years in advance of its time. For various reasons, Gally concentrated on perfecting the principles of the small organette rather than those of the pneumatic piano. Gally and, separately, McTammany laid these foundations. Between the years of 1896 and 1902, the progress and perfection of the external player can largely be attributed to men such as Tremaine, White, McTammany, Gally, Goolman, Doman, Parker, Votey, Kelly, Pain, Brown, Davis, Clark, Hattemer, Winter, Healy, Weser, Salyer,

Klugh, Ball, Wuest, Gulbransen and Welin. In England, Bishop & Down patented a pneumatic system for keyboard playing in 1882, whilst C. A. Custer of New York contrived what must surely have been the first 'expression' device in 1887. His system graduated the power of touch and operated the piano pedals from 'either barrel or perforated roll'.

The so-called American organ, soon to become known almost universally, was developed in the United States* and worked on the principle that air was sucked down through the reed, so producing a sound. This differed from the first harmoniums in which air was blown through the reed. The precursor of the American organ was the organette and in 1881 M. Harris controlled the mechanical performance of one such device by passing a strip of perforated paper across the air passage to the reeds. He mounted his bellows above these passages. Harris later used the same system on a keyboard reed instrument and also a pipe organ and was thus one of the first to follow E. P. Needham's system. In subsequent years, Wilcox & White and the Aeolian Company were to exploit the pressure or blown reed in their paper-playing organs, as this system produced a louder note with a greater purity of tone which could be voiced almost like a pipe-organ sound.

The barrel was now relegated to a third-rate position, superseded by perforated paper and punched card. Barrel organs, however, were still to be made for a number of years to come and, indeed, a wide range of these instruments was included in the 1905 catalogue of Thibouville-Lamy of London and Paris. The barrel piano for street use, as we have seen, was soon to regain its former position in spite of the infiltration by perforated music, such makers as Pasquale continuing in this line of business until the 1930s. However, the 1880s evoked a spate of playing systems which, with but a few exceptions, left the barrel out cold.

Bishop and Down produced a paper-operated piano player in 1882, followed closely by A. Wilkinson, who used a calico tune sheet.

The perforated tune sheet became more sophisticated. The Automatic Music Paper Co. in America made many improvements to the paper roll, starting with such a basic thing as a method of attaching the paper to the wooden spool.

As the paper roll was perfected, so came a demand for a means of making the rolls cheaply and speedily. The Auto Music Co. in the United States devised a machine for punching out music in 1881. This made stencils from which the music rolls themselves could be punched.

The means employed to perforate the paper were indeed diverse. In 1883 J. Maxfield devised a system of perforating organette rolls using an instrument which was equipped with a number of gas jets. The music roll was burned against a template or pattern to produce the holes. The most common system was to use a metal punch to punch closely spaced holes or slots in the paper but in the late 1880s several makers were sandblasting their paper tune sheets against a pattern.

In shotblasting or punching the paper, loose paper fibres would be created and the suction through the tracker-bar would draw this dust, together with any other dust in the atmosphere, into the instrument, ultimately clogging the tiny valves and exhaust ports. F. Engelhardt and A. P. Roth solved this problem in 1901 by splitting the tracker-bar (over which the paper travelled) horizontally and interposing a removable filter which was supposed to trap the dust.

Claude Gavioli in Paris was at this time producing street organs and he perfected a

* In reality, the American organ was a French invention devised by a harmonium maker in the 1840s who sought to improve the tone by using suction bellows. His idea, however, was not taken up in France until many years after its transatlantic perfection. See next chapter.

pneumatic-lever action in which the air valve in a high-pressure windchest was opened by a servo valve in a low-pressure windchest using a key lever moved by the perforated-card tune sheet. This was in 1881.

Gavioli was among the earliest to make serious use of perforated cardboard music and he applied this technique to mechanical organs and pianos, perfecting the zigzag folding of the music into a book which could be fed through the instrument. He patented his piano player which worked on this principle in 1884–5. By 1895 Gavioli was using cardboard music to work the keys of all his show organs and, four years later, was using the servo-pneumatic system which came to be known as the 'keyless' system, in use on some fair organs to this day. This was really just a form of suction tracker-bar.

A number of inventors turned their attention to methods of joining the card into a continuous length and the methods used included metal hinges, cloth strips and wire hinges. Gavioli used a simpler and more practical method. He glued his music strip from machine-creased, overlapped card. This produced a hard, durable board which could be punched cleanly with the music apertures, yet at the same time was capable of easy unfolding and refolding in the organ.

Chiappa applied this music principle to the street pianos he was building in place of the wooden barrel in the early 1890s, using it also in his military band organs. On the continent,

Fig. 31
Thibouville-Lamy's Pianista was a pneumatically-operated push-up piano player controlled by 58-key perforated cardboard music read by a mechanical keyframe.

Bruder in Germany and all other fair-organ makers gradually changed from the pinned barrel to the perforated-cardboard music form.

Paris was at this time the traditional home of the fair organ and thus when, in 1884, Thibouville-Lamy produced their Pianista piano-player, it was not surprising to find that it scorned paper music, but played Gavioli-type book music. The Pianista was matched by the production of the Organina, which applied the same principles to organ playing.

Nevertheless, perforated paper had seized the imagination of many inventors, particularly in America. Organettes were cheap to make and sold well at a price far less than the cheapest average-quality musical box. Hundreds of different styles were made and many inventors found improvements to patent. Ithaca, New York, was the home of the Autophone Company and they produced small organettes from about 1880 onwards. These mostly played paper rolls or endless paper bands, although Autophone also made the Gem roller organette which, in true barrel organ tradition, played small, wooden rollers bristling with pins. These barrels were pinned spirally and made three revolutions to complete the tune – a system well known in barrel-orchestrion making.

F. E. P. Ehrlich of Leipzig made a machine in 1885 for the mechanical playing of an ordinary piano, which used a perforated tune sheet and an escapement-cocking kicking-shoe mechanism worked by small levers to strike the piano strings with sufficient force. He was to produce a number of such interesting variations but all were basically punched-card players. Ehrlich applied these techniques in his many types of organette, which culminated in the successful and widely sold Ariston of 1885 (which played a circular punched card disc), and his little Orpheus disc-playing piano of 1887, which played Ariston cards. Both Ehrlich and Lochmann later made large 'long-case' pianos which were played by metal discs rather like Polyphon's Concerto.

Activity was not restricted to Northern Europe and America, for Italy was a centre of mechanical music and, of course, mechanical pianos. Giovanni Racca of Bologna was a maker of barrel pianos who devised, in 1886, a system of playing a piano using perforated book music. He used a variation of the tremolo system invented by one Signor Caldera in

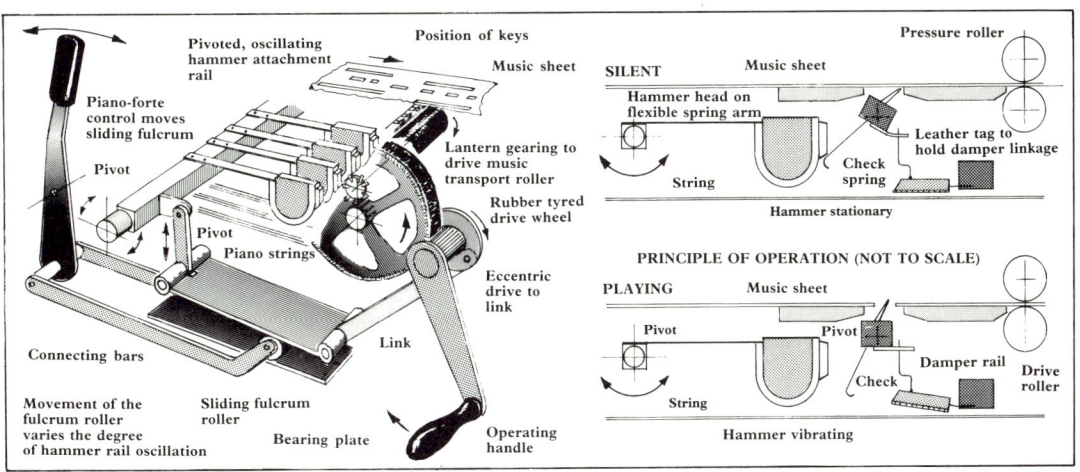

Fig. 32
The mechanical player action of the book-playing Piano Melodico patented by Giovanni Racca and G. Seward in 1886. The instrument was manufactured in a number of different sizes according to the number of notes played and enjoyed quite considerable success.

about 1875, applied in England to the ordinary pianoforte by Kirkman and known as the Melopiano. This was a *sostinente* attachment wherein each hammer was attached by a flat spring to an oscillating rail set in motion by a foot pedal and flywheel. The hammers were restrained by checks which were freed when their respective piano keys were touched, so causing the strings to be struck repeatedly. Racca, with his co-patentee Seward, achieved this with the mechanism shown in Fig 32. Four sizes of these attractive machines were produced under the name 'Piani Melodici' and they were of horizontal layout, the largest one closely resembling a small baby grand. These were operated by small spring-tensioned levers normally pressed down by the card in the same way as Ehrlich's card-operated organettes which were being made in Germany. While at this time many barrel-playing instruments of all types were being converted to book music, for the piano at least this was but a passing phase.

J. M. Grob, A. O. Schultze and A. V. Niemczik in Berlin jointly perfected in 1886 a kicking-shoe-type player for pianos which could also be used with organs. Unlike Thibouville-Lamy's instrument of the same period, this was worked by a perforated tune sheet. Levers were moved mechanically by the cardboard disc, allowing segmented arms to wedge cam-fashion on a rotating drum, thereby cocking the piano hammer and striking the string. It was Grob and, separately, Ehrlich who first applied a variation of the elemental Christofori hammer action to the mechanical piano. This action was a considerable improvement on the direct-striking-hammer principle inasmuch as the hammer mechanism for one note was progressively cocked by the action (with the ordinary piano, the action is cocked by the depressing of the piano key), finally bringing the hammer against the string and allowing it to fall back immediately, regardless of whether or not the operating lever is returned to normal position. This made for a prompt action, allowed notes to be sustained by a separate damper connected to the cocking mechanism and also permitted free and easy repetition of the note. Grob's player acted upon thirty-six of the piano's keys.

Whereas Ehrlich and some of his contemporaries used the progressive movement of a lever, pulled by the tune sheet, to cock the hammer and release it, Grob, and those who favoured this other method, relied on the mechanical fact that a cam can be wedged on a rotating shaft, thereby applying a relatively considerable amount of force for the initial expenditure of a very light force at the opposite end of the cam lever.

A number of very ingenious cardboard-playing pianos were made, particularly those driven by hot-air engines. Of German manufacture and more than likely the products of the Leipzig area, rich as it was with mechanical music expertise, these were intended for domestic use. The Organista, made about 1890, played, in addition to piano strings, a glockenspiel, a drum and a triangle. Another such instrument, the Piano-Orchestrion, was a horizontal instrument and played on strings only. Both these instruments derived their power from a methylated spirits burner and a hot-air engine located in their lower portions, or could be played by turning a handle.

In 1887 C. A. Custer in the United States made a keyboard player for a piano which graduated the power of touch and actually operated the pedals of the piano from the music roll. This was quite probably the first attempt at built-in expression.

Favouring the principle of a device clamped to a piano keyboard, G. P. le Dan patented his key-top player for keyboards in 1887. This worked by a series of metal plates with projections which engaged in levers connected to the keys. It was thus similar to the Antiphonel of Debain.

Crasselt & Rähse,

Pianoforte-Fabrik in Löbau i. S.

Brüssel 1888: Grosse goldene Medaille.   Bologna 1888: Silberne Medaille.

Pianinos und Flügel [322]

in vollendetster Eisenkonstruktion mit aufrechtstehender Stimmschraube (System Rähse).

Ausgezeichnete Haltbarkeit!   **Vorzügliche Klangschönheit!**

Klavierspielwerk.

D. R.-Patent No. 134484.

D. R.-Patent No. 134484.

Dieses Klavierspielwerk, das neueste auf dem Gebiete der Instrumentenbaukunst, mit Gewichtsaufzug, auswechselbaren Notenblättern und Geldeinwurf, ist für Restaurants, Tanzsäle vorzüglich geeignet. Spielt vollendete Concert- sowie vorzügliche Tanzmusik.

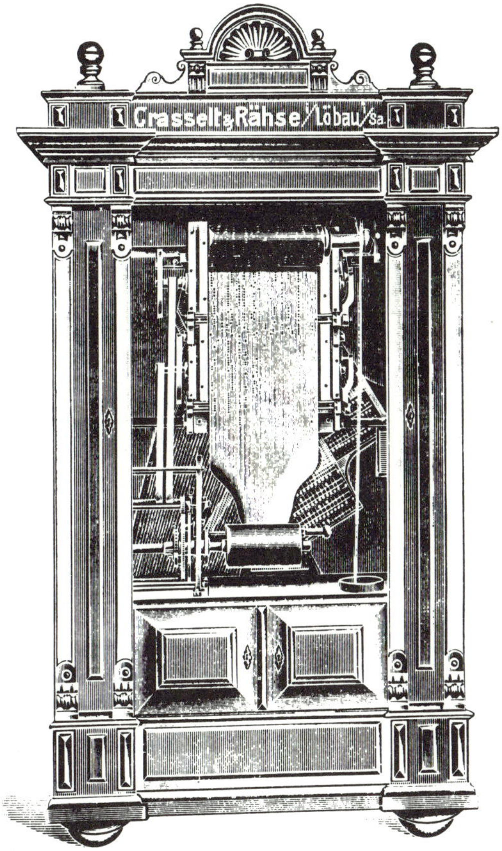

Da sämmtliche Instrumente von uns mit unserer neuen Stimmvorrichtung versehen, so sind dieselben auch sehr gut für den **Export** nach den tropischen Klimaten geeignet. Durch diese Stimmvorrichtung sind die Instrumente unverwüstlich. Wolle sich jeder Interessent selbst davon überzeugen.

D. R.-Patent No. 134484.

D. R.-Patent No. 134484.

Preis mit 12 Noten Mk. 950.—.

☛ *Dieses Klavier-Spielwerk ist das Allerneueste!* ☚

Fig. 33
Housed in a cabinet stylistically similar to those of the upright disc-playing musical boxes made in Leipzig and Berlin, the Crasselt & Rähse piano was keyboardless and played from punched rolls of toughened thin card via a mechanical action.

PIANOLA

The invention of the first proper pneumatic system to be controlled by a perforated paper roll specifically designed to play an organ can be attributed to Emil Welte of M. Welte & Söhne of Freiburg in Germany. Between 1887 and 1889, Welte took out patents for such an action to replace the barrels in their large orchestrions and barrel-playing military bands. Welte produced at this same time an air motor for driving the music roll (a trefoil cam-controlled motor which was, in modified and improved form, to remain a feature of all subsequent Welte mechanical organs and pianos) and made an elementary device to reduce the characteristic tendency of paper-roll music to speed up as it played, due to the driven take-up spool gradually increasing in diameter as more paper was wound on. Welte minimized this by making the take-up spool of large diameter.

ELECTRICITY IN THE PIANO

A handful of inventors gave thought to the use of electromagnetic player actions using the perforated tune sheet. The 1880s saw the production of many of these instruments, which must have been, to say the least, illuminating to watch with their showers of blue sparks as

Modell B.
Nussbaum matt und blank oder schwarz. Höhe 130 cm.

Für Akkumulatorenbetrieb (12 Volt) inkl. Geldeinwurf und elektr. Leuchtern und zirka 50 Meter Noten, nebst 1 Akkumulator, spielfertig . . . . Mk. **1680**

Für Starkstromanschluss (110 Volt Gleichstrom) inkl. Geldeinwurf und zirka 50 Meter Noten, elektr. Leuchtern **spielfertig zum Anschluss an vorhandene Leitung** . Mk. **1530**

Für Starkstromanschluss (220 Volt Gleichstrom) inkl. Geldeinwurf und zirka 50 Meter Noten, elektr. Leuchtern, **spielfertig zum Anschluss an vorhandene Leitung** . Mk. **1580**

Mit Dämpfer-Vorrichtung erhöht sich der Preis um Mk. 50.

Modell C.
Nussbaum matt und blank oder schwarz. Höhe 133 cm.

Für Akkumulatorenbetrieb (12 Volt) inkl. Geldeinwurf und elektr. Leuchtern und zirka 50 Meter Noten, nebst 1 Akkumulator, spielfertig . . . . Mk. **1750**

Für Starkstromanschluss (110 Volt Gleichstrom) inkl. Geldeinwurf und zirka 50 Meter Noten, elektr. Leuchtern, **spielfertig zum Anschluss an vorhandene Leitung** . Mk. **1600**

Für Starkstromanschluss (220 Volt Gleichstrom) inkl. Geldeinwurf und zirka 50 Meter Noten, elektr. Leuchtern, **spielfertig zum Anschluss an vorhandene Leitung** . Mk. **1650**

Mit Dämpfer-Vorrichtung erhöht sich der Preis um Mk. 50.

Fig. 34
Electrically-operated pianos from Leipzig and Berlin all featured the kicking shoe type of action. These two models were similar to the many made by Heilbrunn, Kuhl & Klatt and others.

they played. Tune rolls for these were often of thin brass or special paper, sometimes coated with a non-conducting substance such as shellac. In place of perforations, some of these had the musical 'notes' printed on the roll as electrically conducting portions of the roll where there was no shellac or other insulating material.

To avoid oxidisation of the electrical contacts, silver terminals were used and some even had platinum tips. Perhaps it was the unreliability of the Victorian electricity supply which prevented the hoped-for mass market from developing for these electro-pianos. Special storage batteries in the form of wet-cell accumulators could be used in place of the mains power, but these were cumbersome and had to be re-charged. More probable as a reason for their short life was an understandable fear of the machine for, with its lack of earthing, it was no doubt capable of dispensing electric shocks to those who chose to lean upon it while presenting their party pieces to the family gathering on a Sunday afternoon. Although well promoted, electric players were costly to buy and operate.

One of the more unusual of these electrically played pianos was that thought up by R. K. Boyle in 1884. His piano had no hammers, the strings being set into vibration by energising them in conjunction with an electromagnet.

Another of these monstrosities was the invention of A. P. S. Macquisten, whose piano played an 'electro-magnetic pattern or Jacquard device', using copper wire feelers to make electrical contact through the tune sheet.

The Leipzig correspondent of *Musical Opinion* reported on 22 January 1888 that:

> Herr R. Eisenmann, of Berlin, has brought out a novel kind of piano, with one ordinary hammer action and a second electric action, which can be employed either partially together – that is to say the treble can be played by the electric while the bass is worked by the ordinary hammers, or *vice versa* – or separately. The electric action produces a marvellous change in the tone of the instrument, which, according to the octave used, sounds like an organ, a violoncello, violin or harp. The electric stream is produced by a small battery of eighteen cells.

Henry Klein, of 84 Oxford Street, London, was already established as a musical-box importer when, in the summer of 1898, he secured the agency for the electric pianos manufactured by Hupfeld and distributed throughout Europe by H. Peters & Son of Leipzig. The instrument sold for the sum of £128 – a very costly instrument by contemporary standards. The action was pneumatic, every one of the keys in the seven octaves capable of being played from the music roll. Driving power was provided by an electric motor and, at the end of the roll of music, rewinding was automatic. The piano was coin-operated and represented a considerable advance on the types of instrument available anywhere else in the world at the time. A combined manual and mechanical model sold for £110. For both types the electric power came from storage batteries which provided enough current 'to play a thousand tunes before the need of re-charging'. In Berlin, no fewer than four firms were engaged in producing electric batteries for driving mechanical instruments such as orchestrion organs and pianos.

The United States Krell Piano Co. spent some years in the late 1890s developing an electric piano attachment which, it was claimed, would be one of the most perfect on the market and also would be available at a resonable price. Power could come either from the mains or from storage batteries. The inventor was a Mr Simkins who believed that he had devised something to revolutionise the piano attachment industry. The pious belief of its creator proved unjustified. In 1901, however, a moderately successful if short-lived electric player was devised. This was the Telektra sold by the Tel-Electric Co. of New York. Patented by Timothy B. Powers, two models were made both of which played music from thin brass strip music rolls. This device was unusual in that the player console could be placed on a table at some distance from the piano, a cable passing between the two.

Messrs William Gerecke, of 8 and 9 Goring Street, Houndsditch, London, advertised themselves as manufacturers and importers of musical instruments. In 1901 they introduced the Pneuma, which was a 'self-playing patent apparatus on the Pneumatic Principle – fitted to any New or Old Piano – requires no alteration of the Instrument, which can still be played as a Piano after the apparatus is attached – worked by Storage Battery, or direct from the Lighting Current, or by crank'. The Pneuma, an electrically driven attachment, could be supplied with a piano for £50 or, alternatively, the mechanism could be installed into any existing piano. Gerecke was also a musical box agent and stocked the largest disc-playing musical box ever made – the Komet.

Pianos driven electrically were made by a number of German companies including Kuhl & Klatt, Heilbrunn and others. Heilbrunn & Söhne was founded in Berlin in 1875 and produced a variety of electrically-run pianos, mostly with 'kicking-shoe' player actions. Initially, distribution in Britain was handled by Doremi & Co. of 9 Argyll Place off London's Regent Street. To begin with, the Virtuola expression piano was distributed but by 1905 this model had been replaced by the Virtuoso. It was at Doremi's premises on 15 November 1905 that a private demonstration was given to selected people in the music industry of a special music recording apparatus invented by Heilbrunn and handled by the Heilbrunn Patents Syndicate. No information is available as to how this mechanism operated, but a contemporary report states that 'impressions that had been made by Scharwanka, Ansorge and other celebrated artists were reproduced'. Shortly afterwards, Doremi faded from the scene and in the following year Sydney C. Harper founded the Harper Electric Piano Company in Holloway Road, North London. Later a branch was opened in Paris at 13 Rue Greneta. Harper's business was later reconstructed as a manufacturer of showcards and a new business, Harper Electric Piano (1910) Company, was set up. As well as factoring other pianos, it apparently manufactured its own for a while. The expenditure of a very large sum of money plus time and effort in designing a new electric piano was not rewarded with market success and so the company turned its attentions and manufacturing capacity towards the making of more conventional, pneumatic players. The Harper played 65 notes from 13½-inch-wide perforated paper rolls, most of which were punched out by the Up-To-Date Music Roll Company at Hammersmith.

Electromagnetic action was, however, successfully developed in later years, specifically in America, where the Wurlitzer and Mills Novelty Company made a variety of instruments played electrically from a perforated paper roll.

This popularity of electrically controlled instruments must have been a cause of satisfaction to certain enthusiasts for the new power source. One of these was Dr Henry John Gauntlett (1806–76) who was organist at Olney in Buckinghamshire and thought that one organist might play all the instruments in the county thanks to electricity. That was in 1852 and just eleven years later a man called Goundry actually patented an idea for the playing of organs electromagnetically, projecting that from one keyboard situated in St Paul's Cathedral every organ in London could be operated by one organist! Of all the possibilities

FROM MECHANICAL TO PNEUMATIC ACTION

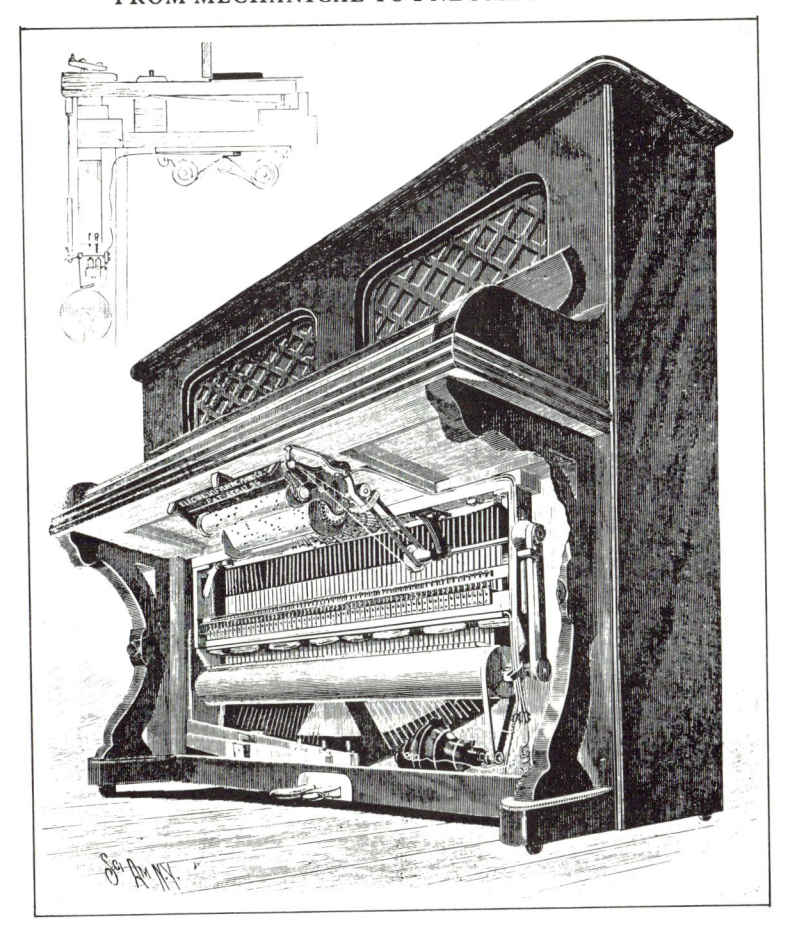

Fig. 35
Patented in 1895 is this American electrically-operated piano with a kicking shoe action. Here the shoe is brought into contact with the operating roller by an electro-magnet or solenoid. The maker was the Electric Self-Playing Piano Company.

which electrical action might have suggested, the one which virtually all inventors overlooked was the potential educational merit of the multiple playing of an instrument as a means of demonstration to students. In fact this is still a development which might lie ahead.

In October 1902, *Musical Opinion* carried the following notice concerning a somewhat advanced player made by Ludwig & Company of 970 Southern Boulevard, New York, a company set up in 1889 to make a novel player:

THE LUDWIG AND CO. PIANO PLAYER

At St. Ermin's Hotel, Westminster, the other day, we were shown this player by the invitation of Mr. J. H. Ludwig of New York. It is a remarkable production, on which thirty-five workmen have been employed for five years; and now we are not sure that the instrument is yet on the British market, for the patents may be offered for sale.

We had the pleasure of hearing much music by means of the player, including 'The Chariot Race' (from 'Ben Hur'), Eilenberg's 'Forest Mill', and a march 'The Coloured Drum Major'. One of the features of the instrument is that the loud pedal is brought into use automatically by means of a music roll; although the performer may use such pedal by touching a stop if desired.

An unique arrangement is that by which (by the addition of six holes in the music roll) the accent to any note required in a treble or bass melody is thoroughly effected. Then, too, the roll is five and a half inches wide – a boon for damp climates.

There are, it is stated, no less than twenty-four new ideas in the construction of the player; and we think that the makers have good 'points', and especially so in this way: the pneumatic tubing to each note is of lead, and even the sides of the sixty-eight tiny bellows are made of steel, the leather portions being painted aluminium colour. All parts (metal) are produced economically by automatic machinery.

Our space is exhausted; or we should have liked to have written about the firm's piano factory, at which twelve instruments are turned out daily.

In the same issue of *Musical Opinion*, a correspondent posed a major question regarding the mechanical player and its music. Needless to say, it was an unanswerable one at that state of the art:

MECHANICAL PLAYER AND ITS MUSIC

SIR, – It would be interesting if some of your readers would give their experience of some of the pianoforte mechanical players which have been brought before the public. In looking through your advertising columns I can enumerate some eight different playing actions, and no doubt there are others in existence. In each it is more or less claimed that, while the execution is done mechanically, the expression is entirely in the hands of the operator. One would like to know whether the expression given is sufficient to overcome the mechanical effect which one cannot but think constitutes a drawback to this class of performance. The cost of the paper rolls, whether loaned or purchased, which is hardly alluded to in the various announcements, must be an important item, in

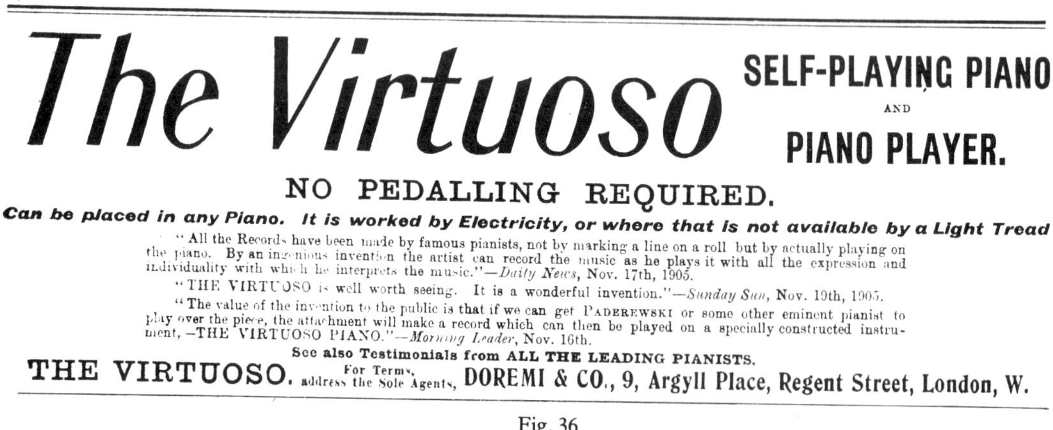

The Virtuoso SELF-PLAYING PIANO AND PIANO PLAYER.

NO PEDALLING REQUIRED.

Can be placed in any Piano. It is worked by Electricity, or where that is not available by a Light Tread

"All the Records have been made by famous pianists, not by marking a line on a roll but by actually playing on the piano. By an ingenious invention the artist can record the music as he plays it with all the expression and individuality with which he interprets the music." – *Daily News*, Nov. 17th, 1905.

"THE VIRTUOSO is well worth seeing. It is a wonderful invention." – *Sunday Sun*, Nov. 19th, 1905.

"The value of the invention to the public is that if we can get PADEREWSKI or some other eminent pianist to play over the piece, the attachment will make a record which can then be played on a specially constructed instrument, –THE VIRTUOSO PIANO." – *Morning Leader*, Nov. 16th.

See also Testimonials from ALL THE LEADING PIANISTS.

THE VIRTUOSO. For Terms, address the Sole Agents, DOREMI & CO., 9, Argyll Place, Regent Street, London, W.

Fig. 36
From *Musical Opinion*, December 1905, comes this advertisement for Heilbrunn's Virtuos electrically-played piano, renamed The Virtuoso for the British market. Agents here were Doremi but by the following year the instrument was being handled by Harper in Holloway.

FROM MECHANICAL TO PNEUMATIC ACTION

THE
ELECTRELLE
Piano Player.

The only Piano-player

capable of expressing

Real Musical

Feeling and Touch.

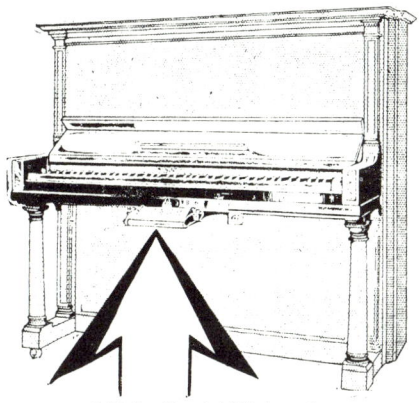

No Foot Pumping.

....

Brings out the

Melody at will.

Roll holder slides out of sight when not in use.

Can be fitted into any Existing Piano

without Structural Alteration:

AND CONSEQUENTLY CAN BE SUPPLIED TO ALL OLD CUSTOMERS.

Expression equal to hand playing.   Absolutely without Musical Limitation.
Standard Music Rolls.   Creased and Defective Rolls can be used.
Exceedingly Durable.   Made entirely of Metal.
Does not affect the tone of the Piano, as there is nothing in front of the sounding-board.
The only Player really adapted for Accompanying.   Very Sensitive Tempo Control.
Music can be instantly transposed into a great number of keys.
Will repeat twice as fast as any other Player.
Does not interfere with Tuning.   Cost of Electricity absolutely trifling.
The Piano Pedals are operated by the feet in the ordinary way.
For Dance purposes will play itself without any attendant and stops automatically.
The Electrelle is as great an advance on Pneumatic Players as the Steam Locomotive on the Stage Coach

INSPECTION INVITED.   Write for Catalogue.   AGENCIES APPOINTED.

ELECTRELLE, Ltd.
30, King Street, MANCHESTER.

Fig. 37
Similar to the action shown in Fig. 35 was the Electrelle advertised in 1908.

PIANOLA

ONLY the artistic interpretation, the musical versatility, and the wonderful scope of the living fingers of a master pianist can compare with the exquisite playing of the TEL-ELECTRIC, the most perfect mechanically as well as the most artistic musically of all piano players. Mechanical music is impossible with

The TEL-ELECTRIC PIANO PLAYER

IT is the *one* player which you, *yourself*, whether an expert musician or not, can quickly and easily learn to play with all the individuality of a master pianist.

It permits you to interpret perfectly world-famous compositions with all the original feeling, all the technique, and with all the various shades and depths of expression as intended by the composer.

In using electricity as the motive force of the Tel-Electric we not only eliminate the tiresome foot-pumping and noisy bellows of the pneumatic player, but we place the instrument under your absolute control—ready to answer, instantly, your slightest musical whim.

The Tel-Electric, though radically different, has proved itself infinitely superior to any player on the market. Consider these exclusive features:—

Requires no pumping—can be attached to any piano—absolutely perfect and instantaneous expression devices—does not obstruct the keyboard—uses indestructible music rolls—totally unaffected by weather-change—has never been replaced by any other piano-player—any piano with a Tel-Electric attached costs less than a player piano of the same grade.

If you cannot call at one of our stores or agencies and learn for yourself the truth of our claims for this marvelous instrument, send for our interesting, illustrated catalog—mailed free on request.

THE TEL-ELECTRIC COMPANY, 299 Fifth Avenue, New York City
Branch Office, CHICAGO   Agencies in All Large Cities

Fig. 38
The advantage claimed for the Tel-Electric was that the action could be worked remotely, the connection to the bank of playing solenoids under the piano keyboard being by electric cable. The music was in the form of a special cassette containing a thin strip of perforated brass. This advertisement from *Country Life in America* appeared in November 1912. Paul Ottenheimer collection.

FROM MECHANICAL TO PNEUMATIC ACTION

The "HARPER" ELECTRIC PIANO

MUSIC IN THE HOME!

The greatest works of the master musicians are brought within the reach of every man, woman, or child by the aid of the "HARPER" ELECTRIC PIANO, and without any question of individual skill. You delight yourself, your family, and friends.

£5 secures this remarkable instrument. The balance may be arranged in easy instalments. The "HARPER" ELECTRIC PIANO does not depend for its action on exhausting pedalling movements. The mere pressing of a button is all that is necessary.

Readers of "The Strand Magazine" are invited to write for an interesting brochure which fully describes its advantages. Your own Piano can be converted into an Electric Piano without the slightest detriment. Particulars free.

THE 'HARPER' ELECTRIC PIANO CO., Ltd., 266/8, Holloway Rd., London, N.

Fig. 39
Advertisement for the Harper Electric Piano, November 1906.

addition to the present high prices of most of the players, which prevent very many from entertaining the idea of possessing one. I note that some 'players' do not by any means act on the full compass of the instrument; one, at least, omitting the lower fifteen notes in the bass in addition to some in the treble.

There is no doubt a future before the mechanical player, which appears to have come to stay; though if they get into common use they would seem to discourage the study of the pianoforte as we have always been accustomed to manipulate it.

Yours &c.,
'OBSERVER'

While expression and other sophistications were the concern of some, other makers were still trying to master the basic properties of paper with holes in. Probably the most unsatisfactory solution to the problem was that contrived by the makers of the Smith Lyraphone, a product from Baltimore, Maryland. These piano players were unusual by virtue of the fact that the 65-note roll openings in the wooden tracker-bar were of varying size, being small and narrow in the centre and quite long on the outside. This was no doubt arranged to allow for mistracking on the paper rolls, yet the inflexibility of the system must have led to its own downfall. The tracker-bar was manufactured by taking two pieces of wood, dividing the note openings with saw kerfs and then gluing in short intercostals. The actual player action was mechanical, being of the 'kicking shoe' variety, using a rotating cork-covered roller and levers. The kicking shoes were drawn up into contact with the rotating roller by pneumatic action – an unnecessarily complex arrangement.

THE NEED FOR SPECIAL PAPER

Meanwhile, the majority of player-action manufacturers were concentrating on the perforated paper music roll. Even this, though, was not without its complications. Certain physical characteristics of the early papers in use had to be taken into consideration, not the least of which was expansion and contraction in varying moisture conditions. Quite often a roll of paper would swell so much as to wedge itself firmly between the wooden spool ends. Again, the paper would not track properly or wind on to the take-up spool in damp weather.

Adjustable spools had to be invented until the introduction, early this century, of music paper which had a low expansion rate. Another problem was fluff, dust and paper fibre from both the surface of the paper roll and also the sometimes ragged edges of the perforations. After a while, the suction at the tracker-bar would dutifully draw any such undesirable debris into the mechanism, upsetting the seatings of the valves and so causing malfunctionings. Filters and dust traps were incorporated until better paper was adopted. The Aeolian Company were the first to fit their piano players with a transparent sliding lid to the spool box to keep out the dust when the instrument was not in use.

Some paper manufacturers, realising how much paper was being used by the manufacturers of music rolls, went to some lengths to produce special paper for this purpose. One of the largest suppliers in Europe was Hoffmann & Engelmann of Neustadt-on-Haardt in Germany. Originally this company supplied its special roll paper to a large number of orchestrion manufacturers but later it was taken over by Hupfeld and so its output was channelled to serving the prodigious roll output of that one major company. This paper-mill always watermarked its music-roll paper at regular intervals with the letters 'H & E' and, further on, the year of manufacture. The production for Hupfeld was always marked with an additional watermark throughout the length of the paper which read, in script, the word *Phonola*.

By the 1890s, the sheer simplicity of the basic principles of the paper-controlled pneumatic piano ensured that the quest for a piano-playing system had been completed. Indeed, the perforated-paper player piano was to be one of the last contributions in the field of musical instruments of the classic generation. The second-generation instruments are, of course, no longer recognisable as musical instruments. Being nothing more than musical noise-generators, they rely on the principles of electronics controlled by perforated-paper computer tape developed from the telegraph transmitting tape perfected as another offshoot from the Jacquard system.

There remained the trickle of odd systems for a few years but, seeing that paper music was easy to make, cheap to sell and quite compact, the piano industry latched on to making pneumatic actions almost overnight. Indeed, far from having his first player piano burned by the gathering of irate music teachers, Needham's principles were warmly welcomed universally. Everyone wanted a self-acting piano and he who made the best and simplest action would be a hero. 'Make a better mousetrap and the world will beat a path to your door!'

With the polished rosewood player pushed up to the piano and a good selection of popular rolls including, perhaps, some virtuoso pieces to impress visitors, every home of 'with it' Victorians was suddenly complete. All that had gone before was relegated to being old-fashioned and valueless. Just as today few, if any, would consider forming a collection of obsolete television receivers, the precursors of the pneumatic piano player were cast out. In but a few short years, the piano player itself was to suffer the same ignominious end.

Before this century was more than a few years old, perforated-paper-controlled pneumatic actions were being made to install inside pianos, upright instruments to begin with and then, as skills developed, grands as well. The sheer convenience and simplicity of the paper roll closed the book on the subject of inventing devices to play the piano. The job was done – almost.

CHAPTER 4

The Evolution of the Player Piano

It is not altogether surprising that the early development of the pneumatic piano followed the same pattern as the street piano and, contemporarily or earlier, the musical box and the barrel organ. Whilst an invention, discovery or improvement would be adopted by one maker, others did not necessarily follow suit for some while. Again, whilst many, many inventions were patented as improvements to almost every conceivable part of the mechanical piano from the disposition of the valves to the shape of manual control levers, other and more important developments are difficult to place as to date of inception. Even the name of the inventor is often shrouded in uncertainty.

This is not hard to appreciate in view of the number of manufacturers on both sides of the Atlantic. Initially, the practical piano player and player piano emanated from the United States, where resources and promotion were already geared to production of instruments. The European players of the time, although probably of better specification, workmanship and performance, were not launched at the market with anything approaching the gusto and financial backing of, say, the Aeolian Company, which published expensive colour brochures, mounted a nation-wide advertising and marketing campaign – and had the production facilities to cater for the resulting demand.

This must not be taken as in any way denigrating the European achievements for, as we shall see, instruments of both musical ability and quality were produced in Germany. The products of Ludwig Hupfeld and Emile Welte, for example, were outstanding in their own right. Significantly, England produced no worthwhile contributions until fairly late on in the story although the British market for American and, to a lesser extent, European products was extremely keen. Such pneumatic actions as were later produced had little to offer over imported products (with the possible exception, as we shall see, of the Boyd Pistonola) and, as with the British-designed and built Carola reproducing action made for Blüthner by the Sir Herbert Marshall Piano Company of Acton, manufacture was soon abandoned. Invariably, imported actions, already produced elsewhere in large quantities, were cheaper and of at least equal performance. Mass-production methods by high-capital-financed special-purpose woodworking machinery also tended towards greater reliability.

Whereas in England the barrel piano found its birthplace in the poorer parts of east London, the player piano came from the much more sophisticated Mayfair showrooms of plush manufacturers whose names and reputations were already firmly established. The Camden Town area of north London was as much the home of the piano-making industry as Hatton Garden that of the jeweller and watchmaker or Shoreditch the domain of the cabinet-maker. But to begin with we must go back and follow the development of the instrument.

The player piano was the result of experiments which took place in three places – France, Germany and the United States. In the beginning France was the scene of much pioneering work and a lot of development study. However, France seemed to lose its early interest and world lead in the mechanical piano several years before America forged ahead. Both Hupfeld and Welte in Germany successfully devised and produced instruments, but it was in America that the commercial know-how and the necessary brains were available to push an idea rapidly through development stages and into production.

Germany's position as the first in the field is not hard to accept when it is realised that the largest mechanical music industry in the world was in eastern Germany, Leipzig being the centre with Berlin a close second. The art of the musical box, first evolved in the Swiss Jura, was systematically developed in Leipzig where the disc-playing musical box was invented and many of the forms of musical automaton which followed were made. Thus Leipzig was in the best possible position to devise a pneumatic action for piano playing. Welte in Freiburg had shown that an organ could be made to play in this manner and the Leipzig industry immediately applied itself to the exploitation and improvement of the system. There was only one dissonant note of any consequence to retard these formative years of Leipzig's self-acting piano and organ industry and this was the antiquated copyright law in Germany which prohibited the making of perforated rolls of musical compositions for which copyright existed. The simple expedient of putting a tax on rolls, later used almost everywhere, had yet to be evolved.

MUSICAL COPYRIGHT

The copyright problem was one which dogged all makers of every type of mechanical musical instrument, not just the piano-roll makers. The major copyright case in Britain was that between George Whight and Boosey (1899) and concerned music rolls for the Aeolian player organ, forerunner of the Orchestrelle. But there were others, each in its way equally significant. It was back in 1865 that Debain became locked in lengthy litigation concerning his *Pianista Debain*. Then music publishers and editors Marquet took action against Thibouville regarding the cardboard book music for his instruments in 1895. The coming of the gramophone served only to intensify the rush for litigation against organette makers such as Ehrlich in Leipzig, piano-roll sellers, Aeolian and others.*

It was partly these omnipresent wrangles that occasioned the formation of a society of German mechanical musical instrument manufacturers at the turn of the century. President of this society was Wilhelm Spaethe, whose organ and piano manufactury was situated at Gera, and it was due to repeated pressure brought on the authorities by the society that the Reichstadt finally passed Paragraph XXII of their new copyright law which decreed that copyright need not apply to the playing of music from a tune sheet, but that the tune sheet or music roll must have a copyright or performing-rights tax levied on it at the time of sale. Spaethe naturally had a personal interest in the matter since his firm was one of the largest manufacturers of pneumatic instruments. It is interesting to note that the Polyphonmusik-

---

* See *L'Exploitation Des Oeuvres Musicales par les Instruments de Musique Mécaniques et le Droit de l'Auteur* by Georges Sbriglia (Libraire Nouvelle de Droit et de Jurisprudence, Paris, 1907).

THE EVOLUTION OF THE PLAYER PIANO

werke in Leipzig, makers of the Polyphon disc musical box, was deprived early on of the rights to make discs of the music of Gilbert and Sullivan because of a dispute over the copyright act prevailing at that period, as applied to their first – and only – disc of their music, which was the Mikado waltz.

The ideas conceived wholly in America were the ones which made the largest contribution, if not necessarily the first, in the field of the player piano and thus it is to America that we must go to start our story. The pneumatic piano player, as distinct from the European cabinet-style mechanical machines, appeared in the States in the late 1890s.

AIR PRESSURE VS. VACUUM

The earliest instruments which operated by changing the pressure of the air had almost all utilised a positive pressure: they had compressed air by means of force bellows. The advantages of a vacuum system were, however, seen as more likely to prove successful to the piano player and so the majority of inventions which followed used air at a negative pressure. Although the invention is generally attributed to one of the employees of the Mustel company in France, it seems that the first use of the principle may have been made by a man from Boston, Massachusetts, named A. M. Peaseley, who is said to have made a reed organ in 1818 operating this way. Reed-organ builder Charles C. Austin of Concord, New Hampshire, applied this style of operation before 1846. However, the first patent specifically directed at protecting an invention for exhaust bellows was granted to Jeremiah Carhart of Buffalo, New York. This was American Patent number 4912 of 28 December 1846. Four years later, Isaac T. Packard was granted a patent for a combined force/exhaust bellows. Carhart was in partnership with Elias Parkman Needham making reed organs in New York as Carhart & Needham. While Bain was only able to foresee the use of air at pressure and so was forced to consider a system of pressure rollers to keep his perforated paper roll in contact with the tracker bar, Carhart's invention meant that the paper was sucked against the tracker bar, so dispensing with the need for any additional means of maintaining the contact seal.

During the life of the player piano, there were very many patents covering developments of the bellows action, in particular with regard to the provision of foot treadles for grand pianos and for treadles that could be folded up and concealed out of the way when not in use. Some of the systems invented were ingenious and others rather impractical. The wind department and its regulation likewise came in for many modifications as makers tried hard to circumvent methods already protected by their rivals.

MUSIC-ROLL DRIVE METHODS

Driving the music roll presented its own problems. With the organette, it was quite sufficient for the roll to be wound on to the take-up spool by hand. With the piano player, however, it was not feasible to expect the performer to pedal with his feet, juggle with levers and at the same time maintain a regular rotation of a handle. Early instruments transported the roll by a mechanical linkage from the foot treadle – a belt, a chain or even bevel gears and shafting. These all suffered from the same intrinsic defects – the speed of pedalling directly affected the speed of the music. Whilst these worked up to a point, they did not make provision for rewinding, unless one was prepared to pedal the roll back again, nor did such systems respond adequately to anything other than regular pedalling.

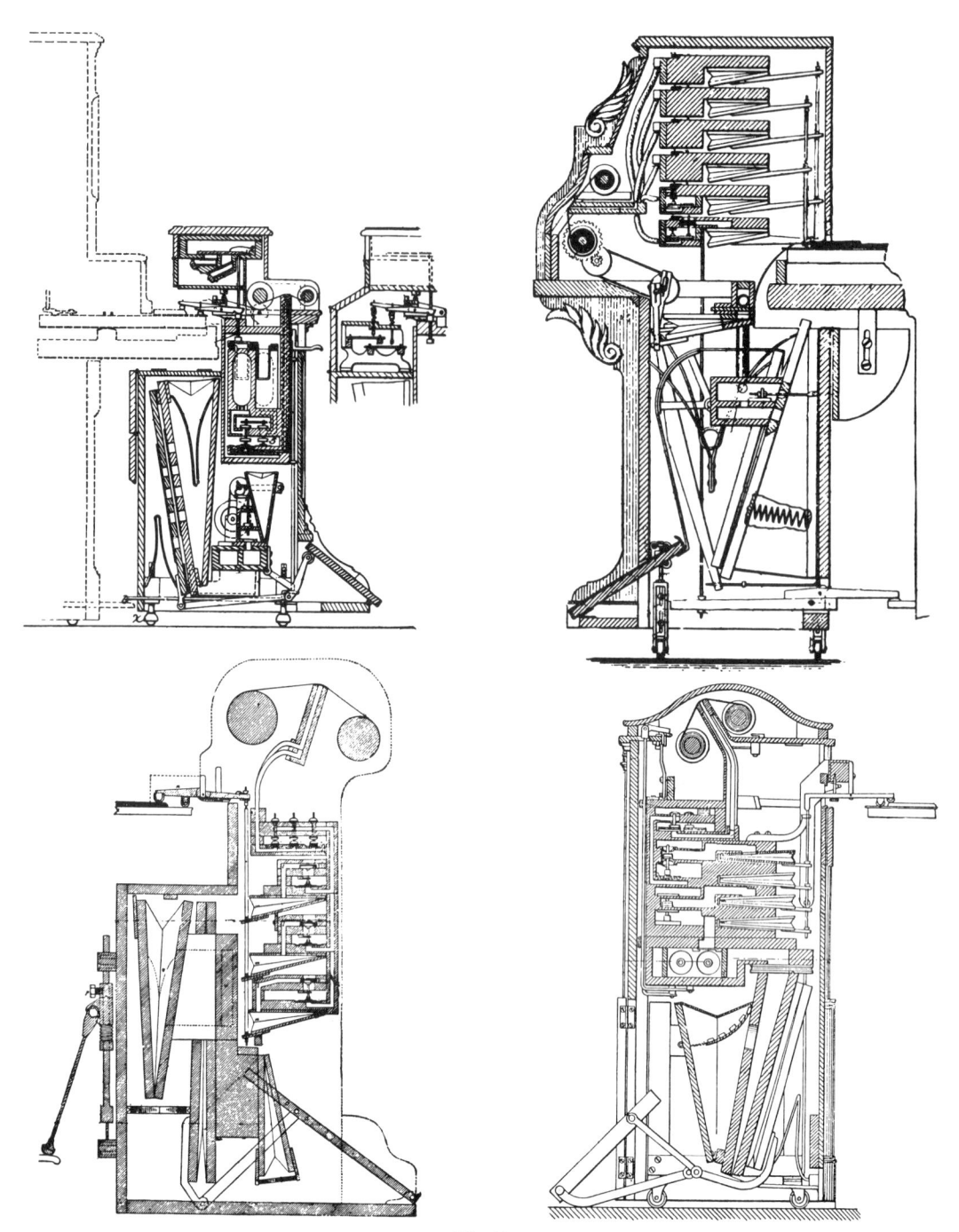

Fig. 40
Four early types of piano player compared. Top left is White and Parker's cabinet player of 1897. This was a novel device in that it included a reed organ so that piano strings and reeds could be sounded together. Like so many similar devices which followed, the main problem was how to keep piano and organ in tune together: the piano strings quickly went 'flat'. Top right is Edwin Scott Votey's first Pianola showing its six banks of pneumatics. Below left is Hupfeld's Phonola of 1902, an altogether neat and practical player. Below right is Aeolian's Pianola push-up of 1901, a four-bank device.

THE EVOLUTION OF THE PLAYER PIANO

The use of the clockwork motor was favoured by several of the early makers and an early piano player was the Simplex, which employed a large three-spring motor to drive the roll. The Simplex – a 65-note player – used rolls which were somewhat narrower than the normal ones and a good proportion of the music for these took the form of accompaniment rolls for vocal songs.

Melville Clark made ingenious use of clockwork in his first Apollo 58-note player of 1899. The action of treadling turned a crankshaft on a train of gears which rotated the take-up spool and also wound up a clockwork motor through a friction clutch. At the end of the roll, a handle was pulled and the gearing was rearranged so that the roll was rewound by the motor.

In spite of the 'innovation' of clockwork, G. H. Davis saw fit to equip his piano player of 1901 with a weight-driven rewind. As the roll was played, so was raised a large weight and the potential energy thus stored was used to rewind the music.

The clockwork motor invented by the Smith Lyraphone Company in America in 1902 could be used for driving the roll and rewinding it independently of the foot treadles, spring winding being effected by a suitable handle on the front of the player.

The first vacuum air motor, in which the action of sucking in air through a system of bellows and valves produced rotary motion, was probably that invented in America in 1884 by J. Morgan for driving the tune sheets in automatic reed instruments.

Air motors on pianos, oddly enough, were sometimes worked by air pressure instead of suction, a small compression bellows being supplied in conjunction with the foot treadles for this purpose, but George Kelly in America devised the most convenient and straightforward suction drive with his slide-valve motor in 1886. Kelly's motor consisted of a series of sliding plates fitted to a board, each with a matching pneumatic bellows fixed to the other side. Inlet and exhaust ports were cut in the dividing board and each slide was linked with a connecting rod to a crankshaft. Suction applied to the exhaust side of the system would cause each bellows to open and close alternately, the slides regulating the admission of atmospheric air into the vacuum chamber of the motor and serving to turn the crankshaft.

An advantage of this system was that the motor could develop a good deal more power than the earlier pressure motors and was also capable of much smoother action by the provision of four or even five sets of bellows and slides, having the effect of a multi-cylinder motor as compared with the erratic low-speed behaviour of a single- or twin-cylinder engine. The wind motor provided more or less constant speed which could be variably controlled by a gate valve. The motor maintained its speed under almost all conditions of pedalling – fast or slow or erratic – so long as there was some pressure differential in the piano system. A flywheel was usually provided on the early three-valve motors to help even out the motion, but the multi-valved successors usually did not need such an addition.

A novel variation was the suction air motor perfected in Freiburg, Germany, by Emil Welte in 1887 and first used to drive his paper-roll-playing orchestrion organs. The Welte motor consisted of a cone-shaped body carrying along its length three pneumatic bellows arranged at 120°. These were linked at their wide ends by connecting rods to a crankshaft which ran through the centre of the body and carried at the opposite end a rotating cam which alternately covered and uncovered the entry and exhaust passages to each of the three triangular-shaped bellows. When suction was applied to the exhaust side of the motor, air would be drawn into one of the three bellows, so causing it to turn the crankshaft via its connecting rod and, at the same time, advancing the inlet and exhaust port cam. When a further inlet port was uncovered, the adjacent bellows would begin to inflate, advancing the crankshaft and so collapsing the previous bellows, the air from which would be passed down the suction exhaust passage to the inlet side of the main bellows assembly of the whole organ. The continuous application of suction to the exhaust side of the motor kept the system working smoothly, the crankshaft turning with sufficient power to drive the take-up spool. A large flywheel fitted on the end of the crankshaft overcame any tendency to jerkiness. So successsful was the Welte rotary motor that it remained a feature of that maker's German-built instruments right through to the electric reproducing pianos Welte made.

A number of inventors tried to produce other forms of suction air motor. One of the more interesting of these was the attempt by C. W. Atkinson to incorporate a motor actually inside the piano roll take-up spool. A feature of Bansall's Universal Piano Player, it was not a lasting success.

TRANSPOSING DEVICES

Transposing devices, thought of as later improvements to the player piano, were in fact used by Melville Clark in his Apollo of 1899. His 58-note tracker bar could be moved to permit the music to be played in any one of the five keys from B^b to D and the change was effected by the turning of a thumb screw to shift the tracker bar laterally, its lower connections being of flexible rubber tubing. This also served to cater for the irregularities in paper and spool width which, with the early players, varied quite greatly. He called it a 'transposing mouthpiece'. Since the early piano player was viewed more as an accompaniment to a vocalist than as a solo instrument, transposing was a vital part of its ability.

In later years, with the introduction of quality-controlled paper music and 88-note actions, tracker bars had to be made of brass and these could be shifted through several keys (in the Hupfeld Phonola pianos through no fewer than nine!) by a small transposing lever. Whilst it was common to shift the tracker bar to transpose, some actions were made wherein the music roll and take-up spool were moved instead.

ROLL TRACKING

Hand in hand with transposing came the problem of maintaining the paper roll in perfect alignment with the tracker-bar holes during playing and this was achieved by an automatic device which moved the spools fractionally. Operation was achieved by special holes in the tracker which aligned with the margin of the paper. So long as these were both covered, tracking was perfect. If the paper tended to drift to one side, it would expose one hole, allowing air to transfer to a bellows assembly which would gently push the spools over until alignment was once more achieved. The Standard Player Action Company in America produced such a system. Aeolian, on the other hand, used a system worked by delicately balanced fingers which followed the edge of the paper and which were connected to bellows as before. Another system ran the paper between two small brass 'fences' set in the tracker bar which performed similar functions. A variation of the 'uncovered hole' method was patented by J. J. Walker in 1909 and this used special music rolls having a continuous line of central perforations, which ran between two holes in the tracker bar. If the roll wandered, so allowing air to enter one or other of the holes, so the bellows would gently ease the roll over the opposite way. This was used by Hupfeld on its early 73-note players.

Players were fitted with wheels to allow them to be pushed up to the piano and all the better ones were fitted with devices for adjusting the height of the player to the keyboard. The Angelus, for example, had two large handles which engaged in a ratchet slot to each side of the front of the case, and so the height of each side of the player could be adjusted independently. Better-class models were fitted with wheel brakes or wedging devices so that, in the middle of a fortissimo passage or when the performer was pedalling hard, the player would not roll away or shift its position on the keyboard.

PIANOTIST – A CLASSIC FAILURE

The Aeolian Company's cabinet-style Pianola Piano player sold for £65 – quite a considerable sum at the turn of the century. The only British-made player of the time was the Boyd, which sold for £27 10s cash or £32 8s by monthly instalments of 13s 6d. But something appreciably cheaper and, by all accounts, easier to work was about to be put on the market. This was called the Pianotist.

The New York firm of Emile Klaber was already well established as a maker of pianos. Emile's son, Augustus David Klaber, worked in London at 29 Queen Victoria Street where Klaber pianos were distributed in this country. On 29 May 1900 he filed a whole series of patents for various details of a mechanical piano, including detachable treadles for a player action which could be fitted to a normal piano, a method of driving the tune sheet from the treadles, a pianoforte system for mechanical playing and a device for playing the piano by hand 'when the feet are not available' – assumedly the mechanical piano. Paradoxically, he concluded this flurry of British patents with one for a tuck-in envelope for printed-paper-rate mail as the normal type of tuck-in envelope was '. . . often cast to one side remaining unopened'.

Klaber's efforts towards the mechanical piano continued and a few months later he formed the Pianotist Company with offices and showrooms at 56 Regent Street, London. His father, Emile, was managing director and the American parent company was the Adek Manufacturing Company of New York. An elaborate machine was produced for punching out music rolls in May 1901 and in September they perfected a device for 'varying the loudness of automatic piano-players by adjusting the force of hammers on the strings'.

During the summer of 1901, Pianotist carried out an ambitious (by contemporary British standards) advertising campaign to popularise their instrument and gave free piano recitals using their player attachment at their Regent Street showrooms. Five styles of the Pianotist were offered, the lowest of which was priced at twenty guineas.

The Pianotist was a mechanism of the 'kicking shoe' variety which played from a roll of thin punched card wound by a handle. Motion for the kicking shoe roller was provided via a single foot pedal and the whole device fitted under the keyboard of the piano. Presumably it was fitted only to uprights. Some patents were taken out for various details of the whole, but it was a mechanism obviously eclipsed by other inventions. Even so, a long article entitled 'Evolution of the Piano Player' in a 1901 issue of *The Illustrated Sporting and Dramatic News* praised the device, saying that it was considered excellent value for £35. Having sung the praises of the ordinary piano-player, the writer continued:

> Hardly are the words uttered in praise and endorsement of these instruments before a veritable genius arises and condenses the whole operative mechanism into such small space that it can be fitted into *any piano, out of sight*, thus not interfering at any time with

the use of the piano in the ordinary manner. Not content with this unquestionable advantage, the inventor of this instrument has provided what he is pleased to call 'melody stops', whereby 'the otherwise fatal accuracy and equal dynamic force' of all the fingers of a mechanical player may be varied at the will of the performer. The bass notes of a composition may be subdued, and the melody in treble accentuated, or if desired a melody brought out in the bass, while the treble provides merely a whispered accompaniment. This is a great achievement hitherto unknown in mechanical piano-players, and in the opinion of those best qualified to judge, it places this instrument far ahead of any other instrument of its kind. A simple frictional device has been substituted for pneumatics, with a consequent result that only 2 lb pressure is required as against 14 lb necessary to operate the cabinet form of piano-players.

In the opinion of some of the greatest artists and musicians who have seen this invention, it is considered artistically superior to anything of its kind, and such artists and musicians as Adelina Patti (Baroness Caderstrom), Mark Hambourg (the great pianist), Henry J. Wood (conductor Queen's Hall orchestra), Wilhelm Ganz, Tito Mattei, Landon Ronald and many others, have not hesitated to put such opinions to paper over their own signatures. From the fact that the *Pianotist* (this is the name of this remarkable instrument) when fitted to a piano in no way interferes with its use, or injures it in any way, it may be reasonably prophesied that the piano of the future will be capable of performing the dual role of 'an old century piano' and a 'new century piano player'. Such manufacturers as Erards, Steinways, Pleyels, &c., &c., are eulogistic in praise of the *Pianotist*, and all those contemplating the purchase of a piano-player would do well to call at the showrooms of the Pianotist Co. Ltd, 56 Regent Street (near Piccadilly Circus), and see and hear this latest invention before finally making their choice.

A strong company has been formed for the manufacture and sale of the *Pianotist*, and as indicative of the success of this instrument it may be stated that a number of prominent people have already availed themselves of an offer made by the Pianotist Company to change their old style instrument for the *Pianotist*, the company making a fair allowance in exchange therefor.

Soon afterwards, the company was liquidated, having lost heavily in trying to perfect its players and repairing those sold to customers. At the time of my first book, *Player Piano*, no complete Pianotists had been found. Now several have turned up but they must be considered both rare and not very convincing as players.

FROM 65 TO 88 NOTES

Melville Clark's masterly stroke of increasing the compass of the player from 65 to 88 notes was another momentous event which so many of the other makers chose to ignore. If ever there was an industry blinkered to the key developments taking place in its midst it was the American player industry. The reasons were in part understandable if not entirely excusable. If a sufficient number of the 'old' style of players were on the market, they stood a chance of forcing out of the way the new (and better) upstart. And with the big investments at stake it was a gamble thought worthwhile taking. McTammany was later to justify the vested interests succinctly:

Personally, the writer was opposed to the change at the time, knowing the loss that would be entailed by those who had so recently embarked in the manufacture of the sixty-five note player. And furthermore, many improvements were being developed, and these could be made more cheaply and effectively on the sixty-five than on the eighty-eight player.

In fact, though, his 88-note player proved a great boon for Clark while at the same time bringing those many others who had only recently started making 65-note models almost to ruin.

The change-over brought about a need for the dual-standard player and many solutions were put forward as to the means of allowing a player to make use of both the old 65-note rolls (of which a prodigious number were still in use, being made and sold) and the new, full-scale 88-note ones.

The news that Melville Clark had perfected a full-scale player was initially greeted by the industry with surprise, then a sort of smug satisfaction that after all nobody would want to buy such a device, particularly as it would be far more complex and liable to disarrangement. What happened, though, was the reverse and the capabilities of the new player were received by the new musical public with open arms. The man who did much to spread the message was Marc A. Blumenberg, the enthusiastic musical critic who bought out William E. Nickerson's *Musical & Dramatic News* from the Lockwood Press. From this, Blumenberg published a strictly trade magazine called the *Musical Courier Extra* and in this he wrote glowingly of the new Clark player. For the trade, however, it was more of a mortal blow than a shot in the arm, for, as McTammany relates, many smaller companies had invested great sums of money in perfecting their 65-note and 58-note players and putting them on the market. Overnight, it seemed, they were obsolete as the trade clamoured for the full-scale player. Many makers sought some interregnum from the inevitable by marketing models with twin tracker bars with various forms of change-over system so that both 65- and 88-note music rolls could be played. Some used two separate tracker bars, the user swinging or swivelling whichever one he wanted into place. Others used one tracker bar with two rows of openings for the different gauge rolls. Today, with plenty of both 65- and 88-note rolls to be found, possession of one of these dual standard players is something very much to be desired. Besides dual-standard players, there was one instrument made which was a triple standard. Hupfeld, which had long produced rolls and instruments for its own 73-note standard, became aware of the fact that the rest of the world was concentrating on 88-note music. In consequence it produced a small number of instruments which would play 73-, 65- and 88-note rolls. The tracker bar was normally 73-note but, by pulling it out of the spool box and reversing it, it would play the other two roll sizes. This also had exchangeable gearing for the spool drive so that, as with the Brinsmead Angelus, bottom-to-top rolls could be played as well as the normal top-to-bottom type by moving the take-up spool.

But there were also attempts to convert the 65-note player to play 88-note rolls and whilst this could be done by exchanging the 65-note pneumatic stack for one with 88 motors it was normally done by fitting an 88-note tracker bar and teeing back the upper and lower notes so that every tracker hole played a piano note – but still only 65 of them! The instruction book describing how to perform this heinous act ran to five editions and was published by *Musical Opinion* and sundries dealer C. F. Baker.

The Angelus player was manufactured by the Wilcox & White Company of Meriden,

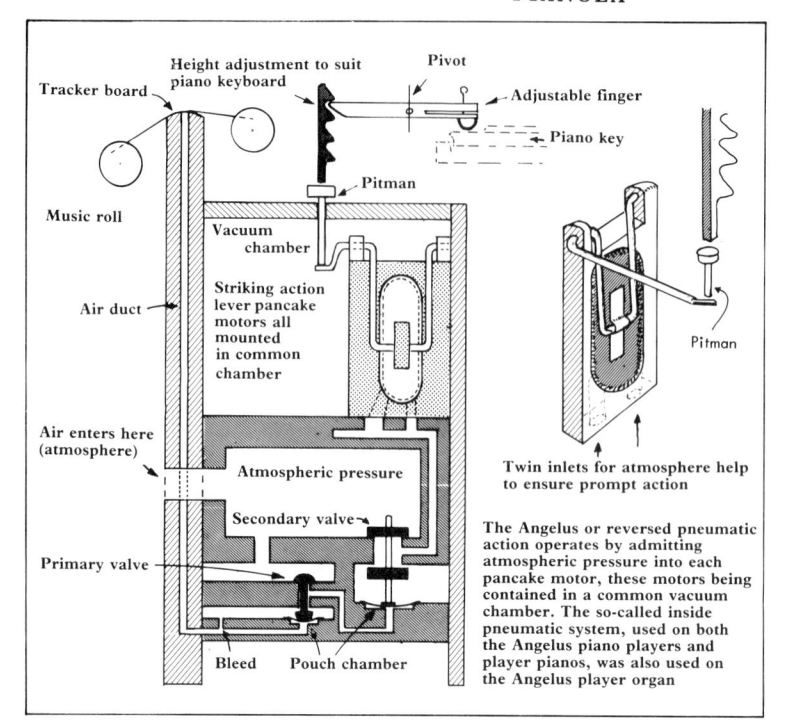

Fig. 41
The Angelus diaphragm pneumatic action as applied to the cabinet or push-up piano player. The Angelus remained with the diaphragm action to the end.

Connecticut, who patented on 8 April 1902 a new approach to the question of how to adjust the height of the player to the keyboard – undoubtedly a problem of great concern to all makers of cabinet players since the fingers had to be at the precise height over the piano's keys in order to do their job adequately. Each note pneumatic of the Angelus after 1902 lifted a pitman which carried a number of notches in its back edge. The keyboard fingers were all carried in a frame which could be moved up and down on guide rails provided at each end, so bringing the adustable fingers into suitable notches on the pitmans. Adjustment, although positive, required careful preparation but, once set, would stay firmly in position. The Angelus also featured a transposing device, as much for the correct alignment of rolls as anything else. This was worked by a knurled screw which moved both the take-up spool and the music-roll chuck laterally across the fixed tracker bar.

However, the dramatic difference between the Angelus and all other pneumatic player actions was that it made use of flat, pressure-powered pneumatics instead of the usual and generally adopted wedge-shaped suction motors. These diaphragm pneumatics were rectangular and they operated not on vacuum like a wedge motor but on atmospheric pressure used to inflate the diaphragm, so moving the piano hammer action through the action of a cranked-lever linkage. The Angelus worked very well indeed and was a good and reliable system, if very fiddly to service when it went wrong.

The Angelus cabinet player was built with a full-scale 88-note action as late as 1909 but this instrument, a specimen of which is in the author's collection, must be a late example. By this time, the 'inner player' was well on the way to perfection and the market for a push-up had dwindled to almost nothing. It was about this time that Wilcox & White changed their name to the Angelus Piano Company with offices in New York.

With the 65-note players and their precursors such as the 58-note early Apollo by Melville Clark, the tracker bar was of wood. Larger scales called for closer, smaller and more accurate holes and the massive expansion of the player market encouraged a gradual adoption throughout the industry of an all-metal tracker bar. Aeolian took out the first patents in 1902 for a tracker bar made of brass tubes, their upper ends flattened into a rectangular shape and cast into a strip of Britannia metal.* Connections from the other ends of the tubes to the valve chests could then be made with rubber tubing. Another advantage of the metal tracker was that it allowed simple registration and transposing devices to be applied to it.

In October of 1903 there was introduced into England a novel and possibly unique instrument called the Simplex Special Piano Player. Heralded by the press as 'the most radical departure in constructive lines from anything in the piano player field since that type of instrument was first evolved', the Special was a small cabinet standing 42 in. high, 24 in. wide and 16 in. deep which was placed next to an ordinary piano. Provided with its own foot treadles and connected to a pneumatic stack built into the piano, this was a short-lived attempt at allowing mechanical or manual playing of a piano without the need to shift around the cumbersome cabinet push-up type of player. None is known to survive and the device was very rapidly superseded by the interior player.

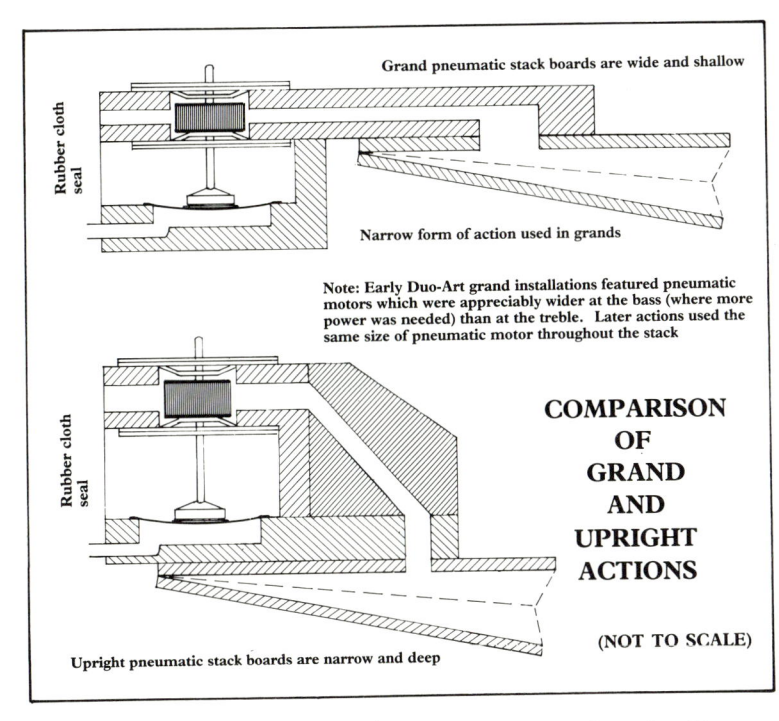

Fig. 42
Comparison of grand and upright player actions. Whereas the upright usually had no restrictions on depth, the width of the action was critical if the piano case was to be kept as slim as possible. On the other hand, the grand presented the opposite set of conditions. Here depth was critical, especially with actions built above the keys. Hence these two basic styles evolved – short and thick for uprights, and long and thin for grands.

Incorporating the player into the case of the piano itself was a major step forward. Whereas initially actions were bulky and were descended too directly from the cumbersome push-up cabinet player, efforts were soon directed to producing purpose-built actions for the so-called 'inner player'.

* Britannia metal: an alloy of tin with antimony and a little copper.

Installing the player action into a grand piano called for a modified type of action. Whereas the upright piano provided at least some vacant space inside the case above the keys and in front of the strings, the grand posed a different set of problems. Some makers placed the entire action beneath the key bed, the best known of these being Ampico. Others divided the action between a top-mounted spool-box and a below-keys pneumatic stack. Aeolian developed a single-valve top stack which was slim enough to fit between the keyboard and the underside of the wrest plank. Several other makers followed with this type of action. One of the most distinctive designs, although an action which was difficult to adjust, came from Reginald H. Collen, Broadwood's works superintendent. He devised a twin-valve action of extreme compactness in which one valve passed through the stem of the other. This was built as a unit action, each valve block and pneumatic being attached separately to the action board and suction chamber in the same manner as the original Broadwood unit player action patented as number 10,084 of 1903. Collen's new action was patented as number 12,724 of 1913.

Around these largely experimental early days of the player piano and piano player, there were many schools of thought as to how many of the piano's complement of notes should or indeed could be sounded by a mechanical or pneumatic action. Actions were being made which played 58, 65, 70, 73, 82 and 88 notes and this complete lack of standardisation did not foster a progressive industry. It was not until 1910 that actions and rolls were standardised at 65-note and 88-note. The decision for this was taken at a convention of player manufacturers at Buffalo, New York. This regularising of the piano and roll industry did not affect player organs, which normally used 58-note rolls.

ATTEMPTS AT ACCENTING

By 1913, there were three systems of music-roll note accenting in use. First was the Themodist type in its various forms (see next Chapter). Then there was the 88-slot (marginal) which had one accent slot for each note on the tracker bar and, finally, the 'Dalian' system of double tracker bar with actual note perforations which determined the playing of accents. This last-mentioned method was used in the Crowley player piano (see below) but was never produced in quantity. The second was used only on a limited scale but it was the first which achieved technical supremacy and wide application.

At the British Music Exhibition held at Olympia in September 1913, a number of manufacturers exhibited player pianos, among them Messrs George Rogers's Rogers Player Piano, William Sames & Co.'s instruments (which were fitted with either Hupfeld or the very successful and cheap Canadian Higel action, London-made and sold by Heckschers of Camden Town), and Malcolm player-piano (Malcolm & Co. used at one time to make a player organ), and the Direct Pneumatic Action Company with their Stems player piano fitted with the Arrow action.

Also on show was the Dalian player piano exhibited by John H. Crowley. This was an unusual type of expression piano which, although of excellent potential, was dependent on costly apparatus with which to manufacture the special paper rolls. Each note was provided with a damping pneumatic and regulator. One common vacuum pressure was used, but the strength of the piano hammer blow to the string was variable by the amount of atmospheric air admitted through the tracker bar. This was regulated by having perforations of different widths in the paper, loud notes having wider holes than soft ones. As an alternative, ordinary

88-note rolls could be played. Here, in theory at least, was the ideal expression piano, indeed *reproducing* piano, where every note was characterised by its very own interpretational value. It was, though, highly impractical and was never produced in any quantity.

The Olympia exhibition also showed the range of mini-player-pianos made by Barratt & Robinson which were small enough to be taken on a small yacht or boat. The Pedaleon was one of the smallest players ever made. Following early organ-building techniques, the keyboards on some of these pianos were both hinged and sliding, folding up out of the way when not in use.

Brinsmead showed examples of their Mignon and Aluminium players, the former being of traditional wood construction and the latter a highly durable all-metal action. From Murdoch, Murdoch & Co., of 461 and 463 Oxford Street, London, came the Connoisseur Player Piano. There was also the Connoisseur Reed Organ and the Connoisseur Pipe Organ, both player instruments. The piano was equipped with all the usual controls. Each maker strove to give his own distinctive names to these expression levers or buttons and to employ these euphemisms in their advertising. Murdoch's instrument, for example, had the Tempola, Phrasiola, Solotheme, Diminuent, Transposa, Automelle (theme isolator controlled by Themodist-type holes), Autoforte and Autotracker. Armed with that lot, it is a bit of a comedown to find that the performer still had to pedal and one wonders why no enterprising manufacturer, tongue in cheek, didn't call his foot treadles 'Pedairolas'.

ROLL REPERTOIRE

By the 1920s, the range of rolls available for the player pianist was enormous. Not only were most of the great piano and orchestral pieces transcribed in roll form, but so were the best of the popular songs, dance music, hymn tunes – in fact the whole gamut of music (see Chapter 11).

Popular songs tended to demand either a knowledge of the words or an additional musical score. Rolls were printed which had the song words stencilled along one side and these were introduced sometime about 1906, although Roehl states that the Vocalstyle Music Company of Cincinatti, Ohio, were the first to make this type of roll 'as early as 1908'. Be that as it may, song rolls were certainly in full production by most companies by 1909. The words were rather disconcertingly printed in lines corresponding to the correct musical note to which they were to be sung. This necessitated their being read virtually from bottom to top and the music-roll songster had to become adept at reading one line above the other – not so simple as it at first seems, particularly with hyphenated words:

> ling
> dar-
> my
> ways
> al-
> love you
> ll
> I'

Along with the 'pedal line' or expression line (which indicated whether a section was to be played *pianissimo* or *fortissimo* and also gave advance warnings of such changes as *crescendo*, *diminuendo*, pause, tempo variance and so on), the words were printed on a rotary stencilling machine which pressed a suitably marked stencil band on to the paper roll as it was passed under it. A similar system was used by the advanced makers of music rolls who printed their tempo lines in different colours (often red or green) and other marks in more colours.

Both player pianos and the concluding production of piano players were made with dual-standard tracker bars and performed using what was by this time the accepted arrangement – a tracker bar with two rows of openings, one for each roll type, and a change-over lever in the spool box to select which row of openings to use. A spool chuck adapter was also provided since 88-note rolls had recessed ends to the spool.

The 88-note or full-scale rolls were much more popular than the limited scale ones but even so there was still a market for the 65-note instruments. To fit into the smaller compass a degree of alteration was required to the score and, in certain pieces, the transformation from the original full-scale to the 65-note roll was nothing short of mutilation. From the mechanical standpoint, though, 65-note actions were more reliable. Component parts were slightly larger and, most important of all, the tracker bar was not so finely pierced and therefore was not so likely to become clogged with dust and paper fluff. Tracking problems were also of less significance.

One of the largest manufacturers of music rolls in England was the Perforated Music Company. With showrooms at 94 Regent Street and a library at 81 Beak Street, off Regent Street, their head office and factory was 197–199 City Road, London. Their trade mark was 'Imperial' and in 1910 they advertised as manufacturing rolls for many instruments, including Pianola, Orchestrelle, Symphony, Amphion, Broadwood, Apollo, Angelus, Hardman, Forte, Metzler, Simplex, Humana, Aristo, Neola, Humanola, Aeriola, Pianotist, Kimball, Chase & Baker, Sterling, Triumph, Rex, Imperial, Electrelle, Cecilian, and Autopiano. All their rolls were made at City Road and, by 1914, their premises were extended with the acquisition of the adjacent buildings, numbers 201 and 203. In March 1918 a disastrous fire gutted the entire factory, destroying all the plant and equipment as well as hundreds of thousands of rolls. The firm subsequently re-established on a much smaller scale at 6 Bride Street, London EC, where it continued for a few years until the general slump in the music-roll trade in the late twenties and early thirties.

THE PISTONOLA

Shortly before the First World War, two young London engineers, H. C. Coldman and C. F. Webb, brought a player piano and took it apart to see how it worked. They were surprised by the seemingly large components and consequently the large amount of air which had to be moved in order to play the instrument. They believed that, by rethinking the entire action, a much simpler, cheaper and more reliable action might be made. The result of their labours was the Pistonola, manufactured by Boyd Limited, whose first head office was at 19 Holborn, London. Boyd had already entered the self-playing piano market with a 65-note piano player of very angular appearance which sold for £32 8s together with six rolls of music.

Boyd showed their Pistonola to the public at a concert held in Ilford Town Hall on 26 November 1913, the programme including both solo and accompaniment pieces for the player piano. April 1914 saw a public demonstration of the Pistonola at the Corn Exchange in London under the auspices of the London music dealers H. Payne & Co. With Mr Stanley

Harris at the controls, the Pistonola performed in concert with a tenor, a contralto and a violin.

The Pistonola was an interesting device, its very name perhaps indicating the principle upon which it operated. Widely acclaimed as the all-metal player action, every function of the player was achieved by the use of a piston moving in a cylinder. The foot treadles drew air out of a master cylinder using pistons. The master cylinder itself had a spring-loaded piston within it through which vacuum tension could be achieved. Pressure-reducing valves provided both low and high vacuum pressures to operate the roll-drive motor (which was again a piston motor) and the valves. The valve chest and pneumatics of the ordinary action were replaced by a compact bank of eighty-eight tiny cylinders each no more than half an inch in diameter and each having a small free-moving piston made of compressed graphite with it. Being self-lubricating, the graphite pistons moved readily under the influence of small charges of air pressure. Each piston was connected to its respective piano-action hammer by a cord. When a hole in the music roll opened a hole in the tracker bar, the piston would move, setting in motion the hammer action. When the tracker bar hole was once more covered, the suction would be removed from the piston which would immediately drop back under its own weight. Appreciably less air was required to be shifted to play the Pistonola as compared with a normal player piano, and when it was launched it was widely acclaimed in the press. Two models were available, one selling for £75 12s 0d and the other, fitted with so-called Modulist and Crescodant manual expression devices, sold at £84 0s 0d.

After the First World War, an improved version was marketed called the Terpreter. Three versions were available, the Models One and Two, each costing 160 guineas, and the Model three at 150 guineas.

When properly adjusted, the Pistonola and Terpreter were very good players and were capable of easy and immediate expression from their controls. The action was, nevertheless, prone to malfunctions which were not always easy to trace and rectify. Mr D. F. Andrews of Boyd Pianos remembers these instruments and relates how some were 'jinx' instruments which were always temperamental. Thus it is perhaps no surprise to find that, by the 1920s, Boyd were producing a more conventional player with imported action. This was the Boyd Autoplayer, available in a number of different-styled pianos for as little as 108 guineas. One of the controls on the Autoplayer was called the 'Deletor'. The advertising literature wrote of this:

> If a section of the music-roll is not required, this wonderful device will allow the roll to travel in silence at high speed . . .

THE QUEST FOR THE REPRODUCING PIANO

The call for the accented piano roll, sometimes referred to as 'hand-played', and the instruments upon which to play them remained right up to the thirties. However, the challenge of making a player piano which could reproduce faithfully the performance of a concert pianist without requiring any dexterity on the part of the owner of the instrument was recognised very early on.

The outcome of much experimentation towards this goal was called a reproducing piano – a name actually patented by the Aeolian Company but one which, as with 'pianola', came to be the generic term for all makes of piano which produced a concert rendition of a piece of music from a music roll recorded by a concert pianist whose name would appear on the roll.

The evolution of the reproducing piano began fairly early in the history of the player piano. I have chosen to devote a separate section to this instrument for such it deserves.

THE DECLINE OF THE PLAYER

As the 1930s advanced, sales of players began to diminish in the face of wireless, which was gaining market penetration, and the gramophone which with the improvements of electric recording could bring an orchestra into the home, albeit in stages of four or five minute between turning the disc. Also at this time, as related in Chapter 1, the depression had killed sales and the trade had lost faith in the instrument. Reginald Reynolds was invited to write about the instrument in the 21st birthday issue of *The Pianomaker, Music & Radio* for June 1934. His words to the trade are worth repeating at length for they spell out much of the unsung history of the player:

> ... the trouble is that you have lost faith in it as a musical instrument and as a selling proposition. So I want to remind you of facts relating to its saleability and superiority to other instruments for the purpose of self-expression. Perhaps few dealers will admit that they are old enough to remember the coming of the piano-player into this country; but I am not ashamed of the fact that I sold some of the very earliest models, while I was in charge of Maple's piano department more than thirty years ago. Those were wonderful days! A short demonstration on the new instrument convinced the client that it was the easiest method of making music. Orders were in excess of production, and some purchsers were so anxious to possess their piano-player that they insisted upon taking it away on the top of a four-wheeler cab, commonly called a 'growler'. Nowadays that term might be applied to some piano dealers! They growl because of the decline in the sale of pianos, just as dealers in harps must have complained about the decreasing demand for those charming instruments, so difficult to play effectively. Doubtless those worthy men were as prejudiced against the newfangled harpsichord (with its mechanical action and keyboard interposed between the fingers and the strings) as the modern dealer who objects to the addition of the pneumatic action to the already highly mechanised pianoforte. Yet the state of passive and active resistance to the harpsichord turned into great popularity, and was only ousted by another form of keyboard instrument, the pianoforte, by means of which greater effects were produced with less effort.
>
> Even so will it be with player-piano. People will find that the pneumatic action enables them to achieve results utterly beyond the capacity of two human hands, with an ease and certainty unknown to the performer upon any other instrument. Then they will insist upon having the 100 per cent of efficacy, whether the dealer likes it or not. Of course, you are not interested in the dim and distant future; you want sales now. Well, you can have them if you stock reliable 'players' at a moderate price, demonstrate them properly, and see that the client knows how to make the best use of his purchase. Remember that many a man, to whom an ordinary piano is useless, can get infinite joy out of a 'player-piano'. There are lots of people who feel the impulse to express their own idea of their favourite music, who have no technical ability. Each one of these is a potential purchaser of a 'player'.
>
> At present this amazing invention is suffering from diminution of propaganda, lack of

enthusiastic exponents, and apathy of the trade. While the public can scarcely be blamed for forming the idea that it is 'a beastly mechanical instrument' if it is judged by its effect when played by novices or unmusical owners. Do you judge a piano when it is being thrashed by a rotten pianist? How would the harpsichord have fared if it had never been taught? In its early days it was played without using the thumbs, and there are plenty of 'player' owners who fail to use the available controls of the instruments. Yet the manufacturers of the players deliberately negatived the necessity for tuition. They advertised that 'a child can play it'. The most misleading statement that could be made about this wonderful music-maker. It is all the worse, because the phrase contains a molecule of truth. For, unfortunately, a child can grind out the notes with appalling precision. But this is the only letting the music-roll play itself, and should be forbidden by Act of Parliament under penalty of death, because it is nothing short of 'murdering' music. With stupidity, the producers of the 'player' introduced an instrument with astounding artistic possibilities as a toy for a child!

Now the child has found other toys, while the adult, who longs to make sweet music in accord with the emotion of the moment, does not know (after thirty-five years of player publicity) that the 'player-piano' is the one and only instrument that will satisfy the cravings of a musical soul for self-expression with the least possible expenditure of time and trouble. The hard-headed dealer will merely say: 'That's only your opinion. You're a "player" crank.' Yes, perhaps I am, but I was a pianist, and it is possible that I still know something about piano playing. So, here are a few facts regarding the capabilities and limitations of a pianist, contrasted with the wider scope of the 'player' pianist.

Eight fingers and two thumbs cannot achieve the same facility of technique as when every note of the piano is provided with a separate unit capable of playing with varying degrees of touch at a speed of repetition equal to the efficiency of the pianoforte action. Thus it happens that all rapid passages can be played more clearly and cleanly by the 'player' pianist than a 'dozen Paderewskis rolled into one'. I am quoting Sir August Manns.

Now for the comparison of hand-touch versus foot-feeling. First, remember that the pianist's finger is not in contact with the string. If you object to the interposition of mechanism, you must go back to the harp! The pneumatic action adds comparatively little to the complexity of the pianoforte action. While the foot-pedals can be so sensitive to variations of pressure, that delicate inflexions of touch can be imparted to successive notes, or sudden accents made instantaneously with a sharp movement of the foot. This being so, the question comes: 'Is it more natural to use the hand or the foot as a means of expressing emotion and as a medium of rhythmical impulse?'

When a person wishes to express 'a big, big D' without using the objectional word, it is more instinctive to stamp the foot, than to thump the table. As for rhythm, the foot taps out the accentuations far more naturally than the hand beats time. From which I am entitled to conclude that the foot is a very suitable part of the human being for the transmission of emotional feeling. In fact, a 'wag' once said that 'suitors for the hand of my daughter had better beware of my foot!' It is true that I try to express every phrase of passionate or subtle feeling through the movement of my feet; and the sensation of doing so gives me even greater gratification than the use of my hands, which were trained as a pianist for six hours a day over a very long period.

This brings me to the most vital comparison between the possible achievement of pianists and of player pianists. The former have to work terribly hard to acquire any considerable proficiency of technique; and then each new solo of any appreciable difficulty must be given a lot of practice before it is fit to play, even to the satisfaction of the pianist. Now see the advantage held by the 'player' pianist who has acquired a fair control of the instrument – a matter of a few weeks' acquaintance with a 'player' piano. The world of music is literally 'at his feet'. Difficulty of technique is of no consequence; there will be no wrong notes, no scrambling and fumbling about. The new solo can be taken at the right tempo, and a really good reading of it can be obtained straight away. This is a joy unknown to the pianist. For I will wager that no one can play faultlessly at sight, such music as I could choose.

Oh! Believe me! The 'player' is the better half of the 'player' piano. But there is still the keyboard for those who want to use their fingers in the old-fashioned way. So why let your clients buy the worst half of the instrument? You have it in your power to persuade them to get the completely satisfying 'player' piano. You say: 'Price counts'. Yes, it does; but the additional cost of the pneumatic action is only a tithe of its actual value to the purchaser. A 'player' piano is worth at least ten ordinary pianos, and viewed from that standpoint is always a good investment.

I am in such deadly earnest about this subject and am so anxious to convert the world to belief in the true type of instrument for the home, that I would submit to be cremated alive up a 'player' piano, if it would have the desired effect. But in these materialistic days it would only make a headline in a sensational journal, and the verdict would be – 'Suicide, while of unsound mind'. Lives are so cheap today, that mine would count for nothing, amid those sacrificed for a more flourishing industry.

If you dealers will only have faith in the musical capacity of the instrument and its unique utility for personal performance, you can bring about such a revival of 'player' prosperity, that not only will it benefit you and the manufacturers, but will bring happiness into thousands of homes.

Reginald Reynolds, whose name appears on many of the later Aeolian patents, was an avowed promoter of the instrument, yet however much he eschewed the merits of the player he could not influence public attitudes and market changes. Even as he wrote, the greatest name in player pianos was crumbling. As related in the next chapter, Aeolian in America was burned out and forced to amalgamate with Ampico, and affairs in Britain had reached a situation from which there was no retreat.

THE END OF AEOLIAN IN BRITAIN

The demise of the Aeolian empire in Britain came about in an unfortunate manner. The player piano was already suffering from the competition created by its rivals the wireless and the gramophone when, in 1927, the company decided to proceed with a grandiose scheme for the publication of a new range of piano rolls under the name Audiographic.

Audiographic rolls contained an immense amount of information printed on the roll which told the pianolist everything he could possibly need to know about the music. To overcome the shortcomings of the Metrostyle markings and the line of dots indicating level of volume (see Chapter 11 for explanation), a special printing press was constructed by means of which

THE EVOLUTION OF THE PLAYER PIANO

expression lines and phrasing marks could be printed with a degree of accuracy never before possible on a piano roll. This printing machine alone set the company back £2,000. Production costs for these rolls were estimated at £5 each – an absolutely fantastically high price. Very few were sold and Reginald Reynolds relates* that ultimately they were placed in the lending library and subscribers used to avoid them. A large and expensive advertising programme – just an extension of the lavish promotional campaigns undertaken during the company's lifetime – did not bring forth the anticipated fruits. The roll library was another activity which became an increasingly heavy overhead, for it is doubtful if this far-sighted venture ever paid off. It was the largest of its kind in the world.

By the time these rolls were ready for the market, however, the state of the world economy was worsening and when in 1929 the depression came this enterprising roll scheme and all the equipment which had gone into its realisation became unsaleable and useless. The enormous loss of capital involved in the Audiographic roll scheme precipitated the company into a major financial crisis and its magnificent premises – the Aeolian Hall in London's Bond Street – had to be put up for auction.

When the crash came, Harrods, the large London department store, bought up the remaining assets and took over some of the Aeolian Hall staff. A much smaller Aeolian Company carried on manufacturing at the Hayes factory and when, on 8 November 1932, Danemann's factory in Northampton Street, Islington, was destroyed by fire, Aeolian was able to lease part of its unused Hayes premises to help Danemann during their rebuild. But Aeolian was no longer a major company in Britain and the company played a diminishing part in player activities. The final winding up was a lengthy process. How different was this from the situation in Australia where the Orchestrelle Company – Aeolian – remained in business repairing instruments and selling rolls from its Melbourne showroom right up until as late as 1976.

THE EFFECT OF THE PLAYER ON THE MUSIC WORLD

The perfection of the techniques of the gramophone, the effects of other entertainments such as wireless and, later, television, and perhaps above all else the gradual trend of the family home to become smaller all set the scene for the close of the pneumatic piano era in Britain. War was the catalyst. What remains today is the afterglow of an age of musical achievement which, in its own scale of sphere, was quite as remarkable as the present space age.

In the space of fewer than forty years, the player piano had been and gone, leaving in its wake two things: a generation of people who had never needed to learn to play the piano by hand thanks to the player, and several generations for whom musical knowledge and experience had been bought pleasurably at the stools of their player pianos. The gentle educator had achieved more than its promoters could have wished even in their wildest dreams.

The impact of the player had been impressive and important. Just how had it achieved this transformation in so short a period? If we go back to the first decade of this century, we start to see the pattern developing.

The extreme popularity of the piano player which could convert a normal instrument into a player immediately – and thereby made sound business sense – was such that

---

* 'Memoirs', *Player Piano Group Bulletin*, No. 65, p. 26.

manufacturers sprang into action in, so it seemed, ever-increasing numbers. Every week, another product was unveiled by another company, and *Musical Opinion* had recourse to headlines such as 'And yet another' and 'Still they come'.

It makes an interesting comparison to evaluate the penetration of the piano as an instrument in the homes of the Americans and the British since, even though the figures are somewhat approximate, they show just how attractive was the market for pianos, so laying open the field for selling players.

UNITED STATES

Year	Population	Households	No. of pianos sold	Equal to market penetration of	Total estimate of pianos	Homes with a piano
1890	62,622,250	10,440,000	72,000	0·7%	200,000	3·0%
1900	76,891,220	13,980,000	220,000	1·6%	460,000	3·3%
1905	82,959,221	15,934,000	305,000	1·9%	760,000	4·8%
1910	89,500,000	18,650,000	370,000	2·0%	1·050m	5·6%

UNITED KINGDOM

1890	34,260,000	6,110,000	50,000	0·8%	170,000	2·8%
1900	38,230,000	7,511,000	71,000	0·9%	205,000	2·8%
1905	40,100,000	8,354,000	75,000	0·9%	270,000	3·2%
1910	42,000,000	8,676,000	78,000	0·9%	335,000	3·9%

These two tables are based on reliable estimations and it will be understood that the arbitrary totals in the second column, when viewed with the production figures in column three, can tolerate reasonable amounts of error without affecting the penetration percentage too greatly. This is important because it clearly reveals that within the space of twenty years the penetration of the piano in the United States increased by some 185 per cent although the number of households only increased by about 78 per cent. In the United Kingdom, however, the same period saw virtually no increase in the penetration of the piano, with manufacture only keeping pace with the increase in the number of households.

The decade which followed saw the massive expansion in player production and, although players in Britain are thought to have represented no more than 30 to 35 per cent of the total output by 1919, in that year 53 per cent of American production was devoted to player pianos – and the peak of production was still four years off.

However, this illustrates how apparently certain success was for the makers of piano players who thronged the market in the early years of this century. Even when the first interior player had come on the market – 'the world's first complete piano' – the cabinet-player makers could not see that their market was to be short-lived. The majority of pianos on the market were relatively cheap, low-quality models and there were still very many wood-framed pianos in regular use that were over fifty years old. Just how much of that alleged market penetration was devoted to the replacement market rather than fresh business is impossible to say, but the fact remained that the public was susceptible to buying a new piano and, if that was to be, then it would be one with the player action built inside. This saved space, inconvenience and the continual risk of damage to the fragile wooden fingers of the cabinet player. Even the arrival of Melville Clark's 88-note player did not galvanise the other makers into reading the writing which was becoming ever clearer on the wall.

The outcome was that a great deal of money was lost by a large number of makers who were still inventing, patenting and building new push-ups as the buyers in the music stores were stocking up on 'complete pianos'. All, historically, had never been sweet and rosy, for Theodore P. Brown's Aeriol Piano was not a great success on the market. McTammany* gives the reason for the failure as 'prejudice, pure and simple', and adds:

> Theodore P. Brown was right, the men who looked with indifference and contempt upon his efforts were wrong, and had Brown received the encouragement and co-operation he deserved, he might today [1915] be at the head of the player procession.

The history of the piano player and the player piano was thus pock-marked with company failures, fortunes lost and, above all, dreams shattered. Sadly, along this path of misfortune there were laid low the ideas of some which should have had better fortunes, more luck, and a chance to make the market big times. The player inventor was never short of ideas and he demonstrated so clearly the old adage that there are more ways to skin a cat than one.

Of course, it would be quite wrong to give the impression that the player piano died with the depression of the 'thirties. It made a few feeble attempts to regain its former glory as a result of the National Player-Piano Publicity Committee (see Chapter 1), but it was to all intents and purposes moribund after 1937. There was, however, a post-war revival (see Chapter 10) and instruments are still being made today but, just like the modern Swiss musical-box industry, the instrument and its numbers represent but a shadow of its former times. From being a consumer product, the player piano is now essentially an enthusiast's one.

* *Technical History of the Player*, p. 76.

METZLER'S "Humanola"

RETAIL PRICE:

£25

Net Cash,

together with offer of £2 worth of Music Rolls to every Purchaser FREE.

Its Popular Price extends its Selling Radius far beyond that of any other Piano Player.

Terms and Particulars on application to: **METZLER & CO. (Ltd.),** [And of all Local Dealers
40-43, GREAT MARLBOROUGH STREET, REGENT STREET, LONDON, W.

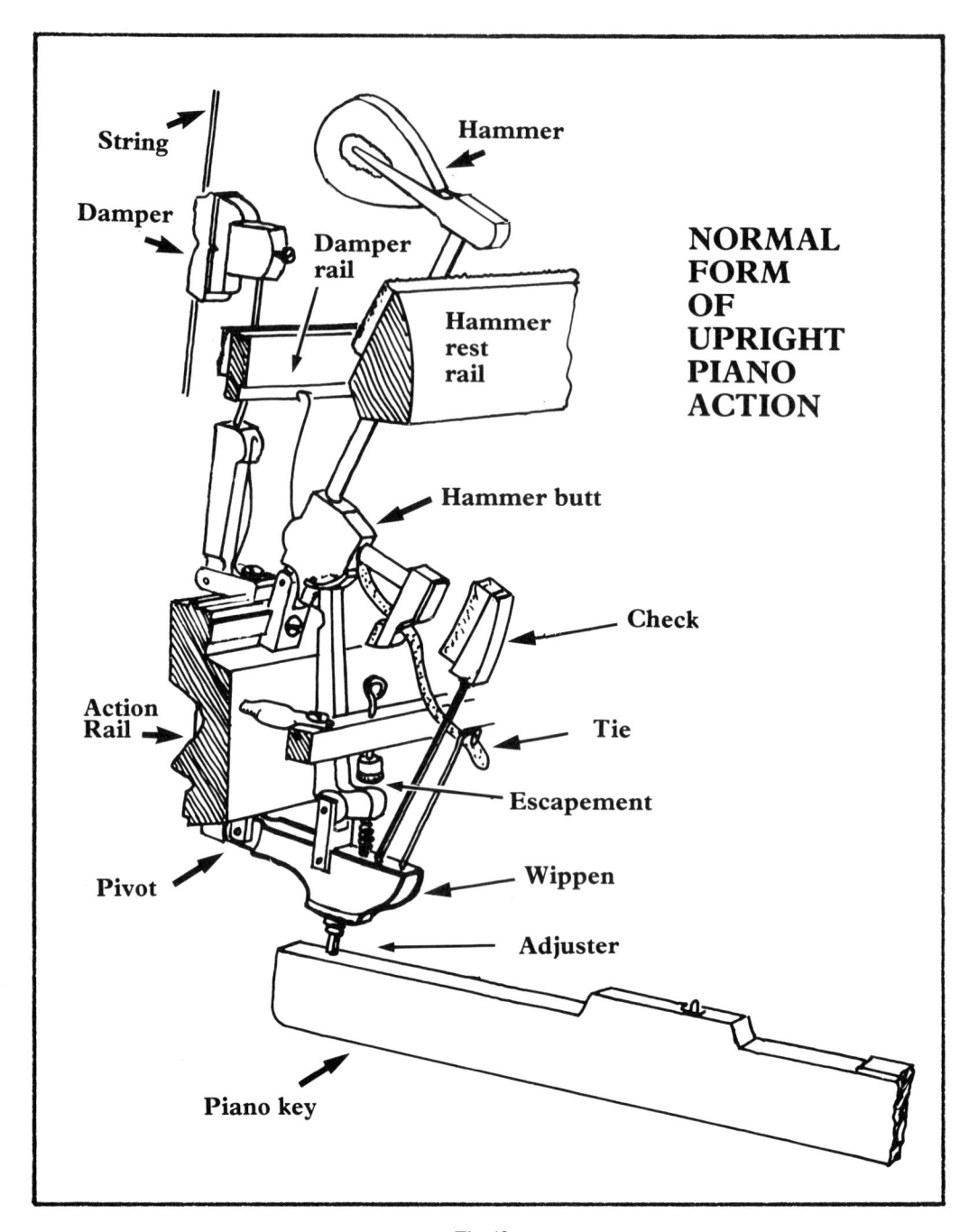

Fig. 43
Action of the ordinary upright piano.

CHAPTER 5

How the Pneumatic Player Piano Works

I shall not be entering into an exhaustive description of how a piano works or detailing the hammer action of the ordinary piano: that is outside the scope of this book. For the amateur who wants to know about such things several good books are available. As for the regulation and adjustment of the piano action, this is covered admirably in a book by Arthur Reblitz (see Bibliography). For these reasons I must suppose that my readers have a basic knowledge of what happens in an ordinary piano so that when a key is pressed down a specific note is sounded. Upright and grand actions differ, so you should know a little of how each works.

However, before looking into what makes a pneumatic player action actually operate the piano, it is as well to have a brief look at the piano action and just see which parts have to be set into motion by the pneumatic system. The illustration of an upright action, Fig. 43, shows the various components which go to making one key action. You can see how when the pianist depresses a key on the keyboard the action is set into motion, causing the hammer to fly forwards and strike the string. Two important features to observe are the rest rail and the damper rail. Even if the pianist holds the key down, the hammer does not stay in contact with the string but falls back clear of it (observe here that when I refer to 'string' I am using this collectively to refer to one note on the piano which may consist of two, three or even four separate wires or strings tuned in unison). By holding down the key, all the pianist succeeds in doing is to hold off the damper which is provided to mute the string before it may be struck again. In holding off the damper, the string is permitted to vibrate for longer duration than if the pianist were to play the note *staccato*. All the dampers can be moved individually in this way, working separately for each note. But all the dampers are freely located upon a rail which itself can be moved away from the string. The action which moves the dampers collectively is called the 'sustaining pedal' – the right one at the lower front of the ordinary piano – which is so often miscalled the 'loud pedal'.

The rest rail is the second of our important features. This is simply the rail against which the individual hammers rest and it can be moved either away from the strings, so allowing the hammer to fly forward a good distance and hit the string hard, or moved closer so that the hammers have only a short distance to travel to do their work and thus hit the strings without great force. This action is controlled by the left-hand pedal at the lower front of the ordinary piano, called the 'soft pedal'. Grand pianos sometimes use a different system which I shall mention later.

Another point has to be considered and that is that the pianist has two hands which normally each play on only half of the keyboard and he can also play loudly or softly by regulating the force with which he strikes the keys. He can also accentuate certain notes, even certain notes in an *arpeggio* or *appoggiatura*, and change with alacrity from delicate tones to strident ones or to *sostenuto*. All these features, separately and collectively, have to be capable of worthy imitation using the pneumatic system.

As we shall see, the execution of these functions by mechanical means is quite easily achieved. But, to return to the ordinary piano action once more, we must make sure that we understand exactly which parts of it have to be set in motion by our mechanical or pneumatic means. It is pointless to try to make something which will move the keys (assuming that we are thinking in terms of an inner player as compared with a piano player), for the keys are, so to speak, a further step beyond the parts we want to move. The key is purely a lever to move the hammer action and the part we have to get at is the hammer action itself. One part of the hammer action lends itself admirably to taking both normal keyboard operation and mechanical inducement in its stride and this is the rocking lever which is called the wippen. Everything above the wippen is required to set in motion the sequence of string-hitting; everything below it is but a means of moving the wippen, which is the starting-point of the chain of sequences which terminates with the striking of a string.

The wippen is also convenient from another standpoint. It is at such a position that it can be pushed or pulled up without interfering with any other function of the piano and, most important, it does not interfere with the manual use of the instrument at other times.

What we have now isolated are the parts of the action which must be moved and also the junction in the road from key to string at which we can build our pneumatic services.

Now we must look into the basic pneumatics and try to see just why the pneumatic player works, what it does and how it does it.

The player piano in essence comprises an assortment of small functional devices connected to a chamber in which the air pressure has been reduced to below that of the surrounding atmosphere. Each device is operated by the controlled admittance of air through it and, because the atmospheric pressure is being allowed access to the reduced state of air pressure within, this air can be used to move a valve on its seat or to deflate a bellows to perform mechanical work, or to permit access of other components to the pressure variations taking place.

Expressed in even more simple terms, the player piano is a machine containing a partial vacuum into which air is continually trying to find access. In entering the instrument, it is made to perform a mechanical function. Place a player piano in an atmosphere which is itself a vacuum, or put it on the moon, and it will not work. Nature abhors a vacuum – and the player piano needs to be able to create a partial vacuum in order to be able to work.

Air has one characteristic which is particularly important to us if we are to use it to power a piano. Regardless of its pressure, it will always fill a given space at an equal density. Suppose you have a box representing a one-foot cube and into this you put a cubic foot of sand. The box will naturally be filled and the sand particles will be tightly packed together. Now supposing we empty out of the box three-quarters of the sand, the remaining sand will lie at the bottom of the box, its particles still tightly packed together, the rest of the box being 'empty'. Supposing that instead of sand we now fill our cubic foot box with air from the atmosphere – all we have to do is lift the lid and then close it again and we can be certain that the air around us is also in the box. The box is now full of air. If we now make the box airtight and, using a pump, begin to draw the air out of the box, as we reduce its pressure relative to that of the atmosphere, the pressure of the air all over the inside of the box falls to an equal level. Air does not pile up, lie in masses of different density or behave in a lumpy way. Air will always fill the space allotted to it and fill it completely, regardless of its pressure and thus its density.

So far, our demonstration of the properties of air has been theoretical, using a proper box. Now we can actually see this interesting property of air at work if, instead of having a box with fixed sides, a top and a bottom, we make one side into a movable diaphragm, or, better still, hinge that side along one edge and make a flexible bellows type of wall between the edges of the side and the rest of the box. If we make a simple non-return valve, such as a leather flap on the inside to cover a small hole, and then blow air into that hole, the increased air pressure inside the box will push out the hinged side. If we now put our non-return valve on the outside of the hole, and suck air out of the box, the hinged side will collapse.

Air exists all around us at a constant pressure of about 14·75 lb/sq. inch. We are accustomed to this pressure and do not notice it. In the same way that deep-sea fish are accustomed to the tremendous water pressures at the bottom of the sea, and, when trawled to surface, expand and actually explode, the human body, to a lesser extent, suffers extreme discomfort if the air pressure around it is greatly varied. Airliners have to have pressurised cabins both to provide the crew and passengers with enough oxygen to breathe and also sufficient air so that the first symptoms of too low an air pressure – bleeding from the ears, nose and eyes – can be averted. Divers rapidly accustom themselves to the increased pressure on the sea-bed, but on returning to the surface have to be reacclimatised slowly to normal pressure. From this we can see not only the importance of air to us to enable us to live, but also that air exerts a pressure.

We can demonstrate another aspect of air with a further piece of schoolboy science. Air can be made to move a cork in a flask or tube. If we take a flask and place a loose-fitting cork in the neck and then draw air out of the flask, the cork will move down the neck of the flask. If we pump air into the flask, the cork will move upwards. It is this desire of air for equality in pressure that causes this to happen. As air is drawn out of our flask, the remaining air is continually expanding to fill the space, becoming rarefied as it does so. The air the other side of the loose-fitting cork, however, is still at 14·75 lb/sq. inch and this pressure pushes the cork down to try to equalise the pressure.

Another vital point appears here. If you place a vehicle with four smooth wheels on a smooth surface, a certain initial effort is needed to start it moving. This is required to overcome mechanical friction. One man can propel a large coal truck in the railway sidings by pushing it, yet it requires three or four men to set it going from a stationary position. If you put an object on a sloping surface, it does not immediately rush downwards, but stays put until the slope is increased beyond a certain point. These two examples illustrate the effect of friction and show that there is a time lag before circumstances change to restore equilibrium, and that additional power is needed to initiate the change from immobility to motion.

Air is by no means so affected by friction. The moment there is a pressure variation at one point, the entire mass of air rapidly sets about adjusting itself either to equal pressure, or to a suitable volume to suit the pressure. A mass of air, suitably contained, can be made to do a surprising amount of work, even when the pressure differential from the surrounding air is only a matter of plus or minus a few ounces per square inch.

It is thus not strictly true to say that a player piano works by vacuum, for were there to be a complete vacuum within the instrument the air pressure of the atmosphere would be so great as to implode the instrument, squeezing up all the tubes, compressing the air passages and chests, and achieving pressure equality in so doing. Of course, you could build a player mechanism so robustly that conditions of almost total vacuum might be achieved and utilised, but it is obviously unnecessary. The conditions whereby the mechanism can and will play are achieved by the development of a *partial* vacuum inside the instrument. The lower the air pressure inside (the greater the vacuum), the quicker will be the response of the instrument and the greater the power exerted by the pneumatic system on the hammers which strike the musical strings. Precise control of the processes of pressure reduction within the instrument is thus very important to make possible the artistic rendering of a piece of music.

We have seen that a high vacuum condition is not necessary to work a player piano. Under ordinary conditions, the instrument will operate perfectly with a pressure difference of eight ounces per square inch, which is equivalent to less than a 4 per cent vacuum. Thus only about one-thirtieth of the air inside the instrument must be withdrawn to set in motion the piano action and produce music of about middle strength. An audible sound can actually be achieved using a vacuum of only half this amount. The average player piano is constructed with an air pump capable of operating for short periods of time at a suction of up to two pounds per square inch. This is far in excess of the amount needed under normal circumstances.

Paradoxically, we speak of the 'pressure' of a vacuum when really we mean the 'suction' of a vacuum. The pressure referred to here is the amount of pressure which the surrounding atmosphere is induced to offer to the mechanism, by virtue of there existing inside it a reduced state of pressure relative to the atmosphere. Thus a working pressure of two pounds per square inch is the same as a vacuum which produces a rarefication of the air to two pounds per square inch below that of the normal atmosphere.

With a player piano, the quantity of air to be moved is comparatively large and does tend to vary over a wide range according to the parts of the piano action which have to be moved at any one time. A loud, full chord, for example, will require the shifting of more air than, say, a *pianissimo* passage for a few short notes. The air pump employed is thus a slow-moving low-pressure piece of apparatus. Its operation, in a piano controlled by the performer's feet, must not require excessive physical effort.

This air pump, commonly referred to as 'the bellows' but more properly termed 'the exhausters', consists, broadly, of a chamber having one wall arranged so that it can be moved inwards and outwards by a linkage from a foot-operated treadle. If the chamber is sealed, as the movable side is pulled outwards so the air inside the chamber is rarefied. The air in the chamber is thus at a lower pressure than the outside, free air, because it has been made to fill a larger area than the space it naturally filled at atmospheric pressure (Fig. 44). Supposing a pipe from the chamber is led to another, smaller bellows assembly, the air pressure difference in the inside of the chamber will also affect this second bellows. This represents the rudiments of the player action.

Hitherto, all we have done is to reduce the pressure in our chamber. But as the action of playing is to admit air, and since air seeps into the chamber however well we try to seal it, we have to devise a way of repeatedly taking air out of the chamber.

A method of flying, fervently believed in by the ancients, was that if you jumped, and then jumped again when you reached the highest point of that jump, you could just keep on going up and up, jumping and jumping. They failed to realise that the action of jumping demanded a reaction to the force – something solid to apply the work of jumping to. You could jump up a flight of steps one at a time, but where there were no steps you could not keep jumping

HOW THE PNEUMATIC PLAYER PIANO WORKS

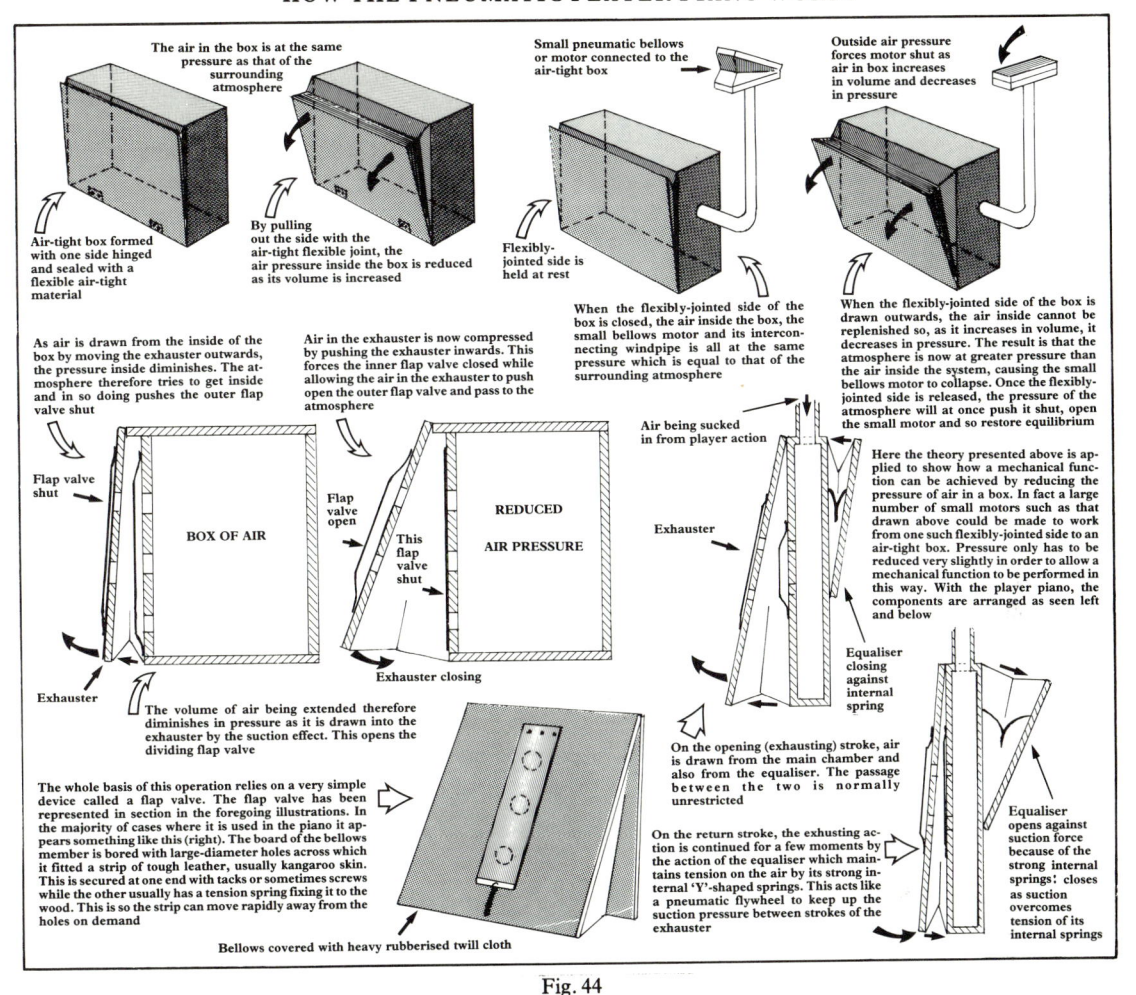

Fig. 44
Principles of pneumatic control and operation.

upwards. Now the player piano poses a problem of similar type. Using the exhausting bellows, we have drawn one lot of air out of the chamber, but we have to keep on doing it. If we just move the movable side in and out all we are doing is alternately stretching and compressing a unit mass of air and doing a lot of work to get nowhere. There has to be a means of taking a bite out of the air and being able to go back for more without replacing the first bite.

One way of making this work is to separate the movable side from the chamber by another compartment. What we will have in effect is a box to which is connected an extra side fixed over an existing side with a flexible diaphragm or bellows. We can now draw air out of the main chamber, through a hole in the proper side, into the chamber created by moving the extra, hinged side away from the box. But still we must solve the problem of the need to take continual sucks without simply pushing the same amount of air in and out.

The answer is the flap valve, surely the simplest and most efficient air valve one could wish for and as useful today as it was when first used two thousand and more years ago – its use was described by the Banu Musa in the seventh century AD – as well as by the earliest of the medieval organ builders as a key component in their bellows. This valve is purely a strip of leather secured at one end over a portion of our movable side which has several holes in it. When the side is pulled outwards, the pressure of air lifts the leather clear of the holes and allows the air to pass through. However, when the side moves the other way, the air pressure now acts upon the other side of the leather strip, pressing it firmly against the holes and so seals them. Fig. 44 shows this and as this is an important fundamental of the pneumatic operation of a piano you must understand how it operates before proceeding further. Air pressing on to one side of a movable seal will move that seal to close an opening against atmospheric pressure; air at atmospheric pressure will close the same opening when there is air at a lower pressure on the other side of the seal. The seal can be a leather flap as we have seen here, or it can be a piston, diaphragm, bellows or pouch which the air can move.

We have now got as far as seeing that we can make a device whereby we can move a side of an airtight box in and out, systematically reducing the air pressure within by the use of a simple flap valve. We can work the movable side with a foot treadle. To make the operation easier, we can fit our main chamber with two movable sides, each quite separate from the other, so that they will work alternately as the piano operator presses first with one foot and then with the other upon the foot treadles. So far so good, but still our pressure-reducing mechanism is short of something. As we pedal, there is a brief moment in each cycle when one of the two movable walls – exhausters as they are called – is at one extreme limit of its position, and the other exhauster is at the other extreme. Under these conditions, the vacuum created inside the chamber will suddenly decrease momentarily. Although this variation is only very brief, it will be quite sufficient to affect the playing performance of the piano. If, for example, this momentary change-over coincided with a rapid passage of music, we would probably lose one or two notes, the music would suddenly change from normal to soft and then back again, and the speed of the music roll, itself driven by an air motor as we shall see later on, might fluctuate.

All these snags are overcome by the provision of a reserve power of suction – a vacuum accumulator. This is another movable wall to the main chamber, only this one is usually on the side opposite the exhausters and it is also larger. When it is at rest, it is normally held wide open by internal springs. Now, as we treadle, air is drawn out of the main compartment still, but the difference in pressure causes the atmosphere to press on the large movable wall and push it in against its internal springs. This makes an air buffer to cater for the moments of lost motion in treadling since it gives an extra quantity of vacuum pressure aided by the internal springs. In operation, assuming there to be no function of the instrument working, as one treadles so the large movable wall begins to close up against the main compartment until finally it is almost completely closed. If we then stop treadling, the large movable wall will gradually open outwards until it comes to rest at its widest open position. During all the time it is opening, a working degree of vacuum is being maintained within the compartment. The duty of this portion of the system is to equalise the suction pressure which would otherwise fluctuate with each stroke of the exhausters. For this reason, the portion is called the 'equaliser'.

The equaliser is thus a stand-by exhauster which comes into operation when, for the reasons already explained, the foot-operated exhausters are momentarily inoperative. The steadier and more regular the operation of the exhausters, the less work there is for the equaliser to do.

Our bellows system, therefore, comprises a central, main vacuum chamber from which vacuum power can be taken to the playing mechanism, two foot-operated exhausters and the equaliser.

Under certain conditions of playing, it is possible to build up an excess of suction power in the bellows system. If we treadle at a steady rate through a roll of music which contains a pause or a soft passage comprising only a few notes, then we might build up so much suction in the exhausters and equalisers that actual damage could result. This is taken care of by the provision of a spill valve – a device to let in air from the atmosphere when the partial vacuum begins to assume excess proportions. The valve is mechanical and is often just a small flap valve somewhere in the system so that, as the equaliser opens to its extreme, a linkage draws back a simple hinged pallet.

The loads imposed on the bellows system during playing are quite considerable. For this reason, the various components of the system are robustly built in hardwood, whilst the equaliser and exhauster panels are made of thick plywood. At a maximum playing pressure of 1½ lb/sq. inch, an exhauster having a surface area of 300 square inches must resist atmospheric pressure equal to a weight of 450 lb, which must be moved by the action of pumping the foot treadles. Whilst constructionally this is a considerable load to resist, the player performer may be truly thankful for the fact that, as already explained, the air in this connection offers but infinitesimal resistance due to friction, and thus his task is readily accomplished.

It is common for the exhausters to be assisted from the open to the closed position by springs. These are V- or gull-shaped and serve to prepare the exhausters for another stroke as quickly as possible. The pressures of these springs vary from 12 to 20 lb. The flexible portions of the bellows are formed in a heavy rubberised twill or duck cloth which is impervious to air.

Player pianos, although working generally to the same system, are all different in detail construction and the first thing which becomes apparent is the wide variations between the proportions of the bellows components. Exhausters and equalisers vary in area and W. B. White has made an interesting study of the reasons why these components do differ so greatly.

The equaliser serves as a pneumatic flywheel to the pneumatic system, supplementing the interrupted action of the to-and-fro cycle with a reservoir of power. This is very much like the flywheel of an engine, where the mass of a solid flywheel is used to take the crankshaft over the top and bottom dead centre positions. The heavier the flywheel on the engine, the smoother will be its running characteristics. But at the same time it will be slow to accelerate (develop power) and also its power output will be diminished by virtue of the amount of power being absorbed in the task of driving a large mass of flywheel.

This same state of affairs can be translated into the interpretation of the duties of the equaliser. Some makers believed that the easier it was for a completely unskilled, insensitive person to play their instrument, the better it was. Others thought it preferable for the player to feel the fluctuations of air pressure beneath his feet. The first approach could easily be satisfied by making the equaliser of large proportions. The second line of thought demanded that the equaliser be small. The same effect could be achieved, of course, by varying the size of the exhausters as well. As it is, the more sensitive a piano is, within certain limitations, the better the instrument is for the serious music lover. Ernest Newman described these variations from the point of view of the listener, and Grew exhorted his pupils to keep one foot always prepared for use to produce a *fortissimo* passage or to accentuate one note – an almost impossible task with a piano having a large equaliser.

Since the equaliser is such a bone of contention, could it not have been dispensed with? The answer is, unfortunately, no, for, no matter how astute the performer, he would be unable to maintain conditions of anything like constant vacuum pressure with his treadles, and his music roll speed would fluctuate considerably. Interestingly enough, this direct-action pedalling was put to good use in the so-called expression stop of the harmonium, and it was also used by both Grenie and Winkel, among others, on pipe organs to vary the timbre of the pipe sound. For the piano, though, it has to be anathema.

Having understood the method of driving air out of a chamber to create a partial vacuum, and accepting that the act of playing a piano by a pneumatic system admits atmospheric air into the partial vacuum (hence the need for continual effort to maintain that partial vacuum), we can turn our attention to how the bellows system already described is made to control musical sounds.

We have, in effect, two pressures of air to play with – one is that of the atmosphere around us and the piano, and the other is a lower pressure which we have created inside the

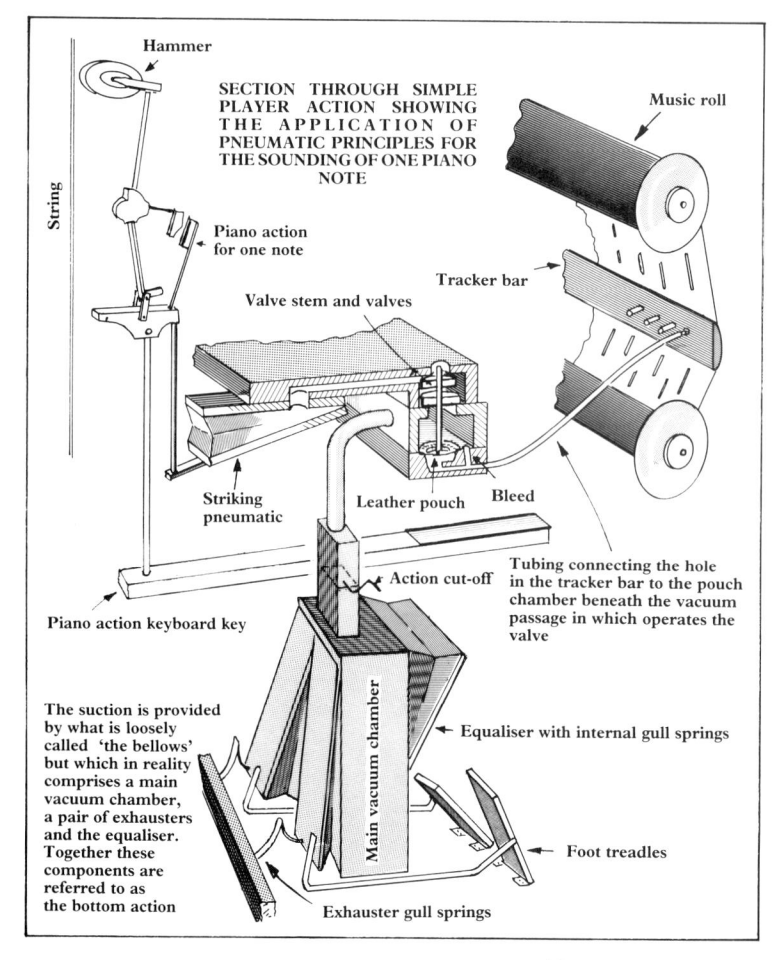

Fig. 45
Section through basic player piano action showing a single-valve pneumatic system.

HOW THE PNEUMATIC PLAYER PIANO WORKS

instrument by using the treadles. It is the difference between these two which is continually applied in various ways to make music.

The piano has 88 notes. As I have already related, in the early days of the player only some of these were played from the music roll but, after 1912, makers standardised on 65-note and full-scale or 88-note rolls. It does not matter which of these we consider – the mechanism is largely the same. Now to play 88 notes we have 88 separate little hammer mechanisms of the piano to be set in correct motion, each one just like the one shown in cross-section in Fig. 45. We have the power to control these since we have an air-pressure-reducing device. What has to be done is to convert one chamber containing air at reduced pressure into a mechanical system which will move those 88 or so mechanisms individually or severally as we ordain to conform to the pattern of the openings in the music roll which correspond to a musical composition. In simple terms, any hole in the paper roll has to result in the sounding of one note of the piano.

This is achieved by using two components. First of all is the valve chest and pneumatic stack. Secondly there is a facility for the provision of a sliding valve to control each of the 88 valves and pneumatics in the stack. The valve chest and the pneumatic stack have a physical connection to the piano-sounding mechanisms (the hammers). The sliding valve device has a terminal block (the tracker bar) at which end all the control pipes for the valves. The sliding valve itself is the music roll.

There are two types of valve chest. First is the simple single-valve system and the second is the double valve consisting of primary and secondary (sometimes called servo and principle) valves. The illustration (Fig. 46) shows a section through a simple, single-valve system. This consists of a pouch in a base-board above which is a suction chamber. Resting lightly on the leather pouch is a stem carrying on it a circular disc which forms a seal on the outside of the suction chamber. By lifting the valve, such as will happen if the pouch is inflated, the suction in the chamber is permitted access to the air contained in an airway above the valve which connects to a pneumatic motor. The air at atmospheric pressure is therefore drawn out of the pneumatic motor causing it to collapse. By connecting the moving part of this pneumatic to

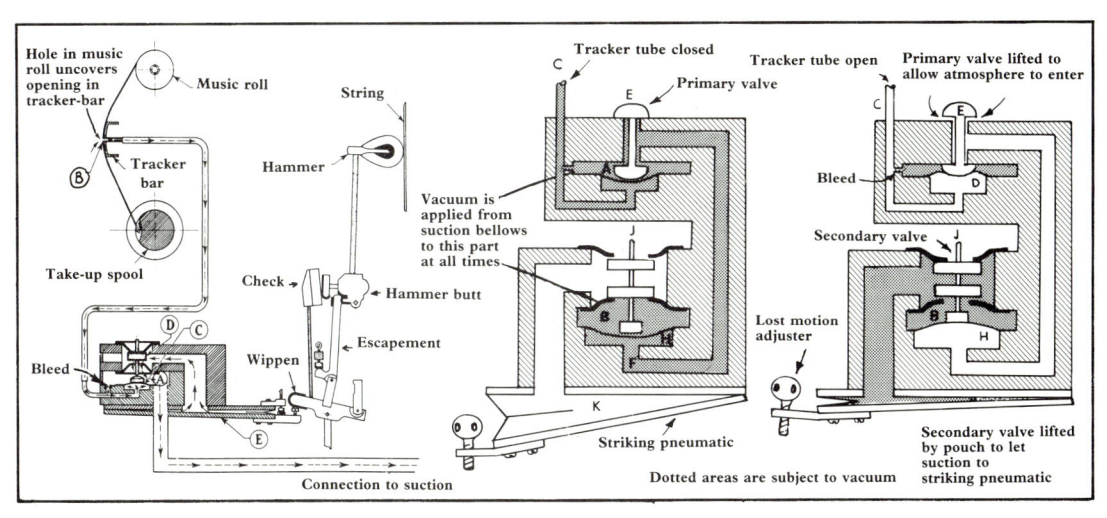

Fig. 46
Two-valve action and Aeolian single-valve action.

135

the wippen of the piano action, using a push-rod or a wire pull-link, a note can be struck. The method of controlling the movement of the valve via the pouch is the perforation in the paper music roll. The pouch covers a chamber in the pouch board, which is connected by a thin tube to the tracker bar. This chamber is connected to the vacuum chamber by a tiny open passage called a bleed hole. This at first seems to nullify the whole purpose of having separate chambers and an inflatable pouch. But let us detail precisely what happens and how the assembly functions.

Because this is an important feature of the player mechanism – the principle of the valve chest and pneumatic motor – I would advise the reader to proceed no further with this chapter until he is absolutely conversant with the workings of the system illustrated in Figs 44, 45 and 46.

The valve stem carrying the valve disc is free to move up and down. It is lightly made and carries a button at its lower end, sitting just a fraction above the pouch, which is made of soft, pliable leather and is glued over the pouch chamber. The main part of the chest through which the valve passes is connected to the partial vacuum produced by the bellows system. The actual sealing disc of the valve is outside this main chamber and in a further compartment which is normally under atmospheric pressure. The valve seal is thus free to move between the aperture in the main chamber and the aperture connecting the upper compartment with the atmosphere.

Beneath the leather diaphragm called the pouch is a chamber which has an outlet to the music-roll tracker bar. This chamber, as already mentioned, is linked to the main vacuum supply by a small orifice – the bleed hole.

Above the main chamber, the further compartment is connected to a pneumatic motor which, by its own weight, remains in the extended or open position under normal conditions.

Now we will apply a suction to the main chest, as in normal use, and close off the orifice in the tracker bar, as by a non-perforated piece of the music roll. The valve closes the chamber at the top both by its own weight and also by the difference between atmospheric pressure and the suction of the vacuum pressure. The air beneath the leather pouch is also extracted, as is that in the tube to the tracker bar, through the bleed hole.

The moment a perforation in the music roll comes into line with the end of the tube at the tracker bar, the partial vacuum in the tube and in the chamber beneath the leather pouch is immediately replaced by air at atmospheric pressure. This at once inflates the pouch, pushing up the valve which now makes a seal between the upper compartment and the atmosphere. The suction from the main compartment is thus applied to the air in the pneumatic motor which, exhausted of air, rapidly collapses. This collapsing of the motor is translated into the operation of one of the piano actions, and thus the sounding of a note, by the use of a connection to the wippen.

Why isn't all this spoiled by the open connection between the two sides of the leather pouch – the bleed hole? This hole is too small to allow the pressures to equalise when faced with the amount of atmospheric pressure rushing in relative to the amount of suction in the main chamber. The quantity of air in movement is always greater than the capacity of the bleed hole because the hole in the tracker bar is larger than the bleed.

However, the moment the hole in the end of the tube at the tracker bar is once more sealed, as by the perforation in the music roll coming to an end, the bleed hole serves quickly to reduce the amount of atmospheric air trapped in the pouch chamber and tube. This reduction only has to be fractional before the atmospheric air pressing on the top of the valve sees a chance to equalise things, and pushes the valve and the pouch down. This seals the aperture in the top of the main chamber and reinflates the collapsed motor, returning the system to equilibrium once more.

This valve system is repeated for as many notes as there are to be played on the piano – 65 or, more usually, 88. The only common passage is the vacuum compartment beneath which are positioned the individual pouches, each with a separate connection to a different hole in the tracker bar, and above which are placed one valve and one pneumatic motor for each note.

The tracker bar serves as the control for the whole mechanism of producing music. Each tube ends in a small orifice in a brass bar over which the sliding or travelling valve of the music roll passes. On early instruments playing 65 notes and less, the bar was often made of wood, but with the advent of the full-scale 88-note action it was impossible to arrange the openings (nine to the inch) accurately or sufficiently airtight from each other, so metal was adopted. Each hole in the tracker bar connects with a pouch in the pouch board, the far left one being the extreme bass note of the piano and successively to the extreme treble at the far right. (Note that this relates to the number of notes played as, particularly with some of the reproducing pianos described later, the scale was not strictly 'full'.)

Because the strings of the piano and the hammers which strike them are fairly close together, it would be impossible to mount a workable action in one straight line, so it is common for the valves and pneumatics to be staggered. Pouches are arranged in staggered lines in the pouch board and pneumatics are arranged in two or three horizontal rows, vertically staggered.*

In the foregoing I have described the device whereby a partial vacuum is created as a wherewithal for playing, and the pneumatic valve system which is arranged to translate a perforated music roll into a musical performance. There are a number of other aspects to be detailed: the roll-driving mechanism, the controls for giving individual interpretation, the double-valve pneumatic system and the reasons for its use, the regulation of speed, the facility for rerolling a music roll after playing and the method of keeping the music roll in perfect alignment with the tracker-bar holes.

The foot-operated upright piano, certainly the most common amongst the breed of player pianos as well as being the cheapest application of the player principles, will serve as a good illustration of the application of the parts already detailed, and as a good vehicle for showing these further aspects to be described. The illustration Fig. 47 shows a side elevation of an ordinary upright player piano. It might be as well at this point to state that, generally speaking, player actions are placed transversely across the front of the instrument above the keyboard. On some players, the action is fitted beneath the key bed (see the cross-section of the Hupfeld piano, Fig. 48). With these, the player action moves the wippen by pushing up under the backs of the keys and, with this and similar actions, the keys are moved in the action of playing. However, piano keys are weighted to provide a balanced action for the manual pianist, and on some actions it is usual for the key to move under its own weight when the wippen is moved by the playing pneumatic. Other makers considered this an undesirable feature and arranged for all the keys to be locked when the player was in operation. Methods of locking the keys varied. On some this was achieved by means of a hinged flap at the front of

---

* In some high quality reproducing actions the pneumatics themselves are scaled, those at the bass end being of larger capacity.

PIANOLA

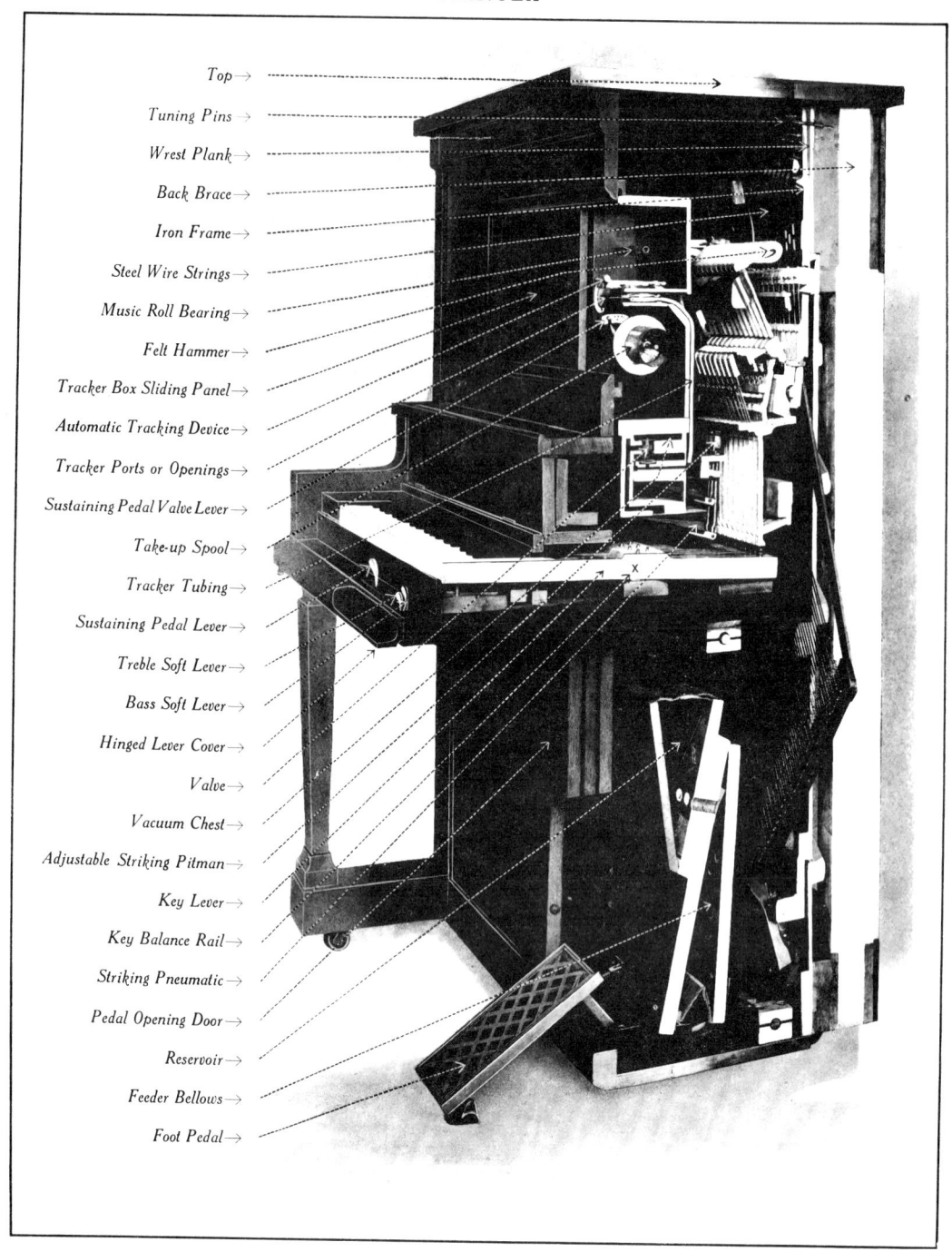

Fig. 47
From an Aeolian promotional catalogue of 1914 comes this sectional illustration showing the parts of an upright Pianola. Note that the exhausters are here termed 'feeder bellows' and the exhauster is called the 'reservoir'.

138

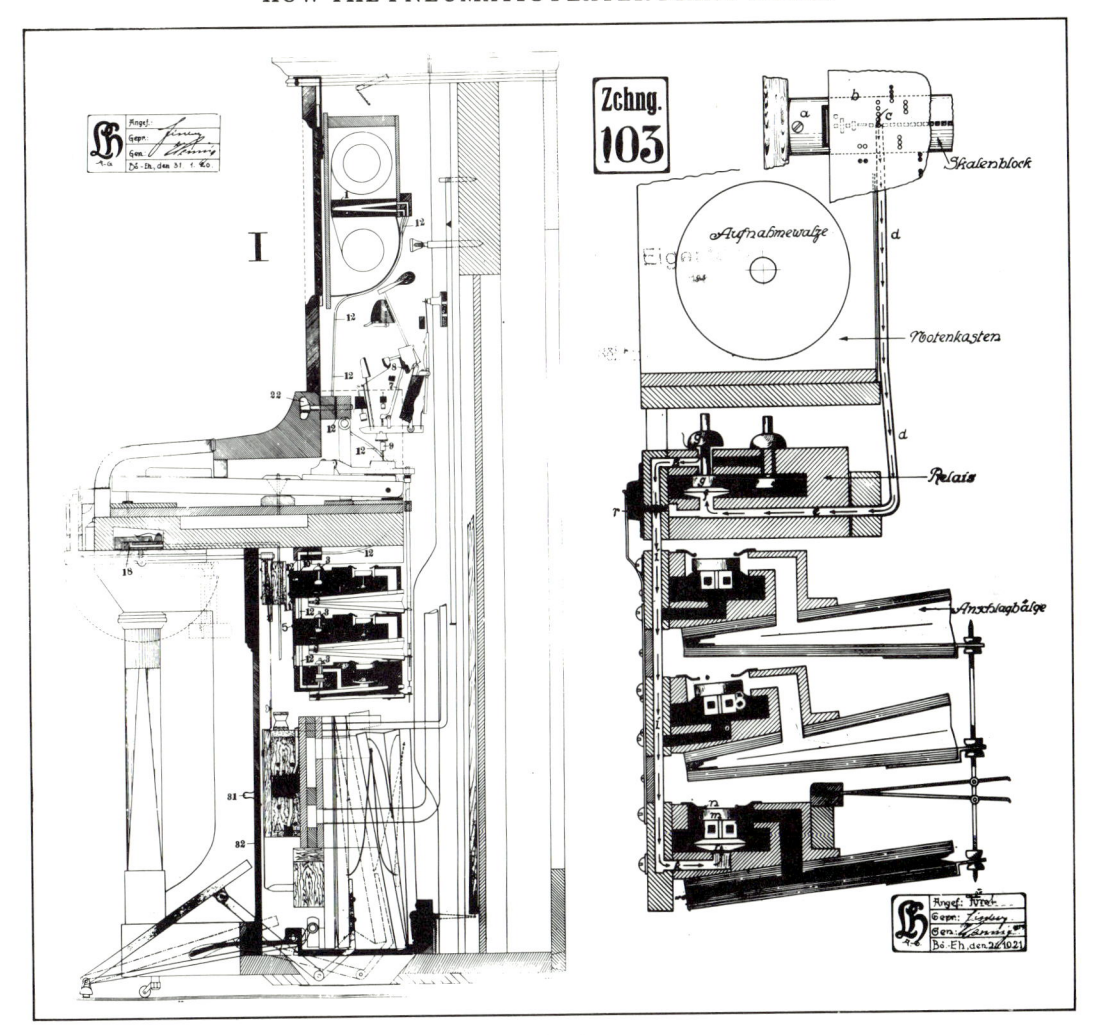

Fig. 48
Section through Hupfeld upright player piano showing double valve chest mounted under the keyboard.

the key bed, which was moved down to uncover the manual expression controls for the player. With the flap open, the keys were locked and the piano could not be played upon by hand. Others such as Aeolian fitted a locking rail in the key bed which was worked by a hand lever under the keyboard.

The bellows system on the treadle piano is always sited beneath the key bed, this being an obviously convenient position. Connections from the tracker bar, which is most commonly situated at a convenient level in the front fall of the piano case so that the music can be watched, are made to the pouch board by rubber tubing or, in the case of better-made models, by lead tubing. It might be worth mentioning here that, whilst a lead-tubed player piano will probably never need to be re-tubed,* it is so alarmingly heavy as to pose a serious disadvantage to the collector.

* Lead tube often oxidises, though. All lead tubing should be replaced by rubber on rebuilding the instrument.

PIANOLA

The connection between the bellows system and the upper or player action is by large-diameter flexible cotton-reinforced rubber hosing.

We have seen that the production of musical sounds is controlled by a perforated paper roll. This paper roll comes wound on to a spool having suitable ends, which engage with a free-turning centre at one end, and a chuck drive at the other, both of these being fixtures of the spool box on the piano. The central feature of the spool box is the tracker bar, whose function we now understand. The roll travels from the top of the box downwards to the take-up spool, which is fixed permanently in the box. (On some instruments the roll travels from bottom to top but the principle is just the same). The end of the music paper has a loop on it to engage with a hook on the take-up spool. When the roll of paper has transferred from the music spool to the take-up spool, to the extent that the music perforations have come to an end, the paper must be rewound on to the music spool. The end of the paper remains stuck firmly to the music spool, so all that has to be done is to disengage the drive to the take-up spool and move a suitable mechanical linkage, so that the music spool is now driven through the provision of the chuck holding one end.

This is nearly always achieved by mechanical means, such as the moving of a free-turning sprocket wheel on a shaft so that it engages with a dog clutch. The spool mechanism is driven by an air motor. This is, in effect, an inlet to the partial vacuum of the bellows system. As the air at atmospheric pressure rushes into the vacuum chamber, it is made to produce rotary

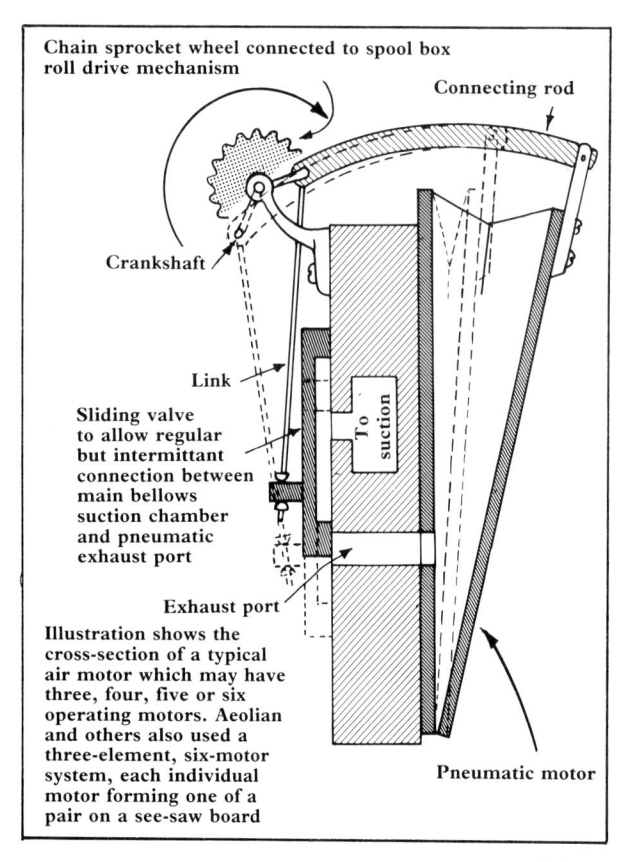

Fig. 49
Section through a typical music roll drive wind motor.

motion which is applied to the spool-box mechanism through chainwheels and sprockets. The air motor is an ingenious piece of mechanism which fulfils its functional requirement under extreme variations of pressure. It is, for example, required to maintain a constant speed from the very gentlest suction up to the maximum suction created for a *forte* passage of music. It must produce a constant amount of power to keep the music roll moving across the tracker bar, against the suction created between tracker bar and paper by the playing mechanism. Above all, the performer must be able to control it to give instantaneous changes of tempo and smooth *accelerando* and *ritardando*, even to the degree of stopping momentarily and instantly restarting at a predetermined speed.

I have already explained how the use of an air pressure differential can cause a simple pneumatic motor to open and close. The music-roll drive works on just this principle and features a number of pneumatics which alternately open and close in sequence. Their motion drives a crankshaft and the cycle of each pneumatic is reversed automatically by a sliding valve, one for each pneumatic. In this manner, the rotary motion imparted to the crankshaft is constant, smooth and continuous.

Figure 49 shows a cross-section of one pneumatic of the motor and from this can be seen the chamber through which atmospheric air is sucked, and the way this is affected by the sliding valve. To ensure perfectly smooth operation, the air motor works in exactly the same way as a car engine except that in place of cylinders the air motor uses pneumatics and for fuel it uses the atmosphere in conflict with the reduced pressure within the system. As with a car where a number of cylinders is used to give smooth motion, the air motor has a number of pneumatics – never less than three, usually four and occasionally five or six.

An important feature of the air motor is this ability to regulate speed within very precise limits. An easy way to achieve this is to throttle the motor, as one throttles the internal-combustion engine, to regulate the amount of air passing though it. If we allow the motor to draw the maximum amount of atmospheric air into the bellows system, then it will move quickly. By reducing the amount of air, we can slow down its performance and adjust the tempo of the music being played from the music roll. This is done by a sliding port linking the suction side of the motor to the suction of the bellows; the port is, in effect, wedge-shaped so that, at one extreme of its movement, it presents the maximum-sized opening, whilst at the other it shows a much smaller hole. Control of this sliding port is by a lever or knob, which also operates a pointer along a scale near the music roll so that the player operator can immediately follow any speed direction printed on the music.

The sliding port also has another feature and this is associated with the reroll mechanism. At the end of a piece of music (or at any other time to suit the will of the player operator), the drive to the take-up spool in the roll box can be disengaged and the music-spool drive engaged, so applying the motor power to rerolling the music. Because the music could still actually play regardless of the direction in which the roll travels, the principal airway between bellows and valve chest is cut off during reroll, so that there is no suction power in the valve chest. To speed up rerolling, the sliding port also has a very large orifice which immediately applies full power to the motor, and this is only brought into operation during the reroll procedure. The air motor always rotates in one direction – the apparent change of direction of drive is achieved by the mechanical gearing. Thus the movement of the reroll control lever (a) shuts off the suction power to the valve chest and pneumatic stack, and (b) opens a very large port between motor and bellows so that reroll can be accomplished in the quickest possible time, and (c) alters the drive to the roll box, through gearing.

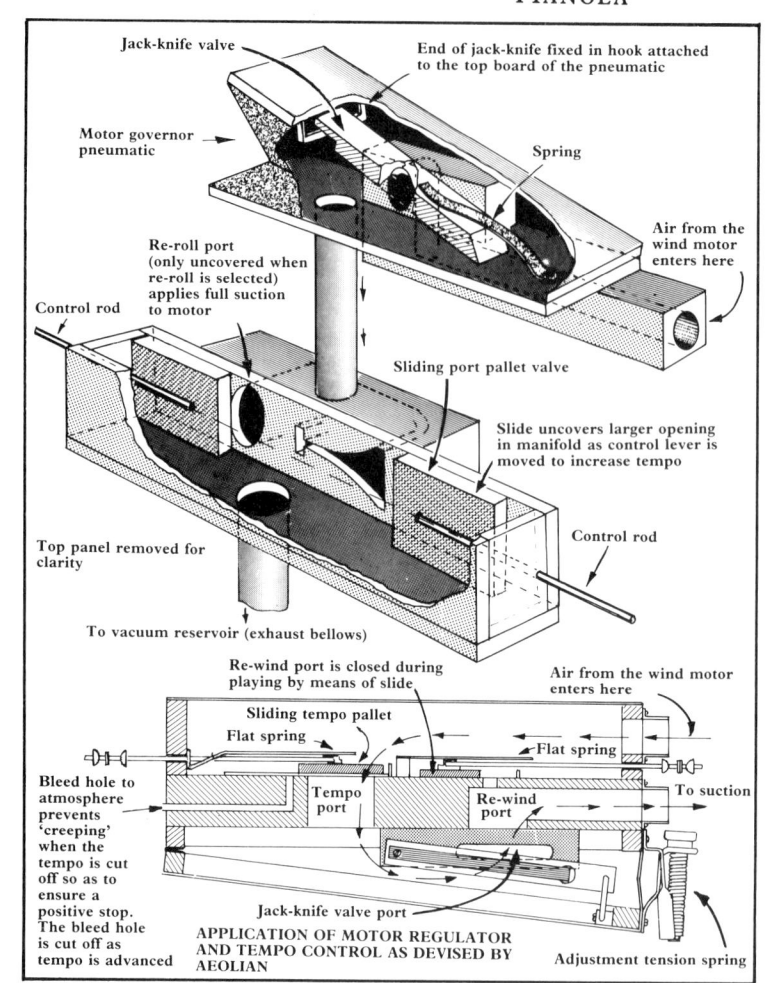

Fig. 50
The tempo governor or regulator.

Now this system of regulating the motor speed would be quite perfect were it not for the fact that, as we have already shown, the amount of suction, and thus the amount of potential power for the motor, is varying continually during playing. So varied is the suction pressure available that were the suction power of the bellows to be connected directly to the roll motor the music-roll drive would fluctuate continuously. Even by the expedient of the equaliser, it is not possible to guarantee the speed of the air motor within the precise limits needed without some other means being brought to bear; for whilst the equaliser 'irons out the bumps' in playing it cannot cope with quantitative differences such as that between soft treadling and hard treadling. This additional refinement is accomplished by the use of a special pneumatic bellows or motor fitted between the motor suction and the bellows, so that the air sucked in through the air motor passes through the pneumatic on its way to the bellows. Its course through the pneumatic, however, is subject to the control of a knife valve. This is a secondary throttling device, only the operation of this one is quite automatic. Whilst the operator of the player can control the general amount of air regulating the overall speed of the motor, the rapid pressure fluctuations are smoothed out by this self-acting valve which is called the tempo governor. Its principle of operation is quite easy to follow and the illustration Fig. 50 shows the components. The pneumatic motor is normally held open by a spring. The air connection into the pneumatic is through a block in one side, across which is arranged a moving pallet valve pivoted on the bottom board of the pneumatic and connected to the top board. This is called a knife valve and we will find it occurring again in other applications, particularly with the reproducing piano described later. When the performer begins to treadle, the amount of suction produced will normally be balanced by the spring force holding the tempo governor open. Supposing now the performer wishes to provide more power to his performance, such as might be required to accentuate a passage, he treadles harder and creates a suction greater than that which the tempo governor spring can resist. The governor closes a little, in so doing allowing the knife to cover part of the inlet hole.

The effect is to allow an increase in the suction force acting on the air motor (which in turn must draw more air from the atmosphere), but to restrict this taking of more air from the atmosphere by reducing the aperture through which it must pass to the bellows. The air motor thus continues to run at a constant speed governed by the overruling control offered by the ordinary tempo control.

It will be appreciated that the setting of this valve is extremely important and indeed, although the pneumatic should always be in a state of partial collapse during playing, it may well be that, for normal setting, the knife valve may be called upon to cover part of the hole so that the player performer can achieve musical effects on both sides of this arbitrary half-way mark.

The paper must 'track' properly as it is drawn over the tracker bar, its holes aligning with the holes in the tracker bar. If the paper is not aligned the right way, the note holes may either miss the tracker-bar openings altogether or partially allow two adjacent holes to open. In either case the effect on the music will be disastrous to the ear. The principles of governing tracking are quite simple. To keep the paper passing across the tracker in the proper position, either you must have a means for moving both music spool and take-up spool from side to side, or you must make provision for the tracker bar itself to move. The amount of lateral shift will be small and should be prompt in operation, without any tendency towards overcorrection. Both the systems hinted at have been successfully applied in player-piano construction although it is more usual to move the spools. Operation is very simple. Two pneumatic motors are used, normally made back to back with one central fixed board and two hinged sides. The tracker bar is provided with an extra opening at each end, larger than the note holes and square in shape. The connection from one side of the tracker runs to one side of the double motor, and that from the opposite end of the tracker to the other. Normally the music roll partially covers the holes. If the roll is warped, unfortunately an all too frequent occurrence, then one of the holes becomes covered, fully opening the other. Previously, the air pressure exerted on each side of the motor was equal, but now it is set off balance and so the motor begins to move. A linkage attached to the moving board of the motor moves the paper spools over until the closed tracking hole is once more opened, restoring the air balance to the motor and bringing it to rest.

To achieve smooth operation, without overcorrection, the airways and openings in the motor are comparatively small so that the air shift is slow. This is important for another reason. Quite often the edge of a roll may become slightly split or damaged. Were the action

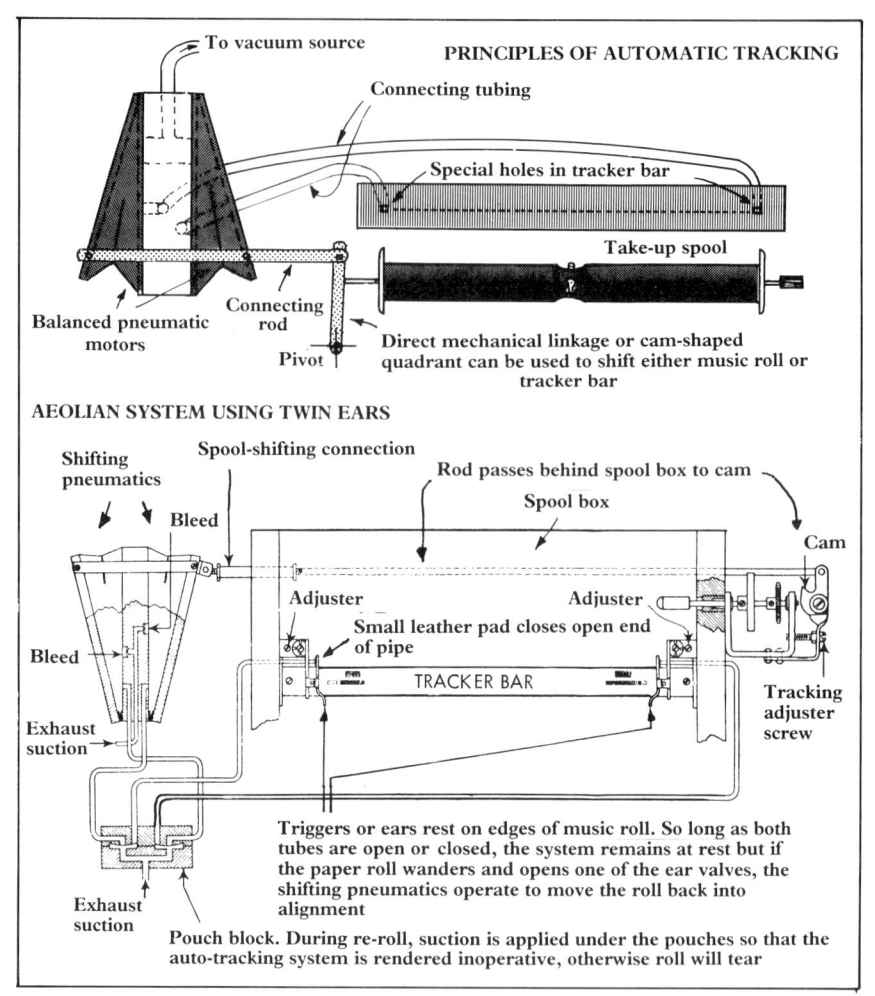

Fig. 51
Principles of automatic roll tracking.

of the automatic tracking to be very prompt, each of these splits would at once cause the music roll to be shifted willy-nilly. Naturally, where the edge of the roll is badly damaged or has been folded over (a feature known to one member of the Player Piano Group as 'the Aeolian pleat'), then the principles of automatic tracking are disrupted and the roll may not play properly at all.

There are at least three common types of automatic tracking device, but all work on this same principle of balanced pressures controlled by the edges of the paper roll passing between certain defined limits. An early Aeolian system used a single metal feeler which rubbed against (and susbsequently wore away!) the left edge of the roll. Any deviation moved the feeler and opened (or closed) an airway. The earlier modes of the Aeolian Duo-Art used two small feelers which gently touched the edge of the roll during playing. If the roll moved, the feeler would also move but, in so doing, a small pallet at its other end would shut off an atmosphere vent, upsetting the balance of pressures in the double-acting motor. Another system employed small fences at the edge of the music. The roll passed between these two delicately adjusted sprung strips and again any tendency for the paper to wander was converted into adjustment of the roll.

Where the tracker bar is itself moved, it is made to slide by the selfsame type of mechanism. Whichever system is used, automatic tracking calls for movement of not more that $3/32$ in. each side of the mean position and usually far less than this.

Automatic tracking must not be confused with *transposition*, where the whole roll is allowed to be played in a different key by realigning it with other holes in the tracker bar. This *en bloc* adjustment is nothing to do with tracking and is usually achieved by moving the tracker bar so that accompaniment for singing can be arranged in a convenient key. It is controlled mechanically by a knob or lever on or in the roll box.

The features we have now examined are all associated one with the other and are thus best considered under one grouping. Starting with the air motor we have (a) the tempo control, governing the speed of the music; (b) the tempo regulator, applying automatic speed conformity to the tempo selected by the tempo control; (c) the system used for rerolling the music; (d) the device for maintaining the proper tracking of the roll; and (e) the transposing control, whereby the key of the music may be changed at will.

Let us now examine how the player performer can play his roll of music with expression and put into it his own shades of colour, accentuation, *forte* and *piano*. To be able to do this, he must have control over those expressive devices which are normally to be found fitted to a piano – the two pedals controlling the position of the hammer rest rail and the dampers. He is prevented from using his feet for these as would a manual pianist, because his feet are treadling to provide the suction power to drive the mechanism. The control has therefore to be left entirely to his hands, buttons or levers. These controls have to be placed within comfortable reach of the player operator and thus it is common practice for them to be mounted in a hinged portion of the forward rail of the key bed. In the majority of player pianos, the controls are found mounted in the control rail. These are exposed by hinging down part of (or all of) the key-bed front rail.

Returning to the fourth paragraph of this chapter, we considered that the pianist playing manually has two hands and can thus vary the force with which he applies the hammers to the strings from one hand to the other. The action of the soft pedal is to move the hammers closer to the strings so that, not having so far to travel before striking the strings, the sound produced is less loud than with the pedal in the normal position. However, the pianist can achieve a combination of tonal effects largely independent of the pedal control by varying the force with which he strikes individual keys or groups of keys on the keyboard. In this way, he can achieve a distinction between a soft accompaniment and an accented melody.

The soft pedal controls the position of the rest rail position relative to the strings and the mechanical operation of this is easily achieved by pneumatic means. However, to make possible the distinction between melody and accompaniment, it is better resolved by dividing the rest rail into two portions, each being free to move independent of the other and each having a separate control. Now this control can be mechanical, by a lever connection, or, more usually, by the employment of a pneumatic motor. One method of pneumatic control is to provide a button on the control rail which controls a small pallet. The pneumatic which controls the rest rail works on exactly the same principle as the motor which is used to move the piano action at each string in normal playing. The difference is that the operating valve, instead of being a travelling one made of paper (the roll) admitting suction to the pedal pneumatic, is a pallet covering the end of the tube open to atmosphere. When the pallet is opened, atmospheric air rushes in, the motor contracts, and the rail is moved.

While the shifting of the rest rail is a feature sometimes found in the upright and occasionally the grand piano, the same effect is obtainable by varying the amount of suction in each half of the pneumatic chest through a 'power governor'. The chest is thus divided more or less in half, the suction level at the bass end being controllable by either a lever or a button, and the treble similarly under the control of variable suction. This is found on all players and occasionally it is found in conjunction with the overall softening which is achieved through rest-rail movement – the soft pedal. The importance of the power governor will become more apparent in a moment.

The soft pedal effect is achieved on some grand pianos (and is reserved almost exclusively for reproducing models) by the shifting sideways of the entire keyboard by a small amount (see Chapter 7). This shift moves the keyboard and the complete hammer action so that the hammers instead of striking the full trichord (three strings of each note) only strike two, so producing a softer sound. This system, operated on a manual piano by a heavy linkage from the foot pedal, can be artificially produced by the use of a large keyboard shift pneumatic, often fitted with twin valves to speed its operation.

The other control which the player piano has to have is a means of operating the dampers. This is the sustaining pedal action and, because all the dampers are moved together throughout the range of notes operated, and because they require considerably more force to move than the rest rail, the operating pneumatic motor is larger than that for the rest rail. Furthermore, since the performance of the music calls for prompt operation of the dampers, it is fairly common for the pneumatic to be governed by two valves. Do not confuse this with the double-valve pneumatic system which I shall describe further on. This is still a single-valve system, but the valve is duplicated in the same chamber so as to provide a more positive and rapid suction connection to the motor. Again, the atmosphere end of the control tube can be closed off by a small pallet valve operated by a button on the control rail. This is shown in Fig. 52.

At this point, you will observe that both the functions of the pedal action of a normal piano can be controlled by pneumatic means and that the method of control is exactly the same as that used to play the piano mechanically. Each pedal-action pneumatic has the same type of control tube leading to atmosphere and governed by a valve, as are the pneumatics in the pneumatic stack. Thus, if we take the ends of the control tubes from their valve pouch chambers to the tracker bar instead of to the control rail, we can operate these functions by punching additional perforations in the music roll instead of having to rely on the player operator to move levers or press the right buttons at the right moment.

Having found a way of doing these things automatically from the music roll, we find that most player pianos have a device – usually a small lever in the roll box – which disengages these features and brings back into operation the buttons and levers on the control rail. This is usually marked 'Pedal On' and 'Pedal Off'.

So far we have dealt with the overall replacement of the pedal action by pneumatic means. The adroit pianist will have detected one major shortcoming – the ability to change very rapidly the playing intensity, perhaps only for one note or a chord. Even the best player performer, operating his foot treadles with the utmost subtlety and understanding, could not achieve this and thus the player piano might soldier on, resigned to being nothing but an obviously mechanical interpreter of music. Happily this is not the case, thanks to the power

HOW THE PNEUMATIC PLAYER PIANO WORKS

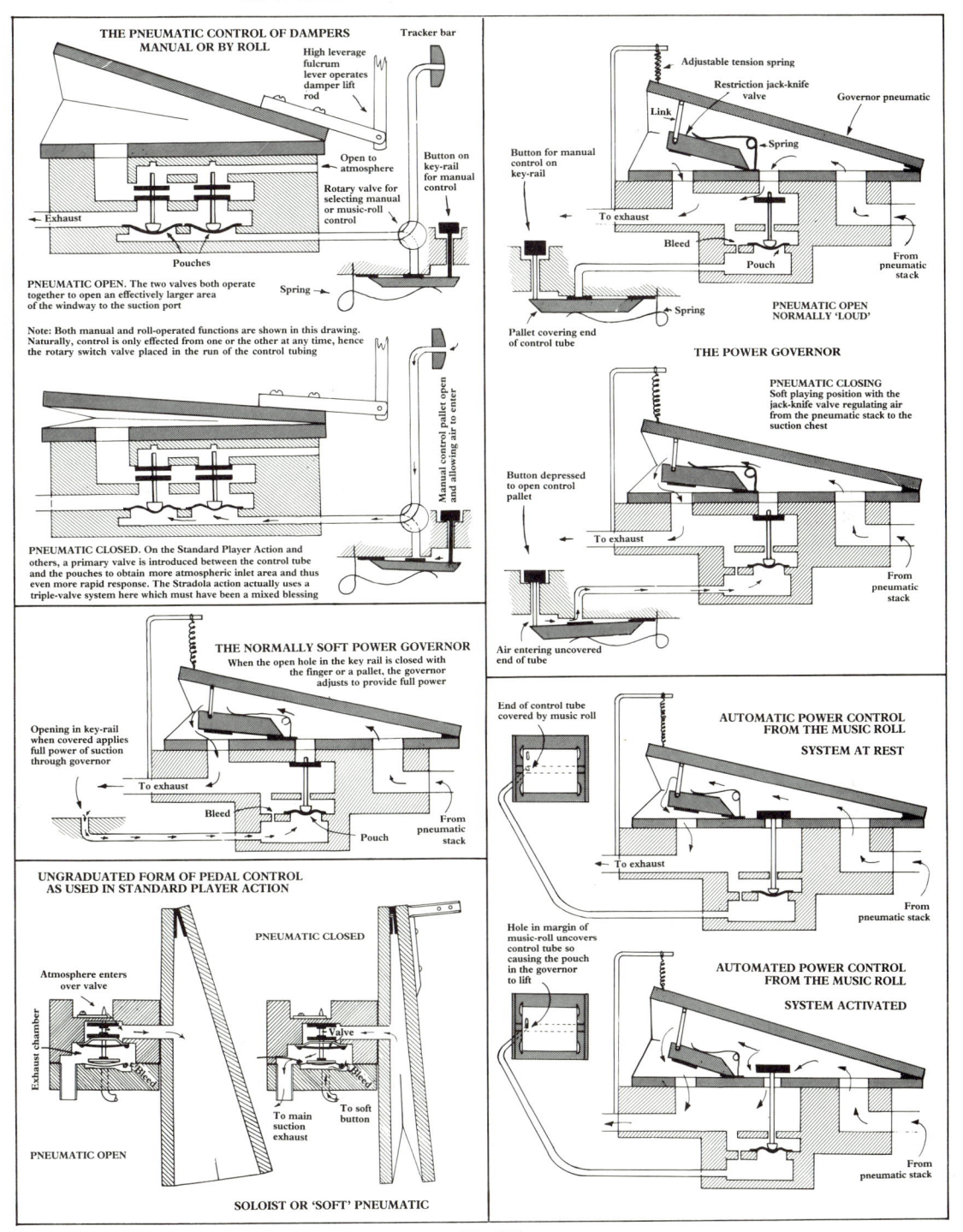

Fig. 52
Methods of controlling piano functions by pneumatic means.

governor. This really holds its own on grand player pianos. In the grand action there is usually no rest rail and thus it is not possible to move the hammers backwards and forwards relative to the strings. In fact, as noted above, the soft pedal action on the better-class grand shifts the whole action sideways.

Let's just see how the power governor is made, but first let me emphasise that this component, in various forms, can be found on virtually all players, even though the details of construction and even function may differ. The parts of the power governor are the single-valve suction system controlled by a pouch operated by a control pipe ending with a valve (either pallet at the control rail or hole in the tracker bar). All these features we have already dealt with. Inside the pneumatic motor we find two openings. The first is above the valve controlled by the pouch, and is so arranged that when the valve lifts it seals off this port altogether. The second opening is smaller than the first and can be restricted by a pallet valve, hinged to the base of the motor and connected with a link to the top in such a way that, as the motor collapses, so the pallet gradually closes up the port. The motor is held in the 'normally open' position by a tension spring which can be adjusted.

In operation, the air from the atmosphere must pass through the large port (under which is the rising valve) on its way to the bellows. Both this port and the valve are of such a size that, even though the pneumatic is in a state of partial collapse against the spring tension, there will be no reduction in the area of opening. So long as the control button is not touched, the system will be doing nothing by way of regulation.

If the button is depressed on the control rail, it will immediately cause the valve to rise and seal off the large port. The air must now pass through the smaller port, which is controlled by the pallet valve. As the pneumatic collapses, so this pallet valve will reduce the size of the port and thus the amount of air which passes through this metered opening is always constant. Remember the tempo governor for the air motor. This is a similar piece of equipment. The operation of the pneumatic is controlled by the tension of the spring, which offers a resistance to the suction from the bellows. The stronger the spring, the greater the resistance offered and the less it collapses under any given condition of suction in the bellows system. From this we can see that the reduction of playing power can be regulated by the adjustment of the spring. The 'steady state' of the automatic governor can be upset at any time by the depressing of the button, permitting instantaneous changes from governed to ungoverned pressure and thus from *piano* to *forte* playing.

So prompt in action is this device that one note or chord in a group can be accented and the dominant note in a bar brought out by its use. The power governor, an important part of the grand action, is fitted to almost all actions and serves to provide this overriding expression control. Its principle is also the key to 'Themodist' accenting, the development of which is related in Chapter 6.

The principle of the power governor is such that, so long as the control button is depressed, the action can be controlled to play relatively softly. When the button is released, the effect is to provide a *forte* crash instantaneously, assuming all other aspects of control and the amount of suction in the bellows system to be adequate. However, it is far easier if, instead of holding down a button for normal playing and releasing it for accented notes, the control is the other way round, the mechanism playing relatively softly at all times, but accents being effected by depressing the button or covering the open end of a normally open nipple (Fig. 52). This is easily accomplished and indeed is the most common principle in use. The playing is at all times relatively soft, no matter how much effort is put into the bellows

HOW THE PNEUMATIC PLAYER PIANO WORKS

system. However, if the open end of the control tube is shut off either directly with the finger or indirectly by a button-operated pallet, the operation of the governor will be reversed and the flow of air will be through the main opening inside the pneumatic, allowing an instantaneous response to the vacuum conditions created by the player operator's feet. Among the makers of player who made use of this version of the power governor was Hupfeld, who employed it in the Phonola pianos.

It is important to fix in one's mind the definition of 'normally soft'. This really means the median of the level of sound being produced; the central path to the left of which is very soft and to the right of which is loud.

If we can control our playing from normally soft to loud by the sudden opening and closing of the vent of a control tube, this can be just as easily accomplished from the music roll, thereby obtaining accented notes quite automatically. If the theme of a piece of music is to be brought out by its being played slightly louder than surrounding accompaniment notes, the operation of the power governor can be achieved by the use of small marginal perforations leading to a common control tube to the valve pouch. With a divided valve chest, there is a power governor at each end and thus their automatic operation is achieved by there being two sets of controlling music-roll perforations, one at each side of the roll. This is a method of control which forms the fundamental means of 'themodising' as well as the mechanisms within the reproducing piano.

To be considered along with the power governor is another device which, although not really in the same category, is also used to create emphasis. This is the *crash valve*, used by a number of makers to enable the player operator to obtain a *forte* accent by the sudden vigorous use of the player treadles. To illustrate this, we will detail the use of the crash valve as applied by the American Standard Player Action Company. In this instrument the crash valve is placed over the opening between the bass equaliser and the main suction chest, where it is connected to the upper action. It consists of what appears to be an ordinary pneumatic motor having a large opening in one side and four small openings in the other. Inside is a fixed valve pad, which is connected to the moving wall of the pneumatic itself and is so arranged that, so long as the motor is at rest, air within the crash valve can be exhausted through the large opening, but it can be replaced by air entering through the four small openings on the

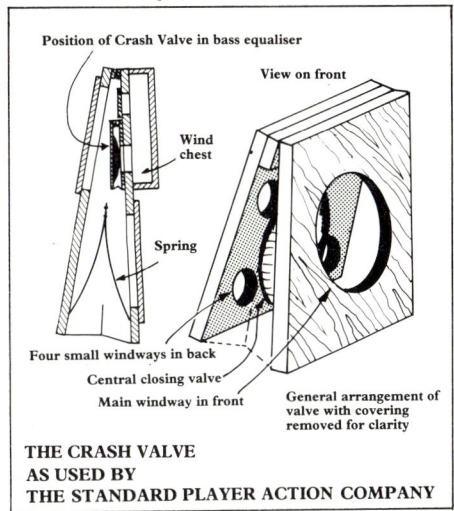

Fig. 53
The Standard Player crash valve, a system for allowing instant note accentuation by foot pressure on an instrument which, because of its provision with a large equaliser, would normally make this almost impossible to achieve.

THE CRASH VALVE
AS USED BY
THE STANDARD PLAYER ACTION COMPANY

other side so that the pneumatic will not move. However, if a sudden pressure is applied to the foot treadles, causing the exhausters to work more quickly, the air within the crash valve is withdrawn faster than it may be replaced, so the pneumatic closes and the valve inside it seals the large opening. The effect now is the complete isolation of that equaliser. The treble equaliser, having collapsed against its internal V-spring and also a special coil spring provided inside, has become momentarily inoperative and so the situation exists wherein the action has no equalisers at all and a sudden forceful push on the treadles operates directly on the channels of the player, without the absorbing and equalising effects of the equalisers. The result is a heavily struck or accented note or series of notes. The instant vigorous footwork is ended, the crash valve opens and the equaliser is recommissioned.

Another control within the player piano is the 'cut-off' or silencer, by means of which the air motor can still draw the music roll over the tracker, but the action will not operate. This is desirable where portions of a roll are not required to be played. All this control does is to operate the slide valve over the large air-transfer port between pneumatic stack and the bellows system. Again, the slide valve cut-off can be made to operate automatically by a perforation in the music roll.

Hitherto, we have only examined the single-valve pneumatic system. In the early days of player-piano manufacture, designers were faced with the virtual non-existence of materials suitable for use in their instruments. Lightness and compactness had to be coupled with the ability to remain airtight. Whilst the principles of the player action were understood, very little of the science had been discovered, with the result that the proportions of various components such as pneumatic motors and valves relative to their weight had not been evolved. It is understandable, therefore, that the makers of such instruments should tend to err on the side of reliability in making their player pianos, contriving a mechanism in such a manner that it would be dependable. By far the main drawback was the lack of suitable materials and, to be able to accept a certain amount of air seepage, it became necessary to use components of such a size that the mechanism could no longer be built practically. In the early years of this century, a 65-note player action took up more space and was considerably heavier and less powerful than the 88-note action of the 1920s.

Much of this problem concerned the amount of air which could be called upon to operate the valves and this was directly governed by the amount of air which the tracker-bar holes could accept. Even with the comparatively large holes in the 65-note tracker bar which came at six to the inch (as compared with nine to the inch in an 88-note action) the intake of air through one hole was often far short of that necessary to raise the valve quickly enough for all conditions of playing, unless the pump or bellows system was operated at a much higher vacuum pressure than was practical or comfortable for the operator. The action worked well on loud playing but poorly when the music was required to be soft. A considerable amount of thought was given to this and the upshot was the provision of a small valve placed between the tracker tube and the valve which operated the pneumatic motor in the stack. This valve would be light enough to lift instantaneously on even a low pressure and it could by this means uncover an air passage large enough to lift the heavier valves which controlled the vacuum supply to the motors. This extra valve was, then, to be used as a 'lever' in the system, so that a light force at one end of the system could be made to move a 'heavy' valve at the other. The tracker-bar hole thus served to move a valve which opened up a much larger atmospheric-air-pressure inlet to the pouch and attendant valve.

The 'double valve' pneumatic system came as the only solution to the problems inherent in the player piano. It was adopted immediately by all makers. However, in the later years, with the gradual availability of better materials, the *raison d'être* of the double-valve system no longer existed and several makers reverted to the single-valve system. Most makers, though, believed that the double-valve system, although more complicated to make, was a good insurance policy against the malfunctioning of their instruments. Today, with modern materials and an understanding of the dynamics of player mechanisms, we might build a thoroughly reliable and prompt action using single valves.

The pneumatic action, whether of the single-valve type or the double-valve type, is extremely prompt and rapid and will repeat its cycle of operations at least ten times per second under normal conditions.

With the double-valve system, the valve chest is divided into two portions – the primary and the secondary chambers. The valves in the first are termed primary valves; those in the other are the secondary valves. The way the system works should be self-evident if the foregoing descriptions of the pneumatic system have been understood. Fig. 46 shows a schematic arrangement of the double-valve pneumatic system, and Fig. 48 a section through an actual system. As the pneumatics are normally arranged in three banks, they are drawn thus.

You will see that there is no vent or bleed hole in the secondary chest. In the single-valve system the bleed is a vital part, being necessary to reduce the atmospheric pressure in the tracker tube so that the pouch will collapse, closing the valve. In the double-valve arrangement, the atmospheric pressure in the secondary channel is allowed to be reduced by leakage into the primary chamber when the primary valve is closed. Remember that the pressure difference has only to be slight before the valve will close. This type of system is considered in greater detail in the companion volume, *Restoring Pianolas*.

Of the pneumatic devices, I have left until last some of the patent systems devised to simplify the valve chest and pneumatic stack. These are usually referred to as 'Unit-block systems' or just 'Unit Valve Pneumatics'. Several American manufacturers devised their own particular variants, among them Amphion Action Company and Simplex. Of the European makers, J. D. Philipps & Söhne and also Kastner produced unit valves, the last-mentioned making a big thing of the fact that their valves and all components were of metal. Briefly the systems all employed valves and pneumatics (or chamber cylinders which served as pneumatics) which, instead of each being installed in a common chest, were individually made and screwed into place so that, for servicing, they could be removed easily. The Standard system is shown in Fig. 54. Large wooden unit valves were used on Broadwood grands *c*. 1910.

Finally to the construction of the chest for the valves. The best actions used maple for the walls of the chambers and, because it was necessary to provide facilities for servicing the double-valve systems, these usually have boards which are faced with buckskin or similar leather so that they may be airtight. Oak and ash are other woods frequently found. Interiors of all chambers and pipes are liberally coated with shellac which fills the pores and minute grain cracks. The leather used for the pouches is a very fine soft kid which meets the need for being airtight yet at the same time extremely flexible. Primary pouches are usually about ¾ inch in diameter and secondaries about 1¼ inch, each being glued over a chamber bored in the pouch board which is slightly smaller than the leather disc. Primary valves are often made by gluing small wooden button-shaped turnings on to a wooden spindle. Secondary valves, on the other hand, have a steel spindle on which are threaded inner and outer discs

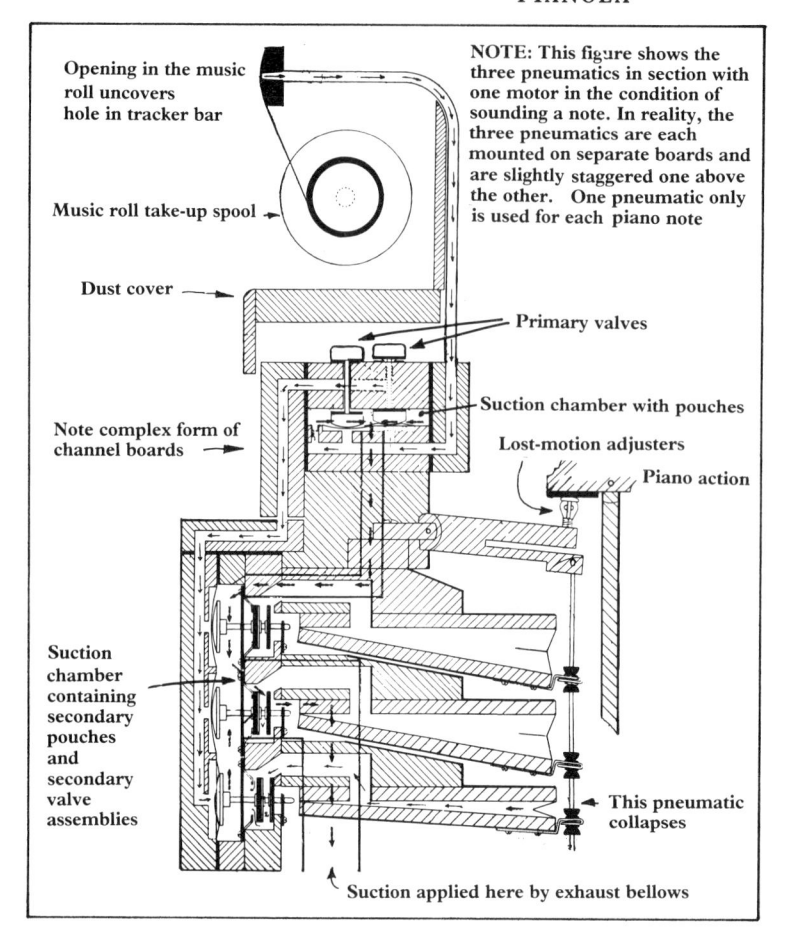

Fig. 54
Detail of the Standard Player action, a two-valve system.

Diagram labels:
- Opening in the music roll uncovers hole in tracker bar
- Music roll take-up spool
- Dust cover
- Note complex form of channel boards
- Suction chamber containing secondary pouches and secondary valve assemblies
- NOTE: This figure shows the three pneumatics in section with one motor in the condition of sounding a note. In reality, the three pneumatics are each mounted on separate boards and are slightly staggered one above the other. One pneumatic only is used for each piano note
- Primary valves
- Suction chamber with pouches
- Lost-motion adjusters
- Piano action
- This pneumatic collapses
- Suction applied here by exhaust bellows

comprising a thick card body faced each side with leather, the thickness of the total not being above $1/16$ inch. A light wooden button is fixed to the end nearest the pouch, and rests just above the pouch. The spindle is carried in guide slots to prevent any distortion in motion and these guides are usually made of fibre bushed with action-bushing felt. Single-valve actions, made in the later years of the industry, dispensed with guides by making the spindles the same diameter as the orifice, and then grooving or scolloping out the spindle to provide an airway, whilst still leaving shoulders to bear on the walls of the hole as a guide. It is probably as well to note that brass screws are used throughout – certainly in the better-made actions – to resist corrosion and to facilitate dismantling and servicing.

I must add that it would be impossible to write a detailed description to cover the mechanism of every type of player piano. Indeed as the motor car has a wheel at each corner, an engine, gearbox, transmission, steering and brakes, so has the player piano a bellows system, a valve chest, pneumatic stack, tracker bar, basic expression pneumatics, roll drive and controls. But makers chose to differ in their approach to problems and so every make of action differs in some way or another. However, an understanding of what the player piano is for and what it does and how it works is the key to the ability to tackle work on any make of

HOW THE PNEUMATIC PLAYER PIANO WORKS

Extra ducts placed in the margins of the tracker bar at each end allow theming of a number of notes in each half of the stack

Open air vent to switch in system by admitting atmosphere to control pouch B which seals vacuum from the ring pouch D

Normal tracker bar holes (often 65-88 note dual)

Primary valve

Striking pneumatic

Suction chamber

The seat of the secondary valve comprises a ring-shaped pouch D into which is arranged the bleed C. The seat itself has bleeds which are closed by the inflation of the ring pouch. The striking force for the individual note is thus variable

THE KASTONOME (Triumph Auto-Piano)

From tracker bar

Primary valve

Link

Piano action lift

Collapsing diaphragm pneumatic motors

Secondary valve

Shape of the cranked lever which is operated by the collapsing diaphragms in order to raise the piano action lift pieces

THE ANGELUS (Diaphragm pneumatics)

All-metal action

From tracker bar

Fixing screws for each of the individual unit valve assemblies

Metal manifold

Metal tube

Suction chamber

Action striker operates in guide

Adjuster

Bleed

Striking pneumatic

THE HIGEL

Ball valve

Cone pin

Low-tension vacuum chamber

Connection to tracker bar

All-metal action

High-tension vacuum chamber

Primary valve

Secondary valve

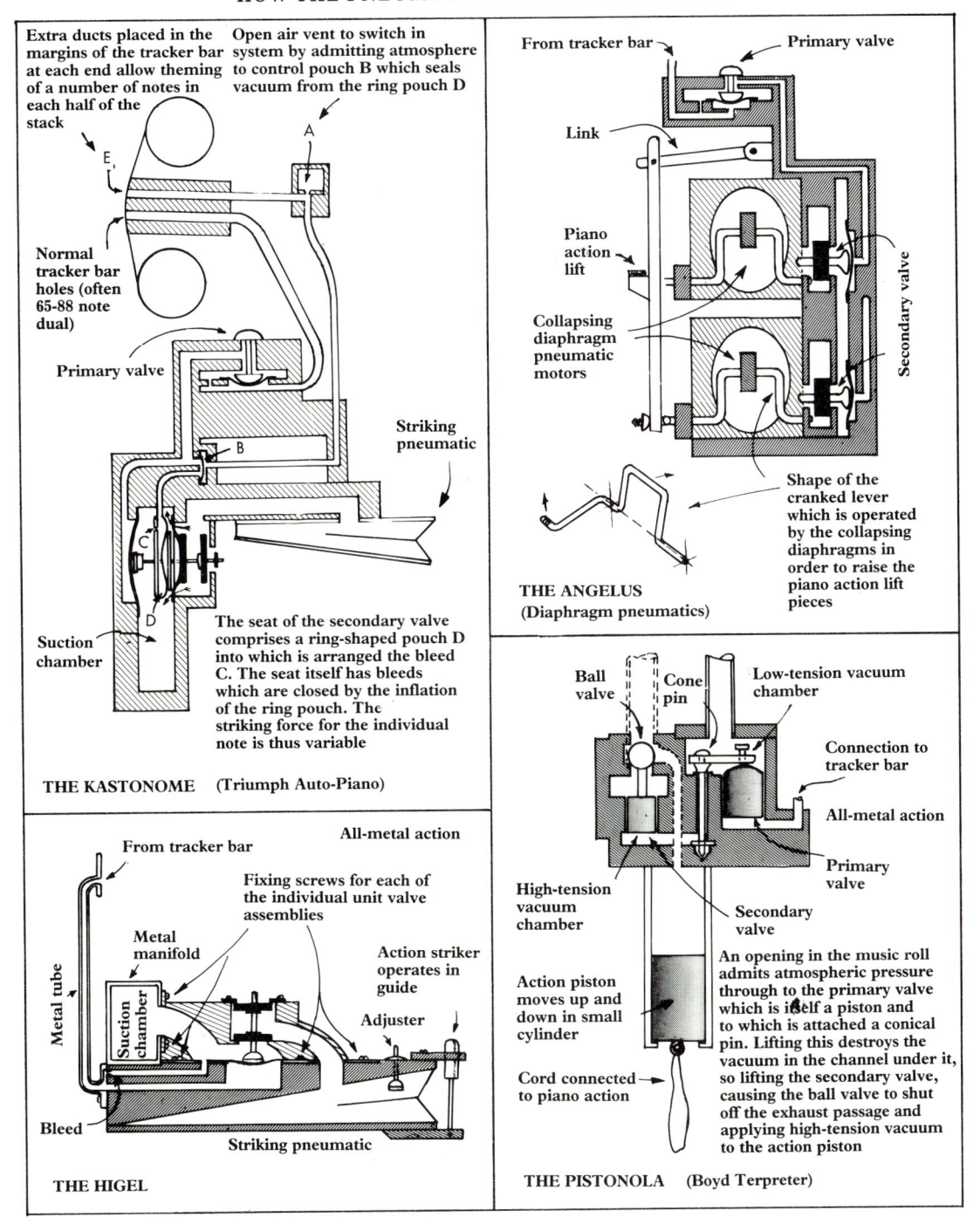

Action piston moves up and down in small cylinder

Cord connected to piano action

An opening in the music roll admits atmospheric pressure through to the primary valve which is itself a piston and to which is attached a conical pin. Lifting this destroys the vacuum in the channel under it, so lifting the secondary valve, causing the ball valve to shut off the exhaust passage and applying high-tension vacuum to the action piston

THE PISTONOLA (Boyd Terpreter)

Fig. 55
Four other types of popular player piano action.

instrument. There are today few specialists in this field. Many piano tuners try to avoid working on player pianos, primarily because to tune a player piano it is advisable to remove the player action first and this can add several hours to the job.* Those who do work on players prefer to work on nothing else and there are at least two firms who will undertake to rebuild instruments as new. Again, the British enthusiast has the facility of the Player Piano Group – a unique association of devotees who, among other more practical aspects of pneumatic piano appreciation, have gathered together a rare assortment of player-piano literature and information. Founder of the Group is Mr Frank W. Holland, MBE, who established the British Piano Museum – an amazing collection of mechanical musical instruments at Brentford, London. Thus the player piano enthusiast may never feel 'out on a limb' and, should he find himself in difficulties, there are always fellow enthusiasts who are willing to advise. Servicing player pianos and barrel pianos is the subject of the companion volume to this – *Restoring Pianolas*.

* Throughout its history, the player piano and its forerunner the piano player has frightened off piano tuners. Glance at almost any piano trade magazine from the turn of the century to the outbreak of the Second World War and you will be almost certain to find some tuner seeking often very basic advice. In the 1930s in particular, many tuners were frankly afraid of the player and letters to the trade press frequently press home the fact that the majority of these men not only had no experience of the player action, but had no idea as to how it worked, let alone anything approaching basic regulation and servicing. It is thus small wonder that owners of players were actively encouraged from a quite early date to 'convert' their players back to regular pianos. At the first sign of a wheeze or a missing note, many a fine action has been removed and burned. I well remember a fine young lady, talented at the violin and a tolerable pianist, whose parents owned a 1930s baby grand – a Steck as I recall – which, at the insistence of a tuner from a highly reputable company, had been deprived of its player action. The felony had been compounded by the affixing to the fallboard of a replacement name transfer bearing the name 'Clementi'.

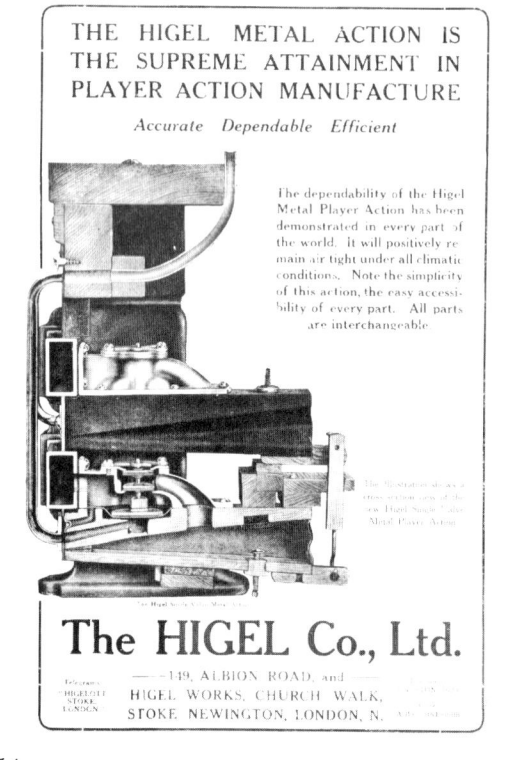

CHAPTER 6

The Perfection of the Player Mechanism

In the previous chapter, I set out briefly the salient points of the player piano and described how these parts interacted to form the automatic player action.

However, the evolution was slow and interesting and, in response to many inquiries I have had as to how this evolution took place, I am devoting this chapter to the story of some of the functions of the player piano and how they came into existence. Much of this will be of value in understanding the next section on the reproducing piano and, indeed, some of it must of necessity anticipate matters covered in that chapter. Some of the very basic parts, such as the suction bellows, have already been described in Chapter 4. While on the subject of the bellows, though, it might be prudent to mention here that several attempts were made to ease the lot of the pianolist who might be feeble of personal wind, or too arthritic to produce a good *forte* with the foot. Several cabinet pumps were marketed in America which could be connected to the player piano and thus dispense with pedalling. The Orchestrelle Company advertised such a device 'for the Pianola and player pianos of various makes' before the First World War, at which time they also sold blowers for the Orchestrelle player reed organ. At the same time, Sir Herbert Marshall & Sons, the Angelus people in London, produced a so-called 'motor cabinet' which could be fitted to 'practically any make of player or player piano'. Later on, better-quality reproducing pianos separated the potentially noisy electric motor and bellows from the instrument and housed them in a cabinet styled to match the piano. It was in America, however, that the ultimate in automatic player piano devices was invented. The Harcourt Moto-Playo Bench was a piano-stool inside which was an electric motor. This drove a crankshaft from which projected two connecting rods attached to pads which were placed on the player piano pedals or treadles. At the throw of a switch, the Moto-Playo Bench burst into life, pumping the piano steadily and ensuring plenty of suction and a thoroughly mechanical performance. Conservatory Player Action Company of 32 East Monroe Street, Chicago, claimed to be the sole licensees and manufacturers. None is known to survive.

HOW THE TUNE-SHEET OR MUSIC ROLL IS DRIVEN

It may seem a strange thing to say, particularly in view of the enormous number of players built with air motors, but the answer to the quest for a perfect roll-drive motor did not come until the very closing years of the instrument, when electric drive was perfected. Indeed, some of the recent home-made drive systems have been considerably better engineered and more efficient than the best of the air engines which consume a very large proportion of the vacuum power.

PIANOLA

As the player piano (or piano player) stemmed from the organette, it is not surprising that the early players relied upon hand-cranking to transport the music over the keyframe or tracker bar. Next came the clockwork motor with various devices for winding the spring from the action of treadling, and then came the air engine or vacuum motor. The first to make and market a player with a spring motor was John McTammany who, in 1884, was granted US Patent number 290,697 for such a device while he also had a wind-operated motor in use to drive the music rolls on his Taber and Tayler & Farley organs.

Melville Clark produced a very practical spring winding mechanism which was wound through a clutch during pedalling and after playing could rewind the roll when a knob was pulled. This was used in the early Clark Apollo players. Meanwhile Theodore P. Brown strove to improve Clark's invention for use on his Aeriol player but finally abandoned the project.

The air motor can be traced back to McTammany's rotary engine which he described in a caveat filed in September of 1876. This he improved with what he called his 'intermittent engine' as described in US Patent number 390,386. On 21 July 1885, Lucius T. Stanley was granted an American patent for a rotary and reciprocating combination engine. William D. Parker now combined with McTammany to produce a very attractive engine patented in December 1886 (US Patent 355,201). With its external valves, crankshaft and connecting rods it would have done justice to a piece of medieval mechanism. It must also have been indescribably wasteful in its consumption of hard-earned vacuum power. But practical success came with George B. Kelly's air engine patented in America on 15 February 1887 (number 357,933). Economic in use, it was smooth and silent in operation and was neat and compact in size and proportions. Kelly's design was thenceforth adopted almost throughout the player industry. The early models had five motors driving a crankshaft; later models with four were widely used and ultimately the double-chamber model was devised by Aeolian. This had three large boards offering the power of a six-chamber motor.

I said that Kelly's design was used almost universally. One major exception was Welte in Germany, who were responsible for one of the most attractive and clever wind motors anywhere in the annals of the player. First used on the orchestrion organs which the company made, it became the motive power for the music rolls in all Welte pianos – see Chapter 4 for description.

The application of electric motors to drive player pianos and keyless pianos did not necessarily dispense with the pneumatic motor-roll drive and even the early Ampico reproducing pianos retained pneumatic drive via a Kelly-type motor.

HOW MUSIC-ROLL TRACKING WAS ACHIEVED

The player piano had, as already explained, developed from the small self-playing organette controlled by a narrow band of perforated paper. The extension of the scale of the player from the average of 14 notes for the organette (a mere handspan in width) up to the necessary width for 65-note playing called for the paper to be much wider. And with this wide roll of paper – initially it was made of a sort of thin cartridge – it was very rapidly discovered that the unrolling and rerolling of a spool of paper, however accurately it was cut, ended up with the paper moving from side to side through a distance which quite often caused adjacent, incorrect notes to be sounded. I quote from the words of John McTammany:*

* *Technical History of the Player*, p. 91.

In the development of every great invention difficulties are bound to arise, and at times the difficulty has seemed almost insurmountable. If ever there was a mechanical problem that tried men's souls it was met in the player, when we were wrestling with the development of the modern pneumatic system. . . . There were many problems difficult of solution, and, next to the pneumatic system, the shrinking of the sheet, the adjustment of the tracker and the feeding, guiding and winding mechanism, proved most distracting. In the early history, prior to the 65- and 88-note scale, sufficient space was allotted to each note so as to preclude the possibility of non-tracking or non-registering of the sheet with the holes in the tracker bar, four notes to the inch being the original scale. Subsequently we reached the 65-note with its scale of six to the inch. Then our tracking problems began.

McTammany himself invented one system – the paper roll had a row of central perforations which engaged in a small pinned wheel mounted close to the centre of the tracker bar, which prevented the paper from weaving from side to side. Of course, ultimately it was discovered that fragile paper which has the will to weave cannot be restrained by such means: the guide holes just tore.

Next was Hartwell R. Moore of Elizabeth in New Jersey who, on 16 July 1901, was granted US Patent number 684,845 for a tracker board fitted with paper guides at the sides plus the ability to use music sheets of different widths by cutting out certain holes at will. Then came James O'Connor of New York (US Patent number 661,920, of 13 November 1900) who devised a tracker board with openings of different sizes. The one in the centre was square-shaped and they became progressively wider as they moved out towards the edges. This was supposed to allow for paper expansion and shrinkage although a few moments' thought will reveal that the claimed advantages (which were the subject of much patent litigation) were of limited practicality. This patent was used in the making of the Smith Lyraphone 65-note player produced in Baltimore, Maryland, in 1902.

There were obviously two different yet related problems to overcome: the weaving of the paper as it unrolled, and the tendency for the paper to change width according to the humidity of the air. Theodore P. Brown of Worcester, Massachusetts, tackled the first of these with his invention covered by US Patent number 735,062, by making the tracker board with a light-wood strip along the centre and into which the ducts were formed. By punching the music roll from thin paper, the position of the tracker holes could be viewed through the paper. All this really did was to allow the user to see what his ears were about to tell him – that all was not well. No means were offered for applying a remedy. Others who tried equally ineffective solutions were Robert A. Gally of Brooklyn, and Joseph Courville and Francis W. Draper of Detroit. But the first man to move in the right direction was a New Yorker, James O'Connor, who spent five years and much of his own money in both patenting and perfecting his improvements in what he termed 'web-guiding devices' and in infringement litigation. O'Connor's successful device, assigned to the Autopiano Company, did not come until 1905. However, I am ahead of the story.

When Melville Clark extended the scale of the player from 65 to 88 notes, the whole problem became much more serious. Robert W. Pain was another of the many who patented a supposed solution: his patent also covered a novel twin tracker board so that 65- or 88-note rolls could be played: each of the two differently pierced tracker boards was provided with a toothed rack on its inward-facing side. Between the boards was placed a small, lever-controlled pinion wheel. Movement of this lever caused one board to advance into the playing position and the other to retreat while at the same time a leather-covered flap swung into position to cover the ducts of whichever of the boards was in the out-of-play position.

George B. Kelly had a go at the problem with his US Patent number 780,356 of 1904 in which the music roll was guided in its travels over the tracker board and to the take-up spool by a system of rollers and flanges. While this appeared to offer a solution, all it really did was to increase the friction and require much more power from the roll-drive motor in order to move the paper. On top of this it must have been an ideal mechanism for pleating the edges of errant rolls.

The answer to the problem of maintaining accurate tracking was to arrange the automatic movement of either the two paper spools or the tracker board itself and the first person to come up with a workable (in theory, at any rate) system was James O'Connor with his patent 789,053. In the first application of his invention he calls for the attachment of two pneumatic edge-sensors to be fitted under the sides of the tracker so that they are normally covered by the music roll. These were connected via a pneumatic valve chest to two small pneumatic motors, one each side of the tracker bar and so placed that they could move the music-roll axis from side to side. In another application of the same system, the shifting was to be carried out electromagnetically. Although the invention of Elihu Thomson of Swampscott, Massachusetts, was the subject of infringement claims by O'Connor because it used pneumatics to shift the paper laterally over the tracker, Thomson produced a much neater and more effective tracking system in which one finger running along the edge of the music roll was able to control a pneumatic motor which moved both take-up and music-roll spools either side of an adjustable norm. At about the same time, Theodore P. Brown came out with a patent for a manually adjustable music-roll spool position by means of a knurled knob: this moved only the music roll, though.

The Autopiano Company was granted a British Patent number 3310 on 10 February 1909 for a pneumatic music-roll-moving system using balanced pressure (vacuum) ducts in the tracker bar. Two extra holes, one each side, were provided and if the lateral movement of the music roll was enough to uncover one of these, one of a pair of pneumatic motors would be set into motion to shift the spool over.

Two systems were subsequently perfected and employed. Besides these two automatic systems, there was the manual form of adjustment either by means of a large knurled brass wheel moving the spools or a screw cam (Angelus action). The pneumatic systems used a variation of the earlier O'Connor system in which two pairs of slightly staggered holes, or a pair of single holes, are covered equally by the travelling roll for equilibrium, or moved back into equilibrium when one is uncovered. The other method was used by Aeolian quite extensively until the middle 1920s and this was a variation of Elihu Thomson's system of using fingers to follow the edges of the paper. Initially, one single finger was used, mounted horizontally inside the spool box so that the left edge of the roll pressed against it during playing. Any variation to the left or right caused the inner end of this lever to modify the otherwise balanced air pressure and so shift the roll. This system had obvious limitations and made no allowances for small tears or folds in the roll edge, which, in fact, it helped to extend. Aeolian then went on to use two fingers as the valves of a balanced wind system, one finger on either side of the roll as it passed over the tracker bar. If one of these fingers was depressed, it uncovered the end of a pneumatic tube, so setting the tracking motors in motion. This technique was standard on all the early Aeolian Duo-Art instruments until the mid-1920s and the two fingers served to move both spools relative to the tracker bar. Later instruments reverted to the use of balanced suction via pairs of staggered holes by the roll margins. These were connected to vertically-mounted shifting pneumatics which operated on the tracker bar itself, the spools remaining stationary.

There were many variations on the schemes. Hupfeld, for example, used horizontal see-saw tracker motors. The problem of bringing the roll back into registration was also solved in many ways. Some moved one spool, others both, while yet others moved the tracker bar (as, for example, on the unit-action Broadwood). There were also variations on the Aeolian ear-type tracking system, one of which was a balanced pressure 'thumbnail' valve actually mounted within the width of the tracker bar and between which the paper roll passed. Ampico used this.

The system of automatic tracking based on balanced pressure in either one or two slightly staggered pairs of holes sensing the edge of the music roll was adopted widely. Although there was no serious competitor to it, Aeolian remained conscious that in the case of a roll with a tattered edge, a pleated edge or any similar damage, this type of tracking device was likely to make tracking much worse since, incapable of differentiating between a damaged edge and a genuine shift of the paper, it would at once attempt to compensate and so throw out the registration of the note perforations with the tracker bar ducts. One answer might be to use the actual note perforations themselves for tracking rather in the same way that Hupfeld had much earlier tracked from a central row of roll perforations. On 17 January 1919, Aeolian in London was granted British Patent number 139,257 (in the name of E. G. Nicholson and Aeolian) for a system which sensed the accurate position of a number of note perforations. Above certain note ducts in the bar were two long and narrow slits so placed that each pair was of slightly less width than the note perforation. When tracking properly, the note perforation would first open both these slits and then the note-playing tracker duct. All the left-hand slits of the pairs of ducts were connected to one side of a tracker-bar shifting bellows of the familiar type, and all the right-hand slits were connected to the other side of the tracker-shift bellows, both being via a usual type of valve block. What this did, then, was to sense the correct relationship of the music roll to the tracker bar at a number of positions across its width so that, regardless of the width of the roll or the state of its edges, the tracker bar could be moved to align correctly before the note was sounded. Occasionally, pianolas are found using this system but they are uncommon and one feels that the high cost of manufacturing the special tracker bar cannot have made the style economic to produce, particularly as many with vested interests in the piano-roll business would rather encourage owners to discard damaged rolls and buy afresh.

HOW PEDAL CONTROL IS ACHIEVED

One of the very basic means of adjusting the playing of a piano is the ability to render it into a *pianoforte* by playing loudly or softly. To a certain degree, this can be achieved by varying the degree of pedalling on the exhausters: soft pedalling produces low vacuum and so the piano is played softly, and vigorous pedalling produces a higher vacuum tension and louder playing results. But a piano has two expression pedals normally operated by the feet. The first is the so-called 'loud' pedal (which should always be given its proper name – sustaining pedal). When the pianist depresses this, it operates a transverse rail in the piano action which holds off all the dampers, so allowing the notes to sound longer (by virtue of letting the string vibrations die in their own time rather than blotting them with the felt damper), and permitting the rest of the piano to come into sympathetic vibration. A second pedal is the soft pedal, which, when depressed by the pianist's foot, moves all the hammers towards the strings so that they have less distance to travel and so hit the strings with less velocity. The proper name for this action, with particular emphasis on the grand piano, is the half-blow rail which may in truth be divided somewhere near the middle to produce a soft bass and normal treble, or vice versa, or wholly soft by operating both halves together.

Under pneumatic action, it becomes easy to put both these functions under automatic control from special ducts in the tracker bar. Initially, the early players were equipped with levers which acted directly on the piano player's action to vary vacuum tension and so produce soft bass/soft treble, and the sustaining pedal was worked by actually depressing the piano's foot pedal using a lever linkage. With the introduction of the inner player, the player piano could be all things automatically (although it was practice to retain the manual lever controls for user control where and when required).

With the push-up piano player, the wholly satisfactory pneumatic control of these functions was difficult if not impossible and as late as 1905 people were still applying their thoughts to levers and buttons for the purpose. Aeolian in some measure acknowledged the difficulties when in 1905 they patented a simple pair of metal levers which protruded from the front of the push-up so that the player's knees could operate them. These operated directly on the piano's pedals, one for sustaining, the other for soft. This was the subject of British Patent number 18,206 of 1905.

Automatic operation of the damper rail from roll perforations – the control of the sustaining pedal – was patented by Ernest Martin Skinner of the Aeolian Company on 21 March 1900. Half-blow seems to have been used first in Germany, probably some time about 1904, by Welte and Philipps, although no positive inventor or date can be assigned. A variation of the half-blow technique for upright pianos was patented by Aeolian in November 1907 and consisted of a pneumatic mounted on the side of the piano case (one at each side) which, when they were deflated by being valved to vacuum, drew up bell-crank arms attached to a pivoted rest rail, effectively moving all the hammers closer to the piano strings. This was patented in England on 10 September 1908 (British Patent number 24,522 of 1907). (See expansion on 'soft' pedal systems in the next chapter on reproducing pianos.)

MANUAL CONTROLS

As regards the physical layout of the controls on piano players and player pianos, few seem to have been evolved with the benefit of an awareness of ergonomics. Perhaps the least well arranged controls are those of the Pianola, an array of little levers which, with cosmetic variations, was a style adopted by many makers. Besides setting out bass and treble subduing levers in such a manner that their functions could readily be confused, the sustaining pedal – a control which should be used frequently – was assigned to the little finger, hardly considered a digit of strength or endurance. Another disadvantage concerns the fairly common type of tempo control, which is a lever moved from side to side. The problem here is that without any fixed reference point the operator has difficulty in varying tempo during playing and returning to *tempo primo* with rapidity and certainty.

This last-mentioned problem was in some measure overcome in the Angelus, where, while a lever was still used to establish tempo, momentary variations during playing could be achieved by the use of a rocking tablet on the key fall: pressing it on the left would slow down the music, while pressing on the right would speed it up. The degree of depression determined the degree of speed variation. Angelus also used buttons for the bass and treble-subduing functions, theoretically easier than levers but again confusing.

A somewhat similar device was tried by Aeolian in America around 1914. This was called the Metrograde and consisted of two buttons placed to the left of the normal tempo lever. Pressing the left one slowed down the roll and pressing the right one speeded it up. This attachment was not fitted in British-made Aeolian actions although it has appeared on American-made actions installed in pianos at Hayes.

The only player action in volume production which really demonstrated careful thought about the position of the hands during operation and took into consideration what movements were comfortable was the Phonola of Hupfeld. Here the sustaining pedal was controlled by a large and unsightly lever which was readily depressed during playing by rocking the left hand outwards, pressing the lever with the left part of the palm. This function could be maintained by the operator even while operating the accenting controls which were in the form of buttons.

All these variations in style of control render it very difficult for the itinerant player pianist to move from one familiar make of instrument to another without a period of familiarisation.

HOW NOTES ARE ACCENTED

The principle of note accentuation was the first step in the development of the basic pneumatic player piano into the reproducing piano. At the time note accenting was first conceived, though, that ultimate goal was as yet undreamed of. The ability to accent a note, that is to make it play louder than any others which might be played at the same time, made it possible to pick out the melodic line – the theme – from a counter-melody or accompaniment.

Recounting the history of theme emphasis, the *Scientific American* of 20 May 1916 wrote:

> There is positively no element in the player that has been made the subject of so much patient investigation and clever invention as that of theme or solo expression, and, during the past decade, some very ingenious devices have been tried out and placed upon the market with more or less gratifying results.

Early attempts at applying expression to the mechanical piano's music were crude and consisted of providing means for varying the strength of blow from one end of the keyboard to the other. Whereas later this was achieved pneumatically and, even in its simplest pneumatic form, could be used with a degree of subtlety, its elemental form was a rocking, swivelling or otherwise adjustable bar to regulate key depression.

The Pianotist mechanical player used a straight bar which, when slid forward at one end under the key bed and pushed backward at the other effectively altered the degree of key depression or dip. A soft bass and a loud treble or *vice versa* was the result, only the effect was graded systematically from one end to the other. Picking out the theme or accompaniment was accordingly an impossible task.

Several inventors tried splitting the bar into shorter lengths. The simplest and earliest attempts at pneumatic expression were already illustrating that a pneumatic solution must be close at hand when Francis Gilbert Webb, described as a music critic of South Kensington,

London, devised his cranked, bowed or otherwise bent bar patented in 1904 (No. 4014 of that year). This ensured that the notes at the centre of the keyboard remained more or less unaffected as the bass became softened and the treble strengthed or vice versa.

The first attempt at melody emphasis, precursor of theme emphasis, came with the division of the pneumatic stack into two separate compartments, bass and treble, so that by means of hand controls the vacuum tension in the two halves could be controlled independently. This enabled one half – usually the accompaniment – to be subdued while allowing the melody (presumably in the treble) to play louder. The idea of dividing the compass of the player in this manner came from Hupfeld and was first used in their Phonola and Claviola pianos, although soon it was taken up by manufacturers world-wide. In operation, it was no different from the earlier systems employed with barrel pianos, wherein a mechanical link could be pivoted about the keyboard centre, notes to the left sounding progressively weaker and those to the right progressively louder or vice versa. But, as with the mechanical subduing control, the system was non-selective in that every note in the half of the stack played louder or softer than the notes in the other half; the melody and accompaniment notes were invariably given the same degree of accent. Other systems were tried out experimentally, one being the provision of every note on the piano with two tracker openings – one for the striking signal and the other to regulate the vacuum tension. The difficulties of manufacturing the tracker bar and punching a roll accurately with perforations of varying widths rendered this impractical for production. However, such a system was the subject of a patent taken out by Robert Williard Pain, described as a manufacturer of 261 West 23rd Street in New York. Pain made use of a special tracker bar having two rows of holes which were staggered, not unlike the 116-note tracker bar of the two-manual Aeolian Orchestrelle player organ. Pain described how in order to adjust the vacuum tension for any note whatsoever all that was necessary was to make that particular perforation slightly wider, or twice the width, so that both upper and lower tracker holes were uncovered. The problems of roll perforating for such a system would have been uneconomical, one feels. However, he was granted British Patent number 19,527 of 1904 for such a system and, significantly, this patent was acquired by Aeolian.

The system adopted almost universally enabled certain theme notes to be emphasised regardless of the overall level of the rest of the notes by means of special theming ducts at either end of the tracker bar and special precisely-cut perforations at the sides of the roll to give pneumatic impetus to the required notes. Aeolian was the inventor of this system, or rather Aeolian acquired the patent for it; the actual inventor was James William Crooks of Boston. The system operated via a single special perforation on the left side of the roll and was intended to be used on a player action having a single, undivided stack. The British Patent for this was numbered 13,715 of 1900. The system was improved in the patent granted to Ernest Martin Skinner of Dorchester in the county of Suffolk, Massachusetts. Here again a single stack was controlled by one hole on the left side of the music roll. The British Patent for this was 15,518 also of 1900.

A very interesting variation was the subject of another Aeolian patent, the British coverage being 17,884 of 1910. So far, accenting had consisted of building up the vacuum tension for a note to sound above its neighbours which had been subdued, and to achieve this the theme note was to be cut slightly after the unthemed notes. Aeolian's experimental system worked exactly the other way about. The note to be themed was cut in advance of the notes not required to be themed and was subjected to whatever was the ruling vacuum tension.

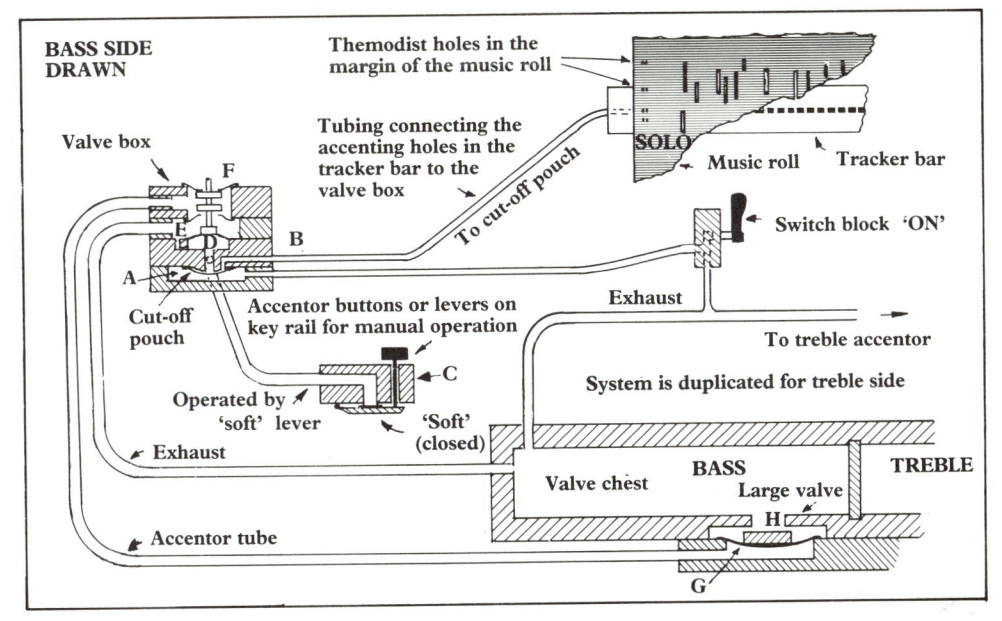

Fig. 56
The operation of the Themodist note accenting system. Fixed to the bottom of the valve chest is a small panel into which runs two rubber tubes and a large exhaust tube. This panel contains the Themodist accenting valve, G. With the Themodist in the 'on' position, the cut-off pouch A is drawn by the exhaust suction clear of the air channels B, thus preparing them for action under the control of the small Themodist perforations in the margins of the music roll. The two 'soft' levers of the manual expression control are then set to the 'on' or 'soft' position, thereby closing the two small pallets C which shut off open air. The pouch D is thus deflated by the bleed-hole E, and the valve F comes to rest. Air enters over the top of F, inflates the large pouch G and closes the port H. All this is achieved in a fraction of a second. When a marginal roll perforation K admits air down the tube B, pouch D is lifted. The valve F is raised and G is instantly deflated, opening H to full suction power. The illustration shows the system in this condition. By cutting marginal holes very slightly ahead of the note to be accented (shown by an arrow), the melody can be picked out very effectively and even individual notes in an arpeggio can be accented. When the Themodist is selected 'off', open air is admitted through the switch block to the pouch A, which is thus drawn against the channels B by the action of the bleed-hole E and the valves F and G can be operated only by the two manual 'soft' levers or buttons. When these manual controls are not in use, they hold pallets C open so that under normal suction power the valve F is raised and the pouch G is lowered. Read this drawing and description in conjunction with Fig. 57.

However, the other notes were subdued to a lower level by means of a sort of anti-theme perforation which subjected the stack to a tension-relieving chamber. In operation, allowing for the resultant different speeds of the action hammers, this must have brought the theme notes considerably ahead of the subdued notes and thereby permitted the possibilities of using varying hammer velocities to work against the satisfactory production of themed music.

Barely a few months later, Aeolian patented the system which was to succeed. This was the Themodist with its familiar marginal twin-perforation theming holes. Now the use of two side-by-side very small perforations, aptly called 'snakebites' by some American collectors, is very interesting and very clever. With the small perforations side by side, operation is certain even if the roll is slightly off track. More to the point, the twin holes admit adequate control atmosphere air pressure for a very short space of time. This ensures very precise theming capabilities. This system is the subject of British Patent 20,352 of 1910, and the system was so successful that it survived thenceforward with many other roll-making companies licensed to use the Aeolian patent. It did, furthermore, make specific allowance for use with a divided stack and thus had theming holes at both roll sides.

The successful Aeolian invention did not mean that theming devices had come to an end or that inventors would not continue to try and improve. The question of the Aeolian licence was another spur to the inventive mind. However, with the gradual standardisation of piano rolls, the sheer size of the Aeolian empire and its massive production of both players and rolls was destined to kill off the other systems.

One of the last to appear in fact harked back to Robert Williard Pain's 1904 patent. This was the work of Paul Brown Klugh of Chicago, who was granted a British Patent number 112,632 in 1916. Klugh's tracker bar had normal openings, but above each opening, and slightly to one side, was a narrow vertical slit. Not only was the system very complex, but it must have been a non-starter on grounds of production costs. It operated by regulating the distance through which the hammer travelled to strike the string. The normal tracker openings worked in the usual way. Mounted above the hammers in the piano were a set of pneumatic motors, one to each pair of adjacent hammers: since piano music normally does not make use of intervals of a minor second, it was safe to assume that adjacent hammers would seldom be called upon to move together, let alone to require theming. These motors controlled an adjustable rest for the hammers, there being no conventional rest rail. The normal location was at a forwards position, but when a note had to be themed, the pneumatic motor was collapsed via its own valve stack, and the hammer rest travelled back from the strings, so allowing the hammer plenty of distance in which to build up velocity. Like Pain's system, Klugh's patent required roll perforations of two sizes. Normal notes were sounded using normal-sized perforations, but themed notes had to be punched with larger openings so as to open two tracker bar ducts.

Another system enjoyed great popularity for a while and this had the ability to accent any note while having none of the complexity of Pain's arrangement. It was the invention of Maximilian Macarius Kastner, the young German who created the Triumph and Autopiano players. The so-called Kastonome was an ambitious system which worked very well. It employed an individual accenting pouch for every note, the accenting pouches being connected to a common windway to which atmospheric pressure could be admitted via special additional openings in the tracker-bar sides and controlled by special music rolls featuring marginal holes for the notes to be accented.

The advantage of the Kastonome system was that it became unnecessary to modify the tension of the vacuum within the whole stack in order to accent one note, as all that was necessary was to alter the tension in a very small volume of space so as to operate the expression pouch. The disadvantage was that the system was difficult to maintain in perfect order and, although perfect when new, deterioration of the Kastonome pouches produced uneven playing – unintentionally accented notes – which was virtually impossible to mask.

The operation was very ingenious. Each of the additional perforations admits air at atmospheric pressure to a cut-off pouch which governs the control of suction or atmosphere to a special ring-shaped pouch which forms a seat for the secondary valves. In the same way that one of Aeolian's patents covered the creation of a subdued piano with the accented notes being given 'normal' conditions, as distinct from a normal piano stack under the overall control of subduing controls through which accented notes were produced by increased vacuum tension, the Kastonome worked on the principle of softening all the notes being played with the exception of the notes required to stand out. A correct musical interpretation required the Kastonome control to be switched on and off according to printed instructions on the music roll. Whereas the Themodist might be described as a passive system in that it did not need to be disconnected when not in use and was only operational when the Themodist perforations dictated so, the Kastonome was an active arrangement because it served to subdue the instrument overall.

Invented jointly by Kastner and C. Katz, British Patents were taken out for the system as follows: 12,761 of 25 May 1910, 8723 of 7 April 1911. The special Kastonome music rolls, characterised by a central pair of parallel tempo-indicator width lines and a series of small green arrows between them to show speed variations, were the subject of British Patent 26,553 of 15 November 1910.

This ingenious system obviously called for special rolls suitable only for the Kastner piano, so, with the pre-1914 spread of 88-note pianos with the Themodist type of accenting system, Kastner dropped the Kastonome and the later Autopianos had what was called the 'Triumphodist' control – the now universal Themodist system.

As demonstrated, then, it was Aeolian's arrangement which was to survive the battle for theme expression with the Themodist and although much later on, with the era of the reproducing piano, expression and theming came in for closer scrutiny and refinement, and although other systems were looked at at the end of the reproducing piano era whereby individual levels of theming were the goal, the snakebites were here to stay.

The principle of operation has already been described in general terms. The theme holes were connected to a regulator pneumatic, the overall level of vacuum tension therein being controlled by means of a knife valve. The instant a theme hole was uncovered, the regulator moved, opened the knife valve and admitted a higher tension vacuum to the half of the stack in which the note to be themed lay. More than one note could, of course, be themed.

In practice, the faster the travelling speed of the roll, within reason, the better the accenting effect. This is a bit of a generalisation, yet it remains true that many of the earlier, slow-travelling rolls (cut at speeds of 40 and below) were intended to economise on paper and therefore far greater accuracy was needed to position the theme holes. Usually, there was insufficient length of music slot to allow creative theming. This will be understood in a moment.

As already outlined, accenting one note calls for increasing the vacuum tension at the moment of exhausting the pneumatic motor to strike a particular string via one of the piano's hammer actions. Although this action takes place almost instantaneously, there is a minute time lag which is only a mere fraction of a second. With a roll cut at, say, 35 speed, this time represents virtually no distance on the paper, but if the roll is travelling at a greater speed, such as 60, then that split second now becomes a noticeable fraction of an inch. It is this literally marginal distance which can now be put to use in a very subtle way.

Consider for a moment a chord of, say, four notes cut into the paper roll so that, as one might assume, all the notes start at the same instant and their starts thus represent a straight line across the paper. If we want one of these notes to stand out louder than the others, there are two ways to do it. One is to cut that note with a longer slot in the paper, leaving the other three very short. This means that the unwanted three will damp quickly, leaving the 'accented' note singing out longer because the damper is held off the string.

Now that system is all very well, but it is not actually making one note physically louder and thus more predominant than the others. If we choose to punch theme holes to line up with the chord, they must affect all four notes and we are back to where we started. The trick is to rely on the fact that the real live pianist seldom if ever will strike four notes evenly all at once. In an exaggerated case, they will sound as an arpeggio, and probably not in the logical order 1 2 3 4, but maybe 4 1 2 3 or what have you. This pianistic shortcoming, though, is seldom discernible to the human ear and only really shows when we have a pianist cutting a roll melographically so that we can actually see his problems in the way the lines of perforations are presented.

So it does not matter all that much if, in cutting our roll, one or more notes are cut marginally late or early relative to our straight line. Remembering that the accenting of a note can only take place at the second when that particular piano action is set into motion, and that once the piano hammer is moving towards the string nothing we can do with a paper roll can alter its velocity (short of thrusting the paper roll down inside the piano), the trick is to select the note to be accented and cut it with a very slight delay – and then theme that note.

This little trick has far greater potential than may at first appear, for it makes it possible for one note to stand out louder regardless of where the 'soft/loud' controls are held – up to a position, of course, of maximum loudness. This means that it is a practical proposition to make one note stand out louder in a chord of apparently simultaneously sounding notes, regardless of whether it is the note at one end or in the middle. Used in its developed form in the reproducing piano, this technique of theming individual notes takes precedence over the general level of vacuum in the stack as controlled by the special perforations for controlling the reproducing action.

Now we come back to my statement about roll speed and the faster speed giving greater effectiveness. It goes, I hope, without saying that absolute precision is a prerequisite of positioning the theme perforations and that this precision is a factor of time rather than distance meaning that the faster the paper travels over the tracker bar the greater the distance in front of the note to be accented the theme holes have to be. If you visualise our fast-travelling roll and come back to our four-note chord within which we want note number three to stand out, the effect is, of course, only noticeable when the piano is being played at a level of sound below maximum loudness – this is the same whether the pianist is live or it is you with a paper roll and, if you think about it, is a very obvious statement. So, with the expression levers in use, we come to our four-note chord. As the paper traverses the tracker bar, the perforations for notes 1, 2 and 4 uncover the ducts in the tracker bar and in the usual way set the hammers for those notes on their course to strike the strings. A split second later, our theme duct is uncovered and note 3's perforation uncovers its tracker bar duct. Under high tension, the pneumatic slams the piano hammer at the string at a greater speed than the other three. Depending on the degree of vacuum tension used for the first set of notes it is now quite possible for all four hammers to strike their strings at one and the same time since three were travelling at a slower rate than the fourth. Hence we can explode the oft-repeated comment from non-aficionados (both concert pianists and laymen alike) that accenting one note in a chord is impossible by player piano.

In this résumé of the history of various methods of note accentuation, I have made specific references to the Kastonome and the Themodist and passing reference to the Triumphodist. These were but a very few of the names used in describing so-called accenting methods and the rolls from which such effects were produced. Of course, there is no doubt that in English-speaking countries the most common was the Themodist of Aeolian which, on the roll and box labels, was always indicated by the word Themodist and the presence of a letter

THE PERFECTION OF THE PLAYER MECHANISM

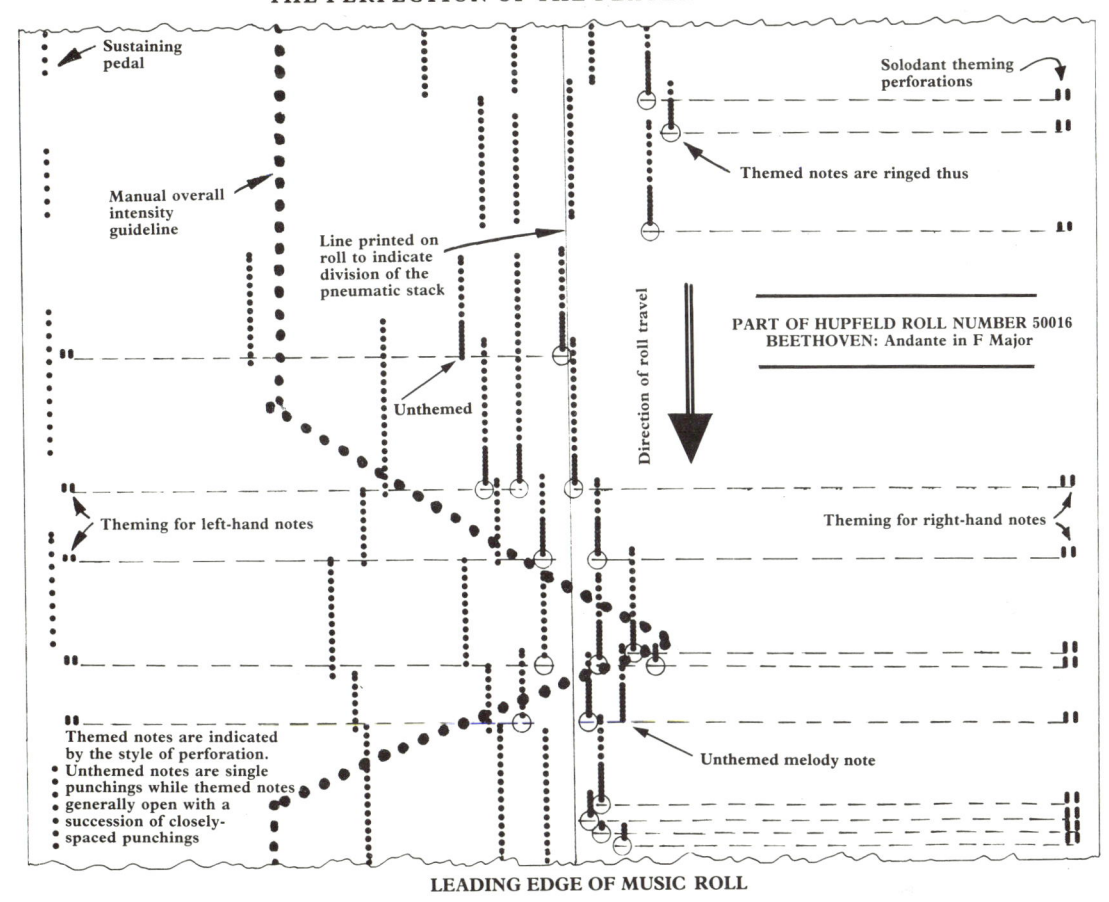

Fig. 57
Part of an actual music roll showing how the notes to be Themodised are cued by marginal perforations cut very slightly ahead of them. The roll is made by Hupfeld and the Hupfeld term for the note-accenting facility is Solodant. The system works virtually the same as the Themodist of Aeolian. Observe how not all of the melody notes are themed, so allowing some to stand out above others.

'T' before the roll number. This was found on the Aeolian rolls produced under the Universal name and, of course, Meloto when Universal changed its name.

Many other rolls equipped with perforations to operate the Themodist-type of accenting were just marked with the word 'Accented', and of course this was a characteristic of the so-called 'hand-played' rolls. In Germany, the word Solodant was used for the same thing.

As distinct from physically emphasising melody notes in the piano roll, Aeolian considered that it was worth making these notes clearer to identify in the roll by punching them with a different type of perforation. British Patent number 14,325 dated 1 September 1904 was granted for a system in which while accompaniment notes are chain-punched, the melody notes have contiguous perforations – separate holes separated by a narrow neck of paper. In fact in the years to come, the system was reversed and the accompaniment often had contiguous perforations while the melody line had slotted openings, in the case of longish notes a slotted opening followed by contiguous holes. Aeolian's differentiation of types of note perforations stood it in good stead when it came to the Aeolian Pipe Organ with its double-row tracker bar wherein upper manual notes were in single perforations and the lower manual ones were in the form of slots, so that the operator of the instrument could see at a glance where the melody was.

All the makers of reproducing pianos (see Chapter 7) made claims for their instruments which were sometimes extravagant,* while standards of advertising were often downright objectionable, particularly in America, where Ampico engaged in a public denigration of its rival, the Duo-Art. How the two companies fared when the exigencies of commercial interest and the depression brought the two systems under one and the same roof has never been related.

One of the things which all the makers made a great thing of was the ability to perform absolutely faithfully in the manner of the original roll. Now it must be said that, thanks to skilful and masterly editing by persons whose knowledge of both music and the pneumatics of their piano systems was second to none, this was a goal more often than not achieved – within the overall limitation that certain types of music were difficult if not impossible to reproduce pneumatically. There were, towards the end of the era, for example, some Ampico rolls which must be rated as interpretational failures not just on the basis of their having been badly played originally – this cannot have been the case – but because the system could not cope with the demands made upon it.

The key to this was the ability to theme any note anywhere in, for example, a rapid arpeggio or counter-theme. In truth, this was just what Pain had done, somewhat arbitrarily, back in the early years of this century, while Kastner had gone a long way towards this with the Kastonome. But both these systems had the disadvantage that, as already stated, they were not passive systems, but fully interactive. And in the intervening decades player actions and music had together come along considerably. With the availability of the Aeolian-created action pattern now used world-wide, whatever new system created had to be fully compatible with normal Themodist and Duo-Art rolls.

The first company to attain this goal would obviously reap a rich reward in the market. Several other systems had been invented. Perhaps the most interesting yet impractical on the grounds of economy was that conceived as early as 1909 by Arthur Ronald Trist of the Trist Piano Player Company. Trist had begun with a push-up player and an under-capitalised company which went into liquidation. He formed a new company and spent much time and money perfecting an isolated theme system. It does seem, though, that he never actually produced any pianos with his invention. Trist felt that the admixture of pneumatics and electricity was the key to isolated theme and between 1909 and 1912 he patented at least five electropneumatic devices – and these were developed from an even earlier Trist patent of 1906. The key to his system was a three-ply music roll made of thin metal sandwiched between paper. Note theming was achieved in the accepted way by marginal perforations which passed right through the roll. However, note sensing was achieved by electric tracker brushes and the music rolls contained 'partial' perforations which only exposed the metal foil, or full perforations which operated the pneumatic chest. One major advantage of the

---

* Although one should bear in mind the large number of testimonials from, apparently, top-quality pianists back in the days of the piano player who claimed that the instrument gave them the satisfaction which only a live player could hitherto provide. Testimonials, one tends to feel, were bought at high prices.

Trist system which no doubt would have been of a certain attraction was that it was possible to control up to three instruments at once from one music roll and spool box and these could be organ or piano. The high cost of making a saleable player on this system more or less killed it off and Trist went on to perfect a three-colour printing process.

It is at this point that Gordon Iles came into the picture. A man of immense talent – he built the Duo-Art Robot described in Chapter 10, spent the war years making pneumatic synthetic trainers for bomber pilots out of Duo-Art technology* and today runs the Artona Music Roll Company at Ramsgate – Iles succeeded where others had failed, only to be beaten by the financial collapse of Aeolian in London.

Born in 1908, he studied music at Cambridge under Dr Cyril Bradley Rootham (born 1865, died 1938), where he had charge of the University's Duo-Art, a Weber Model 12 pedal-electric grand. Dr Rootham, a composer in his own right, used the instrument more as an ordinary piano than as a reproducer and, although he had contributed to the Aeolian 'World's Music' series, he did not have an especially good opinion of it and was never slow to point out the occasional lack of what came to be termed *isolated simultaneous theme* or IST for short. He conceded that it was extremely good in the case of certain recordings, but not all.

Gordon Iles was a pianist of above average ability and he was also aware of its shortcomings. Fortunately he had the time to study the problem in some depth. It should be pointed out that his father, John Henry Iles, had at one time been a journalist and became president of the London Press Club. His prowess as a one-time County cricketer who had played with the legendary W. G. Grace for Gloucestershire brought him to the notice of the managing director of Aeolian in London, G. F. Reed, and they became firm friends. Iles Senior became public relations and advertising adviser to Reed. Through this, the Iles home had every model of the pianola from the 65-note push-up to the most sophisticated electric Duo-Art and all of these instruments Gordon Iles stripped down to the smallest part until he had become thoroughly acquainted with the art and practice of pneumatic action.

Ultimately, Gordon Iles succeeded in producing a prototype Duo-Art action of his own which was credited as being 'remarkably fine'. Both Iles senior and Reed were much impressed and the suggestion was made from his father that Gordon Iles should tackle the problem of IST. Acceptance of the challenge was met with the immediate shipment of a special Weber Duo-Art to Gordon's workshop at his home, and here research and experiments in IST began in real earnest. This was around 1925. Aeolian's chief technical superintendent at Hayes in Middlesex was Harry W. Palmer and he made all the special components designed by Gordon Iles and sent them to his home at Broadstairs in Kent.

Finally Gordon Iles completed his IST Duo-Art in his workshop. At this time Aeolian was spending vast sums of money on special-purpose equipment to manufacture educational music rolls under the label 'The World's Music'. The company had also redesigned the basic piano playing stack and taken out a patent (number 323,005 dated 17 September 1928) in the names of C. F. Cook and H. W. Palmer for an action featuring hingeless, square striking pneumatics as distinct from the usual wedge-shaped ones.† However, the financial collapse of the company was nigh and IST was abandoned.

The entire programme of work on IST had been conducted in secrecy for company policy demanded that the public should be told that the Duo-Art with its Themodist constituted the

---

* See 'How the Duo-Art Won the War', in *The Music Box*, Volume 7, p. 131.

† The use of parallel striking pneumatics had been included in a British Patent number 4804 dated 26 February 1909 in the name of C. Katz and M. M. Kastner.

ultimate in perfection and left nothing further to desire. However, those who heard the IST in operation immediately became aware of the very definite improvement in reproduction that it gave.

The operation of the Aeolian-Iles IST system hinged on the use of a special twin valve chest* employed in conjunction with a tracker bar having a double row of holes, the two rows being very close together. The top row included Themodist ports but were fixed with a minimum (extremely soft) level of accompaniment. The lower row of ducts were accompanimental only and were under the influence of the usual variable Duo-Art level as set by the music-roll accompaniment perforations.† This bottom row was not provided with Themodist ducts.

The tracker bar was made in an ingenious way. Some of the early pre-Duo-Art tracker bars had comparatively narrow slots and so two of these were cut lengthwise and the portions with slots joined together to form a single bar in which the two rows of holes were together very little wider than the single row in a standard bar.

In operation, if a themed note was provided with a theme perforation, as normally found in a roll, and set back by a fraction of an inch corresponding to the space between the two rows of holes in the double tracker bar, then the themed note or notes arrived at the first row at the same time as the forward-cut accompanimental notes. These, having no Themodist perforations, would either not have sounded at all when they passed the first row or at most would barely have played due to the low level setting of that valve stack. The result of this was that themed notes could be played simultaneously with accompanimental notes. In this way it was only necessary to arrange rolls to play at a tempo setting of no more than 100 and sometimes even less in order to provide full IST without losing maximum repetition. An added advantage was that the rolls would also play satisfactorily when used on standard Duo-Art instruments although without, of course, the IST effect.

Conversely, ordinary Duo-Art rolls would also play in the normal way on a special IST instrument. The 'stop' slot position between the treble Themodist and soft pedal slots in the tracker bar was used, in the case of an IST piano, to bring the mechanism into operation, otherwise the lower row of holes only functioned. One or two patents were taken out but allowed to lapse when the Aeolian Company folded up.

This perfection of IST was actually built into a piano as a commercial venture. Iles senior built the Dreamland Super Cinema at Margate in about 1936 and Gordon Iles co-operated with the John Compton Organ Company in designing the organ. Part of the installation was an IST Duo-Art on the stage which could also be played with expressive touch from the organ console. This unique piano and installation was destroyed by enemy action during the war.

Aeolian had also experimented with another method of achieving IST which used a standard tracker bar but had the disadvantage that it required the use of special rolls which could not be used on standard instruments. In this system, each slot in the tracker bar had three functions which, as before, were brought into action through a perforation aligning with the 'stop' position. These three functions for each note-playing hole were: (1) to play a note; (2) to cancel the playing power of the adjacent tracker note-playing hole; (3) to theme

---

* Aeolian had used the twin chest as the basis of a rudimentary, non-automatic theming system as early as 1916 when, on 28 November of that year, it was granted British Patent number 111,349 for variable-tension striking pneumatics under the control of a tune sheet or from special buttons provided for the purpose in the key-slip.

† In truth, the double-row tracker bar used in conjunction with two valve chests, one at a high vacuum tension and the other at low, combined with accenting ducts, had been the subject of British Patent number 7698 dated 26 March 1914, in the name of D. Kennedy.

exclusively the note corresponding to the slot on the left. Spelled out, then, this system used the normal tracker hole next to the one being played for theming by first signalling a cancel to its normal playing function, and then causing it to react to the opening of the note channel to its left. This assumed that in normal music intervals of a minor second are seldom encountered for in such instances the theming of one of the notes would be impossible by this method, although imaginative Themodist cutting could no doubt be used to some advantage. In use, if a note to be themed had a single pip perforation next to it on the left, it would be themed without the production of what might appear to result as a discord. Naturally, the operation of this IST system was achieved in conjunction with a special twin valve chest of similar design to that employed in the twin-bar system described above, and a rather complex bank of cancel membranes was also required.

It is believed that one example of an experimental type of Aeolian IST player survives. Built as a *vorsetzer* and at present owned by Akio Morita of the Sony Corporation in Japan, this plays special rolls which are wider than usual and which incorporate a number of non-standard features. The tracker bar, for example, has two special theming holes above the blocks of four expression-controlling holes at each end. There are also several additional tracker-bar ports outside these.

Although this system proved completely reliable, it had obvious limitations and was restricted for its full effect to using special rolls which could not be used on any other playing mechanism.

And so ended the quest for themed notes. Like so many inventions, it reached perfection at a time when nobody wanted it. Significantly, the demand is there again today. Perhaps some latter-day engineer may resurrect the work of Gordon Iles.

THE **RIALTO ACTIONS**

for every existing Piano are rapidly gaining ground.

RIALTO ACTIONS

have already been installed in hundreds of different styles of Pianos.

A HIGH CLASS PLAYER at a MODERATE Price.

RIALTO PLAYER PIANO CO.
15, Castle Street East, London, W.

Showing Rialto Player when in use.   Showing Rialto Player when not in use.

FIXES INSIDE AN ORDINARY PIANO.   MUSIC ROLL IN TOP DOOR.

THE **Classic** (Patent No. 2852)

A PLAYER OF DISTINCTION (65 or 88), with all Modern Devices, All-metal Tracker Desk, Sound Construction, Excellent Finish, Accessibility, Expressive Pedalling.
COMPLETE INSTRUMENTS A SPECIALTY.

T. H. POYSER, 39, HERMITAGE ROAD, HARRINGAY, LONDON, N.
Phone: Tottenham 2244.
Send your REPAIRS as usual to Repair Department.

THE Pistonola

The Player Piano of the Future.

THE introduction of the all-metal player-piano, The Pistonola, has had a marked effect on the vast player-piano industry of this country. It has nothing in common with any other type of player in that it is operated by suction; and, in place of the unwieldy and inefficacious bellows the Pistonola is operated by diminutive metal cylinders, and compressed graphite pistons.

THE "PISTONOLA" can be fitted inside any normal piano without in any way increasing the size of the instrument.

THE "PISTONOLA" has numerous important features which every dealer and every member of the public should investigate, all of which are fully explained in the new Pistonola booklet, free on request.

BOYD Ltd. MANUFACTURERS OF GOLD MEDAL PIANOFORTES & OF THE PISTONOLA

Wholesale and Export Department: 32, Worship Street, London, E.C.

◀ PLATE 56
The Farrand Organ Company of Detroit, Michigan, introduced the Cecilian cabinet-style push-up piano player. Farrand had wide experience in organ building and with the inventor-to-be of the Pianola E. S. Votey on the staff, the Cecilian was a well-engineered instrument. It was also the first to make use of all-metal action components.

▼ PLATE 57
The Pianola push-up player set new standards not just for quality and performance but for aggressive promotion. This one, fitted with Metrostyle and Themodist, sold for £65 or $350. This view shows the controls.

PLATES 58 & 59 ▼▼
The Pianola with the panels removed seen, left, from the opperator's side and, right, as presented to the keyboard of an ordinary piano. Note the sustaining pedal linkage from the hand lever on the front.

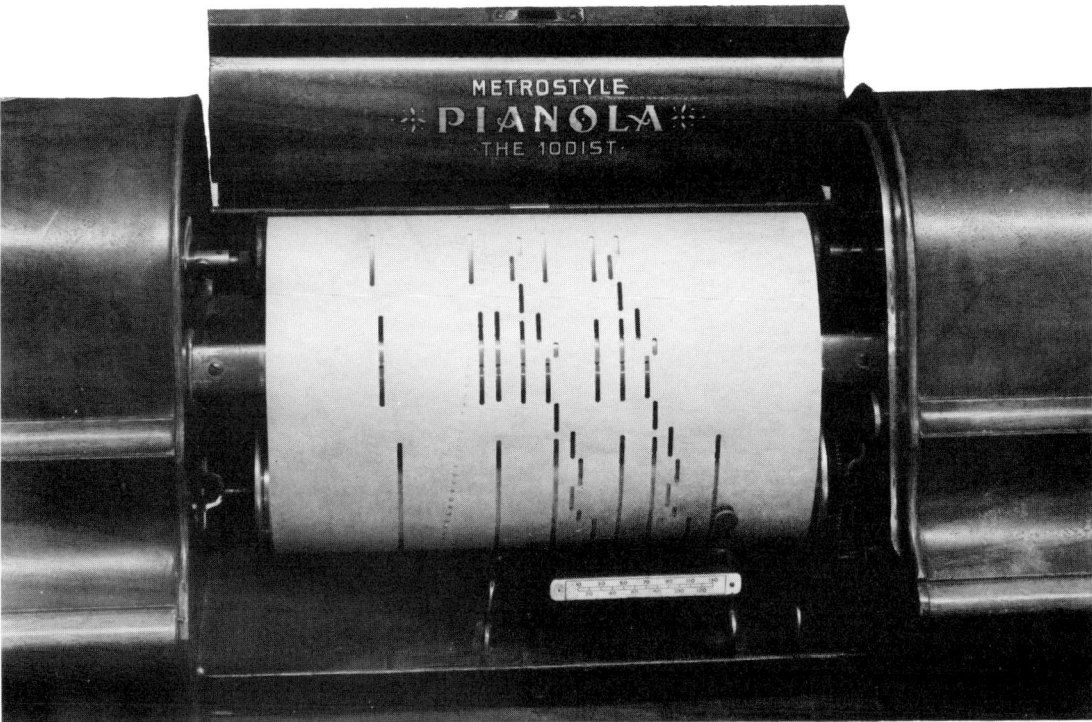

◀ PLATE 60
The Lyraphone was introduced around 1901–2 by the Smith Lyraphone Company of Baltimore, Maryland, formerly the Gilbert Smith Piano Company. Selling at $225, the Lyraphone was lavishly promoted for a very short period. It was designed at a time when artistic lines still held sway in domestic artefact and was a handsome device to behold. The advertisements of the makers claimed it to be 'Nature's only rival' adding that it had 'the marvellous Human Touch' and only needed 'the addition of gray matter behind its wonderful Flexible Fingers to become a sentient being'. The mechanism was that of the 'kicking shoe' or mechanical action.

▼ PLATE 61
Operator's view of the Smith Lyraphone showing the controls. The fact that every make of instrument was different in its method of control meant that a person skilled with one instrument could not play another type without practice. The same applies today.

◀ PLATE 62
The same price as the Lyraphone, Theodore P. Brown's Simplex piano player was made in Worcester, Massachusetts. Again it was a well-made and quite attractive instrument. In England it was marketed by a number of agents at £52.

PLATE 63 ▶
Hupfeld's Phonola cabinet player demonstrated rugged engineering and a serious attempt at evaluating the needs of the performer as regards hand controls. Characteristic of all Hupfeld players was the assignment of the sustaining pedal control to the palm of the hand, a more natural and easier function which left the fingers free to use the other controls. Aeolian, for some reason, expected the pedal to be worked by the little finger of the left hand, neither the most practical nor the most comfortable part of the anatomy to employ for such a purpose.

◀ PLATE 64
The zenith of perfection of the cabinet player came with the introduction of the reproducing piano player, dealt with in depth further on. Here, though, to illustrate the stylistic development of the push-up is an ornate Welte Vorsetzer reproducing player engaged in servicing the keys of a Chickering grand.

▼ PLATE 66
The advent of the so-called 'inner player' inspired a number of inventors to find ways of converting an ordinary piano into a player. A London-made invention was Poyser's Classic which was narrow enough to fit into any piano. The example seen below has been installed with the minimum of alteration. The cut-out and hinged front fall panel can be seen and the key rail has been cut to mount the controls.

▲ PLATE 65
The Angelus Orchestral was unusual amongst players in that it was also a player reed organ and could play a music roll without a piano present. It could also play a piano solo or in duet with the organ contained in its bulk.

▲ PLATE 67
The take-up spool of the Classic folded up out of the way and was swung down for playing. So little room was allowed for the roll drive motor in this installation that the front fall had been gouged out with a chisel to allow sufficient clearance.

◀ PLATE 68
Poyser's Classic relied for its slimness on having the pneumatic chest placed under the keyboard. The rubber tubing from the tracker bar thus had to pass down and between the keys which had to be pared away to allow clearance.

▼ PLATE 69
Most unusual and readily recognisable amongst tracker bars is that of the Kastner Autopiano. This is a dual 65/88-note example and Kastner's patent expression ports can be seen above and below the 88-note tracker. The small lever in the spool box, lower left side, changes from 65 to 88 note action.

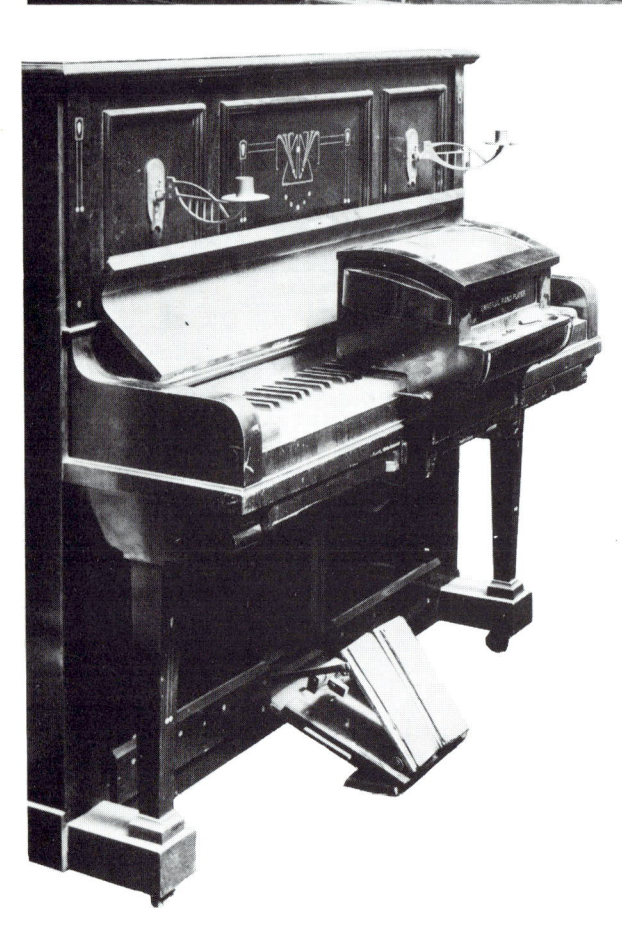

▲ PLATE 70
Another of the strange conversions was afforded by Bansall's Universal Player. The instrument resembles a key-top player but has no contact with the keys, the cabinet merely housing the music roll and its wind motor and tracker bar plus the hand controls. The box is fixed to the front of the piano so that a series of holes in the box corresponds with a matching series in the lower key bed of the piano. A leather seal, suitably perforated, ensures airtightness. The chest is below the keys. Bansall failed to realise that with the player fitted it was no longer easy to play the piano by hand. When not in use, though, the player could be kept in the piano stool.

▼ PLATE 71
Plate 63 showed an early Hupfeld Phonola cabinet player controls. Here is another form of Phonola, this time added to a converted upright. Note again the hinged, folding palm lever for the pedal. This is swung right out for either left or right palm use.

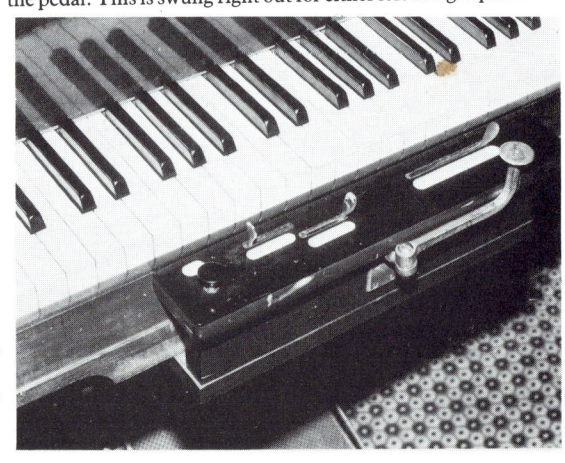

◀ PLATE 72
The early form of Pianola inner player installed in a Steck upright. The six-motor, double-sided roll drive motor is clear here.

▼ PLATE 73
Pianola built into a German Ibach upright. Wide-spaced treadles allow the adroit operator to use the soft pedal, if he wishes, during pianissimo passages.

▼ PLATE 74
The Boyd Pistonola, one of the neatest and most compact of all player actions thanks to its well-engineered piston/cylinder action in place of the more bulky pneumatic motor.

▼ PLATE 75
Another view of the Pistonola showing the diminutive roll drive motor.

PLATE 76 ▼
Angelus diaphragm action in a Brinsmead upright, left. Note the rocking tablet for tempo changes at the right end of the control rail. This allowed a certain return to tempo primo.

▲ PLATE 77
This Angelus will play 65 or 88-note rolls driven top to bottom or bottom to top to suit early European rolls. Roll motor is unique in being placed left.

◀ PLATE 78
Remote control was the main advantage claimed by the Tel-Electric Company of New York for its two all-electric piano players. The instrument comprised two parts: the player itself, seen left, and the box of electro-magnets connected to the underside of the piano keyboard. Between the two passed a cable of whatever length the owner might require. The operator could regulate the voltage passed down the cable so that the piano played soft or loud. Two models were made. Seen here is the Telektra which played music via special perforated brass music rolls 6¾ inches wide. The instrument cost $450 in 1911.

PLATE 79 ▶
The smaller version of the instrument was the Tel-Electric seen here. This played music from brass music rolls 5 inches wide. A feature of these machines was that they were capable of a degree of in-built expression. Each music roll had a number of extra holes for this purpose which automatically controlled the playing level besides allowing the operator a further or over-riding degree of control.

▼ PLATE 80
The rolls for Tel-Electric's piano players were unique. Each was housed in a brass cassette from which it would be drawn out during playing and then rewound back into. The roll itself was made of very thin brass sheet and they were thus very heavy. The 5-inch Tel-Electric roll played 65 of the piano's key compass from 73 perforations, the remaining 15 being used for expression. The Telektra roll was 6¾ inches wide and played the full 88-note compass, again with 15 extra holes for expression. The music roll catalogue was extensive and during the decade or so of its popularity, this playing system presented a strong if up-market rival to the pneumatic players. Both rolls were perforated at 15 to the inch.

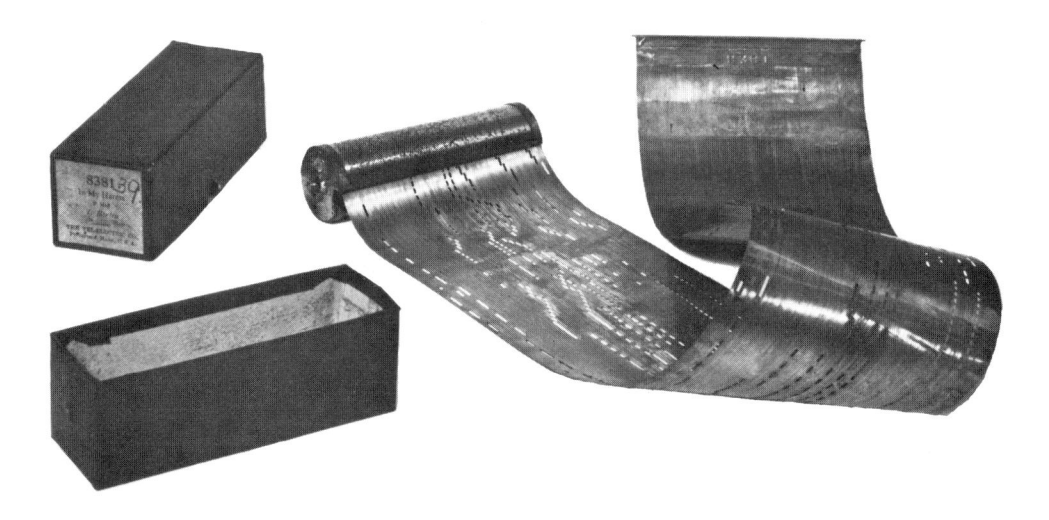

◀ PLATE 81
This composite picture shows the Telektra player in front of a Chickering upright and illustrates the decks of underkey solenoids. The Tel-Electric company was founded in 1905 by John Forrest Kelly, one-time associate of Thomas Edison who was a pioneer in consumer distribution techniques of alternating current. Ultimately he went on to become a founder of the General Electric Co. in Pittsfield.

PLATE 82 ▶
Electricity in the home was initially used as a means of illumination and the early electric pianos and orchestrions were made to be run off wet-cell accumulators. By 1912, however, it was doing other things in the home. In that year, Wolverhampton's West Park was the setting for an electricity exhibition. This particular stand, representing a then-modern home, featured a Hopkinson Electrelle 65-note player piano. This player was an all-British design but its makers were in Receivership by July 1913 through trying to develop an 88-note version. The name Electrelle was also used by an American maker c. 1910–16.

◀ PLATE 83
Playing a well-restored player piano is one of the most satisfying experiences, particularly if possession of such an instrument is supported by ownership of (or access to) a good library of music rolls. Here the author takes a break at the levers of a Blüthner grand Triphonola in the Utrecht museum. Hupfeld's Animatic music rolls are amongst the very best rolls available, superbly arranged and cut for quality which means that there are few interpretational tempo changes needed since the rolls are next best to those for a reproducer.

◀ PLATE 84
Welte's cabinet reproducing instrument, the Welte Vorsetzer, appeared around 1904 and, with its ability to reproduce the performance of a named performer on any piano, rapidly attracted world acclaim. The instrument operated from wide paper rolls, usually red in colour, hence the cognomen 'red Welte' for the instrument. While other makers, particularly Hupfeld, made similar devices on a short-lived enterprise, the Welte Vorsetzer remained in production well up into the 1920s. It was a finely-built and well-crafted mechanism. Emil Welte and Karl Bockisch were the system patentees. In the years to come, both Aeolian and Ampico paid a $2·50 royalty on each of their reproducing pianos for the use of the Welte concept, namely that of using variable suction pressure as a means of providing variations in piano expression.

◀ PLATE 85
In this view of the Welte Vorsetzer – which means 'to sit before' – can be seen the electric motor drive at the bass end running via a large reduction pulley at the treble to a central cross shaft powered by a flat leather belt. This shaft worked the ingenious system of levers which in turn drove the exhausters. The three exhausters can be seen above the wind platform – the coils of their hairpin springs are clearly visible. The equaliser is centrally placed below.

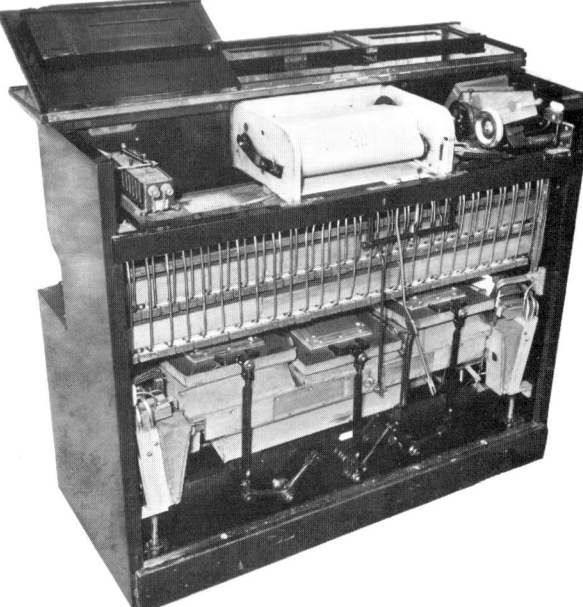

PLATE 86 ▶
Viewed from the front, the Welte Vorsetzer displays the exhauster drive cranks and tie rods to the three exhausters, the use of which ensured perfectly even suction levels at all times. To the right of the music roll can be seen the trefoil rotating motor, virtual trade-mark of all original Welte systems. Note also the metal tubing – there was little or no rubber used for pneumatic connection.

◀ PLATE 87
A real rarity is the Aeolian Duo-Art reproducing cabinet player. Believed to be a unique specimen made to the express order of some wealthy or special customer, this is a late product of the Duo-Art era. It is in the private collection of Sony Corporation's managing director, Akio Morita in Tokyo who is a devoted player piano enthusiast.

PLATE 88 ▶
The keyless 'red Welte' – the Welte-Mignon piano – was introduced sometime before 1910 and remained in occasional production until around 1920. A full reproducing piano playing the wide red paper rolls already encountered on the Vorsetzer, it was made in a variety of styles. Seen here is one which comprises a Feurich piano made in 1908 and sold in Paris by Steinway. The piano was made to suit a room in a mansion and the case was specially panelled and ornamented in oak to match.

▼ PLATE 89
One of the problems of the keyless piano was tuning it and most piano-tuners experience difficulty in tackling an instrument where they cannot work with a keyboard. Welte overcame this by producing a small, narrow detachable keyboard which could be slotted into place and used in a normal way. These attachments are today very rare. Here is one which turned up a few years ago still in its proper storage/transit box.

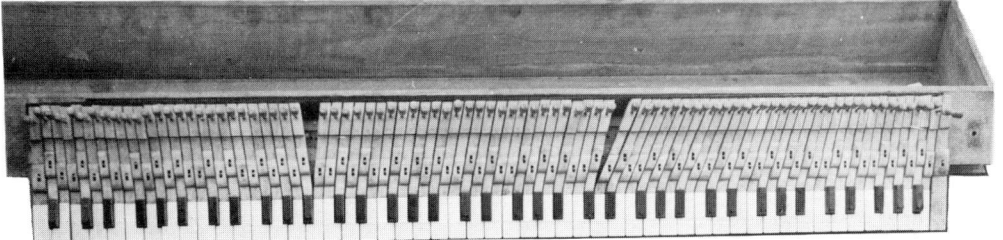

◀ PLATE 90
There were several styles of the keyless Welte-Mignon piano, one of the most popular being the model seen here. The cabinet shows a transition between the classical formalism and the rising *Jugenstil*. The interior mechanism of these instruments was very similar to that of the Vorsetzer and all major components were interchangeable.

PLATE 91 ▶
Besides the cabinet players and the keyless players, the Welte-Mignon reproducing action could be installed in other makes of instrument. Here is a 1922 Steinway grand piano containing the action. Again the characteristic form of roll-drive motor is unmistakably Welte. Note the large flywheel attached to the motor axis shaft.

◀ PLATE 92
Edwin Welte and his associate Karl Bockisch were the brains behind the Welte-Mignon reproducing system. The factory at Freiburg contained a fine panelled recording studio with special Feurich recording piano and the recording machine. The piano's keyboard was provided with a mercury trough beneath it into which carbon contacts dipped as keys were depressed. This made electrical contact with an ink-pen recording machine housed in the tall cabinet next to the piano, the characteristics of the ink marks depending on the force employed to depress the keys. In this picture, itself a rare survivor from the World War II destruction which levelled Welte's factory, Karl Bockisch stands elbow on his recorder. Eugen d'Albert sits at the keyboard and Edwin Welte stands right.

◀ PLATE 93
The year following the arrival of Welte's reproducing piano, Hupfeld introduced the Dea reproducing instrument. This played music rolls a massive 15$^{15}/_{16}$ inches wide using a 106-hole tracker bar. The rolls played from bottom to top as seen here. The machine was extremely well engineered.

PLATE 94 ▶
Introduced by the American Welte company was the Welte-Mignon (Licensee) action using conventional-width rolls and, unlike the top-mounted Welte-Mignon, capable of drawer-mounting in a grand piano. Here is one such installation in a piano by Bauer of Chicago dated 1924.

◀ PLATE 95
Like the Welte-Mignon, Hupfeld's Dea used metal tubing for most connections and was characterised by its use of transverse exhausters and equaliser, clearly seen in this picture. Production of the Dea suffered from the competition by the inventors of the reproducing piano, Welte, and the last one made was around 1913. A small number of Dea Vorsetzers was made but none is known to survive. In spite of its commercial failure, the Dea was an outstanding interpreter and laid the ground for Hupfeld's Triphonola reproducing action.

◄ PLATE 96
Close-up view of the roll drawer on the Welte-Mignon (Licensee) action in the Bauer grand piano. This model has been given a non-standard but practical electric roll drive using grooved pulleys and toothed rubber belts.

PLATE 97 ►
Hupfeld called its player action the Phonola and this was produced in three forms – the ordinary foot-blown Solophonola with Solodant theming, the Duophonola all-electric reproducing piano, and the Triphonola which was a foot-operated or all-electric reproducer of the type dubbed 'pedal electric'. Here is a Bluthner Solophonola with the lid on 'half-stick'.

◄ PLATE 98
The early Duo-Art reproducing actions made by Aeolian took a leaf out of the Welte book and used three exhausters belt-driven from a large electric motor. Here is a Steinway full electric Duo-Art made in Aeolian's factory at Hayes, Middlesex. Subsequently, Aeolian used the familiar square-shaped four-lobe suction pump and at the end of production used a small suction unit rather like a vacuum cleaner. This was the Motora which tended to be noisy and of insufficient power to cope adequately with full expression.

PLATE 99 ▶
The controls of the American Steinway Duo-Art showing third from right the 'accompaniment graduation' lever, subsequently replaced by the sliding and rotating 'Temponamic' knob used on almost all English Duo-Arts (see Plate 101).

◀ PLATE 100
The Steinway Duo-Art Pianola in pedal-electric style. This could be played entirely by electricity using the built-in motor-driven pump unit, or could be pedalled by foot. As a foot-powered reproducer, the full range of expression is often impossible to achieve. This particular style of installation was considered the zenith of the Duo-Art system and it is interesting to note that the pedal-electric concept was not adopted by Duo-Art in America. It is found with Steinway and Weber grands.

PLATE 101 ▶
The Steinway 'pedal electric' in position for foot-playing. Note the position of the hand controls in the key rail and the large circular knob of the Temponamic control. The pedals fold up out of sight in the box which also contains the normal piano pedal controls.

PLATE 102 ▶
Operator's view of the Steinway Duo-Art Pianola with the key fall removed showing one of the Aeolian 'World's Music' series of music rolls in position. These expensive rolls provided extensive written information about the composer and the particular piece of music on the roll leader.

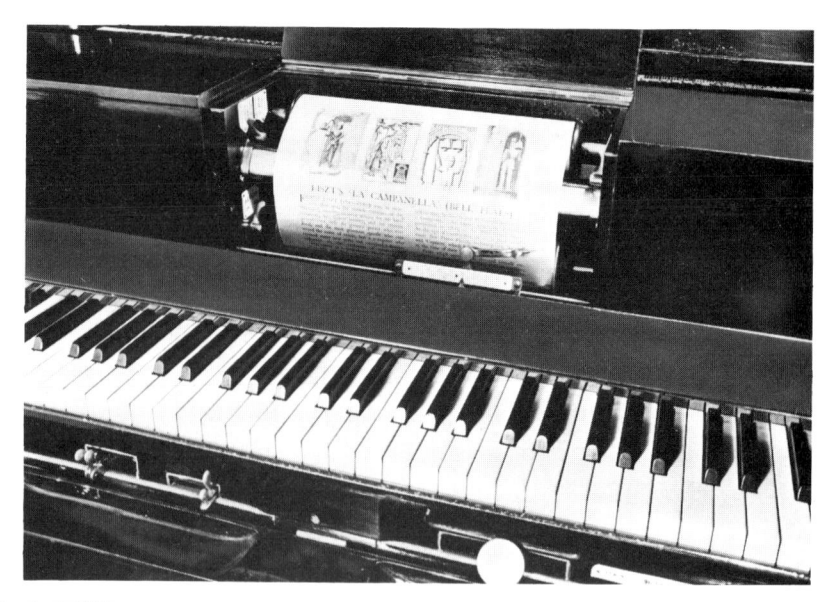

◀ PLATE 103
Aeolian in New York produced a lavish portfolio of case styles available for the Duo-Art. It is not known whether these were ever produced but here are four of these with their original descriptions. This one is Design No. 3010 Spanish: 'This case of Spanish design has as one of its beautiful features contrasting inlays of ebony and boxwood on the leghead, panels and music desk – a detail frequently found in Spanish work. The legs are twisted, with a heavy connecting stretcher that is rather close to the floor. This combination of inlays, carvings, pilasters and panels is exceptionally effective, and great care has been taken to tone it to a soft antique finish.'

PLATE 104 ▶
Design No. 3028 Louis XVI: 'A rare case of Louis XVI design, done in walnut or mahogany. This design is noted for its fine carving and delightful proportions. The rim, keybed, moulding, legs and desk are beautifully carved with motifs of the period. The desk is perforated, with a leaf pattern carved over these perforations and framing a plaque in the center. Throughout the development of this case, from the selection of the veneers to the finishing process, great care is employed to assure a real work of art.'

◀ PLATE 105
Design No. 3027 Louis XVI: 'Delicacy and refinement are reflected in this Louis XVI case in walnut. The legs are very finely fluted and reeded, with an acanthus leaf carving at the base just above the stretcher. The desk, forearm and lyre are carved with the finest of the Louis XVI motifs. There is a beaded band on the rim of the case dividing the field and the delicately toned border.'

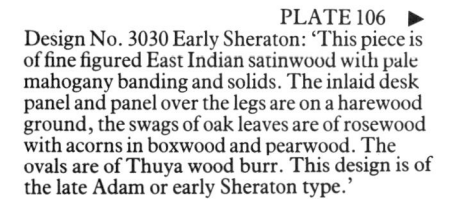

PLATE 106 ▶
Design No. 3030 Early Sheraton: 'This piece is of fine figured East Indian satinwood with pale mahogany banding and solids. The inlaid desk panel and panel over the legs are on a harewood ground, the swags of oak leaves are of rosewood with acorns in boxwood and pearwood. The ovals are of Thuya wood burr. This design is of the late Adam or early Sheraton type.'

◀ PLATE 107
The magic of the reproducing piano now comes home to a new generation of music-lovers with the occasional series of concerts organised in London by The Player Piano Group. Here at the Queen Elizabeth Hall in the autumn of 1972, Percy Grainger (who died in 1961) was the soloist in the Grieg Piano Concerto – via the Duo-Art reproducing rolls he had made half a century earlier.

◀ PLATE 108
The Ampico Model A reproducing action was fitted into a variety of quality pianos. This installation is in a 1927 Grotrian-Steinweg. Here the action drawer is opened and the panels removed to reveal the mechanism.

▲ PLATE 109
The Marshall & Wendell reproducing grand piano seen here has the Ampico Model A action fitted. The action was the invention of Charles Fuller Stoddard and it remained in production until the late 1920s.

▲ PLATE 110
In the late 1920s, the Ampico was redesigned to produce the Model B seen here also in a Marshall & Wendell piano, this one dating from 1931. The penetration of the Model B was curtailed by the economic depression of 1929–31 and so it is today somewhat rare.

PLATE 111 ▶
The neat and uncluttered appearance of the Ampico Model B drawer can be seen in this installation in a William Knabe piano of about 1930. While the Model B was markedly different in operation from its predecessor and its fullest potential was developed with the rolls cut for it, it was also fully compatible with the Model A music rolls. There was some loss of expression, however, because the Model B used a different crescendo system.

CHAPTER 7

The Reproducing Piano

Putting authenticity into piano-roll performances was identified very early as the essential goal for the player makers. The earliest approach was to contrive to subdue the bass while allowing the treble to sing out louder. This was made possible by the division of the pneumatic chest or stack. Next came the various ways of accenting notes which ultimately resulted in the Themodist/Solodant type of control. However, the path to even this achievement was no smooth one. The division of the chest, not unnaturally, is made to coincide with the division of the hammer rail, itself a fundamental affected by the design of the piano frame (in a grand) and in the early days this was not standardised. The Vocastyle Music Company, later to be taken over by Q.R.S., did much to alert the industry to the anomaly of the systems in use in the early years of the industry through its newsletter *Vocastyle Notes*. In one issue is lamented the fact that with three makes of electric expression pianos then on the market (*c.* 1912) the division was arranged between C sharp and D, yet many players were still being made with the division between E and F. Vocastyle wrote to all American piano makers to try to get the system standardised between C sharp and D, 'the logical division point'. In truth, the world industry finally settled for the division between E and F in the centre octave.

PAVING THE WAY

This first major step at rationalisation was the one event which established the groundwork for all that followed: the standardisation of piano roll gamuts at 65 and 88 notes, agreed at a convention held in Buffalo back in 1908, was an inevitable sorting out of a then tangled industry but in itself was not directly responsible for the developments which followed and therefore was not as major a development as the standardisation of the chest division which followed the hammer rail division agreement.

 Electric drive, automatic sustaining-pedal control from the roll, theme accenting and, finally, soft-pedal control from a duct at the right-hand side of the tracker bar were all developments which followed apace. The result was the 'expression piano', fully automatic (even as to rewind) and strongly marketed as an artistic instrument in the United States from about 1912 onwards.

 But the ultimate goal was to encode in the paper roll the veritable spirit of the original performance. This came about with the development of the instrument which was to be known as the 'reproducing piano' although, like the word 'pianola', it was a trade name for one company only. So markedly better than an ordinary player piano were these instruments that each successive improvement became, in the minds of the advertising men and the public who read their notices, closer and closer to the soul of the recording pianist. In truth, the reproducers went a very long way towards that goal but, in spite of their claims, they never quite made it. Had the Gordon Iles isolated instantaneous theme come along a decade earlier (see Chapter 6), the story might well have been different. But the reproducing piano was good, very good in fact, and some musical interpretations on it were without doubt magnificent in every way. Many were extremely fine, and a large number were mediocre. Let's look at the instruments first, though, for we will consider the achievements of the devices towards authenticity in another chapter.

WELTE AND THE MIGNON

Surprisingly enough, the first such instrument came with the so-called 'Keyless Red Welte' made in the opening years of the present century. This piano did not have a keyboard (a feature which undoubtedly cost the Welte company many sales and which led to its having a very restricted market) and performed electrically. Requiring neither pedalling nor touch from its owner, it would perform at the pull of a switch.

The original Welte-Mignon action used remained practically the same from the keyless reproducing piano of 1901 to the end of the 1920s. The system was usually fitted only in grands, particularly the Steinway, and was different from other installations in one major respect – it was fitted above the action on top of the piano as distinct from the later Ampico which was fitted beneath.

Welte was the first maker of reproducing pianos to dispense with the most awkward component in the player action – the pump which created the vacuum. In the non-electric players, the vacuum was manufactured by large exhausters. Electric players used either a four-lobe rotary pump belt-driven by an electric motor or a self-contained electric motor and exhauster pneumatics built into a sealed metal case. With the grand installation, the pump tended to spoil the side appearance of the piano since it protruded below the instrument. The player action itself took up little space. Welte put the pump in a completely separate cabinet, finished in matching style to the piano and connected to it with a flexible rubber hose. In addition to dispensing with the bulkiest part of the player action, this also eliminated any mechanical noise. Separate box-mounted vacuum pumps were made to match many quality pianos and the Aeolian Key-Top Pianola of the 1950s also used a detached vacuum system.

Welte also produced cabinet-style piano players right up until at least 1931. These push-ups were, however, very different from the players of the turn of the century for they were full reproducing players. Tastefully constructed, beautifully finished and driven by an electric motor, these played wide, red-paper music rolls and performed on the keys of a piano with all the sensitivity of a real pianist. Each of the four wheels of the player could be adjusted with a screw-jack so as to position the fingers correctly. The illustration (Fig. 58) shows a 1912 cabinet-style push-up of this type. Known as the Welte *Vorsetzer*, it made any ordinary piano into a 'reproducer'.

As John Farmer relates, the immediate success of the Welte and the very fulsome and doubtless sincere tributes which it was paid by almost every important musical figure impressed the Germanic personalities of the co-inventors, Edwin Welte and Karl Bockisch, with a Wagnerian sense of destiny. The Welte system in its original form became imbued with mystic significance and was seen as the embodiment of perfection. In consequence of this, no important modification was made either to the recording mechanism or to the playback piano action throughout the quarter of a century or so of manufacture.

The Welte reproducing piano-player cabinet first appeared about 1904. It differed from the common player in that it was a full reproducing machine which played on an ordinary piano with 'pianists' fingers'. When not in use, the player could be pushed against a wall where it looked like a tasteful sideboard, there being neither pedals nor doors to belie its contents. It used the Welte system of triple exhausters to the suction reservoir and, of course, used the triple radial wind motor characteristic of Welte. As with the Ampico and Welte internal actions, it performed on eighty of the piano's keys, the remaining holes in the 100-perforation tracker operating the expression and other functions of performance.

The keyboardless style of the Welte reproducing piano was also marketed by the French company Victor Mustel, as the Maëstro. A report in *Musical Opinion* during 1906 suggests that artists recorded for 'Messrs Mustel'. In truth these must have been Welte artists and their rolls were branded with the Mustel name:

> We were glad quite recently to hear, at 41 Wigmore Street, the Mustel Maëstro piano. It is a mechanical instrument, the power for working it being electricity. The price is £220. Here is a pianoforte a long way out of the beaten track, inasmuch as the music which emanates from it possesses the technic of the artist who played whilst the perforated music was being made; and in this connection we may state that forty eminent musicans have already so acted for Messrs Mustel in the manner described. From a booklet issued, we learn that Mr R. Pugno – amongst others – has written in eulogistic terms of the pleasure he had derived in listening to music performed on the instrument; and Dr Gordon Saunders writes: 'I had entertained a decided prejudice to all mechanical musical instruments until I heard the one made by M. Mustel. By means of the wonderful Maëstro piano – an entirely automatic instrument – every *nuance, tempo rubato, una corda* – indeed the most minute detail is reproduced with marvellous accuracy. In a word, this extraordinary instrument seems *to enclose a great artist*.' We may state that, for the purpose of tuning, a key-board is temporarily fitted to the piano.

The detachable keyboard for tuning was an interesting feature of these Welte instruments. Without such a facility, tuning would have been unnecessarily tedious. This keyboard fitted into the front of the piano after the fallboards had been removed. The keys themselves were very short and this keyboard was kept, when not in use by the tuner, in a long wooden case. At least one of these is known to have survived with its original case and piano: this was auctioned at Christie's South Kensington during 1978 and now belongs to a collector in Aalst, Belgium (see Plate 89).

1911 saw the start of the manufacture of the Welte-Mignon in America. However, under the provisions of the Alien Property Act, the company was confiscated upon America's entry into the First World War. It was later reformed as a subsidiary of the Auto-Pneumatic Action Company and named the Welte-Mignon Corporation. The Welte patents were used under licence and a re-engineered instrument produced which was called the Welte-Mignon (Licensee) Reproducing Piano.

In 1924 the Welte-Mignon Corporation of 297–307 East 123rd Street, New York, copyrighted the name 'reperforming piano' as their answer to the 're-enacting piano' of Ampico and the 'reproducing piano' of Aeolian's Duo-Art. It should be noted that all makers of reproducing pianos referred to them as such and, as already pointed out, this became the generic terms for them just as 'pianola' had come to mean a player piano.

The Welte-Mignon Corporation produced the Welte-Mignon (Licensee) action which played standard-width 11¼-inch paper rolls and was generally accepted as being not quite as good as the original German Welte-Mignon with its much wider red-paper rolls. Red Welte music had tended to be almost exclusively of a serious nature, the popular music repertoire being limited. The Red Welte remained in production for some considerable while – it was still being made in the 1920s – and it retained its wooden tracker bar to the end at a time when virtually all other makers had moved over to brass or Britannia metal.

Welte-Mignon Licensee reproducing actions* were fitted in a hundred and twelve makes of American piano including those by Baldwin, Bush & Lane, Conover, Hardman, Kimball, Kranich & Bach, Mehlin & Sons, Packard, Sohmer and Stieff, also Acoustigrande, Hazelton, Ivers-Pond, Kurtzmann. Pianos by Schulz used both the Welte-Mignon and the Aria Divina mechanisms.

In 1927 the Steinway-Welte Grand in a rosewood or mahogany case cost £550 and the upright version £350. The Welte Cabinet Player reproducer cost £195. It is interesting to note that whilst the ordinary 'push-up' piano player went out of fashion by about 1910 Welte's reproducing player was still in production until 1931, in which year they produced their last reproducing instrument. Edwin Welte, son of the great Emil, died in 1957 at the age of eighty-two having lived right through the entire history of the pneumatic piano.

Key to the success of the Welte system was what was known as the floating crescendo. This was a very good description indeed for the Welte expression method which could operate in a totally free and variable manner throughout the whole range from pianissimo to forte. Half-way through this variable system there was provided one fixed reference point: this was the mezzo-forte control. In operation, the degree of loudness of the playing was alterable in two speeds – fast or slow – by the selection of either the 'crescendo' or the 'sforzando' valve assembly. Either motion was programmed from the expression perforations in the music roll. Now the mezzo-forte pneumatic could also be used as a quick-reference point to monitor the movement of the floating crescendo at any moment and so prevent the overreaction of the expression system under certain conditions of playing. This set of expression features was duplicated, one for the bass and one for the treble, and they could be used individually or together to reproduce the original performance's expression. A further feature was borrowed directly from the company's orchestrion organs and this was the use of lock and cancel valves for expression devices. The big advantage of these was that any function such as sustaining or soft pedal could be brought on with only a short perforation, and then cancelled at will later by another short perforation. This avoided the need for long chain perforations which tended either to tear or 'ribbon' and close up.

Now these features were used in all the Welte systems in various guises. The Welte action appeared in three separate and different styles and a further version was that produced in the United States by the Welte-Mignon Corporation of New York. Significantly, because Welte in Germany was the first to make a practical reproducing piano and to make use of variations in vacuum level to achieve expression, and because the patents taken out by Emil Welte and Karl Bockisch virtually covered the world, Welte took the Aeolian Corporation to Court over the use of variable vacuum for expression in the Duo-Art. In September 1921, Aeolian

---

* Givens relates that evidence shows all Welte-Mignon (Licensee) instruments in America to have been made at the Estey Piano Company factory in New York City.

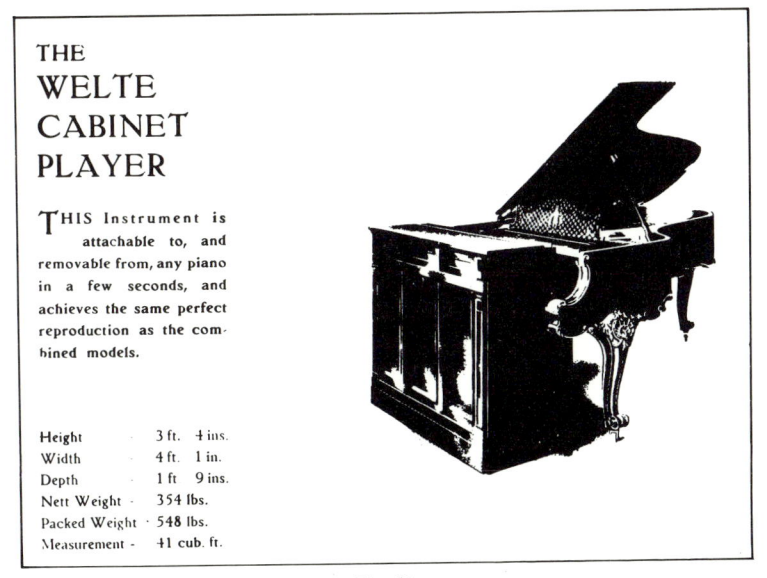

Fig. 58
The Welte *Vorsetzer* cabinet reproducing piano player.

settled out of court and agreed to pay a licence fee of $2·50 to Welte for every Duo-Art piano it made.

The first of the Welte-Mignons was the wide-paper Red Welte, so called because the music rolls were of red paper. The paper width, 12⅞ inches, and texture was identical to that used by the company for its orchestrion organs. Later, some of these wide rolls were also made on a buff paper. The Welte system was also the first to make use of a constant roll speed, so no tempo marking appeared on the roll aprons. Another unusual feature was that to provide extra power for loud passages one perforation was used to activate a pneumatic switch on the electrically driven vacuum pump to speed it up and increase suction.

Noticeable features of the Welte-Mignon are the varnished woodwork and wooden tracker bar plus the three-sided pyramid wind motor – surely the neatest and smoothest roll-drive mechanism ever perfected before the electric revolution.

This Red Welte style was also manufactured in America before the First World War, where it was called the Welte Artistic Player.

THE PHILIPPS & SÖHNE DUCA

Another very solid and well engineered system was the Duca made by the Frankfurter Musikwerke-Fabrik J. D. Philipps & Söhne. This business, established in 1877, later took over the Frati company, makers of the Fratinola electric expression piano. The Duca was introduced quite early on and replaced Philipps' first two player pianos which were the Cäcilia and the Corona. There were three models starting with the Ducanola which was a pedal-operated player piano. The second was the Duca, an all-electric reproducing piano. Finally came the Ducartist pedal-operated reproducer. All three were produced as grands – grand pianos are known in German as *Flugels*. However, the Ducanola could also be found as an upright and also as a *vorsetzer*.

There is an interesting coincidence here. The Duca action bears a strong similarity to that of the Welte and was introduced around 1909 and remained in production through to the early 1930s. It used a wooden tracker bar which was detachable by the turning of two small levers. When removed, it uncovered all the bleed holes immediately behind and was thus extremely easy to service. The Duca action was not provided with any system of roll tracking. Aside from these aspects, it is unusual that both Welte and Philipps should have produced *vorsetzers*.

An examination of the Philipps patents reveals very little in the company name, and certainly nothing connected with reproducing action. I believe that there is a very strong possibility that the Philipps action, although designed and built in the Philipps factory, was designed within the Welte patents. Perhaps Philipps paid a royalty to Welte for the use of the design. Although many Duca pianos were made, they are scarce today. However, they are high quality instruments and the manufacturers produced over 2,000 rolls, including some very ambitious ones such as for 'trios, quartettes, et al., accompaniment' and a number for violin and for cello accompaniment.

HUPFELD'S EARLY INFLUENCE

The firm of Hupfeld was formed in Leipzig and was originally known as J. M. Grob. It was established in 1892. Later it was taken over by Ludwig Hupfeld with the aim of producing on a large scale all types of mechanical musical instruments. In that year he took out patents on the principles of pneumatic action for pianos and organs. Hupfeld is probably better known today in the field of large orchestrions and also for the remarkable Dea-Violina (Phonoliszt-Violina) pneumatic violin and piano (see Chapter 9), yet they were responsible for some very advanced thinking on the subject of the pneumatic player piano. As with all other makers, their first instrument was a cabinet-style 'push-up' player and the factory was engaged in the production of these until about 1901, by which time they had perfected an action which could be fitted to the underneath of the piano keyboard. Adaptable to both upright and grand pianos, the attachment was available as a hand-cranked unit costing £30 or could be driven by a 100 volt electric motor at a cost of £58. A third choice was a model powered by a 25-hour accumulator. This cost £66 inclusive of the battery.

By 1902, Hupfeld was producing pianos with an electrically operated pneumatic player action. The compass was 5 octaves, C to c^3, and models were available which were coin-operated and/or remotely controlled from separate wall-mounted coin boxes.

An electric expression piano capable of playing 73 notes and having five central expression holes in the tracker bar was produced in 1908. At the time of this 73-note expression instrument, the American makers were still producing 58- and 65-note ordinary pianos. Shortly afterwards, Hupfeld had perfected the full-compass or 88-note player and devised melody- and theme-emphasising systems, pedal control and tracking for his ordinary player pianos as well as the fully automatic reproducing instruments.

Europe greeted the Hupfeld player piano with enthusiasm but it was not until 1910 that the first Hupfeld actions, fitted into Blüthner pianos, came into England. They were an immediate success, particularly as the action was far easier to fit to an existing piano than contemporary makes. The Hupfeld technical know-how at this time was extremely advanced – the firm possessed no fewer than 250 patents, the vast majority on the subject of pneumatic actions.

THE REPRODUCING PIANO

By 1920, wood and rubber tubing had been almost entirely dispensed with in Hupfeld construction and the action was largely metal. At this time also they made models which could operate by 'the electric light current'. Remember that at this time domestic electricity was used almost exclusively for lighting and the thought of using it for operating any form of machinery was practically unheard of.

Three models were put on the market – the foot-operated Solophonola, the electric reproducing piano called the Duophonola and the Triphonola, which could be used as a foot-operated instrument playing ordinary rolls, as a reproducing piano with electric drive or as an electrically driven ordinary player. Unlike most other reproducing pianos, the Duophonola played the full 88-note scale, additional holes in the tracker bar taking care of expression facilities in the same manner as the original Welte.

The renowned German firm of Blüthner, which distributed its pianos in England through a London office in Wigmore Street, fitted the Hupfeld action to both their grand and upright instruments. The last Hupfeld installation was made about 1937. In the early part of the 1930s, Blüthner designed their own player action which they called the Carola, and this was built at their factory in Southfield Road, Acton. The Carola, however, was if anything more costly for Blüthner to make than the cost of importing the Hupfeld action and, since there was very little difference between the performance of both actions, the Carola was dropped.

Hupfeld actions showed distinctive characteristics as compared with their American counterparts. The automatic tracking device, for example, used the horizontal see-saw bellows principle and the air motor was a straight-line, three-valve, slide-action unit. The Solophonola and Triphonola models had automatic expression and theme accentuation built in, and the theme emphasis was a patented system called the Solodant.

Each note of the Hupfeld action comprised a self-contained individual unit which could, if need arose, be removed and replaced in a few moments. This system, the so-called unit block board, was used by a number of makers in later years. The one-piece unit valve-assembly was patented in 1929 by player-piano makers Kastner-Autopiano Akt.-Ges.

All Hupfeld music rolls bore the watermark 'Phonola' and also the year of manufacture within the first yard or so. This also applied to their violin-playing rolls.

Blüthner made a great point of the system known as 'aliquot' stringing in their pianos. The system made use of a sympathetic string on each note above the so-called break in the keyboard (bass to treble). This string was not struck by the hammer but was allowed to vibrate in sympathy with the struck strings. In the middle treble register, the Aliquot was tuned an octave above (producing a distinct brightness of tone) and in the extreme treble the Aliquot was tuned to unison. This feature, still used today in Blüthner concert grands, was always emphasised on the Blüthner-Hupfeld grand instruments.

STODDARD AND THE AMPICO

By 1913, the first Ampico action had been produced by the American Piano Company in New York, taking its name from the first two letters of each word in the company's name. Although first made in 1913, it did not make its début until 1916, when it was demonstrated to a distinguished gathering at the Hotel Biltmore in New York (today overshadowed by the giant Pan-Am building) on 8 October. Pianist Leopold Godowsky played four pieces of music which were then repeated by the Ampico playing rolls which he had previously recorded.

The original designer of the Ampico was Charles F. Stoddard and his first system came to be known as the Stoddard-Ampico. It was also known as the Ampico Artigraphic, while an entirely foot-operated version, only marketed for a short while, was known as the Marque-Ampico. A flurry of activity in the Patent office heralded the supersession of the Stoddard Ampico by the Ampico Model A in 1920–1. This was further improved with the introduction of the Model B in 1929.

The Stoddard Ampico made use of pneumatic chests manufactured by the Auto Pneumatic Action Company which also manufactured the Welte Licensee action. The expression system on these was a rather complex affair but the salient features remained constant throughout all three variants as also did the use of the under-keyboard sliding drawer for the roll mechanism and controls in the grand installation. Within the spool box of these models was a power-regulating lever marked 'loud–soft–normal', which is an identifying feature of the system. An odd feature exclusive to this early model was an automatic section repeat system which would replay any section of the roll at will.

The Stoddard-Ampico gave way to the Model A which was manufactured in greater quantities than either of the other two Ampico variants. Action parts for this were made by the Syracuse-based Amphion company, which American Piano Company had recently acquired. Amphion had made the Artecho reproducing action and so the new model Ampico incorporated certain features of that action. Amphion's patented unit valve block, invented in 1912, became a feature of Ampico actions and while the basis of Stoddard's expression system remained it was greatly simplified and improved. The step intensity units, formerly provided with two valves, were changed to a single-valve system and the power-regulating lever was now marked 'subdued–medium–brilliant'.

With the Model B came a host of improvements and refinements, not the least of which was the dubious ability to play the so-called 'jumbo' half-hour rolls. This enlarged spool box necessarily carried a larger take-up spool to reduce the effect of varying paper speed as the roll diameter increased during playing (this feature was first adopted by Welte for orchestrions and later taken to the limit by Bruder, who used some massive spools in his roll-playing show organs). The expression system had been completely revised by Dr Clarence Hickman, who had succeeded in achieving the dual goal of speeding its response and making it simpler. This was achieved while at the same time ensuring that the newly made system with its special rolls would not preclude satisfactory interpretation of the rolls made to be played on the earlier model.

The main difference in the Model B expression system is that it uses but one crescendo mechanism and the special B-type rolls thus carry identical crescendo perforations for both treble and bass.

With the length and bulk of the special Model B Ampico music rolls, it became necessary to make some arrangement for ensuring that the large rolls were rerolled to the correct tension, in particular if the rolls were to be set to repeat, that is play continuously, for example, after-dinner music. This was achieved by a simple yet effective function of the electric roll-drive/rewind mechanism. Every once in a while during rewind, the take-up spool from which the paper was being rewound would be braked, the music spool being allowed to continue rotation. This ensured that the paper was correctly cinched (tightened) and the paper tightly rolled.

Ampico also made use of harmonic effects which were denied to the majority of pianos and player rolls. The three-pedal piano, in which the centre pedal was employed for sostenuto, was the key to the Ampico success. In a sostenuto piano, the centre pedal operates an extra rail in conjunction with the piano dampers. When operated while a chord, for example, is being played, the sostenuto rail will hold the dampers away from the strings even after the fingers have left the keys. In simple terms, the sostenuto pedal is like a sustaining pedal but, unlike its big brother which operates on all the piano dampers, the sostenuto operates only on the dampers which are raised at the time the pedal is operated. This allows the pianist to bring out almost a four-hand harmonic effect on certain types of music.

Ampico found that this same effect could be gained in the player piano by the simple expedient of extending the note perforation so that the dampers remained clear of the strings for the duration of the passage of the perforation over the tracker bar. This allowed a richness of sound which could not be obtained with conventionally cut music rolls where the length of a perforation conformed to the exact value of the note. Strange to say, this was far from a new concept. Precisely this system – and to achieve the same effect – was patented by Aeolian in 1900, the British patent being No. 10,615 of 29 June 1901. Now used on a wide scale for music of the popular type on the later Model A as well as the B Ampico rolls, this feature added a new and realistic dimension to the sound of the Ampico, virtually at no extra cost.

The depression of 1930 ensured that the Model B production was very limited and today it is a scarce instrument. Even rarer was a rather strange mutation of the Ampico Model B and a clock so that the piano could be used as a latter-day cuckoo clock, marking the hours with a short piece of music or simulated chimes. The clock mechanism was called by its makers Telechron, so the piano thus fitted had to be called Ampichron. Very rare today, this must mark the very lowest ebb of the reproducing piano which, although capable of doing better things, earned its bread and butter by imitating the Town Johnny* of the Middle Ages.

Ampico used as their trade mark the words 're-enacting'. Artists, some of whose music, recorded in Europe for Ludwig Hupfeld, had been 'scientifically adapted for the Ampico', included Wilhelm Backhaus, Harold Bauer, Alexander Brailowsky, Ferruccio Busoni, George Copeland, Erno Dohnányi, Edvard Grieg, Mark Hambourg, Fritz Kreisler (whose talents are today better associated with the violin), Theodor Leschetizky, Misha Levitski, Alexander MacFadyen, Pietro Mascagni, Benno Moiseiwitsch, Sergei Rachmaninov, Artur Rubinstein, Camille Saint-Saëns, Artur Schnabel, Alexander Scriabine and Richard Strauss.

In 1923 Rachmaninov, who had scorned the overtures from other and wealthier roll-manufacturing rivals to the Ampico organisation, sat down with the directors of Ampico to listen to the finished master rolls of a recording of his G-minor Prelude. At its conclusion, he puffed a cloud of smoke into the air and calmly remarked: 'Gentlemen, I have just heard myself play.' According to Adam Carroll, American popular music arranger and performer who headed the light music section of Ampico, this one remark caused a sensational rise of Ampico stock on Wall Street. The roll had, of course, been played back on the same piano as that upon which it had been recorded. The significance of this is amplified in Chapter 13.

A few months before his death, the great pianist Moiseiwitsch was discussing recordings for Ampico with a BBC interviewer in London, relates John Farmer. One of the pleasures of working with the company, he said, was that the editing staff with whom the pianist was expected to co-operate closely in the final stages of correction of the master recording were

---

* Town Johnny was the nickname of the person, usually of humblest upbringing and ability, who served the village community by sweeping the marketplace and, at certain times of the day, would ascend the church tower and sound the bell to indicate the time of the day. Obviously the 'time' was a somewhat arbitrary indication of the actual hour and was more geared to the sunset, the call of the church and the mid-day.

not only engineers with complete command of their craft but also consummate musicians. When asked if he considered that the Ampico recording system and the playback piano could adequately and faithfully realise his artistic intentions, he paused a while and then replied, 'Absolutely!'

One of these Ampico technicians was Edgar Fairchild, today living in California. Under the name 'Milton Suskind', Fairchild made a number of Ampico recordings of his own playing for the serious music department, making some superb arrangements of popular music of the 1920s which, as piano transcriptions, would not have done dishonour to Liszt. Fairchild finally assumed responsibility for the editing of all recordings by the great pianists, a course of action largely dictated by the fact that many of these performers, particularly Lhevinne and Rachmaninov, would discuss matters arising out of their performances with Fairchild and no one else.

Ampico's recording apparatus comprised two separate moving sheets of paper on which were recorded all the movements of the piano keys and pedals, together with exact measurements of hammer velocity at the moment of impact with the strings. This was done by the spark chronograph technique, firing one spark through the sheet of paper as the piano hammer approached the string, and a second spark in the final instant of travel before it struck the string. The integration of the data from the two sheets was the work of skilled artist engineers. The men who formed the Ampico team were a uniquely creative and happy band. 'Every day', according to Adam Carroll, 'was a holiday.' This was certainly reflected in the quality of the music rolls produced and in the company as a whole.

The Ampico recording pianos were no 'run of the mill' instruments. Carrying no maker's name, they were built to the special order of Ampico using the best parts of the best makes of American pianos. In this manner was produced a piano with a perfectly even tonal quality throughout the keyboard, ensuring that reproducing of the music roll on other instruments would be the nearest possible to the original.

One reason why relatively few Ampico instruments survive today (particularly outside America) is that the entire player action was attached to the underside (of the grand) by bolts which could readily be removed to return the piano to normal. There being few tuners or repairers who have either the interest or talent to regulate these (or any other player, come to that), owners have long been advised to throw away the player and rolls and restore the piano as an ordinary piano (see the concluding footnote of Chapter 5).

The actions were expensive – Marshall & Wendell, for instance, offered an Ampico baby grand piano in 1929 for $995 – but perfection and subsequent modification enabled the piano firm of William Knabe & Company to produce a 'baby Ampico and piano combination' for $495 in 1938 and made a point of offering to 'exchange your old, silent piano at good allowance'. Some of the finest American-made pianos with Ampico actions were those made by the famous house of Chickering.

A British company – Ampico Limited – was formed with offices at 233 Regent Street, London W1, and the action was distributed in England by Marshall & Rose. The Ampico action cost £200 and a further £200 to install and the 6 foot 1 inch grand Ampico cost 659 guineas. In 1928 the installation was modified by the introduction of the Model B tracking device and electric drive. They ceased production in about 1936 but continued making rolls until 1940.

Perhaps the finest of the Ampico grand installations and also the finest reproducing pianos were the Grotrian-Steinweg and Steinway. The main parts of the player action were mounted in a sliding drawer which ran the full width of the piano under the keyboard. A five-valve slide motor was fitted to the left of the spool compartment and all controls were neatly displayed on the top panels either side of the drawer. The Grotrian-Steinweg Ampico was also one of the most expensive of the reproducing instruments. In 1929 Ampico introduced the so-called Model B drawer, which was intended to replace the standard one where desired. This had electric roll drive through a constant-speed series-wound motor in place of the air motor and was also capable of taking rolls which would play for a full half-hour.

The Ampico reproducing action was fitted into many pianos. In America it was installed in the Knabe, Chickering, Mason & Hamlin, J. and C. Fischer, Marshall & Wendell and Haines Brothers pianos; and the Canadian maker, Willis, also fitted it. In Great Britain, it was used in pianos by Broadwood, Chappell, Collard & Collard, Challen, Hopkinson, Marshall & Rose, and Rogers. Besides the quality German maker Grotrian-Steinweg, another top flight European maker, Bosendorfer of Vienna, selected Ampico.

THE DUO-ART

A rare insight into the American player piano industry was afforded to Musical Box Society International members in April 1981 when Steinway's former board chairman Henry Z. Steinway was a guest speaker at a regional meeting held in Binghamton. I am indebted to Harvey Roehl for these notes, a full transcript of which appeared in the MBSI *Bulletin*, Volume XXVI, pages 146–50.

The relationship between Steinway and Aeolian in America was cemented by the signing of a contract approved on 9 March 1909. Prior to this, Aeolian's top-quality piano was the Weber. This contract, intended to run for 25 years, provided that:

Steinway & Sons agree to discontinue furnishing their pianos to the Welte Artistic Player Piano Co., for the incorporation of their Welte-Mignon players for the United States of America, on and after 1 June, 1910, but the present existing relations, arrangements and contracts between Steinway & Sons, Hamburg, and Steinway & Sons, London, and the Welte Company are to remain in full force . . .
Steinway & Sons agree to supply to the Aeolian Companies a minimum of not less than six hundred new Steinway Pianos per year . . .
The Aeolian Companies agree to officially relegate their Weber Pianola Piano to second place under the Steinway Pianola Piano, and they further agree to withdraw from the artistic concert field and that they will exploit the Weber Piano in public only through such minor pianists as Steinway & Sons may permit.
The Aeolian Companies are to have the exclusive marketing of the Steinway Pianola Piano, both wholesale and retail, throughout the World.

This contract was finally terminated by mutual consent in April of 1933 by which time the player piano market in America had slumped. Henry Steinway recalled that his company took back from Aeolian 241 pianos which had been specially constructed for them as reproducing pianos and these were subsequently sold as regular pianos. 'There must have been hundreds of Duo-Arts from which we removed the player mechanisms, but no records exist to tell just how many,' he added.

The last Steinway player, according to Mr Henry Steinway, was a model L in walnut,

Louis style, serial number 290,000 into which Aeolian fitted an Ampico player. This was after the amalgamation of the interests of Ampico and Aeolian and the piano was sold to a Denver, Colorado, dealer in December of 1937.

The Hamburg factory continued to despatch pianos to the Orchestrelle Company in England through the London branch, and to the Choralion Company in Berlin, both being Aeolian subsidiaries. The Hamburg factory retained its relationship with Welte. Unfortunately, all the Hamburg factory records were lost during the war.

The Steinway Duo-Art, introduced as a result of this liaison, thus became Aeolian's top-market product. The company's other brand names, in descending order of price, were Weber, Steck, Wheelock, Stroud and, finally, Aeolian. In truth, there was little difference in quality and price between the Weber and the Steinway and Aeolian's enforced down-grading of the Weber was tactical rather than indicative of inferiority.

It seems that Aeolian used several methods of recording their artists. A recording piano with electrical contacts was used, movements of the keys, dampers and pedals being traced on a sheet of paper by the action of a series of relays. Although giving an accurate recording of the length and duration of notes, this did not provide for the degree of force given to each note. This was, at one stage, applied to the roll after recording, editors of varying degrees of skill working in collaboration with the recording artist. The company also made gramophone records of performers so as to compare the roll with the actual performance. Later on, though, the direct measurement of the individual hammer velocity in the recording piano was introduced. The technique was probably similar to, if a little less refined than, the spark chronograph method used by Ampico.

The Duo-Art had the advantage of being available on the market several years ahead of the Ampico and scored over the newly introduced Welte-Mignon and Hupfeld in that the music rolls were much cheaper. Multiple-roll-punching machinery at the Aeolian factory worked twenty-four hours a day to keep down costs and also to meet the fantastic demand for this instrument which could play as all the great instrumentalists.

The Duo-Art was in production in America until 1932, when the New York factory was destroyed by fire. At this point, the Aeolian Corporation merged with its former arch rival, the American Piano Company, and moved to the Ampico factory at East Rochester. From that date forward, Duo-Art and Ampico actions were under the same roof and there was much interchanging of rolls, and Roehl states that the very late Duo-Art rolls are sometimes to be found fitted with Ampico labels. Drawer-mounted actions, characteristic of Ampico, now also appeared with the Duo-Art. There were two other centres of production – Hayes, Middlesex, and Berlin. The Orchestrelle Company made its last all-British Duo-Art action around 1936. Meanwhile the Choralion Company in Germany ceased production of Duo-Art parts somewhere around 1934, no doubt because home-made competition on the German market was too forceful.

As with all reproducing piano rolls, Duo-Art had its own selection of the masters and this leads one to wonder whether or not a keyboard virtuoso would go to the bother of recording a roll for, say, Welte, Ampico, Hupfeld and Duo-Art (and probably others), or whether, as Ampico admitted, some of their rolls were 'scientifically adapted' from a master reproducing roll cut elsewhere and for another company. Be that as it may, the Aeolian Duo-Art artists included the celebrated I. J. Paderewski, George Gershwin, Victor Herbert, Harold Bauer and Rudolph Ganz.

The interesting advertising ethics of the period, particularly those practised in America, may come as a revelation to us today. Testimonials, blatantly solicited, were printed from famous artists. Paderewski, so one was led to believe, was perfectly content to have no fewer than two 65-note Pianolas (and countless other makes of player) and sit at the piano with them, pedalling his way through music which he could far better perform by hand. In later years wide publicity was given to the fact that Benito Mussolini had a Weber Duo-Art in his palace at Rome and there was also one to be found at the Élysée Palace, the official Paris residence of the President of the French Republic.

One of the more amusing advertising stunts was pulled off by the Ampico makers. Under a large headline proclaiming 'Becomes so engrossed in the Ampico that he neglects to perform his literary work', the dramatic critic of *New York World* is credited with having written to Ampico Corporation officials saying that he wanted the piano removed at once. 'I shall miss it acutely,' the story goes on, 'but everyone flocks here to play the instrument . . . I never will get any work done while this beguiling attraction remains on the premises.' The scruples of advertising!

Even so, it must be said that the Duo-Art and the Welte-Mignon (Licensee) actions were surpassed in excellence of performance by the Ampico action.

A useful profile of the American player market comes from a table of deliveries relating to the contract between Steinway and Aeolian in America. I am grateful to Harvey N. Roehl of The Vestal Press for this information, provided by Henry Z. Steinway and first published in the *Bulletin* of the Musical Box Society International. The list does not differentiate between ordinary 88-note players and Duo-Art reproducers but if one assumes that all those made after 1913 were actually Duo-Arts, then 6,458 grands and 1,931 uprights were produced for a total Duo-Art Steinway production of 8,389 instruments.

Player pianos shipped to Aeolian, 1911–1931

Year	Grands	Uprights	Total
1911	125	327	452
1912	214	210	424
1913	254	290	544
1914	108	325	433
1915	100	324	424
1916	25	477	502
1917	223	271	494
1918	363	66	429
1919	274	55	329
1920	250	140	390
1921	444	45	489
1922	390	76	466
1923	448	56	504
1924	667	20	687
1925	762	18	780
1926	804	20	824
1927	514	16	530
1928	456	3	459
1929	319	19	338
1930	209	–	209
1931	102	–	102
Totals	7,051	2,758	9,809

PIANOLA

Historically, the only reproducing push-up piano player to be produced in quantity was the Welte Vorsetzer. There are in existence, however, two unique Duo-Art instruments of this type, one contemporary and one modern. The first is a Duo-Art push-up apparently made in the early 1930s to special order. This is currently in the private collection of Mr Akio Morita, chairman of the Sony Corporation in Tokyo, Japan. This one appears to be a unique specimen of the Aeolian-developed IST system, referred to earlier. This has a number of non-standard features which include special music rolls to embrace tracker-bar perforations which extend outwards beyond the usual expression ports used with normal Duo-Art pianos and rolls. The second instrument was hand-built by Britain's Player Piano Group member Gerald Stonehill in conjunction with one-time Aeolian Company inventor Gordon Iles. This so-called Duo-Art Robot has been used to perform at public concerts in London and is a specially-designed one-off machine using a late Ampico-built Duo-Art drawer-type player action. A full description of this machine appeared in *The Music Box*, vol. 7, pp. 75–6, in 1975. There are also details to be found in Chapter 10.

To revert to the production development of the reproducer, the old-established firm of Broadwood (famed for its production of the so-called square piano for which they produced no fewer than 65,000 between 1770 and 1854) made a number of reproducing pianos using several different bought-in actions. They also equipped Steck pianos with Duo-Art actions by arrangement with Aeolian.

SYSTEM COMPARISONS

The basis of the Duo-Art system is a method of expression providing sixteen different degrees of loudness for both theme and accompaniment sides of the stack. These are built about a zero setting for, again, both sides of the pneumatic chest, the zero being contrived so that the instrument is at its softest. It is so arranged that the theme side is set one step or degree louder than the accompaniment side so as to ensure that even in the loudest passages of music the melody can be slightly more predominant. Because the theme may be in either treble or bass sections, theming accordingly can be used in both halves of the stack (this is a normal characteristic of the Themodist system). However, judicious use of the Themodist openings in conjunction with a normally constant level of loudness in both halves of the stack can produce sudden and powerful fortissimo notes or chords. Where these theme-emphasising perforations are arranged in both treble and bass simultaneously, some very impressive fortissimo passages can be achieved.

In the Ampico system, the expression system is duplicated for both halves of the stack and each system offers seven degrees of power which can be used if required in conjunction with a two-speed continuous crescendo or decrescendo control. This crescendo system formed the linchpin of Ampico's promotional campaign, part of which was involved with the criticism of Aeolian's step system. Having said that, though, it comes as a surprise to find that the avowed benefits of this system are by no means fully employed by the majority of Ampico rolls, which still rely on the two sides and their seven-step loudness capability.

While Duo-Art makes use of pneumatic motors pulling against a return spring, thereby tending to be somewhat slow in response, the system scores in admitting very large changes in playing volume by relatively small movements of the accordion pneumatics.

In contrast, the Ampico action has a more delicately balanced pneumatic action with consequent improvement in response speed which allows it to respond at high speed to the

THE REPRODUCING PIANO

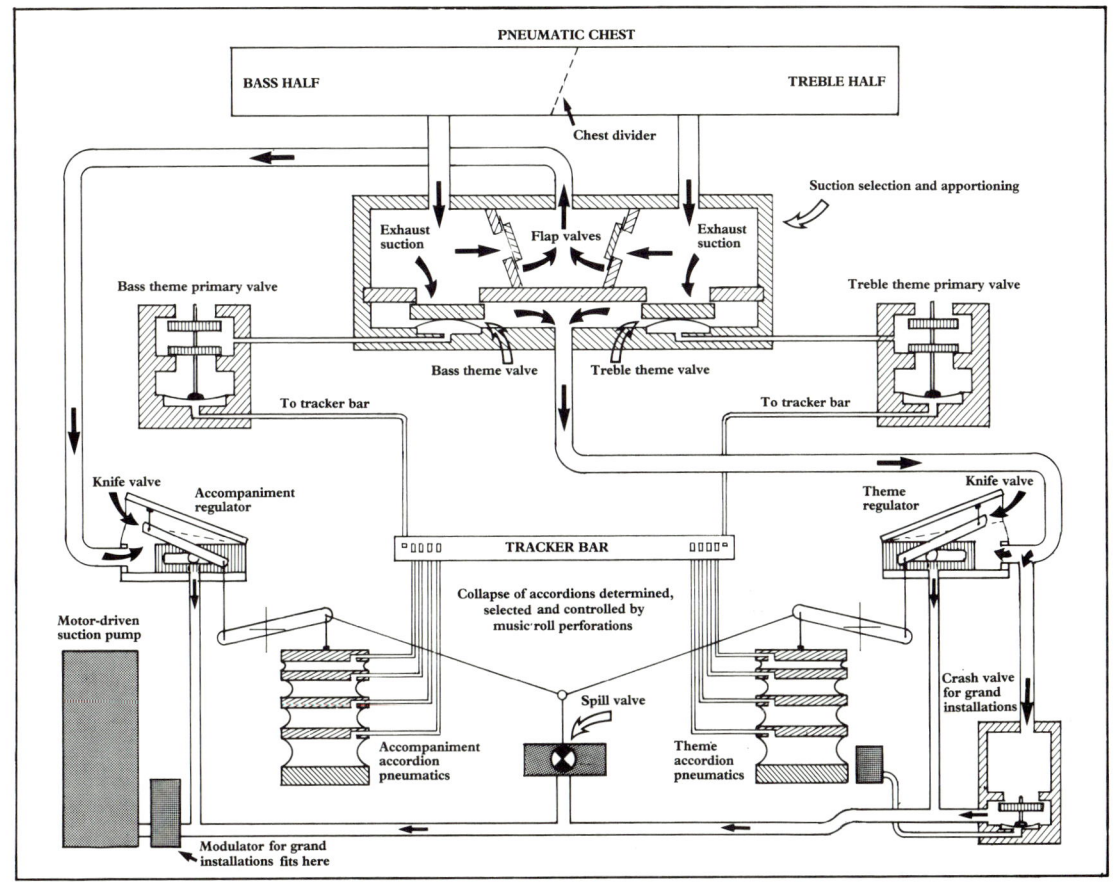

Fig. 59
Schematic illustration of the Duo-Art reproducing system.

loudness requirements of individual notes. In theory, then, the Ampico action can produce a more faithful representation of the pianist – assuming that the pianist was that good to begin with! As for response speed, this is not a great limiting factor, since accordion and theme punchings can be adjusted to be far enough ahead of the notes which they are to affect to allow for delay. One limiting factor of the Ampico is that its crescendo pneumatic opens or closes in one of two speeds – two or eleven seconds. This can produce an almost infinitely variable dynamic for each note, but only in relatively slow music. Since most Ampico pianos also offer the user via a three-position switch lever the choice of playing subdued, normal or brilliant, this setting (no recommendation as to which ought to be used is provided on the roll) will also affect the authenticity of the original performance.

The soft pedal action in pianos takes two primary forms. First is the use of the keyboard shift, popular with the concert grand piano and found on American-made Duo-Arts. With this action, the piano keyboard and indeed the whole action is shifted sideways by something like ¼ inch. This allows the hammers to strike on only two of the three strings which make up the majority of notes, and as far as the bass is concerned allows just one of the two strings to be struck, so producing a softer sound.

Fig. 60
Sir Henry Wood directing the Queen's Hall Orchestra in London at a Duo-Art concert.

The second type of action, almost universal in upright pianos and introduced in some grands (not exclusively the cheaper variety), is the half-blow rail which moves all the hammer actions slightly closer to the strings, so reducing the travel of the hammer to the string and thereby making it possible to play softer.

The half-blow rail presents its own problems in the player action in that the movement of the hammer action alters the distance between the pneumatic action and the action wippen. This problem was first identified by Welte with the keyless uprights. They introduced a lost-motion pneumatic in the system which counteracted it. This feature is also seen in some Ampico actions although in the majority the action is such that operation of the soft-pedal control does not alter the geometry of the action parts by any significant amount.

Reproducing pianos were no cheap devices. Chappells produced an ordinary upright player for 158 guineas and a grand for 240 guineas in the 1930s, yet in February 1927 the price of an average small Ampico grand in Britain was 560 guineas or 476 guineas for cash. By 1931, when prices had fallen, the same piano was listed at under 300 guineas. At the same time, a pedal-electric Duo-Art model O Steinway cost £615, and the Model B £745. The list price of the Mason & Hamlin Ampico in England was 70 per cent higher than that of the cheapest English Ampico grand.

The Artrio reproducing action was used by Broadwood in their quality grand pianos for a while around 1924. Sir Herbert Marshall & Sons, the Angelus concessionaires in the United Kingdom, staged a recital in October 1924 at the Broadwood Galleries, New Bond Street, at which the instrument was compared with the playing of Olivia Cate. A report on the event (Player Piano Supplement to *The Gramophone*, November 1924, p. 4) speaks glowingly of the occasion, adding:

> One can only marvel at the astonishing ingenuity and craftsmanship that go to the making of this product of two such famous houses, and commend it to all those who value artistic merit.

Another famous quality piano maker was Bechstein. However, Bechstein were not believers in the merits of the player or reproducing piano and, although a few Ampico installations were provided to special order, this company did not go out of its way to advertise that it was associated with player production.

Other reproducing pianos were the Solo Carola, the ArtEcho, Apollo, Angelus Artrio, Aria Divina and Celco, all of which stemmed from America. The ArtEcho and the Apollo were mechanically the same and both were developed by the American Piano Company, the former for sale to independent manufacturers and the latter for Wurlitzer. The Solo Carola never sold in great quantities, although, claims Roehl, it was potentially very good. The Angelus Artrio was invented by Wilcox & White, the organ builders of Meriden, Connecticut. It was used in Hallet & Davis, Conway and Merrill pianos, all built by the Conway Music Industries. When Wilcox & White liquidated in 1921–2, the plant was sold to the Conway company which also owned the Simplex Player Action Company. Simplex subsequently redesigned the Angelus Artrio to use the normal Simplex pneumatic motors in place of the diaphragm motors for which the Angelus piano and organ actions were renowned.

The Celco action was incorporated into pianos built by Chase, Emerson and Lindeman. In Germany, the Stuttgart firm of Lipp & Sohn produced the Duca-Lipp using the Philipps action. This sold for £300. The Leipzig firm of Popper made the Stella reproducing piano.

Companies spent out considerable sums in trying to perfect better reproducing actions. The Solo Carola, for example, apparently took two years to develop and cost its backers – The Cable Company of Chicago – $175,000.

Most of the reproducing systems were unable to play the full 88-note compass of the piano. Ampico, Duo-Art, Welte-Mignon (Red) and others depended for their expression systems on the sacrificing of some of the notes at each end of the keyboard when used as a reproducer. The first to provide a full 88-note reproducing system was Hupfeld with its Triphonola in 1918. The expression ducts in the tracker bar were beyond the note compass which allowed normal or standard rolls to be played without the need for switching back in these extreme bass and treble notes. Four years later, Welte made the so-called 'Green' system – the music rolls were green – which also gave 88 playing notes.

As to the dates of the various reproducing systems, in chronological order we have Welte-Mignon (Red) – 1904; Hupfeld Dea – 1905; Welte-Mignon (Licensee) – 1908; Philipps Duca – 1908; Aeolian Duo-Art – 1913; Ampico Model A – 1914; Wilcox & White Artrio Angelus – 1915; Melville Clark ArtEcho/Apollo/Celco – 1915; Hupfeld Triphonola – 1918; Welte Green – 1922; Ampico Model B – 1929.

How good were these non-starters in the world of reproducing pianos? Why did they fail to catch on? And why did the three big names of Aeolian, Ampico and Welte succeed? The simple answer is just that they were 'big names'. The giant Aeolian Company and the American Piano Company together comprised most of the biggest and best of the American piano trade. Welte held a high reputation in Germany. In favour of the Ampico action, Celco, ArtEcho and Apollo – all produced by subsidiaries of the American Piano Company – were not allowed the chance to make much of an impact. Instruments such as the Solo Carola, launched in the summer of 1916, the Artrio and the Aria Divina of the 1920s (whose rolls also played on the Recordo expression piano) all tried to find a chink through which to break into the market. That they did not succeed does not directly imply that they were poor reproducers or in any way inferior actions. They failed due to the fundamental fact that their makers did not have the backing to forge and maintain a standing in the market. Indeed, it is an interesting thought that one or more of these may well have been a candidate for a better action than those produced by the great names – we can never know.

It is worth mentioning again the rival method of musical reproduction of the period – the gramophone. The first electric recordings were in production and a 12-inch 78 r.p.m. record would play for almost five minutes. Tone arm pick-ups were heavy and the essence of reproduction was the steel needle which could only be used once as its passage in the record groove ground it (and, ultimately, the groove) into a different shape. Needles came in tins marked 'loud tone' (fat ones), 'soft tone' (thin ones) and 'medium tone'. A novelty was the dual-purpose spear-shaped needle which could be used as either loud tone or soft tone just by rotating its odd-shaped body through 90 degrees in the sound-box chuck. Commonest defect of all was the ever-present 'needle hiss' caused by the rotation of the disc under the needle and accentuated by the quite ridiculous weight of some of the pick-ups, which seemed more intent on wearing through to the groove on the other side than in concentrating on the one on top of the record. Gramophones worked by clockwork. Records were made to be played at about 78 r.p.m. although several makers produced ones to be played at 80 r.p.m. and one at least at 82 r.p.m. Speed naturally affected pitch and thus pitch was arbitrary. My gramophone-loving colleagues will no doubt accuse me of denigrating the gramophone but all I am doing is showing that as regards piano music, in which field an alternative method of reproduction was available, the reproducing piano was far, far superior since it was in truth a real piano giving forth a real performance by an accredited artist.*

Marshall & Rose fitted the Angelus action made by Wilcox & White and first patented in 1895. Their Model 43 grand had the action in a drawer under the keyboard very similar to the Ampico and it also had foot treadles.

Because player pianos had to reach the public in a mass-market sector in order to be commercially viable, most of the pianos to which player actions were fitted were of the smaller, domestic variety. Since very few homes could accommodate, for example, a 6 ft 2 inch Steinway, the small grand and boudoir grand were the largest usually available.

In recent years in London, an enterprising body of enthusiasts in the Player Piano Group, the body set up by Frank Holland of the British Piano Museum, has staged a number of concerts at the Purcell Room, a post-war concert hall on London's South Bank close by the National Theatre and the Festival Hall. Here it has been possible to give occasional public concerts on instruments such as Duo-Art concert grands, the Steinway Red Welte, the Grotrian Steinweg Ampico, and so on. The recently designed Duo-Art Robot, described in Chapter 10, has been demonstrated playing the concert hall's own Steinway concert grand to perfection, and generally these concerts have done much to stimulate a new interest in these instruments in the eyes of the concert goer. Significantly, several music critics of the British press have been sufficiently impressed as to sing the praises of the instrument in their newspapers; others have been less than charitable, just serving to prove that part of a critic's task is to demonstrate what he thinks to be superior intellect. In some cases, of course, intellect and mental atrophy run together. And prejudice, the destroyer of the true critic's very ability, occasionally rears its gorgon's head.

The high cost of the reproducing piano and the demand for better-quality interpretation from the ordinary-type of player piano – in particular the automatic or electrically driven players used in public places – raised a demand for a sort of low-cost instrument somewhere between the normal pedal piano and the reproducer. These were called expression pianos and very simply what these did was to divide the chest or stack in the normal way and then apply a series of degrees of expression or intensity to each half. Coupled with note theming, these instruments were generally employed only in the playing of light and popular music and in this genre they could perform very well indeed. From the basic expression piano was later to be developed the nickelodeon (see next chapter).

Many companies manufactured expression pianos in the 1920s. There was no common design and most offered between five and seven degrees of expression for each side of the stack. Used in conjunction with multi-tune rolls, instruments of this type rapidly gained favour in that section of the market which specifically had a call for a low-cost provider of

---

* Just as the gramophone and phonograph were not at first seen as a serious challenge to the musical box, which it was so thoroughly to usurp, the player piano industry did not consider this machine to pose worthwhile competition. Even so, the gramophone had one major advantage to offer and that was its unique ability to record and reproduce the human voice. In fact, right from its earliest days, it was a superb reproducer of the voice. While most musical instruments sounded tinny and lacked credible frequency response, the human voice fell most exactly within the optimum band of sound frequencies which best suited the machine. It was, no doubt happily for the player-piano industry, not for many years that the reproduction of piano music became acceptable. As electric recording appeared in the 'thirties, so did the era of the player piano wane not just from the market depression but from the effect of serious competition.

reasonably good music which did not demand too frequent roll-changing. Bars, restaurants and those rather less-respectable places of male entertainment made up the major sector.*

Of the many expression pianos made, one of the most unusual was the Solo Expression Twin Tracker Empress marketed by the Chicago firm of Lyon & Healy. Introduced in February 1923, this instrument featured a double-width music roll which traversed a double tracker bar, the two bars effectively being mounted in one line, end to end. The music roll was perforated with five tunes in each direction. During the first movement of the roll, as it was unwound onto the take-up spool, the right half of the tracker bar would be used on the first five tunes. At the end of the roll, the direction of motion would automatically reverse, and the roll would rewind under the same controlled drive-motor speed, this time playing a further five tunes from the perforations on the left half of the roll. A promotional leaflet located by Q. David Bowers reads:

> The unique features . . . will commend themselves to all who have any acquaintance whatsoever with piano construction. Twin Tracker: The two trackers are end to end . . . Double width roll: The roll plays in both directions, forward and reverse, one tracker for the downward and the other for the upward movement. This means no waste of time or energy for rewinding, no rolls torn from high speed rewinding. Nine degrees of Expression. Seven degrees of expression are considered the extent obtainable in hand playing. The Solo Expression Empress has nine degrees of intensity.

The instrument was offered with a 'steel wind chest of square steel tubing that will last forever'.

Sadly, these interesting and unusual instruments, along with many other unconventional American pianos, have since been converted to play standard rolls in the standard mode. Many of these conversions were done during the working life of the instrument in order to extend their practical utility, but early collectors have likewise been guilty of more than a few transgressions.

* These had a wide application in the houses of ill repute for the entertainment of the drinkers and the clients of the professional women who served their various needs. In so doing, they took over from human performers: remember many great jazz piano players of the era such as Scott Joplin and Eubie Blake owed their early livelihoods to the keyboards of bordellos.

DUPLEX

(Maxfield's Patent) Player-Piano

This Action is fitted to large numbers of the Best Makes of Pianos, and is

THE BEST moderate priced PLAYER ACTION MADE.

We were the first manufacturers of Pneumatic Instruments in Great Britain.

Awarded Diploma of Honour and Gold Medal.

Illustration of the Piano open for tuning.

MAXFIELD Player Piano Co., Ltd., 324-6, Liverpool Road, N
LONDON.

Three minutes from Highbury Tube Station and Highbury North London Railway. Bus No. 62 passes the door.

CHAPTER 8

The Nickelodeon

If the brand name 'Pianola' was to become synonymous with all the products of the entire player piano industry, then the word 'Nickelodeon' came into use to relate to all American pianos operated by a coin. However, unlike 'Pianola', there never was a 'nickelodeon'. The nearest instrument of that name was a strange coin-freed instrument made by John A. Weser around 1913 – the Nickel Player.*

The coin-operated electric piano was conceived in two places independently and more or less at the same time – Germany and the United States. Berlin and Leipzig piano-makers began producing stately uprights which could be played manually or allowed to play automatically by remote control – a remote wall-box would be strategically placed into which customers of the café or bar would be persuaded to insert a coin. Within the box, the coin would make an electrical contact, so switching on the piano.

The coin-operated piano was by no means the first coin-freed musical instrument to be made. Indeed, the Encore Banjo conceived by Charles B. Kendall of Boston, Massachusetts, and produced as early as 1896, takes that honour. But the first electric piano was put on the market in 1898 by the St Johnsville, New York, company of Roth & Engelhardt. This was the cabinet-style 44-note Peerless. With vacuum pump and pneumatic stack it was not only the world's first production electric piano (if not the true progenitor) but a very advanced piece of player-piano technology made at a time when there was still no technical agreement as to how a piano might best be automated. And mechanical players operated by barrels and punched card were still being made and would continue to be invented for some years to come. Indeed, deKleist's Tonophone of 1899 was a hybrid device with pneumatic striking action operated by a pinned wooden barrel.

As Q. David Bowers relates,† Farny Wurlitzer visited the Leipzig Trade Fair in 1902 and saw such a variety of automatic instruments that he immediately contracted to distribute them in America. He signed up with the Frankfurt business, J. D. Philipps & Söhne, to have

---

* Q. David Bowers (*Encyclopedia of Automatic Musical Instruments*) tells the story of the Weser Brothers' business. Founded in 1879 by John A. Weser, the business made a large variety of upright and grand pianos, later turning to players under the Marveola trademark. The Nickel Player was a coin-freed electric piano housed in a case identical to one of the styles of Electrova made by the Jacob Doll company. A 1913 description of an electric Marveola said: 'The Marveola can be played by electricity . . . Its special, unique features include the ability to play with proper expression and tempo any standard 65-note or 88-note player piano roll, with much expression and musical feeling. It has an automatic rerolling feature of great value and the patented Virtuoso accenting system. Bowers relates that the Nickel Player indeed does have an unusual accenting system – a rotating cam wheel which introduces loud or soft expression into the music from time to time at random and not in any way co-ordinated with the music roll.

† *Op. cit.* p. 347.

shipped to the States the Philipps Pianella and the Paganini which were sold by Wurlitzer as the Wurlitzer PianOrchestra, the Concert PianOrchestra and the Paganini. To cover up the origin of the instruments, Wurlitzer went as far as stamping parts with the legend 'Manufactured by the Rudolph Wurlitzer Company'.

DeKleist's answer to the Peerless, the 44-note Pianino of about 1901, was an instant success, according to Bowers, and established the coin-freed automatic piano firmly in the American way of life.

So was born a whole new industry and its centre became Chicago. Here makers such as the Operators Piano Company, J. P. Seeburg Piano Company, Marquette Piano Company and others united with makers scattered elsewhere in the States including The Automatic Musical Company (later to become the Link Piano & Organ Company), the North Tonawanda Musical Instrument Works.*

The America of this era was suffering from growing pains and the majority of these seemed to hail from the events surrounding the San Francisco gold-rush which began in 1850 or thereabouts. The Californian gold-rush was to have a subtle yet profound influence on the development of the nickelodeon. It came about through the avarice and changing social values which the rich supply of gold generated.

As more wealth poured into California, San Francisco developed into a city of big spenders and then as now there was no better way to spend money – or to show that you had money to spend – than to create a luxury home and with it possessions of quality. While the architecture of Old San Francisco developed along certain well-defined if self-indulgent patterns with that finely etched dividing line between sham and folly on the one side and beauty and art on the other being manipulated freely to suit individual whim, it brought to the city, the state and to the nation as a whole aspects of art and artefact that were new. The beauty of stained glass or art glass was one of these. And the burgeoning *art nouveau* and the seeds of *art deco* found their way into America at the end of the nineteenth century.

The richness of California was demonstrated by the immense wealth of goods imported into San Francisco – and the large number of drinking houses and whore-houses. It was in these places of entertainment that the nickelodeon makers sought to place their products. Indeed, so great was the demand that subsidiary companies were set up on the West Coast to try to cater for the demand. And the new-found beauty of stained glass soon became a feature of the instruments, front panels of art glass being fitted. The increasing use of electricity in the early years of this century meant that the nickelodeon, with its illuminated art glass front, could be sold or rented in an increasing number of establishments and the takings were commensurately rich. At thirteen minutes past five on the morning of 18 April 1906, San Francisco was virtually wiped off the map in the earthquake and subsequent fire which did an estimated £60 million of damage. San Francisco did not die, though, and, like London, was rebuilt to live again. And the coin-operated nickelodeon which owes some measure of its origin to that city was to remain firmly entrenched.

As the nickelodeon developed, it gained more musical effects by way of percussion instruments and the addition of ranks of organ pipes. Its musical repertoire was extensive and its playing time increased by long, endless bands of music and by multiple-roll changers.

---

* *Tonawanda* is Iroquois Indian for 'swift running water' and is so named from the Niagara River which surges along the city boundary.

THE NICELODEON

The heart of the instrument from quite early on was the electric expression piano and this, while it never reached the sophistication of the reproducing piano, became a comparative musical marvel in its own right.

In 1920, a Congressman named Volstead succeeded in getting through a private amendment to the US Constitution. His act came to be known by the one word 'Prohibition' and it effectively banned the sale of intoxicating liquor. Overnight, the bars and drinking rooms were out of business and the nickelodeon market virtually wiped out. Prohibition not only resulted in lost revenue; it encouraged smuggling and illicit distilling and it was a long thirteen years before the narrow-minded law was repealed. For the nickelodeon, though, it was too late. Before Prohibition it was facing competition from the radio and gramophone. And after Prohibition the rivals had the upper hand.

But there was one particularly interesting species of roll-playing pneumatic or electrically operated pneumatic instrument which remained almost unknown in Europe.* This was the automatic orchestra of the silent cinema which was known variously as a 'photo-player' or a 'fotoplayer' (the name of a product of The American Photo Player Company). These were produced by several manufacturers to meet a need for music and sound effects to accompany pre-talkie films.

The photo-player was made in numerous styles and instrument combinations. The instrument frequently comprised a piano console with one or sometimes two matching attached cabinets to contain the various other effects. The whole could be operated manually from a keyboard and pedal clavier, or could be operated from roll music. Some could play two music rolls at once, others were made with complex arrangements for selecting instantaneously any part of any one of up to half a dozen or more rolls fitted into a self-changing mechanism.

Typical of the advertising media of the period and a good example of the literature circulated by the makers of photo-players is the following extract from an advertising booklet published by the house of Seeburg, one of the leading makers of this type of instrument. Their Pipe-Organ Orchestra was available in models ranging from $3,500 for a console and one case up to the vast Style A De Luxe with its towering ranks of pipes on either side. 'Price', it added darkly, was 'by arrangement'. But to quote from their publicity:

> It is Tuesday night and you are showing a five reel feature of undoubted merit; but it is more than a film which has filled your theater to the last row. With an orchestra at his finger ends, your piano player sits at his keyboard and watches the film flit across the screen. He is only a single person, an individual, mind you, and yet he has at his instant command the resources of a pipe-organ with its wonderful variety of stops, the tender, true tones of a violin, the brisk notes of a xylophone, the gay click of the castanets, the silver rattle of the tambourine, and the syncopated beats of the drum.
>
> There is no descriptive demand which a film story can make but he is able to meet it – no episode in movie land that he cannot make more thrilling, more touching, more enjoyable to the audience. As his fingers run over the keyboard he is master of every

---

* Several theatre players were made in Europe around the time of the First World War. One was Hupfeld's Clavimonium and another was called the Tyler Apparatus. Both were in the form of large upright pianos and contained, besides a piano, a reed organ, pipe organ and percussion effect. Both were hand-played as distinct from roll-played. The Hupfeld model was advertised as suitable for 'kine theatres' and included a five-rank harmonium. Another was Hofmann & Czerny's Kinophon range. These Vienna-made models were introduced about 1910.

situation. He is the living interpreter of every shade of emotion registered by the silent players. He can express sorrow of the life-stories enacted there in the heart-searching melodies of that great organ's voice; or he can add zest and life to a comedy film with an instrumental accompaniment which puts a new bustle and spirit into the funmaking of the screen comedians.

The silent audience sitting there with eyes glued on the screen as yard after yard of film unwinds may not be conscious that this one man holds their emotions in the hollow of his hand. They may not realise that it is his perfectly fitting accompaniment which make a photo play in your theater twice as enjoyable as in the movie house across the street, but when the final 'close up' of the lovers clasped in each other's arms fades away with the sweet pianissimo tones of the organ giving the scene new meaning, then they turn to one another and say 'What perfect music'.

And that is just what the SEEBURG Pipe-Organ Orchestra is – 'perfect music'. It enables you to have the same sort of music in your theater that only an orchestra and a $10,000 pipe-organ could otherwise give you – and in addition you have all the sound effects which add so much to the showing of any film.

If a messenger dashes up on a foam-covered horse, your pianist presses a single button and hoof beats are perfectly imitated. If the wind is howling around the miner's cabin, the effect is correctly achieved by the SEEBURG – the ring of a 'phone, bird call and any number of other realistic effects are in your SEEBURG instrument at the player's finger tips.

Who can overestimate the value of a perfect musical accompaniment to a moving picture? Who can say what a great effect such music has on the box office receipts?

Isn't that the sort of music you want in your theater? It certainly is. But, you object, the cost is too great. No longer, however, can this objection hold true because since the advent of the SEEBURG Pipe-Organ Orchestra such perfect music is within the range of any good motion picture playhouse. The SEEBURG instrument not only gives you a piano, an organ, the resources and traps of an orchestra, but it has the further advantages of both hand and self-playing operation.

Note that we say 'self-playing' and not 'mechanical' because there is nothing to even suggest the 'mechanical' when the SEEBURG is operated by a roll. It still has the human touch and the human soul found in no other instrument on the market – the quality of tone shading and personal expression which have made the SEEBURG the choice of the proprietors of America's best motion picture theatres.

There were many other photo-players and makers, among them the Cremona made by the Marquette Piano Company of Chicago, the Capital Symphony Orchestra by the Capital Piano Company, New York, the Banjorchestra by F. Englehardt of New York, and the Link produced by the business which was later to pioneer the Link Trainer for instructing aircraft pilots in blind flying. There was also the Reproduco, the Nelson-Wiggen, Coinola, North Tonawanda, Berry-Wood, Wurlitzer, and so on. This was a vast industry the likes of which Europe was never to see.

With the arrival of the 'talkies', it was now the turn of the photo-player business to be struck down almost overnight and the many thousands of theatre orchestras thrown out and destroyed. Thanks to the efforts of present-day enthusiasts in America, such as Q. David Bowers and Harvey Roehl, remaining machines – and their literature – are being preserved.

Nickelodeon scales and hence music rolls were standardised into several sizes and types and could be used on instruments having xylophone and other percussion accompaniments. It was not uncommon to find a row of violin-toned organ pipes to provide a sometimes uncompromisingly transparent chorus, often loud but nevertheless thin.

The keyless nickelodeons, such as those made by the Nelson-Wiggen and Link companies, were much smaller than a comparable player piano and could thus be fitted easily into the smallest bar or diner. Instruments often played an endless 'roll' of music which, without the facility of a spool, would be allowed to uncoil and pack into a compartment provided for it – approaching entanglement but never actually jamming and shredding – several hundred feet of paper in its meanderings preceding and succeeding its passage over the tracker bar.

The point at which the nickelodeon became an orchestrion or piano-orchestrion is not possible to determine with any degree of accuracy. The terminology of the time, both in Europe and America, tended to be imprecise. The Wurlitzer Bijou Orchestra, for example, included a piano, mandolin effect, string-toned pipes, snare drum and xylophone. The same firm marketed a larger model named the PianOrchestra (ex-Philipps) as well as the Mandolin Quartette, which was really a pneumatically operated tremolo piano. Another coin-operated tremolo piano was the Regina Sublima which played from rolls of stiff perforated paper $19\tfrac{5}{8}$ inches wide. This used the same type of beating-hammer action as the Piano Melodici invented by Racca of Italy, only the piano-forte effect was achieved automatically by a ratchet wheel inched back and forth by twin pawls on an eccentric. Generally speaking, the reciprocating cycle of this type of action caused rapid wear so that in some respects the instruments were unintentionally self-destructive.

Nickelodeons with keyboards could be depended upon to entertain even when the resident ivory-tickler was out having a beer and sometimes they were fitted with the famed Wurlitzer roll changer, which systematically played six rolls of music one after the other, rewinding each at its conclusion. Unfortunately, many of the parts of these ingenious and complex devices were cast in a metal alloy which has swollen over the years and thus a number of collectors have experienced various malfunctions, including the miserable results of a roll changer going haywire and attempting to change its rolls in the middle of a tune. However, newly produced replacement parts can now be obtained to restore these.

The nickelodeon represents an interesting byway of player-piano history, and yet it should be rembered that, as I have already suggested, the term 'nickelodeon' is nowhere accurately defined. The term is usually thought to apply to the coin-operated piano with expression and effects and probably keyless, yet it may also be found used to describe almost any make of coin-freed electric piano, including those with facilities for being played manually, those with organ registers and even those coin-operated barrel-piano orchestrions. This problem of definition makes it doubly hard to say with any certainty when the era of the instrument came to an end – or, come to that, when it blossomed. Certainly the era of the electric coin-freed piano seems to lie between 1905 and 1920, with some examples predating and some postdating this.

The electric piano for use in public places was to continue in production for a further decade until the early 1930s. But the heyday of the instrument being considered here, both in the United States and also in Germany, was the period from 1909 to 1914. Throughout these years, new instruments were being introduced to the trade almost weekly. Production of photo-players grew during the years from 1910 to about 1912 and, although some firms continued making models into the late 1920s, the peak of that market was the period between 1915 and 1920.

In assessing the numbers of photoplayers made, Q. David Bowers* says that in 1921 there were 17,824 theatres in the United States exclusively devoted to the showing of motion pictures. It is estimated that 1,000 of these had pipe organs (Wurlitzer alone had installed 500 or more that year), this leaves 17,000 or so theatres which were candidates for an instrument. Most theatres – possibly half that total – provided music by having a full-time pianist play by hand during the shows.† Possibly a few hundred others had more elaborate arrangements for providing music, such as a small group of musicians or an orchestra. Bowers says that he believes that between 8,000 and 10,000 photo-players were made in America and Europe during the period 1910–28 and of these the best sellers were the Reproduco made by the Operators Piano Company, American Photo Player Company instruments, and those made by Seeburg and Wurlitzer. In 1916, Wurlitzer was to advertise that 'every day more than two million people listen to Wurlitzer music'. By 1930, the business was well and truly dead. Sadly, their sheer size and bulk resulted in vast numbers being destroyed and survivors are but few, including several which, remarkably, remained intact through being walled up *in situ*.

* *Encyclopedia of Automatic Musical Instruments*, pp. 352–3.
† So established was the job of film accompanist that in 1924 or thereabouts one Erno Rapée arranged a collection of some 400 pieces of music entitled: *Motion Picture Moods for Pianists and Organists: A Rapid-Reference Collection of Selection Pieces . . . Adapted to Fifty-Two Moods and Situations*. Comprising more than 678 pages, this was published in New York and no theatre accompanist was considered complete without his copy on the music desk.

Kerrobert Sask., Canada

Gentlemen: My "North Tonawanda" Organ is still as good as when I received it, 3000 miles or more from the factory, and though it has been in use Four Years, has not cost us 5 cents for repairs. Some recommendation, what?

Sincerely yours,
Ernest Pepper.

Behind the scenes of "Model G." Note the compactness and accessibility of the interior workings— designed and built by experts and master musicians.

CHAPTER 9

Other Roll-Playing Musical Instruments

Pause a moment and take a tiny silicon chip, the heart of the microprocessor or computer, and marvel at the complexity of its photographically reproduced, minute circuits. Imagine just what the inventors of the player piano would have thought of that! Or better still, had they understood it, imagine what they might have done had the technology been available to them. The electronic synthesiser is another marvel of this age which, like a mechanical musical instrument, can be programmed to produce a complex tune or rhythm. Unlike the paper roll, though, the programme is controlled by miniature time gates and delicate circuitry which would defy visual translation into a musical form. After all, many people can read the music on a piano roll! But perhaps it does not do much good to dwell on the achievements of this new age when we are evaluating a past age of pneumatic control. Just as in the time of William Shakespeare people no doubt gazed in wonderment at Bidermann's clockwork spinet, so did people stare in amazement three centuries later at the Wurlitzer automatic harp and the Mills self-playing violin.

It is a sobering thought that almost every one of the so-called orchestral musical instruments was automated by one process or another between the years 1500 and 1930, from the saxophone of the dance band to the harp of the symphony orchestra, from toy trumpet to banjo, from xylophone to violin. Even the drum could play tattoo or roll from a perforated disc within.

The early mechanical instruments played to the best of their creator's ability by using the pinned barrel, but, with the advent of perforated music, the whole gamut of the orchestra in perfection became a mechanical possibility. Whether the best results were achieved electromagnetically or pneumatically, the programming of the impulses to produce sound was undertaken by paper. From Aeolian's 'reproducing' pipe-organ down to the elementary triangle, paper music encouraged and inspired inventors all over Europe and America.

Strange as it may seem, one of the earliest instruments, other than the piano and organ, to inspire the creative genius of inventors for paper musical adaptation was perhaps the most difficult to mechanise – the violin.

The Paris organ builder, Antoine Corvi, patented in 1854 a method of playing 'violins, tenor violins, violoncellos and other common stringed instruments' using either a pinned barrel turned by a handle or by finger keys. Corvi's system used rubber-tyred wheels as bows to each string and mechanical fingers to stop off the strings. Best known for his fine portable street organs, Corvi went on to patent the playing of almost every orchestral instrument but it is not known whether he actually built such an array of musical automata.

Many mechanical organs contained stops which were named 'violins', but these were hardly stringed instruments, being in truth wooden pipes carefully voiced to produce string tones. All the famed makers of orchestrion organs incorporated violin pipes in their instruments and many of the so-called piano-orchestrions also had a rank of violin pipes for tonal effect.

Among the earliest of the genuine mechanical violins was that which was contrived by Professor Wauters of Binghamton, New York. Wauters was development engineer for the Binghamton Automatic Musical Company, later to be taken over by the Link Piano Co. The Automatic Musical Company, founded by two brothers named Harris, concentrated mainly on modifying pneumatic pianos made by other concerns but they did contribute some considerable research and experimentation in the realm of other mechanical musical instruments, producing in 1903 the Automatic Xylophone which, as Roehl says, was undoubtedly the forerunner of the marimbaphones and xylophones produced by American manufacturers in later years. In Europe makers such as Welte had been using similar accompaniment techniques for some years.

Professor Wauters joined the company in about 1900 and spent seven years perfecting a 65-note pneumatic violin. The resulting instrument was remarkably sophisticated and featured pneumatic devices for the automatic application of rosin to each of the four circular 'crystal' bows, variation of bowing speed and the ability to play on all four strings at once. Wauters's instrument, although contemporary writers speak well of it, was probably too temperamental, too in need of repeated attention to maintain its perfection, for it to be a viable manufacturing proposition. The firm continued selling their other lines which included the Encore Automatic Banjo which played paper music rolls $9^{5}/_{8}$ inches wide. By 1913 they were in debt, as a result of which the firm was taken over and renamed the Link Piano Company (see Chapter 8).

There were three main contenders for the self-playing violin in Europe. Dealing with the rarest first, there was the attempt in France by Émile d'Aubry and Gabriel Boreau. Their instrument, called the Violinista, was said to have had almost perfect bowing from a genuine violin bow moved as required on a carriage over the violin strings. It was built for the personal amusement of the inventors in 1926 and was not intended to be a production mechanism. Next in terms of rarity is the Popper Violinovo of 1929, manufactured by Hugo Popper of Leipzig. A single violin surmounted a player piano and was arranged in a horizontal position. Two of its strings, the A and the E, were played by pneumatic plungers which pressed down on the strings. Bowing was by means of a small circular wheel rotated by a motor. The Violinovo was of the piano orchestrion variety of instrument with percussion effects, all from the control of a perforated roll. Only one of these is known to survive today and that is in the Werner Baus collection in Fuldatal, West Germany.

But by far the earliest production instrument and the one which gained a permanent place in the hearts of collectors was another Leipzig-built instrument. The star attraction at the Brussels Exposition of 1910 was Hupfeld's Phonoliszt-Violina. This consisted of a Rönisch piano with player action above which were mounted three vertically set violins played pneumatically and, like the piano, controlled by perforated-paper roll music. Upon the first violin, sixteen fingers worked on the E string; on the second violin ten fingers worked on the A string, and on the third violin ten fingers worked on the D string – the G string was not used. The fingers were little pads of felt attached to arms fitted to collapsing pneumatic motors. The three violins were arranged vertically with their necks lowermost. Each was pivoted so that it could be moved outwards to bring its single string into contact with the bow. The group of violins was encircled by a horizontal continuous hoop-shaped bow rotated by an air motor. The bow, patented in 1910, consisted of some 1,550 horsehairs, each about twelve inches long and forming a short tangent inside the circular bow. They each overlapped slightly so as to provide, in effect, a complete, circular interior bow. The rotational speed of this bow could be varied automatically by the control of its driving air motor.

Hupfeld had begun experimental work on its self-playing violin in the early 1900s and the first production began around 1907. The first to be marketed, according to Bowers,* was in 1908. It was widely acclaimed and considered by some to be the eighth wonder of the world. Initial production was for instruments playing a paper roll $15^{15}/_{16}$ inches wide. There were two types of roll made for this and the tracker bar had two sets of holes, the upper one for Phonoliszt-Violina rolls, and the lower set for Phonoliszt artists' rolls. Later models played narrower rolls $11^5/_8$ inches wide. Both types were made in limited quantities with two separate spool boxes side by side, and also with duplex or 'double roll-changing' mechanism.

Just before the First World War, the company introduced a model with six violins in two groups, each with its own circular bow. Very few of these seem ever to have been made and although there was most certainly one in the London showrooms it, along with all the others, seems to have disappeared.

After the war was over, the instrument was aimed at the silent cinema as a provider of musical accompaniment.

There were numerous variations: the Dea-Violina in 1909, Clavitist-Violina and Phonoliszt-Violina in 1910 – these names signifying the piano to which the violins were fitted. Both the Dea and the Clavitist were, though, short-lived. Another short-lived variety played on Violin-toned organ pipes in place of the real strings.

The Viennese brothers E. and C. Stransky were connected with Hupfeld in some way as yet undetermined and, in 1911, were granted patents for certain features of violin-playing mechanisms identical to those of the Phonoliszt.

Many thousands of these fine instruments were turned out, yet very, very few are known to collectors today. Throughout the world there are fewer than three dozen known in spite of the fact that tonally these were in the finest automatic violins ever made – much better, for example, than the later and more widely known Mills machines from America.

Those that do exist still demonstrate superbly the sheer quality of their manufacture and the thorough understanding of both the instrument and its music in the setting up of the special paper rolls. An interesting feature of the instrument is that a *sourdine* effect is provided for, yet in most surviving examples it is not complete. During a run-through of rolls one day on the example in the Utrecht museum, one roll was found which operated the sourdine with striking effect. Strange to relate, of the known rolls, this appears to be the only one to take advantage of this facility.

From the instruments made in Europe, we go to the United States to see how the automatic violin player fared in that country of enterprise and development. The abortive attempt to produce a mechanical violin playing fifteen strings, which was the brainchild of J. W. Whitlock, is described later in this chapter, but by far the most outstanding achievement in this field was the work of Henry Konrad Sandell in conjunction with the Mills Novelty Company of Chicago. Sandell was born in Sweden in 1878 and went to America at the age of

---

* *Encyclopedia of Automatic Musical Instruments*, p. 437.

ten. By the time he was eighteen, he was chief electrician for the Adams Westlake Company and at the age of twenty-one he took out his first patents for a coin-operated, mechanically played violin. Up until the time of his death on 29 January 1948, he had secured over 300 patents, mostly on violin-playing machines.

By 1904 Sandell was employed by the Mills Novelty Company, who remained his employers for the following twenty years. In 1907 the first of Sandell's automatic violins appeared. It was called the Mills Automatic Virtuosa and consisted of a normal violin played electromagnetically from a perforated-paper roll. Metal fingers were used to stop off the strings and bowing was achieved by rotating celluloid discs after the fashion of Professor Wauters, whose work was contemporary.

Strange to relate, the public awareness of this Chicago-made instrument came about not in America but in London. One of the then very large department stores was Waring & Gillow, who occupied a fine building in Oxford Street a few moments' walk east of Oxford Circus. This imposing building housed some seven floors of household furnishings, including musical instruments.* An idea of the importance of this store in the world of both furnishing and music can be gleaned from this notice which appeared in *Musical Opinion* of July 1906:

> One of the sights o' London town last month was the series of musical receptions given by Messrs Waring & Gillow (Lim.). The business is so large that there are two and a quarter miles to be traversed should one walk through every room. However, we were content to leave pedestrian exercise alone and so were taken up in the lift to the piano department; it is under the management of Mr Edwin Ashwell. We should have stated that many of the various show rooms contain suites of furniture for many kinds of houses and flats. For instance, the furniture for a cottage is offered at a hundred pounds; and in this case a piano at nineteen guineas is recommended and is on view. On the other hand, in an elaborately furnished drawing room of Louis XV style, there is a Steinway (at eight hundred pounds) to match the surroundings. In the piano room there are grands and uprights by Bechstein, Beckhardt, Blüthner, Bord, Brinsmead, Broadwood, Cramer, Challen, Chappell, Collard, Erard, Förster, Heyl, Ibach, Kapps, Lipp, Obermeier, Rosener and Steinway. In players, those by Chase & Baker, the Cecilian and the Claviola are stocked; and violins, guitars and high-priced gramophones are on view.

In the spring of 1908, this music salon was the setting for the demonstration of a singular musical instrument which had an astonishing effect on London and created a veritable sensation. Let us quote again from *Musical Opinion*, this time the issue for April 1908. Notice the somewhat tongue-in-cheek tone:

AN AUTOMATIC VIOLIN

The problem of applying machinery to the violin, says *The Times*, so as to imitate the performance of the human performer is one that has attracted many ingenious persons

---

* After the 1939–45 war, Waring & Gillow reduced the size of their business dramatically and occupied only the ground floor of their building, the remainder being converted into offices. For several years I had the pleasure of editing a technical journal in one of these offices. Ultimately, in the early 1970s it was decided to replace the building but the Greater London Council put a preservation order on the fine carved-stone façade. The upshot was that Waring & Gillow moved into close-by Regent Street and their old building was gutted and rebuilt as a modern shop and office block behind the fine front. Waring & Gillow have not sold musical instruments for many years.

OTHER ROLL-PLAYING MUSICAL INSTRUMENTS

in the past, but hitherto none has found any permanent favour. A new invention, far the most elaborate of any, is now on view at Messrs Waring & Gillow's in Oxford Street. The Mills Automatic Virtuosa [sic] consists of a large cabinet, the lower part of which contains the roll of perforated music to be performed. In the upper part of the cabinet there is placed an ordinary violin fitted with wire strings and with screw tuning pegs like those of the guitar. The bowing is effected by four small rosined celluloid wheels (one to each string) and the 'stopping' is done by keys which descend upon the keyboard and which are worked upon a principle similar to that of some typewriters. Pizzicato effects are made by jacks like those of the harpsichord.

The whole is worked by electro-magnets and a small motor and at a little distance some of the sounds produced are very like those made by a real player who has learnt a great deal of technique. There is a tremolo arrangement, obtainable by causing the whole tailpiece to shake; and a surprising amount of the usual violinist's tricks can be imitated. The 'automatum', as it is called in the prospectus, is the invention of a Dane [sic], Mr. H. K. Sandell.

Automatum, indeed! Probably confused with some sort of musical ultimatum!

The instrument was subsequently sent on tour and everywhere it went it was loudly acclaimed. During its travels, something like two thousand separate references or news items concerning it appeared in the British press.

King Edward VII commanded that the instrument be brought to Windsor Castle for him to hear but this great honour was never to come to pass, for Queen Alexandra's father, Prince Christian,* died the evening before the command performance and all arrangements were automatically cancelled.

It seems that on the tour pianists were hired on frequent occasions to accompany the concerts which the instrument gave. Word of this got to Sandell and he immediately gave thought to combining the two instruments – a requirement which he rapidly met. The result was the Violano-Virtuoso. The first of these instruments contained a 44-note piano of regular layout, with the bass strings on the left and the treble on the right. However, subsequently the piano was made with a symmetrical lyre-shaped frame having the long bass strings in the centre and the shortest strings on each side, so that the treble was at both ends. This unusual form, proven to pose almost insuperable problems to the ordinary piano tuner, was selected since it distributed the string tension evenly on the iron frame, thereby reducing the need for regular tuning.

News of the earlier Automatic Virtuosa and its successful tour of England reached officials of the United States Patent Office in Washington. They considered the machine worthy of exhibition at the Alaska-Yukon-Pacific Exposition to be held in Seattle and, unaware of the makers or owners, they requested the United States Consul in London to investigate. Patent experts then visited Mills in Chicago where the first Violano-Virtuoso was being completed and, upon invitation to exhibit at the Seattle show, the instrument was hurriedly finished and delivered to the American government. At government expense, it was then taken to Seattle and exhibited together with seven other inventions which received similar honour. These included the steam turbine, the Telepost system, an early colour photography device and the Parallax Stereogram – a stereo projector.

---

* Prince Christian of Schleswig-Holstein Sonderburg-Glücksburg.

Mills cannot be criticised for seizing this excellent opportunity to gain kudos for their instrument, and thus every Violano-Virtuoso to be produced from that date forward carried a legend reading 'Designated by the U.S. Government as one of the Eight Greatest Inventions of the Decade'.

After the Seattle display, the U.S. Patent Office moved the instrument to the National Land and Irrigation Exposition in Chicago – the home town of the Mills company. The company records show that another feature of this particular show was the Mexican National Band. 'The swarthy little bandsmen stood and listened to the Violano-Virtuoso play their favourite and intricate Spanish dances by Sarasate and other composers', relates Mills. From Chicago, the instrument was taken to other exhibitions, all at government expense and at no cost to the Mills concern. Indeed, no finer publicity agent could hope to have been found in the whole country – and entirely free of charge!

The list price of the Violano-Virtuoso was between $2,000 and $2,500. The DeLuxe model, which played two violins, cost $3,000. From its inception until the time when production ceased *circa* 1930 (a specimen in a London collection was shipped in 1930 and remained mint and unopened in its packing case intil 1963), between 4,000 and 5,000 were built. Today it has survived in larger numbers than many of its contemporary mechanical musical instruments and some 200 or so are known to exist. In England there are known to be about a score. The British Piano Museum at Brentford possesses a number, including a fine specimen of the DeLuxe twin-violin instrument.

It now becomes clear to see that the inspiration behind the Mills Violano-Virtuoso came from the Swedish *nyckelharpa* or keyed violin. This folk instrument, known since the fifteenth century, is similar to the North German *Schlüsselfiedel* which it has successfully outlived. As a small boy, Sandell would almost certainly have heard this strange instrument which can be played like a normal violin with a bow. One can imagine that he set about the challenge of producing an improved and automatic version of this memory of his youth. Significantly the method of stopping off the strings is virtually identical in the two instruments.*

The operation of the Violano-Virtuoso was ingenious. The Mills company discovered very early on in their history that the ordinary violin, regardless of make, was unable to stand up to almost continual playing and expensive ones made by famous craftsmen soon went out of tune and became unplayable. The only answer was to make a special violin and Mills set up a production line of instruments. From their literature, it would seem that great pains were taken to produce an instrument that was both mechanically perfect and aesthetically satisfying. The greatest care was taken in selecting timber and in construction. The method of tuning, however, was quite different from that of a normal violin. Instead of turn-keys in the neck, the Mills violin passed its strings over a lever to which was attached a weight on a threaded arm. Tuning was achieved by moving this weight along the arm. Once the correct position was found, the instrument would stay in tune for long periods. Other than this, and the special linkage to provide a most lifelike vibrato effect to the playing, the violin was quite standard in appearance, except that it had no finger board.

Bowing was effected by an electric motor which drove four shafts, each terminating in a pack of small celluloid discs. Each shaft was arranged in line with one of the violin strings and was also universally jointed, so that it could be moved up and down by solenoids whilst

* For a detailed description of the *Nyckelharpa*, see Jan Ling: *Nyckelharpan* (Stockholm, 1967 and 1979). A detailed description of the case for comparing this instrument with the Mills appears in *Music & Automata*, Vol. 1, pp. 134 *et seq.*

rotating. The motor itself had a variable resistance so that its speed could be varied continuously from slow to fast. This permitted the effect of light bowing for pianissimo playing, and strong bowing for forte passages. Before playing each tune, a block of rosin was pressed on to each of the bow wheels.

The tailpiece of the violin was connected by a lever to a cam so that, all the time the instrument played, the strings were in lateral movement. This produced an excellent vibrato effect. Beneath each string was arranged a number of cleft fingers, one for each note and semitone capable of being played on that string. These fingers were each controlled by a solenoid corresponding to the position of a slot in the music roll.

The roll itself was situated in the lower half of the instrument and was driven by a governed motor so that, regardless of the amount of paper on the driven spool, the speed of travel of the paper across the tracker bar remained constant. This was a most important feature since the rolls played five or more tunes each and were of large diameter. A brush of copper finger contacts made the complete electrical circuit between the tracker and the playing mechanism, the paper music passing between. Operating on 110 volts direct current, the playing was accompanied by a shower of bright blue sparks, normally hidden from public gaze by the doors in the base of the cabinet.

The piano part was again fully electrically controlled, each hammer having its own operating solenoid. The rest rail, adjustment of which gave piano and forte playing, was likewise controlled by a solenoid. The only contact between the piano and the player was a thick electrical cable and, since the piano was mounted in the form of a hinged door to the rear of the stoutly built case, it could be removed and stood against the wall several feet from the rest of the Violano-Virtuoso where it would play quite happily. Though in no way an intentional or optional feature of the machine, this characteristic demonstrates the simplicity of the electric action as compared with the pneumatic action.

Having made such a success of the Violano-Virtuoso, the Mills Novelty Company chose to capitalise still further on the mechanism, producing the Viol-Cello in about 1912. This variant had no piano, utilising the violin and playing mechanism of the Virtuoso combined with a vertically mounted cello to the right of the case. Whilst contemporary sources state that 'famous cellists who have heard this instrument have marvelled at its wonderful execution of the great violin concertos which have never before been arranged for cello playing', the machine was not the hoped-for success. Q. David Bowers, who recorded the history of the instruments made by Mills, several years ago had the opportunity to question a man who was a Mills distributor somewhere around 1922–4, and he was told that 'the instrument was unsuccessful as no way was found to finger it successfully'.

Another Mills product was the Viol-Xylophone, which was similar to the Virtuoso but employed a xylophone in place of a piano. This also appears to have been unsuccessful and none has survived.

Accessory cabinets were produced for the Violano-Virtuoso and these, standing alongside the instrument, contained percussion effects which could be 'plugged in' and played from the same standard roll used for violin and piano.

The next Mills product was the 65-note all-electric Expression Piano. This used a design concept similar to the Violano-Virtuoso in that the bass strings were in the centre of the frame. The 'orchestra box' or accompaniment cabinet for the Violano-Virtuoso could also be connected to this piano. There were several variants, including one with a horse-race diorama. Said to have been one of the most complex and intricate devices ever sold by any manufacturer, the Mills Race-Horse piano operated its horses electromagnetically in conjunction with a moving belt. A sophistication of the London street pianos with their moving picture fronts! Even so, the success of the early days was never repeated and little remains now save the Violano – incredible even by today's standards and remaining a focal point and discussion topic amongst collectors in both America and England. A number are still in regular use in the way originally intended and one example in an American tourist resort still earns upwards of $500 in a four-month season. Many were shipped to England and were in use in funfairs and seaside shows right up to the outbreak of the 1939–45 war. Lamentably, with the altered set of values which ruled during the war, many were needlessly destroyed or 'cleared' and left to rot.

Mention was made earlier of one which survived in London in mint order. This machine was discovered still in its original packing crate and complete with its instruction manual and spare parts plus shipping documents which show that it was dispatched from Chicago in 1930 and thus must have been among the last to have been manufactured by the Mills people. Unfortunately, in spite of its outward mint appearance, a large proportion of the metal castings proved to be quite useless. They had been cast in a zinc alloy called mazak and then nickel-plated. Electrolytic corrosion had taken place, reducing the metal to powder. The instrument was carefully rebuilt, new castings being made in bronze from the remains of the originals.

The Mills system for operating violins was later put to use in another application – the Mills Melody Violins. In this instrument, the violin was played by a keyboard and it was claimed that as many as a hundred violins could be played by one operator seated at the keyboard console. Of course, this was not strictly mechanical music.

Other makers of automatic violins included Hegeler & Ehrlers of Oldenberg in Germany whose Geigenpiano was introduced in 1908, and Dienst's Selbstspielende Geige, first made in 1910 and sold in small numbers in 1911 and 1912. The first of these was an upright piano containing one violin mounted flat on top of the instrument at the treble end. It played from the two top octaves of the piano compass via trackers and a belt-driven rotating bow wheel. The music rolls were of 72-note compass. Dienst's model was barrel-operated and was driven by a weight-operated clockwork motor. The price, with two barrels, was 2,200 marks. This, of course, did not have a keyboard. In the Deutsches Museum in Munich is preserved a most unusual electromagnetically played violin mounted horizontally in a cabinet the proportions of which are not unlike those of a push-up cabinet piano player. Believed to be a prototype or one-off experimental machine, this plays very small organette-type paper rolls. Date and maker are unknown, but it seems to have been created as late as the 1950s.

Banjos, mandolins, guitars, harps 'or other stringed instruments' were all embraced in the patents taken out in 1892 by J. Vose for his electromagnetic device worked by means of a roll of perforated paper. Unfortunately it is not known whether or not any of his instruments were ever made. Likewise the 1893 mechanical banjo of the American, W. S. Reed, seems to have come to nothing.

E. Tippmann and O. Keller thought up similar ideas for their automatic harp (or other stringed instrument) of 1895. This was worked by a simple perforated-card tune sheet.

Leipzig's piano makers, J. M. Grob (later to become Hupfeld) and K. A. Gutter, invented the Autoharp in 1884. This was a small zither-like instrument across the strings of which were arranged a number of wooden bars. Each bar was fitted with spring studs, so that it could be moved up and down on to the strings, and carried felt pads in certain positions.

These pads muted certain notes and thus, if one bar was depressed and the strings strummed, only the free strings would sound and these would be arranged into one of the standard accompaniment chords. Each bar would mute different strings and so give forth different chords.

The Autoharp would not strictly be termed an automatic instrument, but it was soon to be modified for mechanical playing. Paul Riessner, who had been one of the founders of the Polyphonmusikwerke in Leipzig, invented many systems for plucking stringed instruments from mechanical linkages. In fact, he and F. E. P. Ehrlich (of the Monopol musical box fame) both individually patented a large number of such devices during the first two decades of this century.

By 1919, Riessner had perfected the Mandoline-Zither, a mechanically played version of the Autoharp. This played twenty-five strings from a narrow paper roll. This was transported across a keyframe by means of a handle turned with the right hand. The left hand was used for the manual plucking of the accompaniment chords. These chords were numbered and the appropriate number stamped on to the music roll at the point at which it was intended to be played. Also known as the Triola, this instrument featured a reciprocating frame carrying short springs which actually plucked the strings when a note was to be sounded.

Another automatic zither was that made by Symphonion and called the Koschat, named after Thomas Koschat (1845–1914), who was a gifted Carinthian singer and vocal composer and who according to the advertisements warmly endorsed this device. A mechanical zither produced by Claus & Co. in Leipzig ought to be mentioned here although this, the Chordephon, was operated not by paper roll but by a metal disc of the same type as that used for the disc musical box. This had a plucking action. Another instrument of similar form was the Guitarophone patented in May 1894 by Menzenhauer of Leipzig. This also used a musical-box-type disc, but featured a hammer action to strike its 47 playing notes. There was, though, a fully automatic cardboard-book-playing mechanical zither. This was the Arpanetta patented also in 1894, this time by E. Tippmann and O. Keller. It was similar to an instrument produced about the same time called the Volkslavier which played a continuous band of thick paper rather like the organette.

The small organette was one of the first practical instruments to make use of the perforated-paper music roll. The instrument stemmed from the brains of several inventors, both in America and in Europe, where J. Carpentier made several machines in the early 1880s. Maxfield and McTammany in the United States probably did more to develop the machine into a worthwhile and cheap instrument, although McTammany was denied the reward of his inventive genius, seeing his expired patents exploited by others. The American Orguinette Company, basis of the subsequent Aeolian Company, was the largest manufacturer. Instruments were made which played endless paper bands, paper rolls, cardboard discs, zinc discs, metal discs and annular rings.

In operation, three systems were used. First there was the type which used mechanical levers, held down by the tune sheet, to lift pallets so as to allow air to pass through a reed. Then there was the style which featured a tracker board over which the perforated paper was drawn. In one type of this style, air from the atmosphere was drawn in through the reed to a chest from which the air had been reduced in pressure by means of exhausters. The other type compressed air in a windchest using bellows and then allowed it to escape to atmosphere through the reed, when a hole in the tracker board was uncovered. The German Ehrlich brothers favoured the use of mechanical levers and produced the highly successful 24-note Ariston played with cardboard discs. Other European types, such as the Mignon, were complex in operation, having a set of 'primary pneumatics', made of thin skin, to operate valves in the reed chamber. In all these, however, driving power was achieved through a cranked handle and there was no other form of motive power.

The English manufacturer, J. M. Draper, was the first to make an organette with two or more stops of reeds and he took out patents for such a device in 1887. It must be added that multiple reed stops were common in reed organs at this time, but nobody had so far applied the technique to the little organette.

The Mechanical Orguinette Company also made some larger organettes, one of which stood in a cabinet some four feet high, and another of which resembled a cabinet-style piano player in that it had foot-operated treadles and a handle to transport a wide band of music across a tracker board. This had two stops or banks of reeds, the second one being controlled by a small knob. A swell effect was also provided. Many small organettes at this time also had this provision, usually in a very rudimentary form and comprising a hinged flap over the reed chamber. The early Aeolian organ was developed by Tremaine from his work with the Mechanical Orguinette Company.

Tremaine came from a family of piano-makers and was, above all else, an astute businessman. He designed and had manufactured a whole range of organettes including a very sophisticated model called the Celestina. He then bought out the invention of Robert W. Pain, an upright reed organ with an interior player mechanism which played 46 notes from a perforated paper roll. This instrument, unlike the small organettes, also had a keyboard and so could be played manually. This was in 1882. Within a few years, Tremaine and his son improved the instrument and coined the name Aeolian. By 1888 he had acquired a factory at Meriden in Connecticut and formed his New York business into the Aeolian Organ & Music Company. He bought out a business called the Automatic Music Paper Company of Boston who were makers of both organettes and paper-roll music for them.

An early tie-up with the Vocalion Organ Company in Worcester, Massachusetts, gave him the necessary volume production to market the Aeolian organ successfully. The purchase of the Munroe Organ Reed Company gave him what would be called in today's business jargon, a 'vertically-integrated' organisation.

In the early 1890s, Tremaine introduced a larger player reed organ, this time using a 58-note compass. It was called the Aeolian Grand and was an immediate market success. In 1897 came the triumph of the Aeolian Orchestrelle. Also a 58-note instrument, the Orchestrelle differed from the Grand in that, instead of operating on suction like a player piano, it worked on air at pressure employing patents taken out by M. S. Wright in 1893.

Constructed along the finest organ-building practices, the Orchestrelle was manufactured in a variety of models, some of the smaller, cheaper variants having mechanical tracker controls for the stops. Later and more expensive models used pneumatic control of almost all the functions.

The zenith of the Orchestrelle was the manufacture of the 116-note Solo model. While still capable of playing standard 58-note Orchestrelle rolls, it had a tracker bar with two rows of extremely small holes, slightly staggered so that special double-compass rolls could be played as well. In the 'solo' mode, one of the tracker bar rows would operate on one set of stops while the second row played on a different registration. With this it was possible to achieve some beautiful two-manual effects with, for example, a melodic line able to stand free within an accompaniment chorus just like a true two-manual organ performance. Subsequently, a Duo-Art version was made which automatically selected its own stop registration and degrees of swell ('shade setting' as Aeolian termed it). In 1905, the company introduced the Aeolienne, a roll-player which had no keyboard and was thus similar to the keyless Welte player pianos. This model is only known today from old advertisements.

Akin to the Orchestrelle of Aeolian was the Symphony built by Wilcox & White whose Meriden factory was literally across the street from Aeolian. Well made but not so thoughtfully designed, the Symphony was also a 58-note organ but nowhere achieved the popularity of its peer.

A number of attempts were made to unite the piano and the pipe-organ other than in the style adopted in the nickelodeon. One of these was that of E. C. Jardine-Smith who, in 1930, was granted British Patent number 333,661 for a player piano combined with a pipe-organ using electro-pneumatic action. This he called the Symphonique and it made use of standard piano rolls or could be played by hand from its player-piano console which was flanked by the stop-jambs of the organ. The inventor had been a partner in his father's organ-building firm – Jardine & Company of Old Trafford, Manchester – along with his brother, but left in 1930 to set up in business on his own at 98a Braemar Road, Fallowfield, Manchester. No instruments of the Symphonique type are known to survive.

In 1887, J. P. Browne devised an 'automatic instrument for teaching bugle or trumpet calls' reminiscent of the mechanical trumpeter made by Kaufmann in the 1840s. 'The calls are played on an automaton reed musical-instrument actuated by a tune-sheet and similar to the Ariston. The number of notes on the instrument is equal to that used for calls.'

I am indebted to Q. David Bowers for his research into the history of a machine which must vie with the Violano-Virtuoso for originality. This machine, the self-playing harp, was certainly a most curious and interesting mechanical musical instrument. In spite of this, and also the claim of the Rudolph Wurlitzer Company that 'as a money maker the Wurlitzer Harp has proven itself the king of them all', Bowers has found that ten years after its introduction in 1905, it had all but disappeared.

The automatic harp was first thought of in the 1890s by a Cincinnati harp player and band leader named Harry Connor. He interested his friend, inventor J. W. Whitlock, in the idea and Whitlock began experimenting. The first patent for the instrument was taken out in Whitlock's name in 1899 and covered an upright wooden-framed harp housed in a rectangular case. Pneumatic action operated by a perforated-paper music roll 8½ inches wide set in motion small mechanical fingers which plucked the strings, there being one finger for each note. The sound produced by this mechanism was not unlike that of a guitar and was softer than that of a piano. Although a most pleasant and mellow sound, it did not sound very much like a harp.

The subsequent years saw the production of a small number of automatic harps by Whitlock in a small wooden building next to his home in Rising Sun, Indiana. In 1905 Whitlock put several instruments out on location in various taverns in Cincinnati, Ohio. Whitlock's choice of Cincinnnati, about 35 miles from Rising Sun, as a trial ground proved happy, for that town was also the home of the Rudolph Wurlitzer Company. Wurlitzer had been in business with coin-operated musical instruments since the 1890s, having begun with the Regina disc-playing musical box which was produced in a coin-freed variant. In 1899 Wurlitzers sold the first cylinder-playing, coin-operated piano (deKleist's Tonophone), followed a few years later by the 44-note Pianino. These were such a success that thousands were sold and the factory could only just cope with the demand. Having introduced coin music to the American public, Wurlitzer was out to corner the market in all types of this music.

And so it was that one day Howard Wurlitzer, then business manager of the Wurlitzer Company, chanced to visit a certain café and was confronted by an ideal machine to add to the Wurlitzer range – an automatic harp. Wurlitzer travelled to Rising Sun and signed a contract with J. W. Whitlock for the purchase of 1,000 instruments. Whitlock constructed a new factory and set up his production line.

The Automatic Harp sold through Wurlitzer for $750 each and music rolls cost $7·50 apiece. Alternatively customers in the neighbourhood of Cincinnati could hire out instruments for a percentage of the profits. By early 1906, 135 different places in Cincinnati alone had the Automatic Harp installed. A year or so later the Style B Harp was introduced and this was built in the shape of a real harp as distinct from the rectangular case of the earlier model. This cost $100 extra. Soon afterwards, though, demand fell and the Style A price was dropped to $650, and then to $500. By 1916 they were being remaindered for only $375. By 1920, the instrument was finished. In all, 1,500 had been built.

Following the success, short-lived though it was, of the Automatic Harp, Whitlock experimented with a self-playing violin which was intended to have fifteen strings, each with its own rosined disc bow. The instrument was never finished and is today in the Bowers collection. Whitlocks subsequently went into business building furniture, which work they still do to this day. J. W. Whitlock died in 1935 at the age of sixty-four, and was succeeded by his son Stewart, who died in 1966.

The forerunner of the accordion, itself played pneumatically in latter years in the Belgian Mortier and Arburo café organs of post-war years, was the concertina. This used a reed plate in which alternate reeds were set facing opposite ways. They were controlled by small pallets worked by finger buttons. Wind was passed through the reed by the inward and outward moving of the bellows and each reed would have a leather flap over the speaking side so that, when the bellows moved inwards, the inner reeds on the plate would speak, the others muted by the flaps. When the bellows were moved outwards the process would be reversed.

Mechanising the concertina, beloved, or so tradition would have us believe, by the mariner and country dancer alike, was attempted by several inventors, among them M. A. Wier in 1883. He used a perforated tune sheet transported across the pallet linkages by springs and bridges between the two ends of the instrument. Wier also made many other mechanical instruments playing perforated music, including a trumpet-shaped reed instrument blown by means of a mouthpiece and playing music by a hand crank. Similar instruments were made in Leipzig by O. Meinhardt from 1886 onwards, whilst G. A. Cole's toy trumpet of 1888 played its tune from a fixed disc against which a handle rotated a reed plate.

L. A. Klepzig shunned perforated music in his mechanical concertina of 1884, favouring a pinned barrel rotated by a linkage between the two ends as used by Wier. G. Richter, probably of the Richter manufacturing empire which produced the Libellion, Imperator and other musical boxes using plucked combs, devised a type of inertia motor to drive his tune sheet. This was in 1885 and the inertia motor was set into motion and boosted on each compression of the concertina bellows. J. M. Farmer's concertina-like instrument of 1889 again played music and was similar to that thought up by M. A. Wier.

The name of Richter, this time Friedrich Adolf Richter, the musical-box maker, appears on another patent dated 1893 for a concertina. In this one he used a coil spring to drive the

OTHER ROLL-PLAYING MUSICAL INSTRUMENTS

Fig. 61
The Rolmonica perforated paper roll-playing mouth organ.

music roll, and wound it by a ratchet lever from the normal playing action of moving the bellows in and out. However, the successful self-playing concertina – as automatic as it could be – was the work of P. Fehling in 1895. Fehling used a motor of the inertia type which had a large flywheel which was driven by a ratchet lever within constant easy reach of the performer's fingers. This lever could be flicked back and forth whilst 'pumping', and the music roll was thereby transported across a keyframe. The music paper held down a row of lightly sprung keys. Where a hole in the paper indicated a note to be sounded, the key rose through the hole, and its other end lifted a pallet. R. Wunsch patented a similar device in Leipzig in 1896.

The mechanical concertinas were produced with 14 or 28 single notes or 28 quadruple reeds and were in production right up until the 1930s. They were known as the Tanzbär or 'dancing bear'.

Many hundreds were built and they were particularly successful in the field of the old music hall where it was often desirable for the comic to be able to play a few bars of music to get himself off the stage. The instrument lent itself admirably to such harmless little pieces of deception. Each bore a small circular emblem showing a dancing bear.

Toy trumpets have been mentioned already, but paper-roll playing toy saxophones (the $2·89 Play-a-Sax) were marketed in America as late as the 1920s. Other instruments were also made such as the Clarola Clarinet and all worked by looping a band of perforated paper around the body of the instrument. The paper covered the 'key' holes and, acting as a sliding valve, played a tune as the holes were uncovered by the passage of the paper. A smaller application of this principle was to be seen in the Rolmonica patented in May 1928. The Play-a-Sax, the Clarola and the Rolmonica – a paper-roll playing mouth organ costing $1 – emanated from America, the first two from the Q.R.S. music-roll company.

DESIGN INFLUENCES

In an earlier Chapter, I mentioned the geographical boundaries to which certain types of instrument strictly adhered. The café piano with drum, castanets and triangle was common in France, Italy and Spain, yet never caught on in England. The coin-operated café piano, common enough in its basic form in the British Isles, was to be developed and perfected, improved upon and embellished almost beyond recognition in America and to find markets where no comparable market existed – or was pursued – elsewhere in the world. Teutonic piano-orchestrions were Europe's nearest counterpart. The habits of people and their conditions of living, their surroundings and temperaments can all be said to have had an influence on this demarcation.

Styles of furniture and also, surprisingly enough, architecture have a considerable bearing in the study of the development and the stylistic appearance of mechanical instruments. I think most of us are familiar with the rich, Gothic-style cabinets of the larger Polyphon musical boxes, frets, curlicues, Stephensonian-order turned columns, richly carved, almost overpoweringly heavy pediments surmounted by spiky finials. This is typical of the furniture and, in fact, of the architecture of the age.

It is obvious that in the eighteenth century, furniture of the cabinet type was largely influenced by the proportions of classical buildings. Work-boxes, automata, and nécessaires became architectural microcosms. They not only simulated town houses and country villas in mahogany and other hardwoods but also portrayed in their façades all the current fashions and conceits of Palladian mansions, Gothic churches, Indian pavilions, Chinese pagodas and French châteaux. Many cages for live birds of the period were examples of this trend and resembled some of the most palatial of the contemporary dolls' houses.

This tendency, to take architectural criteria into consideration when styling furniture, was broadly adopted by almost all of the creative cabinet makers and designers to follow. Indeed it can be argued that even today we still follow this practice in creating modern furniture which is quite as unbeautiful as our modern architecture. One has only to examine a tubular chair or a cocktail cabinet-cum-television receiver to see, in miniature, the influences of those depressing monstrosities of concrete, glass and plastics which are variously scattered about our land as offices and living machines ('homes', other than for the mentally ill and the aged, are dictated no longer to be in fashion).

The Germans brought the trends of the Gothic edifice (often, one finds, even the Hellenic) to bear on their mechanical musical instruments. I have already mentioned the Polyphon cabinet. Indeed, all the disc-playing musical boxes made in Germany displayed a similar Teutonic appearance. When such orchestrion makers as Popper, Hupfeld, Gebruder Weber, Lösche, J. D. Philipps & Söhne, and Welte went to work, they built, no doubt unconsciously, miniature examples of the most solid local architectural constructions as cases for their devices. In Paris, the father of the fair organ – Gavioli the Italian – styled his façades in the rococo and the *art nouveau*. This feature of the fair organ undoubtedly captured a world-wide acclaim, for cases in this style became characteristic of many fair organs the world over, so demonstrating a diversion from our arbitrary geographical limitations. The rococo or Louis XV style became known almost universally. Molinari in New York and Limonaire in Paris and Camden Town, London, built a range in austere cases (perhaps even more Teutonic than Italo-Parisian), as did others in the trade, but Gavioli's display of the ornate had set the trend. The Dutch *draaiorgel* or street organ today displays a charming façade quite in keeping with the best of the Gavioli foundation – the architecture of Louis XV, Versailles, Paris, in the 'eighties.

This treatise on cabinet trends is given to explain in part the great variety of styles to be found over the years and to help in the regional identification of work. Mission oak finish, for example, coupled with casework after the best Colonial pattern, characterised many of the

American products in the field of mechanical musical instruments in the early years of this century.

As both a major producer and major exporter of automatic instruments, it is perhaps not surprising that many instruments came to Britain in the early years of this century. The dance halls and skating rinks, the restaurants and the ballrooms were customers for this sort of instrument. As fashions changed, of course, the instruments were discarded, but there was another and much more determined reason for the loss of many of these instruments.

With the onset of the 1914–18 war, many of the German piano-orchestrions in England were destroyed. With the understandable and emotive atmosphere of the Great War, there was a nation-wide feeling that if a product was German then it must be destroyed: indeed, many people would not have a musical box or other instrument in their homes unless it was British-made. Where families had suffered a bereavement, these actions were easy to understand. And so countless specimens were thrown out and gleefully burned. For those that escaped this treatment, there was another more mundane problem. With Germany and Britain at war, there was no fresh music to be had. One of London's piano makers came to the rescue. This was the old-established company of Keith, Prowse, which had a piano factory in Camden Town. This company advertised that it was in a position to supply British-made music for all 'foreign-made' (carefully avoiding the sensitive word 'German') automatic instruments. The actual volume of business transacted in this department is hard to imagine: one feels that in the climate of war it must have been small, uneconomic and short-lived.

Russia also took very large quantities of these German-made instruments but in the absence of any definite information (and the almost certain non-existence of anything approaching a collectors' association for their preservation) one might assume that most of these have long since been destroyed.

Carillons operated by perforated roll via pneumatics or, more usually, electricity, were first introduced in the late 1920s and indeed there is a large number of smaller instruments so equipped, that at the Quaker settlement of Bourneville in England being a fine early example, although, at the time of writing, the player has lain derelict for many years. A number of new carillons made in Holland today have electromagnetic players using punched music but, unlike the hygroscopic and readily torn papers of the past,* these are today made in plastic sheet.

Perhaps the most unusual musical device to play from a perforated roll, again of plastic (mylar film), is the remarkable percussion 'instrument' formed out of some 64 acres of stalactites in the Luray Caverns, Virginia. Conceived by an electronics engineer named Leland W. Sprinkle in 1954 following a visit to the caverns, the first stage in making this instrument (erroneously called an organ) was to grind thirty-seven stalactites to form the first 'rank' of tuned rocks. The results are most impressive: constant temperature means that the rocks should only need tuning once in a millennium, and, most extraordinary of all, although the sounds are produced by a solenoid-operated ram which strikes the stone, the profile of the resultant sound, instead of showing a 'clang tone' and then a decay, actually shows a pre-peak rise as the stone is excited.

The music for this extraordinary and very beautiful sounding instrument (which must surely rank as the biggest musical instrument in the world) was melted into the plastic using a soldering-iron and comprises, at the time of writing, four popular melodies (*Silent Night*,

---

* The carillon at Bourneville, founded by the Quaker family Cadbury, has a punched cardboard player action which has been out of use for many years although preserved *in situ*.

A mighty Fortress in our God, Christ the Lord is Risen Today and an eighteenth-century Dutch *Hymn of Thanksgiving*).

Roll-playing instruments once ruled the realms of mechanical musical instruments, replacing the cumbersome and expensive pinned barrel. Only a fraction of these remain today – and most of them are player pianos. Significantly, the punched paper tape of the computer has been employed by inventors as a new means of programming instruments such as pianos. So far, though, the greater success has been with specially encoded magnetic tape. This is described in detail in the next Chapter.

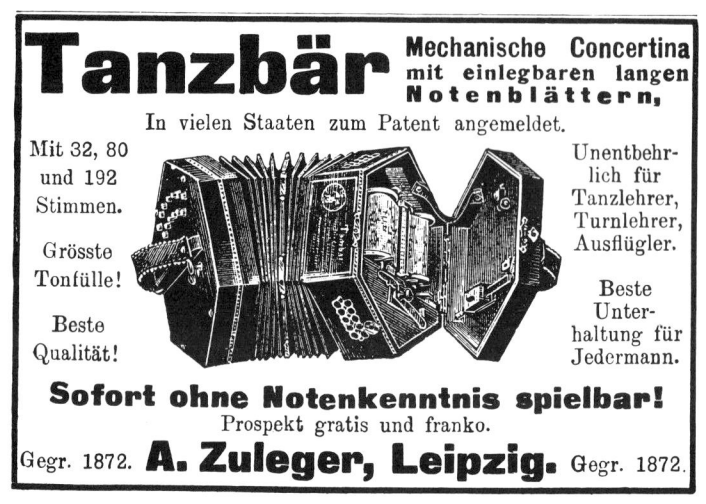

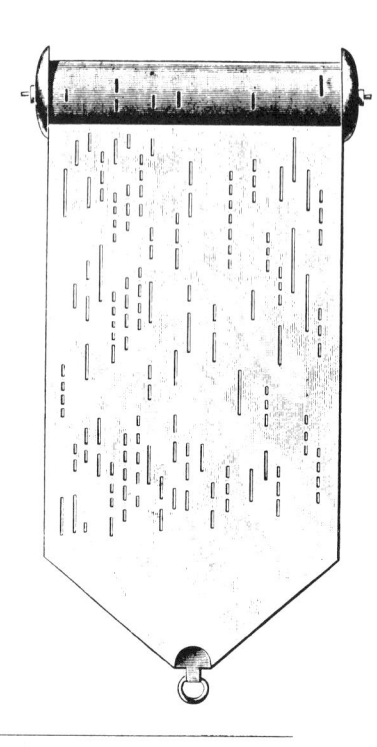

CHAPTER 10

The Post-War Revival of the Player Piano

❧

Since 1945, attempts at reviving the player piano have centred on the application of three techniques. Two are little more than a revival of old ideas, and one is a brand-new approach using technology which was unheard of even in the 1950s.

So far in the story of the player piano, I have made a few references to a strange breed of instrument which has appeared at odd intervals throughout history. I refer to the key-top player – a separate device which is something like a piano player, but, instead of being in a separate cabinet, is housed in a small case which is placed on top of the piano keyboard.

Key-top players have recurred in the post-war years and so it is worth taking a good look at the genus.

The idea of the portable key-top player which could be attached to the keyboard and made to play the keys goes back to the days before 1850. It was in that year that the organ builder Holditch provided the church organ at Easton-on-the-Hill in Northumberland with such a device (see *Barrel Organ*, p. 88) and there is plenty of evidence that they predated this by anything up to a score of years. These were called *dumb organists*.

Of course, Jules Carpentier's Melotrope was also a key-top player using, in place of the pinned barrel of the dumb organist, strips of perforated card. And Debain's Antiphonel (described on page 20) was of this family.

The advantages of the key-top piano-player attachment are obvious: perhaps less obvious are its disadvantages, the biggest of which is where to store it when not in use and how to protect the key contacting plungers or fingers from damage.

Debain's earliest version of the Antiphonel was advertised as suitable for use with the piano, the organ or the French instrument which was at that time extremely popular – the harmonium. But the ability to produce a small and very portable device did not entirely elude subsequent makers. Of course there were exceptions. When, in the first decade of the present century, Chicago department store Lyon & Healy introduced a range of pianos and players under the name Empress Electric, there was a thing called the Little Empress Electric Cabinet Player, said to fit 'any piano and make(s) an Electric out of it'. This enormous box made by Operator's Piano Company fitted over the keys, rested on the piano cheeks and was braced over the top of the piano for security. It must have required two strong men to position it. Not so the attractive little Maestro made in Elbridge, New York, by the Maestro Company and advertised in 1899. Costing $40, this was a rectangular wooden box-like mechanism which played a special 50-note perforated paper roll measuring 9¾ inches in width. The tracker bar was mounted vertically and the take-up spool was situated behind it. The music roll featured a short rectangular pin on the left side and a plain round one the

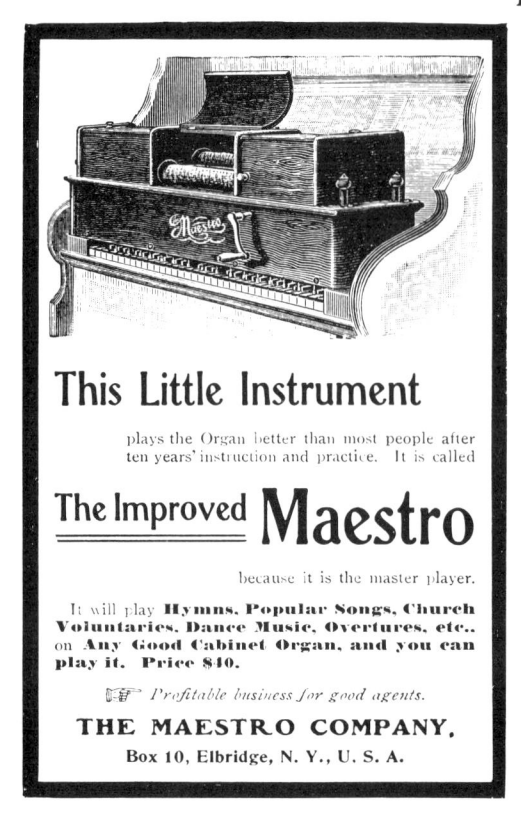

Fig. 62
An advertisement from *Munsey's Magazine* of 1900 shows the Maestro key-top piano player which was pneumatically operated. Turning the handle worked a neat shuttle exhaust system at each end of the cabinet.

other. The roll was inserted left side first and the right hand pin then slotted into its location. As the operating handle was turned, a gear mechanism wound the roll on to the take-up spool while the rectangular pin on the music-roll spool wound up a spring-power motor. The other function of turning the playing handle was to move, by means of a crankshaft and a wooden connecting rod, a reciprocating carriage which traversed from the right-hand side to the left, its side pieces passing either side of the tracker bar. This carriage was attached to a small double-acting bellows no more than 5 inches square which provided the power for the small pneumatic stack fitted directly underneath. With the device on a keyboard, wire plungers with felt end pads played the instrument. At the end of the roll, the pulling of a small knob just above the crank handle disengaged the drive to the take-up spool and brought the roll spool under the direct influence of the spring motor which rewound the roll. Tracking the mechanism was achieved by means of a small lever under the top shelf forming the upper part of the case: this actually moved the tracker bar from side to side.

The post-war revival of the key-top player in the United States was obviously considered to have a potential in the modern home where space was at a premium and many people still owned ordinary instruments. At least three fully electric examples were made, and probably more which were of short-lived duration. One of these three was the Electrone, another the Dynavoice – and naturally Aeolian was not to be left out with the great hopes which the post-war Pianola had.

In 1950, Aeolian introduced an electrically driven key-top version of the Pianola. This was a wooden case which rested on the keyboard of an ordinary piano and into which could be fitted normal music rolls. Vacuum was provided from a large pump box which could be sited under the piano and connected by means of a hose to the key-top player. The retail price was $395.

The Dynavoice was introduced some time in the later 1950s by Dynavoice Inc. of Plymouth, Michigan. Styled as model no. PL 52 (115 volts), one example is to be seen in Bellm's Museum. Bearing the legend 'Patents and Trade Mark Registration applied for', this is a low-cost and rather crudely made solenoid machine housed in a large and supremely ugly brown plastic case. The playing fingers are metal plungers with plastic ends and the back of the case is closed off with perforated hardboard – pegboard. The failure of this instrument to make its way in the market might be attributed to the fact that it emerged at a time when America did not require something which had to be lifted on and off the piano, nor did it want something with two pieces, one of which had to be stored somewhere while the machine was not in use. This second piece was a matching plastic tray which fitted over and so protected the key plungers when the device was not in use. The Dynavoice was provided with a sturdy lifting handle which hinged over the tracker bar. Vacuum was provided by a small electric motor and suction pump built inside the case.

The market circumstances which killed off the Dynavoice also, apparently, finished a second device, this one being the Electrone, made probably around the same time by the Electrone Corporation of Santa Ana, California. Much better engineered than the

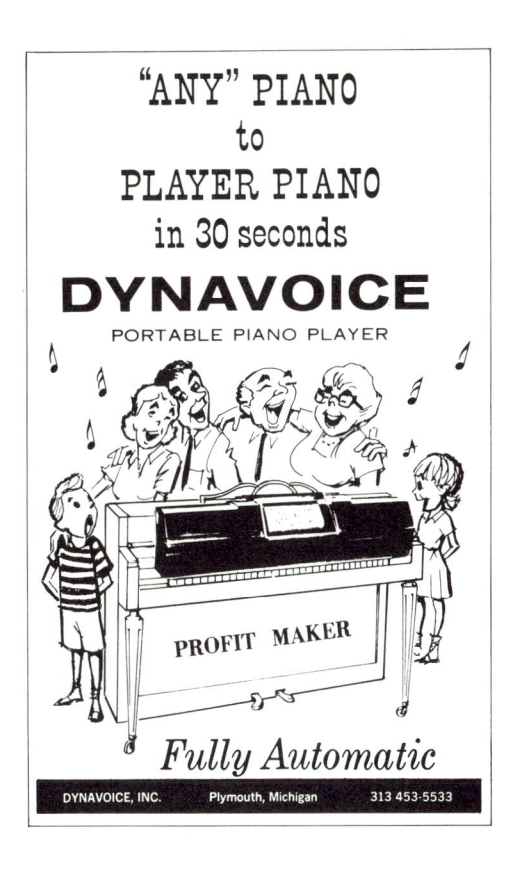

Fig. 63
The Dynavoice was made as recently as 1965, yet this electrically-operated key-top player has already long been forgotten.

Dynavoice, this had proper wooden fingers covered with good quality green piano felt. Again, a detachable tray was provided to protect the delicate fingers underneath.

Magic Fingers was the name selected by the Gribble Music Company of Kansas City for their piano player introduced in the mid-1950s. Unlike the key-top player, this was much more akin to the Pianotist mechanical player with a touch of Ampico added for good measure. The device was intended to be attached more or less permanently to any piano and was electrically powered. Installation took a number of hours and the mechanism was contained in a drawer which fitted under the keyboard. Magic Fingers was an extremely well designed and precision-built system said to have been the outcome of more than three years of research and experimentation by the company in conjunction with the Midwest Research Institute, 'one of America's foremost research and engineering organisations' according to the aggressive marketing and publicity literature.

Perhaps due to its inflexible installation plus its high cost, sales did not match expectations and the enterprise folded. Another equally short-lived device was called the Phantom Player.

Attachable players of the electro-pneumatic type now gave way to the new generation of player pianos, heralded in 1957 by the Hardman Peck Duo. Introduced with a selling price of $1,300, the Duo was of the so-called 'spinet' size of upright piano with the player action incorporated. Late in 1960, Aeolian brought out its new Pianola, a 64-note spinet, which sold for just over $1,000.

Since then there have been several other models launched including one with the name 'Duo Art' – only here this name appears to refer to the ability of this 'straight' player to be played either by hand via the keyboard or electrically 'at the flick of a switch'. Aeolian's latest Pianola is electric or pedal-operated and is now distributed in both England and America. A feature of the more recent American player pianos is what is prosaically referred to as a 'honky-tonk' sound generated by interposing a piece of leather usually with a metal tag on the end between hammer and string. Each note is provided with the dubious merit of such an accessory, the whole set of tags being attached to a rail which can be raised or lowered somewhat like the effects occasionally found on the barrel piano.

In an age when musical appreciation is higher than ever before, the new Pianola does little to ennoble the rich past of the self-acting pianoforte.

The third new type of piano is, as I suggested in my preamble to this chapter, truly new and original and involves the use of computer technology. Before looking into this, though, I think it would be of interest to describe a very special one-off instrument designed and built by Player Piano Group member Gerald Stonehill in conjunction with the one-time Aeolian man and Artona music-roll chief Gordon Iles. My reason for including this is to highlight some of the problems of making a new machine to perform an old function, in this case to design a new way of playing old reproducing piano rolls.

Called the Duo-Art Robot, it was conceived as a portable concert pianist which could perform on any piano – in other words, a latter-day *vorsetzer*. It was built between 1973 and 1974 and the main component was originally an Ampico-built Duo-Art drawer originally fitted to a Pennsylvania lady's Steinway. This roll-play drawer was built around 1936, by which time Ampico and Duo-Art had merged, and features the normal Duo-Art tracker bar with electric roll drive built into a late Model B-style Ampico drawer.

Early on in the project, the inventor Gerald Stonehill thought that it would be a good opportunity to improve upon the original Duo-Art system and so, with the aid of Gordon Iles, who was responsible for the later and final development work at the British Aeolian factory at Hayes in Middlesex, a fresh approach was begun in the interpretation of existing Duo-Art rolls.

A look inside the lower portion of the Robot immediately reveals that this is no recognisable Duo-Art action. In fact, the expression system owes more to the Ampico intensity-valve concept. The inventor of this fresh approach told me that the usual trouble with all Duo-Arts around the world is that, whereas they might have been efficient when they were new and in perfect working order, they have since become more and more sluggish. The system as designed in the Robot is one in which there is no sluggishness. Unfortunately, of course, the original Duo-Art recording system was programmed to allow for a certain degree of sluggishness and so the Robot proved to be so responsive that the expression holes in existing music rolls were too far in advance of the required player response. Stonehill and Iles therefore had to build in special 'inefficiency reservoirs' through which to produce a controllable or adjustable sluggishness to return to the peak intended performance of the Duo-Art.

Achieving the optimum degree of sluggishness was the outcome of much careful examination of music rolls. Certain functions in the Duo-Art roll (in fact, in any music roll) are called for by a perforation in the paper, and then are cancelled at a certain speed – that of the mechanism – which can be perceived in the positioning of the perforations so that they remain in action for a specific period although in effect the 'cancel' signal has been given. An example of this in its simplest form can be seen in the way that ordinary themodising perforations are placed ahead of the notes which they are intended to operate on. When, in the case of the Robot, this switching was found to be taking place during the actual playing of a passage it could be determined that the action of the Robot was too fast and that the rate of slowing down had to be increased.

A capacity bellows – a sort of pneumatic buffer – of the right size for the theme side was made largely by process of trial and error, and a similar capacity bellows capable of producing the same sluggishness was made for the accompaniment side in order to cope with the observable slowness on the solo side.

This prototype unit is housed in a plain cabinet, access to the roll compartment being by a full-size hinged lid. The piano key fingers are all individually adjustable so that an optimum setting for each felt-padded finger can be made for each key. A very large spool box is fitted of the type used at the very end of the American reproducing piano era so that large rolls can be played rather like the half-hour Ampico rolls introduced in the 1930s. Special behemoth Duo-Art rolls have been cut for this purpose by Gordon Iles on his original Aeolian roll perforators. In order to maintain silence in operation, the Robot has a separate pump which can be mounted some distance away.

The Robot has appeared in concert in London demonstrating that it is what it was designed to be – a portable concert pianist.

The Player Piano Group in London has staged a number of player- and reproducing-piano recitals at the Purcell Room in London's South Bank complex. These concerts have attracted a great deal of public attention and, although some of the newspaper reviews have been rather less than charitable (people still prefer to see a live pianist pounding the keys along with the inevitable wrong notes, rather than listen to the infallible machine which has been carefully programmed), the general response has been one of interest, curiosity and satisfaction. At one concert, for example, the concert hall was full and the platform sported an Aeolian piano player of 1910 connected to the hall's resident Steinway concert grand, a 1922 Steinway Red

Welte model O, and a home-engineered conversion of a modern Estonia Russian-made concert grand to Ampico A standard. This concert, the fifth the P.P.G. had staged, was held on 22 April 1977 and was organised by Michael Magnus Osborn. On that Friday night, the audience heard the playing of Paderewski, Pugno, Saint-Saëns, Levitzki, Sauer, Dohnanyi, D'Albert and Moseiwitsch. Indeed an evening to be remembered.

Mentioned above is the Estonia Ampico. This instrument is the work of P.P.G. member Norman Evans, who obtained this brand-new concert grand from the makers in Tallin, Estonia. The piano itself is a top-quality instrument fitted with the proven Schwander hammer action. A key-shift *una corda* is used and, because the Ampico system uses a half-blow rail, the action of the piano had to be modified to accommodate an inflexible box-section extruded aluminium half-blow. The Ampico striking pneumatics had to be repositioned to allow for the bars of the piano's iron frame. A separate exhaust pump is fitted in a soundproofed vibrationless box. The finished piano, the result of very many hours of work, was given its first public showing at the Purcell Room on 3 December 1976.

So far we have been talking about pneumatic instruments and the occasional electric (solenoid) player. Since the 1950s, the computer has become part and parcel of our lives and with it a whole new science of coded information using magnetic tape. The onset of the microprocessor which offers computing and memory capability along with minuscule proportions and very low cost has inspired technicians to take a fresh look at the player piano.

And so to the modern computerised approach to the reproducing piano, which has produced an instrument which, instead of playing a roll of perforated paper, plays from an ordinary Philips-patent compact cassette of specially encoded magnetic tape.

As an introduction to this, remember that there are at least three different types of reproducing piano roll which can be found – four if you add to the list the Welte Mignon Licensee, and many more if you include Aria Divina, Angelus Artrio, and so on. On all these rolls, although the perforations controlling the musical notes remain interchangeable, the perforations which control the reproducing action differ since the systems themselves are different. What a truly vast library of music would be available to the owner of an instrument which had a sort of compound action which would perform equally well from a Hupfeld Triphonola (Animatic-T) roll, that for a Duo-Art, and a Red Welte wide roll! Hitherto such a capability would have necessitated ownership of one piano for each system. Now, thanks to the computer, this is not necessary.

With the increasing interest in reproducing pianos plus the availability of very many rolls for all systems which can now be copied faithfully, there is demonstrably a shortage of instruments and skilled enthusiasts to maintain them in the necessary tip-top condition. To make today a pneumatic reproducing action which might be fitted to a piano would be prohibitive although as I have already said there is a growing market for a piano capable of reproducing those master interpretations by artists long since dead.

The age of the computer and attendant micro-electronics now makes this a commercial possibility by using techniques totally unknown to the design staff of Ampico, Duo-Art and Welte. Furthermore, the necessarily fragile and, it must be said, bulky boxes of spooled perforated paper may now be dispensed with in favour of magnetic tape.

The idea of using recording tape not so much to play piano music as to programme the physical operation of a piano goes back some fifteen years to early experiments conducted by a London piano manufacturer who experimented with the idea of using a tape as a piano-teaching aid. Since that time, very successful techniques have been developed by computer engineers.

One immediately apparent problem is that while the traditional player or reproducing piano is a pneumatic instrument (it uses air at less than normal atmospheric pressure in order to manipulate the 88 separate hammer actions found in the normal piano), the computer, the microprocessor and the magnetic tape all belong to a totally different kind of power – electricity. And another basic thing is that air is a far more simple, cheap and flexible source of motivating power for sounding a piano string than is electricity. Put very simply, an air-operated (and this really means vacuum-operated) system has the ability to be infinitely more expressive under the control of a simple action than does one powered by electricity, which requires a far more complex action to attain the same degree of playing quality.

I have already mentioned the problems which arose with the Duo-Art Robot where the improved action turned out to be so responsive that it was impossible to retrieve from the original Duo-Art recordings the correct interpretational information.

This highlights another problem in attempting to make a modern instrument to play old rolls. The original rolls were made for a system with known shortcomings – if it took half a second for an expression function to work, this did not matter as the roll made allowances for the sluggishness. However, make a modern system without this accepted slow response and you render the music anything but a faithful performance of the original.

All this means that the degree of electronic involvement and the point at which it interfaces with roll and piano action has to be chosen with profound care.

It is so easy to examine, say, the Duo-Art expression system and identify it as a binary code (which it effectively is) while at the same time missing that it is a relatively *slow-acting* function intended to be slow-acting.

Some five years ago, Professor Fred Heath at Edinburgh's Heriot-Watt University applied himself to this problem. He rightly saw that the piano roll is exactly like computer paper tape with the pneumatic action copying the mechanism of a computer printer. The Duo-Art expression mechanism operates on a 4-bit digital-to-analogue converter device similar to the familiar systems found in industrial automation equipment.

'It is true to say', says Professor Heath, 'that player pianos represent a packaged maintainable system which has remained unequalled in terms of reliability until the recent advent of electronic equipment.'

With the advent of the home computer and the availability of low-cost silicon chips which can contain many thousands of circuits, it is not surprising that several attempts have already been made to produce computer-driven player pianos.

The advantages in the way of product potential are attractive since the ultimate goal would be to take all three popular reproducing systems – four if you count the Red Welte and the Welte Licensee – and write a programme which will assimilate the different expression data on each system and unify them into one omnibus data bank which will feature but one system of output.

MELOGRAPHY AND THE COMPUTER

A further potential is to rekindle interest in what was called melography. Melography is the ability to record a keyboard performance as it is being played in such a way that it may immediately be re-played. Back in those heady days before magnetic sound recording, this was a most attractive goal for, with talented extemporisers around, many – both listeners and players – felt it would be a marvellous thing to make some device which would record a mark each time a key was depressed, a mark which indicated the two dimensions of a musical note – pitch and duration. An English clergyman named Creed was the first to theorise on such a machine in 1747 but, although a Frenchman, J. Carpentier, conceived the name 'melograph' in 1880, practical melography did not arrive until the early days of this century with the direct manufacture of piano rolls from a pneumatically driven machine coupled into a 'recording' player piano in a studio.

Melography became the key, of course, to the successful making of artists' rolls for the reproducing systems but by this time it had progressed from being everyman's dream into a reality along with all the attendant complexity that even the piano-roll recording studio managed to muster.

Now, though, the computer makes it possible to store an almost infinite quantity of information – the 16K RAM is now commonplace (this means a random-access memory with a capability of 16,000 pieces of information) and this can easily be expanded to 32K and 64K. In simple terms this means that the master keyboard performer may now melographically record his music onto recording tape. The difference between this recording and that on a tape-recorder, however, is that this new recording will operate his piano for him, so producing an actual performance with each replay. Just as the conventional tape-recorder has been responsible for preserving much mediocre music which should have been allowed to float through the ether into oblivion, so the computer-generated melographic recording will undoubtedly find itself charged with the preservation of digitally encoded musical

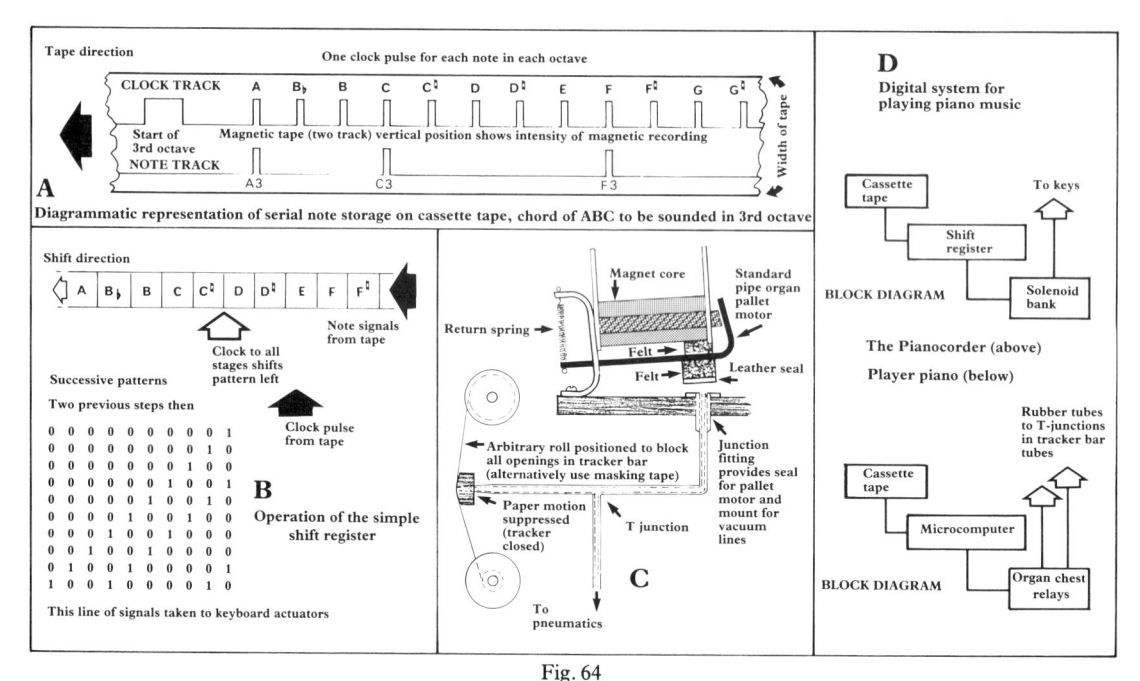

Fig. 64
The principles of the computerised player piano as devised by Professor F. G. Heath of Edinburgh's Heriot-Watt University. Professor Heath converted an old upright by the Berlin maker, Mörs, to play computer encoded magnetic tape in 1974.

excrement. With luck, though, it will be permitted to find itself an undoubtedly important place in the interpretation and study of music.

The magnetically encoded piano-playing system can be subdivided into three components for installation in a piano. The shape and form of these components again can be presented in two forms: the instrument which is already a pneumatic player piano, in which it is intended to install the system as a modification; and the ordinary instrument which is to be 'computerised'. Still further variations will become apparent as we proceed.

In the simplest form – that of the existing player piano which already has a pneumatic means of striking the piano strings – the system requires use of a tape-playing unit, a microcomputer, and a set of electrically operated simple open/shut valves connected into the existing rubber tubing of the player piano somewhere between the tracker bar and the pneumatic stack (see Fig. 64).

For the ordinary piano, the system might compromise the tape-playing unit, a shift-register and a solenoid stack operating on the individual piano-key actions.

The most interesting component here is probably the tape unit and the first point to emphasise is that with modern computer techniques, and given the overall high properties of modern recording tape, a considerable amount of information (more, in fact, than is needed) can be put onto and taken off ordinary domestic recording tape. The half-inch and one-inch tape of the big-time computers is not necessary and the perfected schemes use ordinary Philips-type compact cassettes encoded at conventional speeds. The only difference is that it is preferable to employ the cassette as a full-width tape, which means that it can only be used on one side in one direction. This is usually used in two-track format, track one having responsibility for the time-base requirement and track two for the individual note selection.

Heriot-Watt University made use of this system in its computer conversion of a 1920s Mörs* player piano. Professor Heath takes up the story:

'We use the two tracks of the stereo tape as follows. Track one has a wide pulse to signal "start" for each octave, and eleven short pulses to indicate the time at which the signal for each note will be present on the second track if the note is to be played. We have to send as many pulses as there are notes on the keyboard plus extra pulses for pedals and expression. In general, 100 pulses are enough and a fairly cheap cassette recorder could send more than 1,000 pulses per second, which is 10 keyboard images or lines on a piano roll per second.'

Because each keyboard image can start at any moment in time after the previous one, the performance has the same spontaneity as the piano roll. Indeed, it is worth adding that Professor Heath's 100 pulses for both notation and expression compares very favourably with the number of perforated tracks on a piano roll (the number of openings in the line on the tracker bar).

Most magnetic-tape systems in computer use succeed in mixing clock and data signals on a single track – a version of the now familiar multiplexed recording signal used by the telephone system and by aircraft in flight entertainment systems. The single-track system does offer one major advantage and that is that it avoids potential problems resulting from tape skewing since tape is appreciably more elastic than the paper of a piano roll (which, while capable of expansion and contraction in the critical dimension of width, will usually remain loyal to its perforated data in spite of itself).

There are two principal ways of converting the serial flow of data signals from the cassette

---

* The piano factory of L. Mörs & Co. was founded in Berlin at Reichenberger Str. 142, SO 26, in 1869 and remained in business until the outbreak of the 1939–45 war. Not a company widely acclaimed for its player pianos.

recorder (which emerge as electronic signals in an output wire) into the instantaneous parallel form which must be fed to the keyboard. The first method was used by the Heriot-Watt University and makes use of shift registers which can work in either direction (see Fig. 64). The pattern of digits shifts in from the left one at a time and when the register is full the parallel read-out signal is activated and electric signals can be taken to the piano's pneumatic stack interface.

In the melographic role, if the keys are pressed it can be arranged that a 1 is read into the register for each pressed-key position on the piano keyboard, and then a suitable clock signal generated to move the digits out in series and put them on magnetic tape. Professor Heath found that this system worked very well although it is, of course, inflexible. The circuits must be designed to suit exactly the format on the cassette tape.

The second method of conversion is to use the microcomputer, which can offer extreme flexibility. In other words, for rapid musical passages, it will image the keyboard 'on demand' as frequently as the speed of note depression requires, whereas for slow musical passages, it will image the keyboard only as necessary – on a change in 'steady state', such as a fresh key being pressed, or one released.

It is now possible to buy a complete microprocessor, which is the heart of a small computer system, for as little as £10·20. Using a suitable control programme, these can perform all that the player piano may ever ask of it. With the aid of the microprocessor, it becomes possible to achieve that ideal goal mentioned earlier – the reducing of piano rolls recorded on any reproducing piano system to one common encoded form.

The new melographic reproducing piano at present being developed experimentally by Professor Fred Heath at Edinburgh is to make use of this high-flown technology and, when it is finished, it could be the most sophisticated piano-playing system anywhere in the world today.

One computerised player piano is now in production and this is the Pianocorder currently being manufactured in California by Superscope-Marantz.

There is quite a story behind why Superscope-Marantz should have undertaken such an unusual project. Well known in the hi-fi circles, the company has amassed a great deal of experience in modern solid-state and computer technology. The president of the company is Joseph Tushinsky, who is a self-confessed collector and devotee of the reproducing piano. Indeed, he has a private library of about 18,000 music rolls from the various reproducing systems already listed.

And so, when Tushinsky decided that it was time the old player piano was given a new lease of life, he set about the task from an extremely well founded base – that of top-end audio and electronic equipment, and that of a man who knew a Duo-Art piano roll from a can of beans.

Because the venture had to be 'commercially viable' (which means that it had to sell), the instrument was designed as a mass-market mechanism which could be fitted into a normal piano. And the system chosen was the first one I described – that which centres on the shift register.

Since the Pianocorder is made to fit ordinary non-player pianos (pianos without pneumatic playing stacks) an all-electric system was devised. This posed certain inherent problems for, as is well known, relays which work by magnetism – and this means solenoids or actuators – tend to have a rather soft touch for a piano keyboard. This is because they become more powerful as they close, whereas the human finger and the pneumatic motor (in the form of a wedge-shaped exhaust bellows) start at full power and their force diminishes with the development of the stroke.

The Pianocorder solves this shortcoming by driving the actuators with very high voltage pulses of very short duration. The width of this pulse is accurately controlled for expression. The effect of this is to throw the inertia of the actuator upwards at the back underneath the key action, resulting in a fair approximation of the human touch pattern.

Existing piano rolls are encoded using a system which employs a modified player-piano tracker bar. Behind each hole in the tracker is a sensor which registers that particular hole position and length (remember that on a piano roll the length of the note from initial strike to the return of the damper is indicated by a slot of the required length) and feeds this information into a computer. This computer is equipped with a programme to suit the type of piano roll being 'recorded' and encodes the information on a normal type of C90 cassette. The computer itself, once programmed, can be used to write music since notes and chords can be typed, along with pedal expression information, on the computer keyboard. This can then be processed into cassette format.

The cassette recorder used by the Pianocorder is a special unit offering less sophistication but greater read-out accuracy than a normal audio cassette deck. The signals from this go into a shift-register-type circuit and then generate signals which decide which solenoids on the piano key actions must be set in motion. Since piano rolls only divide expression into bass and treble, the Pianocorder is controlled in the same way for simplicity with the bass solenoids being given a pulse width corresponding to the bass expression bits for the chord in question, and the treble being treated similarly.

Superscope-Marantz's Pianocorder offers the student the ability to make a recording of his own performance and then play it back for critical analysis of piano technique. To be able to do this, though, some sophistication of computer-recording technique has to be applied and the system S-M uses is somewhat limited in capability due, undoubtedly, to the high cost of an ideal or pianistically perfect system.

The recording system for the home user records all the keys which are depressed as a tape signal. There is a small microphone at each end inside the piano and the short period after a chord is struck indicates the sound level in the treble end and so determines the level of expression for the treble. In truth, the word 'expression' is more properly what the old Ampico paper-roll system called 'intensity'. A similar system controls the bass end. The microphones are, of course, suitably signal-attenuated for function inside the piano case close to the hammers and strings.

For the making of a true reproducing/recording piano – the next step in the chain – S-M is still debating whether to calibrate hammer velocity or key velocity, both now being technically possible. It is known that Ampico tried the technique of measuring hammer velocity back in the early days of the reproducing piano. The system they tried was calibrated by measuring electrically the time taken for a golf ball to pass through two thin metal contact plates. It must have been an odd sight indeed to have entered what was then a recording laboratory and been confronted by a man in golfing outfit about to drive a golfball into a piece of electrical equipment.

Welte, by comparison, claimed to have used key velocity as a means of expression calibration, yet the method which they reckon they used – two needle points of different lengths under each key dipping into a pool of mercury – could not have been anywhere near accurate enough.

The Superscope-Marantz development work has so far been concentrated on a lowest-possible-cost domestic system. The company so far prefers to market a factory-installed unit and a price of around $1,800 plus fitting cost is being quoted. Marketing began in June 1978 and the instrument comes with 100 45-minute tapes, the music taken from Duo-Art, Ampico and Welte rolls in Tushinsky's collection.

The only control provided for the user, other than an on/off switch, is a tempo control – an unfortunate paucity of owner participation for the true player-piano enthusiast, for whom individual interpretation is possible by the judicious use of levers or control buttons. There is also a remote switch available to control the tempo when it is used as an accompanying instrument.

The discerning listener will find very little difference between the Pianocorder performance and an original reproducing piano roll played on a good instrument.

The revival of the reperforming piano through this device may well serve to convince the general public that the player piano has never been replaced by the gramophone and the LP record. Given the choice of a record or having your own piano play for you with the hands of a recorded master on the keys, only he who has no room for a piano would opt for the ersatz sound, however well recorded and pressed and reproduced, of an instrument processed electronically and then synthesised by plastic cones excited by a magnet.

True high fidelity must, after all, be faithful reproduction by the best possible way and the computer piano is, after all is said and done, still a piano.

There is another technique which can be applied to electronic musical instruments to enable them to play music automatically. This system is now used by a number of makers of electronic organs but there is no reason why it cannot be applied to any other form of instrument, including the piano. It makes use of short-time, reprogrammable active circuits using a light pen and bar coding. Bar coding is systematically being used in the supermarket industry to 'read' the prices of a variety of mixed products into an electronic cash register. The user simply passes the bar code strip over a special area of the till counter beneath which is a light source. Another and more readily identifiable version is being used increasingly by public lending libraries where the information concerning a library book is contained in one bar code, and that of the borrower in another bar code on his reader's ticket. The library check-out counter features a computer access which first takes the particulars of the reader using a light pen, and then those of the book by the same means – stroking the bar code strip with a special pen which can detect the positions and the widths of the code of lines.

In musical use, one manufacturer of electronic organs in Japan prints the music for the tunes the owner may play in normal staff notation on one side of the music book, and on the other in bar code. While the skilled player can play the tune from the staff notation by hand, when the electronic organ is switched to the 'record' mode, the user can plug a light pen directly into the memory circuit, and then 'load' the memory with the music bar by musical bar by stroking the relevant bar-code strips.

The author spent some while recently evaluating the possibilities of programming a computer to 'read' ordinary staff notation, at once opening up the entire musical repertoire to such an application which, by the aid of the extensive memories available on floppy disc, for example, could accept the massive number of separate instructions needed to perform, say, a Bach organ fugue. The benefits of bar-code analysis, however, were considered easier, even allowing for the limitations therein.

A second system evaluated as far as a working model involved the use of traditional music rolls but dispensed with the tracker bar. In this experiment, the presence of openings in the paper was detected by optical/electronic means. This system had the theoretical advantage that it would allow the enterprising owner to 'write' his own music rolls using a felt-tipped pen on a roll of paper, for the optical/electronic system should be equally at home with paper with a hole in it and paper with a black line on it. This concept with the immense advantages it might offer could not, however, allow for the fact that some piano rolls (particularly modern ones) are punched in an almost transparent paper while others of greater age are to be found in paper of varying opacity and reflectivity. In reality, the sensitivity of the system would need to be fine-tuned for each roll.*

Electricity has not been the only power source to be mated with the piano in the present-day quest for a player piano. Probably the most extraordinary device to have come to my attention was one which emerged in the Far East a few years ago.

The technical publication *Machine Design* published in 1971† a news item and illustration of an 'electrohydraulic piano-playing system' apparently measuring 90 × 43 × 58·5 inches and weighing 660 lb. Manufactured by the Tokyo Keiki Company and unveiled at Japan's Fluid Power International Fair – surely a strange place to show a piano – this used pre-punched tape which was fed into a minicomputer 'which controls the arm, finger, intensity and foot actuators [*sic*]' via what was described as 'a two-unit set of 28V DC interphase controls'. The report went on to say that 'Actuator motions are power-assisted by a hydraulic power supply that includes a 15-kw electric motor and a pump delivering 14 gpm [gallons per minute] at 2,000 psi'. From this it can be appreciated that a leak from the piano would have resulted in a high-pressure jet of hydraulic fluid spraying all over the powerful electrics. Probably built for no other reason than to prove a point, nothing more was heard of this monster nor was there any indication as to the sort of music (if any) which it could play.

The new generation of player pianos for the home as distinct from the theoretical and heavy engineering workshop looks like developing around all-electronic action and the computer. In the world of electronic organs which today are compact enough to be described purely as keyboards, true melographic capability is possible with 'smoothing' ability so that the stumbling one-finger tune created by the novice can be re-timed, given a full orchestral backing and harmonic accompaniment. And one particular maker has gone a step further and fitted a printer to his keyboard which makes a 'hard' copy of the music played in staff notation.

As far as pianos are concerned, the days of huge volume sales can never again be so much as approached, but devices such as the Superscope-Marantz Pianocorder and its successors could well earn for themselves a small and no doubt unspectacular future (in pure marketing terms) among the very small sector of the vast music-loving public which enjoys the luxury of owning a real piano.

---

* See *New Era Automatic Instruments* by Arthur W. J. G. Ord-Hume in 'Bulletin', MBSI, Vol. XXXVII, No. 1, pp. 44–8.
† Volume 43, No. 27, 11 November 1971, p. 46.

PIANOLA

THE HUPFELD
Solophonola Players
are the highest class productions of the world.

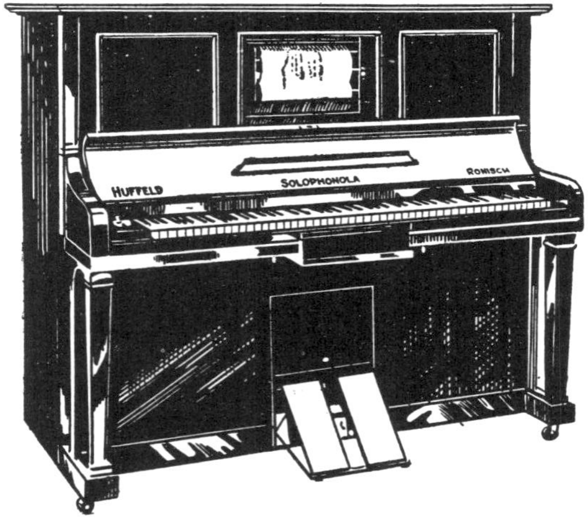

The Hupfeld-Rönisch "Solophonola" Upright Grand.
Prices from £88 4s. 0d. upwards.

"The 'Solophonola' and its Artistes' Rolls are such valuable inventions that we cannot to-day estimate the magnitude of their field."
FERRUCCIO BUSONI.

"Your 'Solophonola' is an invention which offers almost unlimited possibilities of musical expression."
EMIL SAUER.

"The 'Solophonola' with its Artistes' Rolls enables the general public to play the piano artistically."
EUGEN D'ALBERT.

THE HUPFELD-RÖNISCH SOLOPHONOLA GRAND
is the only Perfect PLAYER GRAND PIANO yet produced.

CATALOGUES AND ALL INFORMATION FROM M. SINCLAIR.

SOLOPHONOLA
16-17 ORCHARD STREET, PORTMAN SQUARE, LONDON, W.

The Player-Piano for the Connoisseur

The
HUPFELD PLAYER-PIANO
is the most remarkable invention of our time in the line of musical instruments.

IT disarms every criticism heretofore made against mechanically-played pianos. It enables anyone to play his favourite pieces with a masterly technique, the fullest expression of individual feeling and without a trace of mechanical effects.

Tone-beauty is insured by the incomparable BLÜTHNER and other fine makes of pianos in which the Hupfeld action is incorporated.

A small initial payment secures immediate delivery of any of the three different models in which the Hupfeld Player is obtainable.

Your present piano will be taken in part exchange.

Among the new inventions incorporated in this "Player" are interchangeable metal valve boxes and a turbine wind motor. The SOLODANT, which automatically gives prominence to the notes of the melody. The TRANSPOSER, which permits a song roll to be played in any key. The PIANISSIMATOR, an almost human device for playing very softly.

BLÜTHNER & Co. Ltd. 17-23 WIGMORE St., LONDON, W.1.

CHAPTER 11

Music for the Player Piano

The transcription of music onto a paper roll as a series of perforations could be achieved in two ways. First was the physical marking out of the music using, in simplest form, a pencil, a scale and a ruler. Second was the direct recording of marks onto a moving strip of paper while a piano was actually being played, contacts from the keys making the marks electrically or pneumatically. A variation of this latter method was to be incorporated in the system of the actual perforating machine itself so that a hole was automatically punched whenever a key was depressed.

This latter method, which was to become generally adopted by the music-roll manufacturing industries of the world, was the realisation of the dream of melography, described in the previous chapter. The ability to record a keyboard performer's performance actually while he played had been a cherished goal since earliest times. The trials and tribulations of inventors who sought to achieve this must have been many as they strove to solve the complex problems behind the simple requirement of measuring the two dimensions of a musical note – pitch and duration. These inventors struggled without recourse to such aids as electricity and pneumatics and were forced to work in an entirely mechanical regime using levers, linkages and pens as the means whereby a mark or series of marks might be left on a sheet of paper.

Although the term 'melography' came from the first practical instrument intended for the purpose – Jules Carpentier's Melograph – there were many precursors. The first recorded attempt was as far back as 1745 when Johann Friedrich Unger thought up a device which he later presented to the Berliner Akademie. He called this, somewhat grandly, his 'Machina ad Sonos et Concentus quoscunque ope Clavichordii productos in ipso cantationis actu chartae tradendos', according to his somewhat impressive Latin dissertation for the Berlin Academy in 1752. The device consisted of a supplementary keyboard attached to that of an existing instrument in such a manner that depression of a key moved a series of rods and levers and resulted in a line being marked on an endless roll of paper. The note took the form of a line of the same length as the duration of the sound. It seems unlikely that Unger ever actually built his machine for, although he must have appreciated the heart of the problem as being the means of providing uniform, steady motion to the roll of paper, he gave no indication as to how this might be accomplished. But Unger did invent something practical: he found that the pens which made marks on the paper quickly stopped writing because the ink dried, so he experimented with thin tubes of ink with a spongey end in place of a conventional nib. He thus invented the felt-tipped pen.

Two years after Unger's first claim for his invention, an English clergyman by the name of

Creed entered the field with the first of a number of inventions claimed to make possible the writing down of music as it was being played. His device was to be attached to a harpsichord or clavichord so that every note played was written down. A paper of his was read before the Royal Society in 1747. This was entitled 'A Demonstration of the Possibility of Making a Machine that shall write Extempore Voluntaries or Other Pieces of Music'. This paper will be found in the *Philosophical Transactions for 1747*, number 183. Creed died in 1770 leaving the realisation of his dream to the Frenchman, Carpentier, who exhibited his Melotrope and Melograph at the International Exhibition of Electricity in Paris in the year 1880.

Carpentier's device consisted of a stylus-type recording machine called the Melograph (Latin *melos* meaning melody, *graphium* meaning stylus for writing) which marked out lines on a travelling band of card while a keyboard instrument was being played. After recording, the band of paper was removed, the marks used as a guide for punching holes in the paper, and the resulting band of perforated paper placed on a machine called a Melotrope which would play back the recording via a kicking-shoe type of mechanism. Placed upon a piano or organ keyboard, the music strip was transported across a mechanical keyframe by means of rubber-covered rollers turned by a hand wheel. This piano-player device, of the key-top variety, was later sold in large quantities on its own for playing pre-punched folded strips of thin-card music. There appeared to be a far greater market for this type of player than for its progenitor, the melograph.

A Berlin mechanic by the name of Höhlfeld, said to have been inspired by the work of Unger, produced a similar machine sometime about 1771. All these were the precursors of the numerous recording machines which were to culminate in the ideal system of the player-piano era when direct roll-perforating machinery could be set up to operate under the control of a piano or organ keyboard.

Preserved in the Deutsches Museum, Munich, is a five-octave compound harpsichord inscribed 'Josephus Merlin Privilegiarius Novi Fortepiano N. 80, Londini, 1780'. This is the work of John Joseph Merlin (1735–1804), who was born at Huys near Liège and came to England in 1760, where he later established a renowned museum of his inventions at Princes Street, Hanover Square, London. This instrument is fitted with a copying machine which is brought into operation by depressing a pedal. The keys can then be connected to a series of pencils to mark lines on a roll of paper about nine inches wide. The paper is transported by a clockwork motor. No doubt this device was intended as a guide to the transcription of a performance into manuscript music at a later date. The instrument was restored in 1912 by Carl Pfeiffer of Stuttgart.

In the same museum is an example of the Kromarograph. This is a special harmonium built by the famous Viennese maker Teofil Kotykiewicz (Peter Titz Nachfolger) in the name of Adam Knopf von Kotykiewicz. Each key is fitted with electrical contacts connected by cable to a separate device for writing on a moving strip of paper as notes are played.

At the International Exhibition of 1862 held in London, G. Marzolo of Padua in Italy showed 'an organ with a melographic appliance for recording and repeating music played upon it'. No further details have been preserved.

As early as 1856, the Vicomte Théodose du Moncel, French electrical engineer, had carried out experiments in recording music electrically as it was being played. This he did using sensitised paper rolls upon which marks were made when a current was passed through it. At the Vienna International Exhibition of 1873, a similar device perfected by an engineer called Roncalli was shown. This used paper coated with equal parts of calcium iron cyanide and ammonium nitrate. A steel stylus was provided for each piano note and allowed to traverse the paper. Depression of a key caused a current to pass through the stylus so producing a blue line caused by the production of ferric oxide salt in conjunction with the potassium iron cyanide. A copper stylus would produce a red line; cobalt a brown line; and a bismuth stylus produced a line coloured yellow only when the marked paper was soaked in clean water.

So far, the prime characteristic of these instruments was purely to mark out music on a travelling paper roll so that at a later date it might be transcribed into conventional notation. Thus perhaps the better name for the system was *pianography*. At any rate, 'pianograph' was the name selected by the inventor of a machine described as follows in *Musical Opinion* for February 1889:

> A new pianograph, remarkable for simplicity, as well as inexpensiveness in its working process, has been invented by Captain Furse. The apparatus, which can be fixed to any piano, enables the performer to record the music whilst playing in the ordinary way by simply turning a knob which sets the mechanism and requisite rolls of paper in motion. This paper costs only about threepence per hour of continuous winding, i.e. playing; no less than six hundred consecutive notes per minute (or ten per second) being, if required, marked down by this ingenious invention. The bars are indicated by the easy pressure of a pedal. By the mere turning of another knob, the music played can be transposed into any other key, and yet, by another alteration, can be made applicable to an American organ. This novel contrivance should prove of especial advantage to those who, although clever at improvising, do not possess sufficient depth of technical knowledge for effectually concentrating their ideas into proper musical composition, and, likewise, to a large number of composers who, distraught maybe by other calls upon their time, wish to make an instant record of some happy inspiration, to be taken up at will later on. Captain Furse is prepared to show the working of his new discovery at his rooms, 69, Guildford Street, Russell Square, W.C. As the only drawback to the above, it is to be feared that much music, which had better remain unwritten, will be committed to paper by the presumably extensive use of this the latest, and apparently best, of existing pianographs.

The first masters of practical recording and playback melography were the German engineers who at the turn of the century produced the Welte-Mignon reproducing piano and its recording system using the sliding-paper valve after John McTammany.

Interest in instantaneous recording continued well into the present century and probably the most northerly inventor was C. W. Nyström of Karlstad in Sweden. This man, son of J. P. Nyström who invented the unusual Nyström Reform-Orgel (a reed organ played either by hand or by means of Ariston-type perforated cardboard discs via a playing mechanism on the right-hand side of the case), was granted Swedish patents for his recording device to be fitted to a recording player piano. His British patent for this, number 1579, is dated 29 July 1898. Later he patented further improvements under British Patent number 2418 of 31 January 1910. This related to a device by the use of which the movements of piano pedals could be indicated by a stylus on a wax-coated travelling sheet. Subsequently he patented a kicking-shoe-type key-top player (see Chapter 8).

Until very recently, the practical recording and reproduction of music has rested almost exclusively on the use of perforated paper rolls with the paper serving as a sliding valve in a pneumatic system. During the past few years, though, the digital control of pianos from specially encoded magnetic tape cassettes had made possible a new era of melography. Following initial experimental work which was restricted to the computer laboratory, it is now possible to play an ordinary piano fitted with the computer interface and then have the piano replay the performance electromagnetically using the tape for signalling individual key operation. The first commercially available instrument was the Superscope-Marantz Pianocorder introduced in America in 1978. This is described, along with the experimental principles involved, in Chapter 10.

But the mainstay of the player piano has traditionally been the piano roll and it may come as a surpise to learn that throughout the world there were many hundreds of different labels. Recently, I have been collecting specimens of these different rolls and my 'one of a kind' shelf now has several hundred rolls on it – and that is only the tip of the iceberg!

Every company involved in making piano rolls published its own catalogue and for some while in the burgeoning days of the player the makers of different systems strove to ensure that their rolls would play only on their instruments. Soon, fortunately, the short-sighted aspect of this policy was recognised and, with the rationalising of players to 65 and 88 notes, all makers of rolls sought to garner the greatest possible potential market share by emphasising that their rolls would play on any instrument of the scale to which it was cut.

There was, needless to say, no pattern of order evident between roll catalogues and for this reason I will describe briefly some of the classification systems evident from catalogues in my own collection.

No doubt because of the musical tastes of the early days of the player piano, the repertoire tended to mirror that of the reed organ and so was built on a firm foundation of popular classics, sacred music, popular songs and suchlike.

A glance at one of the early well organised catalogues will show a typical mix. The Farrand Organ Company of Detroit issued in May 1905 its catalogue of music rolls for its Cecilian player, which it offered for sale through its European branch at 44 Great Marlborough Street in London's West End. These rolls were broken down into the following classified sections:

Roll numbers		
1 to 1271	=	Classical
1001 to 1076	=	Sacred
2001 to 2273	=	Operatic
3001 to 3162	=	Songs and Ballads
4001 to 4172	=	Marches, Two-Steps and Cake Walks
5001 to 5178	=	Dances
6001 to 6076	=	Coon Songs and Selections
7001 to 7031	=	National, Folk and War Songs
8001 to 8202	=	Miscellaneous
9001 to 9259	=	Accompaniments
10001 to 10048	=	College and Lodge Songs

This listing bears every sign of having been carefully thought out with the intention of having, apparently, 999 titles in each section as a maximum. However, the first classification proved impossible to keep within these constraints, hence the apparently anomalous numbering which in fact runs from roll number 1 (Chopin's Impromptu, opus 29) through to 999 and then continues from 1201 through to 1271. This situation was materially helped along by the fact that Farrand issued only 76 titles in the 'Sacred' section.

Prices of the Farrand Cecilian rolls ranged from as little as 2s 6d up to a maximum of 8s, the price steps being 2s 6d, 3s 6d, 5s, 6s, 7s and 8s.

Kastner published a catalogue of music rolls for the Kastonone Autopiano and Autogrand some time about 1910. All Kastonome rolls carried the prefix K and the first roll, K1, was Liszt's Rhapsodie Hongroise, No. 2. This was priced at 10s 6d. The last roll in this catalogue was K2933, Mendelssohn's Songs Without Words, No. 2, priced at 6s 6d. However, there appears to be a gap between K2639 and the final just two numbers in the K2900 series.

Kastonome rolls were priced in no fewer than fifteen groups which were not indicated by any prefix or suffix to the roll number. The price of rolls was 2s 6d, 4s, 4s 6d, 5s, 5s 6d, and so on in sixpenny steps up to the most expensive at 10s 6d.

Kastner also manufactured rolls for both 65- and 88-note instruments and a supplement marked No. 30 and dated November 1912 lists 65-note rolls all in the 7700 series and 88-note versions all in the 83000 series. Prices are apparently reduced from catalogue prices – 8s rolls at 6s; 7s rolls at 5s 3d, and so on.

An undated Kastner Triumph catalogue of 65-note rolls runs to 430 pages and starts with roll number 1001 (Bartlett's *Polka de Concert* for 6s) and, with the exception of some random gaps towards the end of each thousand numbers, runs to 7702 and then jumps to what may well have been a new series started at 9012 continuing to 10791 (arias from Handel's *Messiah* for 8s). There is then a major jump to 60217 (a potpourri of music from Mozart's *Zauberflöte* arranged, Lord preserve us, for four hands and exchanged for the sum of 8s). Again there are some pretty major random gaps to the final title in the catalogue, roll number 77239 – Elgar's Sonata, opus 28, fourth movement for 7s. This sonata was presented complete on four consecutively numbered rolls and the immediately preceding roll listed is 76935, the 'Automobil [sic] March' from *The Dollar Princess*, premiered in 1909. Almost all the final rolls were what would be grouped as 'classical', including 'Tschaikowsky', Weber, Wagner, Schubert and so on.

Prices of the Kastner Triumph 65-note rolls were listed at 2s 6d, 3s 6d, 4s, 5s, 6s, 7s, and 8s. Indicating that the catalogue dates from the period when the full-scale piano was making its presence known, the catalogue in my library bears a rubber stamp reading: 'Catalogue prices subject to discount of 3d in the Shilling 6/– Nett being the most expensive roll'.

The earliest Aeolian catalogues were published in New York and these were all devoted to 65-note rolls for the Pianola and its predecessor, the Aeriola.

By April of 1903, The Aeolian Company was advertising that 'there are 9,106 different pieces of music at present available to owners of the Pianola. And new ones are added to this number at the rate of over two hundred a month.' The Pianola at this time cost all of $250 or, at that time, about £65.

The Orchestrelle Company in London issued its 'Catalogue of Music for the Pianola and Pianola-Piano' for June 1910 with a notice on the title page:

NOTICE TO LIBRARY SUBSCRIBERS

All rolls in this catalogue are available to subscribers to our Music Roll Library under Class A. Only rolls in the Pianola column are available under Class B.

The catalogue, containing only 65-note music rolls, is arranged in three columns headed 'Pianola', 'Metrostyle' and 'Themodist'. Not all titles were available under all three columns, which meant that the enthusiastic roll collector occasionally had to compromise. The roll numbering system gives little clue as to the type of roll except in the case of the Themodist rolls. Plain numbers, sometimes but not always with a suffix L or Y are used for Pianola and Metrostyle rolls, but all Themodised rolls bear the suffix T. Where the Metrostyle number already has a letter prefix, the letter T preceded the existing prefix. As an example, Verdi's *Aida* in transcription by Rosellen appears as a Pianola roll number 62931 costing 8s, as a Metrostyle roll number 73781 costing 10s, and as a Themodised roll number T73781 also priced at 10s. However, Cécile Chaminade's *Air de Ballet* appears as Pianola roll number 8683 costing 2s 6d, as a Metrostyle roll number Y8683 for 5s, and a Themodised roll, also 5s, number TY8683. Dubourg's *Valse Chaloupée* comes as a Pianola roll on L2848, as a Metrostyle roll number L12294, and as a Themodist roll number TL15239.

Also available were so-called 'autograph interpretation' rolls either with a plain number or the prefix L. These featured interpretational markings either by the composer or by a named performer (for example, Wanda Landowska annotated roll number 69581, Muzio Clementi's Sonata, opus 26 No. 2 in F sharp minor).

Some measure of clarity appears in the Aeolian numbering system when the numerical catalogue is consulted. Roll number 1, we find, is Glazounov's *Serenade Espagnole*, opus 20 No. 2 in A for cello and pianoforte – an accompaniment roll. Many of these low-numbered rolls are of music for small group or duet and occasionally we find duet music arranged for two pianolas (the Mozart Sonata in D, opus 53, for example, appears on six rolls, two for each of the three movements and marked 'first piano' and 'second piano': numbers are 69a, 69b and so on to 71b).

The extent of Aeolian's musical output is clearly demonstrated by the reversion to number 1 again after the last of the first series numbers in this catalogue – number 77409 being a medley of popular German songs and obviously dating from before the time when German music became anathema. But, after all, this was well after the date of catalogue issue – 1910. However, at this point or thereabouts, the system reverted to 1 again, this time prefixed with the letter L. Roll L1 was Barnby's *The Soft Southern Breeze* in B flat. The last in this catalogue, numbered L3172, is the two-step from the 1909 musical *The Dollar Princess*.

The numerical arrangement of autograph interpretations shows that the numbering system was not substantially different and that number allocations came from the main list; that is to say, numbers in this list (which are, by the way, all Metrostyle rolls) do not appear in the earlier, cumulative list. To begin with, though, the same numbers were used: and these were the ones with a double letter prefix. For example, the *Bagatelle*, Opus 63 Number 1 in D Major by Moszkowski was available as a Pianola roll on 1079 and as a Metrostyle roll on Y1079. However, the 'Autograph Interpretation' with markings by the composer himself was available as YA1079. Fairly early on (after 36 numbers in this catalogue), the system reverted to 'ordinary' numerical, complicated only by the non-conformity of the numbers. Homer N. Bartlett's *Ballade*, not available on Pianola, was on Metrostyle as 72131 and on Themodist as T72131. However, Bartlett's own interpretation was on 63251. Moszkowski's *Pièce Rustique*, Opus 36 No. 8 could be had on Pianola 9382, Metrostyle 70461 or Autograph 63271.

As with the main numerical listing, Aeolian began to run out of numbers and after the 79000s reverted to an L-prefixed series of five numbers. The first roll was L14000, Elinescu's *Scena Pastorala Romana*. Many of the boxes for these autograph rolls bore labels on their lid tops reading 'Interpretation Indicated by . . .' followed by the name of the composer or annotator.

Right at the back of this 1910 catalogue is a small section headed 'Foreign & Special Music' with the warning that 'music listed under this heading will not be placed in the circulating library'. Then there is an explanatory note saying that 'the rolls listed under this heading have been manufactured to meet the requirements of foreign and special trade. As these rolls are not of general interest they are neither carried in our ordinary stock nor included in the Library, but copies can be purchased on giving a few days' notice.' The first of these rolls is *Annie Laurie*, surely one of the best known and most popular folk tunes. Perhaps the decision to segregate this one came from a non-Scots-loving American. Prices in this catalogue run from 2s 6d to 10s.

The compass of the full-scale player piano was from Contra-A to c^7 whilst the range of the 65-note instrument ran from A to c^6. The perforations for the full-scale roll were spaced at nine to the inch while the 65-note roll is perforated at six to the inch.

By the end of the First World War, the 65-note player was completely obsolete although there was of course a very great number of instruments still in the prime of their lives. In June 1920, Aeolian issued its last catalogue of 65-note music. Instead of the rolls being individually priced, they were coded A, B and C, so reducing to just three the different price brackets. This was, certainly as far as the full-scale or 88-note roll catalogues were concerned, a very useful change since any price variation only required the insertion of a revised code price sticker in the catalogue front. With this change, there was also a radical change in the roll-numbering system, for the price code now became part of the roll number as a suffix. For example, Mozart's *Adagio Favori* was a Themodist roll price-coded A (the cheapest and in this case costing just 5s), so the number on the roll was T72763A, this final letter being somewhat smaller than the type size used for the prefix letter and numbers. Rolls with the suffix B were priced at 7s 6d and those with the letter C cost 10s. A roll of one of my own grandfather's compositions, *Soldiers of the Entente*, a military quick march, was numbered T16425B. But to revert to the 1920 65-note catalogue. The Foreword comments:

> Owing to the fact that this Company and the other principal makers of Piano Players have for some time discontinued the manufacture of instruments of 65-note scale, the demand for 65-note music has decreased to such an extent that, in order to maintain a satisfactory output of 65-note rolls, and to provide adequately for those customers who still have 65-note instruments, it is necessary that we should concentrate on the manufacture of one class of 65-note roll only.
>
> Therefore, *all* 65-note music is issued in standard form, i.e. without the Metrostyle line, but with Themodist perforations (with few exceptions).

An example of one of the few exceptions was Weber's *Grande Polonaise*, Opus 21 in E flat major, which, although a C-class roll – the most expensive – was simply numbered 1341C, indicating clearly that it was un-Themodised. A number of L-prefixed numbers still survived. The highest-numbered roll in the catalogue was T104822A, Irving Berlin's fox-trot *My Bird of Paradise*.

In July 1924, Aeolian in London issued a matching catalogue of full-scale music. This followed the same general lines as the pioneering 65-note catalogue, only prices were coded into six sections: A = 6s, B = 6s 6d, C = 11s (these all being Metrostyle-Themodist), and D = 7s 6d, E = 10s, F = 12s 6d (these all being full-scale hand-played). Aeolian song rolls had their own price of 6s 6d. The Foreword warns that hand-played rolls and song rolls are not available from the circulating library.

PIANOLA

The main section of this catalogue is devoted to the Themodist-Metrostyle roll but also includes 76 vocal accompaniment rolls which were Themodist only, and 60 instrumental accompaniment rolls, again Themodist only.

Ballads and light songs plus what were called 'vocal dances' were issued as song rolls, with an introduction advising that:

> Aeolian Song Rolls are issued in the most popular key bringing them within easy reach of most voices but as the compass is stated in most cases it should be noted when selecting titles.
>
> This point does not arise, of course, for those whose instruments are fitted with the Aeolian Transposing Device, which, lying completely out of sight behind the tracker bar enables the player to raise or lower the key by moving a small lever.
>
> Full particulars of this apparatus which may be fitted at a moderate cost, will be sent on application.

Each of the song titles which follows includes the key and the numbers have no suffixes, for example *Asleep in the Deep*, key D – D to B (H. W. Petrie) 26111. Some of the rolls were available with words in French and English, Italian and English, solely in French and solely in Spanish. The vocal dances were intended to be sung and danced to.

A small additional section was provided under the heading 'Illustrated Music Rolls'. These comprised music, words and pictures and there were five in total, numbered consecutively from 26199 to 26203 inclusive. The first four were nursery rhymes and the last one was entitled 'Children's Popular Songs and Games'. This gave the owner *London Bridge* and *Jolly is the Miller*.

Hand-played rolls all had three-figure numbers plus the prefix A. Chopin's *Andante Spianato and Polonaise*, Opus 22, played by Alfred Cortot, therefore carried the number A609F, indicating that it was one of the most expensive rolls at 12s 6d.

The Foreword to this section of the catalogue reads:

> Hand-Played rolls differ from the ordinary roll in that whereas the latter is cut in strict time, the former are produced by a pianist whose actual playing with all its slight variations from strict tempo, is transmitted to the cutting machine. Even in the hands of a not very expert player they are extremely pleasing to listen to while those who study their instrument and give attention to arriving at artistic renditions, will find them interesting and enjoyable to play, as they do not interfere in any way with perfect personal control.

Aeolian's copy-writer, one must conclude, was not particularly good at his craft.

The high cost of music rolls was recognised as the major limiting factor in the popularity of the player piano and its music. The installation of extensive machinery for the mass production of music rolls brought about a dramatic reduction in roll prices. In the July 1928 catalogue, the rolls are arranged in the same manner only this time rolls in price brackets A and D cost 4s, B and E cost 5s 6d, and C and F cost 6s 6d. Aeolian song rolls were also down at 4s 6d, while 65-note rolls were reduced. A rolls were 3s from 5s; B were 4s 6d from 7s 6d, and C were 5s 6d from 10s.

By this time, the growth in interest in dance music necessitated the issue of a separate catalogue for the 'vocal dance' category. Song rolls had also increased and now warranted a larger section in the catalogue. Illustrated music rolls had been joined by a sixth title, *John Peel*, numbered 26430. Hand-played rolls had also multiplied from 4½ pages to more than 11½ pages with a few in the four-figure numbers.

The last complete roll catalogue which Aeolian issued was in July 1932. From then onwards, until the company closed in around 1938, only monthly supplements were published.

The arrival of the Aeolian Duo-Art in 1913 soon produced a catalogue of special reproducing rolls. These were frequently listed alongside Pianola rolls. The last complete catalogue issued was in July 1932. All Duo-Art and AudioGraphic Duo-Art rolls had a small letter suffix which again was a price code. The suffix A was costed at 5s 6d for ordinary Duo-Art, and 6s for AudioGraphic Duo-Art; B was 6s 6d (7s); C was 7s (7s 6d); D was 7s 6d (8s); E was 8s (8s 6d); F was 9s (9s 6d); and G was 10s (10s 6d). An example of the 10s roll was Bach's two-part inventions numbers 1, 6 and 8 played by Bauer (roll No. 6392 G). All Biographical Duo-Art rolls were in this class-G price band. All AudioGraphic roll numbers, whether for Duo-Art or straight Pianola, had the prefix D, and hand-played rolls (naturally not available on Duo-Art) carried the prefix either D or A, then the number and then the usual price code letter. Song rolls were all five-figure numbers with neither prefix nor price code suffix and were all one price – 4s 6d for 88-note, and 3s for 65-note.

The pedal-electric Duo-Art piano was an English market model which is virtually unknown in America. Also made only for sale in the United Kingdom is the pedal Duo-Art, a sort of half-and-half instrument produced only in upright format, which was fully Duo-Art in the treble but which had only one set of expression accordions. Because the theme holes in the accompaniment were not read by the tracker bar in these instruments, special rolls with a boost to the accompaniment were cut for these foot-operated Duo-Arts in England. These rolls are generally unsuitable for use on the fully electric and the pedal-electric models. All London-made rolls carry the figure '0' as the first digit of the number, and in the December 1922 monthly supplement Maurice Ravel's *Miroirs* played by the composer on roll number 082 cost all of 20s.

Among the many types of roll which Aeolian issued were accompaniment rolls divided between vocal and instrumental, the AudioGraphic which came as annotated, analytical, running comment, biographical, children's rolls, playtime series (words, music and pictures), and school songs. Then there were hand-played, song rolls (words and music), illustrated song rolls (words, music and pictures), special song roll (only one issued – *Songs for the Camp Fireside* – which presumably required a player piano to be taken along with the tent and the sleeping bags!), accompaniment rolls (with words) which were intended for use with gramophone records, and so on. On some of the biographical rolls, the first 8 feet of paper was intended to be read prior to producing any music at all.

One of these types of programme roll introduced by Aeolian was the so-called 'World's Music' educational series first introduced about 1925–6. These were printed with particular emphasis on the presentation of extra-perforal (!) information in the way of woodcuts on the apron to depict the composers, plus other illustrations printed throughout the extensive biographical prologue. The rolls, issued with yellow box labels, were the brainchild of Percy Scholes, who was responsible for a major programme of expanding the scope of the piano roll for Aeolian. The rolls were, of course, more expensive and, when the financial crisis heralded by the 1929–30 Wall Street crash came to pass, Aeolian was forced to abandon the scheme.

Aeolian in London introduced its own little magazine called *The Duo-Art and 'Pianola'-piano Monthly* in September of 1924. This 12-page bulletin of new rolls and cameos on musicians and their music is today rare, although it ran for about thirteen years. Prior to this, the company published a monthly pocket-sized booklet of new releases, the first issue being in 1908.

Sometimes the task of the music-roll editor was akin to the pianist's art as he strove to correct the extensive and varied mistakes of some recording pianists. Wrong notes were an ever-present and understandable feature of the master roll which a careful comparison with the score could remove. But sometimes it was more than that. Ignace Paderewski's Duo-Art recordings were a case in point. Although a brilliant and talented performer, Paderewski's almost complete lack of formal musical training had left him with some serious technical faults. This came to a head in his piano rolls when it was found that his hands did not play together. The job of trying to sort out his piano rolls was beyond the capabilities of the editor, so Rudoph Ganz was given the task of trying to make some sense out of them. In fairness it should be pointed out that Paderewski never wanted to be considered a virtuoso pianist, but wished to be remembered as a composer.

Making piano rolls had its lighter side. Duo-Art recording pianist Robert Armbruster (born in Philadelphia in 1896) was at one time in charge of operatic, semi-classical and salon music, and one day a roll appeared labelled *Loof Lirpa*. None of the personnel was able to identify it, but apparently there was some general agreement that it sounded like a Brahms intermezzo. Finally it was discovered that the title was 'April Fool' spelled backwards – and that the unknown Brahms was a roll of 'Peas Porridge Hot' spooled backwards. A technician who had been on the receiving end of numerous studio pranks was having his own back.*

Aeolian underwent a spate of serious problems in the United States. The depression of the early 1930s was bad enough, but then the company sustained a serious fire at its factory, and largely as a result of this in 1932 it merged with the American Piano Company at East Rochester. The fidelity of performance in recording could no longer be economically justified and from about 1934 onwards the rolls were not made on a recording piano but were marked out on special master stencil paper, the marks for notes and expression being made with blue and red pencil. In 1941, all production of rolls ceased and the plant went over to war production. The flagging popularity of the player piano did not encourage the company to maintain any of its old plant and machinery and all was unceremoniously scrapped.

Animatic rolls were manufactured by Hupfeld and these, in my opinion, represent probably the finest of all the 88-note full-scale rolls ever made outside those for the reproducing piano. Properly interpreted, these excellent hand-played-type rolls can be as good as if not better than many a Duo-Art or Ampico roll. The word Animatic, says the catalogue 'is a play on the word "anima" (soul)'.

Animatic rolls were sold in London by Bluthner & Co. Ltd, of 17–23 Wigmore Street. The earliest catalogue in my library bears a pencilled date of May 1927 and contains 144 pages. Animatic rolls could, of course, be used with any make of 88-note piano. The full title was 'Animatic Artists' Roll', and they were the nearest thing to a reproducing type of performance. Each roll bore the name of the recording artist. These rolls were coded with Roman numerals for pricing so that rolls catalogued with the suffix 'I' cost 5s 6d, those with 'II' cost 8s, and those 'III' were 11s. They were thus very much more expensive than the

---

* James Elfers, *Player Piano Group Bulletin*, No. 51, page 23.

three categories of hand-played Pianola roll which sold at 4s, 5s 6d and 6s 6d.

A few rolls had letter prefixes. Those with an 'A' before the number were intended as accompaniment rolls, and those with an 'O' indicated that the roll was not hand-played but was, presumably, metrically cut.

All the rolls in this catalogue have five-digit numbers in the 50000 series and no fewer than 149 separate recording artists' names are listed. Some of the rolls are issued in more than one part, in which case there are small suffix letters, as for example in the case of J. S. Bach's Organ Toccata and Fugue arranged by Stradel and played by Anton Rihden. The three movements provide parts 1, 2, and 3 and are numbered 59385A, B and C, each being a Code III roll selling at the maximum price of 11s.

Ampico reproducing piano rolls came in such a variety of classifications and styles that a detailed analysis of them would take up a volume of its own: in fact it has done so in Elaine Obenchain's monumental *Catalog*. I shall therefore confine myself to a few abbreviated historical pointers.

Before Ampico, rolls were issued on the Rhythmodik label. The product of the American Piano Company, Rhythmodik was a straight 88-note roll with a numerical numbering system which Obenchain considers probably began with the figures '10'. Following the numerical digits was an extra digit which denoted the size of playing length of the roll. Known size numbers range from 2 (the smallest) up to 9 (very large). Preceding the entire number group was a letter used to denote the price code of the roll, 'A' being the cheapest.

The first Ampico rolls were Stoddard-Ampico and these were the reverse of their Rhythmodik counterparts so that the size digit came first, then the reversed number of the roll itself, and finally the price code letter. The last-known Stoddard-Ampico roll is 20721A, *Omar Khayyam*.

The next name used was Ampico-Artigraphic, and finally just Ampico. Between April 1921 and February 1922, the company began to use a dated number system but this was abandoned due to what must have been mounting confusion at all levels. Rolls so numbered included classical, popular and ballad series.

The standard numbering system was introduced as early as 1916 and apart from the brief interlude described above it remained in use up to the demise of Ampico in 1941. The classical series ran from 50004 to 71903; the popular series ran from 200002 to 216673; and ballads from 11 to 3171.

A 'Jumbo' series, introduced in November 1929, was the equivalent of the long-playing piano roll. Packed in 4-inch wide boxes, the roll numbers all began with 10 and all terminated with the number 5. These rolls played for an average of 20 minutes and some up to 30 minutes. Numbers ran from 100005 to 101065. There was also a 'descriptive story' series beginning with the figure 9 with numbers running from 90003 to 90143, the last digit referring to size. These rolls had words printed on them but, unlike song rolls, they were intended for reading rather than singing. They were introduced briefly in 1925, a maximum of fifteen titles being prepared.

A vocal accompaniment series was also issued by Ampico. First seen in mid-1924, the series was virtually discontinued in June 1927 although a final one appeared in 1929. Numbers ran from 30001 to 30751. A violin accompaniment series proved to be the shortest on record, beginning effectively in mid-1925 and ceasing a year later. Only four rolls appeared, numbered 40003, 40013, 40023 and 40031. All bore the suffix letter G. There was also a short run of 'unnumbered' rolls. These were demonstration or free-gift rolls and no numbers appeared on the box. However, by playing the roll through, the number would be found stamped on the end of the roll. The unusual *Christmas Greetings* Ampico rolls of 1925–8 are featured in this list which runs from 4760 to 7133 and comprises a mere nine rolls.

Of the catalogues Ampico issued, the earliest full specimen I have is dated July 1916, and is 'for the Ampico Artigraphic and Stoddard-Ampico Player Pianos'. This has a mere 72 pages, and rolls are priced from 75 cents for *Aloha Oe* (Hawaiian Song), on 28911A played by Andrei Kmita, to $3·50 for Leopold Godowsky playing Chopin's *Polonaise*, Opus 53, on 6566M.

Price code letters on these rolls were A = 75 cents; B = $1; C = $1·25; D = $1·50; E = $1·75; F = $2; G = $2·25; H = $2·50; J = $2·25 (same as G); K = $3; M = $3·50; N = $3·25.

The July 1920 catalogue displays the same confusing pricing suffixes, but once more they are different. Starting this time at D = $1; E = $1·25; F = $1·50; G = $1·75; H = $2; J = $2·25; K = $2·50; L = $2·75; M = $3; N = $3·25; P = $3·50.

The vast 351-page 1925 catalogue, superbly printed with illustrations, short biographies of many of the composers and artists, and notes on the music, reveals that the same Hawaiian song, played by the same pianist and now renumbered 57052D, carried a price of $1, while the Godowsky Chopin was just $2. Indeed, this catalogue reveals that there were only five prices indicated by the code letters as follows: D = $1; E = $1·25; F = $1·50; G = $1·75; and H = $2.

After 1930, the price structure remained in five steps, but the price code letter no longer formed part of the roll number.

Not only were Welte reproducing pianos very expensive as detailed in the chapter on reproducing pianos, but their rolls were extremely pricey. The Welte (Licensee) catalogue of rolls, published in England at London's Steinway Hall in October 1922, listed 3,755 titles of which the most expensive was Fanny Bloomfield-Zeisler's performance of Beethoven's Sonata, op. 111, in C minor (second movement), which cost all of £3 19s. Song rolls and accompaniment rolls were generally cheaper and short pieces of music could be had for as little as 10s 6d.

By 1926, however, Welte perfected new paper-perforating machinery and, in the face of competition from other manufacturers whose roll prices were less and becoming lower still, they lowered their charges appreciably.

Writing in the foreword to the 1927 London catalogue, Wallace Madge (whose position is described further on) commented: 'With the publication of this New Catalogue, our pink Number List of January 1st, 1926, (containing new reduced prices), and our Interim List of Welte Music Rolls of October 1926, become unnecessary, and can be thrown away, as both the new reduced prices for rolls and the Interim List are embodied in this Catalogue.'

Fanny Bloomfield-Zeisler's Opus 111 of Beethoven now cost 24s per movement, and the Welte price structure ranged from 10s in one-shilling increments up to the maximum of 24s. Even so, it was expensive for the music lover to build up a repertoire of Welte music rolls.

The methods by which Welte rolls were recorded are shrouded in mystery. In an article contained in the *Journal of the British Institute of Recorded Sound*, John Farmer states that, unlike Aeolian and Ampico, Welte always insisted that their recording system was fully automatic and did not ask for the services of the pianist in the later stages of preparation of the master roll. It seems that the recording piano had a trough of mercury beneath the keyboard. Each key had a light carbon prong suspended from its lower side which dipped into the mercury when that note was played. This was said to have enabled the recording of the exact force and duration of the note. This does, however, seem unlikely, but the late Richard Simonton, who befriended Edwin Welte during his later years, told John Farmer that the carbon prongs were in fact suspended from the key by a fine coil spring and consequently the depth of penetration of the carbon rod in the mercury would have varied with the force with which the key was depressed. From this, it would follow that the resistance to the flow of current would vary slightly with this depth of penetration and if this could be traced against each note a fairly good idea of the pianist's dynamics would be obtained. But, as John Farmer rightly asserts, the techniques of electrical measurement with the limited knowledge available at that time makes this a little doubtful. Undoubtedly this is not as reliable a recording system as one which directly measured hammer velocity and Farmer suggests that this may be one reason why some of the passages in Welte rolls tend to sound a little rough.

The De Luxe Reproducing Roll Company was a branch of the Auto-Pneumatic Action Company which produced the Welte-Mignon (Licensee) reproducing action for sale to independent piano manufacturers, Roehl relates.

In the late 1920s, Welte (Licensee) rolls were grouped into four price steps, each indicated by the prefix letter to the four-figure roll number, for example C-7690, *Peer Gynt Suite* played by Richard Singer. Cheapest rolls were those with the letter Y prefix. These were $1·25. Those preceded by the letter B were $1·50, X were $1·75, and C were $2.

Prestigious names in the field of music were obviously advantageous to the major roll companies. Aeolian had the services of Leeds-born Percy Alfred Scholes (1877–1958) who advised on rolls, promoted the pianola and Duo-Art and wrote several books for the company. Ampico had the services of Philadelphia-born Sigmund Spaeth (1885–1965). Both these musical polymaths lived into their eighties but, while Scholes is not known to have made a piano roll, Spaeth did record two – a parody of the tune *Yankee Doodle*, and a whimsical medley called *Songs you forgot to remember*. Spaeth served with Ampico between 1920 to 1927 as education musical director. Subsequently, he became renowned for his radio series as 'The Tune Detective', on which for some seven years he invited listeners to tax him with music to which he would almost always find the title. In England, Percy Scholes left a more erudite monument in the form of the *Oxford Companion to Music*, a reference work now in 11th edition.*

Although generally speaking the German companies were content to let the names of their recording artists along with their reputation carry the message to the public, Welte in England could hardly stand by and see its two big rivals move into an area which it couldn't match, and so Wallace J. Madge, FRCO, was hired to edit the roll catalogues.†

MUSIC FOR THE REPRODUCING PIANO

The major makers of reproducing pianos set about cornering the rights to certain pianists whose performances they might alone issue exclusively. The first of these makers was Welte-Mignon, for whom the following signed up exclusively:

---

* The present author is one of the contributors in the latest edition, 1979.
† Little seems to be known about Madge other than that he was born in Devon at North Tawton, and that he was organist at north London's Pembury Grove Chapel between 1912 and 1924 and then at several other churches in north London.

Bela Bartok   (1881–1945)
Claude Debussy   (1862–1918)
Gabriel Fauré   (1845–1924)
Alexander Glazounov   (1865–1936)
Ruggiero Leoncavallo   (1858–1919)
Theodor Leschetitzky   (1830–1915)
Darius Milhaud   (1892–1975)
Raoul Pugno   (1852–1914)
Ottorino Respighi   (1879–1936)

Next came the Aeolian Company which signed up exclusively:

Claudio Arrau   (1903–   )
Cécile Chaminade   (1857–1944)
Georges Enesco   (1881–1955)
George Gershwin   (1898–1937)
Percy Grainger   (1882–1961)
Myra Hess   (1890–1966)
José Iturbi   (1895–1980)   (also Ampico)
Sergei Prokofiev   (1891–1955)
Igor Stravinsky   (1882–1971)

Among the artists which Ampico recorded exclusively were:

Rudolph Friml   (1879–1972)
Fritz Kreisler   (1875–1962)
Mischa Levitzki   (1898–1941)
Benno Moiseiwitsch   (1890–1963)
Mieczyslaw Munz   (1900–   )
Leo Ornstein   (1895–   )
Sergei Rachmaninoff   (1873–1943)
Moriz Rosenthal   (1862–1946)
Sigismund Stojowski   (1869–1946)

There were many artists who recorded for more than one system and others whose rolls made for one system were 'reprocessed' to another. The systems were Welte = 1; Hupfeld DEA = 2; Duo-Art = 3; Ampico = 4; and Angelus Artrio = 5; and the list with systems is as follows:

Eugen d'Albert (1864–1932) Recorded for Hupfeld; issued on 1, 2, 3, 4.
Wilhelm Bachaus (1884–1969) Recorded for Hupfeld; issued on 2, 3, 4.
Harold Bauer (1873–1951) Recorded for Hupfeld; issued on 2, 3, 4, 5.
Ferruccio Busoni (1866–1924) Recorded for Hupfeld; issued on 1, 2, 3, 4.
Teresa Carreno (1853–1917) 1, 2, 3, 4.
Alfred Cortot (1877–1962) Recorded for Hupfeld; issued on 2, 3, 4.
Erno von Dohnanyi (1877–1960) 1, 4.
Arthur Friedheim (1859–1932) Recorded for Hupfeld; issued on 1, 2, 3, 4.
Ossip Gabrilowitsch (1878–1936) 1, 2, 3, 4, 5.
Rudolph Ganz (1877–1972) Recorded for Hupfeld; issued on 1, 2, 3, 4.
Walter Gieseking (1895–1956) Recorded for Hupfeld; issued on 1, 4.
Leopold Godowsky (1870–1938) 3, 4, 5.
Enrique Granados (1867–1916) 1, 3.
Edvard Grieg (1843–1907) Recorded for Hupfeld; issued on 1, 2, 4.
Mark Hambourg (1879–1960) 1, 2, 3, 4.

Josef Hofmann (1876–1957) 1, 2, 3, 4.
Vladimir Horowitz (1904–   ) 1, 3.
Frederic Lamond (1868–1948) Recorded for Hupfeld; issued on 1, 2, 3, 4.
Wanda Landowska (1877–1959) Recorded for Hupfeld; issued on 1, 2, 3, 4.
Ethel Leginska (1890–1970) 3, 4, 5.
Josef Lhevinne (1874–1944) 1, 4.
Pietro Mascagni (1863–1945) Recorded for Hupfeld; issued on 1, 2, 4.
Herma Menth (–   ) 3, 5.
Yolanda Mero (1887–1963) 1, 3, 4, 5.
Elley Ney (1882–1968) 1, 3, 4.
Guiomar Novaes (1896–   ) 1, 3. (also spelled 'Novais'. b. 1899 according to *Grove's Dictionary*)
Vladimir de Pachmann (1848–1933) 1, 3.
Ignace Paderewski (1860–1941) Recorded for Duo-Art; issued on 1, 3.
Maurice Ravel (1875–1937) 1, 3.
Artur Rubenstein (1886–   ) 3, 4.
Camille Saint-Saëns (1835–1921) Recorded for Hupfeld; issued on 1, 2, 3, 4.
Wassily Sapellnikoff (1868–1941) Recorded for Hupfeld; issued on 1, 2, 4.
Xaver Scharwenka (1850–1924) Recorded for Hupfeld; issued on 1, 2, 3, 4.
Ernest Schelling (1876–1939) 1, 3.
Elie Schmitz (1889–1949) 3, 4.
Artur Schnabel (1882–1951) 1, 4.
Alexander Scriabin (1872–1915) Recorded for Hupfeld; issued on 1, 2, 4.
Richard Strauss (1864–1949) 1, 4.

Many of the conversions from one system to another were achieved by editors who were responsible solely for the adjustment of the expression marks for one reproducing system to those of another. With skill and understanding, the results were usually very good indeed: occasionally one finds a roll in which something is not quite right. A number of the early Welte-Mignon recordings were transferred to the Artecho/Apollo, Artrio, Recordo and other systems. Transfers were also made from Duo-Art to Ampico, Ampico to Artecho, Hupfeld to Ampico and Duo-Art to Artrio.

MUSIC-ROLL PAPER

Music-roll manufacturers during the early days were engaged in a constant quest for suitable paper. The quality of available paper was a problem which confronted everybody. The goal was to find a paper which was thin, would not expand and contract excessively on exposure to changes in humidity, would perforate easily and cleanly and which was, above all, plentiful and cheap.

Since all papers of the period were excessively hygroscopic – they readily absorbed moisture from the atmosphere – music rolls were highly susceptible to changes in humidity. This meant that the early music roll could swell so much if stored in damp conditions that it would not unwind from its spool. Even worse, if it could be persuaded to unwind, it would split across its edges on being wound onto the take-up spool. A roll with split, torn and folded edges rapidly became worse until it reached the point where it began to sound marginal notes unintentionally. Used in conjunction with a tracker bar with automatic tracking, the roll would wander from side to side, making its condition even worse and transposing the music with a freedom which was painful on the ear.

The first improvement, more in the way of an acceptance of fact rather than a solution to the problem, was to provide the actual spool with an adjustable flange which could be pushed

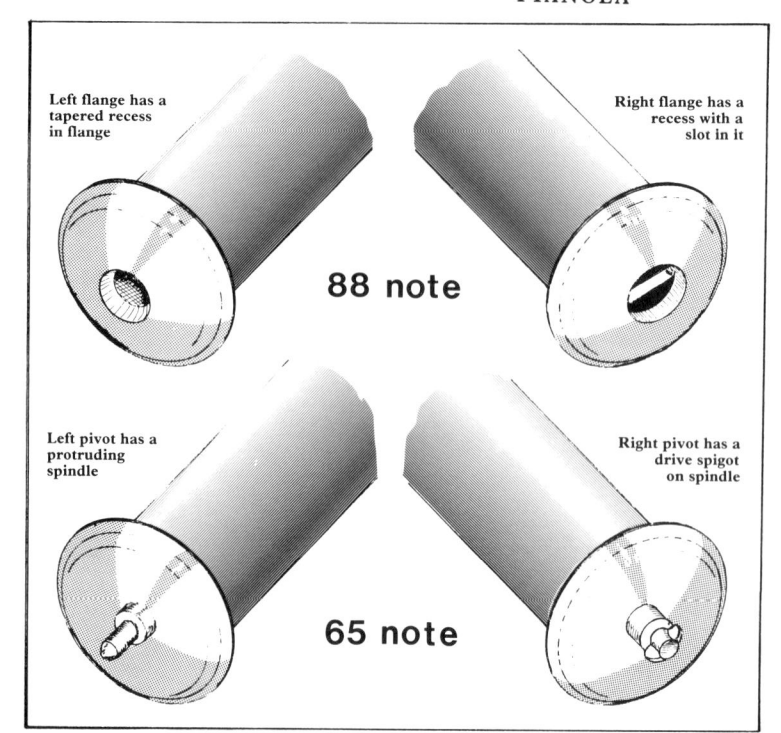

Fig. 65
The main difference between 65- and 88-note music rolls lies in the spools themselves. The 65-note roll is on a spool which has projecting ends while the 88-note roll has a spool with recessed ends, the righthand one having a slot in its bottom. Music rolls for the Aeolian Orchestrelle have the same type of spool ends as the 65-note piano roll.

in or pulled out to accommodate the width of the paper. Aeolian was probably the first with this simple expedient – a loose flange which could be slid along the wooden roll core. However, Welte had used this system for orchestrion paper rolls since the turn of the century, except that these beautifully engineered spools had a telescoping end.

Most of the roll makers later adopted the adjustable spool to allow for paper expansion and, with greater accuracy in both tracking and, subsequently, paper quality, take-up spools did not have to be so close-fitting to the paper width.

In the manufacture of piano rolls, it had been usual to cut sustained notes in the form of one long slot in the paper. These long cuts frequently caused the roll to tear or, where a sustained chord resulted in the paper 'ribboning', discord would sound. These disadvantages were largely countered in 1914 by the introduction throughout the roll-making industry of the so-called 'contiguous' perforation where long notes were represented as a series of closely-spaced yet separate perforations. These were close enough to prevent the primary valves from fluttering, yet far enough apart to offer some resistance to roll tearing. Broadwoods and the Perforated Music Company were among the first to adopt this in England. Often, notes would begin with a short slot and continue with contiguous holes: this was used on many rolls to indicate the melody notes and to ensure accurate themodising.

Since the era of the organette, various attempts had been made at strengthening the edges of the paper but all this did in effect was to alter the physical properties of the paper across its width, either making it stiffer or thicker at the edges and so cockling the paper in the centre. Even so, Hupfeld experimented during the 1920s in reinforcing the edges of the rolls for the Duophonola piano with a band of varnish about ⅜in. wide. This was a mixed blessing since,

MUSIC FOR THE PLAYER PIANO

although it undoubtedly reduced the chances of edge damage, it had the effect of making the rolls spool up loosely. As everybody came to know, loosely spooled music rolls were even more susceptible to attracting moisture and this distorted the paper, made it track badly, and started the problem over again.

But Hupfeld was an enterprising company and its prodigious demands for quality paper began to exceed the quantity available from the suppliers – a mill which was providing music-roll paper to a number of German instrument makers. The matter was resolved by the simple if unusual expedient of buying the paper mill and so acquiring the entire paper production for its own roll-perforating plant. In the heyday of Hupfeld music-roll manufacture, the company employed 2,000 workers in its five factories and used fifty million metres of music-roll paper every year – rather more than would be required to encircle the earth at the equator!

Another company which used large quantities of special paper was Welte, which discovered a particularly fine quality red paper, calendered on both sides, which punched cleanly. This paper was used for both orchestrion rolls and Welte-Mignon piano rolls right up to the outbreak of the 1914–18 war.

Making piano-roll spools was a major undertaking on its own and one short-lived attempt to obviate this onerous task was the so-called Golden Tube music rolls for both 65- and 88-note music. Advertised in 1912 as the Suprema Golden Tube Piano Player Rolls, it was patented in Britain by A. Dow and J. Bennett on 26 July 1910 (UK Patent number 17,757) with improvements on 10 June 1913 (patent number 13,371 in the names of A. Dow and J. Allwood). The idea of these was to dispense with the spool, the roll being supplied in a cardboard tube and then slid on to a special fluted spool core provided with a detachable end. The user of these rolls thus bought only one spool with which to play all his Golden Tube rolls. The patents were the property of Murdoch, Murdoch & Co. of Hatton Gardens, London.

MUSIC-ROLL-LENDING LIBRARIES

Roll-lending libraries were a feature peculiar to the English market. They had no equal anywhere else in the world and were a direct development of the long-standing lending-library system for books which had operated successfully in Britain since the middle of the nineteenth century. Apart from a few isolated instances in America where collections of rolls were made available to the public – the story of the Kansas lending library had already been related* – the United States was too large and diffuse an area for the successful and economic operation of a system similar to that found in Britain. Here the lending libraries were an early innovation. The idea was that, with the very high cost of piano rolls, the opportunity to borrow rolls for a low cost would encourage player sales and above all maintain the owner's interest in his instrument. So popular were the libraries that even after roll costs had been dramatically lowered by the introduction of mass-production machinery, the library remained an important part of many companies' business.

Aeolian operated a lending library for both 65- and 88-note rolls and later for the Duo-Art rolls as well. This was housed at Aeolian Hall, New Bond Street, London. It was originally known as The Orchestrelle Company's Music Circulating Library. All library rolls bore

---

* See p. 36.

TABLE SHOWING TYPES AND WIDTHS OF COMMON MUSIC ROLLS

Instrument	Paper Width	Type of Spool Drive
Aeolian Orchestrelle	10⅛ inches	Projecting pivot on left end of spool, projecting pivot with drive lugs on right end of spool
Aeolian Pipe Organ	10⅛ inches	As above (Reproducing organ rolls are 15¼" wide)
Wilcox & White Symphony	10¼ inches	As above but roll is wound in reverse on spool
Piano, 65-note	11¼ inches	Projecting pivot on left end of spool, projecting pivot with drive lugs on right end of spool
Piano, 88-note, Full-Scale	11¼ inches	Recessed hole in left end of spool, recessed hole with drive slot in right end of spool
Piano, Hupfeld Phonola range	11⅝ inches	Projecting pivot on left end of spool, projecting pivot with drive lugs on right end of spool
Piano, Welte-Mignon (original red paper rolls)	13½ inches	As above

NOTE: The *Orchestrelle* and *Symphony* rolls are for player reed organs. *Symphony* rolls also fit the *Angelus* reed organ/cabinet-style piano-player combination. Both of these instruments play 58-note rolls. The *Aeolian Pipe Organ* plays 116-note music rolls of the same width as the 58-note *Orchestrelle* rolls. The method of driving the music spool on rewinding, perfected by Aeolian, was adopted almost universally. The only variation is the 65-note rolls as described above.

Fig. 66
Types and widths of player music rolls.

labels on the boxes and usually a rubber stamp on the roll apron. This library was probably the first lending library of its type anywhere in the world and its enterprise is just what we would expect from so dynamic a company as Aeolian. Subscribers paid four guineas (£4·20p) for a one-year subscription, or three guineas (£3·15p) for six months. This entitled them to borrow rolls. London subscribers could take out 12 rolls of music every two weeks; country subscribers 24 rolls once every four weeks, there no doubt being some subtle difference other than the fact that these subscribers were responsible for all carriage costs while presumably their London cousins got away with a free delivery and collection.

Other companies soon established similar libraries in London, with Steinway operating a library and approval service for Welte-Mignon rolls from Steinway Hall, and Ampico doing the same from its Regent Street showrooms.

Piano-roll libraries were, though, not all that they were cracked up to be. In the same way as latter-day record-lending libraries tend to have a large proportion of damaged recordings and the ones you particularly want to borrow are out on loan already, they were a cause of some dissatisfaction among subscribers. This is demonstrated by an article in *The*

> A name or label was <u>originally</u> an indication of origin. To-day its use is to disguise origin.
>
> The Perforated Music Co., Ltd., are opposing on independent lines the commercial disease of stencilled music rolls.
>
> It is obviously to the interest of the Roll Dealer to support such action.
>
> An agency, or a divided agency, is of no value if your competitor is selling the same goods under the flimsy veneer of a different label.
>
> Why buy a stencilled or foreign-made roll when you can purchase Rolls with a Reputation direct from a British Manufacturer?
>
> **Imperial Linenized**
> (The Roll de Luxe).
>
> **Songola**
>
> **Omnia**
> (The Roll of price quality).
>
> **Spool End Label**
> (The Revolutionary Roll)
>
> Investigation will convince Music Roll Dealers of the value of mutual support. Special terms for the establishment of Local Libraries. A paying proposition!
>
> **The PERFORATED MUSIC Co., Ltd.,**
> 197-203, CITY ROAD, LONDON, E.C.

Fig. 67
By 1915, British piano roll makers were becoming more and more concerned by the growing practice of 'stencil brand' rolls. This advertisement in *The Pianomaker* for September that year sets out the case for buying only British-made, branded goods. It also shows a novel, if short-lived style of roll-box which The Perforated Music Company tried to introduce. In March 1918, the business was burned out in a major fire. Although it restarted in other premises, it never fully recovered from this disaster and was an early victim of the general slump in the music trade by the late 'twenties.

Piano-maker for April 1919, reproduced in facsimile in *Clockwork Music*, page 311.

The invention of the song roll was a mixed blessing since in the hands of the less scrupulous it could be turned into a valuable piece of commercial advertising or even political propaganda. In America during the 1920s a new type of song roll appeared whose words were not quite suitable for the vicar's tea-party. Suggestive words and ribaldry enabled the dealer who wanted to make a fast buck to sell what at that time must have been viewed in the same light as many view pornography today. As Harvey Roehl relates (*Player Piano Treasury*, page 154) the thought of 'filthy piano rolls' as a latter-day variant of 'filthy pictures' must sound amusing to us today.

But filth in the piano-roll business was a highly contentious subject and many a righteous dealer expressed his disgust eloquently in the local papers in a form which must have increased his legitimate trade encouragingly. Of course, piety and morality had the upper hand at that time and the Q.R.S. roll company saw the potential open to them if they chose to side openly against the pedlars of dirty piano rolls – in both senses of the expression! And so

Q.R.S. launched a crusade against naughty-word rolls and their enterprise received wide coverage in the trade press. Swarms of letters came in from dealers who had been offended. One wrote:

> We think it's demoralising and vicious. How do you feel about it? We are enclosing a few excerpts of a new song, just published. Suggestive songs for grown-ups are bad enough, but when it comes to corrupting the minds of children we draw the line. We don't want profits from such a source.

The vituperation which these rolls generated makes me think they must have been interesting. As collectors' items at least, their rarity must make them worth having. So far, though, in my years of collecting piano rolls I have never come across anything more suggestive than *I Know a Lovely Garden* in E flat by Guy d'Hardelot on Aeolian 26119!

The actual perforating of paper as a means of making a music roll is another subject on which a whole vast chapter might be written. It goes back to the early days when organette makers were trying to find ways of copying from master rolls. Some of the methods tried sound very odd to us today. One was for a master tune sheet to be made in metal and then used as a template in a sand-blasting plant, the sand perforating the paper where the master left it unprotected. Another was to burn the holes against a gas jet, again using a mask. Both these systems presented problems. First they were time-consuming and fiddly, and second they were guaranteed not to produce a clean edge to the holes so perforated, leaving in the first case a paper rag and in the other a charred paper ash residue which, in the case of a suction instrument, would be drawn in to interfere with the rest of the action. Punching was the logical solution but it was far from easy to contrive a machine which would make a perfect, accurate copy from a master each time. Probably the most famous roll-perforating equipment was the Acme machine which would punch up to sixteen copies from a master at one pass. At the other end of the scale, so to speak, was the Leabarjan, a home perforating machine from which the owner might, at the expenditure of infinite patience and care, punch out his own music roll.

Copying an existing roll is not as easy as at first it may appear. Whether 'read' pneumatically or electrically, where the master presents one hole, the perforator has to determine just where that hole is: if it senses it at its leading edge it may punch a hole which is half a hole too far forward: if it then senses it at the trailing edge, it will punch again, so converting a single hole into two or even three. This is just one of the many problems which face the serious experimenter in his quest for a roll-copying machine. Several have been highly successful at designing and building their own machines, perhaps the most enterprising being the work in England of Mr and Mrs Medcraft who, starting out with no engineering experience whatsoever, both ended up, after taking night school classes in shop practice, in designing and building a highly sophisticated machine which can make reproducing piano rolls. For many collectors, though, making your own rolls may be just a shade too esoteric. For those who wish to know more about perforating, the various collectors' societies exist to provide a free interchange of knowledge and experience between members.

MUSIC FOR THE PLAYER PIANO

A SUMMING UP OF THE MUSICAL SCENE

The great era of the player piano is now firmly behind us and enterprising pianolists are now relegated to the realms of the amateur enthusiast and the collector. It is thus as well to take a backward glance at the achievements of the instrument and the shortcomings it demonstrated and the fine, high goals which it never quite made.

The overwhelming feeling on studying the music for the player piano is that a very great opportunity was lost – the opportunity to allow the player piano to stand as an instrument upon which music might be played which could not be played by hand. The New York *Music Trade Review* expressed this back in the 1920s very succinctly when it wrote:

> It is gradually coming to be seen that the player piano mechanism must finally lead us entirely out of the idea of ten-finger music and into a realm of eighty-eight-finger music, where the piano becomes a new instrument and opens up a whole new school of composition which, for melodic, harmonic, colorative and technical wealth, surpasses all imagination.

Harry Ellingham, writing in the *Player Piano Supplement* to *The Gramophone* (December 1924) said:

> Music rolls should also be cut and prepared without the slightest regard to what the hands can do. Only then shall we hear the best possible effects from a player-piano. Consider, what is the object of playing Bach's great G minor organ fugue on the piano-player and slavishly following all the limitations of hand-playing? I believe he would have revelled in its great possibilities, and it is a joy to know that at least Granville Bantock and Josef Holbrooke are among those musicians who want to have the player-piano associated with the performance of their compositions.

The failure of the player piano to live up to these expectations is not entirely its own fault. Roll manufacturers were forced by purely commercial dictates to give their customers the music they wanted and this meant a diet of acceptable classics and light music along with the rather ephemeral popular dance and song melodies of the day. Symphonic transcriptions and hymns were suitable (much more so then than they would be today!) but there was a fear of anything new, radical and untried. The 88-note music scale, which a few visionaries (such as the *Music Trade Review* writer) hoped would come to pass, was deemed never to be.

There were some venturesome attempts at making the player piano do more than just ten-finger music. Cutting in octaves, where possible, was resorted to fairly widely, while arrangements for four hands (in other words, duets) were quite common. Only very rarely did one find the situation where music was transcribed as a concept divorced from the number of hands or fingers available. One example that stands out in my mind was the French company, Pleyel, which introduced (I suspect experimentally because the rolls had typewritten labels and did not appear in the catalogue) rolls of Stravinsky's *Firebird* and *Petrushka* in which, in many places, the entire compass of the piano is used to full dramatic effect with notes being depressed by the handful.*

---

* Since this was written, some observations on these rolls have been published by Rex Lawson in the *Bulletin* of the Player Piano Group (No. 75, January 1980, page 17). He writes:

A number of the classical composers did write for the player piano with varying degrees of success. These included Moszkowski, Malipiero and Stravinsky while in 1918 the foxtrot composed by Casella contained all the notes of the chromatic scale of two octaves sounded at once! In spite of this sort of music, of the fifty or so who wrote for the instrument few really contributed music which is even remembered, let alone compositions which have any merit.

The mechanics of the instrument were in many ways better taxed by those skilled musical arrangers who set up pieces for four hands on one roll or transcribed orchestral works for the keyboard. Two typical examples are the overture *Fingal's Cave*, and also the Suite Opus 15 by A. S. Arensky played by Bauer and Gabrilowitsch. This duet, Duo-Art roll number 5849, contains some remarkable expression shadings between the four hand parts.

Clearly the player piano was viewed by composers in two distinctly different lights: first as a straight musical instrument capable of being played no differently from the ordinary piano, and second as a protean music machine. The first approach was unimaginative: the second often unmusical. Somewhere between the two lay the sort of music which the player piano alone knew all about.

Besides the four-handed music there were a few attempts to develop the total sound resources of the piano. To this end, Edgar Fairchild, Herbert Clair and George Dilworth formed what they called the Original Piano Trio. Dilworth was an Ampico roll editor who was with the company for about a year around 1922. Clair had been with the Republic roll company and joined Ampico as head of the popular music department. Fairchild was a prolific recording artist for Ampico. The three came together for a series of six-hand performances on roll, some two dozen in all. One of these, *Song of India*, number 202491/F, clearly demonstrates the lively light music idiom of these talented three who knew how to get the very best into – and out of – a piano roll. This piece really sets the keyboard alive!

On 8 April 1978, the Nederlandse Pianola Vereniging staged the world premiere of a specially-commissioned *Concerto for Pianola and Orchestra*, Opus 608, by the Dutch composer Jan van Dijk. The pianolist was Lucius Voorhorst, who was accompanied by the Brabant Orchestra, and the venue was the Stadsschouwburg in Tilberg. The instrument was

▶ In 1922, Stravinsky moved into a working apartment in the Pleyel building in Paris, and set the scene for a musical collaboration which was to result in fifty rolls being made of his works, forty of them special arrangements of orchestral or chamber music. Since so many rolls are involved, it is possible that one or two may still remain untraced, but they certainly include *The Firebird* and *Petrushka*, *The Rite of Spring*, *The Song of the Nightingale*, and *Pulcinella*, and they are listed in an appendix to Eric Walter White's excellent book.

He continues:

Five years later, in 1927, the Aeolian Company in London began to issue an expensively produced educational series of Duo-Art rolls. Percy Scholes was the director of this 'Audiographic' series, and his ambitious plans resulted in all the Pleyel transcriptions being purchased by Aeolian. Alas, the slump at the end of the 1920s caused the American Aeolian Company to sell off its overseas subsidiaries, and the Audiographic project, including various sets of Stravinsky rolls, came to an untimely end. Of the special arrangements only *The Firebird* was ever issued in this way, though it was very attractively produced, with pictures and autobiographical articles printed on the six rolls, together with analyses of the music as it unwound.

This is not altogether correct, for Aeolian still had in its AudioGraphic roll catalogue of 1932 the roll entitled 'Sonata, 1st movement' played by Stravinsky in a presentation annotated by Edwin Evans and numbered D231F. The same roll was also available as a hand-played roll, also by Stravinsky, as number D232E. The six biographical rolls Rex Lawson mentions above were D-prefixed, G-suffixed rolls numbered 759, 761, 763, 765, 767 and 769. These were also available for the Pianola, again D-prefixed but this time with the price-code suffix C, numbers 760, 762, 764, 766, 768 and 770 – an interesting numbering exercise! The only other Duo-Art interpretation of any kind was roll number 528G, being the composer's recording of the 'First movement: Largo' of his Concerto.

a 65-note Aeolian piano player in conjunction with a concert grand of unknown make. A description of the work is given in the *Journal* of the Brabant Orchestra for December 1977, mellifluously titled 'Klank en Weerklank', which includes the following remarks:

> Voorhorst became aware [of the possibilities of the player piano] during a visit to Switzerland where he heard a piece of music written for the pianola by Paul Hindemith. . . .
>
> If a real pianist [tried to play this new music] he would have to cope with up to 16 notes at the same time which is quite impossible. Instead these special compositions were programmed on to the paper roll in an entirely mechanical manner by converting the musical notes as indicated by the composer into small perforations.
>
> Voorhorst is kept very busy: he says that he has had to position every single note that he has cut into the roll, obviously a very time-consuming task for it took him more than 200 hours to punch out what he estimates to have been 20,000 perforations. In this way, a roll was made which will occupy nine minutes of the pianola solo in Jan van Dijk's 12-minute-long composition.

So far, though, there is no report as to just how this extraordinary work must have sounded.

Player Piano Performances, the organising company formed within the P.P.G. to stage the Purcell Room concerts, commissioned a piece of music for Duo-Art pianola, three speakers, trumpet and two percussionists. Composed by James Wood and called *Aria*, it was premiered on 4 June 1976. Because of the position of the music roll as part of an ensemble, as in the Dutch piece, it is not a piece of music for private owner and drawing room.

Another shortcoming of the player piano was highlighted by the editor of the *Player Piano Group Bulletin* (No. 70, summer 1978, page 2), when he wrote:

> . . . apart from popular items, very few new rolls have been made since the mid-1930s. Those of us with reproducing pianos can flick a few controls and summon up anyone from Grieg to Gershwin, but our children will have to make do with loudspeakers if they wish to rediscover Ashkenazy or Barenboim.
>
> In the same way, Percy Scholes, Edwin Evans and others saw fit to praise the foot-operated pianola for the way in which it educated its users in music from the sixteenth century to the present day, which at that time meant Stravinsky and his contemporaries. Few of Scholes's successors in the field of musical criticism will pay much attention to an instrument which still stops at Stravinsky, and early Stravinsky at that. If we are to secure the future of the player piano, which gives us such pleasure now, we need engineers to design recording machines and musicians to cut a vast backlog of fifty years of classical music.

A new twist to player-piano music and to the music of the reproducing piano was evolved at the end of 1976 when CBS, the gramophone record company, issued a most unusual long-play disc featuring the Columbia Jazz Band conducted by Tilson Thomas and George Gershwin as soloist in a new disc of *Rhapsody in Blue*. Now Gershwin died in 1937 but he left behind two Duo-Art recordings of the *Rhapsody* – 7094E and 6873C – being parts one and two of the piece, the odd numbering coming from the fact that the ordinary or full-scale rolls which Gershwin recorded are consecutively numbered 30525C and 30526C.

Cut in 1925, these performances by the composer also included a piano reduction of the accompanying orchestral score. Given that the idea was to play these Duo-Art recordings against a full-score band accompaniment, the rolls were scrutinised and every non-piano score perforation was taped over and the result copied as a new roll, giving just Gershwin's piano score. This was then played with the new backing to produce the unusual result of a new record of a fresh performance featuring a soloist dead for almost forty years.

At London's Queen Elizabeth Hall on 13 December 1972, a hushed audience assembled for what was undoubtedly the oddest concert of modern times. The orchestra was the English Sinfonia conducted by Neville Dilkes and the piano soloist was Percy Grainger, who had already been dead for eleven years. The work was the Grieg Piano Concerto in A minor. Grainger (1882–1961) had made a set of Duo-Art rolls of this work in the 1920s as a piano-only rendition. His version thus included not only the normal piano part but his interpretation of the orchestral parts as well. To make this concert possible, the rolls had to be re-edited to bring them back to solo-performance standard. The adjusted rolls were then copied on fresh roll stock using a special machine developed in London by Harry and Sylvia Medcraft, and it was these recuts which were played with most impressive results on a Steinway Duo-Art from the British Piano Museum.

This operation was undertaken afresh in Australia in 1978 when the Sydney Symphony Orchestra under John Hopkins recorded this selfsame work with Grainger's rolls for RCA.

Piano rolls frequently sustain damage and when one considers that these frail sheets may be anything up to eighty-five years old it is surely not surprising. The care of rolls is the finest preventor of damage but where physical damage has occurred it can usually be repaired. First, though, a word of caution. Sticky tape of the Sellotape sort is something never to be used on a piano roll. After a while, the adhesive either turns into a sticky mass which oozes out under the transparent carrier or it dries out and the carrier paper falls off. In either case, the result to the paper is that a brownish gluey substance has been deposited on it which resists any further attempt at gluing.

How do rolls get damaged? Most player pianos today have the speed control pointer removed because this was one of the main causes of roll damage. During rewinding, if the pointer was still up in position and the spool brakes were faulty, if pedalling was slackened it was inevitable that the top spool would go on turning, casting loose paper over that swordlike point – and so producing a long rip. Rolls so ripped are the very hardest to repair as cockles almost invariably remain and so adjacent notes sound.

The next damage is where the rewind slot on an electrically operated piano has not operated for one reason or another, or where a thoughtless roll pedaller has carried on pedalling – and so torn the end of the paper off the spool core to which it is glued.

Far worse really than any of these is the frayed edge which upsets tracking, the roll which weaves from side to side like a streamer in a gale, and the roll with the edges folded over. This last problem, in which the roll edges develop a pleat, is generally a characteristic of the Pianola, hence the sobriquet 'Aeolian pleat'! Torn roll leaders are usually the result of either a bent or deformed take-up spool hook or a bent hook on the roll itself. In both cases, hell-for-leather rewinding will yank the eye end off the roll. Always avoid the temptation to make a quick and easy repair by using sticky tape. You can buy a large packet of new roll end tabs: keep these by the side of the piano and when a roll gets damaged in this way put on a new tab at once.

First, how do we repair tears? Long strips of stuck-on reinforcing paper just will not do since they thicken the roll at that part so that it rerolls unevenly, ultimately developing a tracking problem as it weaves from side to side. Where roll edges have the familiar short tears in them, use a small piece (as small as will do the job) of Scotch Magic Tape – this is used the same way as Sellotape only it does not have the undesirable adhesive characteristics and is used for libary work. In cases where there is a massive tear in the roll from the pointer, stretch out the length of damaged roll and iron out any creases on a flat board with a warm smoothing iron. Now use the same small pieces of tape to make good the tear, recutting any perforations which you have no option but to tape over.

The apron or leader to the piano roll protects the paper from atmospheric attack but on some rolls, particularly early 65-note and Orchestrelle rolls, there was no apron and the leader of the roll was just formed from the ordinary paper. Where rolls have been exposed to damp, this leader portion will often be found to have been eroded by microscopic fungus organisms so that it is left limp and, in severe cases, a little like a lace curtain. Lay this portion of the roll on a clean sheet of glass of ample proportions and paint onto it an even coat of wallpaper paste. Use the cellulose variety and, ideally, mix it in distilled water. Leave it to dry, after which it will separate quite easily from the glass. Dust both sides with french chalk and brush off any surplus with a soft brush.

Pleated rolls are also easily treated only here it is not advisable to use wallpaper paste since the moisture of the paste will cockle the paper. Stretch the roll over a plain wooden table and unfold all the pleats with a thin blunt knife, such as an artist's palette knife. It has been suggested that beeswax rubbed into the folds serves the purpose very well, but I personally prefer to use a spray-on starch of the sort used on shirt collars. Apply this sparingly to the pleats and immediately pass a warm iron over it. Ideally, hold the iron in one hand and the aerosol can in the other.

Rolls which are damp through incorrect storage can often be as much as 3 millimetres wider than normal. Play these on your piano and they will develop edge pleats and splits where they foul the edge of the take-up spool. There are several ways of narrowing a wide roll. Attempts to dry out the spooled roll using heat will spoil the paper. If your piano has an adjustable take-up spool, then open this up to take the roll and play it half a dozen or so times. In a normal dry atmosphere, this will suffice to shrink it while at the same time resisting any chance of its becoming wavy.

An alternative is to make up a roll-spooling board from spare player-piano parts and to place in the centre of this a metal cylinder with a heating element inside. Passing the paper over the outside of the heated cylinder and spooling the roll back and forth a few times will reduce excessive humidity in the paper.

When buying second-hand piano rolls, check the condition of the roll before you part with cash. A roll which is frayed at the edges will seldom play properly. In extreme cases where the edges have torn and folded back, the roll cannot be spooled up tightly, so a good quick test for condition is to squeeze the roll: if it is hard it is a fair assumption that it is in good order, but if it is unevenly spooled and is spongy, then somewhere along its length you can be certain that it is damaged. Rolls with edge damage distort because one side of the roll effectively becomes thicker than the other. In severe cases this will lead to the paper warping, a permanent wave being developed which will cause wrong notes to be played and, as the paper cockles from side to side, it will lift off one side of the tracker bar and sound random notes.

REMOVAL SALE

OF

New and Library Music Rolls.

These Rolls can be used not only for Simplex Instruments, but also for

ANY STANDARD PLAYER OR PLAYER PIANO.

Prior to removing our Music Rolls Department from 244, Tottenham Court Road, W., to our factory premises at 113, Cottenham Road, Holloway, N., we are now offering

New and Library Rolls at a Very Great Reduction

in order to reduce our stock. The selection of New and Library Rolls can be made from our Catalogue, containing over five thousand different numbers. The Library Rolls will be guaranteed to be in good playable condition. When ordering, please state whether you want New or Library Rolls; also whether you require

SIMPLEX ROLLS (for playing Simplex Instruments); or
SIMPLEX STANDARD ROLLS (for playing any other Player or Player Piano).

Particulars of Removal Sale Prices and Catalogues will be sent on application to

THE SIMPLEX PIANO PLAYER CO.
113, Cottenham Road, Holloway, N.

Triumph Auto, Ltd

SUCCESSORS TO
KASTNER & CO., LTD., MANUFACTURERS OF THE
KASTNER AUTOPIANO.

191, REGENT STREET, LONDON, W.1.

Telephone — REGENT 4744.

Telegrams — "KASTOREN, LONDON," or "AUTOPIOLA, LONDON."

F P.A. 95220.

CHAPTER 12

How to Play the Player Piano

To someone uninitiated who is confronted with a player piano and the thought that somebody is going to teach him how to play it, there must be a strong feeling that this sort of education is superfluous. The music, such a person contends, is already there and so are the treadles on the piano, so what could be simpler? Usually this understandable confidence is shattered with the first attempt at getting any musical sound out of the piano. Pedalling and manipulating the piano are admittedly quite non-musical things, but in their own way they require understanding, practice and skill, and a musical awareness. And because every piano is different the ability to operate one does not automatically mean that you are competent to tackle any other instrument without careful evaluation of what it can do beforehand. To the novice and the overconfident, the player piano tends to behave rather in the way of a bucking bronco: it may not physically unseat you, but it will eliminate that overconfidence!

Some few years ago, a talented lady pianist who was capable of eliciting the finest performance from her own Pianola was invited to play her favourite roll before an assembled and admiring audience at the British Piano Museum. The music, I emphasise, she knew well; the piano was the same as hers, but not the selfsame piano. She sat down and within seconds what the experts among the gathered listeners knew and feared was happening. This piano responded very slightly differently from her own model, and she was unable to make it play the way she wanted. Gallantly, she pedalled to the end and everybody politely applauded. The lesson, a painful one, is that when you sit down at a strange player, accept that you must play it for half an hour or more to get the feel of it. Whereas many a garage mechanic can with confidence drive just about any car that comes in for servicing, pianos with paper rolls are a different matter.

But first down to absolute basics. Back in February 1904, *Musical Opinion* reported on a pianola concert at the inauguration of London's new home of players. I quote:

> I wonder what will be the future of the mechanical piano player. The other day I attended the opening of the Aeolian Hall, and in the program of the concert the Pianola took a large part, both as soloist and as accompanist to songs and violin pieces. The instrument was skilfully manipulated by a Mr Schulz, who managed the wind supply with an evenness which the amateur could hardly hope to equal without long practice. That the machine player is capable of expression is evident enough; but it was clear to me that only a musician who knows the music by heart can ever hope to get the best results out of the Pianola. And what applies to the Pianola no doubt equally applies to other instruments of the same type. I shudder to think of the travesty of classical music

which these mechanical players might be guilty of in the hands of a manipulator who had no knowledge of music. Expression would doubtless degenerate into a meaningless contrast of pianissimo with fortissimo and of quick tempo with slow – a contrast, however, by no means confined to mechanical players.

Of course, one misses the different tone colour which a skilled pianist can obtain from the piano with his fingers; but I believe that this can be imitated to a great extent by a careful graduating of the force of the wind supply. The merits of the instrument, on the other hand, are obvious. Its performance is certainly correct with a correctness which is almost uncanny. No pianist ever plays a composition with such note perfection. And then – this opens a very wide field for speculation – it places the lover of music in the position of a conductor of an orchestra, who can hear his ideas realised by his players without playing himself. For those who do not trust their own ideas of a composition, the rolls are marked by well known pianists, whose indications can be faithfully followed by the manipulator when once he has acquired a certain amount of skill. After all, music does not exist for the sake of concert virtuosi . . .

And yet, although this technical perfection is not to be attained by the ordinary amateur, there is all the same a knowledge of what constitutes executive art, in which the tyro may often have finer ideal than the professional, who more often than not has taken up the art of piano playing because he possesses some physical aptitude rather than because he has a mind singularly open to musical impressions. For that reason we are compelled to wonder why many artists who have gained such technical mastery over their instruments exhibit such a misunderstanding of the music that they play. Many an amateur pianist who is baffled by the difficulty of executing rapid passages of arpeggios, and who never hopes to be able to play runs with the evenness which he knows quite well they require, is nevertheless a better judge of how a composition should be played than the professional pianist to whom these matters present no kind of obstacle. The Pianola enables this common type of amateur to realise his ideals. It opens the door for him to a limitless field of artistic enjoyment. The necessity of possessing a knowledge of music prevents the use of the Pianola becoming a mechanical means of degenerating a taste for music, which might happen if just as good results could be obtained by those ignorant of the art as by those who have knowledge of it. And there can be no doubt that the close knowledge of the great masterpieces of art which these mechanical players must give to those who use them will have an influence for good.

Several books have been written purporting to be guides on playing the player piano. To me, though, these tend to ignore the fact that player pianos are often owned by those to whom the ordinary written notation of music is an unsolved riddle, and they are sprinkled with musical extracts which surely may only confuse the pianolist who has only his two slipper-clad feet for musical comfort.

What I will try to do is to offer some very basic advice about how a player piano should be approached by the novice player. But as with so many other things the skills have to be learned and much of it is achieved by practice and experimentation.

Sidney Grew in his book *The Art of the Player-Piano* may have overstressed the matter somewhat when he wrote: 'I find that it takes about three years to make a good player-pianist of a man or woman of average musical intelligence.' Even so, he rightly says that it takes a long while to cultivate true musical nuance in the player-pianist's interpretation.

First, then, how to sit at a player. The proper player-piano stool is a sloping seat and should be placed so that it slopes towards the instrument. If you put the seat on a slippery floor, or on a loose mat, the chances are that as you pedal the piano will get further and further away as you slide slowly backwards, seat and all. Nailing the seat to the floor is not to be recommended except in dire emergency, but if polished floor conditions do exist tack some small rubber heels to the legs of the stool.

Sit comfortably in front of the instrument, slightly further away from it than if you were going to do your actual Rubinstein act by manual playing. Place both feet on the pedals (this means the exhauster treadles, not the soft and sustaining pedals of the piano) so that the heel is more or less on the hinge point of each pedal. You should sit at such a height that pedalling does not cause discomfort, remembering that the act of pedalling is not to be like a racing cyclist with your knees coming up and down all the while, but that you pedal, in general, solely by using your ankle muscles to pivot your foot about the heel.

Now a word of warning. If you have never pedalled a piano before (or if it is some while since you last did), you will very rapidly be fatigued by pedalling. A too-lengthy first attempt will give you sore ankles and tender calf muscles and, if you have an unpadded stool, you could get a sore accompaniment section. This same caution goes for cycling and gardening among other activities and is equally unlikely to prove detrimental to health or sanity.

The player pianist has at his disposal a variety of means by which the music can be controlled. These devolve from four main devices: the foot-operated pedals, the tempo lever, the various accenting/subduing devices, and the control for the sustaining pedal. These controls can be combined in a number of ways the majority of which can only be fully realised by careful practice and experience since demonstration (let alone just description) cannot bring home the full technique of their use.

All player pianos are different in one way or another. Apart from the obvious differences between different makes (for example the Pianola has a sliding tempo control but the Angelus provides an additional tempo control in the form of a rocking tablet on the key rail), at this distance from their original manufacture many instruments within the same family possess differences brought about by age, condition, standard of restoration and so on. Adjustment of an instrument is often an individual thing and one can be a maestro on one's own particular example yet fail completely to wring artistry from another of the same make without practice from scratch again.

The most expressive control on any piano is the foot pedals and once a player has amassed a great deal of practice he should have no difficulty, once the correct tempo is set, in producing a creditable performance of the average roll by sitting on his hands and using his feet alone for power and expression. On some pianos this is easier to do than on others, but believe me it is possible and it is the best test of a pianolist's understanding of his own instrument.

Now these foot pedals perform two functions. First they provide power for the playing mechanism: the greater the suction the louder the instrument can sound, given that all other conditions are equal. And second they produce the power to move the roll by means of the air motor which, as we have seen in Chapter 5, is purely a controlled leak into the system which, in admitting air, is made to drive the roll.

The tempo control is the second master mechanism. The player who sets his tempo lever to the speed indicated at the start of the roll – and then leaves it well alone, is singularly lacking in musical understanding or individuality. In this section, of course, I am speaking of the foot-operated instrument, not the electrically operated reproducing piano where the tempo control need never be touched during play. What the tempo control can do when operated by a sympathetic player is quite amazing. Music comprises a mixture of sound and silence and the tempo lever can be used to vary the performance with great nicety to produce a true hand-played effect. On a Metrostyle roll, for example, you will see that almost continual movement of the tempo lever is called for with some quite sharp operations in places. These movements add reality to the playing and you may well find that your own musical taste will dictate how you control this on your own rolls.

Accenting devices are fundamentally of two types. First are the bass- and treble-subduing levers and second comes the 'solo' control in the form of Solodant, Melodant, Themodist or similar. Some special systems such as the Kastonome operate in a different way but achieve a similar result when used as directed by the piano roll.

The use of the manual subduing levers or buttons is largely self-evident. They can be used in conjunction or individually to affect the portions of the keyboard as required. The solo control, however, works in a different way. When this is switched on by the lever provided (in the spool box in the case of the Aeolian or Angelus), the normal functions of the subduing levers are usurped. On the Angelus, for example, the buttons are automatically depressed and cease to function. With this condition pertaining, the piano will play quietly, but the Melodant or solo notes will stand out. With the Pianola, changing to 'Themodist' from 'normal' should be followed by holding the subduing levers hard over to the left. In this position, it will be impossible to create any marked difference in sound volume by using the foot pedals, but the volume of the Themodised notes will be directly affected by how you master your footwork. On the Duo-Art pedal-electric models, a special detachable brass clip (most frequently lost) is used to hold the hand controls over to facilitate Duo-Art theming. Always switch the solo control off when the roll shows the word 'normal' and on when the word 'solo' or equivalent is shown.

Note accenting on unthemed rolls is achieved by the combined use of the feet and the two subduing levers. Notes to be accented or chords to be played loudly are first of all under the command of the feet and one foot is used to give a sharp, hard push to the respective pedal a split second before the perforation for the note or chord passes the tracker bar. It is impossible to make a note louder once it has played, by the way; the decision to make it louder and, consequently, the hard press on the pedal has to be very slightly before the perforation uncovers the tracker hole. Once it is understood that the foot is the prime accenting medium, the accenting levers can be used in conjunction with the foot to achieve impressive and sudden fortissimo passages. This requires practice but consists of bringing the relevant subduing lever sharply to the right (normal or loud) position at the instant the push on the pedal is made – and then returning the lever equally smartly to its previous position.

Another vital control is the one which is least understood by most pianola players – the sustaining pedal control. First let's explain how vital this function in a piano is. The sustaining pedal controls the dampers on all the piano strings which are provided with dampers – normally all but the upper octave or so. Some very beautiful and outstanding effects can be gained by the use of this pedal and the concert pianist can make his instrument sing by the thoughtful and practised use of this control. It is a control which must be used discriminatingly – it must be used at exactly the right moment and cancelled quickly if necessary. Many pianists practise high agility with this pedal, using taps of very short duration indeed, and sometimes achieving a partial pedal effect called flutter pedalling. It is the use and understanding of this pedal which makes a good pianist.

So what about the mechanical or pneumatic player? To start with, the force needed to perform this function is pretty great. On the upright, the damper rail must be moved at an awkward angle. On the grand, the dampers are even harder to move smoothly. This then calls for the use of a larger than normal pneumatic motor which by its very size becomes slow and not very efficient at rapid movement. Many attempts have been made at trying to get a very rapidly moving damper pneumatic and few have been the successes.

While many player pianos have a little lever in the spool box (usually) for the automatic sustaining pedal (this is worked by the extreme left-hand roll perforations which are usually a long chain), there is also a finger lever provided for this in the key slip along with all the other controls. Because this is invariably a mechanical linkage without any pneumatic intervention, this means that it is usually the little finger of the left hand which is called upon to perform the duties of the left foot! Expert Pianola-players always demonstrate phenomenal strength in this digit as a consequence of this. The Hupfeld action, by contrast, wisely relegates this function in a more ergonomically practical way to the palm of the hand on a special lever. However, the practising player will have to learn how to manipulate this with speed and dexterity. I confess that because the finger can perform this operation speedily and with prompt timing, I prefer to switch off the automatic sustaining pedal (pneumatic) on my Pianola and play my rolls working the pedal control by finger. As much as anything else, the sustaining pedal is a slow control and sometimes one needs to apply a deft dab of pedal which a perforation cannot produce.

So much for the controls and their use: what about the art? The art has to start with the foot work and it is a surprise just how many players believe that pedalling should be regular left–right–left–right with never a variation in beat, and that the beat should follow that of the music! One could imagine a whole army of practising pianolists all moving their feet to the metronome of a sergeant-major! In fact this is absolutely wrong and is fatal to good playing. Remember that the footwork controls the suction power of the player action and that you only need to provide enough power to meet the demand, except when accenting. Foot pumping, therefore, should be a case of 'supply on demand only'. As for regular pedalling, once you get into the habit of the left–right–left business and start unconsciously pumping in time to the music, you will lose the ability to be able to accent notes as required.

I strongly discourage anyone from regular pedalling: it destroys the very soul of playing. Let the feet caress the pedals and make a conscious effort to break any semblance of rhythm. Use the feet to sense the resistance of the bellows and to maintain constant power. Give short dabs with one foot if you like, and long, languorous presses with the other, give the occasional double dab in mid-stroke, put one foot on the floor and pedal adroitly with the other during soft passages – do *anything* but pedal metronomically.

One of my Steck uprights, incidentally, is very easy to pedal and is a very smooth runner. I find no difficulty whatsoever in pedalling all but the loudest and fastest passages with just one foot, while using the other foot to operate the piano's soft and sustaining pedals between the floor treadles. The whole purpose of all these exercises is to get away from that regular rhythm and the more experienced you become as a player the more you will understand why.

And don't ever be seen playing a player piano the way a racing cyclist takes a hill. The head and the shoulders, the thighs and the knees should all be still with the only movement taking place in the ankles. Mind you, I'm not saying that you should sit to attention and not move: there are many (myself included) who find it unavoidable to move as the mood of the music dictates. Concert pianists often sway about like this and I am assured it's not due to piles and an uncomfortable piano stool. What I never want to see is the cowboy player who plays after the fashion of somebody trying hard to get the better of an obstinate mechanism.

Actual player-piano playing calls for a lot of careful practice. Select a roll of a piece of music you know very well and work at this over and over again until you find that it sounds the way you want it to sound. Learn self-criticism and always remember that you can do better.

If you have access to a proper practice roll (the Pianola one is very good), then use this and follow the instructions printed on the roll very carefully. Now I commend these to all pianolists since they provide short lessons in operation of the piano's controls. In lieu of this, select a roll of music which you know. This is important, since playing familiar music will give you confidence at this early stage, and will also offer some basis for self-criticism.

Take the roll from its box and place the box on top of the piano. Cultivate personal discipline about boxes; unkempt rolls are the result of bad box practice, so always keep a roll in its box (except while playing, of course) and, immediately after playing, put it back in its box. Never leave a roll on the piano, half-played or half-unrolled, as this will cause the exposed part of the paper to expand or contract to suit the atmosphere. Tracking problems will surely result.

Hold the roll loosely in the right hand so that the drive end of the spool (the end with the slotted hole in the case of an 88-note, or the end with the spade-shaped spigot if it is a 65-note) is lowermost and now tap the roll gently on a hard surface. This makes sure that the spooled paper is knocked down to one side. Place the 'reroll-play' control on the piano key-slip to the 'reroll' position (it should have been left there after playing the previous roll). Do not move the foot pedals. Holding the spooled roll in the hand tightly so as not to let the paper 'cone' or slip, insert the left end of the roll into the left spool-box chuck, making sure that the roll is the right way round. In the great majority of players this means so that the apron with its tag is coming off the top of the roll at the front. Now gently push the roll to the left, depressing the chuck against its spring so that you can insert the right end of the roll into the drive chuck. Turn the roll slightly until it clicks into place. See that the roll is securely located before letting go of it. Now take a hold of the tag or D-ring on the end of the apron and slowly unwind it until it can be engaged in the hook on the centre of the take-up spool. Turn the take-up spool by its flanges to unwind the music roll across the tracker bar until the whole apron is wound onto the take-up spool and is clear of the tracker. Carefully wind on some more until the start instructions appear, i.e. tempo indication and, occasionally, key signature. Now place the motor control lever to the 'play' position. You are in command of an instrument which is just about to teach you something – that playing a player piano is no easy business!

The secret lies as with everything else in practising your chosen music roll. And it is a mistake to have a large selection of rolls and play them all straight off. Each roll needs practising over and over again. It takes on average a day to learn how to play a piano roll properly and most people take a lot longer over the learning period. Just because the instrument happens to be mechanical does not mean that it requires no skill to operate. You still have to make yourself master of it and make it do precisely what you want it to do.

There are some pedalling pitfalls, too. There is a great temptation to try to vary the speed of the music (the speed of the roll) by pedalling slowly. If this is possible, then the tempo valve on the air motor is not adjusted properly. While I am not discouraging experimentation (and every piano is slightly different and thus controlled in a slightly different manner), do remember that there are proper devices for regulating speed and the feet are not two of them.

I did mention how to accent notes with the feet. There are also many variations of the foot technique which can add distinction and beauty to your playing. One of these is the *un-accent* for adding lyricism to certain types of music. The term 'un-accent' is my own but I think it is a good one for the effect and how it is achieved. I am thinking in particular of many of the Chopin Nocturnes wherein you come across *cantabile* sections with softened chords in them. Now there are several ways of softening a chord, the obvious one being to bring the subduing levers sharply to the soft position at the moment of striking. But the system I use differs in that it allows of greater precision in use although it requires a bit of practice to learn the right moment to apply it. My system is to approach the chord to be subdued quite normally and then, at the moment before it is played, stop pedalling or at any rate make a positive hesitation. This allows the chord to be sounded with but residual vacuum pressure. Practised in combination with the sustaining pedal it can be a most beautiful effect. Do note, though, that the instant the notes have sounded, you must quickly regain power with a few quick foot strokes to return to the original power setting.

By the way, it is worth mentioning that those lines on piano rolls put there to guide you in your tempo and expression should not be relied on as gospel. In the early days, the master roll was marked fairly accurately and then this master fed through a machine with six or ten new rolls. A girl had the task of following the line on the master roll with a pantograph pen which automatically marked all the other rolls. Since the job was done at high speed, errors crept in. This is why many of the tempo markings one finds are, frankly, impossible to follow and unnecessary. Later on, rolls were run through special printing presses but still the markings could be advanced or retarded depending on how they were started in the printer. Sometimes one finds evidence of roll slip – the printed marks are blurred. At other times musical awareness indicates that a *forte* chord is in the wrong place according to the marks. The message is to use these marks as a guide, but to use your own skill (or whim) to make the interpretation yours within this framework. Follow the roll markings slavishly and it may well prove you have very good responses – but little musical common sense.

If one secret of being a good player pianist is practice, another is experimentation. Devise your own systems and effects and thereby learn the things you can and cannot do. A well regulated player is a highly responsive mechanism with which you can perform, note perfect, a vast repertoire of music. But, unless you really know how to extend both you and the piano to the limits, you will never be other than a mediocre player exuding mediocrity from every hole in your tracker bar. If that is the way you would wish it, then I'm sorry for you. You are obviously the sort of person who mows your lawn yet can't adjust the height of the cut, or drives a car but doesn't know how to change a wheel.

THE PERFECT PIANO PLAYER.
THE
Cecilian
is a Piano Player that for
EASE OF OPERATION,
CAPACITY for MUSICAL EXPRESSION,
DELICACY OF CONTROL,
ACCURACY OF TECHNIQUE,
stands alone in its class.

FARRAND
ORGAN COMPANY
Sole Manufacturers & Wholesalers.
24, DENMAN ST., LONDON, S.E.
SEND FOR BOOKLET.

How Mme. Bloomfield-Zeisler played a jest on some friends

Mme. Bloomfield Zeisler, the eminent pianiste, while playing to some friends suddenly rose and left the piano. Her playing, however, continued to the bewilderment of the company.

Mme. Zeisler laughingly confessed that a player attachment on a second grand piano in the studio had been started at a given signal. Mme. Zeisler was acting a part, while the player produced the music. Several guests, however, still objected that the technique and interpretation were Mme. Zeisler's own, whereupon she further explained that the instrument was the Welte-Mignon Autograph Player, which actually rendered her own playing and so exactly that the most delicate musical judgment could detect no difference.

The WELTE-MIGNON AUTOGRAPH · PIANO

brings to your home the personal interpretations of the world's greatest masters of the piano. Seated comfortably in your easy chair you can hear the marvellous technique, the brilliance, the living soul of Paderewski, of Hofmann, of de Pachmann, of Grieg, of Busoni, of all the masters of the pianoforte

M. WELTE & SONS, Inc.
273 FIFTH AVE.   NEW YORK CITY

Welte Mignons built in following styles: Welte Piano, with keyboard; Welte Piano without keyboard; and Welte Attachment to grand pianos.

CHAPTER 13

An Assessment of the Capabilities of the Reproducing Piano

According to all the advertisements of the time, the properties of the reproducing piano were virtually magical. Once the pianist had done his stuff, perforated paper and pneumatic mechanism took over to do for your own reproducing piano what the artist did on his recording piano. Now it is fundamental to the art of the piano roll that certain parameters – limitations, if you like – are accepted first before we can attempt to evaluate the musical interpretations of the rolls themselves in terms of their being 'faithful recordings'.

It is obvious that not all pianists were enamoured of the reproducing-piano system. There is a great story about Artur Schnabel and Aeolian which demonstrates this. On being asked if he would record for Duo-Art, he declined. Pressed by Aeolian with the advice that the Duo-Art offered sixteen shades of nuance, Schnabel replied with the news that in his playing he used seventeen shades.

The fundamental problem with the reproducing systems was a massive one of unknown quantities which, because of their very nature, makers could neither solve nor overcome. The selfsame problem exists today in hi-fi. Hear a test recording in the hi-fi store played back under ideal conditions through a specific pair of loudspeakers, then take those speakers into your home and try to repeat the performance. Assuming that you use the same equipment as you heard in the shop, the chances of hearing exactly the same sound are slim indeed. The accoustics of the room will differ, certain frequencies will be lost or exaggerated, the result will not be absolutely perfect without an adjustment of controls.

With the reproducing piano, the same conditions exist but are compounded by the fact that the sound of the piano itself will more than likely differ from the sound of the original recording piano. And you do not have hi-fi-type controls to adjust that. The import of this at first barely relevant statement will be explained in a moment. The seat of the matter lies in the popular misconception (aided dramatically by those Welte advertisements of ghostly hands on the keyboard) that the reproduction of music lies in replicating the work of the pianist in operating the keys of the piano. This is patently erroneous since what the pianist is really doing is applying himself to a mechanism in order to make a sound. His interest lies in the relationship between strings and soundboard, room acoustic and audience, not in how hard or fast the hammers of the keys strike the strings of an arbitrary studio piano. You can, for example, drive in a 2-inch nail with a tack hammer, but it requires a totally different technique from that required if you used an 8-ounce carpenter's hammer.

In case all this seems a little academic, consider for a moment the different sounds which pianos make. Probably the piano with the loudest tone is the German Ibach, a veritable powerhouse of sound. Imagine, then, playing a roll of Liszt's *La Campenella* with its *glissandi* of notes on a piano as resonant as that! Now turn to a softer-toned instrument such as a Pleyel grand with a bright top end and imagine the difference. The former will sound thick, resonant and objectionable while the latter will be far more acceptable. Yet both are perfectly good, indeed fine instruments.

The pianist, when he plays, adjusts his performance to suit the particular piano he is playing and the room in which it is situated. He judges the tonal relationship between notes and strives to attain a balance which is as subtle as it is difficult. If he is recording a piano roll, his performance will be tempered by these very local studio conditions. The resultant roll is now sold to a buyer with a different type of piano, probably not as well adjusted as the peak performance of the recording piano, and placed in a room which may either be resonant or acoustically dead. Whichever it is, the chances of its matching the conditions in the recording studio which governed the original performance are indeed remote.

As for that comment by Rachmaninov on hearing the Ampico roll of his G Minor Prelude (see Chapter 4) when he said 'Gentlemen: I have just heard myself play', this was because he was sitting in the recording studio listening to the recording piano play back to him the performance he had originally matched to those conditions. I'll wager that if it had been played back on a different piano in somebody's home he'd have had some reservations.

Although the actual fingering of the piano can be achieved very well by the reproducing piano, within the confines of the above argument, there is another aspect which presents fresh difficulties – the operation of the sustaining pedal. Anton Rubenstein called this 'the soul of the piano' and if you think back to *La Campenella* and the Ibach and Pleyel pianos something of his meaning will become evident. Back we go to Beethoven and his *Moonlight Sonata* – and his original manuscript which shows the sustaining pedal held hard down for the entire first movement. Pianists follow no strict rule in pedalling the sustaining pedal. The effects which individual pianists seek to obtain are produced with an interaction between the use of this pedal and the natural decay time of individual notes struck with varying degrees of force. In matters such as these, the reproducing piano suddenly becomes remarkably inept. So-called flutter pedalling can be reproduced with good effect, but for the finest interpretation of serious music the reproducing piano's ability must always be slightly suspect.

I have chosen my words with infinite care here because the many who cherish the avowed abilities of the reproducing piano tend more to be piano experts than musical experts – which is rather like the difference between a highly technical motor engineer and the motor rally driver: one may not automatically have the talents and understandings of the other.

However, I used the words 'serious music' for it is in this area that the greatest problems are found. When it comes to the light classics and to popular music, of course, while the same problems exist, they are, as a rule, demonstrably of less consequence. A roll of popular hits from a musical show, for example, or a once-popular dance melody is, in musicological terms, of lightweight or negligible interest.

In recent years there has been a veritable flood of gramophone records on the market which have given us vintage performances afresh via the reproducing piano. For many, these interpretations have been seen as inviolate indications of how the masters of the past actually played. It must be said, though, that many of these records are very bad – surprisingly so in some cases. In one instance, for example, it is patently clear that the Themodist valves which vivify the Duo-Art were either not working or were switched off – perhaps even the Duo-Art switch was left off, leaving us with a thick bass and a thin and barely distinguishable melody line.

The issue of recordings of this type depends on the use of a piano in absolutely tiptop condition with its piano action regulated to remove all lost motion and with its player action then regulated to the piano action. And then the action may need re-regulating to suit each roll played (see the problems in zero-setting on the Duo-Art as set out in Chapter 7).

For many, these reproducing roll performances are acceptable as gospel, authentic re-performances of the originals. I must say that while they are very good and generally establish an acceptable re-creation of the wishes of the recording artist, their absolute fidelity (which can only be compared with their original performances and which, in most cases then, is an unattainable goal) must be considered with caution. In those cases where gramophone recordings exist it is sometimes (but far from always) possible to discern certain qualities which do not come over in the piano roll. These qualities, to my mind at any rate, stem from differences, the variables and the limitations which I have already outlined.

Some acceptance that this shortcoming existed is to be found in Aeolian's attitude towards its isolated instantaneous theme, described in Chapter 6. Here we have a move towards that final development in recording, yet obviously it was appreciated that no two pianos were ever likely to give the same reproduction and this was a condition which would have to be lived with.

A most interesting letter appeared in the Player Piano Group *Bulletin* at the end of 1978. Written by Patrick Handscombe, it discusses the merits of Duo-Art and Solophonola accenting. I reproduce salient parts here with acknowledgement to the P.P.G. and the author:

> An examination of Duo-Art rolls of serious music (rather than the synthesised dance rolls) will reveal the extensive use made of the Themodist for reproducing superb chord shadings, crescendos and diminuendos, particularly in the late USA recordings, where the editors had long since outgrown the concept of merely using the Themodist to 'bring out a tune'.
>
> Those fortunate enough to listen to a Triphonola in perfect condition can vouch for the even greater subtlety with which it uses the Solodant. As in the Duo-Art, it is contrived that a given solo level is always fractionally above its corresponding accompaniment dynamic, and in my opinion it is not the analogue – as opposed to digital – expression system used, but the extremely careful coding of Hupfeld rolls that makes the Triphonola generally superior to the Duo-Art.
>
> It is interesting to note that the Ampico can produce accents in much the same way by rapid switching of the intensity valves; but with only seven available levels, coding subtleties are not inherently possible. Furthermore, the speed of accent switching is a function of tracker bar hole size, system inertia, perforation length and paper speed, and it is perhaps because of the rather large perforations and *relatively* low speed of Ampico rolls that the pianists seem to break their chords rather more frequently than our parents or gramophone records remember – though few will denigrate the editors' skill heard in all Ampico recordings.
>
> It should be remembered that, even allowing for Aeolian 'engineering', when correctly set up the pneumatic Themodist system can propagate the accent signal at

something only marginally less than the speed of sound; while the small diameter Themodist perforations and *relatively* high roll speed of the Duo-Art allow the accent to be maintained if necessary for only a fraction of a second.

It is also fortunate for the Duo-Art and Triphonola that the human brain can be exquisitely deceived by, and compensate for, only two dynamic levels played at any instant (cf. modern colour TV), which explains why such inherently uncontrived yet sophisticated systems can sound so lifelike.

The various merits of the Ampico and the Duo-Art systems have long been a bone of contention amongst experts and each system has its advocates who assert that the other 'must be inferior'. Assertion is always put forward as dogma in arguments such as this! However, the fact remains that there were fundamental differences between the Duo-Art and Ampico which worked in both directions. To start with, the Ampico was production-engineered to a high standard of repeatable reliability and was factory-installed in no fewer than 100 different types of piano. The Ampico thus had the advantage of being replicated throughout its range and the only variations were the types of piano in which it was fitted. The Duo-Art, on the other hand, tended to be far less of an engineering job with plenty of detached parts and loose components which were installed more or less on an *ad hoc* basis. It is seldom you find two Duo-Arts, even in the same model of piano, which are identical. This did, though, admit of a certain degree of individual setting up of the action to suit the individual piano and there is some reason to suspect that this process of harmonising player to piano was a more lengthy job than in the case of the Ampico. Whether or not this means that the Duo-Art could be that much better purely on the grounds of its installation and regulation is another matter.

Significantly, though, with the introduction of the Ampico Model B, musical tastes directed that most of the repertoire of rolls to be made for this would be of the popular style. Indeed, very few so-called classical rolls were made for the B – the figure is a mere 100 – of which some were altered from Model A recordings. Even so, their performance on the Model B was generally inferior to that on the earlier version. But whereas the Ampico is a better engineered system, and should be capable of better reproduction than the Duo-Art, the whole efficacy is negated by the provision of a volume control lever which allows the user to play his rolls 'loud', 'normal', or 'soft'. Again, no indication is given on the roll of which setting the roll was recorded at in the first place.

The advantage of the reproducing piano roll lies in presenting to us an overall image of the style of a pianist's playing rather than of an absolute re-creation. As regards musicological importance, the reproducing piano roll is nowhere near as vital to our understanding of techniques of times past as is the early barrel organ, or, come to that, the Bidermann spinets. Sadly, the degree of perfection reached in the reproducing roll was too late for it to bring us, say, the performances of Chopin (who died in 1849), Liszt (who died as late as 1886) or Schubert and Beethoven. Had we been able to listen to anything played by these men, then the reproducing roll would emerge as a vital interpretational aid. Now this is not to say that it does not have a measure of importance and this is highlighted when we can hear a composer playing his own music on the system. Here we have a clear insight into what the originators thought their music should sound like and occasionally some gems of advice shine through to us. For example, when Claude Debussy recorded his *La Cathedrale Engloutie* for Welte-Mignon he played the slow central passage at twice the speed indicated by the musical score, so suggesting that he had forgotten to mark the manuscript with the legend *doppio movimento*.

AN ASSESSMENT OF THE CAPABILITIES OF THE REPRODUCING PIANO

So, then, how should one assess these instruments, the Rolls-Royces of the player-piano world? First, I think it is dangerous to describe them as faithfully *re-enacting* the precise interpretations of the recording artists when it comes to classical musical rolls. What one gets is a fairly accurate representation of the shape of their performances, of how they phrased and articulated on the recording piano. The nearest one can possibly hope to get to that original is to have an instrument maintained in absolute perfect order and to spend time checking roll speeds and dynamics.

Some reproducing systems are better than others but before trying to determine which system was better than another several factors have to be taken into consideration. These are (a) the potential of each system; (b) the practical use of the system as an interface between piano and artist; and (c) the adequacy of the recordings available for the system – the special roll interpretations.

Although there is much controversy between Duo-Art and Ampico buffs, from the engineering standpoint I consider the Ampico to be a better-made reproducing system. By comparison, the Welte system is superbly made but its astonishing performance can hardly be attributed to the design of the system, which appears continually in danger of losing its reference points for expression. The Hupfeld system is also extremely well made and, although owing much to the Welte, is better thought out. The Philipps Duca system is similarly very well engineered.

As regards the practical interface between instrument and artist, there we have the first main problem. I suppose it really comes down to the amount of response which the action can produce – given the ideal roll which, as we shall see in a moment, is the big 'if' behind the systems. The response time of the Ampico action is appreciably faster than that of any other system, a fact due in no small part to the smaller volume of the expression chambers which must be adjusted by the intensity valves. Response times with the Ampico, then, are extremely good. Of course, given suitable music and suitable rolls, the minor shortcomings in response times with the other instruments may amount to very little indeed. What I mean here is that the response time of the Ampico is consistently good with any roll and can play with greater flexibility than any other system.

Now for the big question of the adequacy of the recording. A fine performance has to depend on a mixture of qualities, beginning first with the pianist. Since reproducing-piano makers generally employed only the best recording pianists, perhaps it is best to dismiss this aspect and move on to the question of roll editing. This began with the mysterious operation of manual controls on a separate control box as far as Duo-Art and Welte rolls were concerned, so the work of the pianist received its first interference from an outside hand as he was actually playing. Then came the eradication of wrong notes, the correction of imprecise phrasing, the insertion of missing notes and minor adjustments in *tempi*. The final master roll was then a mixture of recording pianist, roll editors and engineers. The proportion of artist that remained obviously varied from roll to roll and from system to system. If we now consider the library of rolls for the recording piano, we find that as far as Duo-Art is concerned some 45 per cent of the repertoire comprises really well-recorded and well-reproducible rolls. With the Ampico, the percentage is a bit higher, being as much as 60 per cent. With the Red Welte, my assessment is that about 75 per cent of the rolls are good recordings. With the Triphonola of Hupfeld, I have never found a 'bad' roll so, applying the reasoning that 100 per cent perfection must be an impossible goal, I will credit Hupfeld with a 95 per cent success rate. I cannot speak with any authority on the Duca of Philipps as I have studied too few of them, but a first assessment would rate this system as not being all that different from the Hupfeld.

You will see that on the assessment of the number of rolls which produce what I believe to be convincing interpretations of an unknown original performance the merits of the systems have altered dramatically, with Triphonola in first place, Duca in second, Welte in third, Ampico in fourth and Duo-Art bottom at fifth place. In terms of capability, though, the Ampico comes first as, indeed, it does in terms of engineering and realisation.

This league table does not, of course, take into consideration types of music – some music lends itself much more readily to recording by a particular system than others. At the same time, I have not allowed my judgement to be too greatly influenced by those artists who were particularly well recorded by a system, nor those who were somewhat less fortunate than that. Josef Lhevinne, for example, was very well recorded on Ampico and his roll (number 63903H) of the Liszt-Busoni version of *La Campanella* is a superb demonstration of how very good an Ampico can be.

A music roll, reproducing or otherwise, is a coded set of information which can only be read back by equipment capable of interpreting that code. A poor initial recording cannot be enhanced by a good piano; and good initial recording cannot be played back on a poor piano. The very best match we can hope for is to have an instrument in optimum condition and accept those remaining limitations.

THE MUSIC TRADES DIARY, YEAR BOOK, AND DIRECTORY

. THE .
"TRIUMPHAUTO"

THE PERFECT
PLAYER PIANO

(SUCCESSORS TO KASTNER & CO., LTD.

Manufacturers of the Celebrated
Kastner Auto-Player Piano

We shall be happy to forward Catalogues and Prices on application.

TRIUMPHAUTO LTD., 191 REGENT STREET, LONDON, W. 1.

◀ PLATE 112
The orchestrion business of Pierre Eich of Ghent, Belgium, seems to have begun in the early 1920s and did not cease until the outbreak of the Second World War. The business was thus one of the last remaining makers of electric pianos and piano orchestrions in the world. Many different instruments were made but one of the most popular was the Solophone. Note that this plays the roll 'inside out', the roll being fed over the tracker bar from the back rather than the front. This served to keep the spool box shallow while at the same time ensuring that the paper was always in good contact with the tracker even when large diameter rolls were in play.

PLATE 113 ▶
This particular Solophone has violin-toned pipes and an extensive xylophone. Instrumentation varied from one Solophone to another and many combinations were built. Rather like the early Welte pipe orchestrions, the Eich instruments featured both suction and pressure wind departments and clearly seen here are the see-saw pressure feeders at the bottom and the smaller see-saw exhausters for suction above the central wind platform. Solophone rolls were 325mm wide.

◀ PLATE 114
The Berlin business of Kuhl & Klatt was founded in 1899 and made a range of electric pianos under the name Pneuma and, later, Pneumatist. After the First World War the firm made a small number of 70-key piano-orchestrions. Although not a major manufacturer, the marque earned a reputation for quality instruments and many examples were sent to Belgium where Eugene DeRoy was one who sold modified machines as jazzband orchestrions. Seen here is one of the products of the early 1920s, an orchestrion containing a front-mounted xylophone (visible above the music roll), and mandolin. This example is contained in a light oak case with two cast brass electric light brackets with the characteristic bead shades of the period. Kuhl & Klatt music rolls were 340mm wide.

PLATE 115 ▶
The Waldkirch orchestrion makers Gebruder Weber was founded in 1880 and produced a very large number of instruments. Among the many popular models made was this, the Weber Grandezza which combined piano with mandolin and xylophone. As with the Kuhl & Klatt seen in the previous picture, the xylophone was mounted at the top of the piano and visible through a glass panel. To emphasise the effect, many of these instruments which were built for use in public places were equipped with lighting effects so that when a register was selected, the particular portion would be illuminated. The Grandezza played music rolls 325mm in width.

PLATE 116 ▶
Another popular product from Gebruder Weber was the Unika. This comprised piano with mandolin attachment and one rank of violin-toned wooden pipes which would play solo. In this illustration the outstanding design and workmanship so typical of many of the orchestrion makers of the era. Notice another method of achieving both suction and wind at pressure, here attained at either end of the wind platform. Unlike many of the American-made piano orchestrions which were to follow, the tone of these instruments with their well-voiced pipework was very attractive even though care was needed to ensure that the piano was in tune with the pipework – a long-lasting disadvantage of piano-organ combinations.

◀ PLATE 117
Weber instruments came in all shapes and sizes, it seems, and this Brabo piano orchestrion of the 1920s is typical of a number produced with names such as Styria, Erato, Otero, Solea, Euterpe, Elite and Maesto. The Brabo was built with a fine range of effects including mandolin, violin-toned wooden pipework and xylophone. Register changes allowed these instruments to play solo with piano accompaniment or in unison and swell shutters were employed to emphasise the effects. The Brabo played music rolls 325mm wide.

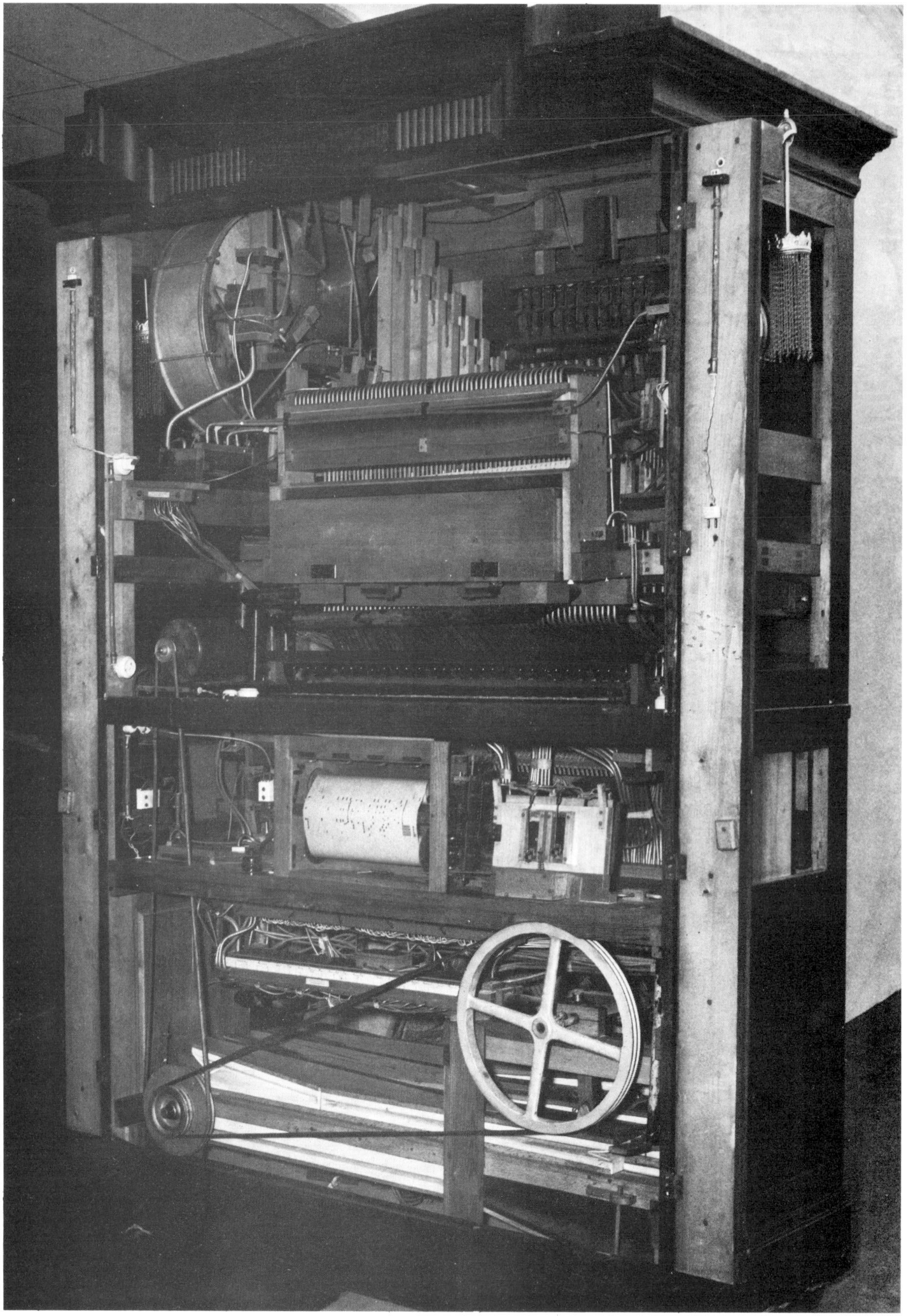

▲ PLATE 119
Johann Daniel Philipps founded the Frankfurter Musikwerke-Fabrik J. D. Philipps in 1886. Here from an original catalogue is a picture of a Pianella-Orchestrion Model 43. This stood 11ft. 9in. tall, had an automatic roll-changer for six 226mm-wide music rolls, and featured an extensive complement of registers including xylophone, chimes and drums.

PLATE 120 ▶
Here is another view of the Kuhl & Klatt seen in Plate 114 to show both the attractive cabinetwork and the beaded electric light shades on the sconces. On top of the piano is a remote control box. These little wall boxes resembled the piano in miniature and when a coin was dropped in it would start the piano playing. In a restaurant, several such coin boxes could be arranged around the room.

◀ PLATE 118
The business of Hugo Popper was founded in 1891, its founder being a close friend of Karl Bockisch of Welte fame. From inception until the early 1930s, the name of Popper was synonymous with quality instruments which included the Stella reproducing piano. The instruments emanating from the Leipzig factory were made to a very high quality. Seen here, left, is a rare surviving example of the Popper Salon Orchestra made between 1912 and the late 1920s. Music rolls were 350mm wide.

PLATE 121 ▶
Automatic roll-changers were often essential when an instrument was sited in a public place such as a restaurant or dancehall. Philipps took out a number of patents for such mechanisms including a system of swivelling tracker bars to allow shift from one music roll to another. The successful 'Revolver System' was invented in 1903 and patented in 1905 and models were made to carry 3, 5, 6 or 10 rolls. Here is a 10-roll Revolver System fitted to a Philipps Paganini piano orchestrion.

◀ PLATE 122
The addition of external percussion effects to pianos was a modification undertaken by a number of instrument factors. Seen here is an example of the Weber Swing, basically a Grandezza piano orchestrion to the top of which has been added a piano accordion, bass drum, snare drum and cymbal. In the majority of such installations, the accordion would be tee'd off the piano notes, the two playing in unison. Only in dedicated instruments would the accordion be allowed its individual melodic line from the piano roll.

PLATE 123 ▶
A late conversion of this type is seen in this Poppers Happy Jazz-Band electric expression piano. These were probably converted after the piano left its manufacturer. Note that the style of the upper casework differs from that of the piano itself.

PLATE 124 ▶

René Seybold established his orchestrion factory in Strasbourg, France. During the between-wars years, he made a variety of unusual instruments influenced by his licence arrangement with the Höhner accordion factory in Trossingen. He arranged music for the Höhner Magic-Organa (an automatic piano-accordion) and built accordions into pianos. His own successful player piano was the Gabriella and this instrument, right, was used as the basis of a family of derivative instruments. Here is the Seybold Piano-Accordeon-Jazz of the 1930s – undoubtedly a centre of attraction in a café or bar.

◀ PLATE 125

Automatic or self-playing violins were produced by a number of makers but the only two brands which succeeded in the marketplace were those of Mills and Hupfeld. One of the rare non-starters in this by-way of the piano-orchestrion came from the works of Hugo Popper in 1930–31 and was probably the last instrument which the business actually produced. Like the Hupfeld Phonoliszt-Violina, it was a pneumatically-operated action which Popper chose for his Violinovo. Only one example is known to survive and this is in the collection of Werner Baus, Fuldatal, West Germany. The applied fretwork to the upper front proclaims POPPERS VIOLINOVO and the legend above the piano keys reads POPPERS WELT-PIANO KONZERTIST. It played music rolls 350mm wide.

PLATE 126 ▶
The interior of the Poppers Violinovo piano, percussion and violin. The instrument was exhibited at the Leipzig Spring Fair of 1930, 20 years after Hupfeld had created a sensation at the Brussels World Exhibition with its Phonoliszt-Violina. Mounted in the upper case above the music roll can be seen the violin. Extensive use of metal tubing for the pneumatic connections makes for a neat and durable construction. The crossed belt suggests the motor is probably not original.

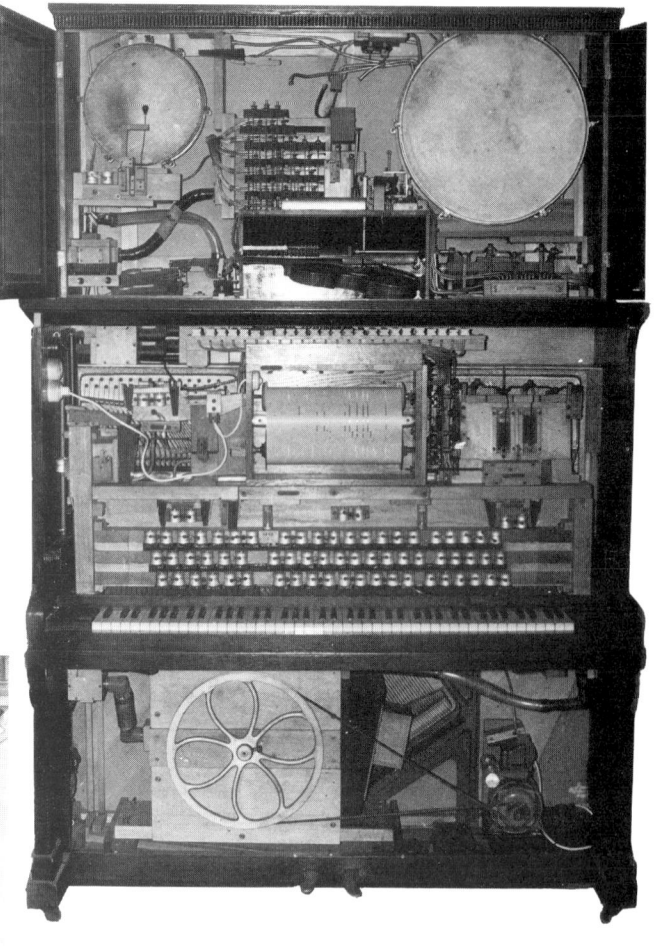

◀ PLATE 127
In this detail view of the actual violin the method of playing can clearly be seen. Unlike the Hupfeld with its tangential finger levers, Popper chose to use direct-acting plungers to push the string down to the finger board. This system was used originally by the Swede Henry Konrad Sandell when he made the first Mills Automatic Virtuosa, forerunner of the Violano-Virtuoso. Subsequently Sandell scrapped this method, rejected the violin's fingerboard and stopped off his strings with small metal fingers which pressed upwards under the strings. While the Popper system may have been more lifelike, allowing for the use of the same type of rotating bow that the Mills Company used, there was still no provision for easy tuning of the violin.

◀ PLATE 128
Ludwig Hupfeld began his first experiments with self-playing violins as early as 1900. Production of the Phonoliszt-Violina, seen left, began around 1907 and the first examples were sold the following year. Bowers relates that the original inventors were, besides Hupfeld himself, Robert Frömsdorf and Johann and Ludwig Bajde. They invented a foot-pedal and keyboard-operated mechanical violin called the Klaviolin and formed a company called Klaviolinfabrik Bajde & Co. in Schischka near Laibach, Austro-Hungary. This business was liquidated in 1913. Gustav Karl and Ernest Hennig were also granted numerous patents for player violins in the years immediately after the First World War. Although many thousands of Hupfeld player violins were manufactured, few have survived. Problems in servicing their delicate pneumatic actions and tuning the single playing string on each of the three violins contained in the upperwork have taken their toll of instruments across the intervening years.

PLATE 129 ▶
The Blessing family retained a prominant position in the Black Forest clock and orchestrion business from the late 1700s through to the 1920s when the last instrument was made. Indeed many of the other famed names in the industry served their apprenticeships with Karl Blessing (1769–1820) including Michael Welte. Blessing made a number of different types of instruments including piano orchestrions with names such as Matador, Jazy, Carmen and Jazz Band. One popular series was the Polyvox made in several styles. Seen here is a 1930 Polyvox Model B with 51-note piano, 27-note mandolin, 15-note xylophone, bass drum, side drum and wood blocks.

◀ PLATE 130
A smaller example of the Philipps' 'Revolver System' automatic roll changer is this six-roll model. Roll-changers were made by several companies including Wurlitzer (who made them under licence from the inventors Verstraelen & Alter of New York City). An idea of the complexity of the mechanism can be gained from this illustration.

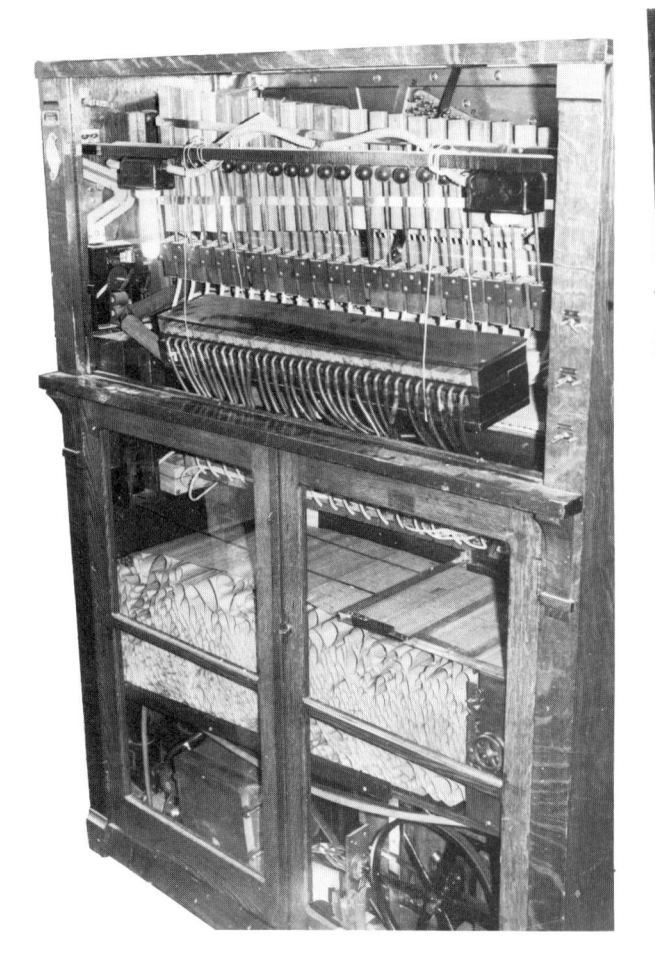

▲ PLATE 131
The North Tonawanda Musical Instrument Works of New York State was founded in 1906 by a breakaway group from the works of Eugene deKleist. Around 1909 the company introduced the Pianolin, seen here. This was a 44-note piano with unison accompaniment flute/violin-toned pipes. The music was in the form of an endless band of perforated paper 6⅝ inches in width which was allowed to fold in a heap in a special music hopper. This form of music was employed by a number of American makers and miraculously the paper never seems to tangle or become jammed.

◀ PLATE 132
The Link Piano Company of Binghamton, New York, was founded around 1910. This Link Model 2-E keyless piano has a mandolin and xylophone as well as the endless paper band type of music. Clear glazed panels were fitted so that saloon bar customers could watch the mechanism. Made *c.* 1925.

PLATE 133 ▶
Brand name of the Operator's Piano Company of Chicago was Coinola. This particular style, the X, cost $1,575 in 1925. Described as 'the most popular orchestrion ever made', the piano was entirely percussion accompanied – there were no organ pipes. Bass drum, drum roll, snare drum, cymbal and triangle combined with either a wooden xylophone or, if the customer preferred, a set of metal orchestral tubular bells.

◀ **PLATE 134**
The Reproduco was also made by the Operator's Piano Company. This was a combined piano and pipe organ and was often fitted with twin roll-drive mechanisms so that one roll could be rewound while the other played. The example seen here has a single roll mechanism. For manual playing, the shorter upper keyboard operates the pipe organ department and the lower keyboard is for the piano. Well over 1,000 were sold during the 1920s and the majority went to the theatres and silent cinemas.

▲ PLATE 135
Another famous name in the world of American piano orchestrions was that of J. P. Seeburg. This Chicago company made a variety of beautiful, high-quality instruments such as this E Special.

▲ PLATE 136
In this view beneath the keyboard of the Seeburg E Special can be seen the xylophone, bass drum and cymbal. Also visible is the variable-speed drive system using a rubber-tyred wheel on a faceplate.

◄ PLATE 137
Ed Link's orchestral pianos were famed for quality and are described by collectors today as playing arrangements which are 'snappy and full of life'. Bowers relates that the case of the Style A piano pictured here was made by the Haddorff Piano Company of Rockford, Illinois, and sent empty to Link who installed the works. Capable also of keyboard playing, the Style A featured mandolin attachment, violin-toned pipework, flute-toned pipework, snare drum, triangle, tom-tom, tambourine and wood block.

PLATE 138 ►
The Marquette Piano Company, yet another Chicago business, made instruments under the name Cremona and seen here is a Style G flute piano orchestrion. Bowers relates that the Style G was one of the most popular makes to emerge from this firm. The business flourished between 1905 and 1920.

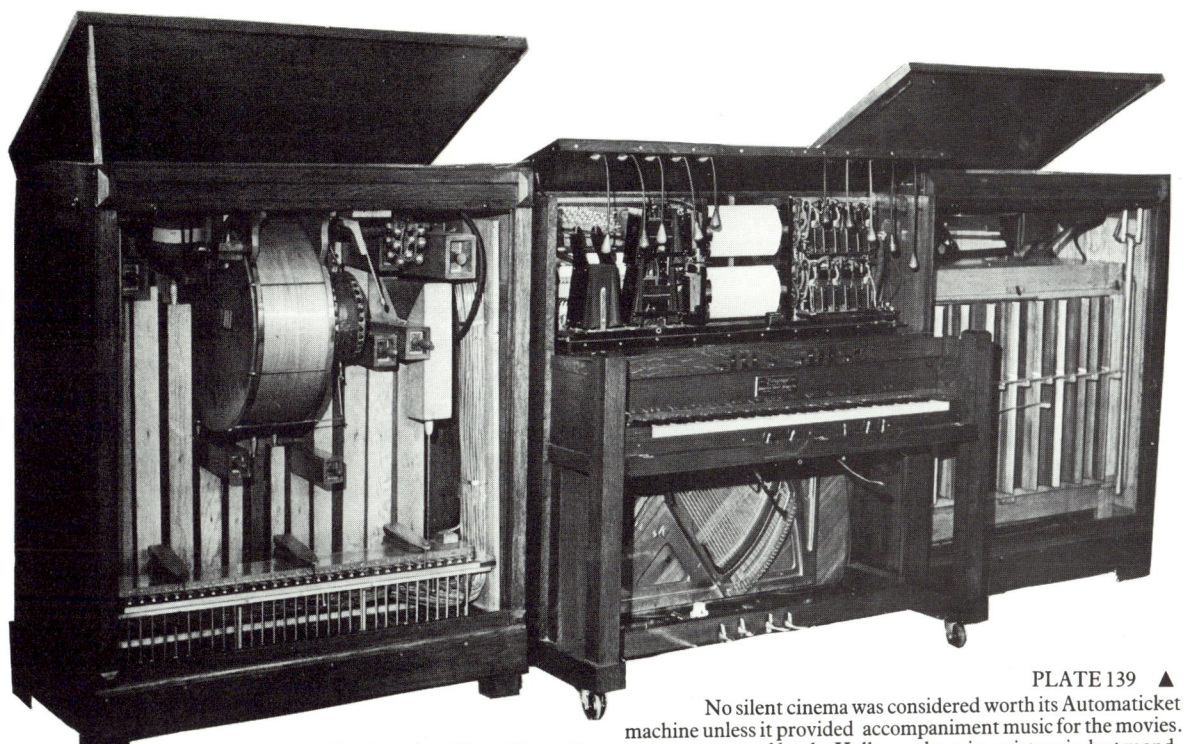

PLATE 139 ▲
No silent cinema was considered worth its Automaticket machine unless it provided accompaniment music for the movies. The American Photo Player Company was spawned by the Hollywood motion-picture industry and invented by two Berkeley, California, brothers named Van Valkenburg. The product which emerged was called the Fotoplayer and many, many models were made until production stopped around 1925. Styles ranged from $2,875 up to $10,750 and some were almost 20 feet wide. With the coming of the talkies, Fotoplayers were scrapped coast to coast. Harvey Roehl owns this rare survivor of the breed.

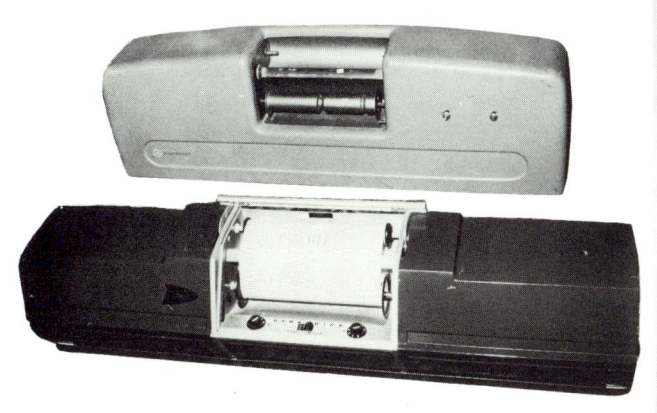

▲ PLATE 140
The post-war revival of the player piano was considered by some to centre on key-top players – separate attachments which could be rested on to a piano keyboard for automatic playing. The majority of these appeared in very recent times – from the early 1950s through to barely a decade ago – yet so fleeting was their impact on the world of the player that today they are all but forgotten. Here are two key-tops, the Electrelle and beneath it the Dynavoice.

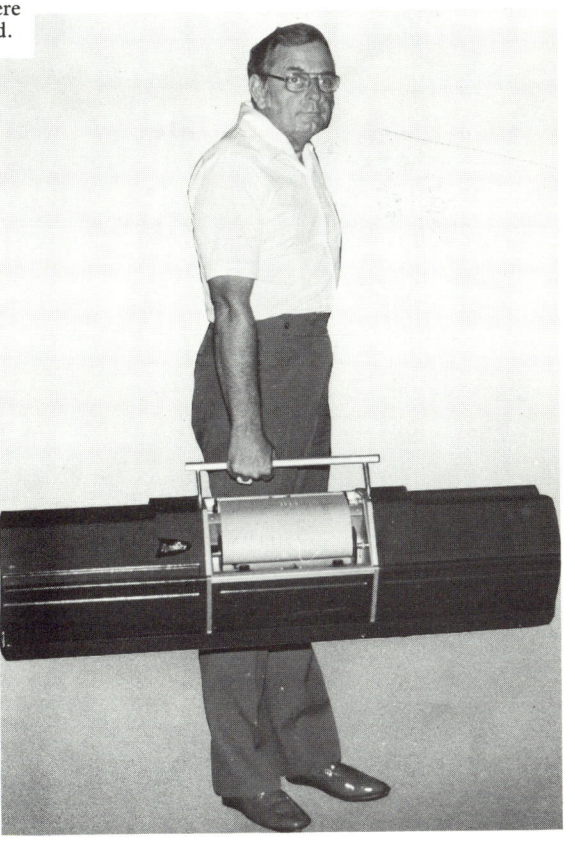

PLATE 141 ▶
A player in search of a piano! Walt Bellm, who owns the key-tops seen here, showing how the Dynavoice was intended to be carried using the protective handle which was attached to the sides of the spoolbox.

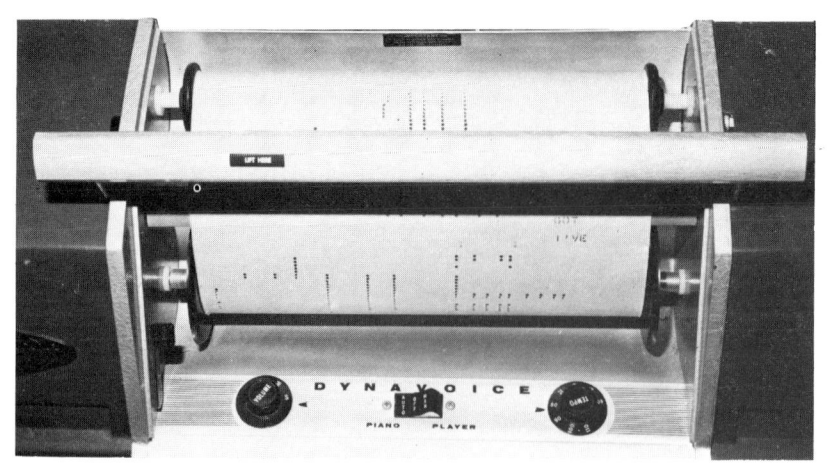

◄ PLATE 142
Detail of the Dynavoice key-top player showing the lifting handle over the tracker bar and the three manual controls – a central rocking on-off switch, a volume control and the tempo control. When not in use, these key-top players all featured a detachable tray into which the machine was clipped. This was in order to protect the plungers which pushed down on the piano keys.

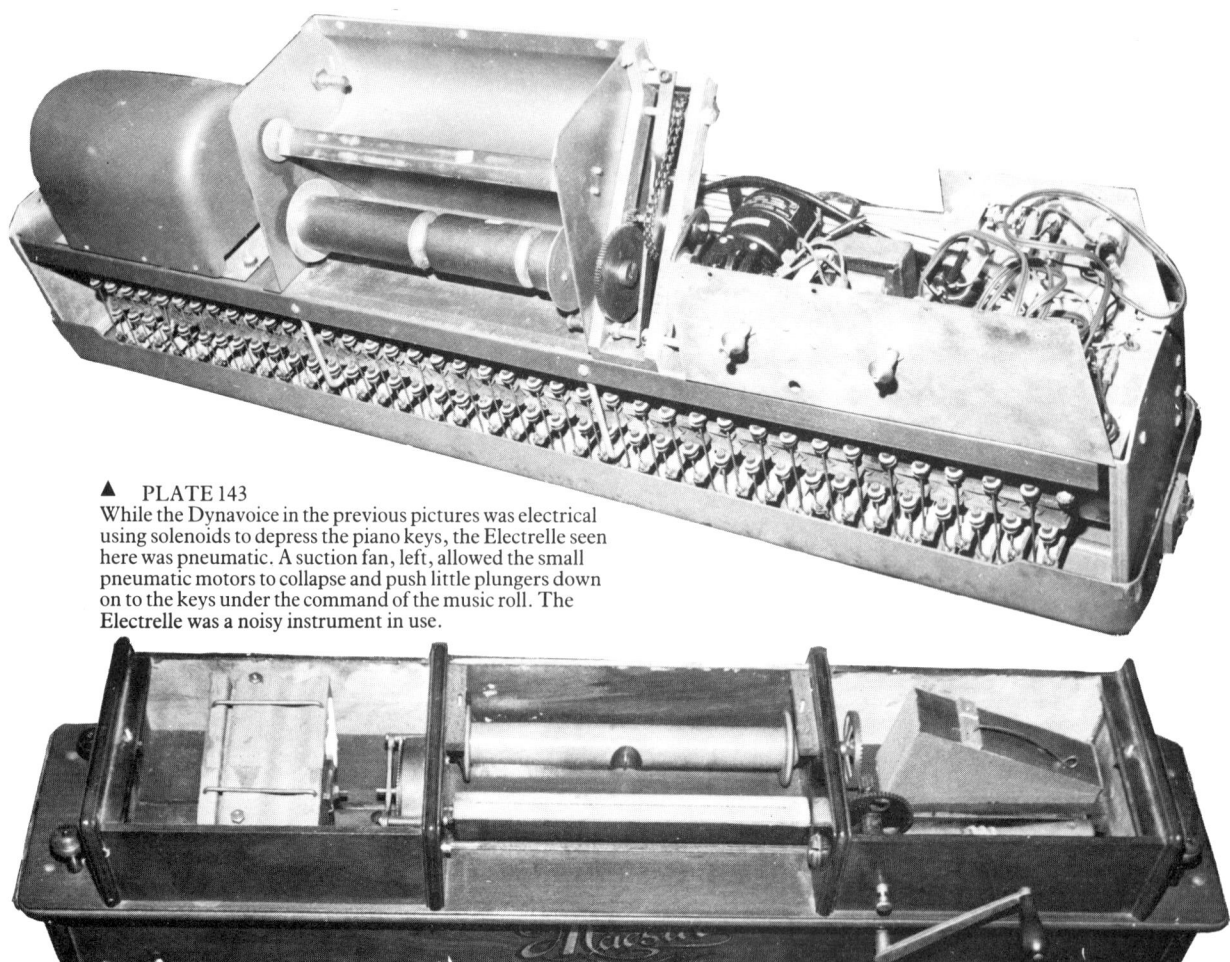

▲ PLATE 143
While the Dynavoice in the previous pictures was electrical using solenoids to depress the piano keys, the Electrelle seen here was pneumatic. A suction fan, left, allowed the small pneumatic motors to collapse and push little plungers down on to the keys under the command of the music roll. The Electrelle was a noisy instrument in use.

▲ PLATE 144
All these key-top players of the post-war era were not as quietly efficient as the little Maestro marketed for a short while between 1899 and about 1901. Whereas the post-war models pictured earlier were all 88-note players, the Maestro was a 65-note instrument and was cleverly engineered. In this picture can be seen the twin parallel-motor exhausters at the left and the wedge-shaped equaliser at the right. Turning the handle operated a small crankshaft which in turn applied reciprocating motion to the exhausters. The power available in these small instruments remained minimal and hence their effectiveness and limited abilities in the way of expression ensured their rapid consignment to oblivion.

◀ PLATE 145
The Duo-Art Robot built to the designs of player piano enthusiast Gerald Stonehill and one-time Aeolian boffin Gordon Iles. This reproducing cabinet player was conceived in 1962, built between 1973 and 1974, and has since performed at public concerts. The core of the Robot is an original Duo-Art drawer-type reproducing player made at the time when Aeolian and Ampico had combined their forces around 1936.

PLATE 146 ▶
The mechanism of the Duo-Art Robot viewed from the back. The Duo-Art system built into an Ampico Model B-type drawer is just visible inside the top of the case. This re-engineering of the Duo-Art system created a number of unexpected problems which are described in Chapter 10.

◀ PLATE 147
The new generation of player pianos relies on techniques completely unknown a decade or so ago – techniques which the craftsmen of the player piano age might have coveted or despised. Rubber cloth, tubing and delicate adjustments of suction have been replaced by computers and magnetic tapes. Here is a new harpsichord made in Boston by Eric Herz converted to automatic playing by Bill Edgerton of Darien, Connecticut. The player is a Marantz Pianocorder seen on the chair at the right and playing via signals from a cassette tape.

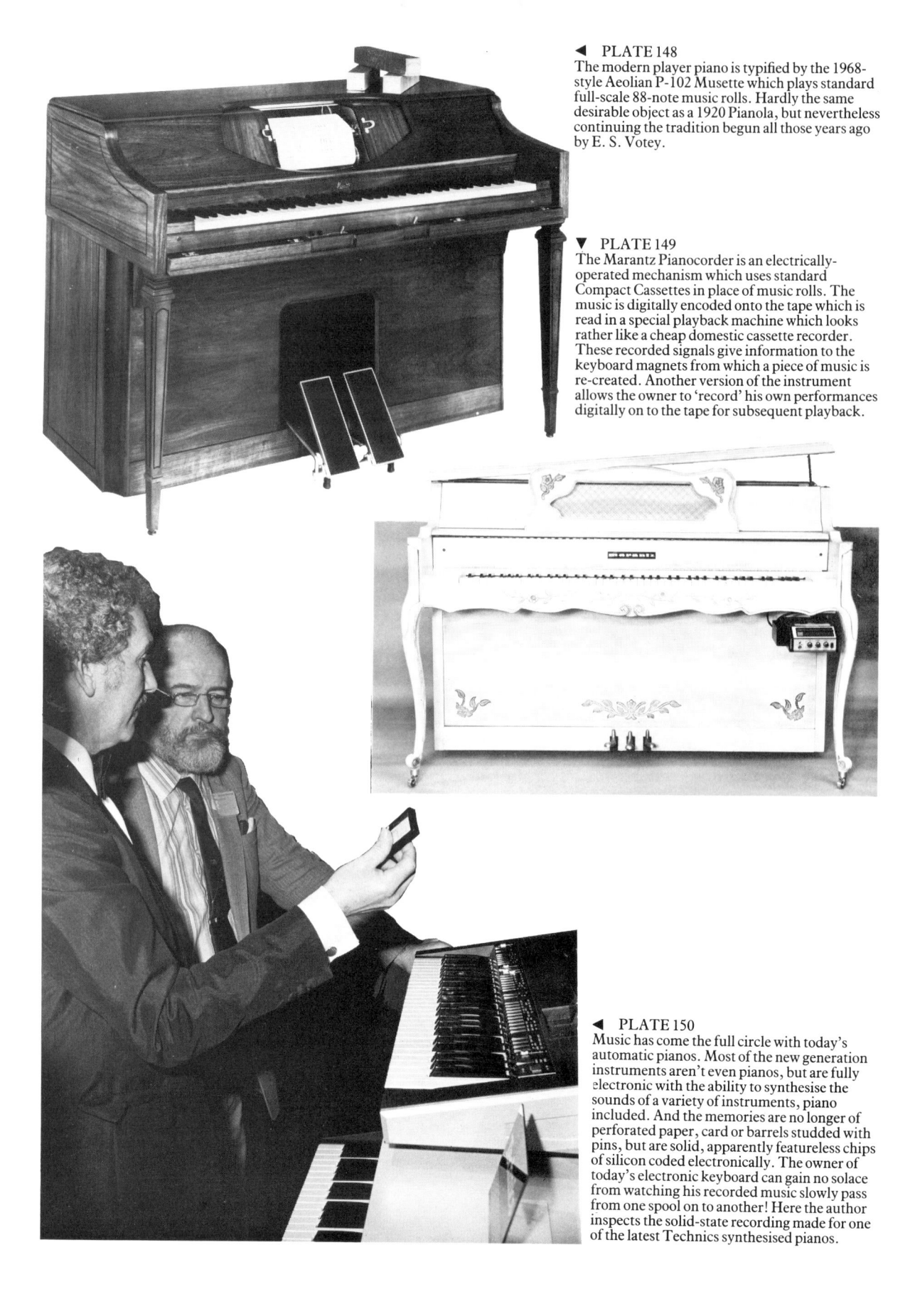

◀ PLATE 148
The modern player piano is typified by the 1968-style Aeolian P-102 Musette which plays standard full-scale 88-note music rolls. Hardly the same desirable object as a 1920 Pianola, but nevertheless continuing the tradition begun all those years ago by E. S. Votey.

▼ PLATE 149
The Marantz Pianocorder is an electrically-operated mechanism which uses standard Compact Cassettes in place of music rolls. The music is digitally encoded onto the tape which is read in a special playback machine which looks rather like a cheap domestic cassette recorder. These recorded signals give information to the keyboard magnets from which a piece of music is re-created. Another version of the instrument allows the owner to 'record' his own performances digitally on to the tape for subsequent playback.

◀ PLATE 150
Music has come the full circle with today's automatic pianos. Most of the new generation instruments aren't even pianos, but are fully electronic with the ability to synthesise the sounds of a variety of instruments, piano included. And the memories are no longer of perforated paper, card or barrels studded with pins, but are solid, apparently featureless chips of silicon coded electronically. The owner of today's electronic keyboard can gain no solace from watching his recorded music slowly pass from one spool on to another! Here the author inspects the solid-state recording made for one of the latest Technics synthesised pianos.

CHAPTER 14

List of Principal Makers, Patentees and Agents

❧

Any attempt at compiling a list of the makers of mechanical pianos must of necessity be somewhat arbitrary since there were so very many makers in all parts of the world. The earliest we can trace is the work of Bidermann, Langenbucher, and Runggel in the sixteenth and seventeenth centuries, whilst the eighteenth century reveals little if anything in the way of positively identifiable makers.

Street pianos or barrel pianos heralded from distant centres such as Italy, Spain, France and Germany. The Italians who sought their fortunes in foreign countries went to London, Barcelona, Nice, Paris, Belgium, New York – in fact they travelled far and wide. These makers, along with those who made similar instruments but who were of British origin such as the Hicks and Distins of Bristol and London, I have listed as fully as possible.

Perforated music, both in the form of cardboard and paper, played such a valuable part in the development of the self-acting piano that I have listed those who played an important part in its evolution and early application.

Pneumatically played pianofortes emanated from France, Germany and the United States, but by far the greatest contribution and the largest volume of player-piano production heralded from America. A number of later British piano manufacturers fitted imported American-made actions, particularly those produced by the Standard Player Action Company, and by the Canadian Otto Higel Company. Significantly, although British-made actions were devised and built, they were soon almost all ousted by American ones. Many British companies who sought to develop new actions did not succeed.

It is thus not only pointless but also quite impossible to list every maker of these later instruments, or to describe every particular modification employed by various builders. I have therefore chosen to deal only with the makers of player and reproducing pianos who contributed something of importance to history, and have also tried to list most of the makers of player pianos, since these were part of the formative period of the vast industry which was to follow.

Music rolls were produced by an equally large number of manufacturers throughout the world and once again any attempt at listing in entirety is quite impossible. It is only to be expected that, with the volume of player pianos being turned out, the largest number of roll makers were American and over fifty companies were engaged in the business of manufacturing rolls in the States. England also possessed quite a few, including subsidiary companies of both American and continental European makers. In the companion volume to this, *Restoring Pianolas*, I have devoted an Appendix to makes and makers of music rolls partly because the name on the roll can sometimes indicate the type of piano for which it was made and occasionally the make of the roll may be mistaken for that of the piano itself.

Throughout this listing, to avoid repetition in the case of the city of New York in New York State, where the city is specifically referred to the name of the state is omitted (for example Fifth Avenue, New York, USA). However, this only applies in that instance and hence Syracuse, for example, is still expanded as New York (the state), USA.

The changes in the names of countries which have taken place this century should also be borne in mind. Austro-Hungary was replaced in Germany by Czechoslovakia, and Russia in Europe became the Union of Soviet Socialist Republics in 1923 with the consequent change of the names of many towns and cities, for example St Petersburg. Because of this, geographical titles should be verified against the status of the date of the entry.

In conclusion, a listing of makers tends, on the face of it, to be about as entertaining as an evening spent reading the telephone directory. I have, I hope, overcome this problem by providing a brief synopsis of the activities associated with the various names, where applicable, usually offering additional data to those given in the preceding chapters. The enthusiast is therefore recommended to include this chapter in his reading, rather than to bypass it as an occasional reference section.

A.P.I. (AUTOPIANI-PIANOFORTI ITALIA), 20 corsa Lecce (17), Turin, Italy. Maker of player pianos, *fl.* 1930.

ACCENTIOLA-ADALBERT PIANO CO. See ADALBERT PIANO CO.

ACKOTIST PLAYER-PIANO CO, Fall River, Massachusetts. Inventors of the Pianotist kicking shoe player action based on the Hupfeld system. Two closely-related companies were the Pianotist Co. in America and the Ackerman Player Piano Co. of New York. See also under PIANOTIST CO. The Adek Manufacturing Co was also under the control of the same operation headed by Edwin D. Ackerman.

ADALBERT PIANO CO., 44 Commerce Road, Wood Green, London, N. Advertised in 1914 as makers of the Accentiola player piano. Previously known as ACCENTIOLA-ADALBERT PIANO CO.

ADAMS, GEORGE. Published in 1747 his *Adams' Micrographia Illustrated* in which is described, in a catalogue, '. . . a particularly new and curious Machine, containing a Movement which plays either an organ or Harpsichord (or both if desired) in a masterly manner'. The precise details of his device are today unknown.

AEOLIAN COMPANY, Aeolian Hall, Fifth Avenue and 34th Street, New York, and, later, 29 West 42nd Street. The empire founded by W. B. Tremaine in 1888 out of the Automatic Music Paper Co. of Boston began as the Aeolian Organ & Music Company making automatic organs. In 1892 he acquired all the patents of the Monroe Organ Reed Co. of Worcester and in 1895 introduced the Aeriol self-playing piano. In 1903 he organised the Aeolian, Weber Piano & Pianola Co. capitalised at $10,000,000 controlling the following subsidiary companies: The Aeolian Co., the Orchestrelle Co. (London), The Choralion Co. (Berlin), The Aeolian Co. (Paris), The Pianola Company Proprietary Ltd (Melbourne and Sydney), Weber Piano Co., George Steck & Co., Wheelock Piano Co., Stuyvesant Piano Co., Chilton Piano Co., Technola Piano Co., Votey Organ Co., Vocalian Organ Co., and the Universal Music Co. (piano-roll makers). These companies employed between them some 5,000 people world-wide and besides extensive piano factories in America included the Steck factory at Gotha in Germany, and Weber at Hayes in Middlesex, England. The total capital under Tremaine's control was $15·5m, which was more than the capital invested in the entire piano and organ industry in America in 1890. Aeolian finally amalgamated with its rival AMERICAN PIANO CORPORATION (q.v.) in 1932 and remains in business to this day. Makers and owners of the Pianola invented by E. S. VOTEY (q.v.). See also under TREMAINE.

LIST OF PRINCIPAL MAKERS, PATENTEES AND AGENTS

ALBAREDA, PABLO, 36 S. Pedro, Villafranca del Panadés, Spain. Agent and hirer for street pianos, *fl.* 1903.

D'ALESSANDRO, MICH, Casalincontrada, Chieta, Italy. Barrel-piano maker, *fl.* 1930.

ALLEVI, FRANCESCO, Corso Carlo Alberto, Porta Milano, Vercelli, Italy. A maker of street pianos who flourished in the early part of this century.

ALMINANA, ENRIQUE, 109 Marquès del Dueco, Barcelona, Spain. Barrel pinner and piano maker who was associated with the business of CASALI (q.v.) around 1920.

ALVAREZ, JOSE, BELMEZ, Cordoba, Spain. Maker of street pianos, *fl.* 1903.

AMBRIDGE & SON, Fountayne Road, Broad Lane, Tottenham, north London. Makers of the Paragon piano player, *fl.* 1909.

AMELIO, GIACOMO, Mondovi, Cuneo, Italy. Barrel piano maker, *fl.* 1930.

AMELOTTI, VVE, Nice, France. An Italian by birth, Amelotti made coin-freed café pianos and large barrel-playing mechanical jazz bands. A specimen of the latter by this early twentieth-century maker has a 39-note wooden-framed, overstrung piano, side drum with four sticks, bass drum coupled with cymbal (one stick), eight tubular metal bells, two temple blocks. The distributor for northern France was S. Rolleau of Nantes, whose name sometimes appears as well as that of Amelotti. See ROBUSCHI, CASTAUD.

AMERICAN PHOTO PLAYER CO., 62 West 45th Street, New York; 64 E. Jackson Boulevard, Chicago, Illinois; 109 Golden Gate Avenue, San Francisco, California. Factory at Berkeley, California. Based in San Francisco, this company was founded around 1908 and named its products 'Fotoplayers'. The last was manufactured around 1925 although models were still being sold from stock as late as 1928. Following financial problems in 1922, the business was restructured and, by 1925, the operators were the Robert Morton Organ Company of Van Nuys, California.

AMERICAN PIANO CO., Knabe Building, 437 Fifth Avenue, corner 39th Street, New York, USA. Formed in the summer of 1908 by the amalgamation of the William Knabe Co., Chickering & Sons, and Foster-Armstrong Co. The new business controlled the manufacture and sale of the following pianos: Chickering (est. 1823), Knabe (1837), Haines Brothers (1851), Marshall & Wendell (1853), Foster & Co. (1892), Armstrong (1893), Brewster (1895), and J. B. Cook Co. (1900). The combined output of the three founding companies with their various brands was said to be 18,000 pianos per year at the time of amalgamation, so making the combine the greatest piano industry in the world. In 1924, the company acquired Mason & Hamlin and later also several other companies including Franklin, Gabler, Holmes & Co., Laffarge, J. & C. Fischer. In 1932 the company amalgamated with AEOLIAN (q.v.) as Aeolian-American, so also acquiring Steck, Stroud, Weber, Wheelock and others. The company moved almost immediately into the design and manufacture of players and in 1914 introduced an electric piano player called the American Electrelle which could be incorporated into any existing grand or upright. This was claimed to have been 'the perfected result of years of work and experiment by the best mechanical skill' and to have cost half a million dollars to perfect. In 1915, the company produced the Flexotone-Electrelle which was a combination pneumatic/electric piano player. The company then introduced the Ampico reproducing piano and formed an operating organisation called AMPICO CORPORATION (q.v.).

AMERICAN PIANO PLAYER CO., 828–840 South 26th Street, Louisville, Kentucky, USA. Founded by George S. Williams in 1909, this company carried a capital stock of $25,000 (according to Q. David Bowers) and purchased a 100,000 sq. ft factory from the American Tobacco Company to produce a player piano with the mechanism, including spoolbox, mounted under the keyboard. Bowers relates that most of the parts appear to have been made by Wurlitzer. The action of the mechanism was, however, not perfected and involved the company in costly repairs. As a result of this, the business became overextended and was declared bankrupt on 1 December 1910. Only one instrument is known to survive.

AMERICAN PLAYER ACTION CO., 2595 Third Avenue, New York, USA. Makers of 'improved' player actions which featured the capability of having all adjustments carried out from the front. Also sometime at 437 Fifth Avenue.

AMERICAN PLAYER PIANO CO., 15–19 Canal Place, New York, USA. Makers of a player with this name c. 1910.

AMPHION PIANO PLAYER CO., Elbridge, New York, USA. Established in 1898 as makers of the Amphion and Maestro piano player. Then as:

AMPHION CO., Syracuse, New York, USA. Specialist in the manufacture of high-quality player-piano actions. Introduced the Artecho reproducing action as well as its own Dynachord 'Art Expression Player'. Was eventually acquired by American Piano Company (the makers of Ampico) and Amphion technology appeared in all the early and Model A Ampico reproducing instruments. Amphion was also a co-owner, with Wurlitzer, of the Apollo Piano Co. Amphion's Artecho reproducing action was also known as the Celco under which name it was installed in Emerson, Lindeman and A. B. Chase instruments. Advertised 'the new Amphion Accessible Action' with demountable valve and striking pneumatic units.

AMPICO CORPORATION, 27 West 57th Street, New York, USA. Established in 1915 by the American Piano Company (hence the name: AMerican PIano COrp). Manufacturers of the Ampico reproducing piano action as initially invented by Charles F. Stoddard. President was George G. Foster and, besides Stoddard, the research and development department included the youthful and talented Dr Clarence N. Hickman and John Anderson from Chickering. The development work was formerly located at 38th Street, but moved into the new Chickering building in 57th Street. During 1925 and 1926, Hickman developed a machine for recording dynamics of the piano using the spark chronograph technique. In 1932, the company merged with Aeolian into Aeolian-American Corporation. A London company was formed in the early years; this was Ampico Limited, 233 Regent House, London W1, and the company survives today, its business being connected with aluminium windows and the building trade.

ANDERSSON, ANDERS GUSTAF and JONES WILHELM. The brothers Andersson lived in the village of Näshult near Vetlanda, Sweden. They produced an improved version of NILSSON (q.v.) Pianoharpa which they patented in Sweden as number 2239 of 13 August 1889. It was shallower than the original instrument. Each barrel played 12 tunes and there was a choice of any three of a total of 12 barrels offered to the customer.

ANELLI (SOC. ANELLI), 3 p. Castello, Cremona, Italy. Player piano makers, fl. 1930.

ANTONELLI, DOMENICO, 59 Great Ancoats Street and 2/4 Blossom Street, Manchester. Described as 'Manufacturer of Piano-Organs', Antonelli produced clockwork barrel pianos and in November 1901 was granted a British patent for a coin-feed, clockwork barrel piano, incorporating a method of removing the barrel for changing without disturbing the rest of the mechanism.

ANTONIAZZI, ANDREW. An Italian who established the B.A.B. ORGAN CO. (q.v.) in Manhattan, having spent six years with MASERATI (q.v.). He made street barrel pianos.

APOLLO MUSIKWERKE MAX ESPENHAIN & CO., Dorotheenstrasse 27, Leipzig-Gohlis. Makers of pneumatic-action orchestrions and orchestrion pianos, fl. 1903.

APRUZZESE, ANTONIO, Carrera de S. Francisco (El Crande) 7, Madrid 5, Spain. An Italian who went to Spain in 1883, Apruzzese settled in Salamanca where he made street barrel pianos or 'organillos', as they are known in Spain. In 1906 the firm bearing his name moved to Madrid where it still exists today under Antonio Apruzzese, who was born in 1906 and is the last surviving member of the family, and is the only barrel-piano restorer left in Madrid.

ARNO, ANTONIO, 17, San Jeronimo, Barcelona, Spain. Street-piano hirer, fl. 1909.

AROSIO, EMILIO, Corso Roma 39, Lodi, Milan, Italy. Founded in 1893 as maker of barrel pianos and musical instrument dealer, fl. 1909.

ARRIGONI & CO., JOHN, 158 Great College Street, London NW. 'Also at Baden Baden, Steam Works, Bruder & Sons, Waldkirch'. Advertised in 1892 as barrel piano and street organ maker. His association with Bruder, a maker of street pipe organs, suggests that he was an agent and probably not a manufacturer of these. By 1896, he had been absorbed by Cocchi, Bacigalupo & Graffigna at the same address and his position with the firm was that of manager. However, two years later, the firm reverted to J. N. Arrigoni & Co. at the same address. By 1912 Arrigoni was at 62 Halliford Street, Islington, advertising as a mechanical-piano maker. A cabinet-maker by trade, he had come from Italy and began by doing street organ and piano repairs. He was still in business in 1922, as witnessed by his signature inside a street organ with that date.

ARTROLA PLAYER CO., 506 Republic Building, Chicago, Illinois, USA. Makers of the Artrola player action for pianos.

ARVATI, CLAUDIO, Mantya, Italy. Maker of barrel pianos, *fl.* 1930.

ASSERETO, ANTONIO, Via Modre di Dio 5r, Genoa, Italy. Agent for barrel pianos, *fl.* 1909.

ATKINSON, C. W. See BANSALL & SONS.

AUBRY, EMILE, 200 rue Lafayette, Paris, France. An engineer who, with Gabriel Boreau, invented the Violiniste pneumatic violin-player combined with a piano in 1926.

AUTO PNEUMATIC ACTION CO., 653 West 51st Street, New York, USA. Manufacturers of the Welte-Mignon (Licensee) reproducing player-piano action, which played standard-width white paper rolls, as distinct from the original or 'red Welte' which was made in Germany and played 13½-inch-wide music rolls of red paper. The parent company was KOHLER INDUSTRIES (q.v.) and the original Welte-Mignon (Licensee) patents were in their name.

AUTONA CO., 23 Court Street, Boston, Massachusetts, USA. Patented an 'inner player' player piano in June 1899, which featured the music roll attached to a hinged spools frame under the keyboard. It is not known if this was ever built or produced, but it certainly was several years ahead of the successful inner player actions.

AUTO-GRAND PIANO CO., Newcastle, Indiana, USA. Established in 1904 by Albert Krell for the manufacture of the Auto-Grand piano player.

AUTOMATIC MUSICAL CO., Binghamton, New York, USA. Founded *c.* 1900 by two brothers named Harris, it produced a number of electric pianos as well as being involved with two violin-playing machines, both called Royal Violista and designed by Professor Wauters. About 1910, the company entered financial problems and a committee of creditors was formed to operate the concern. This was headed by Edwin A. Link who was with the Schaff Piano Company from which the Harrises bought their pianos for conversion. Link saw the potential of the company, left Schaff, and refinanced the business. Now called the Link Piano Company, production restarted in 1913 and in 1916 the business became incorporated. Production was around 300 coin-operated pianos and 12 or more theatre organs a year. The premises were at 183–185 Water Street and there was an office at 532 Republic Buildings in Chicago. Link used basic pianos supplied by Haddorff Piano Co. of Rockford, Illinois. The business ceased in the late 1920s.

AUTOMATIC MUSICAL & DEVICE CO., 22 Fifth Street, San Francisco, California, USA. Dealer in electric pianos, *fl.* 1909.

AUTOMATIC MUSICAL INSTRUMENT COMPANY, 27 Penton Street, London N. Company set up in 1884 to market the Miranda Pianista, a push-up player originally invented by Thibouville-Lamy, Paris. The Miranda, premiered at the Furniture Exhibition at the Agricultural Hall, Islington, London, was to be factored by musical instrument agent, dealer and representative Ellis Parr who was the co-patentee of the Symphonion musical box which played discs. Construction of the Miranda was to be undertaken in Germany by Haake, the German piano makers in Hanover whose pianos Parr already distributed in London. Parr first advertised the Miranda Pianista in July 1885 from his premises at 99 Oxford Street. Immediately Jérôme Thibouville-Lamy of Charterhouse Street in London wrote to the trade press advising that the Miranda was covered by his patents and was a superseded early type of his design. No more was heard of the Miranda and the AMIC and its holding company, Automatic Music Company of 3 Copthall Buildings, London EC, quietly faded away.

AUTOPIANO COMPANY, 12th Avenue, 51st and 52nd Streets, New York, USA. Makers of the Autopiano player piano, also the Triumph and Pianista cabinet piano players. Established in 1903 by R. W.

Lawrence, made only player pianos. Described as being one of the first concerns to market a successful player piano, the first being shipped in 1904. Its premises were also said to form the largest player-piano factory in the world. One model of its player was equipped with the Welte-Mignon action. The Company was described in 1920 as having $1m capital stock, fully paid up. In 1915, made one of the earliest electrically pumped player pianos.

AUTOPLAYER CO. LTD, THE BRITISH, 126 New Bond Street, London W1. Produced 65-note music rolls until the mid-1920s.

AUTO PNEUMATIC ACTION CO., 653 West 51st Street, New York, USA. Manufacturers of the Welte-Mignon (Licensee) action. President of the APAC was W. C. Heaton whose company developed the Licensee, a foot-operated (i.e. non-electric) version of the German Welte-Mignon.

B.A.B. ORGAN CO., 336 Water Street, Manhattan, USA. Founded in 1912 by an Italian, Andrew Antoniazzi, who had been with Maserati for six years. Antoniazzi was joined in partnership by Borna and the firm began by making street pianos. Later on, Dominic Brugnolotti, formerly with Molinari, joined, and the firm converted a number of cardboard-playing organs to a new system of their own using double-track paper rolls. Later still, they took over the old Molinari factory in Brooklyn and built organs. Fried relates that Brugnolotti and Borna died, and Antoniazzi sold the remains of the business to former Senator Charles Bovey of Virginia City.

BACCHETTA, CAMILLO, 4 via Lodi, Crema, Cremona, Italy. Maker of clockwork barrel pianos, *fl.* 1930.

BACIGALUPI, PETER, 1261 Market Street, Nr Hotel Whitcomb, San Francisco, California, USA. Descended from the street-organ-building family of Bacigalupo, this branch of the family altered the name to Bacigalupi. Peter held the San Francisco distribution rights for a number of American mechanical pianos, including Wurlitzer, Cremona and North Tonawanda.

BACIGALUPO, GIOVANNI, 79 Schönhauser Allee, Berlin N, Germany. Born 25 July 1889. Formerly of the Cocchi company in London, he set up in business in 1900 in Berlin and produced six different small street organs. He was also a maker of street barrel pianos. As Bacigalupo-Söhne at 74a Schönhauser Allee as street-organ repairer until his death on 10 July 1978.

BAGA, CONSTANTINE, 5a Bakers Row, London EC. Maker of barrel pianos from 1890 to 1892.

BAILLEUL, L., 23 place de Rihour, Lille, France. Maker of mechanical pianos, *fl.* 1909.

BAKER & CO., LTD, G. F., Xaltona House, Leeke Street Corner, King's Cross Road, London WC1. Established 1897, this sundries house advertised in January 1932 that they had been appointed wholesale distributors for Meloto and Universal Player Rolls. The company already distributed Muvis rolls made by the Up-to-Date Music Roll Co. These full-scale rolls classified as dance, popular and classic, sold at 2s 6d each with a tester at the same price. Meloto and Universals were classified at this time as dance, song and classic at 3s, 4s 6d and 5s 6d each. Baker's information leaflet on converting a 65-note piano to play 88-note rolls ran into a fourth reprint as late as the early part of 1936. At that last stage the company reported that its sales of Muvis and Universal rolls were holding up well.

BALDWIN PIANO CO., 267 Wabash Avenue, Chicago, Illinois, USA. Established 1862. Made the Manualo, 'the player piano that is all but human', advertised in 1920.

BANSALL & SONS, Albert Works, Clarence Road, Hackney, London NE. Made the Universal Piano Player patented in 1909 by C. W. Atkinson (Pat. No. 1439). This novel detachable player fitted against the front edge of the keyboard and when not in use was small enough to fit inside the piano stool. Dual standard 65/88 note rolls could be played. The player action (bellows and chest) remained fitted into the piano. It is illustrated in Appendix A. Bansall also made the Aristos player piano and Atkinson took out many patents including several for roll motors built into spools.

BARRATT & ROBINSON, 288–310 York Way, Kings Cross, London N7. Founded in 1872, this piano maker was set up by the brother of Tom Barratt who built up the famous soap business of A. & F. Pears, and James Robinson who was also a pioneer of amateur photography. The business made a number of small pianos and players for use in boats and yachts, one model being the Pedaleon shown by them at Olympia in 1913. The company also had the distinction of making what was

LIST OF PRINCIPAL MAKERS, PATENTEES AND AGENTS

probably the last player piano in England as late as 1937. This was the Minstrelle Autopiano – a very small instrument indeed. During the 1930s, Barratt & Robinson took over TRIUMPH-AUTO LTD (q.v.). See also under KASTNER.

BASTIDA, RAMON, 21 Pizarro, Valencia, Spain. Street-barrel-piano manufacturer, *fl.* 1909.

BATES & SON, THEODORE CHARLES. Organ builder who also made a large number of quality barrel organs for use in churches and the home. During the second half of the nineteenth century, Bates also made barrel pianos powered by weight-driven clockwork which were either solely mechanical or of the barrel-and-finger variety for normal playing as well as automatic performance. The business of Bates underwent several changes of address and style (see *Barrel Organ* by the present author) but instruments have been seen bearing their address at 6 Ludgate Hill which, from research by Langwill, dates them between 1833 and 1847.

BATTAGLIA, MERCURIO, Ragusa Inferiore, Syracuse, Italy. Barrel-piano maker *fl.* 1930. Also made street organs.

BAYLIS & SON, JOHN, 60 Great Saffron Hill, London. Described on their trade label as being a 'Manufacturer of Barrel Organs', they also advised that they could provide 'Old Barrels re-set to Modern Music'. The label was illustrated with an engraving of a Hicks-style portable street piano (see Fig. 12). No dates have so far been traced.

BECACRIA, LUIGI, Cassine, Alessandria, Italy. Church organ builder who also made barrel pianos, *fl.* 1930.

BECHSTEIN-WELTE, 65 South Molton Street, London W1. The London address of WELTE (q.v.) and that of the make of piano which specialised in the Welte installation, *fl.* 1926.

BEDOS de CELLES, FRANÇOIS. Born 1709, died 1779. A Benedictine of St Maur, Dom Bedos de Celles was both an organ builder and a writer on music and he published his monumental three-volume work *L'Art du Facteur d'Orgues* ('The Organ-builder's Art') between 1766 and 1778. Still a classic reference work, it contained an expansion of the teachings of ENGRAMELLE (q.v.) and devoted considerable space and many superb engravings to the craft of mechanical organ making and the arrangement of music for barrel pinning. His work on barrel pricking has been translated into English (*The Mechanics of Mechanical Music*, Arthur W. J. G. Ord-Hume, 1973).

BEHR BROTHERS & CO., 11th Avenue and 29th Street, New York, USA. Maker of the Behr piano player, *c.* 1899.

BELLOTTI, DITTA, Via Savonarola 17–19, Alessandria, Italy. Established in 1868 as maker of barrel pianos. Exhibited two instruments at the Turin National Exhibition of 1884. Also had premises at Via Alessandria 3, Acqui. By 1930, business was at 27 Via Savonarola making pneumatic pianos.

BENDEL, CARL, Saulgau, Wurttemberg, Germany. Founded in 1892 for the manufacture of piano orchestrions, handling and distribution of mechanical musical instruments and phonographs. Manufactured book-playing pianos operated automatically by hot-air engines as well as clockwork models; *fl.* 1909.

BERETTO, GIUSEPPE, Via Cardano 46, Pavia, Italy. Agent and hirer of street pianos, *fl.* 1909.

BERGEL, JOSEF, Töpferg 9, Rumburg, Bohemia. Maker of barrel pianos and piano orchestrions, *fl.* 1903.

BERLINER ORCHESTRION-FABRIK FRANZ HANKE & CO., GmbH, 39 Chausseestrasse 88, Berlin N, Germany. Established in 1900. Makers of piano-orchestrions and electric pianos.

BERMEJO, VICTOR, 50 Avemaria, Madrid, Spain. Maker of street pianos, *fl.* 1903.

BERNASCONI, GIUSEPPE E FIGLIO, Via Galliari 6, Treviglio, Bergamo, Italy. Founded in 1904 as a maker of barrel pianos and handler of musical instruments. By 1930 the business was at 10 via San Gallo in Treviglio and advertised as makers of barrel pianos and both clockwork and electric instruments. Probably related to:

BERNASCONI, SILVIO, Treviglio, Bergamo, Italy. Maker of street organs, *fl.* 1930.

BERRY-WOOD PIANO PLAYER CO., 20th and Wyandotte Streets, and Southwest Boulevard and 20th Streets, Kansas City, USA. Also offices and factory at 348–50 Canal Place, New York. Makers of coin-operated pianos and orchestrions. Introduced first model in 1911. Opened a branch in San Francisco, but the whole business ceased completely before 1920.

BERTHOLD & CO., JULIUS, Klingenthal, Saxony, Germany. Makers of roll-perforating machinery for making piano rolls.

BERUTTI, LUIGI, 180 bis strada Casale, Turin, Italy. Maker of player pianos, barrel pianos and electric pianos, *fl.* 1930.

BIANCHI, B., Gambolo, Pavia, Italy. Barrel-piano maker, *fl.* 1930.

BIDERMANN, SAMUEL, Augsburg, Germany. Born 1540; died 1622. Maker of small mechanical spinets with keyboards, barrels and clockwork motors. A skilled maker of musical automata who also used water to power some of his pieces. At least three of his clockwork spinets are still in existence.

BIDERMANN, SAMUEL, Jnr. Born 1600; died 1647. Maker of musical automata including a sewing basket with an organ mechanism prior to 1625. Also at work with clockwork spinets. See also reference under LANGENBUCHER.

BIDERMANN, B. Most probably related to the family of Samuel Bidermann, he made mechanical spinets which played from barrels during the 1740s.

BISO & CAMPODONICO, Piazza Verdi 23, Spezia, Genoa, Italy. Founded by Biso and Giuseppe Campodonico for the manufacture of pianos, harmoniums and barrel pianos and the distribution of other musical instruments, *fl.* 1909.

BLESSING, WOLFGANG, Unterkirnach, Germany. The Blessing family became famed for the manufacture of orchestrion organs through Martin Blessing (1774–1847), Jacob Blessing (1799–1879), and Wolfgang Blessing with other members of the family until the main business closed during the 1920s. Repair work was carried on right up into the 1950s. It was around 1910 that Blessing introduced the Beethophon reproducing piano, a short-lived entry into this market. This played special hand-played rolls but never entered volume production: it was discontinued by 1914.

BLUTHNER & CO. LTD, 7, 9, 11 and 13 Wigmore Street, Cavendish Square, London W1. Advertised as 'an English company registered in 1896, and all Shareholders are British-Born Subjects'. Fitted Hupfeld actions into reproducing pianos.

BOCCARENA, GIUSEPPE, Rieti, Perugia, Italy. Barrel organ and piano maker, *fl.* 1930.

BOCKISCH, KARL. Born in 1878 the son of a family of Alsace vintners, Karl Bockisch was brought up in Anaheim, California, which was a community founded by German immigrant farmers. The family was unable to make a success of its new home and so finally returned to Germany where Karl married the daughter of EMIL WELTE. By 1900, Bockisch had become so closely involved with the family business that he had virtually assumed control as manager and decision maker for the Welte company. It was he who first conceived the idea of the reproducing player piano which, despite his protest, became known as the Welte-Mignon. Hugo Popper of Leipzig became a close friend of Bockisch (relates Bowers) and during the first decade of this century they maintained close business ties with collaboration extending to the co-production of orchestrions. The Mignon was introduced in 1905. Popper died in 1910 after which time sales of the Mignon in Germany and America, hitherto largely Popper's province, reverted to Welte and Popper's company promoted its own reproducing piano, the Stella. But it was Popper who organised most of the recording contracts with artists to make rolls for the Mignon. Bockisch died in 1952.

BONAFEDE, GIUSEPPE, 15 via Ricasoli, Rome, Italy. Barrel pianos, *fl.* 1930.

BONINI, U., 4 via Alboino, Pavia, Italy. Maker of barrel pianos, *fl.* 1930.

BORELLA, JUAN, 8 Tabernillas Commandante and 14 Cirujeda, Madrid, Spain. Established in 1860 as makers of street barrel pianos, *fl.* 1903.

BORNO, FRATELLI, Ragusa Inferiore, Syracuse, Italy. Barrel piano maker, *fl.* 1930, also made street organs.

BOUFFIER, Milan, Italy. Exhibited a barrel piano at the National Exhibition held in Turin in the summer of 1884.

BOURQUIN, EDUARD JACQUES, 10 rue des Petites Écuries, Paris, France. Bourquin was a Swiss engineer

LIST OF PRINCIPAL MAKERS, PATENTEES AND AGENTS

who was making mechanical barrel pianos in Paris and musical boxes from about 1885 onwards. In 1922, he applied the so-called revolver mechanism to a mechanical piano. Each of the multiple barrels played one tune or selection and, as the barrel played, it rotated on a spiral, so allowing long musical pieces to be performed. At the conclusion of one barrel, the revolver mechanism would automatically index another barrel into place and so on.

BOYD PIANOS LTD, New Bond Street, London W. Made the only British cabinet-style piano player as:

BOYD LTD, 19 Holborn, London EC. Makers of the Boyd piano player, 65-note instrument sold for £27 10s with six rolls of music, c. 1908. Produced an unusual player-piano c. 1914 which was called the Pistonola. This all-metal action was designed by two university students and employed, as its name implied, pneumatic cylinders and pistons for all the functions of the instrument. Even the foot treadles were coupled to reciprocating pistons in cylinders and the air reservoir was a further cylinder. The method made for a neat and compact mechanism, but it was said to have been difficult to regulate properly. The instrument was later called the Terpreter. Boyds also fitted conventional player actions into their upright pianos. The Boyd Autoplayer was made in several sizes, among them what was called the world's smallest player piano – the Model Six. Full-scale action, accenting device and all controls were packed into a piano just 3ft 9in. high, 4ft 9in. wide and 2ft 1in. from front to back (but see under BARRATT & ROBINSON). The Terpreter was the developed form of the Pistonola and models 1, 2 and 3 were priced at 160 (one and two) and 150 guineas (model 3).

BRAIDA, GIOVANNI, Cuneo, Italy. Barrel-piano maker, *fl.* 1930.

BRAUN, FRANZ, Hutbergasse 8, Rumburg, Bohemia. Established in 1895 as makers of barrel pianos.

BREWER-PRYOR PIANO MFG. CO., Binghamton, New York, USA. Makers of automatic pianos and also harps. Showrooms and shop at 728 Main Street, Buffalo, New York.

BRITISH AUTOMATIC PIANO SYNDICATE LTD. Established at the end of 1901 with £5,000 capital in £1 shares. No further details.

BRITISH PLAYER ACTION CO. LTD, Stour Road, London E3. Makers of the Arcadian player action and Arcadian player upright piano. Advertised in 1930 as 'the latest development and ideal in its responsiveness'. Also had premises at 17 Crouch Hill, Finsbury Park, London N4.

BROADWOOD & SONS LTD, JOHN, Conduit Street, London W. Founded in 1723. Famed pianoforte makers which produced the Broadwood player action (see Chapter 4).

BROWN, THEODORE P., 7 May Street, Worcester, Massachusetts, USA. Maker of reed organs who invented a piano with interior playing mechanism under patents granted on 7 April, 15 June, 7 and 14 December 1897. Went on to make cabinet players under the name Simplex which sold for $225 in 1899.

BRUDER LOOS, 97–8 Seestädtl, Bohemia. Established in 1847 as makers of orchestrion pianos and mechanical organs.

BRUGGER & FURTWENGLER, Staraja Basmannaja, Haus Raichinstein, Moscow, Russia. Established in 1832 as manufacturers of organs and mechanical musical instruments. Were making barrel organs and orchestrion organs in 1903 as well as acting as agents for piano orchestrions and barrel pianos.

BRUN, J. M., 23–27, Cours Victor Hugo, Saint-Étienne (Loire), France. Makers of cylinder piano orchestrions and café pianos under the name Le Brunophone, also electric piano orchestrions which were coin-freed and provided with lighting effects; *fl.* 1920.

BRUSASCO, VITT., Via San Chaira 54, Turin, Italy. Barrel piano agent, *fl.* 1909.

BRUSCO, BARTOLOMÉ, 34 Cadena, Barcelona, Spain. Barrel-piano maker, *fl.* 1903.

BRUSCO, JUAN, 15 Rosal, Barcelona, Spain. Barrel-piano maker, *fl.* 1903–9.

BRUTTAPASTA, CESARE, 15 via Montoro, Rome, Italy. Maker of street barrel pianos with factory at 98 via Flaminia, *fl.* 1930.

BUSSON, Paris, France. Built a harmonium in 1894 which played six Strauss waltzes, among other tunes, and which could be played either by a keyboard or by a pinned barrel.

BUZZI, AGOSTINO, Mondovi, Cuneo, Italy. Barrel piano maker, *fl.* 1930. Also made barrel-and-finger pianos.

CABLE COMPANY, 240 Wabash Avenue, Chicago, Illinois, USA. Established in 1881 as piano makers. Famed maker of player pianos one of which, the Euphona Home Electric, could either be pedalled or operated electrically.

CADINI ET CIE, 13 Rue Assalit, Nice, France. A maker of barrel pianos, *fl.* 1903.

CALAME, ROBERTO V., Calle Uruguay 183, Salto Oriental, Uruguay. Est. 1907 as importers of musical instruments including 'Phonolas and Angelus'.

CALMONT & CO., LTD, S., 83 New Oxford Street, London W. Retailer of the Musetta piano player, *c.* 1909.

CALVO, IGNACIC, 13 Caravaca, Madrid, Spain. Barrel-piano maker and repairer, *fl.* 1909.

CAMPODOMINICO, GIUSEPPE, Via Genova, Spezia, Lugria, Italy. Agent for street pianos *c.* 1903.

CAMPORA, FRATELLI, Vico Orti San Andrea 32, Genoa, Italy. A maker of barrel organs and barrel pianos for street use, *fl.* 1903.

CANOVA, JOSEPH PIANA, 16 Sekforde Street, Clerkenwell, London EC. Patented a tremolo action for barrel pianos on 24 September 1902. He was probably a technician/mechanic working for one of the manufacturers, since his name is not recorded as a maker.

CANOVA, VINCENT, and HARTLEY, HENRY. See under HARTLEY.

CAPDEVILLE, V., SOCIÉTÉ DU 'PIANISTE EXECUTANT', 19 pass. Ménil-Montant, Paris. A maker of mechanical pianos, *fl.* 1903, who may have been in association with ULLMANN (q.v.).

CAPRA & CO., ALEXANDER, 11 & 13 Hatton Yard, Hatton Wall, London EC. Founded by Alessandro Capra, they advertised as manufacturers of barrel pianos in 1890. The firm ceased business in 1894, probably when Capra went into partnership with G. B. RISSONE (q.v.).

CAPRA, RISSONE, & DETOMA, 30 Great Warner Street, Clerkenwell, London EC. A British Patent number 4725 dated 16 November 1880 was granted to A. Capra, J. B. Rissone and S. Detoma for an improvement to a piano action whereby the instrument could be played manually or mechanically via a pinned barrel. Of normal upright piano format, the barrel mechanism fitted under the keyboard in a suitably wide and deep belly with a winding handle at the right. Called the 'Per Omnes Pianoforte'. The inventors advertised in 1881: 'The attention of the Profession and Trade is called to the above Patented Pianoforte, which can be played either by the ordinary Key-board, or by a handle, thus supplying an Instrument suitable alike for the Tutored and Untutored. Any tune can be played on these splendid instruments. The "Per Omnes" arrangement can be attached to any Piano as at a small cost. Barrel Pianos supplied with all the Latest Improvements. Stock always on hand. Great attention paid to Pianos for Export. List and Designs on application.' This is the only reference so far traced to Capra, Rissone & Detoma although RISSONE (q.v.) seems to have remained in business for some while under his own name.

CAPRA, RISSONE & CO., 30 Warner Street, Clerkenwell, London EC. Manufacturers of street barrel pianos who advertised in 1886. Alexander Capra was originally in business on his own until taking Rissone as a partner. Rissone subsequently took over the business in his own name (see RISSONE).

CAPRA & CO., 20 Warner Street, London EC. Alexander Capra was advertising as a barrel-piano manufacturer under this title in 1887.

CARCHENA, ANGEL, 4 & 6 Cabestreras, Madrid, Spain. Maker of street pianos, *fl.* 1903.

CARINZIO, L., Via Ricatti, Treviso, Italy. Barrel piano agent and repairer, *fl.* 1909.

CARPENTIER, JULES. Born in Paris in 1851, Carpentier became a student at the Polytechnique and studied for a career as a precision-instrument constructor. However, he became fascinated by the science of electricity and in particular telegraphy. His early work as a railway engineer was transcended by his electrical inventions and he exhibited electrically operated musical mechanisms at the International Electriciy Exhibition held in Paris in 1880, among his inventions was a recording harmonium or Melograph by the use of which musical notes could be marked for punching into long strips of paper which could later be played back on a key-top piano-playing attachment which he called the Melotrope. He claimed the invention of both instruments although the principle had been used earlier by others. Even so, he did show the first pneumatic instrument of piano form in 1887 in France, in which year he placed it before the French Academy. In 1903 he was selling the Melograph and Melotrope at 16–20 rue Delambre. Carpentier was also involved in the making of the first phonograph designed by Charles Cros, which preceded the invention of Thomas Edison by some months.

CASALI, LUIS, 38 Amalia and 10 Flores, Barcelona, Spain. An Italian who settled in Barcelona during the 1880s and began manufacturing barrel pianos. His partners were Pombia (who owned the business and was responsible for the manufacture of the instruments) and Subiranda (who scored and arranged music for the barrels). Ultimately, Pombia left the business and probably returned to Italy (see POMBIA), whereupon Casali described himself as 'successor to Pombia' on his letterheads. The business was variously at Torres Amati 1 and at Poniente 88. Gold medals for their instruments were awarded in Spain and Brussels in 1886 and 1895 and the business was still functioning in 1909. Makers of some very good instruments.

CAUS, SALOMON DE. A French engineer who, whilst in the service of the Elector Palatine in about 1600, described in his book *Les Raisons des Forces Mouvantes* the method of pinning music to a barrel and illustrated his words with six bars from a madrigal by Alessandro Striggio.

CAZORLA, LUIS, 14 Agula, Madrid, Spain. Barrel-piano maker and hirer, *fl.* 1909.

CAZZULLO, ALBERTO, 24 R. vico Dragone, Genoa, Italy. Maker and repairer of barrel pianos, *fl.* 1930.

CESA, CARLO, Casa Bergonzolli, Novara, Italy. A maker of barrel pianos and organs for street use, *fl.* 1903.

CHANCELLOR & SON, Lower Sackville Street, Dublin, Eire. Advertised as 'photographers, jewellers, watch & clock manufacturers, opticians &c', this firm was distributor of the German Piano Orchestrion driven by a hot-air motor.

CHASE & BAKER, Jewett Avenue and Belt Line, Buffalo, New York, USA. Established by George A. Baker in 1900 for the manufacture of player pianos and music rolls. New York branch at 10 East 34th Street, and one in Chicago at 209 State Street. A prolific and important industry in the early days of piano players and player pianos. New York salesroom: 236 Fifth Avenue.

CHASE & BAKER PIANO PLAYER CO. LTD, 45–7 Wigmore Street, London W. Distributors of Chase & Baker player pianos, piano players and music rolls, the piano players under the name Pianosona, *c.* 1909.

CHIAPPA LTD, 6 Little Bath Street, Holborn, London (now renamed 31 Eyre Street Hill, Clerkenwell Road, London EC1). Fair-organ makers and repairers who are still in business. Founded in 1864 by an Italian, Giuseppe Chiappa, at an address near Farringdon Road. He subsequently went to America and started a barrel-piano and fair-organ manufactory in New York. However, he soon returned to London to organise a factory at the present location. He made street pianos, street organs, street harmoniums, skating rink bands, clockwork pianos and café pianos. These last played an improved form of Jacquard card-music as well as being available with barrels. He was a pioneer in the manufacture of cardboard music for street pianos. Also pinned barrels for Imhof & Mukle orchestrions and mechanical pianos at one time. Giuseppe's son, Lodovico, subsequently took over the firm and his son, Victor, now runs the business, producing punched-card music for fair organs and restoring instruments.

CHIAPPA & FERSANI, 6 Little Bath Street, London EC. Giuseppe Chiappa went into partnership with Fersani, manufacturing street barrel pianos, and in 1878 they jointly patented a street piano with cornet accompaniment, the instrument being both piano and organ.

CHIAPPA & SONS. In 1885, this firm was in business at 5 Jersey Street, Ancoats, Manchester, making barrel pianos. It was the northern branch of the London firm.

CHIAPPA & SON, JOSEPH, 6 Little Bath Street, London EC. In 1881 Giuseppe (Joseph) Chiappa was making street pianos under this name.

CHIAPPO, FELICE, Turin, Italy. Maker of barrel pianos who exhibited three instruments at the National Exhibition held in Turin in the summer of 1884.

CHICAGO PLAYER ACTION COMPANY, Rockford, Illinois, USA. Makers of player actions.

CHRISTMAN PIANO CO., 567–601 East 137th Street, New York, USA. Made a series of player uprights and grands using an action which fitted on the front of the keyboard. Established in 1885.

CICOPERO, FRANCESCO, Corso Buenos Aires 66r, Genoa, Italy. Barrel-piano maker and handler, *fl.* 1909.

CLARK, MELVILLE. With little doubt, Melville Clark was the most influential person in the whole history of the player piano. Its invention and perfection was due in no small measure to his inventive mind. Born in Oneida County, New York State, he began as an apprentice to a piano tuner and then went to California where he began a factory for the production of high-grade reed organs. He sold out in 1877 and finally went to Chicago where he began making reed organs under the name of Clark & Rich. In 1884 he joined with Hampton L. Story (born Cambridge, Vermont, 17 June 1835; famed maker of pianos and reed organs) and his son Edward H. Story in the making of reed organs under the name of Story & Clark. Melville Clark was the inventor of many important improvements in connection with the reed organ. The business grew so much that branches and workshops were set up in London and Berlin. The former was started in 1892 with Charles H. Wagener at its head. In 1900, Clark severed his connections with what was now called the Story & Clark Piano & Organ Company after what Dolge refers to as '16 years of zealous activity', and started the Melville Clark Piano Company with a capital of $500,000, erecting new factory premises at De Kalb, Illinois. From then on, Clark's inventive prowess dominated the world of the piano player and the player piano for almost two decades. A correspondent writing in the Chicago *Indicator* early in 1912 said: 'It is getting to be such a common thing to expect the granting of a patent to Melville Clark of Chicago every week or so, that one is disappointed if a week rolls by without such an event happening.' Over 250 patents were granted to Clark, his first being number 576,032 of 1897. He staggered the piano-player world by bringing out the world's first full-scale or 88-note player in January 1901, the first 88-note interior player in 1902, the first full-scale grand piano, and the transposing device which was used under licence by very many makers. Clark called his player the Apollo, scorning the use of an air motor and applying spring motor roll rewind right up until a very late date. He also invented the Apollophone, an upright Apollo with a phonograph built into the left side of the front fall. He established a piano roll factory at De Kalb – Q.R.S. – which was operated for many years by his brother, Ernest G. Clark. Melville Clark died in 1919. Although his exact dates are unknown, he is thought to have been about seventy-two years of age.

CLARK PIANO CO., MELVILLE, 17 Van Buren Street, Chicago, Illinois, USA.

CLARK PNEUMATIC ACTION CO., 518 Prairie Street, Milwaukee, Wisconsin, USA. Produced a device called the Auto-Namic, 'the reproducing device which turns a player piano into a reproducing piano at a very small cost. The Auto-Namic is a perfect action control for automatic player pianos. Installed with any player action. . . . A New Basic Principle is applied in Auto-Namic – It is the only "single unit" reproducing device in the world.' The device, a hand-sized pneumatic assembly, apparently offered sixteen 'tensions' from a single pneumatic and was piped direct from the tracker bar without any valves.

CLARK-APOLLO CO., 67 Berners Street and 119 Regent Street, London. Established in the summer of 1901 with £12,000 capital to exploit the Apollo piano player in England. The directors were John Beare, Jacques Ullmann (of the Paris firm of Ch. & J. Ullmann), Henry Kaim (of F. Kaim & Sohn, the German piano manufacturers), E. Rink (of Ullmann's London office) and C. H. Wagener (of the Melville-Clark Co.).

CLASSIC PLAYER ACTION. Made by T. H. Poyser of Harringay. Advertised in October 1921 at 39 Hermitage Road, Harringay, London N. Advertised in 1914 as player repairer.

CLAVIOLA PLAYER ACTION. Sole agency held (June 1904 notice) by Klinker & Co. Compass of 72 notes, price of 50 guineas. All tubing was of brass.

CLEMENTI, COLLARD & CO., 26 Cheapside, London. Musical-instrument makers. Muzio Clementi, famed keyboard performer and composer, was formerly a partner with the firm of barrel-organ and piano makers, Longman & Broderip, and on the dissolution of the firm he set up in business on his

LIST OF PRINCIPAL MAKERS, PATENTEES AND AGENTS

own. Finally, he took into partnership John Collard and in about 1820 the firm produced the Self-Acting Pianoforte barrel piano.

CLOUGH & WARREN CO., 213 Woodward Avenue, Detroit, Michigan, USA. Established in 1850. Makers of reed organs who also produced player pianos and player actions for both organs and pianos. Operated by the brothers George P. and Joseph A. Warren in 1909.

COCCHI, BACIGALUPO & GRAFFIGNA, Schönhauser Allee 78, Berlin N, Germany. After their London barrel-piano business failed, they returned to the Continent, setting up business in Berlin about 1898 as makers of street pianos, barrel organs, orchestrions and 'hand organs'.

COCCHI, BACIGALUPO & GRAFFIGNA ('Successors of John Arrigoni & Co.'), 158 Great College Street, London NW. Street-organ and piano makers, 1896. JOHN ARRIGONI (q.v.) was manager for the firm but by 1898 the firm had reverted to the title of J. N. ARRIGONI & CO. at this address and Cocchi, Bacigalupo and Graffigna went to Berlin to set up in business. The son of Giuseppe Cocchi, JOHN COCCHI (q.v.) remained in business in London.

COCCHI, GIUSEPPE, 8–9 Farringdon Road Buildings, London EC. Maker of barrel pianos in 1880.

COCCHI, JOHN, Lychenerstrasse 2–3, Berlin N. Maker of barrel organs and piano orchestrions who was functioning in 1903.

COCCHI & SON, JOHN, 2 Childs Mews, Dirleton Place, West Ham, London E15. Described as 'manufacturers of Mechanical Organs and Pianos', they specialised in the repair of these instruments and were at this address until at least 1935.

COHEN & CO. LTD, PHILIP, 14–15 Little Camden Street, London NW. Makers of the Playetta piano player.

COLDMAN, C. H. See under WEBB, C. F.

COLL Y CARRIGA, 117G Mayor and 6 Peracamps, Barcelona, Spain, Barrel-piano maker, *fl.* 1909.

COLLARD MOUTRIE LTD, 50–52 Southampton Row, Holborn, London. Was agent for the Ehrlich 'Virtuos' piano player (see FABRIK LEIPZIGER MUSIKWERKE).

COLOMBO, GIOVANNI, Sobborgo S. Andrea, Novara, Italy. A maker of street barrel organs and pianos, *fl.* 1903.

COLONIA PLAYER PIANO CO., 72 Wells Street, Berners Street, London W. Makers of the Colonia player piano.

CONNOISSEUR PLAYER PIANO. Sold by Murdoch, Murdoch & Co., 461 & 463 Oxford Street, London, and exhibited by them at the British Music Exhibition, Olympia, in 1913. There was also the Connoisseur Reed Organ and Pipe Organ, both being player organs. Murdochs also made the Golden Tube series of music rolls.

CONSERVATORY PLAYER ACTION CO., 32 East Monroe Street, Chicago, USA. Sole licensees and manufacturers of the Harcourt Moto-Playo Bench which was a piano stool containing mechanical player-piano pedalling feet. 'Solves the Problem of the Home Piano Electrically-Played' (not a very helpful description).

CONTINENTAL MUSIKWERKE HOFMANN & CZERNY, XIII/4, Linzerstrasse 176–80, Vienna, Austria. Founded in 1902 by Julius Carl Hofmann for the manufacture of the 'Continental' barrel-operated piano orchestrion which was handled for them by H. Peters of Leipzig, the big distributors.

COPPLESTONE & CO. LTD, 94 Regent Street, London W. Distributors of the Ideal Mignon player action and the Sterling and Mendel players. Also at 85 Newman Street, Oxford Street.

CORVINO, ENRICO, Via S. Carco 26, and Strada Trinita Maggiore 27, Naples, Italy. A maker of street barrel pianos, *fl.* 1903. By 1909 was at Via San Sabastiano 29.

COSTA, JEAN, 50 rue du Roveray, Eux Viven, Geneva, Switzerland. Repairer of street barrel organs and barrel pianos, *fl.* 1903.

COSTA, BARTOLOMEO, Via S. Maurizio 25, Turin, Italy. Maker of street pianos, *fl.* 1903–9.

COURTEUIL, M. DE. A Frenchman who, in 1852, was granted a patent for a perforated strip of cardboard to replace the planchette type of piano keyboard player invented by Alexander Debain.

CRASSELT & RÄHSE, Neustadt 14, Löbau, Saxony, Germany. Founded by Ferdinand Rähse in 1881 for the manufacture of pianos. By 1909 was advertising electropneumatic instruments. Maker of a piano orchestrion which played perforated-paper music rolls. Housed in an ornate cabinet reminiscent of the style used for the larger Polyphon musical boxes, the instrument sold for 950 marks complete with twelve rolls of music in 1903.

CRIADO, ALEJANDRO, 57 Embajadores, Madrid, Spain. Barrel-piano maker, repairer and hirer, *fl.* 1909.

CROUBOIS, A., 48 rue des Juifs, Granville, France. Makers of good-class clockwork orchestral barrel pianos for use in cafés. One seen is marked 'Pianos Automatiques Croubois' and has 51 notes in a semi-iron frame with drum, triangle and two castanets. The date of this instrument is *c.* 1903.

CROWSHAW, London. A barrel-organ manufacturer *c.* 1790, who produced an instrument (still extant in the Moss collection) which incorporated a 12-note dulcimer in addition to organ pipes and normal percussion accompaniment. The dulcimer was operated from the pins on the organ barrel, using keys on the same keyframe as those of the organ proper. No other example of the work of this maker is known.

CUCONATO, ANTONIO, Via Torino 11, Turin, Italy. Barrel-piano maker, *c.* 1903. By 1930 was making clockwork pianos at 12 via S. Ottavio, Turin.

CUEVAS DE JOSE, 8 Tabermillas, Madrid, Spain. Barrel-piano maker and hirer, *fl.* 1909.

DACHS, JUAN, 41 Rosal, Barcelona, Spain. Barrel-piano maker, *fl.* 1903.

DALE ELECTRONICS INC., Yankton, South Dakota 57078, USA. The Dale Lectronic was a modern key-top player developed in the 1960s using a vacuum to read the paper music roll and pouches to translate the signals into electric signals to solenoids which depressed the keys of the piano. The system was adopted for building into new pianos by Wurlitzer.

DAVIS, JOSEPH, 11 Catherine Street, Strand, London (1819–28), also at Blackfriars Road in 1829 and at 20 Southampton Street, Strand, London (1844–8). Makers of barrel organs who also advertised 'Self-performing piano harp'.

DAWKINS & CO., THOMAS, 205–7 City Road, London EC. Distributor of the Orpheus player piano. Dawkins was founded in 1870. A barrel piano bearing this name, measuring 38 inches by 18 inches, was sold in London by auction at Christie's in 1967. It would appear that Dawkins was agent for a manufacturer of Hicks-style pianos. He was a well-known musical-instrument importer.

DAWSON, CHARLES, Hardinge Street, Islington, Middlesex. In 1848 he produced a mechanical organ worked by perforated cardboard of the Jacquard type in place of the usual barrels. It was not a success, since he used the perforations in the card to effect directly the admission of wind to the pipes, and the gradual opening and closing of the airways which resulted produced a disagreeable wavering at the beginning and end of each note. This organ was shown at the Great Exhibition of 1851.

DE ROY, EUGENE, 20, Longue-Rue Pothoek, Anvers, Belgium. Maker of pneumatic player pianos and piano rolls under the name 'The Symphonia', *fl.* 1930.

DEBAIN, ALEXANDRE FRANÇOIS. Born in Paris, 1809, he trained as a cabinet-maker. In 1825 after completing his apprenticeship he worked in several piano factories, ultimately becoming foreman. In 1834 he began his own factory in Paris, invented several musical instruments and devoted a great deal of time and effort to perfecting and ultimately producing his Antiphonel keytop player for piano or organ, which used pegged planchettes for the music. The Antiphonel was also built into pianos and combined instruments. The Paris address was 15 rue Vivienne and initially sales in London were handled by Novello & Co., 44 Dean Street, Soho. Prices ranged from 55 to 90 guineas. The British Patent for the Antiphonel was number 11,359 of 29 August 1846. Debain died on 3 December 1877 and his business was absorbed into that of Rodolphe as Maison Rodolphe Fils & Debain réunies, at 15 rue de Chaligny, the factory being at Nogent-sur-Seine. Ultimately this business was taken over by the old established harmonium builders, Christophe & Étienne (variously described as founded in 1861 and 1832) as Christophe H. & Étienne, Rodolphe Fils, A. Debain, Cottino (Anciens Etabl. réunis). The Piano Mécanique version of the Antiphonel was a finely engineered instrument.

LIST OF PRINCIPAL MAKERS, PATENTEES AND AGENTS

DEBAIN & CO., 41 Rathbone Place, London W. Founded by Alexandre Debain of Paris, this London office opened during the 1880s and advertised 'pianos-mécaniques' and 'pianos-orgues'.

DEKLEIST, EUGENE, Düsseldorf, Germany. Born Eugene Von Kleist in 1867, he was formerly representative in Belgium and, later, in London for Limonaire Brothers, makers of fair and band organs. He was requested, as an organ expert, to establish the North Tonawanda Barrel Organ Factory in North Tonawanda, New York, USA. The firm was financed by the Tonawanda Carousel Factory and deKleist was its manager. They built their first organ in 1891. DeKleist ultimately separated his company from the North Tonawanda parent company and, in 1903, the barrel-organ factory became the deKleist Musical Instrument Company. Wurlitzer commissioned them to make a coin-freed electric piano and deKleist developed a ten-tune barrel piano featuring pneumatic action which he called the Tonophone. Wurlitzer finally absorbed the firm in 1908.

DELMASTRO & CIA, GIUSEPPE, Corsa Vitt. Emanuele 24, Turin, Italy. A maker of clockwork barrel pianos for use in cafés and public places, *fl.* 1903. By 1909 was at Via dei Fiori 25, Turin.

DEMETZ (CAV. FERDINANDO), Ortisei-Gardena, Trento, Italy. A maker of fronts (façades) for organs and orchestrions with moving figures, *fl.* 1930.

DENIS, CARLO, Via Giovenone 5, Vercelli, Italy. Barrel-organ and piano maker, *c.* 1903.

DENIS, GIORGIO, Via Giovenone 5, Vercelli, Novara, Italy. Barrel-piano hirer, *fl.* 1909.

DEPONTI, CARLO (DITTA), Via Della Rocca 1, angolo Via Maria Vittoria, Turin, Italy. Famous maker of pianos who also made fine-quality barrel pianos. Exhibited three barrel pianos at the National Exhibition held in Turin in the summer of 1884.

DEPONTI, CAROLINA, Via Della Rocca 1, Turin, Italy. Barrel-piano maker, *fl.* 1903.

DETROIT MUSIC CO., 288 Woodward Avenue, Detroit, Michigan, USA. Managed by M. A. van Wagoner. Makers of player actions.

DICRAN, Z., Constantinople, Turkey. Maker of portable street pianos.

DIENST, E., Langestrasse 39–40, Leipzig. Founded in 1871. Dienst made orchestrion organs, orchestrion pianos, played by barrel and pneumatic actions.

DIRECT PNEUMATIC ACTION CO. LTD, 8a Dorset Street, Baker Street, London W. Makers of the Direct Arrow action. Also sole British agent for the imported Standard Pneumatic actions. They produced the Stems player piano fitted with the Arrow action *c.* 1911 and shown at Olympia in 1913. See also KASTNER & CO. LTD.

DISTIN, HENRY, 2 Church Lane, Temple Street, Bristol. Maker of barrel pianos who marked some of his instruments 'Henry Distin (from the late Joseph Hicks)'. He was also a piano tuner. Joseph Hicks died in 1847.

DODDS, ERNEST H. An inventor who, soon after 1914, devised a new type of valve for exhausting the motors of the player action of a piano. This made use of an L-shaped hinged valve flap. Blüthners were so impressed with its possibilities by virtue of its simplicity that they enthusiastically took up its manufacture. Dodds's first British Patent was not granted until 21 May 1919 (number 153,928). He was granted a patent for improvements to it on 12 August 1920 (number 171465). This valve was used in the Blüthner Carola action which also made use of a metal bleed hole with screw adjustment. Dodds was granted a later patent in conjunction with Blüthner for an adjustable take-up spool (number 199,933 of 12 June 1922).

DOGLIANI, PIER NICOLA, Via Caraglio, Angolo via Ospizi, Cuneo, Italy. Piano manufacturer who also made barrel pianos, *fl.* 1930.

DOLL & SONS, JACOB, 117–24 Cyprus Avenue, New York, USA. Established as a piano manufacturer in 1871, Doll formed a business called the Electrova Company specialising in coin-freed pianos. These instruments appear to have been manufactured by others and factored by Doll.

DONADINI & POHL, CESARE, Landsbergerallee 18, Berlin N. A maker of barrel pianos who patented in 1865 a combined manual and barrel piano. This was exhibited at the Melbourne Musical Industries Exhibition in April 1888. Was still in business in 1909. Established in 1880.

DORCHIN, ARMAND, 40 Rosal, Barcelona, Spain. Barrel-piano maker, *fl.* 1903.

DOUILLET, A., 59 rue de l'Ourcq, Paris. Makers of player pianos with 65- and 88-note compass. Successor to the business of A. Gehrling, founded in 1842.

DUCHÁCEK, LADISLAUS, Patackygasse 114, Turnau, Bohemia. A maker of musical automata and mechanical stringed instruments, *fl.* 1903.

DUSART-BOUTEMY, H., 135 rue de Valenciennes, Raismes, France. Makers of mechanical pianos and orchestrions, established in 1897, *fl.* 1920.

DUVAL, RENÉ, 42 rue de la Véga, Paris. Specialist in the restoration and repair of mechanical pianos, *fl.* 1920.

DUWAER & NAESSENS, Kalverstraat 26, Amsterdam, Holland. Agents for Hupfeld of Leipzig and distributors of orchestrions and electric pianos. Founded 1903. Also at Kneuterdyk 20, Hague.

EAST ANGLIAN AUTOMATIC PIANO COMPANY. See WINTLE, CANON A. O.

ECKHARDT, J. C., Pragstrasse 72–4, Kannstatt, Germany. Manufacturer of musical Christmas-tree stands who probably also handled barrel pianos and organs, *fl.* 1903. Was formerly in Stuttgart.

EHRLICH, FRIEDRICH ERNST PAUL, Breitenfeldstrasse 31, Leipzig-Gohlis, Germany. Paul Ehrlich was born on 21 March 1849 and died on 17 January 1925. His inventive genius in the burgeoning days of mechanical music in Germany at the closing decades of the last century cannot be overstated. A prolific inventor of mechanical musical instruments, particularly organettes, he made disc-playing musical boxes, small reed organs and pianos which played from perforated cardboard or paper music. He manufactured the small 24-note Orpheus disc-playing miniature grand piano which played the same discs as the Ariston organette, and also the Automat piano player in the late 1880s. This played from cardboard discs. Some models also used metal discs made of punched zinc. Two distinct models of the Automat were built; one was a push-up style resembling that made by GROB (q.v.) and the second was of similar format but was clamped on top of the piano keyboard. Ehrlich's business was the FABRIK LEIPZIGER MUSIKWERKE (q.v.). In 1904, this became the NEUE LEIPZIGER MUSIKWERKE A. BUFF-HEDINGER (q.v.), at the same time that Ehrlich started a new business with his brother Emil (see EHRLICH'S MUSIKWERKE EMIL EHRLICH).

EHRLICH'S MUSIKWERKE EMIL EHRLICH, Magdeburger Strasse 13, Leipzig-Gohlis, Germany. Established in 1903. Manufactured the Orphobella player piano and a hand-turned machine called 'Ehrlich's Instrument'.

EICH, PIERRE, 5 rue du Roitelet, Ghent, Belgium. Maker of barrel organs, orchestrions and electric pianos. Also acted as agent. Instruments made by Eich included Solophone and the Piano-Jazz. Eich bought in pianos from quality German factories, including Forster. The factory closed in 1939.

ELECTRELLE CO., 30 King Street, Manchester, England. Makers of the Electrelle piano player.

ELIAS, JAIME, Palma de Majorca, Baleares, Spain. Modern maker of miniature street barrel pianos (*manubriet*) complete with dogcart.

EMERSON PIANO COMPANY, 560 Harrison Avenue, Boston, Massachusetts, USA. Established in 1849 as piano manufacturers. Produced the Accompano electric player upright.

ENGLEHARDT PIANO CO., St Johnsville, New York. A subsidiary of the Peerless Piano Player Co. which produced instruments of the same type and under its own name. Also sometime Roth & Englehardt Co.

ENGRAMELLE, MARIE DOMINIQUE JOSEPH. Born 1727, died 1781. An Augustinian monk who became intrigued by the whole concept of setting music on a cylinder. He elevated the practice of the principle to the level of an art and in 1775 published a book in Paris entitled *La Tonotechnie, ou l'art de noter les cylindres* ('Tonotechnique, or the art of placing the notes on cylinders'). It was he who first set out the importance of the *silent* portion of a sound which established the whole character of a series of notes. Engramelle's work was subsequently expanded in the work of BÉDOS DE CELLES (q.v.).

ERHARDT & CO., C., 36 Southwark Bridge Road, London SE. Distributors of the Gehrling player piano.

ESTEY & CO., J., Brattleboro, Vermont, USA. Jacob Estey was making reed organs as early as 1852.

LIST OF PRINCIPAL MAKERS, PATENTEES AND AGENTS

Born 30 September 1814, he was to become one of the most famous of all quality reed-organ makers. The business assumed the title J. Estey & Co. in 1858 and it had a succession of increasingly large factories at Flat Street, Brattleboro. In 1872 it was incorporated as the Estey Organ Co. Subsequently formed the Estey Piano Corporation in Bluffton, Indiana, with premises at 237 North Union Street. Produced a number of player pianos. The business closed in 1959 although the name remains in use as a brand.

ÉTABLISSEMENTS 'ORESTE', 41 Boulevard de Riquier, Nice, France. Manufacturers of player pianos and orchestrions, *fl.* 1930.

ETZOLD & POPITZ, Querstr. 4–6, Leipzig. Founded in 1864. Sole distributor of the barrel piano-orchestrion 'Eldorado' with mandoline, xylophone, etc., and the pneumatic orchestrion 'Serenata'. Also distributors for Polyphon, Symphonion, Kalliope and Lochmann Original. Appear not to have been makers.

FABRICA ITALIANI PIANOFORTI F.I.P., 55 Via Moretts, Turin, Italy. Makers of player pianos, *fl.* 1930.

FABRIK LEIPZIGER MUSIKWERKE, Leipzig-Gohlis. Founded in 1877 for the manufacture of mechanical musical instruments by the brothers Ehrlich, they made the Virtuos pneumatic piano player *c.* 1903.

FABRIK MECHANISCHER ZITHERN 'CHORDEPHON' CLAUS & CO., Waldstrasse 20, Leipzig. Makers of the Chordephon disc-playing mechanical zither which was played by a perforated metal disc. Examples were made which were both hand-cranked and driven by a clockwork spring motor. It was in production in 1903.

FACCINI, A., Ernest Street, Stepney, London E. In business as hirer of street pianos, *fl.* 1930. Described as 'proprietor and dealer in Mandolin & Piano Organs'.

FALCONE, VEDOVA, 5 via Arsenale, Pinerolo, Turin, Italy. Barrel-piano maker, *fl.* 1930.

FANTOSCA, PASQUALE, Avellino, Italy. Street-organ and piano maker, *fl.* 1930.

FARRAND ORGAN CO., 1256 12th Street, Detroit, Michigan, USA. Established in 1884. Makers of reed organs and also the Cecilian piano players. This sold for $250 in 1901. An associate company, the Farrand Company at 12th Street and Grand Trunk Ry, was given over to the making of player actions. The business actually began in 1881 as the Detroit Organ Company, a co-operative which did not succeed. E. S. Votey and Farrand rescued the business. Votey joined Aeolian in 1897 at which time the Farrand & Votey Company supplied the Pianola piano player for Aeolian. The company remained closely allied to Aeolian.

FASCH, JOSÉ, 9 Meliodia, Barcelona, Spain. Barrel-street-piano agent and hirer in business in 1903.

FASSANO, COSTANZO, Largo Tarsia 21–2, Naples, Italy. Street-barrel-piano maker and hirer, *fl.* 1909.

FEILITZSCH ET CIE, HANS VON, 104 rue de Laeken, Brussels, Belgium. Agent for barrel organs, barrel pianos and electric pianos, *fl.* 1903.

FEISS BROTHERS, 240 Chapel Street, Prahan, Melbourne, Australia. Est. 1886. Agents for Imhof & Mukle's Black Forest orchestrions and mechanical pianos in 1888.

FERNANDEZ, ROMAN, 14 Flor Baja, Madrid, Spain. Maker of street pianos, *fl.* 1903.

FERRARI, ANGEL, 4 S. Pedro, Villafranca del Panadés, Spain. Agent and hirer for street pianos, *fl.* 1903.

FERRARI, FRATELLI, Via Savonarola 24, Alessandria, Italy. Barrel-piano agent.

FERRERO, ANGELO, 6 via Losanna, Milan, Italy. Maker of barrel pianos, *fl.* 1930.

FOUCHER, GEORGE. Manufacturer of pianos and organs, 'patent barrel organ, new mechanical pianoforte performing by hand and handle' in 1881.

FOUCHER, GASPARINI, 17–19 rue de la Véga, Paris. Maker of barrel organs and pianos for street use, *fl.* 1903.

FOURNEAUX, NAPOLÉON. A Frenchman who patented in 1863 a mechanical piano player called the Pianista. This is the first known pneumatic player, the action being controlled by a pinned barrel turned by a handle. Each pneumatic, which received its air control from barrel-organ-type bellows, depressed a finger on the piano keys. The instrument, somewhat larger than the pianoforte it was designed to play upon, was exhibited in America at the Philadelphia Exposition of 1878.

FRANCIOLI, ANTONIO, Intra, Novara, Italy. Barrel-piano maker, *fl.* 1930.
FRANCONE, GIUSEPPE, Via Gioberti 27, Turin, Italy. Piano and barrel-piano agent, *fl.* 1909.
FRANCONE, VINCENZO (VEDOVA), Via San Dalmazzo 16, Turin, Italy. Maker of barrel pianos, *fl.* 1909.
FRANKFURTER MUSIKWERKE-FABRIK J. D. PHILIPPS & SOHNE, Solmstr. 9, Frankfurt, Germany. Established in 1877. Makers of barrel and pneumatically played piano orchestrions and player actions for pianos. Players included the Cäcilia and the Corona as well as electric versions. Perfected, in 1912, a motor for winding two tune sheets at once and, in 1916, a special roll-tracking device. Also at Berlin, Essen and Leipzig. See also under PHILIPPS & SÖHNE, J. D.
FRATI, CHIARO, 5 Farringdon Road, London EC. Probably a son of the founder of the famous Berlin firm of orchestrion organ makers, Chiaro Frati advertised as a maker of barrel pianos in 1876. He subsequently removed to 19 Great Bath Street, Farringdon Road, London EC.
FRATI & CIE, 10 place Daumesnil, Paris 12e, France. Branch of the Berlin maker of orchestrion pianos and electric pianos.
FRATI & CO., Kastanienallee 32, Berlin N37, Germany. Founded by Anselmo Frati in 1875 and financed by Giovanni Bacigalupo (1847–1914). Both were barrel-organ builders from Genoa in Italy. Frati had learned his trade with Gavioli in Paris and subsequently worked in London. The business, which the two men jointly owned, prospered until the closing years of the last century when failing health and mental illness caused Frati to return to Italy. The business was continued under various titles by Bacigalupo and his subsequent partners, John Cocchi and Graffigna, until finally it was managed by Heinrich Schmithals. Electric pianos under the name Fratinola were produced in much later years until, with its market failing (the company still made barrel-playing instruments at a time when everybody else was producing paper-roll-playing machines), it was bought out by the FRANKFURTER MUSIKWERKE-FABRIK J. D. PHILIPPS (q.v.). Frati himself had died in the early 1890s. At the International Exhibition held in London at the Crystal Palace, Sydenham, in April 1884, Frati was awarded 'special mention' for barrel pianos.
FUCHS, DIEGO, Wenzelsplatz 13, Prague, Austro-Hungary. Established in 1903 as the Ersten Prager Musikwerke- und Orchestrionfabrik. Makers of barrel piano orchestrions.
FUSCO, GIUSEPPE, p. Pola, Treviso, Italy. Maker of barrel pianos, *fl.* 1930.
FUSELLA, GIUSEPPE, Via S. Dominico 34, Turin, Italy. Barrel-piano maker, *fl.* 1903–9.
FUZELLI, JOSEPH, 379 Great Ormond Street, London W. Maker of street barrel organs and barrel pianos.
GALL, JOHANN, Arnau, Bohemia. A maker of street barrel organs and pianos.
GANTER, KARL, Furtwangen, Bad Schwarzwald, Germany. A specialist in the making of weight-driven clockwork units supplied to many makers of piano and pipe orchestrions, *fl.* 1903.
GARCIA, DOROTEO, 4 S. Cayetano, Madrid, Spain. Barrel-piano and barrel-organ maker, repairer and hirer, *fl.* 1909.
GARCIA, PEDRO, 30 Abades, Madrid, Spain. Barrel-piano and barrel-organ maker, repairer and hirer, *fl.* 1909.
GARGALLO, TOMÁS, 178 Conde del Asalto, Barcelona, Spain. Specialised in pinning music for street pianos, *fl.* 1903. By 1909 was at 154 Conde del Asalto.
GARISCH & CO. (A. & G.), 28 viale Vittorio Veneto, Milan, Italy. Distributor of pianos, player pianos and music rolls, *fl.* 1930.
GAROLACHI, VINCENTE, 6 Sombreria, Madrid, Spain. Barrel-piano maker, *fl.* 1903.
GASPARINI (Successor to Foucher-Gasparini), 17 and 19, rue de la Véga, Paris. Makers of clockwork barrel pianos for cafés and also of book-playing organs, *fl.* 1920.
GAST & CO. See under PIANOFORTE FABRIK 'EUTERPE'.
GATTINO, ONOR, Via Madama Cristina 105, Turin, Italy. Agent of barrel pianos, *fl.* 1909.
GAVIOLI & CO., 1 & 2 Farringdon Road, London EC. Street-organ makers who were producing barrel pianos in 1880.
GAVIOLI & CO., 5 Jersey Street, Great Ancoats, Manchester, and 2 bis avenue de Taillebourg (place de

la Nation), Paris, France. Makers of mechanical organs and pianos c. 1888. In 1885 they were at 55 Blossom Street, Ancoats, Manchester.

GAVIOLI & CO., L., 5 Little Saffron Hill, London EC. Street-organ maker who also advertised mechanical pianos in 1870.

GAVIOLI ET CIE, SOCIÉTÉ. Founded in Paris at 2 avenue de Taillebourg by Ludovic Gavioli, an Italian, with his sons Claude and Anselme; the Gaviolis can truthfully be said to have been the fathers of the fair or showman's organ. Their inventions both in the tonality and mechanics of these instruments, along with the practical improvements in perforated music, were to influence all that came after them. The cardboard-music playing piano was one direct result of their associated work. Ludovic Gavioli was a native of San Geminiano and came to Paris at the end of 1852. He was a meticulous organ-builder who made very fine secular organs, although he did build one for Queen Isabella II of Spain which played hymns. Ordinary barrel organs represented a steady business but the firm was to find its wealth and success in fair organs and, during the late 1850s, the family concern was joined by P. Yver, a financier. After the war of 1870, the Gavioli factory was moved to Alsace in eastern France. There followed a period of decline in business and in 1901 the firm lost its foreman, Charles Marenghi, who was their principal expert. Marenghi established his own successful firm in the same line of business. Earlier, in 1892, Gavioli had introduced 'book music' and the book-playing organ which used perforated-cardboard music folded zigzag fashion to form a thick 'book' of music. This was fed through a pneumatic system named the 'mechanical-pneumatic Touch Key', Gavioli's term for the key frame with its projecting key tips. Gavioli was also responsible for the invention of the portable street organ, many interestingly voiced organ pipes, organs that used two wind pressures from one air source, primary and secondary pneumatic systems for fair organs, and a 'keyless' tracker box along with automatic stop selectors and cancellers. Most of the famous names amongst Italian/French fair organs and their makers served their apprenticeships with Gavioli. In the irony of things, many of these names continued in business long after Gavioli, among them Marenghi and also Chiappa. Limonaire Brothers took over the remains of the Gavioli concern and continued to supply perforated music until they themselves went out of business in 1918. Gavioli built the 'Guitharmony' which was a barrel-operated guitar with plucking mechanism.

GAZZA, GIOVANNI, 71 Roosevelt Street, Manhattan, USA. Took over the barrel-piano and organ business of G. Mina of 2 First Street, Manhattan, on his death. The business did not prosper and was closed by 1902.

GENERALAGENTUR DER CHORALION COMPANY FRANK W. HESSIN, Unter den Linden 71, Berlin NW. The German company representing the Aeolian Company and handling the Pianola and Orchestrelle instruments.

GETTO, FRANCESCO, Via Marsale 5, Ivrea, Italy. 'Pianoforte e Organi a Cilindro.' Maker of barrel pianos similar in style to the portable Hicks pattern, but strung much lighter to produce a most pleasing bright tone. Also made barrel organs; *fl.* 1930.

GIACCHETTI, GIUSEPPE, Cigliano, Italy. Maker of barrel organs and pianos, who exhibited two barrel pianos at the National Exhibition held in Turin in the summer of 1884. Was still in business in 1903.

GIANNINI, GIACOMO, Corso Vitt. Emanuele 132, Bari, Italy. Agent for barrel pianos who also hired and carried out repairs, *fl.* 1909.

GILARDENGHI, J., 12 rue du Fort, Marseilles, France. Barrel-piano agent and hirer, *fl.* 1909.

GILLONE, GAUDENZIO, Via del Ponte, Casale Monferrato, Alessandria, Italy. Maker of barrel pianos, *fl.* 1930.

GILONE, GIUSEPPE, Casale, Italy. Exhibited two barrel pianos at the National Exhibition held in Turin in the summer of 1884.

GIOVANNI RISSONI & CO., 30 Warner Street, Clerkenwell, London EC. Formerly with Capra, Rissone took over the Capra business and continued at the same address from 1887, manufacturing street barrel pianos.

GIULIANO, VITTORIO, Via Monteoliveto 61, Naples, Italy. Barrel-piano agent and hirer, *fl.* 1909.

GIUMMARRA, GAUDENZIO, Ragusa Inferiore, Syracuse, Italy. Maker of barrel organs and pianos, *fl.* 1930.

GÖSSL, JOSEF & ADOLF, VI, Gumpendorfer Str. 81 and I, Teinfaltstr. 9, Vienna, Austro-Hungary. Makers of barrel piano-orchestrions established in 1854.

GRAY, ROBERT AND WILLIAM, '4 New Road, near the end of Portland Road (London). Maker of Barrel Organs, Harpsichords and Pianos.' Probably built barrel pianos or spinets *c.* 1800, but no instruments have been discovered.

GRELLI, GIUSEPPE, 3 via Tornasacco, Ascoli Piceno, Italy. Barrel-piano maker, *fl.* 1930.

GRIBBLE MUSIC COMPANY, 919 Grand Avenue, Kansas City, Missouri, USA. Introduced *c.* 1955 a modern device called Magic Fingers which could convert an existing piano into a player, or could be built into a new instrument. It was not a key-top player, but fitted under the keyboard in a drawer. It was engineered by the Midwest Research Institute.

GRISERI, FRATELLI, Via San Sabastiano, Centallo, Italy. Maker of barrel pianos, *fl.* 1909.

GRISERI & VARETTO, 14 Warner Street, London EC. Producers of street pianos *c.* 1880.

GROB, J. M., Leipzig-Eutritzsch, Germany. Founded in 1872 by J. M. Grob, A. O. Schultze and A. V. Niemczik for the manufacture of mechanical musical instruments. Patented a means of playing a piano or organ by means of a perforated tune sheet in 1886. This employed cam-shaped levers which, when raised through the holes in the music, wedged against a rotating drum and so impelled the piano hammer – this was the 'kicking-shoe' type of action. In 1888, Grob patented a tremolo or staccato action for barrel-operated pianos using a revolving cranked shaft engaging the barrel keyframe key. Also perfected a system of continuously beating hammers and associated check action similar to that used by RACCA (q.v.) of Bologna. Made a disc-operated piano player which operated on 36 notes of the piano. Grob first began making instruments in 1883, having in the previous year secured the sole rights for the Ehrlich Ariston organette. His first patents date back to 1884. Grob died in October 1891 and the following year the business was taken over by HUPFELD (q.v.), the name being changed to Hupfeld Musikwerke. Hupfeld henceforth claimed the date of foundation as 1872 – that of Grob. Grob is best remembered for his work in pioneering the disc-operated mechanical piano player, a device with which both he and Ehrlich were closely associated and which subsequently Nyström in Sweden used for playing a reed organ.

GRÖNDAHL'S FLYGEL- & PIANOLAGER, Karl Johangade 17, Christiana (the old name of Oslo), Norway. Founded in 1904 by Andreass Backer Gröndahl as distributor of player pianos, piano players and electric pianos.

GÜELL, PABLO, 13 Rosal, Barcelona, Spain. Barrel-piano seller and hirer, *fl.* 1909.

GUERIN, CHARLES, 3–7 Boulevard des Vignes, Marseilles, France. Makers of barrel pianos under the brand name Massilia; *fl.* 1920.

GUILBAUD FRERES, LES ETABTS Labaule, 2 rue Charles Baudelaire, Paris, Makers of clockwork barrel pianos which featured overstrung, partly iron frames. This firm also made orchestrions. A label on one 48-note café piano states: 'Mfg. Pianos Automatiques en France & Belgium'.

GULBRANSEN-DICKENSON CO., 3242 West Chicago Avenue, Chicago, Illinois, USA. Makers of the Gulbransen player piano. In 1909 the company was at 37 Union Park Street. Axel G. Gulbransen evolved what was to become the famous trade mark of an upright piano being 'pedalled' by a crawling baby with the words 'Easy to Play'.

GÜNZEL & ROSENBERGER, 7 Victoria Avenue, Bishopsgate Without, London EC. Distributor of Spaethe's piano player, the Pianist.

HAAKE SÖHNE, RUDOLF, Karlsruhe I.B., Furtwangen, Germany. Also at Mannheim. Makers of hot-air engines for mechanical musical instruments, including piano orchestrions. These little engines, set in motion by a spirit burner, developed 1/60 h.p. and cost 38 marks each. These details were advertised in 1897.

HADDORFF PIANO CO., Rockford, Illinois. Makers of 'Clarendon' player piano (1909).

HALL, R., 19b Wilbury Grove, Hove 3, Sussex. 'Piano Organ Specialist.' A restorer of barrel pianos

LIST OF PRINCIPAL MAKERS, PATENTEES AND AGENTS

who also repinned barrels. An instrument by Pasquale of 5 Phoenix Place, London, repinned and restored by Hall, is in the Lancaster House collection in London. It plays the popular American tune *Davy Crockett*.

HALLET & DAVIS PIANO CO., 146 Boylston Street, Boston, Massachusetts, USA. Established in 1839. Became a division of the Conway Musical Industries and distributed Conway and Lexington pianos. Made the Virtuola upright player, and later a fine range of reproducing grand pianos using the Angelus name which earlier had been used for its pedal player pianos.

HANKE & CO., FRANZ. See BERLINER ORCHESTRION FABRIK FRANZ HAWKE & CO., GmbH.

HARDMAN, PECK & COMPANY, Fifth Avenue and 19th Street, New York, USA. Established in 1842 as piano makers. Developed a piano player which was said to have cost the company £100,000 to bring to perfection in 1905. London agents were Hardman & Goetze Agencies (which also handled the German Goetze pianos) of 98 Leonard Street, City Road, London EC. Hardman also produced the Autotone player piano featuring the 'Accentor' control. The company had a branch at 524 Fulton Street, Brooklyn. The Hardman piano player, said in 1905 to have been the smallest on the market, cost £29 (Eclipse model); £39 (Standard model), and £44 for the Perfecta model. The cases were available in a choice of woods.

HARPER ELECTRIC PIANO COMPANY, 258–62 Holloway Road, London N, and 83 New Oxford Street, London W (premises shared with CALMONT, q.v.). Established in 1906 by Sidney C. Harper as distributors of the Premier piano and player. Reformed as:

HARPER ELECTRIC PIANO (1910) CO. LTD, 258–62 Holloway Road, London N. Makers of electric self-acting pianos, who exhibited such instruments in 1911 at the Coronation Exhibition (Shepherd's Bush), at the Earls Court Exhibition and also the Festival of Empire at the Crystal Palace. At the Music Trades Exhibition of the same year (August) at the Agricultural Hall they showed one model fitted with xylophone and mandolin attachment which could be turned on or off at will. This was intended for use in cafés, restaurants and hotels. The firm remained in business through the 1930s although, judging by the rarity of their instruments today, their production must have been small. Most of their music rolls appear to have been made by the UP-TO-DATE MUSIC ROLL CO (q.v.) and were 13 5/16 inches wide.

HARTLEY, HENRY, AND VINCENT CANOVA, 39 Corporation Street, Birmingham. In January 1911, they jointly patented a player-piano system wherein at the completion of one paper roll another was indexed into position for playing whilst an independent mechanism rewound the other regardless of the length of either roll.

HASBROUCK PIANO CO., 539 West 21st Street, New York, USA. Makers of a player piano called the Tone-ola, *c.* 1910.

HAUPT, A. E., Äusere Weberstr. 69, Zittau, Saxony. Established in 1846. Piano orchestrion maker specialising in instruments driven by weights or motor or hand. *Fl.* 1909.

HAYS & CO., ALFRED, 82 Cornhill, London EC. One-time musical-instrument dealers, this firm exists today as a theatre-ticket agency. Their name and former address (above) appears on a small portable barrel piano in a rosewood case similar to the Hicks style and appearing to date from the second half of the nineteenth century. It is likely that, as with barrel pianos bearing the name Keith Prowse, Alfred Hays did not actually manufacture these instruments. Also sometime at 74 Cornhill, EC3, and 26 Old Bond Street (*c.* 1923).

HEDKE, WILHELM, Neu-Lichtenberg, Friedrichstr. 27, Berlin, Germany, Founded in 1890 as piano makers. Produced the 'Artist' piano player and, in 1908, the Ideal player piano.

HEGELER & EHLERS, Blumenstrasse 56–7, Brüderstrasse 20a and Heiligengeiststrasse 31–2, Oldenburg i. Grossherzogt, Germany. Established in 1895 as makers of pianos. Managed by Hermann Hegeler and Heinrich Ehlers, this company introduced in 1908 an upright piano with a violin which played in unison with the two upper octaves of the piano keyboard by means of trackers. The violin, played via belt-driven rotating bows, was mounted on top of the piano and inside the case, where it was hidden from view. Called the Geigenpiano, it seems to have been a short-lived device. Hegeler &

Ehlers also had branches in Bremen and Bremerhaven.

HEILBRUNN SOHNE, K., Keibelstrasse 39, Berlin NO, Germany. Established in 1875 by W. Heilbrunn and S. Blüth. Makers of the Virtuos player piano.

HICKS, GEORGE, 14 Charles Street, St James, Bristol. 'Organ builder and manufacturer of cylinder pianos' reads the label on a portable street piano by this maker. A further example in the Jere Ryder collection has a date, possibly that of a repair, of August 1842. Probably the same as:

HICKS, GEORGE, Brooklyn, Long Island, USA. Probably immigrant, in business between 1848 and 1864. Two small barrel pianos seen labelled 'George Hicks, Hand Organs and Cylinder Pianos'.

HICKS, JOHN, Cobourg Street, Clerkenwell, London EC. A barrel-organ maker c. 1850, related to the Bristol family of Hicks, organ and piano makers, who made the first street barrel piano in England about 1805. Sometime also at Chapel Street, Edgware Road, London. The ramifications of the Hicks family are unknown but various members made many barrel pianos, mainly of the portable, street type, in the first half of the nineteenth century. With the common misuse of the term 'barrel organ' – even contemporarily – John Hicks may indeed have been a maker of barrel pianos. A testimony that he repinned barrels is contained in Vol. III of Mayhew, *London Labour and London Poor*.

HICKS, JOSEPH, 13 Penton Street, Pentonville, London N. Maker of barrel organs and cylinder pianos [sic], whose name appears on a particularly fine 41-key piano in a rosewood case with two barrels bearing the watermark date 1846. This piano is 5 feet 9½ inches high, 39 inches wide and 21 inches deep.

HICKS, JOSEPH, Bristol, 1816–47. Whether related to, or indeed the same as, Joseph Hicks above is uncertain. An early pianoforte has been seen with a label reading 'Henry Distin (from the late Joseph Hicks), Barrel Pianoforte maker, No. 2, Church Lane, Temple Street, Bristol'. Bristol directories, examined by Langwill, list Joseph Hicks as a musical-instrument maker, who was made Freeeman of Bristol on 12 October 1812, at the following addresses: 11 Griffin Lane and Trenchard Street (1816–29); Trenchard Street (1830); 3 St Augustine's Place (1831); 16 Lower Park Row (1832–41); 17 Lower Maudlin Street (1842–4); 17 Montague Street (1845–7).

HIGEL CO. INC., OTTO, Corner Bronx Boulevard and Nereld Avenue, New York, USA. Introduced a new type of player action called the Metalnola, advertised as 'the player action of the future' with 'unique construction of valve castings . . . made in one piece of non-corrosive metal . . . the vertical valve assures positive seating under all conditions . . . accurate . . . dependable . . . efficient'. The Higel metal player action was first patented by Otto Higel and G. C. Heintzman (British Patent No. 21,946 of 1909), improved upon under Patent No 14,572 of 17 June 1914 under the name of W. E. Evans, and finally developed as the two-valve Metalnola by Higel under British Patent No. 100,286 of 15 May 1916.

HIGEL CO. LIMITED, OTTO, 680 King Street, Toronto, Canada. Makers of player actions for pianos. Widely distributed in Britain as well.

HILLIER PIANO & ORGAN CO., 288 York Road, Castle Market, London N. Makers of the Hillier player piano.

HOCH, HERMANN, Kaiserstrasse 313, Solingen, Germany. Founded in 1876. Trade supplier of electric pianos, musicwork and orchestrions.

HOFMANN, JULIUS CARL, 111 Hietzingerkai, Vienna, Austria. Barrel-piano maker, who perfected a pianoforte effect for his instruments in 1905. Also as:

HOFMANN & CZERNY, XVIII/2, Sandleitnerg 79, Vienna. Maker of piano orchestrions 'for public places and private houses', est. 1902.

HOPKINSON LTD, J. & J., 44 Fitzroy Road, London NW. Makers of the Hopkinson Player and Electrelle.

HORVILLEUR, H. & GEORGES PRESBERG, 32 rue des Archives, Paris. Clockwork barrel pianos with interchangeable cylinders. Established in 1893 at 7 rue du Temple, Paris, *fl.* 1920.

HROMADKA, AUGUST, Josefstadt-Sterngasse, Temesvar, Hungary. A maker of barrel pianos, *fl.* 1903.

LIST OF PRINCIPAL MAKERS, PATENTEES AND AGENTS

HÜNDERSEN, A., Dornbush 4, Hamburg. Agent for barrel pianos, *fl.* 1903.

HUNT & BRADISH, Warren, Ohio, USA. Patented a small pianoforte controlled by a perforated paper roll *c.* 1880.

HUPFELD, LUDWIG, A.G., Apelstr. 4, Leipzig, Germany. Established in 1872. Produced barrel piano orchestrions under the name 'Atlantic' and electric pianos under the name 'Phonola', reproducing pianos with the name 'Dea', 'Phonoliszt', 'Konzert-Phonoliszt', and 'Konzert-Clavitist'. The range of player pianos included the Solophonola and Triphonola while the most outstanding instrument of all was probably the Phonoliszt-Violina, a piano surmounted by three violins. Ludwig Hupfeld was born on 26 November 1864 and lived until 1949. His partner in the business was Otto Tetzner, born 20 March 1869. They took over the business of J. M. GROB (q.v.) on 1 July 1892 and in 1904 became 'Aktiengesellschaft'. The company became a renowned manufacturer of mechanical musical instruments and, in 1892, it pioneered a pneumatic action for the playing of pianos using perforated paper music. The firm first produced a cabinet-style piano player and later made the Solophonola, Duophonola and Triphonola player pianos, the last two being reproducing instruments. Also made the Dea which was a pneumatically played violin attached to a piano, and the Dea-Violina which was three violins all played pneumatically. Their association with Blüthner Pianos in London led to their sharing the same premises (7–13 Wigmore Street) in the 1920s. Prior to this, their London agent had been a Mr M. Sinclair, who established the Solophonola Company at 16–17 Orchard Street. By the mid-1920s, the Hupfeld London address and showrooms were at 28–30 Wigmore Street where they displayed the Phonoliszt-Violina, a three-violin and piano unit similar to the earlier Dea-Violina but based on their very fine all-metal player piano, the Phono-Liszt. Their Leipzig factory with its six floors and large wings was the largest in Europe devoted to mechanical musical instruments. During the early 1920s, they amalgamated with ZIMMERMANN (q.v.), becoming Hupfeld-Gebr. Zimmermann and changing their address to Petersstrasse 4, Postschliessfach 215, Leipzig C1, between 1926 and 1928. All Hupfeld music rolls, including those made under their registered trade mark 'Animatic', were made on special paper bearing the watermark 'Phonola' and the year of manufacture – a unique feature indeed. Hupfelds excelled in the production of the all-metal player action in later years, dispensing with wood, rubber tubing and cloth. The Hupfeld reproducing actions were widely used in Bluthner pianos. The firm is thought to have remained in existence until the outbreak of the 1939–45 war. The Vienna address was VI Mariahilferstrasse 9.

ICART, ANTONIO, 23 San Agustin, Tarragona, Spain. Established in 1875 as a maker of street pianos and also a hirer of these instruments, *fl.* 1903.

IDEAL MIGNON. The name of a player action introduced in 1910 by Copplestone & Co. Ltd of 94 Regent Street, London, and fitted by them into their Sterling player piano.

IMHOF & MUKLE. Founded at Vöhrenbach in the Black Forest in 1845, the firm was at 46 Oxford Street, London, in 1870 and at 110 New Oxford Street in 1883. They were also sometime at 547 Oxford Street and also had a 'manufactory' at 9 Sandiland Street, Holborn, London, in 1880. They were the London branch of a famous German musical instrument works which specialised in the manufacture of barrel orchestrion organs. Daniel Imhof took out patents in 1866 for improvements 'in the machinery of chimes and the striking of drums and other instruments of percussion by self-acting organs'. A very handsome drawing-room barrel piano has survived complete with two barrels, each of which bear a pre-pinning barrel label stating 'Imhof & Mukle'. The music dates from *c.* 1846.

IMPERIAL ORGAN & PIANO CO. LTD, 45 King's Road, Camden Town, London NW1. Piano and organ manufacturers who also made a combined piano and organ as well as player pianos *c.* 1930.

INDUSTRIA NAZIONALE AUTOPIANI E PIANOFORTI (I.N.A.P.), 3 via Biella, Turin, Italy. Makers of player pianos, *fl.* 1930. Operated by Giuseppe Cavana.

JACOB, L., Kgl. Hofl, Stuttgart, Germany. A manufacturer of disc-playing piano orchestrions *c.* 1895–1900.

JACQUARD, JOSEPH MARIE, Lyons, France. A straw-hat maker who first conceived the idea of using cardboard strips, suitably perforated, to control functions in a loom. His invention was intended as a means to the production of woven patterned carpets and was to become the Jacquard Loom. He died in 1834. His system was adapted as a means of playing an organ or piano, thereby replacing the barrel.

JANISCH, FRANZ, Newbaugasse 47, Vienna VII, Austria. Franz Janisch succeeded the business of his father Josef as manufacturer of orchestrions, barrel organs and so on as well as handling mechanical musical instruments. His name appears on a large piano orchestrion in the Walt Bellm collection, Sarosota, Florida. His name appears in 1903 and 1909 directories.

JEBAVY, FRANZ, Reichsstrasse 118, Trautenau, Bohemia. Maker of piano orchestrions and barrel organs, *fl.* 1903.

JENKINSON PLAYER ACTION CO. INC., 912–14 Elm Street, Cincinnati, USA. In 1913 advertised 'turn your straight pianos into players' using prefabricated components.

JONES, THOMAS LINFORTH, 53a Franciscan Road, Tooting, London. An engineer who devised and patented in 1905 a method of operating a coin-freed clockwork barrel piano in a public place from remotely situated coin boxes. The slot boxes could be situated anywhere in the building and the release of the piano's clockwork was through 'electro-magnetic contacts'. He was later to improve upon his system in collaboration with G. Phillips.

JORIO, D., Modane (Savoy), France. Maker of barrel pianos, *fl.* 1909.

JORIO, AMEDEO & FRATELLI, Giuliano di Roma, Rome, Italy. Street-organ and piano maker, *fl.* 1930.

KAMENIK, JOSEPH, Prague. A maker of street barrel organs and pianos who was the last maker to follow his trade in that city.

KAPS, ERNST, Dresden. Established in 1858, they manufactured a range of self-playing pianos and other instruments, automata, phonographs, etc. Their London agent was Mr Philip Cohen, 224 Brixton Road, London SW.

KARN & CO. LTD, D.W., 3 Newman Street, London W. Founded in 1867. London arm of Woodstock, Canada, maker of the Pianauto piano player.

KASTNER, MAXIMILIAN MACARIUS. Born in Germany in 1876, Kastner was the inventor of the Triumph piano player, the Auto Piano player piano, and the Kastonome expression piano. Interned as an alien during the First World War, he returned to player pianos after the war only to lose his life in an accident in 1924.

KASTNER-AUTOPIANO Akt.-Ges., 6 Wittenbergerstrasse, Leipzig, Germany. Also called Kastner & Co. Pianos-Apparate Akt.-Ges. Makers of player pianos and actions. They patented a system of unit valves for the player in 1929 in which each pneumatic and motor was fashioned in metal and could be removed and replaced in a few moments. This dispensed with the wooden action components and wooden valve chest. The company also produced music rolls and they had offices at 196 Great Portland Street, London W. (See below.)

KASTNER & CO. LTD, 34–6 Margaret Street, Oxford Circus, London W. Kastner established his business in London in 1903, later expanding it with premises in Germany (see above) and Amsterdam. He manufactured the Kastner-Autopiano expression instrument, later called the Triumph. Manufacturer of piano rolls who made a large quantity of both 65- and 88-note rolls. Other addresses recorded for Kastner in London before the First World War were 196 Great Portland Street, 191 Regent Street and 62 Conduit Street. Under the Trading with the Enemy Act (1916), the business of Kastner was forcibly wound up in December 1916, a receiver being appointed to the Auto-Piano Company. There was considerable resistance to the application of the Act in this instance with the directors of this British company raising strong objection. This was on account of the fact that the company had been manufacturing pianos and players in England since 1912 and fitting them into both British and German pianos. Its Kastonome player was a complex assembly which had a separate theme hole for each note in the tracker bar. The company also made ordinary player actions which it marketed through its associate company, the Direct Action

Company, under the name Arrow. In spite of this strong connection, the Act was enforced and the company wound up. The associate company became the DIRECT PNEUMATIC ACTION CO. (q.v.) and on 11 June 1917 a new company was registered, Triumph-Auto Pianos Ltd – with a capital of £20,000 to carry on the business. One of the directors was Frederick H. Saffell of Teignmouth Road, Brondesbury in north London. Saffell started work for Kastners in 1907 and remained with the business until the last war. He was also associated with the running of piano makers Barratt & Robinson up to the time of his death in 1975. Triumph-Auto Pianos Ltd was to survive until 1929 when it was liquidated, only to be reborn as Triumph Auto Pianos (1930) Ltd with a £150,000 capitalisation. It was later amalgamated with Barratt & Robinson. The complexity of the original Kastner action with its double pneumatic valve seats was ultimately replaced by a more conventional type of player action in which the so-called Triumphodist control was operated by the normal Themodist-type roll perforations. One of the late player products was the Maestrel piano. The Kastonome action was not fitted after 1914.

KEITH, PROWSE & CO. Founded by R. W. Keith, the company first appeared at 131 Cheapside between 1829 and 1832, and then at 42 Cheapside between 1832 and 1846 in which year Keith died. William Prowse, a partner, continued on his own between about 1846 and 1865 when H. Bryan Jones joined Prowse and the title reverted to Keith, Prowse & Co. The business was the manufacture and sale of musical instruments and the publishing of music. The company had its own piano factory making both ordinary instruments and barrel pianos, one of which was a clockwork-driven model for use in public houses and suchlike. This was called the Pennyano, had 48 notes and played 10 tunes. Many other barrel pianos of the coin-freed variety bear this name, sometimes carved on the front barrel fall, but it is thought that many of these were not made by the company but commissioned from other, better known clockwork-piano makers. During the First World War, Keith, Prowse made new music for German piano orchestrions and orchestrion organs. The company is still in business today although activities are restricted to acting as agents for theatre tickets.

KELLY, GEORGE BRADFORD, Jamaica Plain, Suffolk County, Boston, Massachusetts, USA. A builder of reed organs and an early pioneer in self-playing reed instruments, Kelly invented a wind-operated music-roll motor in 1886. This was the subject of US Patent number 357,933 dated 15 February 1887. This made use of sliding valves and closing ports to pneumatic motors. This type of motor was at once adopted and, upon expiration of the patent, was used widely throughout the world with but slight variations. He was a prolific inventor and was finally acquired by Aeolian and in his subsequent patents gave his address as 362 Fifth Avenue, New York – that of his employers.

KIBBEY & CO., H. C., 209 State Street, Chicago, USA. In 1909 were described as makers of automatic pianos.

KINTZING, PETER, Neuwied, Germany. A clockmaker who moved to Paris and c. 1780 made an automaton featuring a young girl playing a stringed instrument, using two sticks as strikers. He was helped by a cabinet-maker named Roentgen. Kintzing also built a musical clock which featured a dulcimer and a number of flutes and this, dated 1780, is preserved in the Museum of Arts and Crafts, Paris.

KLEIN & CO., HENRY, 84 Oxford Street, London W. Agents for mechanical music work, particularly Polyphon musical boxes and Amorette organettes. Also was agent for Peter's electric pianos made in Leipzig. In 1901, these sold for £128.

KLEINSCHMIDT & CO., ADOLF, Herderstr. 4, Braunschweig, Germany. Established in 1902 as makers of piano orchestrions operated by descending weights.

KLEPETÁŘ, HYNEK, 11 Železna ui, Prague, Czechoslovakia. Maker of electric pianos and piano orchestrions, fl. 1930. Possibly successor to:

KLEPETÁŘ, IGNAZ, Eisengasse 11 and Gensengasse 24, Prague, Czechoslovakia. Warehouse and depot for electric pianos and piano orchestrions, fl. 1909.

KLEPETÁŘ, J., Prague. Maker of weight-operated barrel piano orchestrions, early twentieth century. One seen has 37-key piano with iron frame, drum, triangle and cymbal.

KNABE & CO., WILLIAM, Fifth Avenue, Corner 39th Street, New York, USA. Piano manufacturers established in 1837 with factories at Baltimore and Maryland, who produced a range of quality reproducing pianos fitted with the Ampico action.

KOENIGSBERG ET CIE, 28 rue Camusel, Brussels, Belgium. Makers of parts for electric player pianos, established in 1900.

KOHLER & CAMPBELL, 50th Street and 11th Avenue, New York, USA. Producers of the Pianista pneumatic push-up cabinet-style piano player. Their slogan was 'Knows no technical difficulties'. c. 1899.

KOHLER INDUSTRIES, New York City, USA. Manufacturers of the Welte-Mignon (Licensee) action for reproducing pianos. They also controlled the Auto Pneumatic Action Co. and the Standard Pneumatic Action Co. The Welte-Mignon (Licensee) action was installed in over a hundred different American pianos and their slogan was 'The Master's Fingers on your Piano'.

KOTYKIEWICZ, THEOFIL, Straussengasse 18, Vienna. Peter Titz began his musical instrument business in 1852 making reed organs. After his death the business was taken over by Teofil Kotykiewicz, jnr. Invented the Kromarograph recording harmonium c.1900. See Chapter 11 for details. One example survives in the Deutsches Museum, Munich.

KOWATZ, M., Bahnhofstr. 25, Beuthen Ober-Schlesien, Germany. Established in 1893 as makers of piano orchestrions and agents for other mechanical musical instruments.

KRANICH & BACH, 237 East 23rd Street, New York, USA. Makers of quality pianos and player pianos.

KRELL AUTO-GRAND PIANO CO., Connersville, Indiana, USA. Makers of the Krell Auto-Grand upright piano as well as the Auto-Player and the Pian-Auto.

KUHL & KLATT, Wusterhausener Str. 17 and Runge-Strasse No. 18, Berlin SO, Germany. Martin Hesse and Paul Klatt described themselves as manufacturers of pneumatic self-acting musical instruments, but it appears that they were also agents. The business, established in 1899, was renowned for electric pianos, in particular those equipped with accumulators for providing power. These were marketed under the name Pneuma and a similar device was available for church organs under the name Pneumatist. The Vorsteller was the name of Kuhl & Klatt's player action.

LABRADOR, BALTASAR, 127 Toledo, Madrid, Spain. Barrel-piano and organ hirer and repairer, *fl.* 1909.

LACAPE ET CIE, J., Paris. In 1882, patented a treadle-driven mechanical piano, playing either from a barrel or mechanically from a tune sheet. Won a bronze medal for barrel pianos at the Brussels Exposition in 1883.

LAFLEUR & SON, J. R., 15 Green Street, Leicester Square, London WC. Producers of street pianos in 1880.

LAKIN & CO., R. J., 67 Besley Street, Streatham, London SW16. Established at this address in 1934, Lakin came originally from Bristol. He advertised as maker of 'mechanical organs' but it is not known for certain whether or not he did actually make barrel organs or barrel pianos. It is known that he sold both music and mechanical street pianos and organs. He also did repairs until ceasing business in 1943.

LANGENBUCHER. The Langenbucher family was a renowned source of musical automata in the 16th and early 17th century Augsburg. There appears to have been two strains to the family, one headed by Achilles Langenbucher (Augsburg Freeman 1611, died c. 1650) and Veit Langenbucher (born about 1587; died c. 1631). Small clocks with automata, clockwork spinets and automated scenes were produced by these names. An extraordinary insight into the relationship between Balthasar Langenbucher (son of Veit) and the other famous Augsburg automata-makers appears in *Die Welt als Uhr* (edited by Klaus Maurice and Otto Mayr) in a paper by Eva Groiss. An English-language version of this appears as 'The Bidermann-Langenbucher Lawsuit' in *Music & Automata*, Vol. 1, pp. 10–12.

LAUBERGER & GLOSS, Trostgasse 108/110/121, Vienna X, Austria. Established in 1900 as a maker of pianofortes and piano actions. In 1912 was advertising as specialists in 'Konzert-Pianino, Pneuma and other instruments', which appears to suggest that they were agents for Berlin- and

LIST OF PRINCIPAL MAKERS, PATENTEES AND AGENTS

Leipzig-made instruments. Described as 'Grösste u. Leistengsfähigste Pianofabriken der Österr.-Unger.-Monarchie. En-gros-Export'.

LEIDI, ALLESSANDRO, Via S. Lazzaro 9 (Via Osia), Bergamo, Italy. Barrel piano maker, agent, hirer, *fl.* 1907.

LEIPZIGER ORCHESTRIONWERKE PAUL LÖSCHE, Blumenstr. 10–14, Leipzig-Gohlis, Germany. Established 1902. Maker of electric pianos and orchestrions.

LIEBETANZ & RICHTER, Gräbschenerstrasse 85, Breslau, Germany. Established in 1902 and managed by Karl Krause, made piano orchestrions. By 1909 the business had shifted to Gräbschenerstrasse 23.

LIEBMANN, ERNST ERICH, Hainstr. 10, Gera, Reuss, Germany. Established in 1871 as a harmonium builder who also made a self-playing device for harmoniums called the Liebmannista covered by German Patent number 283302. Also made the Kalliston organette.

LINDNER SOHN, JULIUS P., Heilgeiststr. 86, Stralsund, Germany. Piano makers founded in 1825. By 1908 were manufacturing electro-pneumatic player pianos.

LINK PIANO CO. INC., 183–5 Water Street, Binghamton, New York, and 532 Republic Building, Chicago. Makers of coin-operated pianos and instruments with orchestral effects. The firm was originally the Automatic Musical Company, claimed by Bowers to have been one of the earliest makers of coin-operated pianos in the States. They sold the Encore Banjo and the Hiawatha Self-Playing Xylophone. When the firm went bankrupt in 1910, Edwin A. Link was appointed chairman of the creditors' committee, realised the opportunity to re-form the company and so founded the Link Piano Co., later turning out about 300 coin-operated instruments a year. His son, Ed Link, later took over many of the firm's patents and applied them to the manufacture of the famous pneumatically operated Link Trainer still in use with many flying schools.

LIPP & SOHN, RICHARD, Weigenburgerstrasse 32, Stuttgart, Germany. Founded in 1831, this firm produced player pianos including the Duca-Lipp electrically operated reproducing piano. Introduced in the spring of 1910, this cost £300. None is known to survive. Their London showrooms were at 56 Berners Street, off Oxford Street, Mr Fritz Willeringhaus being manager.

LISSI, GAETANO, Piazza Alessandro, Como, Italy. Barrel piano maker and handler, *fl.* 1909.

LLINARES, VICENTE, Castelar, Faventia, Spain. Manufacturer of modern miniature street pianos playing 23 notes on metal rods and known as 'Impuesto de Lujo a Metálico'.

LOCHMANN, PAUL. See ORIGINAL-MUSIKWERKE PAUL LOCHMANN GmbH.

LORENZ, WENZEL, Schillerstr. 176, Trautenau, Bohemia. Established in 1892. Maker of weight-driven piano orchestrions, *fl.* 1909.

LÜNEBURG-MUSIKWERKE. Lüneburg & Co. Musikwerke GmbH was founded in 1908 at Altona on the Elbe in Germany. The office and works were at Rothestrasse 64. The products included the Chitarrone electric expression piano, and orchestrions Bellisore and Annalies.

MACHINEK & SÖHNE, F., XVII/3, Ortliebgasse 5, Vienna, Austro-Hungary. Established in 1882 as makers of mechanical musical instruments. Maker of the International piano orchestrion played by barrels.

MCTAMMANY, JOHN, McTammany is probably one of the most underrated inventors in the history of the player piano. History has not treated him well because, having been cheated of his early inventions and patented ideas, he chose to try to defend himself in the courts. In so doing, he dragged the names of others into the legal limelight and thus acquired the image of a busybody and troublemaker. In truth, McTammany was the real pioneer of the use of the sliding paper valve as applied to the playing of a reed instrument and he made the first player reed organs at Cambridge, Massachusetts. Inventor with a number of patents to his credit, his earliest auto-playing organ dates from around 1864 although it was not to be patented until 1876. Although his claim to be the inventor of the player piano stems solely from his reed organ system, it is true to say that applied pneumatics owe much to his pioneering work. Born on 26 June 1845, he led a hard life and with insufficient funds to renew his patents he had to watch them being exploited by others. He died penniless on 26 March 1915, leaving behind a most unusual yet invaluable reference work called *The Technical History of the Player*.

MAESTRO COMPANY, Eldridge, New York. Produced the Maestro piano-player *c.* 1899 at $125 – half the price of the Pianola and the Cecilian. A utility player which stood on four spindly legs. Also made key-top player of the same name.

MALCOLM & CO., JOHN, Erskine Road, Regents Park, London NW. Makers of the Malcolm piano player.

MANNHEIMER MUSIKWERKE MARIA SCHMID, S.6, Nr 3, Mannheim, Germany. Established in 1908 and managed by Emil Schmid, maker of orchestrions both piano and pipe, as well as gramophones. Handled various makes of mechanical musical instruments.

MARASCHI, FRANCESCO, Corso via Cene, Porta Novara 11 and Via Principe Amedeo 17, Vigevano, Pavia, Italy. Founded 1898. Agent and hirer of barrel pianos.

MARAZZI, ACH., 50 Vico del Governo Vecchio, Rome, Italy. Street organ maker, *fl.* 1930.

MARIANI, LOUIS & ANTONIO, 133 Nueva, Figueras, Gerona, Spain. Street-piano agents, *fl.* 1903. By 1909 Louis was still operating from this address but Antonio was at 15 Nueva, presumably on his own, operating as an agent.

MARKS & HARNETT, 4 & 5 Rosoman Mews, London EC1. Advertised as manufacturers of 'piano-organs' from 1918 to 1919. No other information available.

MARONI, GIORGIO, Varese, Como, Italy. Barrel-organ and piano maker, *fl.* 1930.

MARQUETTE PIANO CO., 415–17 15th Street, Chicago, Illinois, USA. Established in 1905. Makers of electric player pianos, orchestrions and photoplayers under the name Cremona. J. P. Seeburg originally worked for the company before setting up in business for himself *c.* 1907. In the early 1920s, when Marquette was not as successful as the Seeburg company, Cremona-labelled instruments were made using some Seeburg parts. One style of Cremona – the Style 3 – was made for Regina Music Box Co. of Rahway who sold it as the Reginapiano. Some time after 1909 the company moved to 2421–39 Wallace Street in Chicago.

MARROMARCO, VINCENZO, Piazza Arcivescovado 69, Bari, Italy. Street-piano and organ agent and hirer, *fl.* 1909.

MARSHALL & SONS, SIR HERBERT, Angelus Hall, Regent House, 233 Regent Street, London W. Makers of the Artistyle player-piano music rolls which gave printed accenting instructions to the melody notes, to enable the performer to interpret the correct way by reading the roll as he played it. They also made player pianos and extended the music-roll side to include the Angelus Artistyle and the Artist Song Rolls labels. Later a separate company was formed called The Artistyle Music Roll Company with premises at 204–6 Great Portland Street, London W1. Marshall produced the Angelus diaphragm player action which it supplied in pianos by Brinsmead, Winkelmann, Emerson and Knabe as well as in piano-player form.

MARTELETTI, GIUSEPPE, Vicola Giovanni Lanza, Casa propria, Casale Monferrato, Italy. Established in 1860 for the manufacture of barrel pianos and organs. By 1909 he was producing very attractive clockwork instruments. Also operated a depot in Alba.

MARTELETTI, FRATELLI, 31 via Giovanni Lanza, Casale Monferrato, Alessandria, Italy. Maker of barrel pianos, *fl.* 1930.

MARTINEZ, ANTONIO, 19 Mesoneros Romanos, Madrid, Spain. Barrel-piano dealer and hirer, *fl.* 1909.

MARTINEZ, FERMIN, 17 Brava Murillo, Madrid, Spain. Barrel-piano dealer and hirer, *fl.* 1909.

MARYLAND AUTOMATIC BANJO CO., 323 Calvert Street, N. Baltimore, Maryland. Maker of automatic banjos. *fl.* 1909.

MASERATI, CAESAR, 92 New Chambers Street, New York, USA. An Italian organ maker who also built street barrel pianos mounted on carts, which he sold and hired out. He was in business in 1906 and his colleague, Antoniazzi (q.v.), was later to establish the B.A.B. ORGAN CO. (q.v.).

MASSA, ANTONIO, Via Nizza 23 and Via Goito 15, Turin, Italy. The brothers Antonio and Giacomo Massa were makers of street barrel pianos and also had a large business hiring them out, *fl.* 1909.

LIST OF PRINCIPAL MAKERS, PATENTEES AND AGENTS

MASTERTOUCH. Name of piano rolls currently produced by the Mastertouch Piano Roll Company, Box 157, Redfern, New South Wales, Australia.

MAXFIELD & SONS LTD, 324–6 Liverpool Road, London N. Makers of the Maxfield piano player and also piano rolls.

MAZZA, F., 112 via Consolazione, Rome, Italy. Maker of barrel pianos, *fl.* 1930. See MONETTA.

MECHANICAL ORGUINETTE COMPANY, USA. Formed to manufacture Mason J. Matthews' 'Orguinette' table reed organ which played perforated paper rolls. They then made the Aeolian player reed organ at which time they were re-formed into the Aeolian Company (q.v.).

MELNIK, ALBERT, ORCHESTRIONFABRIK, Reichsstr. 61, Trautenau, Bohemia, Austria. Established in 1903 as maker of piano orchestrions, among which was the Delphin. In 1909 advertised: 'Best known and cheapest cylinder-musikworks with weight drawing up. Piano-orchestrions, specialities in mandolin and xylophone-works . . . Unexcelled durability and musical beauty . . .'

MEL-O-DEE MUSIC CO, Meriden, Connecticut, USA. Subsidiary of the Aeolian Corporation devoted to the manufacture of music rolls. Was originally called Universal and by 1923 was the largest music-roll producer in the States.

MELOGRAPHIC ROLL CO., Buffalo, New York, USA. Makers of the Melographic music roll.

MELOTO CO., London. Manufacturers of music rolls for player pianos, particularly 88-note rolls which had automatic pedalling control from extra marginal perforations in the paper.

MELVILLE CLARK PIANO COMPANY, Steinway Hall, 409 Steinway Building, Chicago, USA. Melville Clark, a member of the Storey & Clark Company of Chicago, took out patents for his Apollo piano player in 1899. The first Apollo played 58 notes and used a clockwork motor rewind system for the music roll. This cabinet-style player stood 36 inches high, was 41 inches long and 12 inches wide. Introduced in 1900, it also featured a transposing tracker bar – one of the first. Melville Clark was probably the first to make a piano with the player mechanism inside the case, *c.* 1901. In 1902, he was the first to make a full-scale 88-note player action and was also the first to fit a player action into a grand piano (1904). In 1909, the Clark company was producing a player action to cater for five different sizes of rolls – 58, 65, 70, 82 and 88 notes.

MENZEL, WILHEM, Warschauer Strasse 58, Berlin 0, Germany. Established in 1890 as maker of pianos. Produced a patented self-playing pneumatic player action and also a range of player pianos.

MERLIN, JOHN JOSEPH. Born at Huys near Liège on 17 September 1735, Merlin spent six years in Paris before coming to England in 1760 where he lived in the suite of the Spanish ambassador, Count de Guentes, in Soho Square. A talented musical instrument maker and inventor, he took out a patent in 1774 for a 'compound harpsichord' which was a combined harpsichord and piano with a down-striking action. In this year he was living in Little Queen Ann Street, St Marylebone and describing himself as a Mathematical Instrument Maker. Preserved in the Deutsches Museum, Munich, is a 5-octave compound harpsichord inscribed: 'Josephus Merlin, Privilegiarius Novi Fortepiano Nr. 80, Londini, 1780'. Unusual is the fact that this mechanism is fitted with a copying-machine driven by a clockwork motor which notes the music being played as pencil marks on a long endless band of paper. See description in Chapter 11. Merlin went on to establish and operate a museum of novelties in Princes Street, Hanover Square. He invented an invalid chair (probably the first such device) and also the roller skate. Busby relates in his *Concert Room Anecdotes* (II, 137), how Merlin attended a ball at Carlisle House and traversed the room on his skates while playing the violin, an escapade which came to an abrupt end when he collided with a very valuable mirror which he smashed along with his fiddle while causing himself severe wounds. He died in 1804.

MIGLIAVACCA, ETTORE, 3 via S. Teodoro, Pavia, Italy (factory at 16 via Casa del Popolo). Maker of clockwork barrel pianos, *fl.* 1930.

MIGLIETTI, GIOVANNI, Via Morosini 11, Turin, Italy. Founded in 1905 as makers of components and other parts for barrel pianos.

MINA, GIOVANNI, 2 First Street, Manhattan, USA. An Italian who went to America in 1880 and set up in business making barrel pianos and barrel organs and pinning carousel organ barrels. On his death, the business was taken over by G. GAZZA (q.v.) and moved to 71 Roosevelt Street nearby, but the business did not prosper and soon closed.

MINICUCCI DEL MANZO & CO., Torre del Greco, Naples, Italy. Agent for Piano-Melodicos and other mechanical instruments, *fl.* 1909.

MIOLIS, LINO, 12 via Ormea, Turin, Italy. Maker of barrel organs and pianos, *fl.* 1930.

MIRALLES, ANTONIO, 16 Amazonas, Madrid, Spain. Barrel-piano agent, dealer and hirer, *fl.* 1909.

MODERN INTERACTION PLAYER MANUFACTURERS, 23 South Street, Clair Street, Toledo, Ohio, USA. Advertised: 'Our specialty is Electrical Attachments for Foot-Pedal Player-Pianos . . . Automatic Speed Control Rewinders and Metal Pumps.'

MOJON, MANGER & CO., Bartletts Buildings, London EC. Well-known makers of large-size musical boxes, some with dancing dolls and orchestral effects. Also made coin-freed cylinder musical boxes and, later, mechanical harmoniums and pianos. Their factory, which produced watches and clocks as well as musical boxes, was at Chaux-de-Fonds, Geneva, and they had a branch warehouse at Oxford Terrace, Coventry. Their pianos were most probably manufactured by them in this country. John Manger is described, in a patent application of 1886 relating to musical boxes, as being a 'Musical Box Importer'.

MOLA, CAV. GIUSEPPE, via Nizza 82, Turin, Italy. Founded in 1862 as makers of pianos, harmoniums and church organs who also made barrel pianos, *fl.* 1909.

MOLINARI & SONS, G., 112 32nd Street, Brooklyn, New York, USA. Produced many small barrel organs and barrel pianos for street use. The factory was started during the Civil War and for sixty years the family sustained the business, Joseph Molinari running a shop at 153 Elizabeth Street, Manhattan, where all kinds of mechanical musical instruments could be purchased.

MOLLER, H. P., Copenhagen. Makers of street barrel pianos of the smaller, portable type. A surviving specimen is in the shape of a lyre or guitar and is said to date from *c.* 1850.

MONDINI, VEDOVA LUIGI, Corso Vitt. Emanuele 40, Cremona, Italy. A maker of barrel pianos, *fl.* 1903.

MONETTA, RICCARDO, 112 via della Consolazione, Rome, Italy. Maker of barrel pianos and barrel organs, *fl.* 1909. Shared premises with MAZZA (q.v.).

MONTANINI, ANTONIO, 9 corsa Milano, Novara, Italy. Maker of clockwork barrel pianos, *fl.* 1930.

MONTANINI-CASTALDI & POMELIA, Borgo San Agabia 83, Novara, Italy. Makers of barrel organs and barrel pianos who advertised their speciality as mandolin-pianos, *fl.* 1909.

MORTIER, I. GANDAE A°. This name appears deeply etched, in large letters, on one of the brass side plates of a combined flute-playing and harp-playing clock in the Guinness collection. Whether this Mortier was any relation to the Belgian innkeeper who subsequently became a famed maker of show and fair organs is unknown and unlikely.

MOTOR PLAYER CORPORATION, 536 Lake Shore Drive, Chicago, Illinois. Makers of the Electora vacuum pump for player pianos which 'eliminated foot pumping' when installed in a player. Patented on 28 October 1919, US Patent No. 1,320,224. A mere 7 inches in diameter and 10 inches in height. Marketing began in February 1919.

MÜLLER, EMIL, Friedhofstr. 40–2, Werdau, Saxony, Germany. Established in 1887 as harmonium manufacturers. Produced a harmonium player called the Harmonista.

MULLER, P. A., Pau, France. Built a mechanical recorder *c.* 1907 and an electric piano-roll cutting machine *c.* 1910.

MURDOCH & CO. LTD, JOHN G., 91 & 93 Farringdon Road, London EC. Described as 'sole licensees by Her Majesty's Royal Letters Patent' for the Celestina organette, which played perforated-paper music and was patented in 1887 by A. Maxfield. Distributor of the Minerva piano players.

MURDOCH, MURDOCH & CO., 461 & 463 Oxford Street, London. Agents for the Phoneon cabinet-style piano player first shown in Glasgow at the Musical Trades Exhibition in 1901. They also later handled the CONNOISSEUR (q.v.) instruments.

MUSICUS PLAYER PIANO CO., 2 Salisbury Road, Highgate Hill, London N. Makers of the Musicus piano player.

MUSOLA CO., 2443 Massachusetts Avenue, Cambridgeport, Massachusetts, USA. Makers of player actions and the Musola player c. 1908.

MUSTEL & CIE, 46 rue de Douai, Paris 9e. Factory at 48 rue Pernety, Paris 14e. Established 1853. See MUSTEL, CHARLES VICTOR.

MUSTEL, CHARLES VICTOR. Born at Le Havre on 13 June 1815, Victor Mustel began his career as a musical-instrument manufacturer with Alexandre. In 1853 he set up in business on his own, making harmoniums and pianos, including mechanical instruments. Until the early 1920s, the address was 46 rue de Douai, Paris 9e, with a factory at 14 rue Marie-Anne Colombier, Bagnolet (Seine). His two sons, Charles (born 1840, died 20 May 1893) and Auguste (born 1844, died 16 March 1919), succeeded him on his death in January 1890. Mustel made extremely fine reed organs on the American organ principle and also marketed the Welte Mignon keyboardless reproducing piano under the name Mustel Maestro. The London showrooms were at 80 Wigmore Street. The Paris showroom moved to 16 Avenue de Wagram, where it remains to this day as a showroom for electric organs and hi-fi products. Victor Mustel's grandson, Alphonse Mustel, managed the business for some years and was awarded the distinction of Chevalier de la Légion d'Honneur in 1906.

MUSUMECI, MARIO, via Opificio 4–10, Catania, Sicily, Italy. Founded in 1898 as manufacturer of barrel pianos and an agent for hiring, fl. 1930.

NATIONAL PIANO COMPANY, Boston, Massachusetts, USA. Makers of 'the most up-to-date player in the world' – the Air-O-Player, which was 'the first perfected metal action'. This was in 1913 and it was installed in Briggs, Merrill and in Norris & Hyde instruments.

NEEDHAM, ELIAS PARKMAN. In 1846, Jeremiah Carhart (inventor of the suction bellows for reed organs) and E. P. Needham formed a company to manufacture reed organs. Initially this was at 172 Fulton Street in New York, later moving to a new six-storey building at 99 East 23rd Street. The business became Needham & Sons and later Needham Piano & Organ Co. with a factory at Washington, New Jersey, and headquarters at 96 Fifth Avenue, New York. Accused by JOHN MCTAMMANY (q.v.) of pirating many of his ideas, Needham took out many patents including one for the invention of the upright action used in reed organs and which formed the basis of most organettes and player pianos, wherein a sheet of perforated paper passes over the reed opening. He owned altogether 15 patents which he later sold to the MECHANICAL ORGUINETTE COMPANY (q.v.). He made the Needham Paragon piano player.

NELSON-WIGGEN PIANO CO., 1731–45 Belmont Avenue, Chicago, Illinois, USA. Established c. 1920 for the manufacture of coin-operated electric pianos, the majority of which were of the keyboardless variety.

NEUE LEIPZIGER MUSIKWERKE ADOLF BUFF-HEDINGER, Möckersche Str. 29–33 and Herlossohnstrasse 1–4, Leipzig-Gohlis, Germany. This company was formed in 1904 to take over the Ehrlich business which made disc-playing organettes under several names, the most popular of which was the Ariston, and disc-piano players. Several different types of player action and piano player were introduced, including the Premier pneumatic action, the Premier player piano, piano orchestrions, both barrel and pneumatic, the Primavolta electric piano, the Xylophon-Klavier, and the Toccaphon.

NEW TRIST PLAYER PIANO LTD. See TRIST PIANO PLAYER LTD.

NEWCOMBE PIANO CO. LTD, 121 Bellwoods Avenue, Toronto. Makers of player actions fl. 1909.

NIAGARA FRONTIER MUSICAL INSTRUMENT MANUFACTURING CO., Tonawanda, New York. Makers of self-acting stringed instruments, fl. 1909.

NIAGARA MUSICAL INSTRUMENT COMPANY, USA. Produced instruments similar to those made by the North Tonawanda Musical Instrument Works factory, which was in the same town – North Tonawanda. These included coin-freed barrel pianos.

NILSSON, I. F., Öster Korsberga, Lemnhult, Saxhult, Sweden. Sometime about 1884–5, Nilsson invented an instrument which he named a 'pianoharpa' comprising a table-like mechanism with pinned barrel and a compass of 18 notes. This was subsequently improved upon by ANDERSSON (q.v.).

NIXON, C. E., USA. Built an interesting modern android, in the form of the reclining figure of the goddess Isis playing a zither. The full-size automaton featured an electrically controlled zither, but the fingers actually performed on the strings.

NORTH TONAWANDA MUSICAL INSTRUMENT WORKS, North Tonawanda, New York, USA. Founded in 1893 by EUGENE DEKLEIST (q.v.) as the North Tonawanda Barrel Organ Factory and incorporated in 1906 with premises at Payne Avenue, North Tonawanda, they subsequently produced a range of band organs selling from $250 to $3,000. These had pneumatic action and were played by endless-paper music. They also made coin-freed instruments including the Pianolin and the Mando Piano Orchestrina. Ultimately taken over by the Remington Rand Company, the premises continued as a fair-organ manufactory until the mid-1920s. They produced the Tonophone barrel piano for Wurlitzer.

NYSTRÖM, JOHAN PETTER, Karlstad, Norway. Nyström built a number of attractive reed organs under the name 'Nyström's Reform-orgel' which could be played by means of an Ariston-like cardboard disc. These were covered by certain patents. During the period 1906–9, several patents were issued in the name of C. W. Nyström of the Nyström company for music recorders (melographs), including one which could be used as a key-top player for piano or organ. This model, subject of British Patent number 21,594 of 30 September 1911, was electromagnetic (for detailed description see under Melography in general index).

ODEOLA, 11 rue du 4-Septembre, Paris 2e (factory at 6 rue Marc Séguin, Paris 18e). Makers of player pianos and piano rolls.

OPERATORS' PIANO COMPANY, 715 North Kedzie Avenue, Chicago, Illinois, USA. Makers of coin-operated pianos with percussion and orchestral effects under the name Coinola, and the Reproduco, a player pipe organ and piano. The factory was at 16 South Peoria, Chicago. Founded (according to Bowers) about 1904 (yet in no directory before 1908), the company flourished until the mid-1930s. It also produced the Multitone series of pianos for Welte, and the Empress Electric for the Chicago store Lyon & Healy.

ORCHESTRELLE COMPANY, 225 Regent Street, London W. Formed early in the 1900s, this was a British-owned, American-financed subsidiary of the American Aeolian Company. Was later known as The Aeolian Co. Ltd. By 1904, The Orchestrelle Co. was at the Aeolian Hall, 135–6–7 New Bond Street, London W, and was distributing the Pianola piano player and the Pianola player piano as well as the Aeolian Orchestrelle player organs. The instruments were manufactured in America, shipped to England and assembled at the Aeolian factory at Hayes, Middlesex. The company had agents in Edinburgh (Methven, Simpson & Co.) and Glasgow (Marr, Wood & Co.). Early in 1930 the firm was dissolved, the assets being taken over by Harrods. See also AEOLIAN CO. The first address of the Orchestrelle Company was in Elm Street, off the Gray's Inn Road, London WC. The firm produced a large number of music rolls including the Metrostyle (which referred to the metronome or speed line printed on the roll) and Themodist (accented rolls), as well as music rolls for the Orchestrelle and the Aeolian Reproducing Pipe Organ.

ORCHESTRIONFABRIK ALBERT MELNIK, Trautenau, Bohemia, Austria. Founded in 1903 for the manufacture of barrel-operated piano orchestrions worked by falling weights and marketed under the name Delphin.

ORIGINAL-MUSIKWERKE PAUL LOCHMANN GmbH, Querstrasse 17, Leipzig, Germany. Factory in Zeulenroda. Established in 1900 by Paul Lochmann of Symphonion disc musical box fame and Ernst Lüder. Produced piano orchestrions played by pinned barrel and later by cardboard roll and all bearing the trade name 'Original'.

OROZCO, CARRILLO PRIMO, 97 Bravo Murillo, Madrid, Spain. Barrel-piano agent, dealer and hirer, *fl.* 1909.

ORPHEUS MUSIC ROLLS. See ROLL MUSIC CO.

LIST OF PRINCIPAL MAKERS, PATENTEES AND AGENTS

ORSENIGO, GIOVANNI, via Umberto 1 and Vicolo dell'Arco 27, Casale Monferrato, Italy. Maker of barrel organs and barrel pianos, *fl.* 1909–30.

OTTINA & PELLANDI, via Solferino 5, Casa Propria, Novara, Italy. Established in 1884 for the manufacture of mechanical pianos, barrel organs and street instruments. Also were leading exporters. Probably continued as:

OTTINA, FRATELLI, 30 via Dante Alighieri, Novara, Milan, Italy. Maker of barrel pianos, *fl.* 1930.

OTTO MANUFACTURING CO., 107 Franklin Street, New York, USA. A company formed in 1906 by the brothers Edmund and Gustav Otto and Ferdinand Schaub to produce a disc-playing automatic piano patented by Schaub. Schaub had been responsible for the design of the earlier Capital musical box made by the F. G. Otto Manufacturing Co., which played interchangeable conical tune sheets. The instrument produced was the Pianette which played discs 21 inches in diameter.

PACI, GIOVANNI, Ascoli Piceno, Italy. Maker of barrel pianos, *fl.* 1930.

PACKARD COMPANY, Fort Wayne, Indiana, USA. Founded in 1871 as piano and organ manufacturers. Maker of player pianos.

PADULA, PAOLO, Grassano, Potenza, Italy. Church-organ and barrel-piano maker, *fl.* 1930.

PAIN, ROBERT WILLIARD, 261 West 23rd Street, New York, USA. A manufacturing organ builder who at various times had premises at 157 East 32nd Street and 362 Fifth Avenue, New York. Probably the first to construct a pneumatic self-playing piano in America. In conjunction with Henry Kuster, he built a 39-note instrument for Needham & Sons in 1880. In 1882 he built for the Mechanical Orguinette Co. (which later became AEOLIAN) an inside player with 46-note compass, and in 1888 he made a 65-note electric player.

PALMA, FORTUN, 11 piazza Colombo, Genoa, Italy. Agent for automatic pianos and the Pianola, *fl.* 1930.

PALOP, PEDRO, 99 S. Vicente, Valencia, Spain. Barrel-piano and harmonium maker, *fl.* 1909.

PAPE, JEAN-HENRI. Originally Johann Heinrich Pape, he came to Paris from his home country, Germany, in 1811 and worked for Pleyel as a piano maker. He also at some time worked in London. He introduced no fewer than 137 inventions, among them the first use of cross-stringing in Paris in 1839. In 1851 he made a clockwork barrel and finger piano. Between 1844 and 1848, he was in business at 106 New Bond Street, London. Prior to this, *c.* 1839, he was at 21 Little Newport Street, Leicester Square, and New Bond Street, and in 1846 an address at 75 Grosvenor Square was additional to the one in New Bond Street.

PARKER, WILLIAM D., Meriden, Connecticut, USA. Initially Parker was employed by G. W. Ingalls & Co. of 25 Hermon Street, Worcester, Massachusetts, the company which made the first organettes for John McTammany. He was then with the Taber Organ Co. in that town until finally he joined Wilcox & White Co. Inventor of many improvements to the pneumatic control of musical instruments which led up to the piano player, player organ and player piano. He and NEEDHAM (q.v.) laid the foundations for all pneumatic actions for such instruments.

PARR, ELLIS. See under AUTOMATIC MUSICAL INSTRUMENT COMPANY.

PASQUALE & CO., 73 Basinghall Street, Clerkenwell, and also 9 Phoenix Place, London. Founded by Gregori Pasquale *c.* 1894 to make barrel pianos. Later he devised a means of putting the springs of automatics into the ends of the barrels themselves. A good maker of bright pianos. Partners were Charles Romano of 6 Victoria Dwellings, Clerkenwell Road, and Amato Pasquale of 5 Phoenix Place, Calthorpe Street, Gray's Inn Road. Between 1909 and 1917 business was at 9 Phoenix Place; from 1918 to 1941 was at 12 Poole's Buildings, Mount Pleasant. On 1 February 1907, the business was taken over by Andrea and Germaro Ciniglio who continued to trade as Pasquale & Co. Ltd. (Later history researched by A. G. Bird.)

PASTORE, FREDERICO, Spalto Marengo 4, Alessandria, Italy. Barrel-piano maker, *fl.* 1903.

PEERLESS PIANO PLAYER CO., 2 East 47th Street, New York. Also at Windsor Arcade, Fifth Avenue, New York; St Johnsville, New York; 274 Wabash Avenue, Chicago. Makers of ordinary player pianos as well as coin-operated pianos with percussion and orchestral effects; also photoplayers.

PENNYANO. A clockwork-operated coin-freed barrel piano designed for use in public houses and marketed by Keith Prowse between 1905 and 1918.

PEROTTI, CAV. CARLO, via Ormea e Galliari 41 (showroom/shop), and via Canova e Marocchetti (factory), Turin, Italy. Established in 1870. Large maker of barrel pianos and organs, café pianos, clockwork pianos, etc., *fl.* 1903.

PESARESI, LUIGI, 30 Warner Street, Clerkenwell, London EC. Founder of the firm of Pesaresi & Son, manufacturer of barrel pianos. Later as:

PESARESI & SON, 30 Warner Street, Clerkenwell, London EC. A small maker of street pianos, mostly 40- and 44-note tremolo clockwork and hand-cranked models, who first set up business in 1898.

PESARESI & SON & SPINELLI, 8 & 9 Early Mews, Arlington Road, London, NW1. Spinelli, formerly a partner of ROSSI (q.v.) and latterly working on his own, joined Luigi Pesaresi and his son in 1930 making and hiring street pianos. In the early hours of 12 November 1935, the factory premises were almost entirely destroyed by fire. The business then moved to 12 Field Place, St John Street, Clerkenwell, London EC1, where it advertised 'piano-hire' before finally going out of business in 1941. Their names appear on many barrel pianos and they advertised as 'patentees and makers of Symphonia autos'.

PHILIPPS & SÖHNE, J. D., Frankfurter Musikwerke Fabrik Akt.-Ges, Frankfurt a.-M., Germany. Johann Daniel Philipps had begun making mechanical instruments when he was a mere 23, when he made a barrel orchestrion for a dance hall at Frankfurt. In 1877 he teamed up with one Ketterer with a branch factory in Vöhrenbach in the Black Forest. Nine years later the business changed its name from Philipps & Ketterer to the Frankfurter Musikwerke-Fabrik J. D. Philipps & Sohn of Bockenheim, Frankfurt. The two sons were August and Oswald, who later took over control of the business. Music rolls and, later, piano orchestrions used the trade mark Philag – a simple contraction of the name. Initially the company made barrel pianos and orchestrions and their resemblance to Welte is interesting. Although the company continued to list barrel orchestrions in its catalogue until as late as 1909, the first Philipps paper-roll-playing instrument was introduced in 1896, again closely following the progress of Welte. By the early years of the century, Philipps had become a major manufacturer of orchestrions, many of them incorporating pianos. The company also introduced some special narrow music rolls for the later series of these which were only about 23 cm in width. The company introduced a practical multi-roll revolver-system – believed to be the first in the world – as early as 1903 and this was covered by German patents in 1905. The style and construction of these revolver mechanisms is still considered to be the best of all the types tried. The Duca series of reproducing pianos was introduced about 1921. The fact that Philipps was only ever granted a few patents for player pianos in the United Kingdom, and none of these was for action parts, supports in some measure the belief I have that the similarity between Welte and Philipps reproducing actions is due to the fact that they share a common design for which no doubt Philipps paid Welte a licence fee. In 1923, Philipps acquired the German company FRATI & CO. (q.v.) of Berlin. Frati was making an electric piano called the Fratinola and the Frathymnia. Philipps also acquired in 1925 the Wilhelm Arnold piano factory at Aschaffenburg, which had been founded in 1886. Highly respected as makers of first-class instruments, the business of Philipps was thriving through the 1920s, but as the decade ended so did the era of the piano orchestrion and by 1930 the business closed.

PIACENZA, CIPR., 8 via Belfiore, Cremona, Italy. Barrel-piano maker, *fl.* 1930.

PIANISTA, 64 rue Lafayette, Paris. Company formed to exploit Fourneaux's Pianista piano player.

PIANEX CO., 29, 31 and 33 Station Buildings, Haggerston, London NE. Makers of the Pianex piano player, *c.* 1908.

PIANO, JULES, 30 rue Arson and rue Beaumont, Nice, France. Successor to Tadini & Cie, maker of barrel organs and barrel pianos. At this address *c.* 1908; later at Rouleaux d'Armand Nallino, Nice, where he specialised in large coin-freed instruments which incorporated percussion effects for use in cafés.

LIST OF PRINCIPAL MAKERS, PATENTEES AND AGENTS

PIANOFORTEFABRIK 'EUTERPE' ALBERT GAST & CO., Frankfurter Allee 117a, Berlin, Germany. Piano makers established in 1886 and makers of the Gast's Klavierspielapparate player piano and action.

PIANOTIST CO., 56 Regent Street, London, W. Founded in 1901 by Emile Klaber of the Klaber piano manufactory in America, the parent company was involved with an empire of piano companies all run by entrepreneur Edwin D. Ackerman (see under ACKOTIST). A London factory was set up at Clipstone Street and there was developed and marketed an under-keyboard playing attachment called the Pianotist which played wide, thick paper rolls similar to the early Hupfeld player system. The operation of the Pianotist was virtually the same as that of the Hupfeld, both being of the mechanical 'kicking shoe' variety. The system was technically inferior and few instruments have survived in complete condition. On 16 July 1907, the Official Receiver liquidated the business after revealing that the accounts showed a deficiency of over £31,000 while the assets were valued at just over £1,000 – and they were covered by mortgage debentures. The failure of the company was attributed to the large cash expenditure accompanying efforts to perfect the piano-player, and in repairing them under guarantees given at the time of sale to the public. Early Pianotists were played like the Hupfeld by turning a handle but later variants used foot treadles purely as a means of rotating the kicking-shoe roller and the music transport system.

PILCHER, WILLIAM, Stockbridge Terrace, Pimlico, London. Maker of barrel pianos. In business from c. 1820 until he retired in 1862. Sometime at 23 Upper Belgrave Square, Pimlico. Also made barrel organs and harmoniums.

PITTALUGA E FIGLI, 17 via Gioffredo Mameli, Sampierdarena, Genoa, Italy. Maker of player pianos and electrically operated pianos, fl. 1930.

PIZANO, ROQUE, 8 Cirés, Barcelona, Spain. Street-piano agent and hirer, c. 1903–9.

PLAYANO MANUFACTURING CO., 12 Osborne Street, Cambridge, Massachusetts, USA. Established before 1902 at this address making the Playano piano player. Were purchased by STORY & CLARK (q.v.) in 1905. This was Story's first move into player pianos and the take-over preceded the establishment of a player department at the Chicago factory. Announcing that the Playano interior player as well as the cabinet player would soon be introduced, E. H. Story said: 'I am convinced that the player piano has come to stay; so are my associates in the ownership of the company. We feel that the future prospects of the player business are good enough to warrant us in buying a player business outright, and that the Playano Company was the concern to buy.'

PLAYOLA PIANO CO., 209 State Street, Chicago, Illinois, USA. Makers of player pianos, fl. 1908.

PLEYEL WOLF LYON & CO., 79–80 Baker Street, London W. Distributors of the Paris-made Pleyella player piano and music rolls made by Pleyel.

PLEYEL WOLF LYON & CIE, 22–24 rue Rochechouart, Paris 9e, France. Founded in 1870, Pleyel was an early and highly respected Parisian piano maker with a factory at St Denis, Seine. The company also made the Pleyella player piano and music rolls.

POGGIO, G., 1 via Lodi, Alessandria, Italy. Maker of barrel pianos, fl. 1930.

POLIZZI, DAMIANO E FIGLI, Caltanissetta, Italy. Barrel-piano maker, fl. 1930.

POLYPHONMUSIKWERKE, Wahren, Leipzig, Germany. Produced in 1898 a disc-playing piano called the Polyphon Concerto. Using the expertise perfected in the manufacture of the Polyphon disc musical box, Paul Riessner developed the Concerto which played piano strings, drums and bells from a 32-inch diameter metal disc. See also under REGINA MUSIC BOX CO.

POLYPHON-MUSIKWERKE A.-G., C. Burgstrasse 2, Berlin, Germany. Managed by George Preuss and established as offshoot of the Leipzig company. Sold the Polyphon piano orchestrion, fl. 1909.

POMBIA, PIETRO, Borgo San Agabia 37, Novara, Italy. Barrel-organ and piano maker, fl. 1903–9. May have been related to the Pombia of CASALI (q.v.) connection.

POMELLA, P., 25 corso Milano, Novara, Italy. Barrel-piano maker, fl. 1930.

POOLE PIANO CO., 5 & 7 Appleton Street, Boston, Massachusetts, USA. Founded by W. H. Poole in 1893 as makers of piano players.

POPPER & CO., Reichstrasse 33–35, Leipzig 1. Founded in 1891 by Hugo Popper for the making of

303

pianos and the distribution of orchestrions. Agents for mechanical musical instruments made in Leipzig and also the German distributors for RACCA (q.v.). Makers for a wide range of mechanical pianos, instruments with orchestral effects and so on. Also produced a reproducing piano called the Stella. Branches at rue Nationale 93, Antwerp; Junkernstrasse 4, Breslau, and Bahnhofstrasse 83, Essen.

PORTA, FRANCESCO, Biella, Novara, Italy. Agent for barrel street instruments, *fl.* 1903.

PORTA, SALVATORE DI ROS, Piazza Delle Guardie, Catania, Sicily. Barrel pianos, *c.* 1903.

PORTO & FIGLI, ROSARIO, via Maddem 141A, Catania, Sicily, Italy. Established in 1860. Makers of musical instruments including barrel organs and barrel pianos, *fl.* 1909.

POTTHOFF, LUDWIG, & GOLF, HILMAR, Berlin, Germany. In 1884 they perfected a barrel/keyboard piano which could be played either by hand or by hand-cranked barrel. The piano comprised normal action and the barrel was placed under the keyboard, transmitting playing movement through a series of levers and cams to a secondary key mounted above the normal manual key, thereby setting the complete piano action into motion.

POZZI, EREDI DI FRANCESCO, Treviglio, Bergamo, Italy. Barrel-piano maker, *fl.* 1930.

POZZI, FRATELLI DITTA, 6 via Trieste, Mantua, Italy. Barrel-piano maker, *fl.* 1930.

POZZI & FRATELLI, FRANCESCO, Viccolo Zanda, Treviglio, Italy. Maker of barrel pianos and barrel organs, *fl.* 1903–30.

POZZI & VARESI, via Carloni 7, Como, Italy. Barrel-piano maker, *fl.* 1909.

POZZOULI, VINCENZO, 45 Warner Street, Clerkenwell, London EC. A maker of barrel pianos who patented, in 1906, a street piano producing a mandolin tone by using four bridges, the first being mandolin, the second piano, the third a second mandolin and the fourth a bass piano. He used hammers with hardwood heads.

PRADO, EDUARDO, 10 Torrijos, Madrid, Spain. Maker of street pianos also operating as hirer, *fl.* 1903.

PRADO, THOMAS, 8 Salitre, Madrid, Spain. Maker of street pianos, *fl.* 1903.

PRATT READ PLAYER ACTION CO., Deep River, Connecticut, USA. Manufactured what it called 'an electric bottom unit' which replaced the foot-operated exhausters of an ordinary player by an electric reproducing action.

PRICE & TEEPLE, 206 Wabash Avenue, Chicago. Makers of player pianos including the Symphonola and the Carleton Electric Player Style X for use in public places.

PRIORI, A., 15 via degli Umbri, Rome, Italy. Barrel piano maker, *fl.* 1930.

PROSERPIO, GIUSEPPE M. Monti 40, Como, Italy. Barrel-piano maker who also made and sold organs, *fl.* 1909.

PROTZE & CO. GmbH, JOSEF, Nr 839 Georgswalde, Bohemia, Austro-Hungary. Founded in 1905 as factor and distributor for piano orchestrions.

PROWSE, KEITH. See KEITH PROWSE.

PROWSE, WILLIAM. A barrel piano in the Guinness collection, New York, bears the label: 'Patent William Prowse, late Keith, Prowse & Co., manufacturer, 48, Cheapside, London'. See also KEITH PROWSE.

PUGLISI, GIUSEPPE, Catania, Sicily. Established in 1820 as a maker of barrel pianos, Puglisi was the only maker of these instruments in Sicily. He also made or handled other automatic instruments, *fl.* 1903.

PUSTERIA, FREDERICO, Varese, Como, Italy. Barrel-piano maker, *fl.* 1930.

PYROPHON-MUSIKWERKE ERNST BERGER, Tauchaerstrasse 9, Leipzig 25, Germany. Established *c.* 1905 as makers of electro-pneumatic pianos and orchestrions. No instruments known.

QUAGLIA, BATTISTA, & CO., via Mondovi, Cuneo, Italy. Barrel-piano maker, *fl.* 1930.

RACCA, GIOVANNI, via Milazzo 18, Bologna, Italy. Maker of barrel pianos, who produced some unusual grand-format pianos playing barrels and, later, folded cardboard book-music. He patented an unusual beating-hammer system for his bookmusic piano in conjunction with G. Seward in 1886 and the trade name for his instruments was 'Piani Melodici'. Four models were produced, ranging

LIST OF PRINCIPAL MAKERS, PATENTEES AND AGENTS

from four to six octaves, fully chromatic, and these mostly played serious music from beautifully arranged scores. These were true pianofortes, having both sustaining and soft controls. He also made a piano orchestrion called the Verdi. His products were distributed in Germany by POPPER (q.v.) and in France by STRANSKY FRERES (q.v.). In England, Racca pianos were sold by Guldman.

RACHALS & CO., M. F., Glockengiesserwall 18, Hamburg, Germany. Piano makers founded in 1832 and manufacturers of the Triumphola piano player and Triumphola-Piano player piano.

RAGONE, MICHELE, Cava dei Terreni, Salerno, Italy. Maker of church organs who also manufactured barrel pianos, *fl.* 1930.

RAMOS, MANUEL, 16 Dupl. Palma, Madrid, Spain. Maker and agent for street pianos in business in 1903.

RAMPONE, ALFREDO, 17 via Mazzini, Omegna, Novara, Italy. Barrel-piano maker, *fl.* 1930.

RASERO, F. ILLI, Corsa Alfieri, Asti, Italy, Maker of barrel pianos, *fl.* 1930.

RATTI, FRATELLI, Fabbrica Durini, Como, Italy. Barrel-piano maker, *fl.* 1909–30.

REGINA MUSIC BOX CO., Rahway, New Jersey, USA. Makers of disc-playing musical boxes who produced, in about 1900, a very large mechanical disc-playing piano called the Automatic Regina Concerto. This weighed 950 lb, stood 8 feet 2 inches high, 45 inches wide and 27 inches deep. In addition to the piano, the 32-inch diameter steel disc played bells, cymbal and snare and bass drum. With its quadruple spring motor, this enormous machine changed its discs from a storage rack of ten contained in the base, in the same way that the Regina and Polyphon musical boxes changed their discs. The Regina was developed from the single-play, 32-inch disc size Polyphon produced in Leipzig. The Regina Company was an offshoot of the POLYPHONMUSIKWERKE (q.v.) and both instruments were from the brains of Gustave Brachhausen and Paul Riessner. Also produced the Sublima Piano Junior which was a piano played using '. . . a large roll of heavy and very durable paper, the power being furnished either by Spring Motor or Electric Motor as desired'.

RESTAGNO, CAV. VINCENZO, 90 corsa Vittorio Emanuele, Turin, Italy. Maker of player pianos with factory at 5 via Romagnosi. *fl.* 1930.

RICCA & SON, 881–903 Southern Boulevard and 884–904 East 134th Street, New York. A maker of piano players and piano orchestrions and also an agent for similar instruments, *fl.* 1903.

RICCI, CHARLES, 21 Merlin's Place, Wilmington Square, London WC. Also known as Carlo Ricci. Manufacturer of 'piano organs', established in 1914. In 1917, we find . . .

RICCI, CARLO & SON, 37 Claremont Mews, Clerkenwell, London EC. Barrel-piano makers who ceased trading in 1925.

RIEMER, BERNARD, Chrastava, Northern Bohemia. A maker of barrel organs which featured a separate drive for the barrel and the bellows, to enable music to be played at any speed desired, without losing wind. In 1896 his three sons, Robert, Julius and Jindrich, took over the company and made barrel organs of fine tone and attractive appearance. Then barrel pianos were produced and, after 1903, pianos played by perforated music. Their products were exported to France, Belgium, Germany, Switzerland and Russia. They also made and patented an invention called Automaton, which made mandolin music to the accompaniment of lighting effects and which was driven by an electric motor. This was allegedly a great success and sold well. They won a gold medal for automatic musical instruments at an exhibition at Usti on the Elbe. They also made some fine orchestrions at Chrastava and, later, sold radio sets and ordinary pianos.

RIGONI E FIGLI, DITTA, via Inferiore, Treviso, Italy. Maker of clockwork pianos, *fl.* 1930.

RISSONE & CO., J. B., Poole's Buildings, Mount Pleasant, London WC. Maker of barrel pianos established under this title in 1902. Formerly in partnership as ROSE, COOP & RISSONE (q.v.), and as CAPRA, RISSONE & DETOMA (q.v.). Clockwork pianos by this maker are frequently found with Keith Prowse motors incorporated. Receiving order made against Rissone on 28 September 1905. PASQUALE (q.v.) was later at this address.

ROBAZZA, BENEDETTO, via Cavour 143, Rome, Italy. Agent and hirer of barrel pianos and organs, *fl.* 1909.

ROBINO, SIMON, 59 Oldham Road, Manchester. Described as a musical-instrument maker, he took out a patent in 1906 for producing a tremolo effect on a barrel piano. In his system, bell-cranks pulled the hammer down against a rotating star wheel, to impart the beating motion (British Patent number 14,977, of 2 July 1906).

ROBUSCHI, CASTAUD ET CIE, 5 Chemin de la Madeleine, Nice, France. By 1920 this firm was advertising as successor to VVE AMELOTTI (q.v.) as makers of automatic pianos with interchangeable cylinders. Makers of mandolin and piccolo pianos.

RODRIGUES, ANTONIO, 2 S. Cayetano, Madrid, Spain. Hirer of street pianos, *fl.* 1903.

ROENTGEN. A cabinet-maker who assisted KINTZING (q.v.) in making his female android which played a stringed instrument with hammers, *c.* 1700.

ROGNONI, ERCOLE, 8 via Conchetta, Milan, Italy. Street-organ and piano maker, *fl.* 1930.

ROLFE, WILLIAM, 112 Cheapside, London. A music seller and publisher who also made pianofortes in 1796. In 1806, the business became William Rolfe & Sons and, in 1813, additional premises were to be found at 28 London Wall. In 1850, the business moved to 61 Cheapside, and from 28 to 31–32 London Wall. It seems that there were three subsequent addresses until 1890, after which date the name disappears. With Samuel Davis, William Rolfe patented improvements to barrel-operated pianofortes. On 11 August 1829, Thomas Hall Rolfe was granted British Patent number 5831 for such improvements, one of which was for a method of pinning barrels so as to play 'piano' or 'forte'.

ROLL MUSIC CO. LTD, 1 & 3 Sun Street, Finsbury Square, London EC. Makers of the Orpheus music rolls.

ROLLEAU, S., Nantes, France. Distributor of mechanical pianos and mechanical jazz bands. See AMELOTTI, VVE.

ROMANO & BOUFFEAUX, 21b–23 rue du Pont-de-l'Avenue, Laeken, Brussels, Belgium. Maker of automatic pianos. Was listed in 1909 directories and later became:

ROMANO-BILOTTI, S., 23 rue du Pont-de-l'Avenue, Laeken, Brussels, Belgium. Listed in directories *c.* 1930 as maker of automatic pianos. Several have been seen bearing the legend 'Romano-Laeken'. A Charles Romano was a partner in the business of GREGORI PASQUALE & CO. (q.v.) in the closing years of the last century.

ROSE, COOP & RISSONE LTD, 135 Regent Street, London W (1902) and 71 Mount Pleasant, Clerkenwell, London EC (1905). Manufacturers of barrel pianos, who subsequently took out patents covering an action operated pneumatically from cardboard music. In 1906 the firm was making piano players. John Rose was described as 'mechanic' and Thomas Coop as 'musician' and the secretary of the company was Reginald Albert Goodman. See also RISSONE.

ROSENER, F., Schönhauser Allee 157, Berlin N. A maker of barrel pianos who exhibited at the Melbourne Musical Industries Exhibition in April 1888.

ROSSI. Italy. Rossi returned to Italy from London where he had worked with PASQUALE (q.v.) and also SPINELLI (q.v.) and, *c.* 1920 onwards, produced an attractive range of clockwork barrel-playing café pianos which incorporated percussion effects. Probably same as:

ROSSI, N., via S. Marria 11, Turin, Italy. Maker of barrel pianos, *fl.* 1903.

ROSSI, PASQUALE & CO., 49 Warner Street, London EC. Barrel-piano makers *c.* 1896. This short-lived partnership ended when Pasquale set up on his own the following year and SPINELLI took his place with Rossi.

ROSSI & FILS, 385 rue du Progrès, Brussels, Belgium. The Belgian branch of this firm of barrel-piano makers. They received gold medals for barrel pianos at exhibitions in 1906 and 1907.

ROSSI & SPINELLI, P. C., 49 Warner Street, London EC. Makers of barrel pianos from 1897. Later, after Rossi returned to Italy *c.* 1919, Spinelli was in business on his own until he united with PESARESI (q.v.).

ROSSI & SPINELLI, 22 Baker's Row, Warner Street, London EC. Barrel-piano makers established at this address in 1915 and remaining until 1919, when Rossi returned to Italy. They made both wooden and iron-frame barrel pianos.

LIST OF PRINCIPAL MAKERS, PATENTEES AND AGENTS

ROSSI & TULLIO, 385 rue du Progrès, Brussels (Schaerbeek). Maker of mechanical pianos, *fl.* 1909.

ROTH & ENGLEHARDT, Windsor Arcade, Fifth Avenue, New York, USA. Owned by the Peerless Piano Player Co. of 2 East 47th Street, New York (founded in 1889). Made a number of electric player pianos including the Harmonist.

RÖTTIG, JOSEF, Rumburger Str. 612, Georgswalde, Bohemia, Austro-Hungary. Sole agent for piano orchestrions by FRANZ SIMCH (q.v.), *fl.* 1909.

ROURA, AGUSTIN, 20 Arco del Teatro, Barcelona, Spain. Street-piano agent and hirer, *c.* 1903–9.

ROVIRA, JOSÉ, 9 Monserrate, Barcelona, Spain. Barrel-piano maker, *fl.* 1909.

SÄCHSISCHE REVOLVER-ORCHESTRION-FABRIK F. O. GLASS, Markneukirchenstrasse 160 M, Klingenthal, Germany. Manufacturers of a 'revolver'-type barrel orchestrion in 1903 and also an attractive, large piano orchestrion.

SALENGO, LUIGI, Pinerolo, Turin, Italy. Maker of street pianos, *fl.* 1903.

SALVONI, PINDARO, Cortona, Arezzo, Italy. A maker of barrel pianos, *fl.* 1903.

SANCHEZ, ANTONIO, 30 Abades, Madrid, Spain. Hirer of street pianos, *fl.* 1903.

SANCHES, MARIA, 15 Alinendro, Madrid, Spain. Barrel piano and organ dealer, and hirer, *fl.* 1909.

SANDELL, HENRY KONRAD. Born in Sweden in 1878, Sandell went to Chicago, USA, at the age of ten. When he was twenty-one, he took out his first patents for a coin-operated automatic violin, played electromagnetically. He joined the Mills Novelty Company of Chicago in 1904 and for the next twenty years concentrated on the automatic violin, producing the first practical instrument in 1906 called the Violano. By 1912, he coupled his Violano to a 44-note piano and so was born the Violano-Virtuoso, which was designated one of the eight greatest inventions of the decade by the US Patent Office. Roehl suggests that the Violano-Virtuoso must first have appeared in 1909. Sandell went on to develop instruments with two and three violins and then the Violano Orchestra – a separate cabinet containing percussion instruments which could be coupled to the Violano. The instrument was operated by a perforated paper roll. Next he devised the Melody Violin, which was not roll-operated but could be played like a piano from a keyboard. Sandell, who accumulated something like 300 patents for violin-playing mechanisms during his lifetime, died on 29 January 1948 at the age of seventy. A deeply religious man, he refuted claims made on his behalf that he was a genius, claiming dedication to an ideal as being his motivating force. See also Chapter 9 and Index references.

SARRACENI, BENEDETTO, Angri, Salerno, Italy. Maker of barrel pianos, *fl.* 1930.

SASSI, P., via Vescovado 7, Alessandria, Italy. Street-piano builder and hirer, *fl.* 1909.

SASSO, GIOVANNI, Piazzetta del Carmini 3–4, Vercelli, Novara, Italy. Barrel-piano maker and hirer, *fl.* 1909–30.

SAWIN, MICH., Domnikowskaja, Haus Tscheswiakoff, Moscow, Russia. Maker of orchestrion organs as well as church organs who also handled piano orchestrions, *fl.* 1903.

SCAVARDA, DITTA, 8 via Ottolenghi, Asti, Italy. Maker of barrel pianos, *fl.* 1930.

SCHAUB, FERDINAND. See under OTTO MANUFACTURING COMPANY.

SCHMIDT, JOHANN GERHARD GOTTFRIED, Köpenick, Berlin, Germany. Improved on Potthoff & Golf's system for playing a piano both manually and by a barrel mechanism and, in 1887, took out patents for a barrel action of great simplicity, wherein the barrel mechanism was called upon only to move the piano hammer when playing mechanically, instead of the complete hammer action.

SCHRÖDER, AUGUSTE, Ackerstrasse 68a, Berlin N. A maker of mechanical pianos and organs, *fl.* 1903.

SCHÜBBE & CO., Uferstrasse 5, Berlin N. Claimed to be the oldest established firm of piano-orchestrion builders as well as the largest in Berlin; they produced an instrument resembling, in appearance and specification, the American 'photoplayer' style of effects piano. Founded by Friederich Schübbe and Wilhelm Schnürpel in 1894.

SCHULZ COMPANY, M., 373 Milwaukee Avenue, Chicago, Illinois, USA. Established in 1869 as makers of pianos. The Schulz Reproducing Grand was a quality instrument available with either the Welte-Mignon action or the Aria Divina.

SCHWESINGER PIANO PLAYER CO., 81 Park Place East, Detroit, Michigan, USA. Makers of player pianos, *fl.* 1909.

SCIALANTI, ALESSANDRO, Piazza Principessa Margherita 161, Rome, Italy. A maker of fair organs, *c.* 1910, who also made barrel-operated street pianos. By 1930 was at 175 via Cavour making barrel pianos.

SEEBURG PIANO CO., J. P., Seeburg Building, 419 W. Erie Street, Chicago. Makers of coin-operated pianos with percussion and orchestral effects; also photoplayers.

SEIFERT MUSIKWERKE-FABRIK, GEBRUDER, Domstr. 56, Cologne, Germany. Founded in 1908 as makers of electric pianos and orchestrions.

SEYBOLD, RENÉ. Manufactured player piano called Gabriella. In 1923 began making orchestrions at Strasbourg-Neudorf. Later opened a factory at Bischwieler and secured licence from Höhner of Trossingen to make music rolls for the Magic-Organa and to incorporate accordions in piano orchestrions. Produced a large variety of piano and percussion-based accordion-accompaniment instruments and perfected a 42-note player action from an 8-inch wide roll. René Seybold died aged 82 in 1972.

SEYTRE, CLAUDE FÉLIX, Lyons, France. In 1842 patented a Jacquard-type perforated card system for playing music and made an instrument named the Autophone.

SHARP, THOMAS, Manchester. Thomas Sharp appears to have been in business for less than a decade making Hicks-style portable street pianos. Local directories show the first entry as 1850–51, 'T. Sharp, Piano-forte Manufacturer, Chapel Street, Salford'. The 1852 entry shows the address as 6 Hall Street and in 1855 he is listed as being at 50 Great Ducie Street, Strangeways. There is no entry for him in 1858. One piano has been seen bearing the label: 'T. Sharp. Piano-forte Maker, 48 Great Ducie St., Manchester'. This is on a well-preserved instrument in the Queen Victoria Museum and Art Gallery, Launceston, Tasmania.

SIMCH, FRANZ, Rumburger Str. 458, Georgswalde, Bohemia, Austro-Hungary. Importer of piano orchestrions, est. 1902, *fl.* 1909. See also RÖTTIG, JOSEF.

SIMMONS, WILLIAM, London. Granted British Patent number 4030 dated 14 May 1816. This covered a barrel piano or harpsichord with interchangeable pegs on the barrel. No further details available.

SIMPLEX PIANO PLAYER CO. Company formed by THEODORE P. BROWN (q.v.).

SIMPLEX PLAYER PIANO CO., 244 Tottenham Court Road, London. Maker of the Airmatic piano player, *c.* 1909.

SMEETZ, P., 10 place du Concordat, Curghem, Brussels. Agent for orchestrions, barrel organs and barrel pianos, *c.* 1903.

SMIDT & CO., ED., Georgstrass 48, Hanover, Germany. Maker of piano orchestrions, who was in business in 1903.

SMITH, BARNES & STROHBER COMPANY, 471 Clybourn Avenue, Chicago, Illinois, USA. Later at 1875 Clybourn Avenue. Makers of the Chicago Electric-brand coin-operated pianos which appear to have been built using parts from other instruments or may have been bought in complete. Similar to instruments made by the OPERATORS PIANO COMPANY (q.v.).

SMITH LYRAPHONE CO. Originally the Smith Piano Company formed by Gilbert Smith at 210 Charles Street North, Baltimore, Maryland, the company manufactured the Lyraphone 65-note cabinet player invented by James O'Connor, which featured a tracker board with holes of increasing width either side of the centre. By 1909, the business had adopted the heading title and was located at Hanover in Pennsylvania. A Lyraphone is preserved in the Bellm collection, Sarasota, Florida.

SOCIÉTÉ DES PIANOS PNEUMATIQUES FRANÇAIS, 47 rue de Rome, Paris. Makers of the Monola player piano, a full-scale instrument advertised *c.* 1920.

SOCIETÀ ITALIANA PER GLI ORGANO A CILINDRO, via Torniolli 285, Milan, Italy. This name, associated with street barrel organs and pianos *c.* 1903, is probably that of an agent or distributor rather than a maker or repairer.

SOLAVAGGIONE, DITTA G., 9 via S. Dalmazzo, Turin, Italy. Maker of barrel organs, barrel pianos and

LIST OF PRINCIPAL MAKERS, PATENTEES AND AGENTS

clockwork pianos, *fl.* 1930.

SOLÉ, JOSÉ, 18, 21 and 23 Arco del Teatro, Barcelona, Spain. Street-piano agent and hirer, *fl.* 1903–9.

SPADARI E FIGLI, MICH., Affile, Rome, Italy. Maker of cylinder pianos, *c.* 1930.

SPADARO, FRATELLI, via Baraccha, Reggio Calabria, Italy. Barrel-piano maker, *fl.* 1930.

SPAETHE, WILHELM, Bismarckstr. 11, Gera, Reuss, Germany. Piano maker founded in 1859. Factory in Langenberg. Makers of the Pianist player piano and piano player. Spaethe made player pianos and organs and was also president of the mechanical musical-instrument makers' society, formed in Leipzig to fight the restrictions of the old German musical copyright laws governing music rolls. Opened a London office at 7 Victoria Avenue, Bishopsgate Street Without.

SPERANZA, FRATELLI, Vico 2, Montesanto, Italy. A maker of barrel pianos, *fl.* 1903.

SPIEGEL & SOHN, L., MUSIKWERKE-INDUSTRIE, Kaiser-Wilhelm-Str. 18, Ludwigshafen, Germany. Founded in 1862, Spiegel was an agent, repairer and retailer of mechanical musical instruments including disc musical boxes, electric pianos and orchestrions. By 1909, the Ludwigshafen address was managed by Fritz Karl Spiegel. Other addresses at E.2, Nr 1, Mannheim (est. 1903); Bahnhofstr. 4, Pforzheim (est. 1908), and an office under the name Schweizer-Musikwerke-Central J. Spiegel & Sohn at Freie Str. 103, Basle, in Switzerland (established in 1908).

SPINELLI, LORETO, 49 Warner Street, London EC. Barrel-piano maker who was variously associated with PESARESI (q.v.) and ROSSI (q.v.). By 1926 his address was 40 Hollingsworth Street, Barnsbury, London N1, and he advertised as 'maker of automatic pianos'. He made barrel pianos until 1930, by which time he had united with Pesaresi.

STANDARD PNEUMATIC ACTION COMPANY, 638–52 West 52nd Street, New York, USA. The Standard pneumatic player action, mass-produced by this company, was installed in a large number of American-built player pianos as well as roll mechanisms for photoplayers by makers such as Wurlitzer and American Photo Player Co. President of the company was A. W. Johnston. The company advertised that on 9 October 1916 it shipped its 100,000th Standard player action six years to the day after the shipment of the very first.

STANDARD PLAYER ACTION COMPANY, 638 West 52nd Street, New York City. President W. A. Mennie. Associate company of above.

STANGALINI, ANGELO, via Gal. Ferreris 16, Vercelli, Italy. Maker of miniature barrel pianos, *fl.* 1903.

STANGALINI, GIUSEPPE, Milan, Italy. Exhibited two barrel pianos at the National Exhibition held in Turin in the summer of 1884.

STARR PIANO COMPANY, Richmond, Indiana, USA. Established in 1872. Produced the Starr player piano.

STEENBEKKEN, FELIX. Maker of mechanical pianos *c.* 1890–1900. An instrument in a private collection in France has drum, cymbals, castanets and xylophone accompaniment.

STERLING COMPANY, Derby, Connecticut, USA. Established in 1860, this company produced the Sterling player piano action, *fl.* 1909.

STERNBERG-ARMIN ès TESTVERE, Budapest, Hungary. This firm was a general agent and distributor for the Piano Melodici. The name has been seen deeply engraved on the hinged front fall of a 30-note instrument. See also RACCA.

STEUER, WILHELM, Warschauerstrasse 18, Berlin O. Maker of piano-orchestrions. Established in 1894. By 1909 was at Memeler Str. 14, Berlin O, 34.

STICHEL, FERDINAND, Sophienstr. 43, Leipzig, Germany. Established in 1877 as piano maker. Produced the Claviola piano player.

STINGL, GUSTAV, VII, Mariahilferstr. 17, Vienna, Austro-Hungary. Described as the largest piano-orchestrion maker in Austro-Hungary, Stingl was granted both Austrian and German patents for improvements to barrel piano-orchestrions.

ŠTOČEK, HYNEK, Trautenau, Bohemia (Austria). Made an electrically driven keyless piano with percussion accompaniment, *c.* 1920 (see Buchner).

STODDARD, CHARLES FULLER, born in Chicago on 26 December 1876, son of a furniture dealer,

Stoddard developed an early interest and ability in pneumatic control. Around 1910, he decided that the player piano could be improved upon and so he gave up his $8,000 a year job with American Pneumatic Service Company of Boston to concentrate on the project. Within 18 months, he had developed a system which could re-create piano dynamics and expression by automatic pneumatic means. Although piano makers who were invited to hear his system remained unimpressed, George G. Foster, head of the AMERICAN PIANO CO. (q.v.), was sufficiently interested to buy both it and the services of the inventor. After the crash of the stock market in 1929 and the resultant slump, Stoddard moved into the restaurant business and opened what was probably the world's first 'automatic' catering business in New York where food was scientifically prepared, the numbers of guests accurately recorded and the progress of individual diners' dishes displayed by lights from kitchen to waitress. He went on to distinguish himself in this new field until he suffered a stroke in 1956, a second stroke causing his death on 29 April 1958 at his New York apartment in Riverside Drive. Stoddard was a man of great genius, entirely self-taught, to whom is owed the entire success of the Ampico system which, although subsequently improved from the Stoddard-Ampico of the late 'teens in conjunction with Clarence Nichols Hickman, was the first reproducing action which could be mass-produced without losing quality.

STORY & CLARK PIANO COMPANY, 315–17 South Wabash Avenue, Chicago, Illinois, USA. Maker of player pianos including the Repro-Phraso accenting device. Also made a 'miniature' full-scale upright only 50 inches high. See also under PLAYANO MANUFACTURING COMPANY.

STRANSKY FRERES, 20 rue de Paradis, Paris. Main agent for RACCA (q.v.) mechanical pianos and other similar instruments, including the Autopianiste mechanical player, *fl.* 1903.

STRANSKY, Vienna, Austria. This name is associated with HUPFELD (q.v.) and in particular with the Phonoliszt-Violina. May have been an agent or distributor, *c.* 1911 (see Buchner). There was, *c.* 1930, an Anton Stransky in Graslitz working as a maker and exporter of stringed musical instruments (63 Rathausg.).

STRIDENTE, via Antonio 22, Naples, Italy. Name seen on barrel piano; not in 1903–1909 directories.

STRIXIONE, FERRUCCIO, 60 via del Fico, Genoa, Italy. Barrel-piano maker, *fl.* 1930.

STULTS & BAUER, 738 Broadway, Brooklyn, New York, USA. Established in 1880 as piano makers. In 1909 advertised as makers of player piano actions. The company finally moved to 338–40 East 31st Street, New York.

STYCHA, J., Prague. Produced a barrel-operated piano orchestrion *c.* 1890.

SYMANSKI & SÖHNE, Chlodna 34, Warsaw, Poland. A manufacturer of street and fair organs who also built barrel pianos.

SYMPHONION-FABRIK AKTIENGESELLSCHAFT, Schkeuditzer Str. 13–17b, Leipzig-Gohlis, Germany. Founded (as Akt.) in 1889 as manufacturers of musical boxes and other automatic musical instruments. In 1908 introduced an electric piano called the Symphoniola.

TAGLIABUE, GIUSEPPE, via Sambuco 15, Milan, Italy. A maker of 'barrel keyboard instruments', *fl.* 1903.

TAYLOR & CO., C. R. Established in 1903 at 26 Runton Street, Elthorne Road, Holloway, London N, after the 1914–18 war the business moved to large premises at 34 Commerce Road, Wood Green, London N22. Made cheap uprights and grands and from around 1929–34 period produced players using the British-built Higel action of Canadian design. On 21 February 1936 the factory was severely damaged by fire and, already hit by the economic depression, the business did not resume.

TAYLOR, SAMUEL, Bristol. A cylinder piano in the F. F. Hill collection bears a label reading: 'Samuel Taylor, Musical Instrument Maker, No. 26, Host Street, next to Colston's School, St. Augustine's Place, Bristol. Manufacturers of Barrel Organs and Cylinder Pianofortes. N.B. County Orders punctually attended to'. *Mathews Directory* for 1854 and 1855 lists S. Taylor at 27 St Augustine's Place and describes him as an organ and pianoforte maker. In the Bristol rate books for 1855–7 he is listed under Host Street but without a number.

TAYLOR, THOMAS, Sheffield. A cylinder piano with this name and inscribed 'Maker, No. 79' (no doubt the serial number of the instrument) and also bearing on the pleated silk front the Royal Arms in brass, exists in the F. G. Turner & Son collection at Horsham. It is likely that this maker was related to the Bristol family but this has not been corroborated. Another is in the J. F. Young collection, Lincs.

TAYLOR, WILLIAM, Bristol. A cylinder piano in the G. Planus collection bears a label reading: 'William Taylor, 57, Broad Quay, Bristol. Manufacturer of Cylinder or Handle Piano-Fortes and Organs. Extra cylinders set to Piano-Fortes, Organs and Musical Clocks – Old Ones re-set. Harps and Piano-Fortes Tuned and Repaired'. A barrel organ of the same outward appearance and case design was recently rebuilt by the Author. *Mathews Directory* for 1837 lists William Taylor as a musical-instrument maker of 69 Stokes Croft, at which address he remained until 1840. In the 1841 *Directory* he is listed as 'musical instrument maker and nautical stationer' at 57 Broad Quay where he lived until his death at the early age of 39. He was buried on 10 December 1847. His home was continued in the name of Ruth Taylor but her precise relationship is unknown. See also

TAYLOR, W. F., Bristol. A cylinder piano dated 1848 in the F. F. Hill collection bears a label reading 'W. F. Taylor, Musical Instrument Maker, No. 57, Broad Quay, Bristol'. The classified Bristol trades directory lists W. F. Taylor at this address as a musical-instrument maker. He was contemporary with S. Taylor but is also listed elsewhere in the same directory as a music teacher. Whether W. F. is the same as William or was brother or father to the latter is not certain. The Taylors were a large family, it seems, with various members in the profession of music in one aspect or another. All Taylor-named cylinder pianos closely resemble the Hicks pattern and it could be conjectured that the Taylors, like Distin, may at some time have worked under Hicks.

TEL-ELECTRIC COMPANY, Pittsfield, Massachusetts, USA. Formed in 1905 to produce an electrically operated player piano called the Telektra which could be operated remotely from a detached spool box console complete with function controls. Patented by Timothy B. Powers in September 1901, the Telektra comprised a bank of solenoids attached beneath the piano key bed and connected by a cable to the remote console. The action was very simple, being entirely electro-magnetically controlled, the tips of metal fingers making contact with a 'tracker bar' through perforations in the tune sheet. Originally the music rolls were made of thick, semi-waxed paper but later the music was provided in the form of a metal cassette from which was drawn a long strip of perforated brass strip. Two models were made, the Tel-Electric with a 5in wide roll, and the Telektra with one 6¾in wide. The former played 65 of the piano's notes using 73 holes to include expression and accent. By 1911 the company had offices and showrooms at 299 Fifth Avenue, New York. The instrument was quite successful and many thousands were sold until around 1915 or so.

TENOUDJI, ANDRÉ, 20 rue de Paradis, Paris, with factory at 3 rue Lafitte. Makers and repairers of player pianos and cylinder pianos, *fl.* 1920.

TESTE, J. A., Nantes, France. A mid-nineteenth-century instrument maker, who invented the Cartonium which had forty-two free metal reeds and played music from perforated Jacquard-type cards. Patented in 1861, it incorporated a device which could also cut cards for the instrument to play.

THIBOUVILLE-LAMY, JÉRÔME, 68, 68bis & 70 rue Réaumur, Paris, France, and 10 Charterhouse Street, Holborn Circus, London. Old established musical-instrument manufacturers, who were makers of musical boxes of the cylinder-playing type from about 1865 onwards and, later, were agents for makes other than their own. In 1884 they advertised two devices. One was the Pianista described as 'an apparatus which can be placed before any piano or organ to perform songs, dances, operatic and sacred music mechanically with the greatest exactitude of expression by means of perforated cardboards'. This instrument, of the push-up player style, played book music by turning a handle. Felt-covered fingers played the piano keys pneumatically, there being a bellows system operated by foot treadles. This device, although superseded by paper-roll music, was still being advertised in 1905. At the same time was offered the Organina Thibouville which 'possesses the tone of a harmonium' and won two gold medals at the International Exhibition of 1885. This again played perforated 'cardboards'. The firm also manufactured barrel organs for street use and, in 1890, they produced reed organs playing Gavioli's design of book music which they called the Organophone Expressif, and another smaller device called the Coelophone. Their American office was at 15 Great Jones Street, New York.

THIÈBLE, LÉON, Ruyaulcourt (Seine-et-Oise), France. Maker of piano-player action named the Autopianiste.

THIM, JOHANN, Trautenau, Bohemia, Austro-Hungary. Maker of piano orchestrions, *fl*. 1905.

THOMPSON-U'NETTE PIANO CO., 2652 West Lake Street, Chicago, Illinois, USA. Maker of the U'nette player-grand advertised as 'Music with you in it'.

TINEL, A., 14 Marché aux Oeufs, Antwerp, Belgium. Agent for electric pianos and orchestrions.

TOMASSO, A., & SON, 17 Colne Road, Winchmore Hill, London N21. Clockwork and street barrel-piano manufacturers in business repairing and hiring out street pianos at 4a The Broadway, Palmers Green, London N14. In 1936 the firm was at 18½ Douglas Place, Clerkenwell, London EC, from where they advertised as repairers of 'automatics' (clockwork barrel pianos). Victor Tomasso died in 1968 and the business was dissolved.

TOMASSO, EMILIO, 69 Cherry Street, New York City, USA. Barrel-piano manufacturer who advertised himself on his instruments as 'successor to Cesare Maserati & Co., Mechanical Organ Manufacturer'.

TOMASSO, ERNESTO, 1 St Mary's Lane, Quarry Hill, Leeds, Yorkshire. Barrel-piano maker related to Antonio Tomasso who, with his brother Benedetto, took out patents in 1908 for a tremolo device employing a rotating shaft having four concave flutings.

TOMASSO & PHILLIPO, A., 5a Baker's Row, Clerkenwell, London EC. Antonio Tomasso, Luigi Vincenzo Tomasso was born in 1862 at Cassino and was brought to England in 1867 with his sister, Niccolina (aged seven), and brother, Antonio (aged three). He became a street musician playing the concertina at the age of eight and, from 1876 until 1882, he was apprenticed to Chiappa making barrel organs and pianos at their Clerkenwell factory. In 1882 he started his own factory making these instruments at Baker's Row. His brother Antonio worked for him. In 1883 he married Domenica Capaldi and, in 1889 at the age of twenty-seven, he started a factory at 1 St Mary's Lane, Leeds 9. The Clerkenwell factory was continued by his brother, Antonio. There was also a factory at Pea Street, Glasgow (1892–3). There were now five sons, all of whom worked in the trade. Although clockwork pianos were made in large numbers, they also produced hand-operated street pianos on carts, and these may frequently be found with a tremolo arrangement on the treble strings as well as travelling picture fronts. Later, electric player pianos were built. Luigi Vincenzo Tomasso died on Good Friday, 1944, at the age of eighty-two, and all the pianos which had been hired out were sold by auction excepting one which still remains with the family.

TONK & BROTHER, INC., WILLIAM. Established in 1879 at 259 Wabash Avenue, Chicago, by 1909 the business had moved to New York City. Makers of player pianos.

TREMAINE, WILLIAM B. Born in 1840, he entered the piano business in America (relates Dolge) in 1868, organising the Mechanical Orguinette Company in 1876 to market Mason J. Matthews' paper-playing reed organ or Orguinette. In 1883 he acquired the Aeolian Organ Co. and in 1888 the patents and stock in trade of the Automatic Music Paper Company of Boston, Mass. He then established the Aeolian Organ and Music Co. making automatic organs and music rolls. In 1892 he purchased all the patents of the Monroe Organ Reed Company of Worcester, Mass., and in 1885 introduced the Aeriol self-playing piano. He was succeeded as president of the Aeolian Company in 1899 by his son, H. B. Tremaine, who was also president of the Weber Piano Company. The groundwork of the Tremaines did a great deal to foster the player-piano industry and the ascension of the Aeolian Company, which went from strength to strength, was due entirely to the foresight of William B. Tremaine at a time when there was neither encouragement nor demand for such instruments. He appreciated the power of money, buying not only the patents he needed to put his company in the forefront but also the best brains, such as Kelly, Pain, Votey and others. See also

LIST OF PRINCIPAL MAKERS, PATENTEES AND AGENTS

AEOLIAN COMPANY. Tremaine died in 1907.

TREVISAN, A., 183 borgo Aselo, Castelfranco Veneto, Treviso, Italy. Maker of automatic pianos and cylinder pianos, *fl.* 1930.

TRIST PIANO PLAYER LTD, Gresham Street, London EC. Arthur Ronald Trist invented a system of playing a piano or organ using an electro-pneumatic player action in which special music rolls, made of layers of different substances, could be perforated in part to expose electrically conductive layers beneath. When 'read' by a metal contact finger, a solenoid was energised, so opening the airway controlling a fairly conventional twin-valve (or triple-valve) system. Trist patented his music roll system and a number of different types of player action. Trist Piano Player Ltd was formed in 1908 to exploit his patents. The factory was at St Albans in Hertfordshire. This company carried on until September 1911 when a voluntary winding-up was agreed to although apparently the company was not insolvent. The liquidator contacted Maximilian Macarious KASTNER (q.v.) and as a result a new company was formed, called the New Trist Player Piano Ltd, on 11 December 1911, with Kastner as managing director. Meanwhile Chase & Baker had filed a claim against the company for £1,000 in connection with music rolls made and supplied to the old business. Besides Kastner, the other directors were the Right Hon. Earl of Plymouth (who resigned on 13 June 1913), Sir Ernest Clarke (who resigned on 5 March, 1913), Count Alexis de Toper and A. R. Trist. There was an agreement with Kastner's own company, Kastner & Co. Ltd, under which Kastner & Co. had the rights to sell Trist products. The ramifications of Trist came to a head at the end of 1913 when the creditors' meeting was held following a net loss in the year ended 12 December 1912 of £706. The factory ceased working in March 1914 through lack of working capital and persistent disagreements among the directors. Trist himself attributed the failure to the inability of the directors to agree about methods of conducting business. The relations between Kastner and the other directors became so strained that harmonious working was impossible. Although no products of the Trist business are known to survive – indeed there is little evidence that it ever produced anything – the story of this small business is typical of several which were founded on one man and his inventions. What makes this one the more interesting is that Kastner should have been involved with it.

TRIUMPH-AUTO PIANOS LTD. See KASTNER & CO. LTD.

TURCONI, JOSEPH, Galata, rue Camondo 11, Constantinople, Turkey. Maker of street pianos who was in business in 1903. Exhibited a barrel piano at the National Exhibition, Turin, summer 1884.

UCCI, GINO, corsa Vittorio Emanuele, Castellamare Adriatico, Penne, Italy. Maker of barrel pianos. 'Successor to Chieti', *fl.* 1930.

ULLMANN, CHARLES & JACQUES, Paris, Ste Croix and London. Described as makers of musical boxes and also the Piano Executant Artiste, a 54-note book-playing instrument. Believed more likely to have been distributors. Charles Ullmann also founded the Société du Zonophone and was a part-owner of the Fonotipia record company. By 1930 business was styled L'Industrie Musicale 'Ancien Etablissement Ch.-J. Ullmann' at 11 rue du Faubourg-Poissonnière.

UNGER, J. F. Invented mechanisms for recording pieces of music for mechanical instruments using a keyboard and pens on a paper strip (melography) in 1752.

UNITED STATES NOVELTY CO., 121 11th Street West, Kansas City, Missouri, USA. Maker of automatic pianos, *fl.* 1909.

VALENTE, ANTHONY, 42 Thompson Street, Oldham Road, Manchester. In 1885 he advertised himself as 'mechanical organ maker' although whether this was barrel organ or barrel piano ('piano-organ') is unknown.

VAN ROY, PIERRE PAUL, Aalst, Belgium. Maker of large clockwork barrel pianos, *fl.* 1920–30.

VANROY, P., Hamburg, Germany. Barrel-piano makers who built large orchestrion-type instruments with percussion effects.

VARETTO BROTHERS, 17 Milton Street, Lower Broughton, Manchester. Described as organ builders and repairers, they were agents for Chiappa music books and fair organs. They also specialised in the repair of street and fair organs, pianos, etc. A German street organ has been seen bearing the above address and the date August 1931. They were finally bought out by Chiappa.

VARETTO, PETER, 87 Oldham Road, Manchester. Described as a mechanical-organ maker in 1885, he was also a repairer of street pianos.

VARETTO, PIETRO, 14 Warner Street, London EC. A maker of barrel pianos who advertised as such in the *London Directory* for 1881. Most probably connected with, if not the same as, the 'Pietro' (Peter) Varetto later in Manchester.

VASSALO, VINCENTO, 1 via Michele Angelo, Turin, Italy. Maker of street barrel organs and pianos, *fl.* 1930.

VELA, BENITO, Pueblo Español, Barcelona, Spain. Makers of modern miniature barrel pianos, which are more novelties than practical street instruments. These are mounted on detachable dogcarts with shafts and the whole is gaily painted. Termed *pianos a Manubrio*, these have iron frames and are well made using modern materials and methods such as nylon bushes and moulded parts. They have 32 notes, two clapper blocks and a triangle.

VELAZQUEZ, ISABELO, Los Molinos 5, Bajoiqda, Madrid 20, Spain. Repinner of street piano barrels.

VERBEECK & SON, J., 85 Barnsbury Road, London N1, and 79 Copenhagen Street, London N1. Advertised as makers of mechanical organs, Verbeeck was an organ builder by trade. He sold book music for both fair organs and book-playing pianos between the years 1924 and 1942, when he ceased trading.

VERBEECK, PIERRE, 109 Duinstraat, Antwerp, Belgium. Fair, band and street organ maker. At the outbreak of the 1914–18 war he came to England as a refugee and opened a fair-organ factory in Birmingham, selling also book music for both fair organs and book-playing pianos. He advertised as a maker of mechanical organs. In 1924, he moved to 85 Barnsbury Road, London (see VERBEECK & SON), finally selling out to Chiappa in 1942. He died about 1954.

VIAZANNI. Clerkenwell, London EC. An Italian who used to do maintenance and repair work on organs and, in particular, Imhof & Mukle orchestrions. He is likely to have been associated with the repair of barrel pianos as well.

VICTORIA-MUSIKWERKE TISMAR & BURR, Anklamerstrasse 32, Berlin N. Founded by Berthold Tismar and Willy Burr, this firm produced an electromagnetic piano orchestrion in the early part of this century.

VIETTI, PIETRO, via Madama Cristina 18, Turin, Italy. Maker of barrel pianos, in business in 1903. By 1909 was at via Ormea 12, Turin.

VILLA, LUIGI, 18 Granville Square, Farringdon Road, London EC. Manufacturer of automatic barrel pianos, who patented in 1903 a method of displaying advertisements in the front fall of a street piano. The front fall had a glass central panel and a system of levers and linkages converted the continuous rotary movement of the barrel into an intermittent motion to display signs in the window.

DA VINCI, LEONARDO. Italy. 1690–1730. Is said to have made a mechanical spinet 'with drum' (barrel operated?).

VIORA, MICHELE, Pinerolo, Turin, Italy. Maker of fair organs and street pianos.

VITTORE, Vicola Consolata 3, Turin, Italy. Maker of barrel pianos, *fl.* 1903.

VOGLIAZZO, PALMINO, 8 via Quintino Sella, Asti, Italy. Barrel-piano maker, *fl.* 1930.

VOSE & SONS PIANO CO., 158–60 Boylston Street, Boston, Massachusetts, USA. Established in 1851. Made the Vose Player Piano.

VOSGIEN, LUIGI, Fuori Porta Milano, Strada per Pernate 121, Milan, Italy. Advertised as 'successor to I. Colombo', was maker of street barrel pianos, *fl.* 1903.

VOTEY, EDWIN SCOTT, Summit Union County, New Jersey, USA. A practical organ builder, with experience of both reed and pipe instruments, he took over the Detroit Organ Company and, later, with the partnership of Farrand formed the Farrand & Votey Organ Company which later also made pianos and players. Votey is credited with being among the first to make a practical pneumatic piano player although Theodore P. Brown was granted patents for an 'inner player' in 1897. Votey's invention was the first Pianola push-up and he applied for a patent on 25 January 1897, a patent being granted on 22 May 1900. His device was acquired by Aeolian along with his services.

WALLIS, JOSEPH, 133 & 135 Euston Road, London NW. A maker of mechanical pianos who, in 1876, was classified in the London Trade Directory as a maker of 'street and saloon' pianos.

WARNIES, LEON, Amsterdam, Holland. In 1875 he started renting out street organs and pianos which he repaired and maintained. He died in 1902 but his widow continued the business until competition from the phonograph forced closure.

WAUTERS, PROFESSOR, Binghamton, New York, USA. Worked for the Automatic Musical Company of Binghamton, which produced self-playing banjos and xylophones playing paper rolls. The firm ultimately became the Link Piano Co. making coin-operated paper-roll-playing, keyless café pianos. Professor Wauters produced a self-playing violin for the company in 1907. Pneumatically operated, the instrument took seven years to develop and played special 65-note music rolls.

WEBB, C. F. Collaborator with H. C. Coldman in the design and development of the Boyd Pistonola player piano. See under BOYD.

WEBER, GEBR, GmbH, Waldkirch-im-Breisgau, Baden, Germany. Makers of orchestrion organs, who also produced mechanical pianos and piano orchestrions such as the Unika, the Grandezza and the Brabo, which were basically roll-playing pianos with mandolin, xylophone, string-toned organ pipes and timpani accompaniment.

WEGENER, J., Leipzig, Germany. Built mechanical virginal in 1619 which played three tunes on a barrel and had moving figures. The instrument is now preserved in the Paris Conservatoire.

WEIGEL, C. H., Reichstrasse 30–31, Leipzig 10, Germany. Makers of mechanical musical instruments, who were also agents for Symphonion and Adler disc musical boxes, piano orchestrions and electric orchestrion pianos.

WEISSER, AMBROSIUS, Unterkirnach, Baden, Germany. Formerly the firm of Hubert Blessing established in 1849, this firm made orchestrion organs and also, at the beginning of this century, piano orchestrions, among them being the Germania.

WELTE ARTISTIC PLAYER PIANO CO., 18 East 17th Street, New York, USA. When the Welte reproducing piano began to be marketed in the United States around 1907, this was the name of the company established for the purpose. Advertisements read: 'The Welte Artistic Player-piano – in Europe the Mignon. Gives the Absolutely True Reproduction of the Individual Play [sic] of the World's Most Famous Pianists'. Later at 273 Fifth Avenue, New York. Established by:

WELTE, EDWIN. Born in 1876, the grandson of Michael Welte who in 1832 founded the famed firm of orchestrion builders at Freiburg in the Black Forest, Germany. His father was EMIL WELTE who founded the American arm of the company in 1865. Edwin and his brother-in-law, KARL BOCKISCH, perfected the Mignon reproducing piano which first appeared in 1904 and was marketed the following year.

WELTE, EMIL. Eldest son of Michael Welte Snr, he took out the first patents for 'the use of paper music rolls in connection with a pneumatic action' in 1887. This was to replace the expensive and cumbersome organ barrel with its accompanying paraphernalia and limited repertoire. His work opened up the way to the player piano. Left Germany for America in 1865 and opened a shop on East 14th Street, New York City, opposite Steinway Hall. This was known as M. Welte & Sons Inc. Later a studio was opened at 557 Fifth Avenue. This showroom remained open until the start of the First World War, when it was compulsorily sold by the Alien Properties Custodian.

WELTE-MIGNON CORPORATION, 297–307 East 133rd Street, New York, USA. This company, established in the 1920s, copyrighted in 1924 the title 'reperforming piano' as a description for the 'Welte-Built Welte-Mignon'. This played the original wide red-paper rolls.

WELTE & SÖHNE, M., Lehener Str. 9, Freiburg-im-Breisgau, Germany. Founded by Michael Welte (1807–80) at Vöhrenbach and established in Freiburg in 1832, the business became world-famous for its orchestrion organs and later for the invention of the Welte-Mignon reproducing piano which was largely the work of KARL BOCKISCH (q.v.). The perforated-paper-roll pneumatic system was then applied to Welte's orchestrion organs and the Welte Philharmonic Autograph Organ – a full reproducing-action pipe organ. The firm of Welte produced a wide assortment of mechanical musical instruments incorporating pneumatic action and paper music rolls, including a 'motion picture and cabaret midget orchestra', Brass Band Orchestrion and Concert Orchestrion. Later, offices were opened at 273 Fifth Avenue, New York, USA. Later reformed as the WELTE-MIGNON CORPORATION (q.v.).

WEYDIG PIANO CORPORATION, 133rd Street and Brown Place, New York, USA. In the latter days of the player-piano era in the United States, this company, established in 1880, produced an upright player called the Radi-O-Player which was a combined player piano and radio. The venture was a failure and the company dissolved in 1926.

WIEDEMANN, HUGO, van Woustraat 114, Amsterdam, Holland. Founded in 1900 for the distribution of electric pianos and piano orchestrions. Agent for Frati & Co. Branches in Antwerp, Amsterdam and Ghent.

WILCOX & WHITE CO., Meriden, Connecticut, USA. Founded in 1876 by Horace C. Wilcox, a silver-plate manufacturer, and Henry Kirk White, an organ builder from Brattleboro, Vermont. Wilcox provided the financial backing. White had been building organs for forty-eight years and his three sons joined him in making instruments (James, Edward and Howard). The company's first automatic instrument was the Symphony roll-playing organ, introduced about 1888. In 1891, one of the company employees, WILLIAM D. PARKER (q.v.), took out a patent on a roll-operated player piano but there are some doubts as to whether it was ever produced. Six years later, Edward H. White invented the Angelus piano player, produced from 1898 until at least 1906. Several versions were made, including one with a reed organ built in: this was called the Angelus Orchestral. The Angelus was different from all other players in that it operated by means of flat action motors or 'diaphragm pouches'. These were pressure-operated. James White's son Frank invented the Angelus Artrio reproducing piano in 1915. The company produced music rolls under the name Voltem, having for some years contracted to the Mel-O-Dee roll factory of Aeolian which was situated across the street from the Wilcox & White factory. The company went bankrupt in 1921 and was taken over by the F. G. Smith Piano Co., with the plant and machinery going to the Conway Company, owners of the Hallet & Davis Piano Co. Simplex redesigned the Angelus action, which was then marketed under the name Super Simplex. (Information largely researched by Alan R. Pier.) Henry Kirk White died on 13 January 1907.

WILDBREDT, ERNST, Grosse Frankfurterstrasse 44, Berlin N. Manufacturers of electrically operated pneumatic-action pianos and piano orchestrions as well as ordinary player pianos. Made instruments with flute and percussion effects. Patented automatic roll rewinding, *fl.* 1908.

WINTLE, ALGERNON O. (Canon), The Old Rectory, Lawshall, Nr Bury St Edmunds, Suffolk. During the agricultural depression following the First World War, Canon Wintel provided employment for many men home from the war in the repair and renovation of barrel pianos. No new pianos were actually made, it is thought, but many very old ones were restored, tuned and provided with newly repinned barrels. Wintle made a speciality of converting former clockwork public-house pianos into hand-operated street instruments which were then sold or hired out to charitable organisations. The name of the original maker of the piano was almost always obliterated and the name of Wintle's company marked in place. The barrels were all stamped before pinning with an oval, blue rubber stamp. Canon Wintle, who confessed that he 'couldn't read a note of music', made many new programmes for barrels, his own confessed masterpiece being the setting of Mozart's *Eine Kleine Nachtmusik* on a barrel. He was largely self-taught and acquired a healthy mastery of his work. His trade mark in musical arrangement was what he fondly termed his 'bang in the bass' which was an accompaniment feature when, to emphasise the music, he would arrange to have some six or eight adjacent hammers all strike their strings at one and the same time to produce a bang. Wintle died in 1959 and the business closed. Most of his remaining stock was sold and much of his paperwork and records were destroyed by his family, who had not shared his interests. Some 130-odd pianos and many crates of spares were examined by the author in 1973 prior to their sale to the then West Cornwall Museum of Mechanical Music. Among the copious spares was ample evidence that Wintle had been planning to produce a number of new, small street pianos of about 30 keys. A quantity of cast aluminium key frames and their pattern were found along with some small barrels. Plans to complete the restoration of many of these instruments were set back when many of the case parts were damaged in a warehouse fire at Penzance.

WRIGHT PIANO CO., Queen Street, Camden Town, London NW. In 1906 introduced a piano player and a player piano under the name Regal.

WRIGHT & HOLMES BROTHERS, Forest Street, Rochdale Road, Manchester. Describing themselves as 'mechanical organ builders and repairers', this firm flourished between the two wars and a fairground barrel organ has been seen with a repinned barrel bearing the date 1929, written before the barrel paper was pinned. They probably serviced street barrel pianos as well.

WURLITZER, FRANZ RUDOLPH, Schöneck, Germany. Went to America in 1853 at the age of twenty-two and opened a factory in Cincinatti in 1861 to manufacture military band instruments. Later he undertook selling coin-freed Regina disc-playing musical boxes. He was joined by his three sons, Howard E., Rudolph H. and Farny R. They began by making military band organs in 1907–9. Wurlitzer commissioned the first coin-freed electric player piano – a 10-tune barrel instrument – from deKleist, which firm he subsequently bought up in 1908 (see NORTH TONAWANDA MUSICAL INSTRUMENT WORKS). He made extensive use of electric, electromagnetic and pneumatic action, paper-roll-actuated, for a wide variety of mechanical instruments. The company had warehouses in Cincinatti, Chicago and New York as well as a large factory at North Tonawanda, New York, where the firm still exists.

ZANONI, GIACINTO, Canneto Sull'oglio, Mantua, Italy. A church-organ builder who also made barrel pianos, *fl.* 1930.

ZARI, FRATELLI, 13 via Carducci, Milan, Italy. Maker of player pianos, *fl.* 1930.

ZIMMERMANN, GEBRUDER. The piano-making business of Zimmermann, properly entitled the Leipziger Pianofortefabrik Gebruder Zimmermann A.-G, was founded at Stötteritzer Weg, Mölkau-Leipzig in 1885. Founder Max Zimmermann learned his trade at the factory of Steinway in New York and in 1884 with his brother Richard first set up to make pianos. The following year the business became a limited liability company. In 1926, Zimmermann's business absorbed that of LUDWIG HUPFELD (q.v.) and remains in existence today as Hupfeld-Zimmermann. Max Zimmermann died in Dresden on 31 May 1937.

ZIMMERMANN, JULES HEINRICH, Leipzig, Germany. Manufacturer of the Fortuna disc-playing musical boxes, small portable barrel organs and street pianos. Exhibited an electric piano at the Crystal Palace in 1900.

ZORDAN, DITTA, Cogollo del Cengio, Vicenza, Italy. Maker of church organs who also made barrel pianos, *fl.* 1930.

ZYOB, A. Said by Chapuis to have built a book-playing piano in 1842. No further details have been traced.

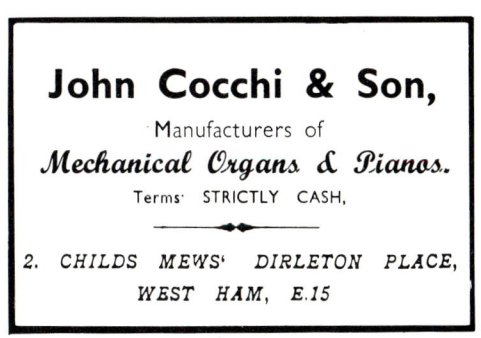

John Cocchi & Son,

Manufacturers of

Mechanical Organs & Pianos.

Terms: STRICTLY CASH.

2. CHILDS MEWS, DIRLETON PLACE,
WEST HAM, E.15

The METZLER PIANO PLAYER

£35 NET CASH.   **£35 NET CASH.**

SIR FREDERICK BRIDGE
On MECHANICAL PIANO PLAYERS at the SOCIETY OF ARTS.

DISCUSSION.

The CHAIRMAN said the examples of mechanical players which had been explained and demonstrated by Mr. James Coward had given the meeting a great deal of pleasure, and he thought that many persons in the audience had been considerably surprised. They had heard a piece of Beethoven played without any wrong notes, and as they must admit, a most remarkable amount of expression. Then they heard an accompaniment played upon the instrument, and the singer was allowed to sing the song with just as much expression as she thought fit to put into it; and as far as he could judge the piece was accompanied by Mr. Coward so well, that if he had not been looking at the instrument he should not have known that Mr. Coward was not playing in the ordinary way with his fingers. He did not think that there had been much to complain of in that accompaniment. At any rate it was better than was got ordinarily from a young lady in a drawing-room, when asked to accompany a song. It would be a perfect blessing to many people if they were able to have a song with an accompaniment played in a decent way. This would no doubt be a tremendous gain; so it was impossible to gainsay the fact that the machine might be extremely useful, and would supply a genuine want. It would enable people to play classical music which they could not hope to play at all fairly with their hands, and it would enable them to have a properly played accompaniment to a song. There was no doubt that those things were not possible in the ordinary state of musical education. Many people could be found to play classical pieces fairly well, but there were very few people who could play the accompaniment to a simple song. This showed that there must be something wrong in the way that pianists and children at school were being educated. The power to read a simple piece of music such as the accompaniment of an ordinary song, was hardly to be found, and yet some people could sit down and play half-a-dozen extremely difficult pieces such as ballades of Chopin and sonatas by Beethoven. He had heard this admirably done by children, and he had given the same children a small piece from an album, and they had been unable to read it. To be able to play the difficult pieces without being able to read the simple ones, was not being a musician, it was being a machine. He would rather buy a machine than have his child turned into a machine. One of the things that the inventor and advocates of the machine for playing the piano ought to be most proud about, was the fact that they had got the machine into such a position that it demanded from the performer the exercise of his own brain. It was not a thing where they had simply to turn on a tap, so that they could sit down and smoke while they listened. That had been done many years ago. But here was an instrument into which the performer could put his own musical feeling if he had any. This was a fact which made the machine worth considering, because if people had been taught to play on the wrong system—and, of course, they all found out when they went to a new teacher, that they had been taught to play on the wrong system—they could make use of one of the mechanical players, and do all the work with two or three fingers and their feet. I wish to record my very high appreciation of the lucid way in which Mr. Coward has put it before you, and the general result of the evening has been a surprise of great interest to me, and I am sure that there is no reason why the invention should not be an immense factor in the spread of really good music.

The Piano Player, as illustrated, was used on the above occasion, and possesses four levers, including the accentuator, loud and soft pedal, transposing spool to take not only 58 and 65 note Music Rolls, but enabling the performer to transpose accompaniments to any Songs or Violin Pieces, &c. into eight different keys.

£35 Net Cash.

METZLER & Co., 40 to 43, Great Marlborough Street, London, W.

APPENDIX A
Player Piano Pot-Pourri

Within this section I have gathered together a miscellany of oddments which the discerning reader may well find of interest. Particularly I have sought to grasp the immediacy of the player-piano era through the pages of the London trade paper *Musical Opinion*. This one journal is a mine of contemporary news and views, some of the marketing attitudes expressed then sounding remarkably topical in other connections even today. The order I have chosen is not quite chronological.

THE PIANOTIST COMPANY (LIM.)

Mr Emile Klaber, managing director of the above company, returned from New York on Jan. 23rd, having been in America for the purpose of arranging for the transfer of a 'music cutting' plant to London. The demand for pianotist music has been so enormous that it has been quite impossible to carry a sufficient stock on hand to satisfy the customers: hence the decision to manufacture music for the instrument in this country. The pianotist, we are informed, continues to meet with great success, and the firm's handsome shop in Regent Street is seldom to be seen without visitors. The premises, however, now in occupation have proved so inadequate that arrangements are being made for the company to occupy a large shop at 94 Regent Street.

The detachable style of Pianotist – to be called the Pianoti – will be ready for the trade, it is hoped, in a month's time. It is made in the same vogue, the same to fulfil the requirements of the

---

THE MUSETTA PLAYER-PIANOS and PIANO-PLAYERS
are the Cheapest High Grade Instruments on the Market. They stand first for Durability, Appearance, Price, Simplicity of Construction and Absolute Control. There is no complicated mechanism; and the Pneumatic Tubes being Metal, they cannot perish or crack.
Particulars and Catalogues post free on application.

S. CALMONT & CO., Ltd. SHOW-ROOMS— 83, New Oxford St. **London, W.**

Manufactured by A. BUFF-HEDINGER, Leipzig.

319

The Cecilian — The Perfect Piano Player

PRICE 50 GUINEAS CASH.
PRICE 60 GUINEAS 3 YEARS.

Enables one to play the Piano with wonderful expression and accuracy.
Requires no musical knowledge.

SEND FOR BOOKLET.

Sole Manufacturers and Wholesaler:—
FARRAND ORGAN CO.,
24, DENMAN ST., LONDON, S.E.

..THE.. PIANOTIST IS THE ONLY PIANO-PLAYER

that does not at any time interfere with the use of the Piano in the ordinary manner.

Can emphasize a melody in any desired part of the keyboard.

Can be operated without physical exertion.

Can be fitted to any piano without ultimate injury.

When fitted to a piano is unnoticeable and not an unsightly and clumsy addition.

Is universally endorsed by all prominent piano manufacturers.

Can be conscientiously warranted for 5 years, there being no perishable rubber used in its construction.

MARK HAMBOURG says: "Far superior to any other."
ADELINA PATTI says: "Most effective."

FREE RECITALS DAILY. WRITE FOR CATALOGUE T.

Price **35 Guineas**, Fitted Complete.

94, REGENT STREET, LONDON, W.

---

makers' patrons, who desire a movable attachment in lieu of one fitted inside the piano. We think that the progress of this house will be watched with interest.

(Musical Opinion, January 1902)

CREDITORS' AND CONTRIBUTORIES' MEETINGS

Meetings were held on July 16th, at Carey Street, in the liquidation of the Pianotist Company (Lim.), of Clipstone Street and Regent Street, W., manufacturers of pianoforte-players. The accounts showed a total deficiency of £31,379 3s 7d, of which £15,000 related to shares issued by the company. The assets, valued at £1,010 14s 8d, were covered by mortgage debentures: there were no assets available for the unsecured creditors. The failure of the company was attributed by its officers to the expenditure of large sums of money in attempting to perfect the company's piano-players and in repairing them under guarantees given at the time of the sale. The liquidation remained in the hands of the Official Receiver.

(Musical Opinion, August 1907)

The Apollo piano player has a first-class showing in the building occupied by the Apollo Company in Regent Street. Mr S. Lorraine (managing director) is a musician of experience and is therefore well qualified to substantiate his opinions of the Apollo. The warerooms are arranged in an attractive manner, and daily recitals are given. The endorsements of the Apollo by the crowned heads of Europe, the late pope and distinguished musicians are taken full advantage of by the manager, with the result that the Apollo maintains its prominent position in London.

(*Musical Opinion*, December 1903)

The most popular form of pushing the sale of a piano player seems to be in the giving of recitals at the warerooms, although a number of firms are now branching out with extensive advertising in the principal magazines and best circulated weeklies.

The handling of the British trade, either for the sale of American piano players, pianos or organs, presents an entirely different proposition from the methods employed on the American side of the pond. The manufacturer who intends to make a bid for British trade must conform his ideas largely to existing conditions, and although his enterprise may be well appreciated, he will find at all times that British sentiment and British tradition must be considered.

(*Musical Opinion*, December 1903)

The competition at times is keen, but up to now it has not partaken of that aggressive nature which is characteristic of the American trade. It is understood that two or three manufacturers of players propose placing on the British market new styles at prices considerably less than for their present line.

403—4,'11   MUSICAL OPINION & MUSIC TRADE REVIEW.   525

Plays any Existing Piano,

WITHOUT ALTERING APPEARANCE OR TONE.

The UNIVERSAL

Piano=Player.

It is the most recent Player to appear before the public and its success is already assured on account of its utility, simplicity and price.

The demand is likely to be very great indeed, owing to the number of pianos already in existence that are never played on account of the scarcity of musicians.

Piano=Player.

It therefore meets the demands of a great number of people who are anxious to have a Player fitted to their own pianos.

The whole apparatus is so beautifully compact that it can be lifted off instantly when desired and placed in the piano stool.

The Largest Makers of Pianos in the British Empire.

Bansall & Sons, ALBERT WORKS **Clarence Road, Hackney, N.E.**

LET US SEND YOU PARTICULARS.

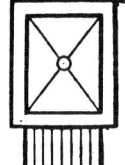

Endorsed by Musicians.

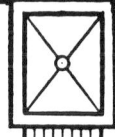

THE PIANOLA

EXACTLY how many homes in this country possess a piano we are unable to say—certainly many hundreds of thousands. We may assert, however, without fear of contradiction, that only one piano of every three is opened oftener than half a dozen times in the course of a year. There must be some reason for this, and it is not difficult to seek. Nowadays one cannot afford the time necessary to learn the technical, or finger work, part of piano playing. Long years of constant practice and drudgery must be undergone before one acquires but moderate proficiency. Even then one's repertory is confined to very few pieces, and every addition to it means more practice and hard work.

THE PIANOLA is an instrument which enables one to skip those years spent in overcoming the physical or finger playing work, while it allows one to have full mental control over one's playing; that is, to infuse just as much individuality as one possesses into one's efforts, and thereby create true music. The Pianola is not automatic, and that is the secret of its success, and why the world's greatest musicians appreciate it.

FAULTLESS TECHNIQUE.

I. J. PADEREWSKI writes: "It executes the masterpieces of pianoforte literature with a dexterity, clearness, and velocity which no player, however great, can approach."

MAURICE MOSZKOWSKI writes: "Anyone hidden in a room near by who hears the Pianola for the first time will surely think it is a great virtuoso playing; but after a time he will perceive his error, because your instrument never plays false notes."

A FACTOR IN MUSICAL EDUCATION.

V. DE PACHMANN writes: "I wish to add my testimony as to its excellence, both for professional use in reading elaborate piano compositions and for private use in educating the musical tastes of people who have pianos and are unable to use them for want of a thorough musical education."

JEAN DE RESZKE writes: "It will certainly have the results of popularising good music, of giving us more educated listeners, and also probably fewer indifferent performers."

LENDS ITSELF TO TRUE ARTISTIC EXPRESSION.

EMIL PAUR writes: "Nothing of the kind I have heard before can approach it. In the hands of a competent player all the shading, crescendo, as well as modification of *tempi*, are remarkably accurate."

LUIGI MANCINELLI writes: "It is a wonderful instrument. Nothing I have ever heard before could be called artistic in the true sense of that much-abused word. It will have a great influence on the future of piano playing."

The above extracts are sufficient to indicate the nature of the reception which the Pianola has met with among leaders of the musical world. Those who possess Pianolas, or have heard them in use, express similar opinions. Have *you* heard the Pianola? If not, and you will favour us with a call, we shall be delighted to demonstrate the instrument to you. We do not plague you to buy. Should you, however, not be able to visit us, please write for fully illustrated and descriptive Catalogue T, which will be sent post-free on application.

The Price of the Pianola is £65.
It may be had on Instalment System.

The Orchestrelle Co.
225 Regent Street, LONDON, W.

THE PIANOLA IS SOLD AT NO OTHER ADDRESS IN LONDON.

PLAYER PIANO POT-POURRI

Maples, Whiteleys and Harrods, the large department stores of London, all keep piano players in stock; but apparently no special effort is made at any of these establishments to push the sale of any particular make.

It is the trade custom, both in London and in the provinces, for several dealers in one town to handle the same makes of pianos and piano players, unless the manufacturer finds it to his interest to appoint a dealer in a particular section as sole representative.

(*Musical Opinion*, December 1903)

THE MECHANICAL PLAYER.
DOES IT INJURE A PIANO?

At Brompton County Court, on March 6th, before Deputy Judge Clement Lloyd, Mrs Seaton Chisholm, 1 Iverna Gardens, Kensington, W, brought an action against Mrs Drew Mercer, Marloes Road, Kensington, claiming six pounds for alleged damage to a piano owing to a mechanical player having been used upon it.

Plaintiff's counsel stated that on June 14th last, his client let her flat to the defendant for three months, at a rental of three guineas a week, with a guinea a week for the use of plate. A provision of the agreement was that at the end of the tenancy all the goods, etc., should be delivered up in as good a state as they then were, the effects of reasonable use excepted. Among the furniture was an upright grand piano by Cramer, which had cost fifty pounds about four years previously. On returning to the flat, at the expiration of the three months, the plaintiff found the piano practically worn to pieces, Subsequently she ascertained that the defendant had used a mechanical player with the piano.

The plaintiff bore out her counsel's statement, and in cross examination said that she certainly considered that a mechanical player would do more damage to a piano than ordinary playing by hand.

Two daughters of the plaintiff stated that the piano was in perfect condition when they left the flat with their mother.

Mr Percival D. Steel, an assistant with Cramer's, stated that on inspecting the piano after the expiration of the three months, he found one hammer broken, one note stuck owing to displacement (evidently by hard playing), and the centre notes were all loose. He considered that the wear on a piano by a mechanical player would be greater than by ordinary use by hand.

The defendant stated that when she first went into the flat she discovered that one of the notes of the piano was broken, and that all the keys were loose. She engaged Hopkinsons of New Bond Street to attach the player to the piano.

Mrs Gates, sister of the defendant, gave similar evidence.

Mr Charles W. Poole, from Messrs John Malcolm & Co., of Regent's Park, stated that the player in question had been supplied by his people. Witness maintained that the mechanical player would not injure a piano any more than ordinary playing by hand, no matter whether the 'fingers' on the player were adjusted too high or too low.

His Honour come to the conclusion that the mechanical player had done some damage to the piano by undue strain, and he assessed the damage at three pounds. Judgment accordingly, with costs.

(*Musical Opinion*, April 1905)

THE ANGELUS AND BRINSMEADS

In answer to the query, Will not the future of the inside piano player in Europe depend largely upon the adaptation of the European piano to the American player action? Mr Marshall replied, 'I have no hesitation whatever in stating that this must and will be the case; in fact, I have acquired

The ANGELUS DIAPHRAGM PNEUMATIC and the HUMAN FINGER

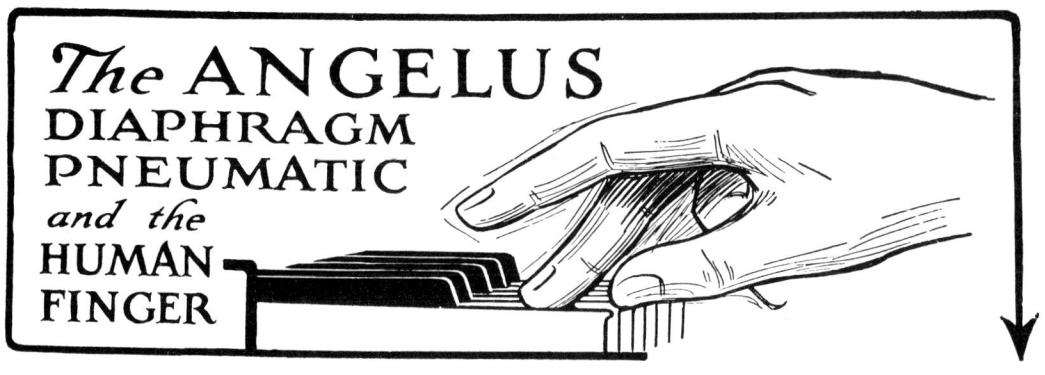

The Diaphragm Pneumatic when in action or "striking" is filled with buoyant air, which gives a resilient touch, just like the human finger. Note the absence of creases or corners, which insures greater durability.

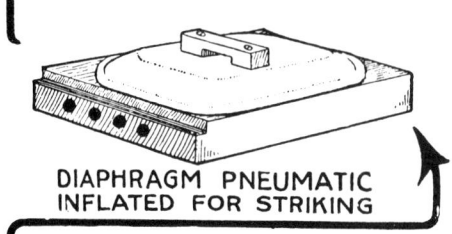

DIAPHRAGM PNEUMATIC INFLATED FOR STRIKING

The Bellows Pneumatic is worked by an exhaust; that is, when it strikes a note the air is entirely withdrawn from it, which causes it to collapse with a hard staccato touch, in no way resembling the pliancy and flexibility of the human finger.

BELLOWS PNEUMATIC WITH AIR EXHAUSTED FOR STRIKING

THE Diaphragm Pneumatic is the only means ever devised to give the real human touch. When in action it is an air inflated cushion, with the same firm but resilient and buoyant touch that characterizes the human fingers. All other pneumatics are collapsed when in action, withdrawing from them the buoyancy of the air, resulting in a hard, mechanical touch.

The

Diaphragm Pneumatic

is an exclusive feature of the

ANGELUS

and together with the famous Phrasing Lever (patented) and the wonderful Melodant (patented) have made the ANGELUS pre-eminently *the* artistic piano-player.

KNABE-ANGELUS	EMERSON-ANGELUS	LINDEMAN & SONS-ANGELUS	ANGELUS PIANO
The Peerless Knabe Piano and the Angelus.	The sweet-toned Emerson Piano and the Angelus.	The original and celebrated Lindeman Piano and the Angelus.	An excellent piano made expressly for the Angelus.

THE WILCOX & WHITE CO.,   **MERIDEN, CONN.**

Pioneers in the Piano-Player Industry

ANGELUS HALL   REGENT ST.   LONDON

the sole right for attaching the Angelus piano player mechanism to the celebrated pianos of Messrs John Brinsmead & Sons – one of the greatest firms in the world.' (*Musical Age*, N.Y.)

(*Musical Opinion*, July 1905)

A week ago we edged our way through a little crowd of dealers who were studying the effects of solos being produced by the aid of an Apollo player of eighty-eight notes, which was combined in an American overstrung, the retail price of the combination being a hundred and twenty-five pounds. The instrument – the first of its kind to arrive at 67 Berners Street – attracted much attention, and commendatory remarks were certainly 'in the air'. Mr Wagener informed us that arrangements had been made so that the player will speedily be combined in some of the company's English and German pianofortes – to be sold at a low price; and, further, that the Apollo player (with transposing arrangement) can be supplied with as few as fifty-eight notes or to the full compass of a seven and a quarter octave piano. Here we may state that particulars of this (amalgamated) company will be found in another column.

(*Musical Opinion*, August 1905)

THE U.S. PERFORATED MUSIC SUITS

In the two actions brought by the White-Smith Music Publishing Co. of Boston against the Apollo Co. of New York City, charging infringement of copyrights on sheet music, Judge Hazel (of the United States Circuit Court) has handed down a decision dismissing the suits for want of equity.

The alleged infringement consisted in selling perforated sheets for playing music by automatic piano players, and the decision of Judge Hazel held that such perforated sheets of copyrighted

PIANOLA

music for use on piano players and self playing organs and other automatic instruments did not infringe the copyrights on such music. The suits were nominally brought against the Apollo Co. of New York City, a merchandising corporation, and were defended by the Melville Clark Piano Co. of Chicago, makers of the Apollo piano players. It is estimated that millions of dollars are involved in the question raised by the litigation.

This is a matter in which the makers of metal discs for music boxes and phonograph rolls are interested quite as much as those who cut the music for the larger automatic instruments. The principle contended for by the complainants would apply to the makers of discs and phonograph rolls as well as to the perforated sheets for the larger automatic instruments; consequently, those who sell them as well as those who make them have a vital interest in the final adjudication of the subject. Judge Hazel's decision until reversed gives the field for perforated music to any that may choose to cultivate it.

(Musical Opinion, August 1905)

MECHANICAL PIANO-PLAYERS
(from the *Daily Telegraph*)

That the mechanical piano-player has come to stay is very evident; and good reasons undoubtedly exist for its advance in public favour. It will be generally agreed that the piano is the most popular of all musical instruments; there is scarcely a home in this country which does not shelter one. But not many people in these homes can play sufficiently well to afford pleasure to cultured listeners; or, if they do perform passably, their repertory is as a rule so strictly limited as to become a weariness to the flesh.

PLAYER PIANO POT-POURRI

With a view to finding out who are the chief purchasers of mechanical instruments, enquiries have been made of the principal agents connected with the trade in London.

It seems that the demand comes largely from the London districts and from elderly people, or rather from those whose children have married or have gone out into the world, taking much of the interest out of the lives of their parents. The piano remains; but there is no longer anyone who can play it. Then it happens that attention is drawn to the mechanical instruments, which anyone possessing a little patience can soon master, and to the tempting offer of the principal American firms doing a large business in London to buy the old piano and deduct the sum from the cost of the piano-player. Small wonder that many people leading dull lives in the country jump at such a proposal; and soon a new instrument, capable of yielding a vast amount of pleasure, is installed in place of what had become a dumb piece of furniture.

How great is the competition that now exists in this particular line of business may be gauged from the fact that there are nearly fifty varieties of detachable piano-players on the market and no less than thirty different instruments which can be used either as an ordinary piano or as an automatic player. It may be mentioned that the combination instrument is no larger than the ordinary piano, as the mechanism is stowed way in the lower portion of the case – a space hitherto not utilised.

Price and Output

The cost of the mechanical player, when built into the instrument as it were, is by no means excessive, the additional cost being about sixty to seventy per cent. A thoroughly serviceable specimen will, it is stated, shortly be placed on the market by a prominent firm at less than seventy pounds. We have spoken of the sale of second-hand pianos; but it is necessary to utter a word of warning (so preventing disappointment) with regard to forming an exaggerated estimate of the value of even well-preserved grands. Truth to tell, there is nowadays very little demand for them in London. The reason is that so many people who formerly dwelt in good sized houses and bought large pianos have now moved into flats containing small rooms and have been compelled to part with their grands. These have indeed become a drug in the market and fetch less than a good upright piano, almost the only buyers of the large instruments being school proprietors.

Hundreds of pianos are turned out in this country every week and many more are imported (mostly from Germany); but, though the trade has not been in a very flourishing condition for the last two or three years, there is no inclination to attribute this dullness to the competition of the piano-player. Nevertheless, the Orchestrelle Company estimate that they are selling about ten times as many mechanical players in this country as were disposed of five years ago; and this organisation – the largest of the kind in London and controlling no less than three hundred and sixteen patents – is only one of many offering such wares. Messrs Broadwood, who only commenced to manufacture the combined instruments last January, have every reason to be satisfied with their output. They claim, by the way, that their piano-player has this important feature: that the wood work, metal work and action are all entirely constructed in one factory. In America the expansion of the industry has been very striking; the production of mechanical piano-players and of piano-player attachments – as certified in the bulletin on the manufacture of musical instruments just issued by the United States census bureau – having advanced from 607,873 dollars in 1900 to 2,029,754 in 1905.

High Class Music

The piano-player was invented about thirty years ago; but for a long time – in fact, until comparatively recently – the only kind available was of the detachable description, an instrument which occupied a considerable amount of room. Now, however, numerous inventors have succeeded in perfecting various kinds of mechanism, which can be placed inside the piano and be operated at will without interfering with the ordinary use of the instrument or affecting the touch or action. The automatic

No Xmas Gift is Comparable in Pleasure giving to the ANGELUS PLAYER PIANO

THE ANGELUS is the one gift that makes instant appeal to every member of the household. From the oldest to the youngest, each can find a special joy in its coming, because it can be personally used and enjoyed by all alike.

The ANGELUS is the universal means for musical enjoyment, requiring no finger skill or knowledge of musical technique.

THE ANGELUS IS THE ONLY PLAYER PIANO WITH WHICH YOU CAN PLAY LIKE AN ACCOMPLISHED PIANIST.

The reason is fundamental; it is because of the three exclusive and patented features which have made the ANGELUS world famous. The Phrasing Lever—the most valuable and important expression device on any player piano, giving a control of tempo only equalled by the human fingers. The Melodant—that emphasizes the theme or melody, and the Diaphragm Pneumatics—through which the perfect human touch is obtained.

"The ANGELUS Player Piano offers the possibility of producing any desired shading in expression, dynamics and color of tone."

FRITZ KREISLER.

KNABE-ANGELUS—Grands and Uprights.   CHICKERING-ANGELUS—Grands and Uprights.
EMERSON-ANGELUS—Grands and Uprights.   LINDEMAN & SONS-ANGELUS—Uprights.
ANGELUS PIANO—An upright made expressly for the Angelus.
In Canada—The GOURLAY-ANGELUS and ANGELUS PIANO.

Any of these instruments can be played by hand in the usual manner.

The WILCOX & WHITE CO.

Business Established 1877   MERIDEN, CONN.   233 Regent St., London

Agencies all over the world.

playing mechanism, forming an integral part of the pianoforte, is indeed brought into operation with practically no difficulty. A great point in favour of the piano-player is the opportunity which it affords to acquire a knowledge of an immense variety of music. People living in the country at a distance from a large town have few chances of listening to high class music. To these the piano-player must needs be a great boon; for it enables them not only to hear music which in the ordinary way would be quite out of their reach but, by studying the indications supplied on the music rolls, to obtain instruction as to the proper method of presenting it. Madame Chaminade, Mr Paderewski, Mr Moritz Moszkowski, Mr Harold Bauer and Dr Richard Strauss – to mention only a few distinguished musicians who have recognised the artistic possibilities of the mechanical instrument – have not disdained to furnish Metrostyle music roll interpretations. These obviously must afford splendid assistance to many intelligent amateur pianists who have studied with a local teacher and who have acquired a technique sufficiently advanced to enable them to play difficult compositions but who are unable to attend the recitals given by notable artists. The Orchestrelle Company's library places at the disposal of the public some eighteen thousand pieces and this collection is being added to at the rate of fifty to a hundred compositions a month. It may almost be said to contain the musical output of the world; for even some soul-subduing examples from Chinese sources have recently been placed on the rolls. Although many subscribers are content with ragtime effusions and frivolous pieces at first, it is noticed that a taste for music of a more elevated character is gradually developed and many amateurs ultimately manifest a liking for the works of the classical masters. There is no difficulty in obtaining fresh supplies of musical fare; for, like the books from the library, parcels containing music rolls can be forwarded by post.

Question of Copyright

In connection with the piano-player companies, there is however a serious grievance which will have to be dealt with and removed before long. It is that of the reproduction of compositions by means of music rolls without any payment being made to the owners of the musical copyright. The unfairness of such a proceeding is admitted by most of the piano-player companies and they would be willing to come to an arrangement with those who consider themselves unfairly treated. At the same time, they maintain that the publicity given to a work by means of the wide circulation of the music among their clients often leads to an increased sale of the composition by the publishers. The law – which the Lord Chancellor in *Iolanthe* declares is 'the embodiment of everything that's excellent' – affords protection to the vendors of music rolls; for it holds that the perforated music sheets come within the scope of the article of the Berne convention exempting mechanical musical instruments from the range of the ordinary copyright law. But that particular clause of the Berne convention was merely intended to apply to musical boxes, toys and things of this kind; piano-players were not then invented.

As the result of the muddle, any composer who writes a piece that engages the popular ear finds that it is immediately reproduced by the piano-player companies and that the revenue derived from it goes into other pockets than his. The better class of trading companies have no desire to act shabbily towards the composers, but they do not see their way clear to pay for wares which would not be protected from piracy. There would, of course, be nothing to prevent their trade rivals from reproducing without fee the compositions upon which royalties had been paid. It has been suggested that publishers might possibly recover penalties under the Copyright Act of 1902, but it seems more than doubtful if this measure applies to the music as utilised in piano-players. That further legislation is required there is no doubt; and, as the majority of the piano-player companies have adopted a reasonable attitude, there should not be much difficulty in arriving at an understanding equally honourable and satisfactory to all concerned.

(republished in *Musical Opinion*, November 1907)

A NOTE ON THE TECHNIQUE OF RECORDING
BY R. REYNOLDS, A.G.S.M.

Very many pianists perform at the Aeolian Hall, in London, leaving no trace of those delightful sounds with which they have charmed their audience during a brief recital; yet fortunately other and greater pianists have found their way to the top storey of the Aeolian building, and there discovered a means of perpetuating their interpretation for all time.

In a secluded room stands a Weber grand piano, in tone and in outward appearance not different from the usual model, nor does the touch betray the magic power beneath the keys. Upon closer inspection the secret is partially revealed by the electric cable which can be seen coming from beneath the instrument; and if it were possible to trace this back into the piano, there would be found 160 wires, half of them leading to specially devised contacts under the keys, the remainder running to positions near the point where the hammers strike the strings, while the cable itself passes through the wall of the room, coming out into a soundproof chamber, in which is installed the amazing mechanism that constitutes the Duo-Art recording apparatus. Here the other ends of the wires are attached to electro-magnets, which operate the punches in the powerful perforating machine, each punch corresponding with each key of the piano. The pianist plays – the punches perforate – the record is produced!

This method of recording ensures absolute accuracy of reproduction, the length of the perforations being determined by the period for which the key is held down. Thus staccato notes produce little round holes about $\frac{1}{32}$ of an inch in diameter, a tribute to the agility of the fingers and also to the rapidity of the recording punches which are working at 4,000 pulsations per minute. The rhythm is determined by the spacing of the perforations in the music roll as it passes through the recording machine at a uniform speed (usually 8 feet in one minute), and this spacing

The Fallacy of Seven Years

Something more than eight years ago when the original 88-note Apollo Player was offered to music lovers, Mr. Melville Clark, with the 88-note stood alone. Other makers jeered at the idea of an 88-note Player being necessary. They did not, however, explain why pianos were made with 88 notes, if only 65 notes were necessary to produce the classics. These makers hung to their fallacy for seven years, insisting that the 65-note was the perfect piano player. We were right, as is abundantly demonstrated in the fact that all leading manufacturers have within the past two years discarded the 65-note instrument whose praises they sung for seven years, and adopted the 88-note.

A real seven years' revolution took place. This revolution is now past history, and we only mention it to show that through a constant leadership we have been able to develop **the Melville Clark**

APOLLO-PIANO OF TODAY

In order to attain a true human touch in a player piano, the player action must strike down on the keys in front, just as the fingers of the performer strike. Any other method of striking the piano key is impracticable and does not secure the human expression.

The down-stroke on the keys in front, making possible a true human stroke, is as necessary as was the 88-note range. The APOLLO-PIANO of today is the only player piano retaining this human attribute, producing that APOLLO-PIANO tone quality which delights all artists. We are right again, even though it may take seven years for other makers to bring themselves to acknowledge it.

A booklet about the APOLLO-PIANO that retains all of the human and discards all of the mechanical effects, will be sent to those interested.

Melville Clark Piano Company
415 Steinway Building
CHICAGO

is in exact accordance with the interval between the notes played by the pianist, so that when the music roll is placed upon a Duo-Art piano, and caused to play at the same speed, there must result an exact reproduction of all the most subtle nuances of rhythm.

Similarly the touch of the pianist is recorded and reproduced; still by means of perforations in the music roll, in conjunction with the most ingenious mechanism, both in the recording machine and in the Duo-Art piano. By the use of only 8 'dynamic controls' no less than 32 variations of touch can be produced, extending over the whole range of finger power, from the lightest pianissimo to the strongest accent, and in combination with the well-known 'Themodist' device ('Pianola' patent) the melody is differentiated from the accompaniment, each having its own free modulation of tonal effect.

THE PIANOLA.

By virtue of its artistic merit the PIANOLA has gained for itself the position of the Standard Piano Player. It is the criterion by which all similar instruments are judged. This high place in the music world could not have been secured unless the PIANOLA had successfully met all the claims which have been made for it. Not only has it done this, but it has achieved the recognition and enthusiastic endorsement of Paderewski, Rosenthal, Moszkowski, Sauer, and nearly every other great musician. Such testimony—the opinion of the expert—is unique. No other instrument has met with such unanimous approval, and for you personally to understand the reason for it and to appreciate the possibilities of the PIANOLA it is only necessary to call at our showrooms and see the instrument in use.

The PIANOLA will enable you and every member of your family to play any composition on the piano, with full control over expression.

The price of the PIANOLA on the hire system is £65, or £53 net cash.

Send for Catalogue AA.

The Orchestrelle Company.

Note our New Address:

ÆOLIAN HALL,
135-6-7, New Bond Street,
London, W.

PLAYER PIANO POT-POURRI

Such fidelity of reproduction will not only perpetuate the artist's performance, but will also show any errors of technique, and will record the stray wrong notes from which no pianist can entirely escape when playing passages requiring great force and extreme rapidity. One of the finest artists in playing a single composition recorded no less than 360 false notes!

Fortunately there is a means by which the 'Duo-Art' music roll can be edited under supervision of the pianist, and every blemish easily and effectively removed, while omitted notes can be cut into their proper places; nor do the possibilities of editing end at note corrections; the touch itself

MELVILLE CLARK'S APOLLO Player Piano

When someone asks you if you've read the decidedly unusual offer in Paragraph 5 of this adv. what will you say?

1. The Solo Apollo is the only player-piano in the world that *correctly* accents the melody.

2. The Apollo is the only player-piano in the world made with a motor that runs and rewinds the music without pumping—a motor so perfect mechanically that it will run immersed in water!

3. The Apollo is the only player-piano in the world that touches down on the keys—as a *human* musician.

4. The Solo Apollo is the only player-piano in the world that *instantly* omits the melody and plays the accompaniment only or omits the accompaniment and plays only the melody.

5. We will pay $1,000.00 to anyone (other manufacturers included) who will produce a player-piano that will do the above. *Do you want an instrument that won't?*

Above are not *all* the features of the Apollo Player-Piano. It has enough *more* to make our brochures and literature so well worth sending for that you can't afford not to. So send your name today.

These 2 Books Gratis Write for them. Reading the books is the *next* best thing to hearing the Apollo play. Send today.

MELVILLE CLARK PIANO CO.
403 Fine Arts Bldg., Chicago   New York Show Rooms, 305 Fifth Ave.

Tone qualities of the Melville Clark Piano are exceptional and even the rhythm can be improved upon if the artist so desires. These alterations are made by means of paper patches over the perforations to be eliminated, or by neatly cutting such notes and 'dynamic control' perforations as may be required. The origianl record (signed by the artist) is then duplicated upon a 'stencil', from which all future copies are produced.

It is obvious that when this revision of the record is carefully carried out under the direction of the pianist there will result a most finely finished interpretation. This is why Percy Grainger was moved to confess that his records represent him not merely as he did play, but – as he 'would like to play'! While Paderewski paid the greatest tribute to the artistic effect when, referring to the

Do You Understand 'em?

Auto Pneumatic Expression and Reproducing Actions are Used in More Different Kinds of Pianos Than Any Like Mechanisms

If you do not understand the Welte-Mignon (Licensee) and Auto Deluxe actions you are passing up a tremendous amount of business.

The entire reproducing and expression output of 115 different piano companies is equipped with this type of action.

The kind of people who own reproducing and expression pianos are anxious to keep them in good condition. These people have made a large investment in music—they will spend liberally to keep this equipment in condition.

Can you afford to neglect this large and prosperous clientele?

You cannot—come in and find out what you need to know in order to serve the owners of Auto Pneumatic action equipped instruments efficiently.

Welte-Mignon
(Licensee)
THE MASTER'S FINGERS ON YOUR PIANO

AUTO PNEUMATIC ACTION CO.
WILLIAM C. HEATON, Pres.

653 West 51st Street   New York, N. Y.

'Duo-Art' record of his well-known Minuet, he said that listening to this gave him the same feeling in his heart as when he played it himself.

Almost all the great pianists have recorded for the 'Duo-Art' either in London or New York, and many interesting personalities have revealed themselves to the person in charge of the recording department. Pachmann's quaint self-appreciation was delightfully illustrated when he prefaced his recording by saying: 'I have heard Rubinstein play this piece, and Liszt also; they both played it beautifully – very beautifully, but – I shall play it much more beautifully!' Busoni stated that he used to be extremely particular about the accuracy of his technique, but now he did not care how many wrong notes he played providing he obtained an artistic effect. This sounded a little alarming to the 'Duo-Art' editor, who foresaw shoals of false notes which would have to be eliminated, because, although not very noticeable at a concert performance in a large hall, they would be rather too obvious in a drawing-room where the 'Duo-Art' is usually heard. However, the Busoni records were quite as free from blemish as those of the other great pianists.

Lamond has taken much care with the editing of his records, and during his several visits has shown the versatility and wide vista of his thoughts by discussing many subjects, even extending to the immensity of astronomical investigation. Harold Bauer and Hofmann are both enthusiastic recorders for the 'Duo-Art'; while the latter declares that he is greatly indebted to his own records which have revealed certain points in his playing he had not previously realised; and, by taking advantage of the knowledge thus gained, he has attained even greater artistic success in his public performances.

This is perhaps the highest compliment payable to the 'Duo-Art', that it not only serves as a most valuable educational medium, already in use at the Royal College of Music, the Royal Academy of Music, the Guildhall School of Music and many other similar establishments throughout England and America, but it had also proved to be of real value to the recording artists by enabling them to hear themselves as others hear them.

The lecture given by the author at the Royal Institution on February 19th, was in the nature of a demonstration of the following article; and included charts showing the comparative rhythms and touch-values in two records of the first four bars of the Raindrop Prelude (Chopin), as played by Busoni and Pachmann. Miss Lilian Southgate played a duet for two pianos with a Duo-Art Cortot roll; and M. Jean Pouguet played a violin sonata (César Franck) with another Duo-Art roll.

(From the Player Piano Supplement to
The Gramophone, February 1924)

Rex Lawson of the Player Piano Group, writing in the *Bulletin* of that society, commented on the achievements of Reginald Reynolds and unearthed some interesting information on a Pianola Festival:

Reginald Reynolds was nothing if not industrious. What with broadcasts, talks and concerts (including the world premieres of at least six works), plus all the Duo-Art dynamics and Metrostyle lines that he arranged, it is understandable that he preferred to take in sandwiches for lunch!

One little-known project with which not only he, but also his elder daughter, was closely associated was the Wimbledon Festival of 1930, which is the only British festival ever to have introduced classes for the pianola. Since Reginald Reynolds lived nearby in Barnes at that time, it seems very likely that he was the moving spirit behind these classes, for the organiser of the Festival, Willoughby Walmisley, although open-minded, was not a particular supporter of the player-piano. Also, it was Reginald Reynolds who performed the winning entry from the pianola composition class at the Festival prizewinners' concert.

The METROSTYLE PIANOLA

The PIANOLA, by providing correct key striking, enables anyone to play the piano. The addition of the METROSTYLE to the PIANOLA makes it possible to render a composition exactly as it has been played by a great musician. The METROSTYLE PIANOLA is a combination, therefore, of technique and interpretation.

IN itself the METROSTYLE consists of a finger or guide attached to the tempo lever of the PIANOLA, with which the performer is able to follow a line marked on the music roll by an authority, say Paderewski, or d'Albert, or Busoni. By guiding his playing according to this marking anyone can reproduce in its entirety the interpretation of the artiste in all its changes and effects of tempo, accent, and expression. The METROSTYLE PIANOLA is the most remarkable achievement in the whole history of pianoforte playing. A pamphlet will be sent to anyone who writes for Catalogue AA. You are invited to call.

THE ORCHESTRELLE CO.
AEOLIAN HALL
135 · 6 · 7 · New Bond Street · W.

PLAYER PIANO POT-POURRI

Certainly, the establishment of such a competition for the pianola and its music was new; in an article in *Musical Times* for September 1930, Harry Ellingham quotes Wimbledon as a pioneering venture, and this is echoed in the *Wimbledon Borough News* for 28th March 1930:

> A striking innovation was the introduction of two classes for the pianola. This is probably the first time that such classes have been included in any music festival, and it is gratifying that there were twelve entries in the two classes. The judge, Dr G. Oldroyd, remarked at the conclusion of these classes that they showed the pianola could be regarded as a musical instrument, even if there were mechanism between the player and the desired effect. This could be discerned in the different renderings of the competitors. He could think of no greater source of pleasure for those who had learnt a little music in the past and wished to pick it up again.

It is not clear who all the twelve competitors were, though no less than eight of them received medals or certificates. Here are the complete lists of those mentioned:

Saturday (22.3.30):
Pianola Solo (pieces, 'Arabesque', Debussy, and 'Nocturne', Chopin).
Silver Medal, Vera Reade (Mitcham) 88 marks; Bronze Medal, William Emuss (Balham) 84 marks; Certificates, James Munden (Balham), Frederick Emuss (Balham), Cecily Clark (Balham), Harry Duffil (Harlington), John Clapham (Forest Hill), and Jane Wood (Wimbledon Park).

Pianola Song Accompaniment (pieces, 'Sea Fever', Ireland, and 'Love went a-Riding', Bridges).
Silver Medal, Vera Reade (Mitcham) 84 marks; Bronze Medal, John Clapham (Forest Hill) 82 marks; Certificates, William Emuss (Balham) and Cecily Clark (Balham).

The Vera Reade who was winner of both classes was the daughter of Reginald Reynolds.
On the following Saturday the compositions for pianola were judged by Dr Oldroyd again, but this time with the assistance of Percy Scholes, propagandist of the player-piano and editor of all those expensive Audio-Graphic music rolls. The results were as follows:

Solo for Pianola (open) – Gold Medal, Harry Gill (Leeds) 88 marks; Silver Medal, William McNaught (Chancery Lane) 82 marks; Certificates, William McNaught, Maud Emily Marshall (Kensington), and Dorothy Cranston (SW17).

Harry Gill's 'Caprice' was in fact made into a roll and performed at the prize concert at the Wimbledon Baths Hall on the evening of Thursday March 13th, by Reginald Reynolds of course, as mentioned earlier. It seems that it was then issued in May as a commercial Aeolian roll, for it is reviewed in *Musical Times* for June 1930. The number of the roll of Harry Gill's *Caprice* is T30479.

One other development of the Wimbledon Festival was that a Pianolists' Club was formed by some of the competitors, holding monthly meetings at Aeolian, and later Angelus Hall.

Mysteries in the world of players are many and the Patent Office is filled with weird and wonderful schemes for which no surviving machinery exists. What happened, for example, to the large numbers of pianophones (gramophones united with player pianos) which were invented and, presumably, made? I know of only one and that is in Walt Bellm's collection in Florida. But what about Aeolian's scheme for a piano roll with 'sound track' down one side so that a needle and horn could produce sound from it?

Perhaps I can offer a solution to another mystery – that of the reason why Q.R.S. piano rolls were called 'Q.R.S.'. The factory has no notion today and nowhere in the recorded history of this great business is there a clue. The company did, for a while, make radio valves (tubes) and if one looks into the world of wireless one finds the so-called 'Q-code' used by transmitters. This consists of a number of stock phrases used between transmitters over the air, all of which are reduced to a small group of letters starting with the letter 'Q'. And one of these is QRS, which means either 'Shall I transmit more slowly?' or, as a response to a message, 'Please transmit more slowly'. Could this be the real answer? Or does it stand for Quality, Reliability and Service?

Finally, what about somebody making a piano roll for those who wish to impress their neighbours? It is a bit suspicious letting the neighbours hear faultless performances of the classics all the time. Why not make a repeating roll of practicing scales or phrases, complete with intended mistakes and tantrum-like thumps on the keyboard. The roll could be issued with special effects such as one-finger themes developing into four-hand accompaniments, the occasional reversion to 'Chopsticks', and odd snatches of Chopin, Bartok and Beethoven. The test-roll and practice roll came close to achieving this, but the notion would stand development – even if only for the sake of one's standing with the neighbours!

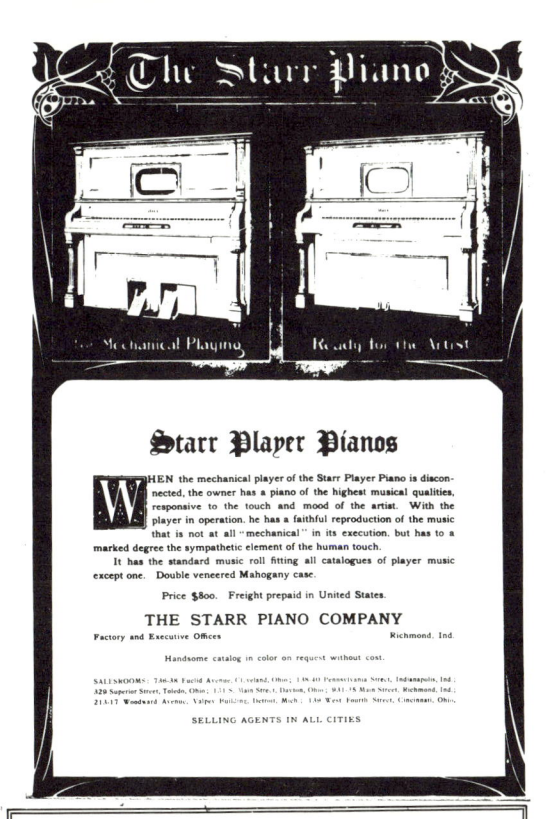

The Starr Piano

Starr Player Pianos

WHEN the mechanical player of the Starr Player Piano is disconnected, the owner has a piano of the highest musical qualities, responsive to the touch and mood of the artist. With the player in operation, he has a faithful reproduction of the music that is not at all "mechanical" in its execution, but has to a marked degree the sympathetic element of the human touch.

It has the standard music roll fitting all catalogues of player music except one. Double veneered Mahogany case.

Price $800. Freight prepaid in United States.

THE STARR PIANO COMPANY
Factory and Executive Offices — Richmond, Ind.

Handsome catalog in color on request without cost.

SALESROOMS: 7-66-38 Euclid Avenue, Cleveland, Ohio; 138-40 Pennsylvania Street, Indianapolis, Ind.; 329 Superior Street, Toledo, Ohio; 131 S. Main Street, Dayton, Ohio; 931-33 Main Street, Richmond, Ind.; 213-17 Woodward Avenue, Valpey Building, Detroit, Mich.; 136 West Fourth Street, Cincinnati, Ohio.

SELLING AGENTS IN ALL CITIES

Kranich & Bach
Ultra-Quality PIANOS and PLAYER-PIANOS

These superb instruments—*the finest that human hands can fashion*—make their appeal only to persons of fine tastes whose intelligence impels them to exercise common sense and a sane appreciation of mercantile values in making a purchase of any high-class article.

Kranich & Bach Prices Represent True Values—
Reasonable Partial Payments for Prudent Buyers

The most beautiful and instructive Piano Catalog ever published and an amusing storiette—"Mascagni and the Organ Grinder," free on request.

KRANICH & BACH
237 East 23rd Street, New York

PLEASING REFLECTIONS

The Emerson Player Piano

with all its faithfulness of interpretation is the means of such reflections. Behind it, however, is the true instrumental worth that produces the famous Emerson tone—a tone that perfectly reflects the conception of the musician.

Over a hundred thousand purchasers have felt the inspiration of the sweet toned Emerson.

Dealers in principal cities and towns.
SEND FOR OUR BEAUTIFUL CATALOG.

EMERSON PIANO CO.,
BOSTON   Established 1849   MASS.

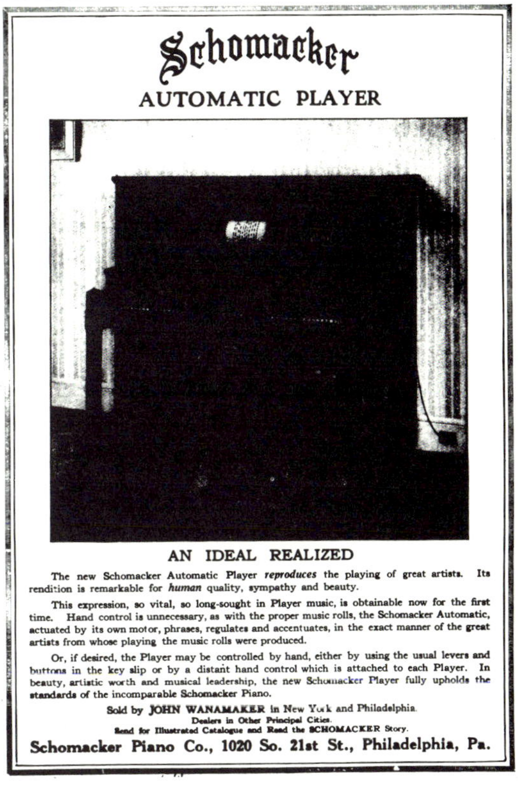

Schomacker
AUTOMATIC PLAYER

AN IDEAL REALIZED

The new Schomacker Automatic Player *reproduces* the playing of great artists. Its rendition is remarkable for *human* quality, sympathy and beauty.

This expression, so vital, so long-sought in Player music, is obtainable now for the first time. Hand control is unnecessary, as with the proper music rolls, the Schomacker Automatic, actuated by its own motor, phrases, regulates and accentuates, in the exact manner of the great artists from whose playing the music rolls were produced.

Or, if desired, the Player may be controlled by hand, either by using the usual levers and buttons in the key slip or by a distant hand control which is attached to each Player. In beauty, artistic worth and musical leadership, the new Schomacker Player fully upholds the standards of the incomparable Schomacker Piano.

Sold by **JOHN WANAMAKER** in New York and Philadelphia.
Dealers in Other Principal Cities.
Send for Illustrated Catalogue and Read the SCHOMACKER Story.

Schomacker Piano Co., 1020 So. 21st St., Philadelphia, Pa.

THE PIANO DE LUXE.

The Grand 'Pianola' Piano represents the highest and most luxurious point of development ever reached in the piano-making industry.

To the rare depth and quality of tone that characterizes only the most costly of grand pianos, to the most distinctive design and richest of casework, is added the inestimable advantages of the 'Pianola.'

The Grand 'Pianola' Piano

(Steinway, Weber, or Steck)

may be played in the ordinary way by hand or by means of music-roll. The inclusion of the 'Pianola' action in no way affects its splendid tone or alters the artistic lines of its appearance.

The Grand 'Pianola' Piano is obtainable upon easy payment terms. It is illustrated in Catalogue "AA," which is free on application.

THE ORCHESTRELLE CO.,
Æolian Hall,
135-6-7, New Bond St., London, W.

"The Marseillaise"
is the greatest war-song ever written.

Written by a soldier for soldiers, its inspiring words and martial strains have cheered French soldiers into battle for over a hundred years. To play it is a fit tribute to our gallant Allies, who, side by side with our own indomitable Army, are fighting the greatest fight that has ever been fought for liberty and honour.

If you owned a "Pianola" Piano you could render "The Marseillaise" with all the fire and vigour that has made it famous, even though you possess no musical knowledge.

The "Pianola" Piano
enables you to play the National Anthems of the Allied Nations as well as all the marching tunes of our "Tommies."

You could not choose a better time at which to buy a "Pianola" Piano: the gloom of the dimly lighted streets, the anxieties through which we are passing, would be forgotten in the pleasure that awaited you in your own home.

The "Pianola" Piano (Weber Model) is made in our factory in England, and is not and never has been—a German instrument. This and the famous Steck and Farrand models are all offered on **SPECIAL WAR TERMS**.

Write for the Illustrated Catalogue "H" and the particulars of the liberal allowance we make on ordinary pianos if given in part exchange for a "Pianola" Piano.

THE ORCHESTRELLE CO.,
Æolian Hall,
135-6-7, NEW BOND STREET, LONDON, W.

Distraction from thoughts of war.

"Talk of anything but the war," said an officer just returned from the front. It is good advice, for, whilst the war must inevitably take first place in our interests, it is very easy to dwell too much upon it—to the disadvantage of our nerves.

The "PIANOLA" PIANO relieves the mind from the stress of war.

Seated at a "Pianola" Piano, you are transported to a sphere where only peace exists—the great masters, whose works outlive all war, voice the softer moods of mankind, and preserve, through these grim days, your faith in the survival of the beautiful and good.

Write for Catalogue "N" and full details of the SPECIAL WAR TERMS which now bring the "Pianola" Piano within the reach of every home.

The Orchestrelle Company,
ÆOLIAN HALL,
135-6-7, NEW BOND STREET, LONDON, W.

Because the future holds danger in the field for some, and long days of waiting at home for others, the pleasures of the passing hour are all the more precious. The music of

The 'Pianola' Piano

will fill these flying moments with happiness, and provide fragrant memories for many a day to come.

The 'Pianola' Piano enables you to play music to suit every mood, and in times of anxiety proves a true friend, for it effectually distracts the mind from gloomy thoughts.

You may now obtain the 'Pianola' Piano on SPECIAL WAR TERMS, and a liberal allowance will be made upon your present piano.

Ask for Catalogue "N."

THE ORCHESTRELLE COMPANY,
ÆOLIAN HALL,
135-6-7, New Bond Street, LONDON, W.

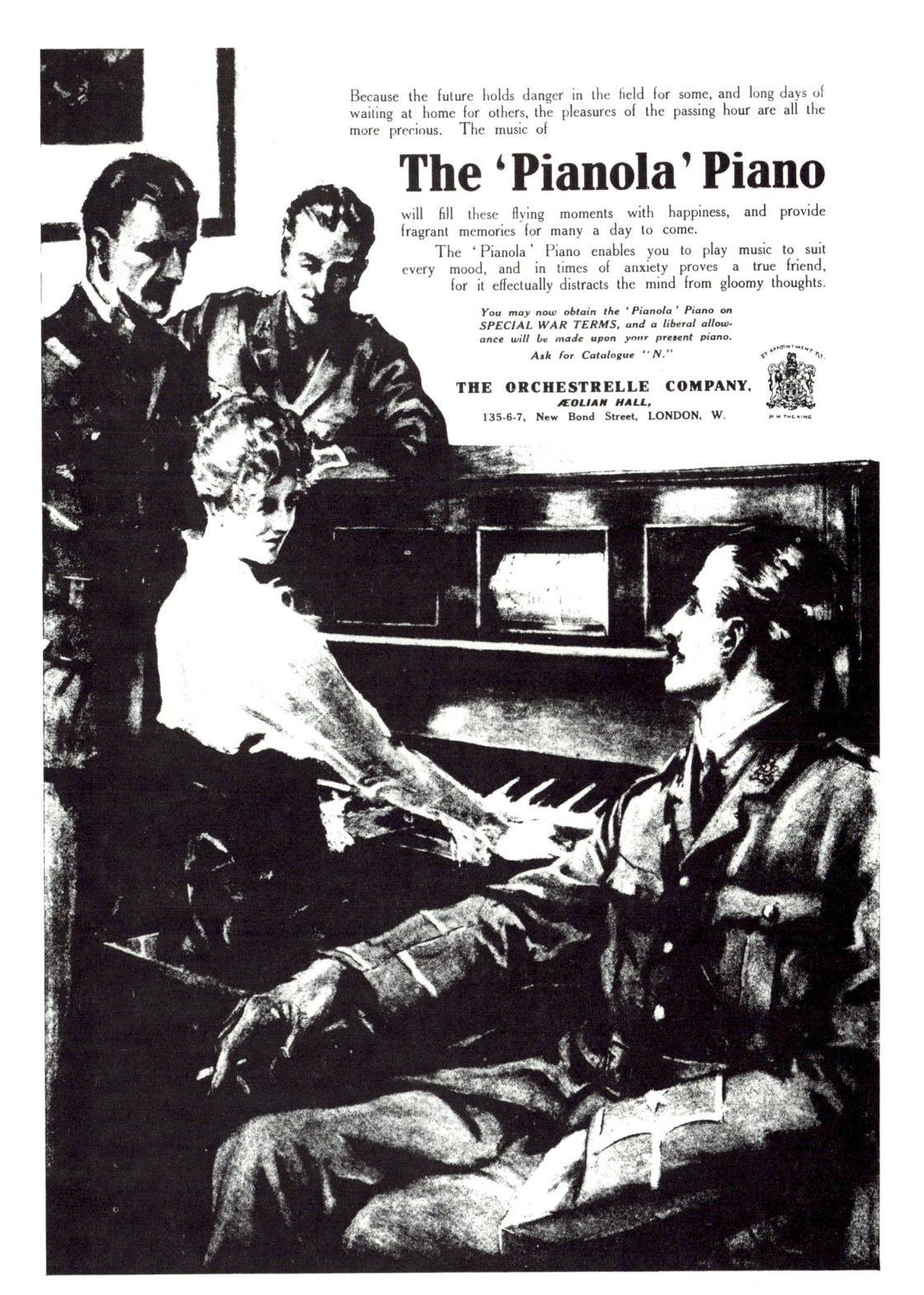

If Beethoven

could be heard by us today playing his Sonatas, what would not the musical world give to KNOW the master's own interpretation?—Today, the works of composers are preserved exactly as played by them. Also the works of the classicists as interpreted by living masters are preserved and brought to homes of refinement; thanks to modern science which has *perfected* the art of a truly absolute pianistic reproduction in

The APOLLO Reproducing PIANO
TRADE MARK REGISTERED

The Apollo reproducing piano is *not* a player piano: it is the true reproducer of the artist's playing. The world's music masters now declare that a perfect pianistic reproduction, giving every shade of tone, color and interpretation has been accomplished.

Make Your Grand a Reproducing Piano
It is possible for us to install the Reproducing Action in certain types of Grand pianos. You may own one of those types. If so, you may convert your own grand piano into a Reproducing Piano and have the exact interpretations of the world's master pianists at your command. We will gladly send you full information about this service upon request. Tell us the make and type of your piano when you write.

Apollo Catalog on Request
This catalog illustrates and describes in detail the Apollo styles, upright and grand, with and without the reproducing action. For those who are considering the purchase, either now or later, of a piano, player piano or reproducing piano, this catalog gives the FACTS *frankly*. It is important to *know* these *facts* before purchasing. Sent upon request, without obligation, of course.

The APOLLO Foot-Power Upright

This Upright is made in several styles; and each style at the lowest possible prices consistent with utmost quality—prices now practically as low as those of ordinary player pianos.

Please note: this foot-power instrument is equipped with a metronomic spring motor which is independent of the pneumatic mechanism. Therefore, the pumping does not affect the tempo of the roll; thus and thus only is correct, true interpretation made possible.

Incidentally, this motor makes pumping easy, because all the air is used to play the music and none to run the roll; you need not watch the tempo of the roll. The roll is rewound without the use of pedals; also more durable and more dependable than a pneumatic motor because it is not affected by climatic changes.

```
┌──  USE THIS COUPON! ──┐
│   APOLLO PIANO COMPANY │
│   Dept. 2647    De Kalb, Illinois │
│                                   │
│   Without obligation, send me your│
│   catalog. I would like information, par-│
│   ticularly on the following, as checked:│
│   ☐ Grand Piano                   │
│   ☐ Upright Piano                 │
│   ☐ Upright Reproducing Piano     │
│   ☐ Grand Reproducing Piano       │
│   ☐ Foot Pedal Player Piano       │
│   ☐ Installation of Reproducing Action│
│     in my piano                   │
│                                   │
│   Name_____   │
│   Address_____   │
└───────────────────────────────────┘
```

The APOLLO PIANO CO., Dept. 2647, De Kalb, Illinois [Pacific Coast Branch, 985 Market St., San Francisco]

Que faites vous cet après midi ?

Vous sentez-vous l'âme musicale ?

Allez entendre le fameux PIANOLUDE RÉGY, un quart d'heure vous suffira pour vous rendre compte de ses merveilleuses qualités, de sa sonorité incomparable, de la facilité avec laquelle il vous sera possible, sans étude préalable, d'interpréter les chefs-d'œuvre classiques aussi bien que les danses modernes.

**N'attendez pas demain....
Allez-y dès aujourd'hui......**

L'accueil le plus cordial vous est réservé.

R. C. Seine 308.028.

"Pianolude Régy"

PARIS — 12, Rond-Point des Champs Elysées.
45, Avenue Victor Emmanuel III.

R.C. (Seine) 308.028 Agent à Nice, Félix Faure, 51, Avenue de la Victoire, Nice

Freiburger Musikapparate-Bauanstalt G. m. b. H.
Freiburg i. Br., Haslacherstrasse 145

Evola

für Private und gewerbliche Betriebe
wird auch als loser Einbauapparat zum Selbsteinbau geliefert.
Lieferung einzelner Bestandteile

Eigene Notenrollenfabrik
Anfertigung fast aller Systeme

Spezialität:
Evola-88er Notenrollen spielbar auch auf Weltelnstrumenten
88er Einheits-Notenrollen für elektrische Klaviere

Freiburger Musikapparate-Bauanstalt G. m. b. H.
Freiburg i. Br., Haslacherstrasse 145
Telephon 7340 - Telegr.-Adr. Evola Freiburgbreisgau

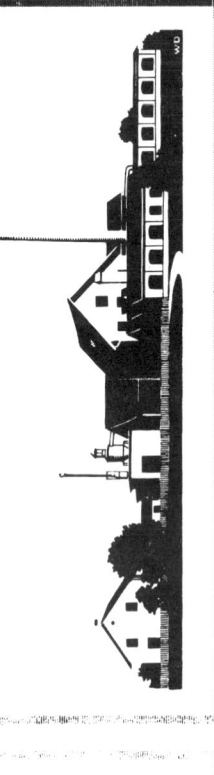

Freiburger Musikapparate-Bauanstalt G. m. b. H.
Freiburg i. Br., Haslacherstrasse 145

Evola

Kunstspiel-Piano und -Flügel
Evola-Notenrollen

Innenansicht
Einfachste Zugänglichkeit und Bedienung

Guests have learned to expect so much—

In the drawing rooms of New York and other metropolitan centers guests have learned to expect great music played by famous artists. Today, all over America, enraptured listeners hear those same artists play through the Ampico.

The Ampico places boundless resources at the modern host's command. For in the Ampico are combined a beautiful piano, a miraculous device that transports great artists to your drawing room, and an inexhaustible store of music.

At the turn of a lever your Ampico will spring into life under the touch of Rachmaninoff, of Rosenthal—or of any one of hundreds of world-famous pianists. The great man will be playing for you as truly as if he were there before your eyes. An Ampico recording of an artist's playing differs from his concert playing only in the fact that the artist is not visibly, physically present. Here is a modern miracle that is past belief—until you have heard the Ampico!

Perhaps your guests may include an accomplished pianist, who will consent to play for you. The moment his fingers touch the keyboard he will feel a keen delight in the piano's action, in its tone. For the Ampico is, first of all, a fine piano, intact for playing by hand. No detail of its construction is altered. When the ingenious device within the piano case is not in use it does not touch the strings or even the keys.

A few of the hundreds of famous artists the Ampico brings to you

TERESA CARREÑO
GEORGE COPELAND
ERNO DOHNÁNYI
ETHEL LEGINSKA
MISCHA LEVITZKI
JOSEF LHÉVINNE
SERGEI RACHMANINOFF
MORIZ ROSENTHAL
ARTHUR RUBINSTEIN
GERMAINE SCHNITZER
E. ROBERT SCHMITZ
FANNY BLOOMFIELD ZEISLER

The Ampico may be had only in pianos bearing these names of present and established reputation—names which for generations have stood for instruments of quality: Knabe; Chickering; Fischer; Marshall & Wendell; Haines Bros.; Franklin; and, in Canada, the Willis also. Note that the Knabe and the Chickering are two of the four great pianos in general use on the American concert stage.

Exchange your piano for an Ampico

Your present piano will entitle you to an allowance in buying an Ampico. The dealer will also be glad to arrange convenient terms of payment. Foot-power models, $795. Electric models: uprights, $985 to $1800; grands, $1975 to $5000. With freight added.

Hear the Ampico!

If you have not yet heard the Ampico, you must do so at your first opportunity. Any dealer who sells any of the pianos mentioned above will be glad to have you hear the Ampico at his store.

If you are not near a store where the Ampico is sold, or if you want to know more about the Ampico before hearing it, write to the address below. You will receive a booklet descriptive of the Ampico and information as to where you may conveniently hear it.

The AMPICO

THE AMPICO COMPANY · 437 FIFTH AVENUE · NEW YORK

LE DUO-ART

ÉLECTRIQUE OU A PÉDALES

est un instrument qui reproduit automatiquement les exécutions des Maîtres du clavier enregistrées sur des rouleaux de papier perforé au cours de ces exécutions mêmes et par eux mêmes

LE DUO-ART
DANS LE SALON PARTICULIER DE S.E. LE CARDINAL GASPARRI SECRÉTAIRE D'ÉTAT DE S.S. PIE XI

THE ÆOLIAN Cᵒ
32 Avenue de l'Opéra, Paris

CATALOGUE IG FRANCO SUR DEMANDE

TÉLÉPHONE : CENTRAL 70-03

IMP. MARECHAL - PARIS

Magasins d'exposition et d'auditions :

PARIS
11, rue du 4 Septembre
Téléphone : Louvre 31-15

MUSIQUE PERFORÉE
pour tous appareils.
Abonnements.

Rouleaux 88 notes.
Prix :
12 et 13 fr. le rouleau.

JE CHANTE ET TIENS BON

MARQUE DÉPOSÉE

Succursales à :

BORDEAUX
9, rue Sainte-Catherine

LILLE
51, boulevard de la Liberté.

LYON
30, rue de l'Hôtel-de-Ville.

MARSEILLE
7, place de Rome

NANCY
19, rue Gambetta

TOULOUSE
5, rue Saint-Pantaléon.

BRUXELLES
14, rue d'Arenberg.

Catalogue descriptif A sur demande.

ODÉOLA

L'ODÉOLA est le seul piano pneumatique dont le pédalage est si agréable et si léger qu'il peut être joué par les dames et même *par les enfants*.

══ FABRICATION FRANÇAISE ══

PIANO DEPARTMENT

Library System Available for Music Roll Supply

ROGERS

PLAYER PIANO
In Rosewood or Mahogany case. Height 4 ft. 4 ins., width 5 ft. 2 ins. depth 2 ft. 4 ins., compass 7¼ octaves. Fitted with all the latest expression devices including Divided Treble and Bass, Automatic Solo, Tracking and Transposing devices
Net cash price
157 guineas
12 quarterly payments of £15 2 3

UNIVERSAL

PLAYER PIANO
Height 4 ft. 1½ ins. width 4 ft. 9½ ins., depth 2 ft. Dark Mahogany case, compass 7 octaves. Overstrung, full iron frame, metal standard tape check action. Fitted with Aeolian Co.'s player action, comprising Expression Controls, Bass and Treble Automatic Solo and Tracking devices together with Silent, Tempo and Re-roll levers
Net cash price
86 guineas
12 quarterly payments of £8 5 9

HARWOOD

PLAYER PIANO
Dark Mahogany case. Height 4 ft. 3 ins., width 5 ft. 1 in., full scale 'Standard' Player action, Divided Treble and Bass, Solo, Accenting, Bass and Treble levers, Silent stop, Retard, Accel.
Net cash price
84 guineas
12 quarterly payments of £8 1 9

PLAYER PIANETTE
In Mahogany case. Height 4 ft., depth 1 ft. 11 ins., width 4 ft. 3 ins., compass 6 octaves, overstrung. Fitted with full-scale Triumph-Auto action, Automatic Solo, Bass and Treble Levers
Price, **75 guineas**. £7 4 6 per quarter.

BLUTHNER-HUPFELD

PLAYER GRAND
In Rosewood case, Aliquot scaling. Length 6 ft. 3 ins. Fitted with the Hupfeld Solophonola player action with Transposing, Auto Tracking, Auto Solo, Auto Pedal, and device for graduating accompaniment
Net cash price
540 guineas
12 quarterly payments of £51 19 6

CRAMER

PLAYER PIANO
In Mahogany case. Height 4 ft. 4 ins., width 5 ft. 2 ins., depth, 2 ft. 5 ins., full scale 7¼ octaves. Automatic tracking, Transposing device, etc.
Net cash price
103 guineas
12 quarterly payments of £9 18 3

CHALLEN-ANGELUS

PLAYER GRAND
In Mahogany case. Length 5 ft. Fitted with the Angelus player action with Auto Solo, Transposing and other expression devices including the Registered Phrasing Lever
Net cash price
275 guineas
12 quarterly payments of £26 9 6

ALL PRICES ARE SUBJECT TO MARKET FLUCTUATIONS

HARRODS LTD

Telephone SLOANE 1234
Telegrams 'EVERYTHING HARRODS LONDON'

LONDON S W1

PIANO DEPARTMENT

The Player Piano Combines the Piano and the Means to Play it Perfectly

JOHN BROADWOOD

PLAYER PIANO
In dark Mahogany case. Compass 7¼ octaves. Overstrung, ivory keys. Height 4 ft. 1½ ins. depth 2 ft. 4 ins., width 5 ft. 4 ins. Fitted with the new Broadwood full scale Player, Transposing device, Automatic Sustaining Pedal, Solo device, Divided Treble and Bass, etc.

Net cash price
109 guineas
12 quarterly payments of £10 9 9

PLAYER PIANO
In dark Mahogany case. Height 4 ft. 2½ ins. width 5 ft. 1 in., depth 2 ft. 3½ ins. Fitted with the celebrated 'Strauch' Player action embracing Transposing device, Automatic Tracking Automatic Solo, Divided Treble and Bass, etc.

Net cash price
108 guineas
12 quarterly payments of £10 7 9

BRASTED

BLUTHNER-HUPFELD

PLAYER PIANO
In Mahogany, Rosewood or Ebonized case bright or dull finished. Height 4 ft. 4 ins., width 5 ft. 3 ins., depth 2 ft. 7 ins. Fitted with the Hupfeld individual metal double pneumatic player action, with Transposing, Auto-Tracking, Auto Solo, Auto Pedal, and device for graduating accompaniment

Net cash price
315 guineas
12 quarterly payments of £30 6 6

PLAYER PIANO
In dark Mahogany case with ivory keys. Overstrung full iron frame, underdamper tape check action. Height 4 ft. 2½ ins., depth 2 ft. 5 ins., width 5 ft. 1½ ins. Fitted with the Hupfeld metal action with interchangeable Pneumatics, Transposing device, Automatic Tracking, Automatic Solo, Accenting lever, etc.

Net cash price
129 guineas
12 quarterly payments of £12 8 9
This instrument is guaranteed by the sole concessionaires, Messrs. Bluthner & Co., Ltd.

LANGHAM HUPFELD

HOPKINSON

'MIGNON' PLAYER PIANO
In dark Mahogany case with ivory keys. Height 4 ft., depth 2 ft. 3 ins., width 4 ft. 11¾ ins. Fitted with full-scale player action, Divided Treble and Bass, Transposing device, Automatic solo and Accenting lever

Net cash price
118 guineas
12 quarterly payments of £11 7 3

PLAYER PIANO
Model 61. In Mahogany case. Height 4 ft. 1 in. Fitted with Divided Treble and Bass, Automatic Solo, Tracking and the special Angelus Phrasing Lever

Net cash price
107 guineas
12 quarterly payments of £10 6 0

ANGELUS

LIBRARY SYSTEM FOR MUSIC ROLL SUPPLY
Harrods have made arrangements whereby some of the largest Libraries of Music Rolls are accessible to owners of Players
Terms for subscription for 12 months
65 note .. .. £2 2 0   Full scale (88 note) .. £4 4 0
Duo Art and Full scale .. £5 5 0
Subscription payable in advance   Prospectus giving full particulars and Lists of Music Rolls may be had on application

ALL PRICES ARE SUBJECT TO MARKET FLUCTUATIONS

HARRODS LTD

Telephone SLOANE 1234
Telegrams 'EVERYTHING HARRODS LONDON'

LONDON S W 1

PIANO DEPARTMENT
Harrods Piano Salon Displays all the Newest Models
AMPICO ELECTRIC RE-ENACTING PIANOS

THE AMPICO is the most highly perfected reproducing piano in the world. It is found only in fine pianos of quality and recognised reputation—MARSHALL & ROSE, JOHN BROADWOOD & SON, COLLARD & COLLARD, CHAPPELL, ROGERS, HOPKINSON and CHALLEN, GROTRIAN-STEINWEG

A piano containing the AMPICO brings the living art of the great pianists into the home, and all the music of which the piano is capable

The device is so skilfully incorporated into the piano, that when played by hand a pianist could not possibly detect its presence, for it in no way interferes with the action or touch of the instrument

Only when a roll is inserted, a button pressed, and the strings sing under the unmistakable touch of a great artist do the wonderful tones of the AMPICO become believable

Almost every great pianist of modern times may be heard. Rachmaninoff, Moiseiwitsch, and many of the greatest artists have recorded their playing exclusively for the AMPICO

Only on the AMPICO can be heard dance music played by Vincent Lopez himself, and the stars of the Paul Whiteman Orchestra

The AMPICO may be supplied foot blown and electric reproducing, and may be installed on any voltage, D.C. or A.C. private or district circuit. The AMPICO is also adapted to play all standard 88-note music rolls and they can be operated according to one's individual ideas of expression

BROADWOOD AMPICO

Upright in Dark Rosewood or Mahogany case, height 4 ft. 4½ ins. width 5 ft. 2½ ins. Overstrung, ivory keys, compass 7¼ octaves

Net cash price .. 306 guineas

12 quarterly payments of

£29 9 3

ROGERS AMPICO REPRODUCING PLAYER-GRAND

Length 5 ft., width 4 ft. 10 ins. Compass 7¼ octaves, ivory keys Mahogany or Rosewood case, on twin legs

Net cash price .. 476 guineas

12 quarterly payments of

£45 16 6

MARQUE AMPICO

Foot-power Upright Model in finely figured Mahogany case, height 4 ft. 4½ ins., width 5 ft. 1 in. This instrument has been specially designed for those who prefer a foot-power model, and besides being an Ampico Reproducing piano, it is a piano on which any Standard full-scale rolls can be used

Net cash price .. 178 guineas

12 quarterly payments of

£17 2 9

Electric or foot operated, as desired, Upright model

Net cash price .. 225 guineas

12 quarterly payments of

£21 13 3

ALL PRICES ARE SUBJECT TO MARKET FLUCTUATIONS

Telephone SLOANE 1234
Telegrams 'EVERYTHING HARRODS LONDON'

HARRODS LTD   **LONDON S W 1**

CAPTIONS TO ILLUSTRATIONS IN APPENDIX A

Page 318:   March 1904 is the date of this full-page notice in *Musical News* regarding the Metzler player which, at £35, was considerably cheaper than the £65 Pianola.
Page 319:   May 1907 is the date of this advertisement for the Calmont Musetta player made in Leipzig by Buff-Hedinger, the company originally founded by Monopol musical box and Ariston organette maker, Paul Ehrlich.
Page 320:   Two advertisements from the *Strand Magazine*, May 1902, the first for Farrand's Cecilian and the other for the ill-fated piano playing attachment, the kicking-shoe Pianotist.
Page 321:   Bansall's Universal Piano player was made to C. W. Atkinson's patents. The pneumatic action and bellows were built into the case, but the roll mechanism was fitted into a box which connected to the front of the keyboard, the tracker bar ducts being carried through a row of holes in the front of the piano. When not in use, the player could be removed and placed in the piano stool. This rare advertisement appeared in *Musical Opinion*, April, 1911.
Page 322:   The Pianola advertising was in a class of its own. This example, from The Orchestrelle Company in London, appeared in *The Sphere* in September, 1901.
Page 324:   An example of the technical message in an advertisement is this Angelus notice published in 1912. From the Ottenheimer collection.
Page 325:   In terms of promotion, the Angelus was second only to the Pianola in Britain as a piano-player and, later player piano. This notice appeared in *The Sphere* for September 1903.
Page 326 *(left)*:   The American organ company, Wilcox & White, made the Angelus Orchestral seen here in this advertisement from *McClure's Magazine*, 1898. From the collection of Paul Ottenheimer.
Page 326 *(right)*:   In October, 1904, this advertisement appeared in British magazines. Little is known about the Humana push-up which was marketed by Metzler in London.
Page 328:   Seasonal sales copy for Wilcox & White with the Angelus. The seal, at the top of this advertisement, became a trade mark on all the company's piano literature. Dated 1915. From the Ottenheimer collection.
Page 330 *(left)*:   An important maker of electrically-operated player pianos was Kuhl & Klatt. This advertisement, c.1909, is for an instrument operated by a box of wet-cell accumulators.
Page 330 *(right)*:   The merits of the push-up cabinet player were still being sung well into the first decade of this century. From *The Sphere*, this time September 1903, comes with the news of the move to Aeolian Hall, Bond Street.
Page 331:   Melville Clark's Apollo advertisement from 1909 was used to get a message across – namely the maker's early identification of the merits of a full-compass player. From *The American Magazine* in the collection of Paul Ottenheimer.
Page 332:   Another of Orchestrelle's graceful advertisements for the Pianola push-up, this one from *The Connoisseur*, 1903.
Page 333:   Bold claims by Melville Clark in this 1912 advertisement in *Scribner's Magazine*. From the Ottenheimer collection.
Page 334:   A pertinently phrased notice in the *Tuner's Journal* for August 1927. From the Ottenheimer collection.
Page 336:   Pianola's high price was justified by the introduction of refinements such as the Metrostyle, announced here in *The Connoisseur* for 1905.
Page 338 *(left)*:   Krell's upright grand player piano was acclaimed 'totally different' by its makers in this undated advertisement in the Ottenheimer collection.
Page 338 *(right)*:   Royal patronage was always a good sales aid as demonstrated by this notice in *Country Life in America* for 1910 in the Ottenheimer collection.
Page 339 *(top left)*:   The American Starr Piano Co. stressed the artistic merit of the player in this 1906 advertisement from *Country Life in America*. From the Paul Ottenheimer collection.
Page 339 *(top right)*:   Pushy advertisement copy goes back a long while as this *Harper's Magazine* ad from 1913 reveals. From the Ottenheimer collection.
Page 339 *(lower left)*:   In America, Emerson used mirrors to promote their player in *The Etude* for 1915. From the Ottenheimer collection.
Page 339 *(lower right)*:   Another 1915 notice is this one for the Schomacker Automatic Player. Note the claims for expression. From the Ottenheimer collection.
Page 340:   Grand pianos which were 'grand' rather than 'upright grands' were for the well-to-do music lover. This May, 1914, advertisement in *The Connoisseur* has the trappings of style and wealth in those pre-Duo-Art days.
Page 341:   War in Europe afforded special opportunities for the advertisement copy writer and designer in 1915. This notice appeared in *The Connoisseur*.
Page 342:   War and relaxation from its pressures was the continuing theme into 1916 in this notice, also from *The Connoisseur*.
Page 343:   There is a piquant naïvety about this advertisement, also from *The Connoisseur* of about 1916. Notice the offer of a 'liberal allowance' on your old piano.
Page 344:   In America, meanwhile, quality advertising depended on the association between the player piano and the great composers. Here, the Apollo reproducing piano is linked with Beethoven in this 1921 advertisement.
Page 345:   Player pianos were not just the province of German, British and American makers as this advertisement from *L'Illustration* in 1924 shows. From the Ottenheimer collection.

Page 346: A very late instrument was the Evola expression piano which was powered by an electric motor. The date of Bauanstalt's instrument is unknown.

Page 347: A copy line to explain how 'keeping up with the Jones's' began? From *Country Life in America*, September 1924. Ottenheimer collection.

Page 348: Aeolian had its offices around the world. Here is a notice from a Parisian magazine around 1924.

Page 349: French manufacturers also went in for big presentations, although none quite matched Aeolian. This *L'Illustration* notice is also from 1924.

Pages 350–52: Three pages from the 1929 catalogue of Harrods of London show the styles and prices available at this late stage in the history of the player piano. Within a few years, the player was virtually dead, its demise being triggered off by the depression although already tastes were changing and the degree of mobility provided by the car meant that more people preferred to spend their money on a motor vehicle.

THE STRADOLA PLAYER ACTION.

The ONLY Player Action in the WORLD which will
GO completely INTO any ordinary EXISTING PIANO
with either OVER or UNDER-DAMPING ACTION,
WITHOUT enlarging or building out the CASE of the Piano.

NO constructional ALTERATION.

With the MUSIC-ROLL BOX fitted BEHIND THE TOP-DOOR and level with the eyes.

Which does NOT ALTER THE DESIGN of the Piano, and requires NO EXTERNAL ADDITION.

It is INTERCHANGEABLE, and can be REMOVED and REFITTED into ANOTHER PIANO.

The "STRADOLA" Action is the Perfection of Pneumatic Action, and finally disposes of the necessity for making large and clumsy Piano Cases.

MUSICAL COMPONENTS, Ltd. Medlar Street, Camberwell, S.E.

Phone: Hop 1293.

APPENDIX B

The Player Piano in Flying Training

The impact of the player piano on flying training may at first seem surprising, yet it is a demonstrable fact that had it not been for the sophisticated pneumatic control devices perfected within the player industry earlier generations of pilots would have had a harder time and the cost of pilot training would have been that much higher. It is worth pointing out that at this present time so perfect are modern aircraft flight simulators that airline aircrew can safely convert from one type of aircraft to another after only a few hours of actual flying, having mastered all the handling characteristics in the safety of a highly developed simulator which, while replicating the complete performance and specification of a given type of aircraft, never leaves the special room in which it is housed.

In the beginning, though, so-called ground trainers began as aircraft with no wings in which would-be pilots could charge around on the ground to get the basic feel of the controls. These were of limited value and as early as 1917 patents were being taken out for artificial trainers in which air motors imparted movement to a stationary 'aeroplane' in response to control movements. Now the science and art of pneumatic control is no way solely the province of the player piano, but it was directly from the player industry that the most significant strides were made during the late 'twenties through to the early days of the 1939–45 war. Edwin Link, who gained his early engineering experience with his father's company, the Link Piano & Organ Co. of Binghamton, New York, took out a number of patents for improvements in pneumatic control for pianos. When the United States Air Force put out an invitation to tender for a trainer for pilots, among the tenders was one from Link. Although his tender was for a machine much less complicated than some of the others, he won the contract on the strength of the fact that his device used standard player piano parts which were already in production, and pneumatic technology which was proven in players. The Link Trainer was developed in the period 1927–9 in the basement of the Link factory. The first trainer, advertised as 'an efficient aeronautical training aid – a novel, profitable amusement device', was described in his American Patent number 1,825,462, filed in 1930. This was an enclosed-cockpit device mounted on four sets of pneumatic bellows which could impart pitch, roll and yaw movement under the control of the trainee pilot's control column. An electrically driven suction pump mounted in the fixed pedestal base provided power while another motor-driven device produced a repeated sequence of attitude disturbances. In the serious flying training model, this last feature, was of course, dispensed with.

The reaction to Link's trainer was slow and despite many costly improvements to the original, including the provision of instruments and control 'feel' to the joy-stick, it was not until the early 'thirties that his brainchild began to catch on in a big way. It was soon being supplied to Japan, the USSR, France and Germany, while American Airlines was the first airline to take delivery of one in 1937. In that year the Royal Air Force also took delivery of its first models and within four years the Link Trainer School had been set up at Elstree Aerodrome in Hertfordshire.

Constantly improved and in production right up until the 1950s, the Link contained large numbers of recognisable player-piano parts, including valves, knife-valves and reworked expression devices. It was, though, a 'beast' to fly and many a pilot who could operate the trainer tended to be a bad flier, while many a reasonable pilot was reduced to a nervous wreck by the Link. My own performance in the Link, a mandatory session at depressingly regular intervals, was very undistinguished.

Quite obviously the Link Trainer had certain shortcomings, although it proved its worth in simulated cross-country and navigational exercises when the course being 'flown' could be monitored by the instructor who had a large map table over which a remotely controlled walking pen (given the apt sobriquet of 'the crab') traced the flight.

When it became necessary to speed up the training of bomber pilots during the war while at the same time coping with an extreme shortage of real aircraft, the player piano, this time in the form of the reproducing piano, once more came to the rescue. This was the so-called Silloth Trainer, which was developed by the Aeolian Company engineer Gordon Iles, then elevated to the ranks of Wing Commander, at R.A.F. Silloth, south of Carlisle.

The Silloth could be set to operate in the manner of whatever machine it was programmed for and consequently variants were made which could simulate the handling of the Blenheim and Halifax bombers along with many other types.

The story goes back to 1935, when Gordon Iles learned to fly at the Cinque Ports Flying Club. With the gathering war clouds on the horizon he joined the Civil Air Guard and became the second officer to be commissioned into the squadron. In 1939 he was called up into the Royal Air Force and by 1942 was serving as chief flying instructor at Blackpool's Squires Gate aerodrome. Meanwhile at Silloth in Cumberland flying crews were being converted to fly the American Lockheed Hudson, an exercise which was proving very expensive in aircraft since this twin-engined bomber had a nasty habit of 'swinging' on take-off. Iles, seeing the aircraft as a supreme example of a pneumatic instrument, came to the rescue and proposed to make a pneumatic trainer for the modest sum of £40,000 – then equal to about $150,000.

The result was a sopisticated crew procedure trainer, the prototype being completed in 1943. Since the mechanism was tailor-made to the detailed performance of the aircraft it simulated, the project was accorded top-security and remained secret until the story was told for the first time in *The Music Box*.* Construction of the trainers was undertaken at Southall, Middlesex, by Automatic Player Piano Actions Ltd under the direction of Aeolian Pianola and Duo-Art mechanics. The sound-producing section which reproduced the in-flight noise of the aircraft was made by the Rank Organisation using Hammond Organ technology. By mid-1945, fourteen of these trainers were either in existence or on order. Partly because they were pneumatic devices and partly because the R.A.F. was entering the electronics age, servicing the trainers was largely the task of their inventor and other player-piano-trained engineers and in consequence by about 1947 the trainers were pensioned off to be replaced by the next generation of electric trainers. Even so, expression pneumatics and valve chests,

---

* Gerald Stonehill, 'How the Piano Won the War', *The Music Box*, volume 7, pp. 131-3.

THE PLAYER PIANO IN FLYING TRAINING

rubber cloth and tubing, all were united into the Silloth, giving credence to the claim that the player piano did help Britain to win the war.

The only other aeronautical aspect of player-piano technology worth recalling is an American experiment in aerial advertising carried out by Ed Link's Link Aeronautical Corporation and called the Link Sky Sign. Suspended beneath the wings of a Fairchild monoplane was a frame containing illuminated advertising messages, the light bulbs controlled by a perforated paper roll and switched pneumatically using a player-piano tracker-bar system. Link went on to provide music from the air with a similar system using high-pressure loudly voiced organ pipes. The venture appears to have been short-lived.

PIANOLA
The Connoisseur

The PIANOLA

Supposing you possess a piano, and are desirous of making it the source of pleasure it is intended to be, two courses are open to you—either you must learn to play by hand, or purchase a Pianola. The first means years of drudgery before you can attain any degree of proficiency. If, on the other hand, you decide on having a Pianola, the ability to play any and every kind of music becomes yours immediately.

The command which the Pianola gives over expression is such that you can play a composition exactly as you think it should be played.

You would enjoy hearing the Pianola in use, and if you will call at Aeolian Hall, it will afford us great pleasure to demonstrate the instrument to you.

Write for catalogue A.A.

The Orchestrelle Co.,
═AEOLIAN HALL,═
135=6=7, New Bond Street,
LONDON, W.

Bibliography

Adlung, Jacob, *Anleitung zu der Musikalischen Gelahrtheit*, Erfurt, Saxony, 1758.
Ampico Reproducing Piano, *Inspector's Reference Manual (1923)*. Facsimile reprint by Frank Adams, Seattle, Washington, U.S.A., 1973.
Ampico Service Manual 1929, Facsimile reprint, Frank Adams, Seattle, Washington, 1973.
Armstrong, Durrell, *Player Piano Co. Inc, Catalogue* (a most valuable source of reference for the American player piano – AO-H), Kansas, 1981.
Association des Amis des Instruments et de la Musique Mécanique, *Bulletin*, Le Vesinet, 1976, *et seq.*
Atta, H. L., *The Player Piano*, 1914.
Baines, A., *Musical Instruments Through the Ages*, Penguin Books, 1961.
Barbour, J. Murray, *Tuning and Temperament, A Historical Survey*, Michigan State College Press, 1951.
Bedos de Celles, D. François, *L'Art de Facteur d'Orgues* (Quatrième partie), Paris, 1778.
Boalch, Donald H., *Makers of the Harpsichord & Clavichord 1440–1840*, 2nd ed., Clarendon Press, Oxford, 1974.
Bowers, Q. David, *Put Another Nickel In*. New York, Vestal Press, 1966.
Bowers, Q. David, *Encyclopedia of Automatic Instruments*, New York, Vestal Press, 1972.
Bowers, Q. David, California, USA. Private collection of mechanical music ephemera.
Brinsmead, Edgar, *The History of the Pianoforte*, London, 1879.
British Patent Office, *Musical Instruments, 1694–1933*. Abridgement Class 88, London.
Buchner, A., *Mechanical Musical Instruments*. London, Batchworth Press, *c.* 1954.
Busby, Thomas, *Concert Room and Orchestra Anecdotes*. London, 1825.
Chapuis, A., *Histoire de la Boîte à Musique*. Lausanne, Edition Scriptar, 1955.
Chapuis, A., and Droz, E., *Atomata*. Transl. Reid. Neuchâtel, Editions du Griffon, 1958.
Chapuis, A., and Gelis, E. *Le Monde des Automates*. Paris, 1928.
Clark, J. E. T., *Musical Boxes – A History and Appreciation*. 3rd edn, London, Allen & Unwin, 1961.
Conservatoire Nationale des Arts et Métiers, *Automates et Mécanismes à Musique*. Paris, 1960.
Conservatoire Nationale des Arts et Métiers, *Les Boîtes à Musique de Prague*. (Catalogue) Paris, 1966.
Debain, A. F., *Antiphonel-Harmonium Suppléant de l'Organiste*. Paris, 1873.
Devaux, P., *Automates et Automatisme*. Paris, Presses Universitaires, 1941.
Dolge, Alfred, *Pianos and their Makers*. Covina Publishing Company, California, 1911 (facsimile: Dover Publications, Inc., New York, 1972).
Dolge, Alfred, *Men Who Have Made Piano History* (described as Vol. 2 of *Pianos and their Makers*), Covina, California, 1913 (facsimile: Vestal Press, New York, 1980).
Drake, Harry, 'The Pneumatic Player', *Musical Opinion*, London, 1921.
Drake, Harry, 'The Player Piano Explained'. *Musical Opinion*, London, 1922.
Duo-Art Reproducing Piano Service Manual, 1925, Facsimile Reprint by Frank Adams, Seattle, Washington, USA, 1973.
Duo-Art Reproducing Piano Service Manual, 1927, Facsimile Reprint by Tuners Supply Co., Boston, Massachusets, USA (n.d.).
Edgerton, Bill, Darien, Connecticut, USA. Private collection of ephemera.
Ehrlich, Cyril, *The Piano, A History*, Dent, London, 1976.
Ellis, Alexander J., and Mendel, Arthur, *Musical Pitch* (a series of monographs by), Frits Knuf, Amsterdam, 1968.
Engramelle, Father Marie Dominique Joseph, *La Tonotechnie ou l'Art de Noter les Cylindres*. Paris, 1775.
Exhibitions, Historic, *Collection of catalogues*, British Museum Shelfmark 07902 b.1/7.
Fair Organ Preservation Society, *The Key Frame* (Journal). Northampton, 1966 *et seq.*
Fetis, Francois Joseph, *Biographie Universelle des Musiciens*. Paris, 1860.
Flight, Benjamin, *Flight's Practical Tuner for the Organ or Pianoforte*. London, *c.* 1880.
Fried, Frederick, *Pictorial History of the Carousel*. New York, A. S. Barnes, 1964.

Galpin, Francis W., *Old English Instruments of Music – Their History and Character*. 2nd edn, 1911.
Galpin, Francis W., *A Textbook of European Musical Instruemnts – Their Origin, History and Character*. 1937.
Gesellschaft der Freunde Mechanischer Musikinstrumente E.V., *Das Mechanische Musikinstrumente* (Journal) 1976 *et seq*.
Givens, L., *Rebuilding the Player Piano*. New York, Vestal Press, 1963.
Grew, Sydney, *The Art of the Player Piano*. London, Kegan Paul, Trench, 1922.
Grove, G., *Dictionary of Music and Musicians*. 5th edn. Ed. Blom. London, Macmillan, 1954.
Grover, David S., *The Piano*, Hale, London, 1976.
Harding, Rosamond E. M., *The Piano-Forte: Its History traced to the Great Exhibition of 1851*, Cambridge, England, 1933.
Harmonicon, periodical, London, 1823–33.
Harrison, Sidney, *Grand Piano*, London, Faber, 1976.
Heinitz, Wilhelm, Extract: 'Mechanische Musikinstrumente der Instrumentenkunde' in *Handbuch der Musikwissenschaft*, Potsdam, 1928.
Howe, Alfred H., *Scientific Piano Tuning and Servicing*, American Piano Supply Co., New Jersey, 1941 (revised edn 1966).
Hupfeld, L., *Dea-Violina*. Leipzig, 1909.
Jacquot, Albert, *Dictionnaire – des Instruments de Musique*. Paris, 1886.
Journal of the Musikhistorische Gesellschaft für selbstspielende Instruments in Deutschland, E.V., Hanover, 1978–82.
Kircher, Athanasius, *Musurgia Universalis*, Rome, 1650.
Kobbe, Gustav, *The Pianolist – A Guide for Pianola Players*, London, Sidney Appleton, 1908.
Langwill, L. G., and Boston, Canon Noel, *Church and Chamber Barrel Organs*, Edinburgh, 1967.
McCombie, Ian, *The Piano Handbook*, New York, Scribner's, 1980.
McFerrin, W. V., *The Piano – Its Acoustics*, Edward Lyman Bill, 1925 (facsimile Tuners Supply Co., Boston, 1971).
Maingot, E., *Les Automates*, Paris, Librairie Hachette, 1959.
Marini, Marino, *Museo di Strumenti Musicali Meccanici*, Marino Marini, Ravenna, Italy, *c.* 1972.
Matetzki, J., *Uber die Behändlung und Instandsetzung von Pneumatischen Musikwerken*, Leipzig, 1913.
Mathot Library, Brussels, Belgium. Private papers, catalogues & ephemera.
Van Der Meer, Dr J. H., 'Beiträge zum Cembalobau im Deutschen Sprachgebiet bis 1700' in *Anzeiger des Germanischen Nationalmuseums 1966*, Nürnberg, 1966.
Mersenne, P. M., *Harmonie Universelle*, Paris, 1636.
Michel, N. E., *Michel's Piano Atlas*, U.S.A., *c.* 1963.
Michel, N. E., *Historical Pianos, Harpsichords & Clavichords*, Pico Rivera, California, 1970.
Music & Automata, London, 1983.
Music Industries Directory, London, 1914, 1924 and 1929.
Musical Box Society of Great Britain, *The Music Box* (Journal). London, 1962–82.
Musical Box Society International of America, *Bulletin* (Journal). U.S.A., 1966–82.
Musique Adresses Universel, Paris, 1919–20 and 1930.
Musical Opinion, London, 1877–1930.
Nalder, Lawrence M., *The Modern Piano*, Unwin Brothers, Old Woking, 1977.
Nettl, Paul, 'Ein Spielender Musikautomat aus dem 16. Jahrhundert' in *Zeitschrift für Musikwissenschaft* II, 1920.
Newman, E., *The Piano-Player and Its Music*, London, 1920.
Obenchain, Elaine, *The Complete Catalog of Ampico Reproducing Piano Rolls*, William H. Edgerton, Connecticut, 1977.
Ord-Hume, A. W. J. G., *Collecting Musical Boxes and How to Repair Them*, London, Allen & Unwin, 1967.
Ord-Hume, A. W. J. G., *Player Piano*, London, Allen & Unwin, 1970.
Ord-Hume, A. W. J. G., *Clockwork Music*, London, Allen & Unwin, 1973.
Ord-Hume, A. W. J. G., *Mechanics of Mechanical Music*, London, Ord-Hume, 1973.
Ord-Hume, A. W. J. G., *Barrel Organ*, London, Allen & Unwin, 1978.
Ord-Hume, A. W. J. G., *Joseph Haydn and the Mechanical Organ*, Cardiff, University College Cardiff Press, 1982.
Ord-Hume, A. W. J. G., *Restoring Pianolas and other self-playing pianos*, London, Allen & Unwin, 1983.
Ord-Hume Library, London. Piano roll catalogues, early advertising literature, player piano and related

BIBLIOGRAPHY

material, US, UK and European patent extracts (collection, shelfmark 2/87.b to 3/24.b inclusive).
Ottenheimer, Paul D., Thorofare, New Jersey, U.S.A. Private collection of catalogues and ephemera.
Paulucci di Calboli, R., *I Girovaghi Italiani*, Castello, Italy, 1893.
Perry, Adelaide Trowbridge, *Compendium of Piano Material*, Schirmer Music Stores, Los Angeles, 1929 (copy in Logan Library, Philadelphia).
Player Piano Group, *Newsletter*, London, 1964–7.
Player Piano Review, Birmingham, 1912–14.
Player Piano Supplement, *The Gramophone*, London 1924–5.
Presto Buyer's Guide (to) Pianos, Players, Reproducing Pianos and their Manufacturers 1926, Facsimile edition Frank Adams, Seattle, Washington, 1972.
Protz, Albert, *Mechanische Musikinstrumente*, Kassel, 1943.
Reblitz, Arthur A., *Piano Servicing, Tuning & Rebuilding*, Vestal Press, New York, 1976.
Reblitz, Arthur A, and Bowers, Q. David, *Treasures of Mechanical Music*, Vestal Press, New York, 1981.
Rees, Abraham, *Cyclopaedia of Arts, Sciences & Literature*, London, Longman, 1819.
Roehl, H., *Player Piano Treasury* (1st edn), Vestal Press, New York, 1961.
Roehl, H., *Player Piano Treasury* (2nd edn), Vestal Press, New York, 1974.
S. G. E(arl), 'How to Repair the Player Piano', *Musical Opinion*, London, 1920.
Sachs, Curt, *Handbuch der Musikinstrumentenkunde*, Leipzig, 1920.
Sachs, Curt, *Real-Lexikon der Musikinstrumenten*, Berlin, 1913.
Saul, David L., *Rebuilder's Illustrated Guide to the Model B Ampico*, Vestal Press, New York, 1982.
Schlosser, Julius, *Kunsthistorisches Museum* (catalogue). Vienna, 1919.
Schmitz, Hans Peter, *Die Tontechnik des Père Engramelle*, Kassel and Basle, 1953.
Scholes, P. A., *Oxford Companion to Music*, London, Oxford University Press, 1942.
Schonberg, Harold C., *The Great Pianists*, Simon & Schuster, New York, 1963.
Shead, Herbert, *The Anatomy of the Piano*, Unwin Brothers, Old Woking, 1978.
Simmen, Rene, *Mens & Machine*, Van Lindonk, Amsterdam, 1968.
Spillane, Daniel, *History of the American Pianoforte; Its Technical Development, and the Trade*. New York, 1890.
Stephen, James Leslie, *Collection of Miscellany on Pianos, 1876–1947* (collection, British Library, Shelfmark 07902.b1/1 to 1/12 inclusive).
Suidman, Peter; Speetjens, Frits; and Mathot, Gustave, *Pianola's*, Nederlandse Pianola Vereniging, Holland, 1981.
Travis, John W., *A Guide to Restringing*, Middleburg Press, 1961.
Tushinsky, Joseph S., *The Pianocorder Story*, Superscope Inc., California, 1978.
de Waard, R., *Van Speeldoos Tot Pierement*, Amsterdam, 1965.
Wainwright, David, *Broadwood By Appointment*, London, Quiller, 1982.
Weiss, Eugene H., *Phonographes et Musique Mécanique*, Librairie Hatchette, Paris, 1930.
Weiss-Stauffacher, H. and Bruhin, R., *Mechanische Musikinstrumente und Musikautomaton*, Published by the author, Seewen, Switzerland, 1973.
Welte-Mignon, *Instructions for Testing & Regulating the Original Welte-Built Welte-Mignon Reperforming Instrument*, (n.d.) Facsimile reprint by Frank Adams, Seattle, Washington, USA, 1973.
White, William Braid, *Piano Playing Mechanisms*, 1st edn, Lyman Bill Inc., Chicago, 1925.
White, William Braid, *The Player-Pianist*, New York, Edward Lyman Bill, 1910.
White, William Braid, *A Technical Treatise on Piano Player Mechanism*, New York, Edward Lyman Bill, 1908.
White, William Braid, *Regulation and Repair of Piano and Player Mechanisms*, New York, Edward Lyman Bill, 1909.
White, William Braid, *The Player Piano Up to Date*, New York, 1914.
Wilson, David Miller, *The Player Pianist*, Perforated Music Co., London, 1911.
Wilson, David Miller, *An Introductory Book on The Piano-Player and Player-Piano*, London, c. 1918.
Wilson, David Miller, *Instruction Book on the Piano-Player and Player-Piano*, J. M. Kronheim & Co., London, 1911.
Wilson, David Miller, *The Player-Piano, Its Construction and How to Play*, London, Pitmans, 1923.
de Wit, Paul, *Weltadressbuch der Musikindustrie*, Leipzig, 1903 and 1909.
de Wit, Paul *Zeitschrift für Instrumentenbau*, Leipzig, 1881–1890.
Wolfenden, Samuel, *A Treatise on the Art of Pianoforte Construction*, Unwin Brothers, Old Woking, 1977.
Woodman, H. Staunton, *How To Tune a Piano*, New York, Corwood Publishers, 1960.

PADEREWSKI
ORDERS ANOTHER
Pianola

7th of November, 1900.
Gentlemen,—I desire to order another Pianola for use in my residence. Will you kindly select an instrument in rosewood, and have packed with it rolls of music, and shipped via steamer.
Yours very truly,
I. J. PADEREWSKI.

It is not mere chance which makes composers, pianists, and musicians of all classes unite in endorsing the Pianola, nor is it lack of artistic temperament which causes Paderewski, Sauer, and Rosenthal to select this dexterous little piano player for their own use. But as the history of the Pianola is full of such acknowledgments of merit, it is evident that the Pianola must give a return in pleasure for the expenditure made, and that this pleasure must be of a pronounced character. Also, the Pianola must afford enjoyment to every one, whether he be a skilled musician or the veriest novice; for each is equally enthusiastic in its praise.

Within a month after Sauer took a Pianola home with him he ordered two more for friends in Germany, the home of pianoforte playing.

Now Paderewski orders another for his residence in Switzerland.

If the appreciation of the Pianola by all musical authorities is a coincidence, thousands of non-professional music lovers are enjoying the coincidence with them, and the movement is spreading with unprecedented rapidity. You cannot afford to ignore the Pianola if you are interested in your home pleasures.

With its aid any member of your household may play upon the piano even if he or she literally does not know one note from another,—not only one or two selections, but every piece of music ever written for the pianofo Grand and light operas, Liszt's rhapsodies, Sousa's marches, and the latest popular hits are practically "at your fingers' ends." You have all the pleasure of hand playing because you control the expression which is the soul of music.

Estimate for yourself the profit in pleasure the Pianolo would bring you in a single year.

Price £65.
Can be purchased on the Hire System if desired.

The Pianola being placed in position to play upright Piano. It does not mar or injure the Piano in any way. When not in use it can be removed to another part of the room.

The Orchestrelle Company,
225, REGENT STREET, LONDON, W.

Picture Credits

I would like to express my thanks to those who have allowed me to photograph instruments in their collections for publication in this book. These include Graham Webb; Gustave Mathot, Belgium; Norman Evans; Ron Benton; Simon Haskel; Mary Belton, Frank Holland, Harvey Roehl, New York; Gerald Stonehill, the late Dr Bottomley and the late Dr Cyril de Vere Green. Two museums are singled out for their joint major contributions to the illustrations – the Nationaal Museum van Speelklok tot Pierement in Utrecht, Holland, and the former West Cornwall Museum of Mechanical Music run by Douglas Berryman and now, sadly, disbanded. Walt Bellm of Bellm's Cars & Music of Yesterday, Sarasota, Florida, has allowed me extensive access to his truly vast collection.

This book is also enriched by the extremely friendly co-operation received from London's two leading auction houses, Christie's South Kensington (Christopher Proudfoot) and Sotheby's (Jon Baddeley) both of which have allowed me to use pictures which are their copyright and additionally permitted me to visit their rooms to photograph some of the rare items which have passed through their hands.

The following is a complete list of sources who have supplied pictures or permitted me to take my own pictures on their premises:

Adams, Dr Frank: 103, 104, 105, 106
Aeolian Co., New York: 148
Baines, Dick: 65
Baus, Werner (Mechanisches Musik Museum, Fuldatal): 58, 59, 73, 124, 125, 126, 127
Bellm, Walt (Bellm's Cars and Music of Yesterday, Sarasota): 56, 57, 60, 61, 62, 63, 64, 78, 79, 81, 140, 141, 142, 143, 144
Belton, Mary (Originala Pianola Shop, Brighton): 45, 46, 47, 48
Benton, Ron: 74, 75
Bird, Tony: 21
Birmingham City Museum & Art Gallery: 90
Bottomley, Dr: 69
Bowers, Q. David: 93, 95, 118, 133, 134, 138
Carlsen, Jens (Museum der Mechanischen Musik Braunschweig): 23, 24, 129
Christie's, South Kensington: 11, 15, 19, 20, 22, 36, 37, 66, 67, 68, 70, 89, 112
Deutsches Museum, Munich: 8
Electricity Council, London (Tony Byers): 82
Evans, Norman: 86, 88, 91, 108
Germanisches Nationalmuseum, Nuremberg: 3, 4
Green, Dr Cyril de Vere (now Utrecht museum): 9, 10
Haskel, Simon: 76, 77
Kijk en Luister Museum, Bennekom: 44

Lawrence, Henry: 40
Lindwall, Bill: 16, 18, 32, 33, 34
Marantz Pianocorder: 149
Mathot, Gustave: 13, 14, 41, 71, 72
Montgomery, David: 12
Musical Museum (formerly The British Piano Museum), London: 100, 107, 117
Nationaal Museum van Speelklok tot Pierement, Utrecht: 5, 25, 31, 49, 50, 51, 53, 83, 101, 102, 112, 113, 121, 128
National Panasonic (Technics Organs): 150
Phelps Pianos, London: 98
Planus, Gerry: 80
Player Piano Workshop, Glendale, Pennsylvania: 135, 136
Roehl, Harvey (The Vestal Press, New York): 94, 96, 99, 110, 111, 131, 132, 137, 139
Science Museum, London: 30
Sony Corporation, Tokyo: 87
Sotheby's: 27, 28, 35, 39
Stonehill, Gerald: 145, 146, 147
Walden, Lord Howard de: 1, 2
Webb, Graham: 21
West Cornwall Museum of Mechanical Music (Douglas Berryman): 6, 7, 38, 52, 54, 84, 85, 97, 109, 114, 116, 120, 123
White, The Revd. Jonathan R.: 42, 43
Ziff, Paul: 17, 55

All other pictures are from my own collection or from instruments which have passed through my workshop during the past quarter of a century.

MUSIC ROLLS FOR ALL PIANO PLAYERS.

The following latest pieces at the prices marked, or 25 per cent. discount if the dozen are taken.

BY THE SIDE OF THE ZUYDER ZEE	Scott	1/-
GIRLS OF GOTTENBERG SELECTIONS	Monckton and Caryll	4/-
GOLD AND SILVER VALSE	Lehar	4/-
LA SIRENE VALSE, OP. 36	Thomé	3/-
MERRY WIDOW WALTZ	Lehar	4/-
MERRY WIDOW, SELECTION 1	Lehar	4/-
MERRY WIDOW, SELECTION 2	Lehar	4/-
NELLY NEIL	Caryll	4/-
POPPIES, A JAPANESE ROMANCE	Neil Moret	2/-
SILVER HEELS, INDIAN INTERMEZZO	Neil Moret	2/-
VALSE ENCHANTÉE	Berger	2/-
WHISTLING RUFUS	Kerry Mills	3/-

These Rolls are made by us under our own Patents, and are British manufacture throughout. Our Catalogues, which can be had on application, are made up of the most popular and up-to-date pieces on the market, the prices ranging from 6d. to 4s.

We have a large number of "top sheet rolls," the music of which is correct, but the perforations are not so clearly cut as the perfect Rolls, the price of these are **6d.** to **2s.**; list can be had on application.

Terms, cash with order. Carriage paid on all orders of over 10s.; on orders of less, carriage will be charged at 4d. for the first Roll, and 1d. for each subsequent Roll.

COLLEY'S PATENTS, Ltd., 3-12, Marine Street, London, S.E.

Index

This index embraces the text of Chapters 1 to 13 and the Appendices. While the List of Makers (Chapter 14) is self-indexing, this index also includes incidental references therein. References to illustrations are shown in bold type. Note that many German instrument names beginning with the letter 'K' were also sometimes spelt with a 'C', particularly elsewhere in Europe and in America.

Abdank, Charles, inventor 14
Accented music rolls 167
Accenting, attempts at 116
    device, Repro-Phraso 310
    devices, how to use 258
    how notes are accented 161
    random system 193
    and 'un-accenting' in piano rolls 261
    with the feet 133
Accentor control 289
Accompano electric player 284
Accordion, its forerunners 210
    mechanical 210–11, 214
Accumulators for pianos 97
Ackerman, Edwin D., Pianotist Co 303
Acme music roll perforating machinery 248
Acoustigrande piano with Welte Mignon 176
Actions, 65-note more reliable 118
    timber used for 151
Adams, Frank xvii
Adams Westlake Company 202
Adaptor, spool chuck 118
Adek Manufacturing Company 111
Adjustable spools for music rolls 104
Adjusting player height 110–11
Adler disc-playing musical box 315
Adolf collection, Gustav, Uppsala 11
Advertising, player makers' standards of 168
Advertisement display on barrel piano 62
Aeolian-American 271
Aeolian Company xx, 2, 44, 90, 91, 104, 105, 106, 110, 116, 139, 156, 158–60, 175, 207, 250, *see also under* Orchestrelle Co
    Ampico amalgamation with 184
    annotated music rolls 37
    artists who recorded for 242
    assets acquired by Harrods 123
    Audiographic roll venture 122–3

Aeolian in Australia 123
    cabinet Pianola 39
    concerts in Aeolian Hall 34
    Aeolian Corporation xvii, 297
    Duo-Art 34, 158, *see also under* Duo-Art
    cabinet player **87**
    date of introduction 190
    French advertisement for 348
    history and development of 183–9
    music rolls 237–8
    piano styles **103–106**
    tracking system 144
    upright piano **98**
    use of gramophone recordings 184
end of in Britain 122
factory at Hayes 123
first use of sostenuto effects 181
Grand player organ 35, 39, 208, *see also under* Orchestrelle
'Great Removal Sale' 47
Hall 255
    concerts at 34
Halls throughout world, list of 39
key-top Pianola 174
    player 216–18
leases factory space to Danemann after fire 123
merger with Ampico 184, 238
Musette player piano **148**
music roll catalogues 233–8
music rolls, 'Aeolian pleat' 144
    last complete catalogue 237
    many different types of 237
    price of 233–7
    with sound-track 337
'Orchestrated' music rolls 35
Orchestrelle xx, 35, 39, 208, 246
    tracker bar 162, *see also under* Orchestrelle

Aeolian organ 208
    of 1883 26
    46-note 39
    patent for note-accenting 163–4
    patents, Reginal Reynolds name on many 122
    pays royalties to Welte 176
    Pianola cabinet style player 111
        advertisement 322, 332
    Pipe Organ music rolls, 246
        tracker bar 168
    player piano brands 184
    printed tempo line 36
    'purveyor to the Papal Palace' 38
    recording methods 184
    reproducing pipe organ 199, 300
    roll library, largest in world 123
    Silloth Trainer 356
    slogan 'reproducing piano' 119
    song rolls 25
    Themodist accenting system 163–7, 169, 171, *see also under* Themodist
    top piano, the Weber 183
    tracking system 144
    'Transposing Device' 236
    vs Welte Court case 176
Aeolian harp 1
Aeolian-Iles IST system 169–70
Aeolian Organ & Music Co 26, 208
Aeolian/Steinway contract, numbers of pianos 185
Aeoline, Aeolian 35
Aeoline organ-player, Aeolian 209
Aeriol self-playing piano 26, 270, 312
    market success of 125
    music roll drive for 156
    music rolls 118, 233
Agricultural Hall, London 22
Air, controlled by paper 24
    discovery of its capability in musicwork 24
    its characteristics explained 128 *et seq.*
    motor 140
    pressure *vs* vacuum 107
Aird, E. H., Harrods 44
Airmatic piano player 308
Air-O-Player 'first perfected metal action' 299
Aiuton 'ever-tuned organ', Clagget's 17
Alaska-Yukon-Pacific Exposition 203
D'Albert, Eugen, pianist 220, 242
Alexandre, harmonium maker 299
Alien Property Act, Welte assets seized under 175
Alien Properties Custodian and Welte 315
Aliquot stringing, Blüthner 179
'All About Organs', article quoted 74
Allen, J. C., Steinway Pianos xvii
All-metal player action, Brinsmead 117
        Pistonola 119
Allwood, J., inventor 245
Aluminium, Brinsmead player piano 117
Amato, Pasquale, inventor 60
America, coming of Prohibition 36
    plans player revival in 1937 49
American Electrelle piano player 271

American organ 91
    played by perforated disc 68
    replaces harmonium 44
American Orguinette Company 207
American Photo Player Company 195, 198, 309
American Piano Company 179–83, 189, 239, *see also under* Ampico
American player makers and the depression 47
American Pneumatic Service Co 310
American reed organ 35, 91
American Society of Composers, Authors and Publishers 46
Amman, J., inventor 83
Amorette organette 293
Ampichron, Ampico with clock system 181
Amphion Action Co 151, 180
    Amphion Accessible Action 272
    music rolls 118
Ampico and Aeolian, amalgamation of 184
Ampico-Artigraphic 239
Ampico Ltd, British company 182
Ampico reproducing piano 31, 40, 116, 156, 159, 174–5, 190, 218, 220, 226, *see also* American Piano Company
    advertisement 347
    advertising campaign against Aeolian 168
        stunt 185
    Artigraphic reproducing piano 180
    artists who recorded for 242
    artists' rolls adapted from Hupfeld 181
    automatic section repeat system 180
    clock system, Amphicron 181
    cost of instruments 182
    vs Duo-Art, merits of 266–8
    Grotrian-Steinweg installation 182-3
    high quality of some performances on 268
    history and development of 179–83
    Marque-Ampico reproducing piano 180
    Marshall & Rose pianos, cost of 183
    mergers with Aeolian 238
    Model A **108–109**
        introduction of 180
        date of 190
    Model B **110–111**
        introduction of 180
        date of 190
    music roll lending library
        'jumbo' half-hour 180
    pianos, pages from Harrods catalogue 350–3
    Rachmaninov's comments on hearing his roll 264
    recording pianos 182
        techniques 225
    recordings transferred to Artecho 243
    roll-recording apparatus 182
    rolls adapted from Hupfeld 181
        made in Britain until 1940 182
        some interpretational failures 168
    speed of accenting with 265
    staff, comments by Moseiwitsch 181
    Stoddard 179
    system evaluated 186–90
    testimonial from Rachmaninov 181

INDEX

Ampico, types of piano fitted to 183
    use of harmonic effects 180
    volume control for playback 180
Amras collection 11
Analytical Roll 37
Andersson, Anders Gustaf and Jones Wilhelm 68, 69, 70, 71
Andrews, D. F., Boyd Pianos xvii, 119
Android, Isis playing zither 300
Angelus Piano Company 114
    piano player with reed organ xx, 36, 155, 158, 189, 257–8, 278
    advertisement 325
    Artistyle piano rolls 296
    Artrio 220
        reproducing piano 189
        types of piano fitted to 189
    Brinsmead 113
        letter quoted 323
    diaphragm pneumatics 114
        pneumatic player 114
            advertisement 324
        pouches, inventor of 316
    manual controls on 160–1
    music rolls 118
    Orchestral piano player **65**
        advertisement 326
    piano player 36
        height adjustment 111
    player action 296
        adjustable for height 114
    player piano, price of 351
    transposing device 114
    Wilcox & White advertisement 328
Animatic Artists' Roll 238
    music rolls 238, 291
Animatic-T music roll 220
Annalies orchestrion 295
Annie Laurie 234
Annotated music rolls 37
Ansorge, Conrad, pianist 98
Antiphonel piano player, Debain's 20 *et seq.*, 56, 94, 215, 282, **49–53**, *see also* Debain
Antonelli, D., piano maker 61, 77
Antoniazzi, Anton, BAB Organ Co 274
    partner with Maserati 296
Apollo Co, copyright case against 326
    vs White-Smith Music Publishing Co 325
    Melville Clark 115
Apollo piano player 110, 297, 320
    music rolls 118
    58-note player piano 109
        advertisement 331, 333
    player, music roll drive 156
    player piano and the Pope 3
    reproducing piano 189
        advertisement 344
Apollonicon organ 15
Apollophone piano and phonograph 280
Appreciation of music 1
Apruzzese, Antonio, maker of barrel pianos in Spain 68
Arburo café organ 210

Arcadian player action 277
    player piano 277
Arensky, A. S., composer 250
Aria Divina reproducing action 176, 307
    reproducing piano 189, 220
Ariophon mandolin piano 30
Aristo music rolls 118
Ariston organette 83, 93, 208–9, 284, 288, 299
Ariston-type cardboard discs 231
Aristos player piano 274
Armbruster, Robert, pianist 238
Arnold, William, piano factory 302
Arpanetta mechanical zither 207
Arrau, Claudio, pianist 34, 242
Arrow player action 116, 293
Art nouveau style 212
Art of the Player-Piano, quoted 256
ArtEcho reproducing piano 189
Artecho/Apollo 243
Artigraphic reproducing piano, Ampico 180
Artist piano player 289
Artist Song Rolls music rolls 296
Artists who recorded for Duo-Art 184
Artistyle player piano 296
Artistic Player, Welte 177
Artona Music Roll Co xvii, 169, 218
Artrio reproducing action, Broadwood 189, 243
Ashkenazy, Vladimir, pianist 251
Ashwell, Edwin, Waring & Gillows 202
Atkinson, C. W., inventor 110, 274
    Bansall's Universal advertisement 321
d'Aubry, Emile, and Boreau, Gabriel 200
Audiographic music rolls 26, 122–3, 250
AudioGraphic music rolls 237
Augsburg 9, 10, 11, 12
    City Council, 1632 acquisition 11
    importance of in 16th-17th centuries 10, 11
Augusta Vindelicorum, Roman colony 11
Augustus, Roman Emperor 11
Austin, Charles C., reed organ builder 107
Australia, Aeolian company in 123
    position of player in 49
Austro-Hungarian improvements 71
Auteola player piano xx
Autoforte control 117
Auto-Grand player 294
Autogrand music rolls 233
Autographic interpretation 234
Autoharp 206–7
    Mandoline-Zither mechanical 207
Automat piano player 284
Automata, Chapuis, quoted 13
Automatic Hand Guide, Bohrer's 8
Automatic harp 206
    Wurlitzer 209–10
        cost of 210
Automatic instruments, primitive 79
Automatic Music Company 23, 194, 295, 315
    name changed to Link 194
Automatic music industry of Augsburg 9, 10, 11
Automatic Musical Instrument Company 23

Automatic Music Paper Co 26, 91, 208
Automatic Player Piano Actions Ltd 356
Automatic Regina Concerto 305
Automatic tracking systems 144
    trumpet or bugle calls 209
'Automatic Violin', article quoted 202
Automatic Virtuosa, Mills 202
Automatic Xylophone 200
Automatic zither 207
'Automatics' clockwork barrel pianos 63, 76
Automaton scenes in piano orchestrions 90
'Automatum' 203
Automelle control 117
'Automobil March' from *Dollar Princess* 233
Auto Music Co 91
Auto-Namic reproducing device for players 280
Autophon, Seytre's 84
Autophon Improved Organ 81
Autophone organette 308
Autophone Company 93
Autopianiste piano player 310, 312
Auto-Piano Company 292
Auto Piano player piano 292
Autopiano 164–5
    music rolls 118
    tracking system 157, 158
Autoplayer player piano, Boyd 119, 277, 294
Auto-Pneumatic Action Co 175, 180, 241
Autotone player piano 289
Autotracker control 117

Babbage, Prof. Charles, mathematician 52, 53
Bach, J. S., piano roll played backwards and reversed 37
    Great C Minor Organ Fugue 249
    Organ Toccata & Fugue arr. Stradel 239
    Two-part Inventions 237
Backhaus, Wilhelm, pianist 4, 181, 242
Bain, Alexander, player action inventor 81
Baker, C. F., publisher of book on converting actions 113
Baker, George A., piano maker 279
Balakirev, Mily Alexeievitch, pianist 4
Baldwin piano with Welte-Mignon 176
Balfe: *The Bohemian Girl* 56
Ball, early pioneer in pneumatics 91
Banjo, mechanical 206
Banjo, *see under* Encore Automatic
Banjorchestra, F. Englehardt's 196
Bannister, Charles W. 43, 44, 46, 47, 59
Bansall's Universal Piano Player 41, 110, **70**
    advertisement 321
Bantock, Granville, composer 249
Banu Musa, teaching of the 132
Barcelona Exhibition, 1888 88
Bar code principle and music 226
Barenboin, David, pianist, 251
Barker, Charles Spackman, inventor 24
Barker pneumatic lever 24
Barlow, Alfred, patentee 83
Barnby: *The Soft Southern Breeze* 234
Barratt, Tom, A. & F. Pears 274

Barratt & Robinson, player makers 48, 293
    mini-player piano 117
    Pedaleon mini player 117
Barred music rolls, plea for 41
Barrel, development of the pinned wooden 9
    features of Bidermann's spinet style 12
    poplar wood used to make 54
Barrel Organ, quoted 9, 13, 15, 18, 81, 215, 275
Barrel organ 1, 51
    combined with piano 57
    oldest surviving 9, 14
    on Pianoharpa principle 71
    term defined 16
    tune changing system 77
Barrel organs, church 73
Barrel piano 4
    with advertisement displays 62
    bells and drum 60
    clockwork driven 56, 59
        motor in barrel end 60
    combined with organ 57
    compass of Spanish 68
    its development 51 *et seq.*
    on donkey cart 68
    with fortune-telling device 62
    how built 74–5
    for indoor use 68
    industry in Spain 68
    with iron frame 60
    mandolin effect in 59
    mechanism illustrated and described 75 *et seq.*
    with moving picture front 62
        ornate fronts and mirrors 63
    percussion effects 63
    pinned to play Mozart 74
    played by punched cylinder 66
    with revolver mechanism 73
    tune-change system 76
    wrist *vs* clockwork power 61
    zenith of popularity 67
    'zither-banjo' 65
Barrel pianos, electric coin-freed in Japan 36
    in London 7
    unusual types of 65
Barrel playing instruments, disadvantage of 79
Bartlett's Ballade 234
    Polka de Concert 233
Bartok, Bela, pianist 242
Bassermann-Jordan, quoted 13
Bassil, W. J., J. & J. Goddard xvii
Bates, T. C., organ builders 56, 73
Batteries for electric pianos 97
Bauer, Harold, pianist 4, 181, 184, 237, 242, 250, 329, 335
    in Chicago at time of New York concert 34
Bauer, Max, pianist 37
Baumes, André xvii
Baus collection 200
Baus, Werner xviii
Baylis, piano maker 54
    trade card 56
Baynes, Anthony, inventor 24

INDEX

Beare, John 280
Beckhardt piano 202
Bechstein pianos 202
    Ampico 189
Beecham, Sir Thomas, quoted 2
Beeswax, use of on music rolls 253
Beethophon reproducing piano 276
Beethoven Moonlight Sonata 264
    Sonata opus 111
Beethoven and the Apollo, advertisement 344
Belgian Order of Leopold awarded to Tremaine 38
Bellisore orchestrion 295
Bellm's Cars & Music of Yesterday museum xviii
Bellm collection, Walt 66, 217, 292, 308
Bellows system described 130
Belton, Mary xvii
Bennett, J., inventor 245
Berlin: *My Bird of Paradise* 25
Berlin Philharmonic Orchestra 2
Berliner Akademie 229
Berryman, Douglas xvii
Berry-Wood, piano-makers 196
Berthold & Co, advertisement 214
Bibliothèque Nationale 9
Bidermann, Samuel 9–13, 59, 269
    characteristics of barrels 12
    clockwork spinet 199
    inscriptions on instruments 11
Bidermann-Langenbucher Lawsuit quoted 10, 11
Bijou Orchestra, Wurlitzer 197
Biltmore, Hotel, New York 179
Biographical Roll 37
Bird, A. G., historian 301
Birmingham University Society 2
Bishop, James C, organ builder 24, 73
Bishop & Down 91
Blake, Eubie, composer 192
Bland, Charles, and Gillet, William, inventors 56, 59
Bleed hole, its purpose described 136
Blessing, Hubert, orchestrion builder 15, 315
    Polyvox orchestrion **129**
Bloomfield-Zeisler, Fanny, pianist 240
    advertisement re her 'joke' 262
Blumenberg, Mark A., music critic 113
Blüth, S., piano-maker 290
Blüthner Pianos xvii, 40, 202, 238, 283, 291
    aliquot stringing 179
    Carola reproducing action 105, 283
    player action 179
    Duophonola **83**
    pianos, Hupfeld actions in 178–9
    piano on Hindenburg airship 49
    Hupfeld player advertisement 228
    price of 350–1
Boalch, Donald H., quoted 11
Bockisch, Karl, inventor 174
Bohemian Girl, Balfe 56
Bohrer's Automatic Hand Guide 8
Book-music piano vogue 65
Boosey *vs* Whight copyright case 106
Bord piano 202

Borna, BAB Organ Co 274
Bosendorfer, piano makers 183
Bouchon, loom inventor 80
Bourneville carillon 213
Bourquin, Edouard Jacques, inventor 73
Bovey, Senator Charles 274
Bow for automatic violin, horsehair 201
Bowers, Q. David, quoted xvii, 192, 193, 194, 196, 198, 201, 205, 209, 210, 271, 276, 295, 300
Boyd Ltd, player piano makers xvii, 118
    Autoplayer player piano 119
    Pistonola 105, 315, **74, 75**
        advertisement 172
    player recital 41
    Terpreter player piano 119
Boyle, R. K., electric piano inventor 97
Brabant Orchestra journal, quoted 251
Brabo orchestrion 315
Brachhausen, Gustave, inventor 305
Bradish, James S., inventor 82
Brailowsky, Alexander, pianist 181
Brass Band Orchestrion 316
Brasted player piano, price of 352
Brauers, Jan xviii
Bridge, Sir Frederick, comments on mechanical players 318
Briggs pianos 299
Brinsmead & Sons, John, player piano makers 202, 296, 325
    player pianos 117
    Angelus action 113
    player piano **76, 77**
Britannia metal used for tracker bar 115, 176
British Broadcasting Company, agrees to player concerts 44
    use of reproducing piano 37
    support for player piano week 44–5
British Broadcasting Corporation, Alexandra Palace TV studio 48
British Industries Fair, player shown at 48
British Institute of Recorded Sound, Journal of 240
British-made music for German pianos 213
British Museum 17
British Music Exhibition, 1913 116
British Piano Museum xvii, 154, 191, 204, 252, 255
Broadcasts, first use of player piano in 44
Broadwood Pianos xvii, 40, 183, 202, 244
    Ampico player piano, price of 352
    'combined instrument' production 327
    music rolls, 118
    player action 151
    piano, price of 351
    reproducing pianos built by 186, 189
    roll tracking system 159
    unit player action 116
Broadwood Galleries, reproducing piano recital 189
Broadwood's works superintendent, R. H. Collen 116
Brown collection, George 52
Brown, J. P., inventor of automatic bugle-call 209
Brown, Theodore P., inventor of pneumatic systems 90, 314
    Aeriol player piano 125
    music roll drive 156
    Simplex piano player **62**

Brown, Theodore P., tracking system for music rolls 157–8
Bruch, Max, composer 4
Bruder, organ builder 93
    use of large take-up spools 180
Brugnolotti, Dominic, BAB Organ Co 274
Brunophone, Le, café piano 277
Brussels Exposition, 1910 200
    1883 294
    1895 68
Buchner, Alexander, quoted 85, 309
Buffalo, music roll convention 173
Buff-Hedinger's Musetta player piano 278
    advertisement 319
Bugle, Distin discovery of keyed 54
Bulletin, MBSI, quoted 183, 185, 227
Bulletin, Player Piano Group, quoted 238, 249–50, 335
Burr, Willy, inventor 314
Busby, L. K., Blüthner Pianos xvii
Busby, Thomas, quoted 18, 19, 297
Bush & Lane piano with Welte Mignon 176
Bush Televisor television 48
Busoni, Ferruccio, pianist 4, 32, 34–5, 181, 242
    letter to wife re gramophone recordings 33

Cabinet Pianola 39
Cabinet player 'would not lose favour' 27
Cabinet pumps for players 155
Cabinet-style piano players 26, 174, *see also under* Piano-players
Cabinet style Pianola piano player 111
Cäcilia player piano 177, 286
Caderstrom, Baroness (Adelina Patti) 112
Café pianos 19
    Le Brunophone 277
    in Japan 36
    advertisement for Marteletti's 67
    stylistic development of 211 *et seq.*
Caine, W. R. Hall, quoted 42
Caldera, inventor of tremolo action 93
Californian gold-rush, importance of to mechanical music 194
Calmont & Sons Musetta, advertisement 319
Canova, Joseph Piana, tremolo action improver 62
Capacity bellows 219
Capaldi, Domenica 312
Capella orchestrion 30
Capital musical box 301
Capital Symphony Orchestra 196
Capra, Alexander, inventor 57, 58, 59, 60
Cardboard disc player 87
    music, perforated 22
Cardboard-music street piano 65, 66
Carhart, Jeremiah, inventor of exhaust bellows 107, 299
Carhart & Needham reed organ makers 107
Carillon 79
    Bourneville 213
Carillons, roll-playing 213
Carleton Electric Player 304
Carlson, Jens xviii
Carlyle, Thomas 52
Carnot, scientist and inventor 80
Carola player action, Bluthner 179

Carola reproducing action 105
Carolino Augusteum Museum, Salzburg 11
Carothers, Wallace, nylon inventor 48
Carpentier, Jules, inventor 14, 85–6, 207, 215, 222, 229
Carroll, Adam, music arranger, quoted 181
Carreño, Teresa 4, 242
Cartonium reed instrument 311
Casali, Louis, barrel piano maker 68, **27**
Casella, Alfredo, pianist and composer 250
Cate, Olivia, pianist 189
Cathedrale Engloutie, La, incorrect manuscript 266
Caus, Salomon de 14
Cavaille-Coll, organ-builders 24
Cavana, Giuseppe, player piano maker 291
CBS new record with soloist Gershwin 251
Cecilian piano player, Ferrand 285
    cabinet player advertisement 261, 320
    music rolls 118
    player piano 202, 232, 233
Celco reproducing action 271
    types of piano fitted to 189
    piano 189
Celestina organette 26, 208, 298
Chain-punched roll perforations 167
Challen piano 183, 202
    Angelus player piano, price of 350
Chaminade, Cecile 2, 242, 329
Chaminade: *Air de Ballet* 234
Chappell, piano maker 183, 189, 202
    maker of special player for King Edward VII 2
Chapuis, Alfred: *Automata*, quoted 13, 317
Charing Cross Road, barrel pianos 7
Chariot Race from 'Ben Hur' 100
Chase, A. B., piano makers 189, 272
Chase & Baker music rolls 118
    player piano 202
Chevillard, Camille, conductor 4, 31
Chiappa, Giuseppe, street piano maker 57, 60, 65, 92, 313, 314
Chicago, centre of electric piano production 36
Chicago Electric coin-operated pianos 308
Chicago Indicator, quoted 5, 28, 280
Chicago, major centre for manufacturing 28
Chicago *Presto* quoted 29
Chickering pianos 40, 183
    Ampico 182
    grand piano 22
Chieti, barrel piano maker 313
Children's Popular Songs and Games 236
Chime 79
Chitarrone electric expression piano 295
Chopin, Frederic, composer and pianist 6
    Andante Spianato & Polonaise 236
    Impromptu opus 29 232
    Nocturnes 261
    Polonaise opus 53 240
Choralion Co, 184
Chordephon disc-playing zither 207
Christ the Lord is Risen Today 214
Christian, Prince of Schleswig-Holstein 203
Christie's Old Organ, illustration 16

INDEX

Christie's, South Kensington, auctioneers 175, 282
Christmas Greetings music rolls, Ampico 240
Christmas-tree stands, Musical 284
Christofori, inventor of piano action 9, 94
Christophe & Etienne reed organ makers 282
Cinema, age of 45
    Margate's Dreamland Super 170
    orchestra pianos 195
Cinema orchestras, decline in number of musicians in 46
Cinematograph soundtrack on piano roll 39
Ciniglio, Andrea and Germaro 301
Cinque Ports Flying Club 356
Civil & Military, quoted 42
Clagget, Charles 17
    Aiuton 83
Clair, Herbert, Original Piano Trio 250
Clarinet, Clarola mechanical 211
Clark, Ernest G., piano roll factory 280
Clark, John, quoted 52
Clark, Melville, inventor 27, 28, 90, 109, 110, 326
    effect of his 88-note player on market 124
    expansion of roll scale 157
    perfector of 88-note action 112, 113
    spring winding music roll drive 156
Clark, 58-note Apollo 3, 115
    advertisement for 331, 333
    music roll drive 156
Clark & Rich, reed organ maker 280
    Connoisseur 117
Clarke, Sir Ernest 313
Clarola Clarinet 211
Classic piano player action, advertisement 171
Claus & Co, manufacturers of Chordephon 207
Clavichord, player mechanism for 230
Clavimonium, Hupfeld 195
Claviola piano player 162, 309
    player piano 202
Clavitist-Violina, Hupfeld 201
Clementi, Muzio 17
    false name on piano fallboard 154
    mechanical piano 19
    Sonata opus 26 234
Clementi's Celebrated Duet 19
Clementi, Collard & Co 17
Clock, Amphicron Ampico piano 181
    flute-playing 13
    harp 13
    Trautmanndorf 79
Clocks incorporated into piano orchestrions 71
Clockwork driven barrel piano 59, 60, 61
    manufacturing centres 63
    in pubs, cafés, etc 64
    cylinder piano 56
    motor in barrel end, inventor of 60
    to drive music roll 109
    roll drive 156
Clockwork motors, how wound 77
Clockwork Music, quoted 74, 247
Clockwork pianos 19
    with iron frame 60
    spinets 10, **1, 2, 3, 4**

Clockwork spinets, Bidermann 199
Clockwork spinets, surviving examples of 11, 12
Cocchi, John 286
Cocchi & Sons, John, trade card 317
Coelophone, Gavioli 312
Cohen, Philip, agent 292
Coin-freed automatic pianos 77
    barrel pianos in Japan 36
    piano 60
    pneumatic piano-player 63
Coin mechanism in barrel pianos 77
Coinola piano orchestrion 196, 300, **133**
Coldman, H. C., inventor 118, 315
Cole, G. A., inventor 210
Collard, John 281
Collard & Collard 18, 183, 202
Collen, Reginald H., Broadwoods 116
Colley's Patents, advertisement for music rolls 364
Colombo, I., street piano maker 314
Colonia player piano 281
Colonne, Judas (Edouard), conductor 4
Coloured Drum Major, The 100
Columbia Jazz Band with George Gershwin 251
Commercial advertising music rolls 247
Commons, House of, comment by Dan Leno 2
Compact cassette 39
Company failures in player industry 30
Compass of largest player organs 36
    player actions, standardisation 116
    pianos, 65 and 88-note 235
Composers who wrote specially for player piano 250–1
Compton Organ Co, John 170
Computer and melography 220 *et seq.*
    used in player technology 220
    tape 104
    technology 199
Computers and bar-coded music 226
Concert of Liszt shared by Cortot and player piano 34
Concert Orchestrion 316
Concert PianOrchestra, Wurlitzer 194
Concert Room Anecdotes, quoted 18, 19, 297
Concertina, mechanical 210–11
    player, street 312
Concerto for Piano & Orchestra by Jan van Dijk 250
Concerto piano orchestrion 303
Concerts in Aeolian Hall 34
Conner, Harry, harp-player 209
Connoisseur pipe organ 117
    Player piano 117
    Reed organ 117
Conover piano with Welte Mignon 176
Conservatoire des Arts et Metiers 80
Conservatory Player Action Company 155
Contests in player piano proficiency 37
Contiguous roll perforations 167–8, 244
Converting 65-note to 88-note, booklet 43
Conway Music Industries, piano makers 189, 289, 316
Cook, C. F., Aeolian patentee 169
Copeland, George 181
Copyright case, American 325
    Debain 106

371

Copyright case, Whight vs Boosey 106
Copyright Law, Germany's antiquated 106
Copyright in mechanical music 106
Corn Exchange, London, Pistonola concert at 118
Cornet accompaniment to street piano 57
    players, female 6
Corona player piano 177, 286
Coronation Exhibition, 1911 289
Cortot, Alfred, pianist 236, 242
    performance of Liszt rhapsody shared with pianola 34
    his wrong notes 35
Corvi, Antoine, inventor 199
Cost of Ampico instruments 182
    reproducing pianos 189
Couched harp 9
Courcell, John, barrel organ maker 18
    push-up player 20
Courville, Joseph, inventor 157
Cramer, piano maker 202, 323
    player piano, price of 350
Crash valve, its purpose 149
Crasselt & Rähse advertisement 95
Creed, English clergyman 222, 230
Cremona orchestrion 196, 296
Crescendo and *sforzando*, Welte 176
Crescodant control 119
Cromwellian dictum 'strike until you make it hot' 44
Crooks, James William, note theming system 162
Cros, Charles, phonograph inventor 279
Crowley, John H, player piano 116
Crubois, café piano maker 67
Custer, C. A., inventor 91, 94
Cut-off or silencer control 150
Cylinder piano 51
    clockwork 56
Cylindrichord mechanical piano 18

Daily Chronicle, quoted 3, 42
Daily Mail, quoted 42
Daily Telegraph, article 326
Daimonion, Leipziger Musikwerke advertisement 89
d'Albert 4
Dalian note-accenting system 116
Damper rail 127
Damrosch, Walter 38
le Dan, G. P., inventor 94
'Dancing Bear' mechanical concertina 211
    advertisement 214
Dance of the Hottentots automaton 13
Danemann's factory fire and Aeolian's help 123
Daughter with good foot for music, story 3, 38
David, Samuel, inventor with Rolfe 306
Davis, early worker in pneumatic actions 90
Davis, G. H., inventor 109
Davy Crockett on barrel piano 289
Dawkins, musical instrument agent 282
Dawson, Charles, inventor 81
Dea-Violina, Hupfeld 178, 201, 291
Dean Castle, clockwork spinet at 10
Debain, Alexandre, inventor 20, 56, 82, 94, 106, 281

Debain, Antiphonel piano player and player piano 21, 215, **49–53**
    copyright case involving 106
Debussy, Claude, composer and pianist 4, 31, 242, 266
Decline of the player 120
Dekyndt, Danny xviii
Deletor control 119
De Luxe Reproducing Roll Company 241
Delphin piano orchestrion 300
Design influences of instruments 211 *et seq.*
Destruction of unwanted pianos xix
Detachable keyboard for tuning Welte keyless 175
Detoma, S., inventor 57, 59
Detroit Organ Company 314
Deutsches Museum xviii, 206, 230, 294, 297
Development of barrel piano 51 *et seq.*
Diaphragm pneumatics, Angelus 114
    pouches, *see also* Angelus
Dickens, Charles, quoted 6
Die Welt als Uhr quoted 294
Dienst, E., orchestrion manufacturer 30
Dienst's Selbstspielende Geige 206
Dijcks, Anton van, painter 12
Dijk, Jan van, Dutch pianola composer 250
Dilkes, Neville, conductor 252
Dilworth, George, Original Piano Trio 250
Diminuent control 117
Direct Action Company 292–3
Direct Arrow action 283
Direct Pneumatic Action Company 116
Disc-playing musical box 39
    Adler 315
    Fortuna 317
    Imperator 210
    Komet 98
    Lochmann Original 285, 300
    Monopol 207
    Polyphon 106, 212, 282, 285, 293
    Regina 209, 317
    Symphonion 23, 273, 285, 300, 315
    piano, Orpheus 83, 284, 35
    piano-player 83, 93
Disney, Walt, cartoon of player piano 3
Distin, Henry, piano maker 51, 54, 68, 269, 290
Distin, Snr, discoverer of keyed bugle 54
Division of player action for expression, inconsistency of 173
Dohnanyi, Erno von 4, 181, 220, 242
Dolge, Alfred, piano supplies' empire head 26–7, 312
Doll, Jacob, piano makers 193
'Dollar Princess, The', musical 233, 234
    Automobil March 233
Doman, early pioneer in pneumatic actions 90
Doremi & Co 98
Double tracker bars in reed organs 35
Double valve pneumatics 150
    system 135
Dow, A., inventor 245
Drake, Harry, author 43
Draper, Francis W., inventor 157
Draper, J. M., inventor 208
Dreamland Super Cinema, Margate 170

INDEX

Drum, automatic 199
Drumroll, development of in p. orchestrions 71–2
Dual standard tracker bars 118
Dubourg's *Valse Chaloupée* 234
Duca, J. D. Philipps & Sohne reproducer 177
    reproducing action 177–8
        quality of 266–8
Duca-Lipp reproducing piano 189, 295, 302
Ducanola player piano 177
    vorsetzer 177–8
Ducartist, pedal operated reproducer 177
Dulcimer 9
    clock 13
    mechanical 51
Dulcitone, Machal's 17
Dumb-organist key-top player by Holditch 215
Dundee Advertiser, quoted 42
Duo Art player piano, post war 218
Duo-Art reproducing piano, Aeolion 31, 39, 40, 158, 168, 190, 220, 226, 264, 266–8, **98–106**
    action, last British 184
    Ampico's advertising campaign against 168
    vs Ampico, various merits of 266–8
    concert, London 39
        at Queen's Hall 213
    concerts 191
    educational use of music rolls for 37
    history and development 183–9, 190, 191
    'how it won the war', article quoted 169
    music lending library 245
        roll recording 35
        rolls with Ampico labels 184
    Mussolini's 185
    Orchestrelle 209
    pedal electric 237, 258
    performance of Paderewski's *Minuet* 38
    recording artists 184
    recordings converted to Ampico 243
        to Artrio 243
    reproducing push-up players 186
    Robot, vorsetzer 169, 186, 191, 218, 221, **145–6**
    rolls in Melbourne 49
    royalties paid to Welte on each 176–7
    Schnabel declines recording contract for 263
    vs Solophonola accenting 265
    system evaluated 186–90
    tracking system 144
    vorsetzer, a unique 171
Duo-Art and Pianola Piano Monthly 238
Duophonola reproducing piano, Hupfeld 179, 244, 291
Duplex Player Piano, Maxfield's 192
Dutch street organ 212
Dynachord Art Expression Player 271
Dynavoice, Inc, manufacturers 217
Dynavoice key-top player 216–17, **140–2**

Eagle Tavern, mechanical piano at 19
Earls Court exhibition hall, London 22
Early Mechanical Pianofortes, article quoted 17
East Anglian Automatic Piano Company 73–4
Edgerton, Bill xvii

Edison, Thomas, phonograph inventor 279
Editing music rolls 168
    importance of 267–8
Edward VII, Chappells' special player for King 2
    endorses Chappells' player 2
    and Mills Automatic Virtuosa 203
Ehrlich brothers, manufacturers 207–8
Ehrlich, F. E. P., inventor 83, 93, 94, 106, 207, 299
    Ariston organette 288
Ehrlich's disc-playing piano player 83
    Instrument piano player 284
Eich Solophone **112–113**
'Eight Great Inventions of the Decade' 204
Eighty-eight finger music, lost opportunity 249
Eine Kleine Nachtmusik on barrel piano 316
Eisenmann, R., inventor 97
Eldorado piano orchestrion 285
Electora vacuum pump 298
Electrelle key-top player **140, 143**
Electrelle music rolls 118
Electrelle piano player 101
Electric drive for pianos 173
    expression pianos 34
    gramophone recordings, first 190
    piano, first 193
    pianos 78
        Harper 103
        Peter's 293
Electric pianos at Leipzig Fair 30
    oust piano orchestrions 73
Electrically-driven nickelodeon 36
Electrically-operated piano, first 26
Electrically-played pianos, Berlin and Leipzig styles 96
    New York style 99
Electricity in the piano 96
Electrohydraulic piano-playing system 227
'Electro-magnetic energization' of coin-freed pianos 64
Electromagnetic player action 96
    piano with metal music rolls 36
    player system 81
    piano-playing system 83
Electrone key-top player 216–17
Electronic keyboard **150**
    with music printer 227
Electronics in modern pianos 104
Electropneumatic roll-playing systems 168
Electrova Company, coin-freed pianos 283
    player pianos 193
Elfers, James, quoted 238
Elgar, Sir Edward 4
    quoted 2
Elgar: *Sonata* opus 28 233
Elinescu: *Scena Pastorala Romana* 234
Ellingham, Harry, quoted 43, 249
Elstree Aerodrome, Link Trainer School at 356
Elysee Palace, Duo-Art at the 185
Emerson, piano makers 189, 272
Emerson Player Piano, 296
    advertisement 338, 339
Empress Electric pianos 215, 300
    cabinet player 215

Encore Automatic Banjo 193, 200, 295
Encyclopedia of Automatic Musical Instruments, quoted 193, 198, 201
Enescu, Georges 242
Engelhardt, F., inventor 91
English Review, The, quoted 41
English Sinfonia orchestra 252
Engramelle, The Rev. Father 14
Enthoven Collection (V & A Museum) 19
Equaliser, its function 132
Erard, piano manufacturer 112, 202
Ersten Prager Musikwerke- und Orchestrionfabrik 73, 286
Estey Piano Company, makers of Welte-Mignon 176
Estonia concert grand piano 220
Euphona Home Electric player piano 278
Euterpeon Rooms advertisement 50
Evans, Edwin, quoted 251
Evans, Harry, music adjudicator 41
Evans, Norman, PPG member 220
Evans, W. E., inventor 290
Evans, William, Piano Manufacturers' Association, chairman 45
Eves, George, quoted 74
Evola expression piano advertisement 346
Evolution of the player piano 105 *et seq.*
Evolution of the Piano Player, article quoted 111
Exhaust bellows, inventor of 107
Exhausters, function of 130
Export trade, Britain's loss of 45
Expression device, first 91
    investigation into means of providing 161
    left to piano operator (letter) 100
Expression pianos, electric 34
    Hupfeld, early producer of 178
    inconsistency of stack divisions 173
Expression player piano 36, 173, 191–2
    Fratinola 177
    ideal system 117
    Mills 205
    Recordo 190
    Virtuola 98
    Virtuoso 98
Expression steps, Duo-Art 186
Expression stop in harmonium 134
Expression systems, different names for 117

Fairchild, Edgar, Ampico technician 182
    Original Piano Trio 250
Fairchild Monoplane, Link Sky Sign fitted to 357
Falcon, loom inventor 80
Farmer, John, quoted 174, 181, 240
Farmer, J. M., inventor 210
Farrand Organ Co 232, 233
    advertisement 261
    Cecilian **56**
    piano player advertisement 320
Farrand & Votey Organ Co 314
Farringdon, London home of street musicians 7
Farringdon Road, watch and clockmaking centre 57
Fauré, Gabriel 4, 242
Faust Waltz on gramophone record 33

Fawn, A. H. 44
Feet, correct pedalling with 257–9
Fehling, P., inventor 211
Feldmann, Herman of Haake Pianos 23
Fersani, G., street organ maker 57
Festival Hall, London 191
Financial Times, quoted 41
Findley, representing Aeolian 44
Fingal's Cave by Arensky 250
'First perfected metal action' – Air-O-Player 299
First pneumatic piano 90
Fischer, J. & C., piano makers 183
Fisk, Roger 10
Flap valve, function of 131
Flexotone-Electrelle piano player 271
Flight, Benjamin, jnr 18
Flight & Robson, organ-builders 15, 18, 24
    auction catalogue 18
Floating crescendo concept 176
Fluctibus, de (*alias* Robert Fludd) 14
Fludd, Robert 14
Flugels 177
Fluid Power International Fair, Japan 227
Flute-playing clock 13
Flutter pedalling, how achieved 258, 264
Flying, artificial trainers for 355
Flying trainer 356
Flying training and the player piano 355–7
Foot-operated barrel piano 57
    Duo-Art players 237
Foot pedals, importance of in playing 257
Foot-treadle barrel piano 57
Ford trucks modified for piano delivery 28
Forest Mill by Eilenberg 100
Förster piano 204, 284
Forster & Andrews, organ builders 73
Forte music rolls 118
Fortuna disc-playing musical box 317
Fortune-telling device in barrel piano 62
Foster, George G., Ampico head 310
Fotoplayer silent cinema orchestra 195
Fourneaux, J. B. Napoleon, inventor 83
Fourneaux Pianista 20, 60, 83, 84, 302
Frankfurter Musikwerke-Fabrik J. D. Philipps & Söhne 177–8
Franklin Institute xviii
Frati & Co 316
Frati, taken over by Philipps 177
Fratihymnia 302
Fratinola expression piano 177, 302
Free reeds, table organette playing 24
Freiberger Musikapparate-Bauanstalt advertisement 346
French Legion of Honour awarded to Tremaine 38
French player industry, its early demise 48
Friedheim, Arthur 4, 242
Friml, Rudolph, pianist 242
Fuchs, Diego, orchestrion maker 73
Full-orchestra theatre organs 67
Furse, Captain, melographic experimenter 231
Fürstlich Oettingen-Wallenstein'sche Bibliothek und Kunstsammlungen 11

INDEX

Gabriella player piano 308
Gabrilowitsch, Ossip 4, 242, 250
Galerie d'Horlogerie Ancienne 13
Gallopade by Weber 19
Galley, Robert A., musicaroll tracking system 157
Gally, Merritt, inventor 90
Galpin collection 17
Ganz, Rudolph 184, 242
    work on Paderewski's rolls 238
Ganz, Wilhelm, pianist 112
Gaslight, first street to be lit by 54
Gast's Klavierspielapparate player piano 303
Gauntlett, Dr Henry John 98
Gavioli, Anselme, inventor 86
Gavioli, Claude, street organ builder 61, 88, 91, 92, 212, 312
Gavioli Coelophone 312
    Organophone Expressif 312
    'Piano Executant' 88–9
Gebruder Weber (Weber Gebruder) 212
Gehrling, A., player actions 284
Gehrling player piano 284
Geigenpiano, Hegeler & Ehrlers 206
Geigenpiano violin/piano 289
Geissler, Bruno, self-playing harmonium 30
Gem roller organette 93
General Motors dispute in America 48
George III, King, street music in time of 54
Gerecke, William, importer 98
Gerhardt, Elena, singer 4, 31
German band 'monstrosities' 5
German Honorary Committee for the Promotion of Musical Studies 37
German instruments in England, effect of First World War on 213
    mechanical musical instrument manufacturers 106
    musical instrument exports 44, 45
    pianos, import duty increase 45
Germania orchestrion 315
Germanisches Nationalmuseum, Nuremberg 11, 12
Germany, largest mechanical music industry in world 106
Gershwin, George 184, 242, 251
    posthumous soloist in new recording 251
Getto, Francesco, inventor 59
Gieseking, Walter 242
Gilbert & Sullivan, copyright case against Polyphon 107
Gill, Harry: *Caprice*, music roll 337
Gillet, William, and Bland, Charles, inventors 56, 59
Givens, Larry, quoted 176
Glazounov, Alexander 4 242
    Serenade Espagnole opus 20 234
Globe, The, quoted 42
    player piano page in 41
Goddard, J. & J. xvii
Godfrey Ltd, piano-makers 44
Godowsky, Leopold, pianist 240, 242
    Ampico demonstrator 179
Golden Tube music rolls 245, 281
Gold-rush, effects of on mechanical music 194
Gold standard, abolition of 43
Golf, Hilmar, inventor 59

Goodall, H. R., Aeolian Corporation xvii
Goodman, Reginald Albert, executive 306
Goolman, early pioneer in pneumatics 90
Goundry, inventor 98
Grace, W. G., cricketer 169
Graffigna, barrel piano maker 286
Grainger, Percy 242, 334
    posthumous concert soloist 252
    statement on quality of rolls 35
Gramophone, 'cheaper than a piano' 6
    its ability to reproduce human voice 191
    copyright infringements 106
    early recordings 190
    first use in radio broadcast 44
    growth of 44
    industry, improvements in 49
Gramophone records of reproducing pianos, quality of 264
    recording studio, early 33
    recordings, Busoni's letter to wife 33
    recordings used in roll-making 184
    records 32
    sales in America 46
    sales affect player market 120, 122
    technical limitations of recording 32
Gramophone, Player Piano Supplement to, quoted 189, 249
Gramophones built into player pianos 39
Granados, Enrique 242
Grand, Aeolian organ 39
Grand piano, first player 28
Grand player organ, Aeolian 35
Grandezza orchestrion 315
Gravicembalo col piano 9
Great Exhibition, 1851 20, 81, 282
Greater London Council 202
Grecian Hall, mechanical piano at 19
Grenie, organ builder 134
Grew, Sidney, quoted 133, 256
    agitates for barred music rolls 41
Gribble Music Company, manufacturers 218
Grieg, Edvard 4, 31, 181, 242, 251
    Peer Gynt Suite 241
    Piano concerto in A minor played on player piano 4, 31, 252
Grinder, Italian street 6
Grinder organ 51
Grob & Co, J. M., inventors and patentees 59, 60, 65, 87, 94, 178, 206
Groiss, Eva, quoted 10, 11, 294
Grotrian-Steinweg Ampico 182–3, 191
Grundig International Ltd xvii
Guentes, Count de, Spanish ambassador 297
Guildhall School of Music 335
Guinness collection 298, 304
Guitarophone automatic zither 207
Gulbransen, piano makers 91
Guldman, distributor 305
Gutter, K. A., inventor of Autoharp 206

Haake, Karl, piano maker 23, 273
Haines Brothers, piano makers 183
Hainhofer, Philip 11

375

Half-blow control 160
    rail 189
Hallet & Davis Piano Co 189, 316
Hambourg, Mark, pianist 4, 112, 181, 242
Hamilton, Scottish organ builder 24
Hammond Organ, Silloth Trainer involvement 356
Hand guide, Bohrer's Automatic 8
Hand-played music rolls 167
Handel: *Messiah* 233
Handscombe, Patrick, author, quoted 265
Harcourt Moto-Player Bench 155, 281
Harding, Rosomond E., quoted 82
Hardman & Goetze Agencies, pianos 289
Hardman Peck Duo player piano 218
    music rolls 118
    piano player 289
    with Welte Mignon 176
Harfenuhr 13
Hargreaves, James, his Spinning-Jenny 80
Harmonist electric piano 307
Harmonista harmonium 298
Harmonium 68, 91, 215
    expression stop in 134
    folding 88
    Harmonista 298
    Kromarograph recording 230, 294
    perforated tune sheet patent 83
    player 86
    playing Strauss waltzes 277
    replaced by American organ 44
    self-playing by Bruno Geissler 30
    silent cinema use 195
Harmoniums, barrel 52
Harp clock 13
    couched 9
    Wurlitzer Automatic 199, 206, 209–10
Harper Electric Piano Co 98
Harper Electric Piano (1910) Co 98
Harper electric piano 103
Harper, Sydney C. 98
Harpers Magazine 28
Harpsichord with Pianocorder player **147**
    player mechanism for 230
Harris brothers, inventors 200
Harris, M., inventor 91
Harris, Stanley, pianolist 119
Harrods department store 44, 300, 323
    acquire Aeolian assets 123
    Piano Department xvii
    player piano department catalogue 350–3
Harwood player piano, price of 350
Haspels, Dr. J.-J. L. xvii
Hattemer, early pioneer in pneumatics 90
Hazelton piano 176
H & E watermark on music rolls 104
Healy, early pioneer in pneumatic action 90
Heath, Prof. Fred, inventor 221–6
Heaton, W. C., APAC president 274
Heckscher, D. R., Heckscher & Company xvii
    agent for Higel actions 116
Hegelers & Ehrlers Geigenpiano 206

Heilbrunn Patents Syndicate 98
Heilbrunn Söhne 98
    electric pianos advt. 78
    Virtuoso electric piano 100
Heintzman, G. C., inventor 290
Henry VIII, King 10
Herbert, Victor 184
Heriot-Watt University 220, 224
Hess, Myra, pianist 242
Hesse, Martin, inventor 294
Heyl piano 202
Hiawatha Self-Playing Xylophone 295
Hickman, Clarence Nichols, Ampico improver 310
Hicks family, piano makers 51
Hicks, George, piano maker 52
Hicks, John, piano maker 52
Hicks, Joseph, piano maker 51, 52, 54, 68, 269, 311
Hicks, Peter, cabinet maker 52
Hicks, trade card 56
Higel Co, Otto 269
Higel action 310
    Metalnola player action 290
    player action 116
Hill, F. F., collection 310, 311
Hindemith, Paul, pianola music by 251
Hindenburg airship, special piano on 49
Hoffmann & Engelmann, paper makers 104
Hofmann, Josef, pianist 4, 243, 335
Hofmann & Czerny Kinephon 195
Hofmann, Julius Carl, inventor 65
Höhlfeld, mechanic and inventor 230
Höhner Magic-Organa 308
Holbrooke, Joseph, composer 249
Holditch, organ-builder, 'dumb organist' 215
Holland, Frank W., MBE xvii, 154, 191
'Honky-tonk' sound in players 218
Hopkins, John, conductor 252
Hopkinson player piano 183
    price of 351
    Electrelle piano **82**
Horowitz, Vladimir 243
Horsehairs, number in Hupfeld bow 201
Horse-race diorama, Mills 205
Hose, rubber 140
Hot-air engine 94
    makers 288
Hotel Biltmore, New York 179
Hotel de Provence 19
Hottentots, Dance of the, automaton 13
Hottentottentanz, Der, automaton 13
House of Commons, comment by Dan Leno 2
'How the Piano Won the War' article quoted 356
How to play the player piano 255–61
Hrubes, Wenzel, orchestrion maker 73
Hull College of Music principal's words on player 42
Humana music rolls 118
    piano player advertisement 326
Humanola music rolls 118
    piano player, advertisement for 125
Humperdinck, Engelbert, composer 4
Hunt, Adoniram F., inventor 82

INDEX

Hupfeld & Co, Ludwig, mechanical musical instrument makers 30, 40, 59, 87, 97, 105–6, 137, 149, 162, 178, 184, 190, 201, 206, 212, 244–6, 259, 284, 303
    actions in Blüthner pianos 178–9
    Animatic music rolls 238
    artists who recorded for 242
    artists' rolls re-worked for Ampico 181
    buys paper mill 104, 245
    Clavimonium cinema instrument 195
    Clavitist **41**
    Clavitist-Violina 201
    Dea reproducing piano **95**
        date of introduction 190
    Dea-Violina 201
    Duophonola reproducing piano 179
    early influence on reproducing piano 178–9
        producer of electric expression pianos 178
    electric pianos 179
        reproducing piano 31
    kicking shoe player action **42–4**
    last player installation 179
    metal actions, use of 179
    music rolls, 73-note 113
        Phonola 179, 246
            precision in making 265
    number of patents owned by 178
    Phonola 110, **63, 97**
        piano player controls **71**
    Phonoliszt-Violina 200–1, 310, **128**
    piano with triple roll standard 113
    player action 116
    player-piano advertisement 228
    prolific exhibitor of orchestrions 30
    recordings converted to Ampico 243
    reproducing system, quality of 266–8
    roll tracking system 159
    Rönisch Solophonola upright grand advertisement 228
    Solophonola player piano 179
    Triphonola reproducing piano 179
        date of introduction 190
        violin-playing music rolls 179
Hupfeld-Gebr. Zimmermann, piano makers 291
Hupfeld's Pianoplaying Apparatus **36, 37**
Hurdy-gurdy 16, 51
Hymn of Thanksgiving 214

I do like to be beside the seaside on barrel piano 7
Ibach piano 202
    comparison of sound 264
    Pianola **73**
Ideal Mignon player action 281
Ideal player piano 289
Iles, Gordon, Artona Music Roll Co xviii
        inventor 169, 186, 218
        IST 174
        Silloth Trainer 356
Ilford Town Hall, Pistonola concert at 118
    player piano recital in 41
Illustrated London News 28

Illustrated Music Rolls 236
Illustrated Sporting and Dramatic News, quoted 111
Iles, John Henry 169
Imhof, Daniel, inventor 57
Imhof & Mukle, organ builders 56, 279, 314
    advertisement 50
    domestic barrel piano **11**
    'leaf-system' 90
Imperator musical box 210
Imperial music rolls 118
Import duties on German pianos 45
Indicator, Chicago 28
Industrie Musicale Ancien Etablis. Ch.-J. Ullmann 313
'Inefficiency reservoirs', need for 219
Ingalls & Co, G. W., organette makers 310
'Inner player' action, invention of 115–16
Intermittant engine, music roll drive 156
International Duo-Art Week 38
International Electricity Exhibition 1880, 86
International Electricity Exhibition, Paris, 1880 230, 278
International Exhibition, London, 1862 230
        London, 1884 286
International piano orchestrion 295
I.O.M. Weekly Times, quoted 42
Iron frame in clockwork piano 60
Iroquis Indian language 194
IST, *see* Isolated instantaneous theme
Isabella II, queen of Spain 287
Isis, zither-playing android 300
Isolated instantaneous theme, Iles' 169, 174, 265
Isolated theme system, Trist's 168
Italian influence in barrel piano 57
Italian street grinder 6
Iturbi, Jose 242
Ivers-Pond piano 176

Jacquard, Joseph Marie, inventor 22, 23, 79–81
        loom 80
        card system 83, 97, 279, 282, 308, 311
Japan, player piano industry in 36
Jardine & Co, organ-builders 209
Jet engine, first 48
Ji-do pianos, Japanese player 36
John Peel, song 237
Johnston, A. W., Photo Player executive 309
Jolly is the Miller, song 236
Jones, H. Bryan, Keith, Prowse & Co 293
Jones, Thomas Linforth 'electro-magnetic energization' 64
Joplin, Scott, composer 192

Kaim, Henry, piano maker 280
Kalliope 285
Kalliston organette 295
Kansas City music roll library 32, 245
Kapps piano 202
Kastner, Maximilian Macarius xviii, 168, 169, 313
        note accenting system 164–5
Kastner-Autopiano Akt.-Ges. 179

Kastner music rolls 233
    Autopiano **69**
    Triumph music roll catalogue 233
        music rolls, prices of 233
    Triumphauto music roll label 254
        advertisement 268
    unit valve system 151
Kastner, Prof. M. S. xviii
Kastonome 164–5, 166, 168, 292, 258
    Autopiano rolls 233
Katz, C., inventor 165, 169
Kaufmann, automaton maker 15, 209
Keith, R. W., piano maker 293
Keith, Prowse & Co, piano makers 213, 289, 302, 305
    barrel piano **20**
Keller, O., inventor 206, 207
Kelly, George B., inventor of roll drive motor 90, 109, 156, 312
    roll tracking patent 158
Kemble Pianos xvii
Kendall, Charles B., inventor 193
Kennedy, D., inventor 170
Ketterer, Philipps' partner 302
Keyboard, detachable, for tuning Welte 175
    hinged or folding for yacht pianos 117
    sideways shifting of 146
Keyed bugle, its discovery 54
    violin, Swedish 204
Keyframe of barrel piano, how made 76
Keyless Welte reproducing piano 31
Keyless organ system 92
    pianos 31
    'red' Welte 174
Key-top kicking-shoe player 231
    piano-player 94, 278
    player, Antiphonel 21
        Dale Lectronic 282
        Magic Fingers 288
        Pianola, 1950s 174
Key-top players 215–18, **140–144**
Kicking-shoe player action 86, 93, 94, 98, 103, 111, 231, 288, 303
    drawing of 87
Kicking-shoe electric piano 99
    Pianotist action 270
Kimball piano with Welte Mignon 176
    music rolls 118
Kine theatres, instruments for 195
Kinephon, Hofmann & Czerny 195
Kircher, Athanasius 14
Kirkman Melopiano 94
Klaber, Augustus David 111
Klaber, Emile, inventor 111, 303
    Pianotist executive 319
Klank en Weerklank, quoted 251
Klatt, Paul, manufacturer 294
Klatt, Kulh & 98
Klein, Henry, importer and agent 97
deKleist, Eugene, inventor 60
deKleist's Tonophone 63, 67, 193, 194, 209, 317
Klepetar, Ignaz, orchestrion main agent 73

Klepetar, J., piano orchestrion maker 72–3
Klepzig, L. A., inventor 210
Klugh, Paul Brown, 91
    note accenting system 164
Kmita, Andrei, pianist 240
Knabe & Co, William, cost of Ampico 182
    player pianos 183, 296
Knife valve, its purpose described 142
'Knows no technical difficulty' slogan 294
Komet disc-playing musical box 98
Konzert-Clavitist 291
Konzert-Phonoliszt 291
Koschat, Thomas, singer & composer 207
Koschat automatic zither 207
Kotykiewicz, Adam Knopf von, harmonium builder 230
Kotykiewicz, Teofil, harmonium builder 230
Kranich & Bach piano with Welte Mignon 176
Kreisler, Fritz 181, 242
Krell, Albert, inventor 273
Krell Piano Co, makers of player pianos 97
    player piano advertisement 338
Kromarograph recording harmonium 230, 294
Kuhl & Klatt electric pianos 98
    advertisement for electric pianos 330
    jazz piano **114, 120**
    Pneuma advertisement for 330
Kunsthistorisches Museum xviii, 11, 12
Kurtzmann pianos 176
Kuster, Henry, inventor 90, 301

La mi Aspada 19
Lacape, inventor 87–8
Lacape barrel and finger piano 88
Lambeth Walk on barrel piano 7
Lamond, Frederic 4, 243, 335
Lamoureux Orchestra 4, 31
Landowska, Wanda, pianist 4, 234, 243
Langenbucher 10, 269
    clockwork spinet 5
    Viet 13
Langham-Hupfeld player piano, price of 351
Langwill, Lyndesay G., quoted 52
Largest mechanical instrument in world 213
Laskarewski, Charles Adbank de, inventor 83
Lässig, Jörg xvii, xviii
Last Stoddard Ampico roll 239
Lawrence, R. W., Autopiano Co 273–4
Lawson, Rex, quoted 249–50, 335
Leabarjan home perforating machine 248
Lead tubing 139
Leaf-system, Imhof & Mukle 90
Lecape & Co, J., inventors 57
Lectronic key-top piano player 282
Leech, John, Victorian writer 52
Leginska, Ethel 243
Leipzig, centre of electric piano production 36
    Trade Fair 30, 193
Lengnick, Alfred, wholesaler 87
Leno, Dan, comment on House of Commons 2
Leo XIII, Pope 2
Leoncavallo, Ruggiero 242

INDEX

Leschetizky, Theodor 4, 31, 32, 181, 242
Levitzki, Mischa 181, 220, 242
Lexington player pianos 289
Lhevinne, Josef 31, 182, 243, 268
Liapounov, Serge Michailovitch, conductor 4
Libellion musical box 210
Library, New York Public xviii
        Patent Office xviii
Libraries, music roll lending 245
Liebmannista organette 295
Light pen and bar-coding 226
Limonaire Brothers, organ builders 212, 283
Lindeman, piano makers 189, 272
Lindwall, Bill xviii, 68, 70, 71
Ling, Jan, quoted 204
Link, Edwin A. 273
        Link Trainer 355
Link Piano & Organ Company 72, 194
Link Piano Co 196, 197, 200, 315
        Model 2-E keyless piano **132**
        orchestral piano **137**
Link Sky Sign 357
Link Trainer 196, 295, 355
Link Trainer School 356
Lipp & Sohn, piano makers 189, 202
        Duca-Lipp action 189
Liszt, style of roll recording on Ampico 182
        La Campanella 264, 268
Little Empress Electric Cabinet Player 215
Lochmann, Paul, inventor 300
Lochmann disc-playing piano 93
        hollow-cylinder clockwork piano 64, **32-4**
        Original 285, 300
        Original Walzen-Orchestrion 67
        string orchestral instrument 30
Lock and cancel valves, Welte 176
Lockwood Press, publisher of *Musical & Dramatic News* 113
London Bridge, song 236
London Directory, 1881, quoted 314
London Duo-Art concert at Queen's Hall 39
London Symphony Orchestra 4, 31
London Trades Directory quoted 36
London, use of barrel pianos in 7
Longman, John, upright clockwork piano **9, 10**
Longman & Broderip, musical instrument manufacturers 17, 280
Loof Lirpa title on mystery music roll 238
Loom, Jacquard's invention for 80
Looms and mechanical music 22
Lorraine, Spencer, managing director, Apollo Co 3
Lorraine, S., Apollo Co executive 320
Lost-motion pneumatic 189
Louis XV style 212
Luche, Charles, clockwork café piano **19**
Ludwig & Co piano player 99
Ludwig, J. W., inventor 99
Luray Caverns stalactite-player 213
Lyon & Healy, Chicago 192, 215, 300
Lyraphone, Smith, piano player 103, 157, 308, **60, 61**

McClure's Magazine, Angelus advertisement 326

MacDowell, Edward Alexander, pianist and composer 32
MacFadyen, Alexander 181
Machals, Thomas, Dulcitone-inventor 17
Machine Design, quoted 227
Mackenzie, Duncan, inventor 81
Macquisten, A. P. S., inventor 97
McTammany, John, inventor 90, 112, 113, 125, 207, 231, 301
        music roll drive motor 156, 157
Madge, Wallace, organist 240, 241
Maestro Company, key-top piano player 215, 216, 272, 296, **144**
Maëstro reproducing piano, Mustel 175, 299
Magic Fingers key-top player 218, 288
Magic-Organa, Höhner 308
Magnetic tape in player piano systems 39, 220
Makers of the Harpsichord and Clavichord, quoted 11
Malcolm & Co, John, piano makers 323
        player reed organ 116
        player piano 116
Malipiero, Francesco, composer 250
Manchester Courier quoted 41, 55
Mando Piano Orchestrina 300
Mandolin effect in barrel piano 59
        rotating shaft 65
Mandolin harp piano 58
Mandolin Quartette, Wurlitzer 197
Mandoline-Zither, mechanical Autoharp 207
Manger, John, musical box importer 298
Manns, Sir August, quoted 121
Manual controls, types of 160-1
Manualo player piano 274
Maple used for making actions 151
Maples department store 323
        piano department 120
Marantz Pianocorder 223, **149**
Marimbaphones 200
Marini collection, Marino 51
Marque-Ampico, reproducing piano 180
        price of 352
Marquet, music publishers' editors 106
Marquette Piano Company 194, 196
        orchestrion Style G **138**
Marr, Wood & Co 300
Marshall & Rose 101, 183
        Ampico, cost of 182
Marshall & Wendell 183
        Ampico, cost of 182
Marshall Piano Co, Sir Herbert 105, 189
        Angelus advertisement 325
        'motor cabinet' 155
Marteletti's café piano, advertisement 67
Martin, Easthope, pianolist 4, 31
Martin, William, inventor 83
Marveola player pianos 193
Marzolo, G., inventor 230
Mascagni, Pietro, pianist 4, 181, 243
Maserati & Co, Cesare, barrel piano maker 312
Mason & Hamlin 40, 183, 271
        Ampico, cost of 189
'Master's Fingers on your Piano' slogan 294
Mastertouch music rolls 49

Mathews Directory, quoted 310, 311
Mathot, Gustave xvii
Mattei, Tito, pianist 112
Matthews, Mason J., orguinette inventor 26, 297, 312
Matthias, Emperor 11
Maurice, Klaus, and Mayr, Otto, quoted 294
Maxfield, J., inventor 91, 207
Maxfield reed organ 25
Maxfield Player Piano Co 192
Mayhew: *London Labour and London Poor* quoted 290
Mechanical Autoharp 207
    banjo 67, 206
    dulcimer 51, 52
    guitar 67
    harp 66
    jazz-band 67
    music for silent pictures 67
        largest industry in world, Germany 106
    notation, history and description of 14
    piano at Grecian Hall 19
        early example 17
    pipe organ 51
    playing, technical difficulties 15
    to pneumatic action 78 *et seq.*
    virginal of 1619 315
    zither 67
Mechanical Orguinette Company 26, 90, 208, 312
Mechanical Piano-player, article 326–9
'Mechanical Player and Its Music', letter quoted 100
'Mechanical player – does it damage piano?', article 323
Mechanical-pneumatic touch-key, Gavioli 287
Mechanics of Mechanical Music, quoted 74, 275
Medcraft, Harry and Silvia 248, 252
Medical Press & Circular, quoted 5
Medieval organ builders 132
Meer, Dr van der 11, 12
Mehlin & Sons piano with Welte Mignon 176
Meinhardt, O., inventor 210
Melbourne Musical Industries Exhibition, 1888 283, 306
Melodant 258
Mel-O-Dee music roll factory 316
Melody emphasis 162
'Melody stops' on Pianotist 112
Melody Violins, Mills 206, 307
Melograph 86, 229, 278–9
    creation of word 222
Melographic roll-marking 166
Melographic trace of performance 34
Melography 14, 86, 229, 300
Melography and the computer 220 *et seq.*
Melopiano, Kirkman 94
Meloto music rolls 167
Melotrope 86, 215, 230, 278–9
Melville Clark Art/Echo/Apollo/Celco, date of introduction 190
Mendel player piano 281
Mendelssohn: *Songs Without Words* 233
Mennie, Prof. W. A., Standard Action head 309
Menth, Herma, pianist 243
Menzenhauer, Guitarophone makers 207
Merklin, organ-builder 24

Merlin, John Joseph, instrument maker 230
Mero, Yolanda, pianist 243
Merrill piano makers 189, 299
Mersenne, Marin, quoted 9
Metal action, 'first perfected' Air-O-Player 299
Metal player actions 151
    used by Hupfeld 179
Metalnola, Higel player action 290
Methven, Simpson & Co 300
Metrically cut music rolls xix
Metrograde control 161
Metropolitan Museum xviii
Metrostyle 233
    markings, shortcomings in 122
    music rolls, how to play 258
    Pianola, advertisement 318
Metzler & Co 88
    music rolls 118
    Humanola piano player advertisement 125
    piano player, advertisement 318
Mexican National Band 204
Microprocessor 6, 199
Midwest Research Institute 218, 288
Mighty Fortress in our God 214
Mignon, Brinsmean player piano 117
Mignon organette 208
Mikado Waltz, copyright case concerning Polyphon 106
Milhaud, Darius 242
Military band organs 92
Mills Novelty Company 98, 201–6, 307
    expression piano 205
    horse-race diorama 205
    Melody Violins 206
    Race-Horse piano 206
    Self-playing violin 199
    Violano Virtuoso 201–6
Mina, advertisement for street piano 67
Minerva piano player 298
Minnen, Dick van xvii
Minstrelle Autopiano 48, 275
Miranda Pianista piano player 22, 23, 273
Mistracking, problems of 103
Modulist control 119
Molinari, street organ and piano maker 212
Molyneux, E., inventor of reed organ electric action 83
Moncel, Vicompte Theodose du, electrical engineer 230
Monington & Weston 44
Monkey, colourfully-dressed 16
Monola player piano 308
Monopol musical box 207
Monroe Organ Reed Co 26, 208, 270, 312
Moon, Sidney, piano dealer 44
Moore, Hartwell R., roll tracking system 157
Morita, Akio, Sony Corporation 171, 186
Morgan, J., inventor 109
Morgan, Tony xvii
Morley, John Sebastian 10
Mörs & Co, L., pianomaker 224
Mortier, Belgian organ-builder 210
Moseiwitsch, Benno, pianist 181, 220, 242
    comments re Ampico staff 181

INDEX

Moskowski, Moritz 250, 329
    Bagatelle opus 63 234
    Pièce Rustique 234
Moss collection 282
Motion picture theatre orchestras, employment in 46
Motor cabinet pump for players 155
Motor car, affecting player sales 44
Motor, inertia type 210–11
Motoring, effect on piano sales 45
Mouth-organ, Rolmonica mechanical 211
Mozart, barber's shop lodging 7
    on barrel piano 316
    Adagio Favori 235
    Eine Kleine Nachtmusik on barrel piano 74
    Sonata in D opus 53 234
    Zauberflöte 233
Multiple roll changers, coin-freed pianos 194
Multitone pianos, Welte 300
Munz, Mieczyslaw, pianist 242
Murder of Music, leaflet quoted 46
Murdoch, S. J., Harrods xvii
Murdoch, Murdoch & Co 117
    Golden Tube music rolls 245, 281
Musetta piano player 278
    advertisement 319
Musette, Aeolian **148**
Museum, Bellm's Cars & Music of Yesterday xviii
    British 17
    British Piano xvii, 154
    Carolino Augusteum, Salzburg 11
    Deutsches xviii, 206, 294, 297
    Germanisches Nationalmuseum, Nuremberg 11, 12
    Kunsthistorisches xviii, 11, 12
    Metropolitan xviii
    Nationaal Museum van Speelklok tot Pierement xvii, 13, 201
    Queen Victoria M. and Art Gallery 308
    Schlesisches, Silesian, Breslau 11, 12
    Victoria & Albert xviii
    (Enthoven Collection) 19
    West Cornwall Museum of Mechanical Music xviii, 317
Music & Automata quoted xviii, 10–13, 69, 204, 294
Music book, hot-air engine to drive 94–6
    zig-zag folding of 91
Music Box, The, quoted xviii, 17, 22, 52, 67–8, 74, 169, 186, 356
Music for the player piano 229–54
    a lost opportunity 249
Music played on barrel pianos 74
Music repertoire 117
Music represented by bar code 226
Music roll, air motor to drive 96
    Animatic-T 220
    Biographical 37
    brass 97
    changer **121**
    clockwork drive 109
    compass, standardisation of 173
    copying 49

Music roll, drive 155
    air motor 141
    inventor of 109
    motor inside spool 110
    first vacuum motor 109
drive methods 107
editing to remove wrong notes 35, 168
    importance of 266
editing and correcting, comments re Ampico 181
expression line marking 117
how words were printed 118
drive motor, George Kelly's 90, 109, 156, 312
large take-up spools, use of 180
lending library in Kansas 32, 36, 245
    Aeolian's 233
    Harrods, details of 351
    largest in world 123
    Orchestrelle 329
lending libraries 245
Ludwig's 5½-in system 100
maker, advertisement 214
    QRS 211
    Republic 250
motor inside spool 110
note accenting 116
paper 243
    mill bought by Hupfeld 245
    quantity used by Hupfeld 245
perforating machinery 34
    Acme 248
    punches, speed of 34
    systems tried 248
perforator for home use, the Leabarjan 248
recording 330–1
    speed of paper 35
recording apparatus 182, 225, 240–1
sale, Simplex advertisement 254
'sandwich' of metal and paper 168
special practice type 260
tendency to speed up in playing 96
tracking 110, 156 *et seq.*
with optically-scanned sound track 39
Music rolls, a vast backlog of new ones needed 251
    accented 167
    adjustable spools for 104
    Aeolian 234–8
    Ampico made in Britain 182
    Analytical 37
    Angelus Artistyle 296
    Animatic 291
    Artist Song Rolls 296
    Artona xvii
    attention to pleats in 253
    Audiographic 26
    'autographic Interpretation' 234
    Christmas Greetings 240
    Colley's Patents advertisement 364
    contiguous perforating 244
    copyright tax on 106
    curing expansion problems 253
    double width, playing forward and reverse 192

Music rolls, edges reinforced with varnish 244
    electromagnetic player using sheet metal 36
    electronic reading of 227
    endless bands 197
    extra large Duo-Art 219
    fidelity of, Grainger & Paderewski quoted 35
    for Aeolian pianos 233–8
        Magic Organa 308
        violin player, Hupfeld 179
    hand-played 167
    high cost of 236
    how to handle in use 260
    how recorded 34, 184, 225
    Hupfeld capable of playing three standards 113
    'jumbo'-sized Ampico 239
    Kastonome 165–6
    lack of standardisation 116
    machine for punching out 91
    Maestro 50-note 215
    making a respooling jig 253
    Mel-O-Dee factory 316
    Meloto 167, 274
    metrically cut xix
    multi-tune 191
    Murdoch's Golden Tube 281
    Muvis 274
    need for special paper 103
    newly made 49
    number of Philipps 178
    optical reading of 227
    'orchestrated' 35
    Orpheus 306
    pedal line markings 117
    Philag 302
    Phonola water mark 104
    pitch of early 157
        holes in tracker bar 150
    plea for new reproducing ones 251
    printing with bars 41
    'Popular-Puzzle-Roll' 31
    printed tempo lines 36
    problems of paper fibres 91
    'red' Welte xix
    repairs to 252
    repertoire 117
    reproducing, converted to other systems 243
        signed by artist 34
    ribboning in 244
    'Riddle-Roll' 31
    Running Commentary rolls 37
    sandblasted 91
    'scientifically adapted' 184
    song 117
    special for IST system 170
    specially composed for player piano 250–1
    their educational value 37
    Themodist, how marked 166–7
    tips on buying 253
    types of perforation 167
    Universal 167, 274, 297
    unreliability of tempo markings on 261

Music rolls, use of gas jets in making 91
    value of xix
    various types made by Perforated Music Co 118
    with recording track down one side 39
    with sound-track 337
    'World's Music' series 37
Music setting on barrels, systems used 74–5
Music Student, quoted 42
Music Trade Review, quoted 249
Music Trades Association 44, 46
Musical Age, quoted 325
Musical appreciation 1
Musical box 83, 105, *see also* Disc-playing musical box
    book-playing, Libellion 210
    Capital 301
    cylinder 79
    disc-playing 39
        Adler 315
        Fortuna 317
        Imperator 210
        Komet 98
        Lochmann Original 285, 300
        Monopol 207
        Polyphon 106, 212, 282, 285, 293
        Regina 209, 317
        Symphonion 23, 273, 315
    disc-playing developments 106
    Libellion 210
    modern Swiss industry 125
    tune change system 76
Musical box agent, Klein 97
Musical Box, A History and Collectors' Guide, quoted 23, 39
Musical Box Society of Great Britain xviii
Musical Box Society International xviii, 183, 185
Musical Boxes, quoted 52
Musical boxes, types of music programme 79
    Christmas-tree stands 284
    clocks 79
    dulcimer clock **6, 7, 8**
Musical Components Ltd, advertisement for Stradola 354
Musical copyright 106–7
Musical Courier Extra, trade paper 113
Musical & Dramatic News, quoted 113
Musical Instrument in the Great Exhibition, quoted 81
Musical movements, modern Swiss and Japanese 79
Musical News, Metzler piano player advertisement 319
Musical Opinion, quoted 2–3, 5, 17, 28–30, 42–3, 45, 55, 87–8, 97, 99, 100, 113, 124, 175, 202, 231, 255, 319–21, 323, 325–6, 329
Musical scene, a summing up of 249
Musical Times, quoted 337
Musical Trades Exhibition, 1901 298
Musicus Piano Player Co 31
Musique et Instruments, quoted 48
Mussolini, Benito, Weber Duo-Art owner 185
Mustel, Victor 107, 175
Mustel Maëstro reproducing piano 175, 299
Muvis piano roll 44
Mylar film, use of in mechanical music 213

INDEX

Nahe-Kussen automatic music industry 10, 12
Napoleon 80
National Museum van Speelklok tot Pierement xvii, 13, 201
National Exhibition, Turin (1884) 275–6, 279, 283, 287, 309, 313
    Land and Irrigation Exposition 204
    Music Week 46
    Player-Piano Publicity Committee 48, 49, 125
    Player Piano Week 43, 44, 46
    Theatre 191
Nederlandse Pianola Vereniging concert 250
Needham, Elias Parkman 90, 104, 107
Needham & Sons 26, 90
Nelson Wiggen, electric piano makers 72, 196–7
Neola music rolls 118
Nettl, Paul, quoted 12
New Age, quoted 42
'New Era Instruments', article, quoted 227
Newman, Ernest, music critic 3, 34, 41, 133
New Penny Magazine, quoted 74
New Symphony Orchestra 2
New Trist Player Piano Co 41, *see also under* Trist
New York Public Library xviii
    style of electric piano 99
    Symphony Orchestra 34
New York World, quoted 185
Ney, Elley 243
Niagara River 194
Nicholson, E. G., roll tracking system 159
Nickelodeon development and refinement 194
    electrically-driven 36
    history of 193
    rolls, newly available 49
Nickel Player, coin-freed instrument 193
Nickerson, William E., owner of Lockwood Press 113
Niemczik, A. V., Grob founder 94, 288
Nikisch, Arthur, pianist 4, 31
Nilsson, I. F., inventor 68
Norris & Hyde player piano 299
North Tonawanda Barrel Organ Factory 60, 283
North Tonawanda Musical Instrument Works 194, 196
    advertisement for photoplayer 198
    Pianolin **131**
Notation and mechanical music 14
    of barrels, systems used 74–5
Notation, mechanical, history and description of 14
Note accenting in player actions, systems for 116
    Dalian system 116
    how effected 161
    Themodist system 116
Notes played, lack of standardisation 116
    by reproducing pianos 190
Novaës, Guiomar, pianist 243
Noyes, Thomas Herbert, inventor 83
Number of player piano manufacturers 36
    in London, 1922 36
Nyckelharpa, Swedish instrument 204
Nylon stockings, first 48
Nyström, C. W. 231
Nyström, Johan Petter, inventor 68, 288
Nyström Reform-Orgel 68, 231

Obermeier piano 202
Obenchain, Elaine, quoted 239
O'Connor, James, inventor 308
    roll tracking system 157–8
Octave spinet **1, 2, 3, 4**
    virginals 12
Odeola player piano advertisement 349
Old Savoye Collection 11
Oldroyd, Dr G., pianola-contest judge 337
Oloha Oe, song 240
Olympic Games, ill-fated 1940 49
Omar Khayyam, last Stoddard-Ampico roll 239
Operators Piano Co 194, 198, 215
    Coinola **133**
Opportunity lost on player piano music 249
Optically-scanned music track on piano roll 39
Orchestra, Berlin Philharmonic 2
    Lamoureux 4
    London Symphony 4, 31
    New Symphony 2
    New York Symphony 34
    Royal Albert Hall 2
Orchestrated music rolls, Aeolian 35
Orchestrelle Co 327
    advertisement for Pianola push-up 322, 330
    its profits in 1914 41
    Metrostyle Pianola advertisement 336
    Music Circulating Library 245
    Paderewski pianola testimonial 362
    Pianola grand advertisement 340
    separate pumps sold by 155
    war-time Pianola advertisements 341–3
Orchestrelle, Aeolian xx, 35, 39, 106, 184
    music rolls 118, 246
    roll library 329
    rolls, damage to 252–3
    separate blowers sold for 155
    tracker bar 162
Orchestrelle Company in Australia 49, 123
Orchestrion, Brass Band 316
    Concert 316
    Germania 315
Orchestrion makers and architectural styles 212–13
    organs, music roll drive motor 109
    Welte 176
    roll drive system in Welte 156
Ord-Hume, Arthur W. J. G., quoted 9, 15, 23, 227, 275
Organ, every one in London played electromagnetically 98
    pipes, violin-toned 197, 200
    Welte Philharmonic Autograph 316
    with melographic device 230
Organ combined with player piano, pipe 209
Organ-builders, medieval 132
Organ-grinder 16
Organ-grinder's 'public enemy number 1' 52
Organette 30, 39, 91, 156, 207
    Amorette 293
    Ariston 83, 93, 288
    Celestina 26, 298
    copyright threat 106
    free-reed 24

Organette Gem roller 93
             Kalliston 295
             Liebmannista 295
Organettes, patents for perforated tune sheets 83
Organillos 272
Organina Thibouville player 93, 311
Organista, Thibouville-Lamy organ-player 22
Organista hot-air piano 94
Organophone, Gavioli 312
Organophone Expressif, Gavioli's 312
Organs, electronic 226
      reed, a developing industry 35
Orguinette, Mason J. Matthews 26, 297
Original, Lochmann piano orchestrions 300
Original Piano Trio 250
Original Pianola Shop, Brighton xvii
Ornstein, Leo, pianist 242
Orpheus disc-playing piano 83, 284, **35**
Orpheus music rolls 306
      player piano 282
Orphobella player piano 284
Osborn, Michael Magnus, concert impressario 220
Ottavinos 10
Ottenheimer, Dr Paul D. xvii
Otto Higel Co 269
Oxford Companion to Music, quoted 2, 52, 241

Pachmann, Vladimir de 243, 335
Packard, Isaac T., inventor 107
Packard piano with Welte Mignon 176
Paderewski, Ignace 48, 121, 184, 185, 220, 243, 329, 334
    difficulties in making rolls 238
    his Duo-Art performance of his Minuet 38
    Pianola testimonial 362
    quote re quality of music rolls 35
    story of immersing hands in hot water 3
Pagani's restaurant, meeting at 44
Paganini, Philipps 194
'Paganini's Set of Quadrilles' 19
Pain, Robert W., inventor 26, 90, 157, 162, 163, 168, 208, 312
Pall Mall Gazette, quoted 42
Palmer, Harry W., Aeolian technician 169
Pape, Jean-Henri, inventor 82
Paper used to control air 24
Paper for music rolls 243
Paper mill bought by Hupfeld 245
Paper, need for special 103
Paragon piano player 271, 299
Parallax Stereogram, US honours for 203
Paris Exhibition, 1801 80
Parker, William D., inventor 25, 90
    roll drive motor 156
Parr, Ellis, inventor 23, 273
Pasodoble on Spanish barrel pianos 68
Pasquale & Co, Gregori, piano makers 60, 76, 91
    street piano **29**
Patent Office Library xviii
Patent Office, United States 203
Patents, number owned by Hupfeld 178
Patti, Adelina (Baroness Caderstrom) 112

Payne & Co, H., music dealer 118
Pears Soap, Tom Barratt, founder 274
Peaseley, A. M., inventor 107
Pedairolas, suggested name for foot treadles 117
Pedal control, how achieved 159–60
Pedal-electric Duo-Art 237
Pedal operated reproducing piano, Ducartist 177
Pedal, sustaining 161
Pedaleon player piano 274
    for yachts 117
Pedalling, flutter 258, 264
    ungraduated in expression piano 34
Peerless Piano Player Co 284, 307
Peerless, 44-note Pianino electric piano 193, 194
Pennyano barrel piano 293
Percussion instruments in barrel piano 60, 63, 68, 71
Perfection of player action 155 *et seq.*
Perforated cardboard music 22
    disc used to play reed organ 68
Perforated Music Company 32, 41, 118, 244
    advertisement 247
    destroyed by fire 118
    piano-roll makers 31
Perforating machine punches, speed of 34
    machinery, music rolls 34
    mechanism, hand-driven 86
    music rolls, systems tried 248
        types of hole 244
Perla orchestrion 30
Per Omnes Pianoforte 59, 278
Pesaresi, Luigi, fortune-telling piano 62
Pesaresi & Son, mandolin & tremolo pianos 63
Peters & Son, H., distributors 97
    electric pianos 293
Petrushka, Stravinsky 250
Pfeiffer, Carl, restorer 230
Phelps Pianos xvii
Philadelphia Exposition 1876, 83, 285
Philag music rolls 302
Philipps & Ketterer, orchestrion makers 302
Philipps & Sohne, J. D. 30, 160, 199, 212
    Cäcilia player piano 177
    Corona player piano 177
    Duca reproducing piano 177
        date of introduction 190
        system, quality of 266–8
    Ducanola player piano 177
    Ducartist pedal reproducer 177
    Paganini 194
    Pianella 194
    Pianella-Orchestrion Model 43 **119**
    player piano action 189–90
    revolver mechanism roll-changer **121, 130**
    unit valve system 151
Philips-patent compact cassette 220
Phillips, G., inventor 292
Philosophical Transactions, quoted 230
Phoneon piano player 298
Phonograph 39, *see also* Gramphone
    built into piano, Apollophone 280
    Charles Cros, inventor 279

INDEX

Phonograph, Thomas Edison, inventor 279
    usurper of musical box market 79
Phonola piano, Hupfeld 110, 149, 160–1, 162, 278, 291, **63**
    manual controls 161
    music rolls, Hupfeld 179
    watermark on music rolls 104
Phonoliszt-Violina, Hupfeld 178, 200–1, 291, 310
    horsehair bow 201
    sourdine effect 201
Phonopectines 39
Photography, colour, US honours for 203
Photo Player theatre organ 36, 67, 195, **139**
    number made 198
Phrasiola control 117
Pianauto piano player 292
Pianella, Philipps 194
Pianette, disc-playing piano 301
Pianino, Peerless 194, 209
Pianist piano player, Spaethe's 288, 309
Pianist played 360 wrong notes 1
Pianista piano player, Autopiano 273
Pianista Debain 106
Pianista, Fourneaux's 20, 83, 84, 285, 302
Pianista player, Kohler & Campbell 294
Pianista, Thibouville-Lamy piano-player 22, 92, 93, 311
Piano, case re damage caused by player 323
    continuously-beating hammer action 56
    delivery, modified Ford trucks for 28
    discoveries about the earliest 9
    driven by falling weight 56
    electricity in the 96
    'the first complete player' 28
    first player grand 28
    the first pneumatic 90
    fronts, proscenium style 63
    Gavioli's book-playing 88
    hammers, made of hardwood 65, 68
    'House of Commons would go better with a' 2
    the 'household god' 6
    iron frame 54
    lightweight, on Hindenburg airship 49
    paper-operated player 91
    piano and *forte* effects from pinned barrel 55
        barrel pinning 59
    played by book music 65
        metal disc, Pianette 301
    playing, generation never taught 7
    quality of instrument and player 29
    reproducing 1
    sales in America 46
    salesman, 'better than professional pianist' quote 1
    tension of strings in 54
    tuners avoid player pianos 154
Piano-Auto player 294
Pianocorder 39, 223–6, 232
    harpsichord **147**
Piano Executant Artiste, Ullmann's player 313
Piano Forte, The, quoted 82
Piano/forte effect by variation of hammer force 111
Pianoforte Manufacturers' Association 45
Pianograph 231

Pianography 231
Pianoharpa barrel piano xviii, 68, 69, 70, 71, 272, 299, **15, 16, 17, 18**
Piano-Jazz, Eich 284
Pianola Piano 39, 233–8
    advertisement 38
        push-up 322, 330
        war-time 341–3
    'a bad form of musical self-indulgence' 42
    educational use of music rolls for 37
    first model 58 notes 26
    grand piano advertisement 340
    key-top style 174
    Metrostyle, advertisement 336
    music rolls 118
        practice roll 260
    'Pianola piano – the First Complete Piano' 28
    Pianola piano player 26, **57–9**
    registered trademark xx, 6
    Votey's first 21, 25
Pianolin coin-freed piano 300
Pianolists' Club, formation of 337
'Piano machine' for loom 80
Pianomaker, Music & Radio, quoted 120
Piano-maker, The, quoted 247
Piano Mecanique 20 *et seq*., 82, 282
Piano Melodico action 93, 94, 197, 298, 304, 309, **38, 39, 40**
Piano orchestrion 71
    losing favour to electric pianos 73
    Polyphon, advertisement 357
    with punched cylinder 67
    Verdi 305
Piano-Orchestrion hot-air engine piano 94
Piano-organ 4
    effect of war on 5
Pianophones, introduction of 337
Piano player, Airmatic 308
    Antiphonel 56
    Bansall's Universal 110
    coin-freed pneumatic 63
    detached, Simplex Special 115
    Ehrlich's disc-playing 83
    Metzler, advertisement 318
    'a soulless machine' 4
    using barrel and stickers 59
    using cardboard disc 87
    would not be ousted by 'inner player' 27
Piano players, cabinet style 174
    'filip to business' 5
    fitted with wheels 110
    transparent lid for 104
PianOrchestra, Wurlitzer 194
Piano-roll, *see also under* Music roll
    accented 119
    cutting machine, electric, Muller's 298
    hand-played 119
    maker, advertisement 214
    Muvis 44
Piano-rolls, Britain's largest manufacturer of 32
    damage to 252

PIANOLA

Piano-rolls, how recorded 34
    repairs to 252
    relatively high cost of 43
Pianos a manubrio 75, 314
Pianos, cardboard music playing 94
    clockwork-powered 19
    destruction of unwanted xix
Piano-smashing competitions 7
Pianosona piano player 279
Pianoti, detachable style of Pianotist 319
Pianotist Co, report 319
    creditors' meetings 320
Pianotist piano player 112, 218, 270, **45, 46, 47, 48**
    advertisement 320
    a classic failure 111
    expression system 161
    'melody stops' 112
    music rolls 118
    Pianoti version 319
    promotion 111
Piano Trade Magazine, quoted 47
Picture display on barrel piano front 62
Pier, Alan R., historian quoted 316
Pietro, Volontè, piano maker 51
Pike England, George, organ builder 54
Pinfold, representing Godfreys 44
Pinned barrel, origins of 9
    wheel 9
Pinning barrels for *piano* and *forte* 55
Pipe organ, mechanical 51
    Connoisseur 117
    with expression stop 134
    with reproducing action 35, 36
Pistonola, Boyd, player piano 105, 277, 315, **74, 75**
    advertisement 172
    its history 118–19
Pius X, Pope 3
Planchette method of piano playing 20, 56, 89
Planus, G., collection 311
Plastic film, use of in mechanical music 213
Playano Manufacturing Company 30
Play-a-Sax mechanical saxophone 211
Player action, *see also* Kicking-shoe player actions
    increase from 65 to 88 notes 112
    modified for grand piano 116
    perfection of 155 *et seq.*
    pressure-powered 114
    quality of affecting piano 29
    Stradola, advertisement for 354
Player, converting 65- to 88-note 43
    French explain its demise 48
    first action in a grand 28
    'How to build an up-to-date', article 42
    industry in France, its early demise 48
    makers and company failures 30
    makers reopen production lines 46
Player organs 116
Player piano in Australia 49
    cheapest on the market claim 31
    classes, Sir Henry Wood quoted 41
    comparison of sound 264

Player piano compass of 65-note instrument 235
    88-note instrument 235
    composers who wrote specially for 250–1
    concerts, provincial 41, 42
    controls, use of 256–9
    direct selling methods 28
    its decline 120
    Ducanola 177
    its effect on music world 123
    electric 90, 174
    expression 36
    English advertisements 28
    its evolution 105 *et seq.*
    fitted with wheels 110
    first electrically-operated 65-note 26
        pneumatic 39-note 26
        used in radio broadcasts 44
    in flying training 355–7
    Gabriella 308
    with gramophones built in 39
    'greater significance than the gramophone' 32
    how it works 127
    how promoted 105
    how to play 255–61
    its immediate popularity 123
    'important an invention as the cinematograph' 32
    industry in Japan 36
    inventors, great number of 36
    last in Britain to be made 48
    makers erred by making piano automatic 48
    manufacturers, number of 36
    market penetration in US and UK 124
    mass production of 105
    with metal music rolls 36
    mini 117
    modern **148**
    Monola 308
    motor cabinet for 155, 281
    music for 229–54
    number sold 1900–30 28
    with optically-scanned music rolls 39
    to oust ordinary piano 44
    its peak of popularity 39
    Philipps Cäcilia 177
        Corona 177
    Pleyella 303
    post-war revival 215
        of market 125
    proficiency contests 37
    with radio combined 316
    result of developments in three areas 106
    revival in America in 1937 49
    sales fall off 120
        affected by motor car 44
    separate pumps for 155
    social history of 39
    sociological effect of 37
    stool for playing 257
    tuners avoid 154
    with violins, Hupfeld 178–9

INDEX

Player piano for yacht or boat 117
Player Piano, quoted xix, 112
Player Piano and Its Music, quoted 3
Player Piano Group xvii, xix, 144, 154, 186, 191, 218–19, 220, 251, 335
Player Piano Group Bulletin, quoted 123, 251, 265
Player Piano Performances 251
Player Piano Review, quoted 41–2
    trade boycott 41
Player Piano Supplement to 'Gramophone' quoted 189, 249, 335
Player Piano Treasury, quoted 37, 247
'Player Piano Vogue', article 28
Player Piano Week 44, 45–6
Player reed organ, *see under* Reed organ
Playetta piano player 281
'Plea for the Player' pamphlet 48
Pleyel, piano manufacturer 112, 249
    connections with Stravinsky 250
Pleyella player piano xx, 303
Plymouth, Earl of 313
Pneuma electric piano 294
    piano-player 98
Pneumatic action, promptness of 151
    development of 84 *et seq*.
Pneumatic barrel piano, deKleist's 63
    flywheel system 133
    lever action 92
    piano, first 39-note 26
    player piano, how it works 127
    playing mechanism, birth of 24
    reiterating motor, use of 72
    square-shaped striking 169
    stack, *see* Valve chest
    systems described 128
Pneumatics, scaled in size 137
Pneumatist organ player 294
Pole, William, historian, quoted 81
Political music rolls 247
Polyphonmusikwerke 207
    copyright dispute 107
Polyphon musical boxes 106, 212, 282, 285, 293
    piano orchestrion advertisement 357
    'Concerto' 93
    Rossini 54
Polyvox orchestrion **129**
Pombia, barrel piano maker 68
Poole, Charles W., representing Malcolm & Co 323
Poole, W. H., piano player maker 303
Pope Leo XIII and the player piano 2
Pope Pius X 3
    awards Tremaine as 'purveyor to Papal Palace' 38
Poplar wood used for barrel 54
Popper & Co, Hugo 30, 200, 212, 276
Poppers Happy Jazz-Band 123
    Salon Orchestra **118**
    Stella reproducing piano 190
    Violinovo 200, **125–7**
Popular-Puzzle-Roll music rolls 31
Popular song, sales of killed by radio 46
Pornographic song rolls 247

Portable street piano, in *Christie's Old Organ* 16
Post-war revival of the player piano 215
Potthoff, Ludwig, inventor 59
Potthoff & Golf player system 307
Pouch, purpose described 136
Power governor, its function 146–8
Powers, Timothy B., inventor 98, 311
Poyser & Co, T. H., advertisement for player 171
Poyser's Classic piano player **66–8**
Pozzouli, Vincenzo, barrel piano maker 65
Practice roll, use of 260
Premier piano player 289
    player piano 299
    pneumatic action 299
Press Club, London 169
Presto, Chicago, quoted 29
Preuss, George, Polyphon executive 303
Price of Steinway Welte grand 176
    Welte Cabinet Player 176
    reproducing instruments 182, 189
Primary valve described 135
Primavolta electric piano 299
Prince of Wales, player advocate 44
Prohibition in America 36
    start of 195
Prokofiev, Sergei 242
Promptness of pneumatic action 151
Propaganda song roll 247
Prowse, William, piano maker 293
Public houses, first barrel piano for use in 59
Public libraries of music rolls 32
Pugno, Raoul, pianist 4, 175, 220, 242
Pulcinella, Stravinsky 250
Pump, four-lobe rotary 174
Punch, quoted 3, 28
Purcell Room, player concerts in the 191, 219, 220, 251
'Push-up' piano-player 26, *see also under* Piano Players, Cabinet Players
    reproducing players 186, *see also under* Vorsetzers

Q-code 340
QRS, music roll makers 49, 173, 211, 247–8, 337, 340
Queen Elizabeth Hall pianola concert 252
Queen's Hall 31
    concert with piano player 4
    Duo-Art concert 39
    Orchestra 112
Queen Victoria Museum & Art Gallery 308

Racca, Giovanni, inventor 59, 93, 94, 197
Rachmaninov, Sergei 31, 181, 182, 242
    Ampico testimonial 181
    comment on hearing his Ampico roll 264
Radio Athlone, support for player piano 45
Radio audience, growth of in America 46
Radio broadcasts, first use of player 44
    combined with player piano 316
Radio Paris 45
    player piano support from 44

Radio, popular song killer 46
    its progress pre-war 49
    set sales in America 46
Radi-O-Player player piano and radio 316
Rähse, Ferdinand, inventor 95, 281
Rank Organisation, Silloth Trainer parts made by 356
Rapee, Erno, silent cinema music collection 198
Ravel, Maurice 243
    Miroirs 237
Reade, Vera, Reginald Reynolds' daughter 337
Reblitz, Arthur, quoted 127
Recording artists with roll makers 242–3
    methods used by Aeolian 184
        used by Welte 225, 240–1
    pianos, Ampico's 182
    studio, early 33
Recordo expression piano 190, 243
Records of reproducing pianos, quality of 264
're-enacting' artists on Ampico 181
'Re-enacting piano' slogan 175
Reed, G. F., Aeolian managing director 169
Reed instrument player, Barlow's patent 83
Reed organ, inventor of upright 208
    Maxfield's 25
    Peaseley's 1818 model 107
    played by perforated disc 68
    separate pumps for Orchestrelle player 155
    Symphony 25, 35, 209
    upright player action 90
Reed organ maker Clark & Rich 117, 280
Reed organs, a developing industry 35
    Taber 156
    Taylor & Farley 156
Reed, W. S., inventor 206
Reeds, table organette playing 24
Reform-orgel, Nyström 68, 300
Regal piano player 317
Reger, Max, composer 4
Regina Music Box Co 296
    disc-playing musical box 209, 317
    Reginapiano 296
    Sublima 197
Regy player piano advertisement 345
Reichstadt passes copyright law 106
Rejlander, O. G., picture of boy with street piano **22**
Remington Rand Co 300
Remote wall box for coin-operation 193
Repeating melograph 86
'Reperforming piano' slogan 175
Reproducing action, the Carola 105
Reproducing device for players, Auto-Namic 280
Reproducing piano 1, 31 *et seq.*, *see also under* Ampico, Duo-Art, Welte
Reproducing piano – Aeolian slogan 119
    Beethophon 276
    Ducartist pedal-operated 177
    on gramophone records, quality of 264
    history and development 173 *et seq.*
    music for the 241 *et seq.*
    the quest for 119
    Stella 276

'Reproducing piano' slogan 175
Reproducing pianos, assessment of qualities 185
    capability assessment 263–8
    cost of 189
    dates of systems 190
    types of 189
Reproducing pipe organs 35, 36
Reproducing push-up players 186
    reed organs 35
    rolls converted to other systems 243
    systems compared 186–90
        fundamental problems 263
Reproduco player piano/organ 196, 198, 300, **134**
Repro-Phraso accenting device 310
Republic music roll company 250
Respighi, Ottorino, composer 242
Rest rail 127
    divided 145
Restoring Pianolas, quoted xx, 77, 151, 154, 270
Revival of the player piano post war 215
Revolver mechanism for barrel piano 73
Rex music rolls 118
Reynolds, Reginald, quoted 43, 44, 120–3, 335
    his daughter 337
Rhapsody in Blue recorded posthumously 251
Rhythmodik music rolls 239
Rialto Player Piano Co, advertisement 171
    player actions 171
Ribboning in music rolls 244
Richter, Friedrich Adolf, inventor 210
Richter, G., inventor 210
Riddle-Roll competition 41
    music rolls 31
Riessner, Paul, inventor 207, 303, 305
Rihden, Anton, pianist 239
Rimsky-Korsakov, Nicolai Andreyevitch, composer 4
Rink, E., Ullmann Ltd 280
Rissone, J. B., inventor 57, 59
Robino, Simon, barrel piano maker 65, 74
Robinson, James, pioneer of photography 274
Rococo style 212
Rodgers, J. A., quoted 41
Rodolphe, reed organ maker 282
Roehl, Harvey, quoted xvii, 37, 117, 183–5, 189, 196, 200, 241, 247
Roentgen, cabinet-maker 293
Rogers, George, player piano makers 116, 183
    player piano, price of 350
    reproducing piano, price of 352
Rolfe, Thomas Hall, musical instrument maker 54, 59, 71, 83, 306
Rolfe, William, musical instrument maker 54
Roll changers, multiple 194
    Wurlitzer 197
Roll drive, clockwork motor for 156
    motor, inventor of 109
Roll-playing musical instruments, types of 199
Roll-punching machinery 184
Roll repertoire 117
    tracking 110
Rolleau, S., Nantes café piano maker 271

INDEX

Rolmonica automatic mouth organ 210, 211
Romano, Charles, barrel piano maker 60, 301, 306
Romano-Laeken, piano maker 306
Ronald, Sir Landon, quoted 2, 4, 41, 112
Roncalli, music recording machine 230–1
Rönisch piano 200
Roosevelt Organ Company 26
Rootham, Dr Cyril Bradley, music tutor 169
Rose, Coop & Rissone, coin-freed pianos 63
Rosellen transcription of Verdi's *Aida* 234
Rosener piano 202
Rosenthal, Moriz, pianist 4, 242
Roskopf watch barrel 13
Rossi, C., inventor 60
Rossi, P., inventor 60
Rossi, café piano maker 67
Rotary engine drive motor for music rolls 156
Roth, A. P., inventor 91
Roth & Engelhardt 284
    first electric piano 193
Rouleaux d'Armand Nallino, barrel piano maker 302
Royal, The, quoted 28
Royal Academy of Music 335
Royal Air Force bombers, pneumatic trainers for flying 356
Royal Albert Hall Orchestra 2
Royal College of Music 335
Royal Grecian Saloon, mechanical piano at 19
Royal Society 230
Royal Violista violin-player 273
Royalties paid by Aeolian to Welte 176
Rubber hose 140
    tubing 139
Rubinstein, Anton, pianist 264
Rubinstein, Artur, pianist 181, 243, 257
    his name for sustaining pedal 264
Rubes, Jan, orchestrion maker 73
Rück collection, Dr 11, 12
Runggel, Matthäus 10, 13, 269
Running Commentary music roll 37
Russia, German instruments exported to 213

Saffell, Frederick H., action maker 44, 293
Saffron Hill, home of street musicians 7
St Denis, organ in church of 24
St Paul's Cathedral 98
Saint-Saëns, Camille, quoted 1, 4, 181, 220, 243
    G minor piano concerto on Duo-Art 39
Salyer, player action pioneer 90
Salzburg, oldest surviving barrel organ at 9, 14
Sames & Co, William, player piano makers 116
Sandell, Henry Konrad, inventor 201–4
    number of violin patents 202
San Francisco, destruction of 194
    gold-rush 194
    wealth of goods imported to 194
Sapellnikoff, Vassily, pianist 243
Sarasate, composer 204
Saturday Evening Post cartoonist 38
Sauer, Emil, pianist 4, 220
Saunders, Dr Gordon, quoted 175
Saxophone, toy mechanical 211

Schaff Piano Co 273
Scharwenka, Franz Xaver, pianist and composer 98, 243
Schaub, Ferdinand, inventor 301
Schelling, Ernest 243
Schillings, Max 4
Schlesisches Museum, Breslau 11, 12
Schlosser, quoted 11, 12
Schlüsselfiedel 204
Schmid, Emil, manufacturer 296
Schmidt, J. G. G., inventor 55, 59
Schmithals, Heinrich, Frati & Co 286
Schmitz, Elie 243
Schnabel, Artur 181, 243
    declining Aeolian recording contract 263
Schnürpel, Wilhelm, of Schübbe & Co 307
Scholes, Percy A., quoted 2, 37, 52, 237, 241, 250–1, 337
Schomacker Piano Co, player piano advertisement 339
Schübbe, Friederich, head of Schübbe & Co 307
Schubert, music rolls of works by 233
Schuhknecht, Peter Georg xviii
Schultze, A. O., Grob founder 94, 288
Schulz piano 176
Schulz, Aeolian Hall pianolist 255
Scientific American, quoted 161
Scotch Magic Tape, use of in roll repairs 253
Scottish Music Merchants Association 45
Scriabine, Alexander 4, 181, 243
Secondary valve described 135
Seeburg, J. P., orchestrion maker 296
Seeburg Piano Company, J. P. 194–5, 198
    Pipe Organ Orchestra, advertising booklet for 195
    E Special orchestra **135–6**
'Self-Acting Pianoforte' 18
Self-Acting Pianoforte, Clementi's 281
'Self-acting piano or seraphine' player patent 83
'Self-Performing Pianoforte' article 55
Serenata piano orchestrion 285
Seward, G., inventor 59, 94, 304
Sewing machine, piano player inspiration from 87
Seybold Piano-Accordeon-Jazz **124**
Seytre, C. F., inventor 84
Seytre, Autophon 84
Sforzando and crescendo, Welte 176
Shakespeare, William, playwright 199
    Cymbeline 10
Sharp, piano maker 54
Sheet music sales in America 46
Shellac, use of as wood sealant 151
Sheffield Telegraph, quoted 41
Shorter Oxford English Dictionary xx
Silencer or cut-off control 150
Silent cinema, automatic orchestra for 195
    music collection, Erno Rapee's 198
Silent Night 213
Silicon chip 6
Silloth Trainer 356
Simkins, inventor 97
Simonton, Richard, historian 241
Simplex Player Action Co 189
Simplex piano player xx, 277, **62**
    advertisement 254

Simplex and the Angelus 316
    music rolls 118
    Special Piano Player 114
    Super action 316
    unit valve action 151
Sinclair, W., Hupfeld agent 291
Sinding, Christian, composer 4
Singer recorded own accompaniment roll 32
Singer, Richard, pianist 241
Single-valve system 135
Skinner, Ernest Martin, inventor 160, 162
    note theming system 162
Smith, Dr, his words on future of player 42
Smith, J. Y., inventor 57
Smith Lyraphone Company 109
    piano player 103, 157
Smith Piano Co, F. G. 316
Smithsonian Institution xviii, 26
Snakebite perforations 163
Social history of the player piano 39
Société du Zonophone 313
Sociological effect of player piano 37
Soft pedal control from music roll 173
    keyboard shifting 146
    and rest rail control 145
Sohmer piano with Welte Mignon 176
Soldiers of the Entente 235
Solo Carola reproducing piano 189–90
Solo Expression Twin Tracker Empress piano 192
Solo Orchestrelle, Aeolian 35, 208
Solodant control 167, 173, 258, 265
Solophone, Pierre Eich 284, **112–113**
Solophonola player piano, Hupfeld 179, 291
    advertisement 228
    vs Duo-Art accenting 265
Solotheme control 117
Song of India, Original Piano Trio 250
Song of the Nightingale 250
Song rolls, advertising, political, pornographic 247
    Aeolian 235
Songs for the Camp Fireside 237
'Songs you forgot to remember', radio programme 241
Sony Corporation 171, 186
Sostinente attachment 94
    effects used on Ampico 180
    on music rolls, first use of 181
'Soul of the piano' sustaining pedal nickname 264
Sound-track on music rolls 337
Sourdine effect on Hupfeld 201
Spaeth, Sigmund, polymath 241
Spaethe, Wilhelm, president of mechanical music manufacturers 106
Spaethe Pianist piano player 288
Spain, barrel piano industry in 68
Spark chronograph recording technique 184
Sphere, Pianola advertisement 322, 325, 330
Spiegel, Fritz Karl, manager 309
Spiegl, Fritz 10
Spill valve, its function 133
Spinelli, Loretto, inventor 60, 65
Spinets, automatic 59

Spinets, development of 9
    clockwork-driven 10
Spinning-jenny 80
Spool box, piano roll 140
    chuck adaptor for 118
Spool, music roll drive inside 110
Springs, bellows 133
Sprinkle, Leland W., inventor 213
Square pianos, number made by Broadwood 186
Square virginals 12
Stalactite-player, Luray Caverns 213
Standard Player Action Co 110, 149, 269
Standard Pneumatic Action 283
Stanley, Lucius T., reciprocating roll drive motor 156
Starr Piano Co advertisement 339
Stavenhagen, Bernhard, pianist 4
Steam turbine, US honours for 203
Steck player piano, Aeolian 154, 184, 259
Steinway, piano manufacturer xvii, 40, 112, 202, 218–19
    contract with Aeolian 183
    numbers of pianos 185
    Duo-Art concert 252
    controls **99–102**
    the last 183
    New York factory 317
    piano roll lending library 246
    Pianola Piano, contract re 183–4
    Red Welte 191
    grand, cost of 176
    Welte-Mignon action in 174
    Welte Model O 220
Steinway Hall, London 240
Steinway, Henry Z. 183, 185
Stella reproducing piano, Poppers 190, 276
Stems player piano 116, 283
Sterling music rolls 118
    player piano 281, 291
Stieff piano with Welte-Mignon 176
Stoddard, Charles F., Ampico inventor 179–80
Stoddard-Ampico 180, 239
    last roll 239
Stojowski, Sigismund, pianist 242
Stonehill, Gerald xvii, 186, 218, 356
Stool for player piano 257
Story, E. H., piano maker 30, 40
Story & Clark Piano & Organ Co 280, 297
    player piano 30
Story, Hampton L., reed organ maker 280
Stradel, arr. Bach's *Organ Toccata and Fugue* 239
Stradola player action, advertisement 354
Strand Magazine, advertisements for piano players 320
Stransky, E. and C., Phonoliszt connection 201
Strauss, Richard 4, 181, 243
    waltzes on automatic harmonium 277
Stravinsky, Igor 242, 251
    connections with Pleyel 249–50
    Firebird and *Petrushka* on music roll 249–50
Street barrel organ 54
    piano industry in London 57
Street Music, article 52
Street music 52

INDEX

Street music and its legacy 16
    resurgence at time of George III 54
    organ-type piano fronts 63
    organs 91
Street piano 4, 51
    combined with organ 57
    defined 16–17
    earliest definable 51
    its Italian roots 51
    name given to Pianoharpa 68
    New York advertisement for 67
    Rejlander's photograph of 22
Street pianos, music played 74
Striggio, Alessandro, madrigal by 14, 279
Strikes, first sit-down labour dispute 48
Stringed instruments, earliest 9
    keyboard instruments, technical problems in mechanising 15
Strohmenger, W. H., quoted 45
Stroud player piano 184
Stychs, J., orchestrion maker 73
Subirands, music transcriber for barrel pianos 68
Sublima Piano Junior, Regina 305
Summing up of the music scene 249
Super Simplex piano player 316
Superscope-Marantz 223, 232, 336
Supernatural attributes to player piano 6
Suprema Golden Tube Piano Player Rolls 245
Suskind, Milton, recording *nom-de-plume* 182
Sustaining pedal 161
    action 146
    control from music roll 173
    Rubenstein's name for 264
Sweden, King of 11
Swedish folk tunes on Pianoharpa 70
Sydney Symphony Orchestra 252
Symphonia, De Roy's player piano and music rolls 282
Symphonia auto, clockwork barrel piano 302
Symphoniola, Symphonion, player piano 310
Symphonion automatic zither 207
    disc playing musical box 23, 273, 285, 300, 315
    player piano 310
Symphonique player piano/pipe organ 209
Symphonola player piano 304
Symphony player reed organ 25, 35, 209
    music rolls 118, 246
System of tracking using balanced air 110
Szántó, Theodor, pianist 4

Taber Organ Co 301
    drive motor for rolls 156
Tadini & Co, barrel piano maker 302
'Talkies', arrival of cinema sound films 196
Tanzbär mechanical concertina 211
Tanzbar advertisement for 214
Tax on music rolls, copyright 106
Tayler & Farley organs, drive motor for 156
Taylor, piano maker 54
Taylor, Ruth, cylinder pianos 311
Technical History of the Player, quoted 125, 156, 296

Tel-Electric Co 98
    piano player 102, **78–81**
Telechron, clock in Ampico piano 181
Telegraph transmitting tape 104
Telektra piano player Tel-Electric 98, 311
Telepost system, US honours for 203
Teleprinter principle 86
Television, first showing of 48
Tempo control 145, 160
    governor described 143
    marking on piano rolls, unreliability of 261
    Tempo regulator 145
Tempola control 117
Terpreter, Boyd, player piano 119, 277
Testimonials, blatantly solicited 185
    how sought 168
    Paderewski and the Pianola 362
Theme accenting from music roll 173
    or expression, investigation into 161
Theming system, non-automatic 170
Themodising 219
Themodist accenting 116, 117, 148, 168, 173, 186, 233, 258, 264, 265, 300
    invention of 163–4
Thibouville-Lamy, Jerome 23, 91, 93, 94, 273
    copyright case against 106
    Pianista piano-player 22
Thomas, Tilson, conductor 251
Thompson, Elihu, tracking system 158
Three-colour printing process, Trist's 169
Timber used for making actions 151
Times, The, quoted 17, 41, 202
Tippmann, E., inventor 206, 207
Tismar, Berthold, inventor 314
Titz Nachfolger, Peter, harmonium builder 230
Titz, Peter, musical instrument maker 294
Toccaphon 299
Tokyo Keiki Company, electrohydraulic player 227
Tokyo Olympic Games 49
Tomasso, Ernesto and Benedetto, barrel piano makers 65
Tonawanda, meaning of 194
Tone-ola player piano 289
'Toni pins a barrel' article, quoted 74–5
Tono-Bungay (H. G. Wells) quoted 3
Tonophone clockwork barrel piano 60, 63, 67, 193, 209, 283
Toper, Count Alexis de 313
'Town Johnny' bell-ringer 181
Tracker bar 135
    Aeolian Pipe Organ 168
    change from wood to metal 110, 114, 176
    compass of largest player organs 36
    double row 162, 168
    pitch of holes 150
    removable filter for 91
    transposing 48
    with different-sized holes 103
Tracker bars, dual standard 118
    reed organs using double 35
Tracker board, twin 157
Tracking systems, automatic 144
    principles governing 143

Trade label, Baylis 56
    Hicks 56
Trading with the Enemy Act (1916) 292
Transcription of music to paper roll 229
Transposa control 117
Transposing devices 110
    Aeolian 236
    Angelus 114
    tracker bar shift 145
'Transposing mouthpiece' 110
Transposition, transposing tracker bar 145
Trautmanndorf clock 79
Treadle-operated barrel piano 57
Tremaine, Harry B. 26, 38, 90, 208
    awards in 1922 38
    empire crumbles 39
Tremaine Tribute Committee 38
Tremaine, William Barnes 26
Tremolant piano orchestrion 30
Tremolo actions, inventors of 61 *et seq.*
    various 63–9
Tremolo pianos, pneumatic 197
Triola mechanical Autoharp 207
Triphonola reproducing piano, Hupfeld 179, 190, 220, 291
    superiority of performance 265–8
Triple standard action, Hupfeld 113
Trist, Arthur Ronald, inventor 168–9
Trist Piano Player Co 41, 168, 313
Triumph music rolls 118
Triumph piano player 164, 273, 292
TriumphAuto company 44
    music roll label 254
    player piano advertisement 268
Triumphodist accenting system 165–6
Triumphola piano player 305
Triumphola-Piano player piano 305
Trumpet, automatic toy 199
Trumpet or bugle calls, automatic 209
    mechanical toy 210
Tschaikowsky, music rolls of works by 233
Tubing, lead 139
    rubber 139
'Tune Detective, The' 241
Tune sheet, calico, use of 91
    drive for player pianos 155
    with wedge-shaped holes 83
Tuning-forks, instrument playing on 17, 83
Tuner's keyboard for keyless Welte **89**
Turner & Son, F. G., collection 311
Tushinsky, Joseph, Superscope Marantz 223, 226
Tyler Apparatus cinema piano 195

Ullmann, Jacques 280
U'nette player grand piano 312
Una corda 220, *see also* Keyboard shift
Un-accenting in pianola playing 261
Unemployment in America 42
    in Britain 43
    in Germany 43
Unger, Johann Friedrich, inventor 14, 229
Unika orchestrion 315

Unit-block systems 151
Unit valve pneumatics 151
Unit valve system, Hupfeld 179
    Broadwood's wooden 151
United States Air Force, Link Trainer specifiers 355
    patent office 203
    Perforated Music Suits, article 325–6
Universal Music Company 44, 45
Universal music rolls 167, 297
Universal Piano Player, Bansall & Son 41, 110, 274
    advertisement 321
Universal player piano, price of 350
Up-To-Date Music Roll Co 98, 274

Vacuum accumulator 132
Vacuum *vs* air pressure 107
Vacuum pump, Electora 298
    roll drive motor, inventor of 109
Valve chest, its function 135
Vanroy, Pierre, café piano **31**
Varnish used to strengthen music roll edges 244
Vatican player piano 2, 3, 38
Vaucanson, inventor of automata 80
Verdi piano orchestrion 305
Verdi: *Aida*, transcription by Rosellen 234
Vestal Press, New York xvii
Victoria, Queen 15
Victoria & Albert Museum xviii
Vienna International Exhibition, 1872 230
Villa, Luigi, inventor of advert display system 62
Violano, Mills 307
Violano Orchestra, Mills 307
Violano-Virtuoso, Mills 201–6, 209
    cost of 204
Viol-Cello, Mills 205
Violin, automatic, patents for 199–206
    electromagnetically played 206
    Hegeler & Ehrlers Geigenpiano 206
    played by keyboard, Mills 206
    self-playing, Whitlock's 210
    65-note pneumatic 200
Violin-players, Wauters 273
Violin-toned organ pipes 197, 200
Violinista, d'Aubry & Boreau 200
Violinovo, Popper 200
Violins, Hupfeld player piano with 178
Viol-Xylophone, Mills 205
Virginal, mechanical 9, 315
Virginals, octave 12
    square 12
Virgynalles reference 10
Virtuola expression piano 98
    player piano 289
Virtuos piano player 281, 285
    player piano 290
Virtuoso electric piano, Heilbrunn's 100
    expression piano 98
    accenting system 193
'Vocal dances' on music roll 236
Vocalion Organ Co 208
Vocalstyle Music Company 117

INDEX

Vocastyle Music Company 173
    Vocastyle Notes, quoted 173
Volksklavier automatic zither 207
Volstead, instigator of Prohibition 195
Voorhorst, Lucius, pianolist 250
Vorsetzer, 174, 186, 218
    Ducanola, Philipps 177–8
Vorsteller player action 294
Vose, J., inventor 206
Votey, Edwin Scott, Pianola inventor 26, 90, 312
    his first patent 26
    first Pianola 21, 25

Wagener, Charles H. 3, 280
Wagner, Siegfried 37
    music rolls of works by 233
Wagoner, M. A. von, player action maker 283
Walden, Lord Howard de 10
Walker, J. J., roll tracking system inventor 110
Wall Street crash 43
    effect on trade 37, 39
Walmisley, Willoughby, festival organiser 335
Walter, Bruno, conductor 37
Waring & Gillow, department store 202–3
Warren brothers, founders of Clough & Warren 281
Watch barrel, Roskopf 13
Water Witch Quadrilles 19
Watts, representing Monington & Weston 44
Wauters, Prof, inventor 200, 202
Weaving machinery, link with musicwork 22
Webb, C. F., inventor 118
Webb, Francis Gilbert, inventor 161
Weber Piano Co 312
    Aeolian's top piano 183
    Duo-Art owned by Mussolini 185
    Pianola Piano, second under Steinway 183–4, 185
Weber Gebruder 212
    Brabo **117**
    Grandezza **115**
    Swing jazz band **122**
    Unika **116**
Weber: *Grand Polonaise* opus 21 235
    music rolls of works by 233
    'Weber's Last Waltz' 19
'Web-guiding devices' patent for 157
Weigel, Erhard, quoted 10
Weight-driven pianos 56
Welin, early pioneer in pneumatics 91
Wells, H. G.: *Tono-Bungay,* quoted 3
Welte Artistic Player 177
Welte Artistic Player Co, Steinway contract with 183
Welte, Emil 96, 105–6, 176, 241
Welte & Söhne, M., reproducing piano makers 15, 24–5, 31, 34, 40, 96, 156, 174, 184, 200, 212, 276
    advertisements 263
    vs Aeolian Court case 176
    artists who recorded for 242
    assets seized under Alien Property Act 175
    Cabinet Player, cost of 176
    detachable keyboard for tuning 175
    expression facilities 179

Welte floating crescendo concept 176
    'green' system 190
        date of introduction 190
    keyless 31, 220, 221
    piano, tuner's keyboard **89**
    Multitone piano 300
    music rolls, value of xix
        very high cost of 240–1
    Philharmonic Autograph Organ 316
    recording operation 240–1
        techniques 225
    roll drive motor 109
Welte-Mignon Corporation 175–6
Welte-Mignon reproducing action and pianos 190, 220, 226, 231, 266–8, 307
    action 180
    advertisement 334
    Autograph Piano, advertisement 262
    date of introduction 190
    its development 174 *et seq.*
    first reproducing piano 241
    keyless 'red' **88**
    music rolls 246
    paper for making rolls 245
    pianos which used the 176
    recordings converted to other systems 243
    similarity to Philipps Duca action 178
    Steinway contract terminated 183
    Vorsetzer piano player 174, 177, 186, **84–6**
Welte-Mignon (Licensee) reproducing action 175–6, 185, 220–1, 241, **90, 92, 94, 96**
    date of introduction 190
    Estey Piano Company tie-up 176
    music rolls 240–1
Weser, John A., inventor 90, 193
Weser Brothers 193
West Cornwall Museum of Mechanical Music xviii, 317
Wheelock player piano 184
Wheels fitted to players 110
Whight *vs* Boosey copyright case 106
White, early pioneer of pneumatic action 90
White, Edward H., Angelus inventor 316
White, Henry Kirk, of Wilcox & White 316
White, William Braid, quoted 27, 133
Whiteleys department store 323
White-Smith Music Publishing Co *vs* Apollo 325
Whitlock, J. W., inventor 201, 209–10
Whittle, Frank, jet engine inventor 48
Widths and type of music roll, table of 246
Wier, M. A., inventor 210
Wilcox, Horace C., of Wilcox & White 316
Wilcox & White, organ-builders and makers of Angelus 25, 36, 91, 113–14, 189, 209, 301
    Angelus advertisement 324, 328
    date of introduction 190
    early Angelus player 191
    Symphony reed organ 35
    music rolls 246
Wilkinson, A., inventor 91
Willis, Canadian piano maker 183
Wimbledon Borough News, quote 337

Wimbledon Festival, pianola contest at 335
Windsor Castle 203
Winkel, D. N., Dutch organ builder 134
Winkelmann player pianos 296
Winter, early pioneer in pneumatics 90
Wintle, Canon A. O. 65
    enterprise, 74–5
Wippen, convenience of for player action 128
Wireless, growth of 44
    effect on player sales 120, 122
Wolverhampton, classical song recital at 41
Wood, Sir Henry J., conductor 4, 112
    quoted 41
    conducts Duo-Art concert 39
Wood, James, composer 251
Work magazine 'How to build a Player' 42
World's Fair, quoted 74
'World's first complete piano' slogan 124
World's largest mechanical musical instrument 213
World's Music series of Aeolian rolls 237
'World's Music, The', series 37
World's Music series of rolls 169
Wright, M. S., inventor 208
Wrong notes in music roll, removing 35
    performance, number of 35
Wuest, early pioneer in pneumatics 91
Wunsch, R., inventor 211
Wurlitzer, Farny 193
Wurlitzer, Howard 210

Wurlitzer Co, Rudolph, mechanical musical instrument-sellers 60, 72, 98, 189, 198, 209, 282–3, 300, 309
Wurlitzer Automatic Harp 199, 209–10
    Bijou Orchestra 197
    Concert PianOrchestra 194
    Mandolin Quartette 197
    PianOrchestra 194, 197
    range of instruments 67
    roll-changer 197
    selling Hupfeld orchestrions 194
    stamping name on Hupfeld parts 194
Wyke, T. J., quoted 52

Xylophone, Automatic 200
    Hiawatha Self-Playing 295
Xylophone-Klavier 299

Yankee Doodle, song 241
York Minster, organ in 24
Yorkshire Observer, quoted 41
Youens, William, inventor 56
Young, J. F., collection 311
Yver, P., financier 287

Zimmermann, Max, piano maker 317
Zither, automatic 207
Zoppa, A. E., inventor 39
Zuleger's Tanzbär automatic accordion 214

For those readers who are interested in the restoration of player pianos, there is a companion volume to *Pianola* which is called *Restoring Pianolas and other self-playing pianos*. Also written by Arthur W. J. G. Ord-Hume, this 143-page volume contains chapters covering: (1) Equipment for the job; (2) Rebuilding the Barrel Piano; (3) Rebuilding the Player Piano; (4) Understanding the Reproducing Piano; (5) Player Organs and their overhaul. There are also three valuable appendices, one devoted to music roll makers and brand names, a second to the trade names of player pianos and a third devoted to how to date player pianos by their serial numbers. An extensive bibliography is included together with a detailed cross-referenced index.

This volume is indispensable for the serious player piano enthusiast and is one of the ten books the author has written to date on mechanical music and its instruments.